CANADIAN MAVERICK

The Life and Times of Ivan C. Rand

PATRONS OF THE SOCIETY

Blake, Cassels & Graydon LLP

Gowlings

McCarthy Tétrault LLP

Osler, Hoskin & Harcourt LLP

Paliare Roland Rosenberg Rothstein LLP

Torkin Manes Cohen Arbus LLP

Torys LLP

WeirFoulds LLP

The Osgoode Society is supported by a grant from
The Law Foundation of Ontario.

The Law Foundation of Ontario
Building a better foundation for justice in Ontario

The Society also thanks The Law Society of Upper Canada
for its continuing support.

CANADIAN MAVERICK

The Life and Times of
Ivan C. Rand

WILLIAM KAPLAN

Published for The Osgoode Society for Canadian Legal History by
University of Toronto Press
Toronto Buffalo London

© Osgoode Society for Canadian Legal History 2009
www.utppublishing.com
www.osgoodesociety.ca
Printed in Canada

ISBN 978-1-4426-4070-2

Printed on acid-free, 100% post-consumer recycled paper
with vegetable-based inks.

Library and Archives Canada Cataloguing in Publication

Kaplan, William, 1957–
Canadian maverick : the life and times of Ivan C. Rand / William Kaplan.

Includes bibliographical references and index.
ISBN 978-1-4426-4070-2

1. Rand, Ivan C. (Ivan Cleveland), 1884–1969. 2. Canada. Supreme
Court – Biography.   3. Judges – Canada – Biography.   I. Title.

KE8248.R36K37 2009   347.71'03534   C2009-902849-2

University of Toronto Press acknowledges the financial assistance to its
publishing program of the Canada Council for the Arts and the
Ontario Arts Council.

University of Toronto Press acknowledges the financial support for its
publishing activities of the Government of Canada through the
Book Publishing Industry Development Program (BPIDP).

To the loves of my life ~
Max, Simon, and Hannah

Also by William Kaplan

NON-FICTION

Everything That Floats: Pat Sullivan, Hal Banks and the Seamen's Unions of Canada

State and Salvation: The Jehovah's Witnesses and Their Fight for Civil Rights

Bad Judgment: The Case of Mr Justice Leo A. Landreville

Presumed Guilty: Brian Mulroney, the Airbus Affair and the Government of Canada

A Secret Trial: Brian Mulroney and the Public Trust

CHILDREN'S BOOKS

One More Border: The True Story of One Family's Escape from War-Torn Europe

EDITED COLLECTIONS

Moscow Despatches: Inside Cold War Russia (with Dean Beeby)

Law, Policy, and International Justice: Essays in Honour of Maxwell Cohen (with Donald McRae)

Belonging: The Meaning and Future of Canadian Citizenship

Contents

Contents

Foreword

THE OSGOODE SOCIETY
FOR CANADIAN LEGAL HISTORY

Ivan Rand had a long, varied, and remarkable career. He is best known for his Supreme Court of Canada judgments in a series of cases emanating from Quebec in the 1950s and dealing with civil rights, cases that established limits on the government's ability to persecute unpopular religious minorities. To labour lawyers he is also an icon for his invention of the 'Rand formula,' one of the defining features of Canadian labour law. Rand was also a member of the United Nations special committee on Palestine in 1947, the founding Dean of the University of Western Ontario law school, and three times a royal commissioner. William Kaplan traces Rand's life and career in all its richness and controversy, through many seminal events of the twentieth century in Canada. The Rand that emerges is variously inspiring, frustrating to understand, sometimes contradictory, always complex.

The purpose of the Osgoode Society for Canadian Legal History is to encourage research and writing in the history of Canadian law. The Society, which was incorporated in 1979 and is registered as a charity, was founded at the initiative of the Honourable R. Roy McMurtry, formerly attorney general for Ontario and chief justice of the province, and officials of the Law Society of Upper Canada. The Society seeks to stimulate the study of legal history in Canada by supporting researchers, collecting oral histories, and publishing volumes that contribute to legal-historical scholarship in Canada. It has published seventy-eight books on the courts, the judiciary, and the legal profession, as well as on the history of crime and punishment, women and law, law and econo-my, the legal treatment of ethnic minorities, and famous cases and sig-nificant trials in all areas of the law.

Current directors of the Osgoode Society for Canadian Legal History are Robert Armstrong, Christopher Bentley, Kenneth Binks, Patrick Brode, Brian Bucknall, David Chernos, Kirby Chown, J. Douglas Ewart, Martin Friedland, John Honsberger, Horace Krever, C. Ian Kyer, Virginia MacLean, Patricia McMahon, R. Roy McMurtry, W.A. Derry Millar, Jim Phillips, Paul Reinhardt, Joel Richler, William Ross, Paul Schabas, Robert Sharpe, James Spence, Richard Tinsley, and Michael Tulloch.

The annual report and information about membership may be ob-tained by writing to the Osgoode Society for Canadian Legal History, Osgoode Hall, 130 Queen Street West, Toronto, Ontario, M5H 2N6. Telephone: 416-947-3321. E-mail: mmacfarl@lsuc.on.ca. Website: www. osgoodesociety.ca.

R. Roy McMurtry
President

Jim Phillips
Editor-in-Chief

Preface

About twenty years ago, I began this biography of Ivan Rand when I was a professor at a law school. Today, few law students and fewer still Canadians could identify Rand, although they might have heard about something called the Rand Formula. It was not always so. Rand was my hero in law school (1980–3). As a puisne judge of the Supreme Court of Canada (1943–59), he expanded federal authority, strengthening the centre and preserving the union. But it was his great civil liberties judgments that really attracted my attention: the Japanese Deportation case, *Boucher v. The King*, *Saumur v. The City of Quebec*, and *Roncarelli v. Duplessis*. Together with at least two generations of law students, I sat in the law library and read in awe as Rand acknowledged the legitimate rights of Japanese Canadians, brutalized and robbed by their government during the Second World War and threatened, at war's end, with removal to a country most of them did not even know. It was Rand who stood up for the Jehovah's Witnesses during the dark years of Maurice Duplessis's authoritarian rule in Quebec in the 1940s and 1950s, when Witnesses were beaten and imprisoned by Quebec authorities, acting with the blessings of the Roman Catholic hierarchy, for the crime of going door to door and peacefully spreading their version of the word of God. It was Rand who upheld the rule of law by calling Premier Duplessis to account for his gross abuse of power. And it was Rand, at the height of the Red Scare, who defended communists and their lawful right to free speech. 'Who is this guy?' I used to ask myself, and I resolved to find out.

'My father was a private person,' one of Rand's sons told me soon after I began work on the project in the summer of 1988. Rand's public life has been relatively easy to document. His private life presented greater challenges. The truth is that while there are telling glimpses, we do not know a lot about the private Rand: the papers do not exist. Fortunately, however, Rand had a long and varied public career and often found himself at the centre of some of the great events in the history of the country. As a young lawyer, he participated in the opening of the Canadian West. He was a reformist attorney general of his native New Brunswick, and he worked at the headquarters of one of Canada's biggest companies, Canadian National Railways, serving as commission counsel responsible for the legal affairs of a Crown corporation with 100,000 employees from coast to coast and carrying millions of passengers a year. None of this would merit a biography, although it does provide some context for Rand's later public life. What makes Rand so interesting is his work as a judge, together with his extra-judicial engagements after he joined the Supreme Court in 1943.

Most important of all is Rand's monumental contribution to Canadian law, especially to what is called the implied Bill of Rights. In the face of repeated transgressions from governmental authorities, mostly in Quebec, Rand implied a Bill of Rights into our Constitution. It was, as one scholar and future Supreme Court of Canada judge has written, an intimation 'of what might be.'[1] Some freedoms, Rand held, are fundamental to society and beyond the scope of legislative power. If the Supreme Court of Canada has had a heroic age, it was the 1950s, and Rand was the hero who defined it. Extra-judicially, Rand, in 1946, helped to solve the first major post–Second World War labour dispute, and his formula for doing so became, without doubt, one of the defining features of Canadian labour law. In 1947 Rand served as Canada's representative on the United Nations Special Committee on Palestine: he was one of the major contributors to the majority report, which recommended partition and led to the creation of the modern state of Israel.

At a time when many think of retiring, Rand, having reached the age of seventy-five in 1959, did not return home to his beloved New Brunswick but became the founding dean of law at the University of Western Ontario. His tenure as dean was interrupted by a telephone call from Ottawa. Would he study the Cape Breton coal problem? The fate of the entire population of the island, it seemed, was at stake as the coal-mining industry, propped up for years by government subventions of various kinds, was in decline, if not already dead. Rand was asked to find a solution to this long-simmering social, political, and economic catastrophe, just as he would later be called upon to make recommendations to deal with the fate of an errant judge named Leo A. Landreville (1966) and labour disputes in Ontario (1968). If there was a problem in the 1960s, Ivan Rand was among the first people governments turned to for solutions. There was a Rand mystique.

Like many people, Rand was confounding and inconsistent. He was a great civil libertarian. He loved his country, and he believed in social progress, rationality, duty, responsibility, and above all, civilization. He hated greed, frivolity, conspicuous consumption, tax avoidance, and luxury. He was also, not uncommonly for the times, an intolerant bigot having little use for French Canadians, Roman Catholics, Jews, and other persons with ethnic-sounding names. So deep rooted was his prejudice against Acadians that, when his sister married one, he did not meet her husband for more than thirty years. But Rand was also brave – as in the Japanese Deportation case, when other judges were timorous and befuddled at best, and, at worst, quiet and complicit.

How much did Rand's private views influence his public ones, such as the reversal after reversal of Quebec judgments in the 1950s? While the outcomes in those key cases – *Boucher*, *Saumur*, and *Roncarelli* – were defensible, indeed praiseworthy, did Rand's negative feelings towards French Canadians and Roman Catholics influence his judgment, making the results easier for him to reach? Likewise, with Leo A. Landreville, the flamboyant ex-mayor from Sudbury, Ontario, appointed to Ontario's Supreme Court by Prime Minister Louis St Laurent and later found to have taken stock options in questionable circumstances when he was a chief magistrate, Rand's conclusions about Landreville positively radiate stereotypical English distrust of things French and Roman Catholic. Speaking about Landreville, Rand wrote, 'His emotions are active and he can be highly expansive. He is fascinated by the glitter of success and material well-being ... He presents the somewhat versatile character of a modern hedonist of vitality whose philosophy is expressed in terms of pragmatic opportunism.' Landreville, by his bad judgment, was his own worst enemy. But Rand played an important role in the demolition of Landreville and his career. Was that in part based on ethnic and religious prejudice?

Twenty-five years ago, there was virtually no modern Canadian judicial biography. Canadian judges, even those who served on the Supreme Court of Canada, were largely marginal figures and their rulings rarely became part of the national conversation (although a handful of Ivan Rand's judgments were an exception). The *Charter of Rights and Freedoms* changed everything. What judges say governs. Who they are and where they come from now matter a great deal. Naturally, people are curious about the men and women who populate the bench, especially about the membership of the Supreme Court of Canada. Almost overnight, judicial biography proliferated.

David Williams's readable life of the tormented, alcoholic, indebted, sycophantic, and impotent Sir Lyman Duff came first in 1984.[2] Dennis Gruending's biography of Emmett Hall appeared one year later, and, in 2004, Frederick Vaughan followed with his interpretation of a grandstanding, activist, domineering, abusive, and, strangely, humanitarian Hall.[3] W.H. McConnell published his study of William McIntyre in 2000,[4] and Ellen Anderson's reverential, authorized account of Bertha Wilson appeared in 2001 and deserves an award for detail.[5] Robert Sharpe and Kent Roach published their biography of Brian Dickson in 2003, a book that tells us less about who Dickson was and a lot about what he did, mostly on the Supreme Court and particularly at the dawn of the *Charter of Rights and Freedoms*.[6] In many ways, Dickson followed a traditional path to the bench: middle-class family, distinguished war service, corporate lawyer, trial judge, judge of the Court of Appeal, appointment to the Supreme Court of Canada – just one more steady climb to the top. There would have been little that was exceptional except that, when the *Charter of Rights* arrived, Dickson became the premier elaborator of the fundamental values underlying the Canadian Constitution.

Philip Girard's impressive study of Bora Laskin is the best of these judicial biographies to date. Laskin did not pursue a typical career path to Ottawa, and his journey is all the more interesting because of the barriers he faced. As a young professor, Laskin was an iconoclast, calling for better judges and judging. But once he got the top job, he proved to be not so much a leader as a dissenter, and, in the end, an increasingly reactionary one at that. Girard's book works well because it is about Bora Laskin, an outsider who became an insider, and not just about courts and cases – although Girard manages to bring them to life too.[7] Contextual, well-rounded, and interesting, this achievement is all the more remarkable because it was written without the cooperation of the Laskin family.

Ivan Rand, the son of a railway mechanic from Moncton and a graduate of Harvard Law School, was the first Supreme Court judge whom Canadians got to know to some degree. There is much to praise about

Rand's career. To date, except around the edges, Canadian judicial biography has been, with a few exceptions, mostly uncritical and largely celebratory, written by unabashed admirers. To my great surprise, this book turned out to be different.

As might be expected in an endeavour of this kind, particularly one extending over twenty years, I have had a lot of help.

A number of friends and colleagues read all or some of the manuscript and made many valuable comments: Irving Abella, Eric Adams, Constance Backhouse, Blaine Baker, Jamie Benidickson, David Bercuson, Earl Cherniak, Bruce Feldthusen, Judy Fudge, Doug Gray, Ian Holloway, Horace Krever, David Mullan, Donald Bruce Nerbas, Jim Phillips, Marshall Pollock, Bruce Stewart, Eric Tucker, Robert Sharpe, and Michael Wright. I also thank two reviewers for the Osgoode Society: Russell Brown and Philip Girard. The chapter on the Ford Strike and the Rand Formula was presented at a conference held in Victoria in June 2008, 'Putting the Law to Work,' and I benefited greatly from the comments of all the participants, especially David Huxtable.

Research assistants, many of whom are now lawyers, include Josh Arnold, Jennifer Danahy, Anthony Dale, James Gotowiec, Derek Ground, Celia Henslowe, Kris Heshka, Paul Jones, John Koh, Lynn Lovett, Laura Madokoro, Jane Meadus, Mike Morgan, Roxanne Noel, Linda Parker, Graham Rawlinson, Kathleen Rasmussen, Joy Saleh, Mari-Anne Saunders, Charmaine Stanley, Rebecca Thompson, Cameron Tiesma, Steven Williams, Wendy Warhaft, Jeannine Woodall, and Katrina Wyman. I thank them all. Alice Palumbo, a law student at the University of Toronto, and Christine Davidson of Halifax, edited the endnotes.

Ivan's sons, Charles and Robert, were gracious hosts in Kitchener and Shediac. They shared freely their memories and made Ivan's Harvard Law School notebooks and a large and diverse body of personal papers available to me. Ivan's sister Ruth Hébert invited me to her home and helped fill in many personal details about the Rand family. Horace Pettigrove gave me several long interviews and shared his personal papers with me.

At the University of New Brunswick Law School, then dean Wade MacLauchlan welcomed me to his congenial faculty, where I spent my one and only sabbatical as a university professor researching this book. Marion Beyea, the provincial archivist of New Brunswick, was of great assistance. Professor John G. Reid at St Mary's University pointed me to references to Rand in the *Argosy*, Mount Allison's student newspaper. Alphonse Girard, QC, general counsel of the CNR, removed roadblocks to access to the company's records and arranged for the railway to make an important contribution to the cost of research. Ken Mackenzie, a former CN archivist, drew my attention to several key sources. At Harvard Law School, Paul Weiler arranged for access to the Griswold papers and to Rand's student file. Carl Baar shared his Rand clipping file with me. Jean Dryden, the chief archivist for the United Church of Canada, and Ruth Dyck Wilson, the reference coordinator, were extremely helpful in guiding me to relevant documents on church union and the role played by Ivan Rand. David Bercuson made available to me the supporting documents he acquired during his research for his important book *Canada and the Birth of Israel*. I also benefited from Anne Hillmer's superb master's thesis, 'Canadian Policy on the Partition of Palestine, 1947.' The late and very great Gordon Henderson introduced me to Leo Landreville, and that meeting led, in turn, to a book about the former judge who came under Rand's microscope.

At the Faculty of Law at the University of Ottawa, a number of colleagues and friends supported this project from the outset, including deans Don McRae and Bruce Feldthusen. Barbara Main provided excellent secretarial assistance, while the elegant Madeleine Glazer was always helpful and efficient. As usual, archivists at Library and Archives Canada and at the Archives of Ontario were professional and helpful.

At the Osgoode Society I would like to thank the late Peter Oliver, who gave this project his support from its inception. Marilyn Macfarlane was also encouraging. Very special thanks, however, go to editor-in-chief Jim Phillips: I have never worked with a managing editor who gave a manuscript, and an author, as much care and attention as he has. More than twenty years ago Robert Bothwell introduced me to Rosemary Shipton, Canada's finest editor. Since that time, she has edited almost all my books. For all of that, and especially for this book, I owe her a great debt of thanks. Len Husband at the University of Toronto Press was always enthusiastic and supportive.

Financial support for this project was provided by the Law Foundation of Ontario, the Ontario Arts Council, the Faculty of Law at the University of Ottawa, the Osgoode Society, and the Social Sciences and Humanities Research Council of Canada.

William Kaplan
Toronto, February 2009

CANADIAN MAVERICK

The Life and Times of Ivan C. Rand

1

The Right Start

He was born on 27 April 1884, in Moncton, New Brunswick, with a caul. For hundreds of years, the birth of a veiled child – his head covered by a thin membrane – was believed to be an omen. 'This boy,' the attending physician prophesied, 'will have a great and worthwhile life.'[1] From his modest beginnings, Ivan Cleveland Rand, the first-born son of Nelson and Minnie Rand, would build a remarkable career of professional accomplishment and success. He studied law at Harvard, participated in the opening of the Canadian West, returned to his home province, served as a reformist attorney general there, and rose to be commission counsel of Canadian National Railways before being appointed, in 1943, to the Supreme Court of Canada. Undoubtedly, and perhaps improbably, Canada's greatest civil libertarian judge, Rand, in his sixteen years on the bench, took time away from his judicial career to resolve a bitter labour dispute at Ford of Canada by imposing a formula that soon became one of the defining characteristics of Canadian labour law. He served as Canada's representative on the United Nations Special Committee on Palestine and was one of the drafters of the majority report that led to the creation of the State of Israel. In 1959, when he retired from the Supreme Court of Canada, he became the founding dean of the Faculty of Law at the University of Western Ontario. He was a one-man royal commission into the coal industry, the conduct of Judge Leo A. Landreville, and labour disputes in Ontario. The attending doctor was right: Ivan C. Rand had a great and worthwhile life.

There have been Rands in the new world for four hundred years. Nelson, Ivan's father, was born in Shediac on 28 October 1843.[2] At the age of sixteen he apprenticed with the recently founded European and North American Railway, working the almost 31 kilometre Shediac-Moncton line. In 1866 he was promoted to locomotive driver and, nine years later, moved to Moncton, where he became roundhouse foreman of the Intercolonial Railway (ICR) – the meandering line built for political and military purposes that had persuaded New Brunswick to enter Confederation. Nelson's first wife was Mary Ann Hawkins. They had five children, but only three sons survived: Willard L., Silas J., and Nelson C. After Mary Ann died in 1880, Nelson married Minnie, the eighteen-year-old daughter of Cornelius and Carolyn Ward Turner, who was twenty years his junior.

Fair skinned, attractive, and deeply religious, Minnie Rand spent her life in service to her family. A Baptist through and through, she deferred to her husband while he was alive and worshipped as a Methodist. When he was gone, she returned to her religious roots. A daughter, Roxanna, came first (1883) but did not live long. Ivan followed next. Then came Daisy Sangster in 1885, Charles Whitney in 1887, Minnie Marcella in 1889, Wilfred Lawrence in 1897 (who died before his first birthday), and ten years later, the baby, Ruth Carolyn. The family, though working class, could claim distant kinship to Sir Charles Tupper, the former premier of Nova Scotia and, briefly, prime minister of Canada, as well as a great-uncle named Silas Rand, a missionary who translated the Bible for the Mi'kmaq Indians.[3]

Two years after moving to Moncton, the headquarters for the Intercolonial, Nelson was promoted to the position of road foreman. Railway employment conferred social cachet and status but also carried responsibility. In 1883 all ICR operating personnel were required to take the pledge – on pain of instant dismissal if they indulged in an alcoholic drink. Nelson was active in community life, particularly as one of the first stewards of the Central Methodist Church, dedicated in November 1891, and as a member of the Masons, the Order of Oddfellows, and the Loyal Orange Order. In his spare time, he liked to play cards at the Brunswick Hotel.[4]

While Moncton is short on physical and architectural beauty, it does enjoy 'location.' It was, and is, at a crossroads of sorts – located at the geographic centre of the Maritime provinces, with nearby water access to the Bay of Fundy and, if the timing is right, via the Petitcodiac River tidal bore, which arrives twice a day. The building of the ICR in the 1870s gave Moncton sudden new life. Forty hectares of land were acquired for a huge sprawling yard where offices, a car shop, a storehouse, a machine shop, and an engine house were built. There were even tenements for employees and, most conspicuously, an elegant railway station. By 1872 it was possible to travel from Moncton to Saint John and Halifax. Later the route was extended from Moncton to Quebec City and Montreal. Moncton, as planned, was at the centre.[5]

The community benefited handsomely from the feverish economic activity. The town got its first daily paper in 1877 and soon had two, the daily Conservative *Moncton Times* and the weekly Liberal *Moncton Transcript*. The population just kept on growing, from 1,200 people in 1872 to 5,000 in 1882 (the year Oscar Wilde included it on his North American lecture tour) to more than 7,000 in 1887 – about one-eighth of whom worked for the ICR.[6] In the 1880s the telephone and electricity arrived, just as the last remnants of the old Maritime staple, the wood shipbuilding industry, all but disappeared. Bank branches proliferated, and new stores seemed to be opening every day. John A. Macdonald's National Policy appeared to be working: high tariffs kept American and other foreign manufactured goods out and gave Canadian manufacturers a competitive advantage while, at the same time, low freight rates encouraged primary and secondary manufacturing. Moncton already had a cotton mill and a sugar refinery, and several new foundries opened for business. From there, 'stoves, furniture, pianos, mining cars, soaps, shoes, textiles, confectioneries, and even a few farm tractors found their way to the Prairies and British Columbia.'[7]

At the centre of it all was the railway. By the end of the decade more than one million passengers a year travelled on the ICR, and more then 30,000 of them used the Moncton station. In 1879 a local referendum on alcohol was held and Moncton went 'dry,' although the law, when it came officially into effect several years later, was violated more in this town than anywhere else in New Brunswick. Moncton, one travelling journalist observed, was a 'veritable free-whiskey paradise.'[8] In 1880, when it became a city, it adopted as its motto the Latin term *Resurgo*: 'I rise again.' Unlike the phoenix, there was no reason to believe that it would fall back to earth, at least anytime soon.

Moncton, like much of the rest of New Brunswick, was divided first by language: English or French. The linguistic differences were reflected in religious ones: a Protestant majority and Roman Catholic minority. In the 1870s these differences came to a head in a long, sometimes violent, and extremely bitter dispute over the adoption of a free nonsectarian public school system. A compromise of sorts was reached, but the bitterness remained: English and French, Protestant and Catholic – two communities living in isolation from each other in a single city in a small province. 'Amiable apartheid' was the way another Moncton boy, Northrop Frye, later described relations between the two founding peoples.[9] Regardless, Nelson Rand considered it the perfect place to raise a family.

There was a piano at home, and Ivan learned how to play from his mother. He could also sing, after a fashion. The kitchen was often crowded with railway men engaged in lively debate, usually fuelled by illicit whiskey. It was obvious to Ivan how well respected his father was, as the railway men talked until late at night debating the issues of the day. The subject matter was always compelling, but so too was the process through which the 'ideas were stripped bare and left to stand naked in the snow. Only the *most* hardy could survive.'[10] In 1902 Nelson received yet another promotion; as master mechanic, he was responsible for the entire line east of Campbellton.

Rand graduated from Aberdeen High School on 26 June 1900. The following November, now sixteen years old, he began work as a messenger in the audit department of the ICR in Moncton – employment undoubtedly secured by his father. His salary was $96 per year. Railway travel then regularly involved passage on a number of different lines, and Rand's job was to allocate the fare among the different carriers – an exacting task that, once mastered, was hardly the basis for a career. The following year he got a raise to $120 annually, and in 1902 he was promoted to a clerk's position, at the princely sum of $192 per year. Like his father and his brother Charles, Rand could have probably stayed with the railway his entire working life. By 1905 he was earning $480 a year. But he had higher sights. At the age of twenty-one, with his savings in hand, he left Moncton for Sackville and Mount Allison University, 40 kilometres down the road, but really a universe away.

The Mount Allison Wesleyan Academy had opened its doors in 1843, founded by Charles Frederick Allison, a successful Methodist merchant who believed the biblical injunction that, if you trained a child in the way he should go, he would not depart from it. Located in Sackville, New Brunswick, a very small town at the head of the Bay of Fundy, Mount Allison set out to educate the children of the three Maritime provinces at all three levels – primary, intermediate, and collegiate. By the time Ivan Rand arrived in September 1905, Mount Allison had just over one hundred students, but the fundamentals had not changed. It was still a school run by Methodists imbued with John Wesley's beliefs. Salvation required a lifelong process of service to God through personal faith, moral uprightness, and service to others. Not surprisingly, discipline and morality were strict, relations between the sexes were diligently supervised (the ladies' residence was known as 'the penitentiary'), tobacco and alcohol were prohibited, and everyone was required to attend morning chapel and church on Sunday. Above all, academic standards were rigorous.[11]

Initially, Rand had been uncertain of his direction. 'What should I study?' he asked Clifford Robinson, a well-known Moncton lawyer, leading Liberal, and fellow Methodist. 'Avoid law,' Robinson advised; 'engineering is the ticket.' And so Rand enrolled in the two-year engineering certificate program. He was one of sixteen freshmen at the school that year. 'Entered Mt. Allison,' he wrote in his diary on 23 September 1905. 'Weight 158 lbs, Height 6 ft (with boots on).' A new and larger drawing room was 'fitted up' to accommodate the increasing number of students, and a laboratory was furnished with all sorts of 'experimental apparatus.' The first-year program consisted of courses on surveying and mapping, kinematics of machines, materials of construction, and free-hand drawing. Most courses came under the supervision of the newly appointed professor, John William Crowell, a Dartmouth graduate, who, in turn, had two assistants, F.S. Swaine in the laboratory and J.M. Clindinnin in the shop. 'At 21,' Rand wrote in his diary,' 'just beginning to see things a little. Believe everything has its course to run – sooner it gets there the better ... Am quite pleased that I at least am not a fool – that I have awakened (whatever I may come to).'[12]

Rand had not come to university to loaf, and he immediately set himself apart from his classmates by his total devotion to academic work. As the *Argosy*, the student newspaper, described Rand's academic progress, 'From his lamp the midnight oil poured in continuous stream – result, a place in the class lists which any student would be glad to hold – a place, too, which he faithfully maintained throughout his course. His second year showed a slight and desirable weakening in his devotion to his books, and, at the same time, a gradual awakening to the other attractions of our college life. And as his course went on, this change continued to take place.' Rand was increasingly seen at the rink, where he played hockey, and at receptions and social functions. But he made his name in debates held under the auspices of the Eurhetorian Society.

Organized in 1861, the Eurhetorian Society held its first public debate in Lingley Hall the following year. Members met weekly for debating and public speaking. It was, one commentator observed, 'well fitted to be a preparatory school for those who, in pursuing a course of study, look forward to forum, bench, or pulpit as the future scene of their labors.'[13] Three years before Rand arrived, intercollegiate debating was introduced and became an important means of maintaining Mount Allison's honour. There Rand played a major role. He signed up in the fall of his second year, and was immediately elected treasurer. The following March, Mount Allison met its archrival, Acadia, at the university's imposing college hall in Wolfville. The attorney general of Nova Scotia, a judge of Nova Scotia's Supreme Court, and the local post office inspector were the judges. The subject under debate was that old bugbear: 'Resolved: That legislative union of the Maritime provinces on terms alike equitable and agreeable to the provinces concerned would be advantageous.'

Mount Allison spoke for the affirmative, and its team leader, J. Norman Ritchey, opened the discussion with the observation that there was strength in numbers and that the three Maritime provinces made a natural territorial unit. The people, he said, were alike in racial characteristics and traditions, they shared similarities of interest, and union would bring about a better commercial climate and achieve economies of scale in administration, particularly in education. Ritchey, the *Argosy* later reported, gave a speech that was methodical and well delivered.[14] Responding to Mount Allison's first speaker was A. Burpee Balcom, who opened the discussion by maintaining that there was a limit to the size of the provinces and that there was nothing wrong with the status quo. Moreover, he observed, the provinces and their peoples saw themselves as different and were best equipped to deal with local issues themselves. Balcom's voice and complete self control roused the audience to rapt attention. Then it was Rand's turn to talk.

Under the present administration, Rand observed, we pay large salaries to three lieutenant governors, three premiers, three attorneys general, and so on. Union would reduce government and rationalize it. There would be greater efficiency in the result. 'Mr. Rand had a fine platform appearance, phenomenal control of a difficult speech, and a compelling and effective delivery,' the *Argosy* reported. Then James M. Shortliffe rose to answer Rand. The provinces had different laws, he argued, laws that varied because of local conditions and different notions of the people being governed. Not only did this make sense, but it followed the constitutional scheme set out in the *British North America Act*, whereby the provinces were charged with legislative authority over local matters and the common interests were within the purview of the federal government. Shortliffe's speech was, according to the *Argosy*, 'full of logic and especially forceful in the closing.' After more speakers and further rebuttals, it was decision time: Acadia won. But a good time was had by all, and the winners entertained the judges and the visitors at a banquet at the Acadia Villa Hotel.

The next academic year it was Mount Allison's turn to play host, and the debating partner this time around was King's College. Rand was no longer on the executive of the Eurhetorian Society – he was now business manager of the *Argosy* – but he was chosen leader of the Mount Allison team. Assigned the negative, Mount Allison's debaters had to refute the resolution: 'It would be in the interests of the Maritime provinces to secede from the Dominion of Canada.'

On Friday, 27 March 1908, the crowds began to gather at Mount Allison's Lingley Hall. William Morley Tweedie, an English professor who had taken a real interest in Rand and his career, was in the chair. King's got to go first, and J.F. Tupper led off. There were, he argued, no natural trade relations between the Maritimes and Upper Canada. That being the case, better transportation arrangements would not lead to increased trade. Confederation, he continued, created an un natural connection, one that, in practice, was depriving the Maritime provinces of their fair share of the spoils. Secession could change that. We would, he said, enjoy all that we presently enjoy except our grievances and high taxes. 'Mr. Tupper's address,' the *Argosy* reported, 'was well arranged and clearly delivered and he proved perhaps the most convincing speaker of the affirmative.'[15]

Tupper was clearly a hard act to follow, but Rand appealed to reason. We can't afford it, he explained, pointing out that if the provinces separated from Canada, they would be unable to sustain their financial obligations except through deficit financing. Is that, he asked, what the people want? The answer was obvious, and Rand gave it: no. He showed, the *Argosy* reported, remarkable control of very difficult subject matter, and he built up a strong argument.

The King's College team harkened back to the good old days before Confederation, while speakers for Mount Allison asked who would buy Maritime goods if not fellow Canadians – certainly not the Americans. Outside Canada, the provinces of Nova Scotia, New Brunswick, and Prince Edward Island would be a small and insignificant part of an empire with no real power, quite unlike the influence they could exercise as part of a strong and united dominion. Rand closed the debate for his side, arguing that the affirmative had failed to prove that the Maritime provinces would be better off going it alone. They might well not be receiving all that was their due, but that was a different question and for another day. The issue before us, he said, was whether we should leave Canada, and those who proposed that we should had failed to advance any facts, only abstractions, in support of their submissions. 'Our duty,' Rand argued, 'was with Canada.'

On home turf, with a favourable crowd, Mount Allison won the debate, but only by a whisker. The debaters and honourees were then guests of the Eurhetorian Society at a Sackville restaurant. After 'full justice' was done to the meal, several non-alcoholic toasts were exchanged. The gathering broke up at 'the mystic hour of one a.m.,' with all joining together to sing 'Auld Lang Syne.'

That semester Rand also participated in the mock parliament put on by the Eurhetorian Society. He was a member of the Liberal Party, bringing in a heavily criticized budget in the second session. Politics obviously attracted him, and in the *Argosy* he set out some of his views on reform of the upper chamber: The Senate, he observed, serves no useful purpose. If it was to be retained, senators should be elected and limited to a term of office of eight years or two general elections: 'Such a Senate, truly representing the highest intelligence of the people of Canada, removed as far as may be from partisanship and the cry of the demagogue, closely in touch with local interests and national affairs, is in all respects fitted to perform the functions of an Upper House and to exercise a real and guiding hand in moulding the Canada to be.'[16]

Rand's transformation from bookworm to a man of prominence on the campus was in part due to the fact that, in his second year, he switched to Arts from Engineering. Rand did not care much for forging, a mandatory course, and he decided that he would rather work with words than with metal. This other program of study opened up a new world and expanded his horizons. He became an associate editor of the *Argosy* and, in his final year, 1908–9, served as president of the Eurhetorian Society. Under his leadership, more than forty new members were elected, and he directed a program of interclass debates as well as the usual intercollegiate debate. That year, Mount Allison squared off against the University of New Brunswick in Fredericton with a topic that flowed naturally from the previous year's debate: 'Resolved: That free trade with the United States in coal and lumber would be profitable to Canada.' Mount Allison was assigned the affirmative, and Rand again took the lead.

The debate was presided over by the lieutenant governor of New Brunswick and attracted a large crowd. Rand characteristically appealed to facts and logic in advancing the case that free trade made sense and that Canadian producers would do just fine if allowed free access to American consumers. But what of the political consequences? Mr Orchard of UNB argued that selling renewable resources such as trees was not necessarily a good thing, and selling non-renewable staples such as coal was not wise – it should be preserved for Canadians. But, even more important, he stated, free trade would merge the Canadian and the American economy together, imposing a host of new problems on us. Mount Allison debaters ridiculed the notion of a Canada without trees, while UNB speakers suggested that Canada should sell manufactured goods instead of just the raw materials to make them. The heart of the debate, though, could be found in the remarks of Rand and Orchard. Was free trade good for Canada or bad? Would it make Canada more of a country or less? Rand argued that, at the end of the day, protective tariffs could not work. He even took the debate further than the resolution under discussion, arguing in favour of removing all tariff restrictions in order to give Canada a strong and healthy economic base.

It was not a popular argument, but it was persuasive and it carried the day. Mount Allison won the debate, and Rand was its hero. As his university career came to a close in the spring of 1909, he was elected valedictorian of his class and, with Elaine Borden of the ladies' college, assisted by the university president and his wife, hosted the annual 'at home' – a most important social event that was attended by more than 600 students, professors, and alumni. Although a star, Rand's social skills still left something to be desired. 'His history,' the *Argosy* wrote in his graduating class profile, 'is mainly that of a crusader against all that, to his searching glance, appeared counterfeit or insincere. Armed with unsparing sarcasm, his Excalibur, he ranged through all our college world, while dealing everywhere the same deep-cutting blows ... there was no word more frequently upon his lips than the word "inconsistency."'[17] Rand was no easier on himself, confiding to his diary, 'honour lies in making others happy (which I don't practice much). Am able to see myself ... always criticizing ... consider myself a first class ass.'[18]

Rand's valedictory address, pure Allisonian Methodism, embodied much that he had learned and much of what he was to become:

The honesty, the courtesy, the dignity, the flush of modesty, the purity of thought, these are characteristics which are not the exclusive property of the possessor. To the extent that we recognize them in others and make them our own, we become possessors of each other. To these and such as these, let us pay homage; they are the best things in the world; they point out the drift and tendency of things; and we should seize them. It is only on the basis of a common attitude towards them that we can meet in friendship. To this common attitude, independence is essential; without it we are chasing shadows, and it is the recognition of these truths and loyalty to them; it is such a triumph of principle that brings satisfaction; nothing else can. As we go out let us take as a working principle, do the duty that lies nearest you – and let it be done honestly and thoroughly. If we do this, perhaps our living here will not be altogether vain.

As Ivan Rand's career was just beginning, his father's was coming to an end. In January 1909, after fifty years on the job, Nelson Rand retired from the railway. There was a ceremony, with many fine speeches, after which his men presented him with 'a purse' in recognition of his long and exemplary service to them and to the railway. In reply, he said that he was most proud to be able to say that, during this long period, he had not had one single employee hurt through his neglect and not one explosion. Moreover, he had 'a clean sheet since entering the service – never an hour's suspension or fined 10¢.' It had been, he concluded, a 'busy and hard life,' but one 'filled with friends and with thanks.'[19] Two years later Nelson Rand ran for alderman in Moncton's Ward 3 and was elected at the head of the poll. It was not a surprising result, as he was popular with the men. He died on 6 August 1912, one of 'Moncton's oldest and most highly respected citizens.'[20]

Ivan Rand would later recall his time at Mount Allison as the university's 'golden age.'[21] It was also his own. After briefly 'reading law' in the office of a prominent Moncton barrister, Robert W. Hewson, KC,[22] Rand left for Harvard Law School, preparing for what the

Argosy accurately predicted 'will assuredly be an unusually brilliant career.'[23]

Rand did not have to go to Harvard to study law: he could have continued to work in Hewson's office, attending occasional evening lectures by leading practitioners and eventually being called to the bar. He could have attended the Saint John Law School, which had been founded in 1892, but Rand quickly ruled that option out. 'Until the 1920s,' critics said, 'it was easier to become a student-at-law – and hence gain admission to the Saint John Law School – than it was to get a high school diploma.'[24] He could also have enrolled at Dalhousie Law School, which was a real law school at a university, with a library, a faculty, and a dean. But Harvard Law School, established in 1817, was, by the time Rand enrolled, the best law school in the United States if not the world. It attracted the best faculty and boasted about seven hundred students, all of whom had to be university graduates to be admitted. In September 1909 Rand was one of three Canadians in his class: he was joined by New Brunswicker Frederick Charles Squires and Nova Scotian James Henry Fraser.[25]

Rand, like all incoming students, registered for his first year in residence. In his second year, however, he would take a room at 12 Oxford Street, which was also the home of the Canadian Club. The law school estimated that rent and care of a furnished room cost between $40 and $150 per academic year. Board for thirty-eight weeks ran between $133 and $266, 'fuel and lights' between $11 and $25, and textbooks between $25 and $35. Tuition was $150 each year. Although good cheap meals could be had at Memorial Hall, Rand had barely enough money to survive, and his main daily meal was a bowl of soup – the crackers were free! Back home in Moncton, the Rands put a mortgage on their house and took in roomers to help pay his way, and Clifford Robinson also lent a financial hand.[26]

To prepare for his new life as a law student, over the summer of 1909 Rand read Blackstone's *Commentaries on the Laws of England* several times, and learned that English common law was more than a collection of disjointed rules. Rather, Blackstone argued, the law was a rational and coherent whole that was best studied in an academic institution: 'Law can be systematically taught, not merely as a body of practical rules, but as a science; as a science, law can be taught only in a university setting surrounded by teachers and students of the other sciences.'[27]

At Harvard, Rand quickly realized that, while some straight lecturing was inevitable to provide information, context, and structure, the students there spent most of their time not simply memorizing rules but figuring out how to find them. The case method was primarily about digging and depth. Law, under this case method, was thought of as a science. The law students were the practitioners, the law library their laboratory. Classroom work consisted of Rand and the other men analyzing mostly appellate decisions in response to questions from the professor – questions directed at exposing the steady evolution of the law through the study of precedents and developing the students' power of reasoning. Through this 'Socratic method,' the cases making up the common law were identified, penetrated, and distilled. The faculty was not large, but from their first day at Harvard Law School, Rand and his classmates were exposed to powerful and brilliant academic legal minds.

Edward H. Warren, Rand's property law instructor, explained the system on the first day of class, and Rand recorded it in his notes: 'Make abstracts of cases. State facts in few words and decisions. Read case through hurriedly. Get atmosphere. Find out points. Read facts very carefully. Write down essentials. Read third time. Read their opinions carefully. Put down decision and reasoning necessary to decision. Put down dicta. Then ask: Do I agree? Examine carefully and put down ... 1. Facts. 2. Decision and Reasoning. 3. Dicta. 4. Own views. Write out summary of each subject: 1. What is the existing state of the authorities? 2. What, in principle, do you think the law ought to be?'[28] In property law, Warren observed, the central question was what rights does the law permit in situations of less than absolute ownership? And how does the legal system afford protection to those rights? In criminal law, Joseph H. Beale described how to brief cases, and then went on to explain on the first day of class that 'nothing can happen ... which is not either according to law or contrary to law.' 'Law is practical,' Rand wrote on the first page of his contract law notebook, 'therefore changes must be adapted to conditions. Practically no contract law in the Anglo-Saxon period due to no commercial engagements. Credit system requires power to enforce obligations. In early periods there were assuredly sales by exchange: but this is not really a contract. Buying a cigar for cash is really an exchange. No obligation on either side.' The modern way of life, however, required a mechanism for the enforcement of promises, and that is what this contract class was to be all about.[29] Rand's excitement, his zeal for hard work, and his sense of embarking on a voyage of discovery were all conveyed in his Harvard notebooks. And he would maintain this habit of recording his thoughts for the rest of his life.

In addition to the mainstays of criminal law, property, contracts, and torts, Rand also had several hours of agency and civil procedure every week. In his second year, he had bills of exchange, promissory notes, and equity with the famous Professor Roscoe Pound, a Harvard Law School dropout with a doctoral degree in botany from the University of Nebraska. One of Pound's best-known essays, 'Liberty of Contract,' made the case against dogmatic interpretations of the Constitution, insisting that consideration be given to the practical effect of those decisions on daily life. At the time, the idea that the law should serve people was not commonly accepted. There were also classes on insurance, advanced property, public service companies (especially common carriers), sale of personal property, and damages and the law of persons. In his third year Rand studied conflict of laws, constitutional law, corporations, equity and quasi-contracts, partnership, more property, suretyship and mortgages, trusts, bankruptcy, and municipal corporations. Ezra Ripley Thayer, a perfectionist who taught Rand evidence, succeeded the scholarly James Barr Ames as dean in 1910. The course of study, including optional courses, was designed 'to afford such training in the fundamental principles of English and American law as will constitute the best preparation for the practice of the profession in any place where that system of law prevails.'[30]

Like all Harvard men, Rand took his studies very seriously. He had to. Although anyone with an undergraduate degree could enroll in first-year Harvard Law, provided the degree came from a respectable school, a 'gentleman's C' could not keep you there. At the end of each year, the school's professors graded the 'blue books' – the four-hour examinations worth fully 100 per cent of the final mark in each subject. These books were assessed anonymously, and when the results were posted, a third of the class could be let go. One professor compared the system to the pioneer men and women who set out in wagon trains to settle the Far West: 'The cowards never started, and the weak died on the way.'[31] Second year was less of an ordeal, but there was additional wastage there too. Students were assigned seats and were expected to be prepared, to have read the cases in advance and to respond when called on in class to recite the facts, principle, and holding. Rand focused almost entirely on his studies. He made no contributions to the *Harvard Law Review* in his three years on campus, though he did attend meetings of the Law Club. His marks were good, but he was nowhere near the head of his class. He obtained a 76 per cent average in his first year, 73 per cent in his second, and 78 per cent in his final year, graduating *cum laude*. His graduation photograph shows a handsome, determined young man with two things on his mind: a call to the New Brunswick bar and marriage.

American Ivy League schools have a way of creating lasting impressions, and Rand never forgot his Harvard roots: 'I had been one of the most favoured persons on earth to have been privileged to spend three years in such a surrounding and atmosphere. When one thinks about it, what an insignificant percentage of this world's population ever do enjoy such a privilege?'[32] Undoubtedly, Rand's time at Harvard was deeply formative, inculcating in him a specific way of looking at the world. After graduation, he returned to Moncton and was admitted to the New Brunswick bar on 12 November 1912. It was time to get to work: he was now twenty-eight years old.

Rand moved to Regina. There he was admitted to the Saskatchewan bar on 20 December 1912, though he did not remain in the prairie capital for very long. 'I was in Saskatchewan only a month and a half,' he wrote at the time.[33] After that he went further west to Medicine Hat. Gainfully employed there, he could carry through on his second goal: getting married.

Five foot five with dark hair and unusually large hazel eyes, the striking Iredell (Dell) Baxter was a doctor's daughter from New Brunswick who was studying at the New England Conservatory of Music. It was music that brought them together. They met at Harvard's Canadian Club, and they soon discovered that they both loved to play the piano. Even though Rand was broke all through his years at Harvard Law School, he knew he had something better than money and the opportunities it provides: Iredell.

Dell had been born on 15 October 1881, the granddaughter on her mother's side of James McAllister, a cashier of the Westmorland Bank; her other grandfather was the Reverend John I. Baxter. She was the daughter of Dr Robert Gordon Baxter and his wife, Jean, of Moncton. Dell, like Ivan, was an Aberdeen High School graduate but had matriculated two years earlier than he. She even gave him the pen he used when he asked her to marry him. As she wrote at the time she made the gift,

It seems to me that you said once that you found it difficult, or a tremendous nuisance, or some such thing, to write down all you knew: we are referring to examinations etc, of course. I hope you will take up this pen often and find it a help in transferring more easily your vast knowledge to paper. There are several injunctions I would give you. Firstly, be very careful how you begin with this pen, for it is bewitched and will only write one thing ... I know because I've tried it. Secondly, if it does not exactly suit your hand, you are to please exchange it till you get one that does. Thirdly, if you already have a fountain pen, you must throw it away – the other one, I mean.[34]

Ivan knew exactly what to write with his new pen. Dell had taken a teaching post in South Carolina, so in his letter he began by listing her fine qualities. He then turned in a lawyerly way to make the case for himself:

Let me see: tall, thin, fair, awkward, rather slouchy, lazy, dislikes companies and crowds, a conceited air about him, inclined to be honest but quite capable of humbug ... likes music, a taste for literature, inclined to envy men and chafes under subordination or restraint, has enough philosophy and ability to see somewhat below the surface of things but not enough for a strong faith – oh, he has a thousand such ordinary qualities which I won't enumerate but which make me wonder how he could so get the start of this majestic world to hold your hand alone. I'll admit this; I think he loves you – but who wouldn't? or couldn't?

... What I want most to tell you is this: What you should require of him from your first day together till the last. In the first place, you will have to remember that he has all the faults of men, or at least the most of them. He is inclined to be selfish – he must not be so toward you. Should he ever lapse into that state and forget that you are a sweetheart, and not a means for his entertainment, just take out one of his effusive offerings – written during these past years – and ask him if he meant what he said or was merely frothing as other fools have done since the beginning of the world. Just let him understand that it is for him to give to you all that lies within his power to give – that his purpose should be to offer a life as nearly as possible complementary to that of yours in which you find the full expression of your rich nature.

In the next place, never let him forget the respect he owes to you. Almost every man has, at times, a tendency to treat women as 'adjuncts' – though perhaps he has never done so with you; but no person has a right so to treat another. Do not be afraid of hurting his vanity – I fancy he has had it pummeled rather thoroughly in his time and he is perhaps capable of being rational.

He will have promised to love you always. Now if he should do this, he will give to you the courtesy and chivalry he now gives, as to the first girl in all the world: the best things in literature will he share and enjoy with you; flowers too, will he bring, roses and mayflowers and violets which you love; his hours will he give to you, all of them, as well when working as when not; his best efforts will be made for you – he should give some accomplishment for the privilege which is his, or at least he should try; and then he should love you, only you, tenderly, deeply, should be happy in your happiness and darkened in your pain, should ask only for the kiss and the hand of his sweetheart. For him, home and to you should be the first thought after each day with the world and there he should find the sweetest delight in life. Must go to a club for entertainment? Let him stay with his sweetheart – she can supply him with all the intellectual strength and keenness he will have need for, and with a sparkling clearness he should be glad to enjoy ...

You wonder why I have written so much tonight, a great deal of which you may consider dull. Well, I'll tell you. I just think you are too exquisite a girl to be treated other than as a queen ... Take this as my last word. You are a girl of strength and beauty; it is his duty, as it should be his supreme happiness, to love and cherish you through life as he has loved you during these few years.[35]

Rand had only one hurdle standing in the way of marriage to Iredell: his prospective mother-in-law, who he thought might object to his working-class roots. But Rand soon turned Jean Baxter around: 'You are quite right in supposing that my little girl is very dear to me,' she wrote. 'For a long time I felt as if I was losing my last treasure, and I suppose on that account I failed to be very enthusiastic about this arrangement. But now I will say "willingly and sincerely" that I am glad to know Dell has such a good friend – even if he does happen to be a Liberal.' Jean was concerned about their plans to move west. It was not, she wrote, 'what I would have wished, but since that cannot be helped I shall say no more about it.'[36] The couple were married on Friday, 3 October 1913, at the historic Old South Church in Boston. Dell then returned with Ivan to Medicine Hat.

It was the place to be, some said. The *Medicine Hat News* certainly thought so, predicting that 'Medicine Hat will shortly take its place amongst the greatest and possibly largest cities in the North American Continent.'[37] The optimism was not entirely unfounded, for Alberta – a province only since 1905 – was, like much of Canada, experiencing a boom. Medicine Hat was doubly blessed because it was also located on a huge field of natural gas.

The discovery was accidental. Water was what was wanted, but systematic drilling discovered an unparalleled reservoir of natural gas. The gas was used for street lighting – lights that were kept on day and night because it was cheaper to leave them burning than to hire a man to turn them on and off. When Rudyard Kipling visited the city, these constantly burning gas lights led him to observe that it was a town 'born lucky' but that it had 'all hell for a basement.' It was a small price to pay. Pottery and brick manufacturers were the first to take advantage of the low-cost fuel, followed by milling interests turning out flour, cereals, and animal feed from the locally abundant high-quality grain.

Some of the key ingredients for a metropolitan centre were there. Medicine Hat was close, by Canadian standards, to Calgary; closer still to the United States; and midway between Winnipeg and Vancouver. It was also an important divisional point for both the CPR's main line and its Crow's Nest line. There was talk around town that the CPR had chosen 'the Hat' for its brand new maintenance shop. Looking ahead, obviously attracted by the region's economic prospects, the Canadian Northern Railway purchased a station site and right of way. The climate could not be described as good, but the city was surrounded by fertile farmlands and prosperous ranches. The site, on the banks of the South Saskatchewan River, was an attractive one. But it was the inexpensive energy that promised a bright future for Medicine Hat – a promise that would not be kept. When Rand moved to town, Medicine Hat and Alberta were actually coming to the end of an economic cycle with a long period of little or even negative growth.

No one knows when one economic cycle is going to end and another begin, and few could have predicted the outbreak of war and the impact it would have on industrial development. In early 1913 all the evidence suggested continued prosperity. Rand was among the almost one million newcomers to the Prairie West in the first dozen years of the twentieth century, as new towns emerged out of nowhere and existing ones, like Medicine Hat, grew at a phenomenal rate. In the twelve months before he arrived, sixteen new companies, employing more than one thousand men, had set up shop in the small city, and negotiations were under way with dozens of other manufacturers from across Canada, the United States, and Great Britain. Indeed, some real estate promoters laid out a town site on the outskirts, advertising it widely and offering almost free gas.[38] New businesses were promised free land, free gas, free water, a spur line, and electricity at cost. 'Give it away for nothing and they will come,' claimed the two industrial commissioners who had been hired to spread the word. 'Hatters,' the *Medicine Hat News* confidently predicted, could expect continued growth: 'In place of our thousands, we are going to have hundreds of thousands.'[39]

Medicine Hat rejoiced in its success. The local paper, a key civic booster, regularly trumpeted the increase in building permits and, in terms of percentage, compared it with that in other Canadian cities. Medicine Hat always came out near the top, though when actual expenditures were examined, the city came out closer to the bottom. The Board of Trade was a veritable propaganda machine, setting new standards in its use of superlatives. In 1913 it distributed 40,000 pamphlets and folders, 16,000 copies of the *Medicine Hat Manufacturer*, and 10,000 envelope slips, all extolling the virtues of the Hat, along with 200,000 gummed letter seals adorned with a drawing of a flaming gas well. There was a kind of mindlessness to the hoopla. Nevertheless, even after the Rands arrived, the population continued to grow. By the end of 1913, approximately 15,000 people called a bursting Medicine Hat home, many of whom lived in a tent city hastily erected on the north side of town.

New schools were planned and built; a new water system with the capacity to serve a city of 50,000 was constructed; and the 'finest' telephone service in Canada was installed, with poles kept off the main street and a telephone immediately available to anyone who wanted one. City Council hired a 'traffic officer' for the first time, and a constant stream of by-laws regulating social life crowded its agenda. To be sure, the growth created social problems – the prosperous times, the *Medicine Hat News* reported, has attracted 'a rough and undesirable element.' There was also an increase in public intoxication and street fighting. Nevertheless, looking at Medicine Hat as Rand would first have seen it, it appeared to be a city about to take off. For a young man with debts to pay and a career to build, going west made sense. Rumours that New Brunswick native and international financier Sir Max Aitken, later Lord Beaverbrook, had bought property in the area were confirmed, driving already inflated real estate prices even higher. All in all, Medicine Hat was the perfect place for a young lawyer starting out. Economic activity attracts lawyers, lots of them. And between 1908 and 1912, the Alberta bar more than doubled in size.[40]

Rand joined two other young lawyers, Lorne Nelson Laidlaw and Charles Henry Stewart Blanchard, in the practice of law. Born in

Kitchener, Ontario, in 1882, Laidlaw had trained in law in Manitoba before making his way to Medicine Hat around 1911. He was, reputedly, a fabulous hockey player. Blanchard, a renowned practical joker, though born in Winnipeg in 1885, had been educated at Upper Canada College in Toronto and then at McGill University in Montreal. He was also a newcomer to Medicine Hat, arriving the same year as Rand. In light of the reciprocal rule with the Law Society of Saskatchewan, Rand was admitted to the practice of law in Alberta simply by paying a $310 fee. As soon as he was sworn in, the firm changed its name to Laidlaw, Blanchard & Rand. The three men set up shop in the downtown Merchant's Bank Building. Rand soon developed an eclectic practice of small-town fare.

One day he represented a man charged with maiming cattle. The next, he was acting on behalf of the owner of three horses and a colt that had wandered over to a neighbour's property and so gorged themselves on his wheat that they died.[41] On another occasion, he was acting for management in a very small wrongful dismissal claim, and the day after that for the defendant in a real estate deal gone bad (there were many of those once the economy declined and purchasers desperately sought reasons not to close). Rand also represented plaintiffs and defendants in wrongful death suits, sometimes he initiated actions to obtain insurance proceeds in cases of suspicious fires and other times defended against them, and he also acted in claims for damages brought by wronged husbands in cases of 'criminal conversation.' The wife's consent was no defence for the accused, for a wife, regarded as the chattel or property of her husband, could not consent to her own adultery.[42] Plaintiffs, defendants, it did not really matter – Rand represented just about anyone who came through the door, although, over the years, he received an increasing amount of upper-end work. He acted for retail merchants before a provincial commission studying the operation of the *Factory Act* and, occasionally, took on criminal work, though that was mostly done by his partner Blanchard.

There were some relatively big cases, especially after the City of Medicine Hat became his client. Rand's first action on behalf of the municipality arose when the city found itself on the wrong side of a lawsuit filed by the former mayor. F.G. Forster was asking for $2,500 in damages, claiming that the city, when it re-graded the road in front of his house, had wrecked his front yard – 'previously one of the prettiest houses in town' – and made it difficult to get from the street to the house. Forster testified that he was ashamed of his residence, had moved out, and could not obtain a decent rent. When the city witnesses testified, however, they stated that the improvements to the road increased the value of the ex-mayor's house and that he, like many of his neighbours, could simply build a retaining wall at his own expense. Rand won the case. The judgment noted that the former mayor had been in office when the by-law was passed providing for the re-grading and that it had received his full consent.[43]

The law firm was doing well and added two more men on staff. Other city cases followed, but that did not stop Rand from acting for clients who needed something from the city. In early July 1916 he represented a group of hotel proprietors seeking concessions from City Council. Their bars had just been put out of business by prohibition and their very survival, Rand told the city councillors, depended on local tax breaks and free gas, water, and electric lights. Good hotels, he continued, were essential to the economic well-being of the city. The city had previously offered economic inducements to all sorts of other industries. All the hotels wanted was 'serious consideration' of 'a fair request.' The request was referred to a committee for study after the mayor observed that tax cuts were out of the question, although 'the matter of fuel could ... have the consideration of the council.'[44] The prospect of free fuel proved enticing; the day after Rand's presentation to City Council, the city solicitor received a request for equal treatment from the boarding-house keepers.

Obviously concerned about establishing a precedent, City Council rejected Rand's request. The hotels fought back. After not getting the concessions they believed they deserved, the hotels flexed their economic muscle at the end of July and decided to go on strike. 'Hotels will close doors on Saturday,' was the headline in the paper, with the hoteliers promising that it was no 'bluff.' It was not just guests, they pointed out, who benefited from access to good hotels with fine up-to-date dining rooms but local residents as well, and the demand for free energy was entirely justified. The strike worked. City Council capitulated, dropping the water rate immediately and putting a further reduction on electricity costs to a municipal plebiscite (natural gas was already almost free). The hotels then reopened their doors and business returned to normal. There was no secret to Rand's method: 'I am often reminded of a line in Emerson to the effect that everything made by God has a crack,' he said. 'When you tackle a problem you must look for the crack.'[45]

The twenty or so lawyers in town would, when required, square off against each other, but they also socialized together. Two local lawyers, Gordon Fraser and Norman McLarty, became Rand's life-long friends. After the Medicine Hat Bar Association was established in 1913, there were dinners at the Assiniboia Hotel. 'The members ... had a royal time last evening ... Mr. Rand proposed the toast,' the local newspaper reported on one such occasion.[46] Rand also played tennis on the clay courts along the Saskatchewan River. Most social events, however, took place in private homes, though the Rands never seem to have entertained. At Blanchard's surprise birthday party in April 1915, 'Mr. Rand gave special pleasure with his piano selections.'[47] In mind-numbing detail, the paper recorded everyone's comings and goings: 'Mr. I.C. Rand, barrister, returned yesterday from Calgary' or from Edmonton or from summer vacation. The birth of Rand's sons – Robert, nine months and one week after the wedding, and then Charles – made the newspaper. The family returned home to New Brunswick every summer, often for several months at a time: 'Mrs. I.C. Rand, with small sons, Bobbie and Charles, left last night for an extended visit to her old home in Moncton, N.B. Mrs. Rand has taken a cottage at Shediac for the summer months.' They regularly made it back east for Christmas too.[48]

Whether it was serving as a judge when Alexandra High School debaters fought the competition or speaking on behalf of the local YMCA, Rand became part and parcel of the local life of Medicine Hat. He participated in the annual corn feed and played the piano at events organized by the Cypress Club. At the same time, he was a person apart, always keeping a distance. According to local gossip, 'when Rand would go down the street in Medicine Hat, no one would do any more than nod to him.'[49] The odd star would pass through town – Charlie Chaplin gave several performances at the Monarch Theatre in August 1915 – and on these occasions the local gentry generally turned out. Before long, however, there was no difficulty in getting tickets. Medicine Hat was in trouble.

The city had simply stopped growing. The CPR's decision to locate its shops in Calgary, not Medicine Hat, was the first blow. Long-standing rumours that Medicine Hat was at the top of the list, compounded by wishful thinking, had fuelled land speculators and driven prices up substantially. The market quickly corrected, and land prices, despite all the inducements offered to residential and industrial purchasers, rapidly declined – with much attendant litigation.[50] In one important case, Rand realized that the vendor had promised to convey land for a proposed subdivision without 'encumbrance.' His client, wishing to avoid the transaction because real estate prices had fallen so badly, instructed Rand to get him out of the deal. Rand, searching the title, discovered that the promise could not be fulfilled because the coal rights attached to the land belonged to someone else. The vendor sued and, initially, won, the trial judge having determined that neither party cared about coal rights. The only thing they really did care about was 'flipping' the land and profiting by it. Rand appealed.

'We have here,' Mr Justice Stuart of the Alberta Court of Appeal wrote, 'another example of the common case of the purchaser of real estate at a highly inflated price during the boom times becoming unable, due to the collapse of the boom, to meet the enormous obligations which the vendor has, in the midst of the boom, secured from him, and then seeking to escape from them by means of a point of law which he would no doubt have overlooked if the boom had continued.' It was also true that both the vendor and the purchaser had engaged in a similar enterprise: 'The parties were both in the same game – speculating in real estate and doing no useful service to the community.' Rand's client offered to settle: In return for dropping the claim, the purchaser would let the vendor keep the land and the deposit, some $12,000 on a $50,000 deal. The vendor, foolishly, rejected the offer. In the aftermath of the action being commenced, the vendor had acquired the mineral rights and so was now in a position to convey the land as originally promised. But it was too late: 'When the defendant discovered that the plaintiff's title was subject to a reservation of all coal, what were his legal rights? Had he not a right to assume *then* that there really was coal in existence which had been reserved and to repudiate the contract because the plaintiff could not give him what he had contracted to give?' The answer to that question was yes. In the result, Rand got his clients the $12,000 they had been prepared to leave on the table to get out of the deal gone bad. They were not the only ones seeking to escape transactions made improvident by the passage of time, but they were among the fortunate ones, beneficiaries of an approach Rand successfully deployed on several occasions in a town that had run out of luck.[51]

In 1915 the population of Medicine Hat had dropped to a little less than 9,000, barely more than what it had been when the Rands arrived two years earlier. Almost none of the development earlier prophesied had occurred; there were almost no new businesses coming to town, and many had departed, leaving the city with a large inventory of serviced land – the land earlier purchased, improved, and offered as inducements to attract industry. The city planners had grossly overestimated future needs: Medicine Hat had utilities for four times its population. It had hundreds of vacant buildings, thousands of vacant lots, perhaps 400 men unemployed, hundreds of thousands of dollars in tax arrears, and a city debt approaching $4 million and growing daily. One fight over taxes took Rand for the first time, in 1916, to the Supreme Court of Canada.[52]

City Council, unable to sell municipal debentures and finding it hard to meet its ongoing obligations, belatedly decided to retrench. But it was too little and too late. 'A movement began to stop paying taxes and to let the city go bankrupt ... in late 1915 ... a dozen major industries ... were all dead ... and the glass bottle plant was now a stable.'[53] The war relieved the city of some of its unemployed – Alberta had one of the highest enlistment rates in the dominion, and the highest casualty rate. While there were a few lucrative munitions contracts to keep other men, and increasingly women, working, the Hat was still a long way from the front and no one's first choice for military procurement. To make matters even worse, there was a drought. Bumper crops in 1915 and 1916 signalled the end of the good times, not the beginning of an economic recovery. 'Around the Hat it was bone dry for years ... The disaster constituted the worst farm abandonment in Alberta history – over four times that of the same parts during the Great Depression, and worse by far than anywhere else in Canada at the time.'[54]

Things may not have been going well at home, but domestic difficulties paled in comparison to the problems overseas. The war was raging on. The triumph at Vimy Ridge cost dearly: 10,602 casualties, 3,598 of them fatalities In October 1917, 15,654 Canadian troops were left dead or wounded on the bleak, waterlogged battlefield at Passchendaele. The allied struggle was a crusade for freedom and, at its end, more than 60,000 Canadian soldiers were left dead. It was impossible not to have a point of view about the war, and in December 1917, just before the general election, Rand spoke at a rally in favour of union government – the coalition government proposed by Prime Minister Robert Borden for the duration of the war which would include both Liberal and independent representatives.[55]

The principle of union government had been accepted by all Canadians, Rand began his address to a packed house in an election eve rally, and the onus was on its opponents to establish that it was not in the national interest. He ridiculed Liberal leader Wilfrid Laurier's statement that union government was actually Tory government camouflaged with a Liberal veneer, noting that a significant number of prominent and able Liberals had signed on. They had done that, Rand alleged, because of their honest desire to work in the best interests of the dominion.

Rand then touched briefly on the matter of Quebec: 'If we can't take any action except to the satisfaction of Quebec, then the sooner we know it the better.' It was a fair point. The more critical matter, however, was conscription – the *Military Service Act* of 1917 had been introduced in the House of Commons the previous June, providing for compulsory military service and setting off a firestorm of protest in Quebec. Rand was in favour – for others, that is. His younger brother served in the artillery and was wounded in battle. But, at least according to one account, Rand believed that he could 'serve his country better in the courtrooms of Medicine Hat than in the trenches of France.'[56] He had turned thirty in 1914, was married with two children, and was well down on the list to be called up for military service. Nevertheless, many men his age and older, with wives, families, businesses, and professions, did sign up. Rand's reason for not enlisting is unpersuasive.

Conscription, he explained in his speech, was all about applying scientific methods to the prosecution of war. 'It is absurd to suppose that those methods should be used by autocratic Germany, and that democratic Canadians should be too stupid to avail themselves of the scientific principles of placing the manpower of the Dominion in the situations where the object in view could be best obtained: winning the war.' They say, Rand thundered, obviously gaining momentum, 'it is not democratic, but are we in this war for pleasure? The fundamental obligation under law is that, when the state is in danger, every member should place his services, and if necessary, give his life in its defence. If we enjoy the privileges and liberty, we must also assume our responsibilities in connection with it.' The audience, the *Medicine Hat News* reported, 'seemed to be satisfied with Mr. Rand's presentation of the case for unionism.' Well satisfied, in fact. Medicine Hat returned A.L. Sifton, the minister of customs, to office with a large majority. The government of Robert Borden was victorious.

The war had done little economically for Medicine Hat, and neither did peace. Returning military men swelled the ranks of the unemployed. City Council had not yet pulled itself out of debt. The people of Medicine Hat would suffer for years from the foolishness of their civic leaders. There was the odd flurry of economic activity suggesting better times ahead, but it was just more blind boosterism. The crop failures continued. The city was flooded. The water became undrinkable.

Farmers left their farms. Rand's partner Blanchard departed to become a Crown prosecutor in Calgary and, after a time, resumed the private practice of law. Rand's friends McLarty and Fraser moved away. Medicine Hat continued to shrink. 'I came in touch with big thinking, big ideas, in the west,' Rand later recalled, but it became harder and harder to make a living.[57] There was really no reason to stay, and then, suddenly, events back in Moncton gave Rand a reason to return to New Brunswick.

One of Rand's younger sisters, Minnie, killed herself. 'I will try and tell you a little of the awful catastrophe that has come to us,' Daisy wrote her brother in June 1919. 'Minnie, as you know, has been very miserable for weeks ... I may as well tell you, perhaps bluntly, but there is no other way, that Minnie was mentally deranged and took her own life.' There was, Daisy continued, 'no stopping her even though mother watched her constantly.' But it wasn't enough. 'You will wonder and wonder but you will know that we did all that could be done and it was better that Minnie should die as she did ... than living in an institution until the end came. Dr. Bourque said her trouble came on so gradually: we don't know *when or why* it came to her. She had a fear of someone taking her and giving her some awful punishment – and it was when she was suffering from this terrible fear that she made these different attempts on her life.'[58] Daisy had trained as a nurse, but there was nothing that she, or anyone, could do to help. Minnie was undoubtedly suffering from a psychotic depression. Nothing short of constant observation in special psychiatric units can prevent a determined depressed person from committing suicide. Electroconvulsive therapy sometimes helps, but it was not introduced until the 1930s and antidepressants only in the 1950s. Most depressive episodes, even the ones that last years, eventually burn out on their own. Putting Minnie in an asylum had been considered but, unfortunately, ruled out.[59]

It was time to go home. His mother was in Moncton; his brother and two remaining sisters were there, as was his wife's family. In Medicine Hat there was nobody and, increasingly, nothing. With a young family to support, there was, of course, the matter of a job. Rand wrote to Clifford Robinson, the man who had urged him to avoid law and study engineering instead. In the middle of September 1919, Robinson wrote back: 'I think you could safely count on a fair business at Moncton if you come here.' The practice, Robinson said, was 'pretty brisk,' although a few of the younger men were ruining the situation by drawing deeds and other documents at 'bargain prices.' More

important, however, was the prospect of an association: 'I would feel
in favor of coupling our names together if you came here on any fair
and reasonable arrangement.' You would, Robinson continued, have
to do 'practically all of the legal business,' but Robinson promised to
make rain: 'I would be like the commercial traveler and no doubt bring
considerable business to the firm.' I am willing, Robinson concluded,
'to make an arrangement with such a man as yourself. I think Moncton
is a promising location and that the class of business in the future will
be on a little broader scale than it has been in the past. Suppose we
make a try?'[60] Rand replied, yes.

There was another reason too. Dell suffered terribly from hay fever,
and at times was reduced almost to invalid status.[61] 'Owing to Mrs.
I.C. Rand's health being impaired,' the *Medicine Hat News* reported but
gave no details, 'Mr. Rand left last evening to join her at Moncton, N.B.
for an indefinite period of time. It is pleasing to learn that Mr. and Mrs.
Rand expect to eventually return to reside in Medicine Hat.'[62] Intentions change, and the Rands never came back. He filed declarations of
non-practice with the law societies of both Alberta and Saskatchewan
and began his new life back home.

2

The Young Lawyer Tries Politics

Looked at from Medicine Hat, New Brunswick seemed a far better place to be. But appearances were deceiving. In 1920 New Brunswick had about 390,000 people living in a region of fertile valleys, unending forests, and numerous lakes and rivers. The forests were rich in hard and soft woods, the fishery rated second among the province's abundant natural resources, and considerable mineral reserves awaited development. As always, there was the potential of water power. Still, most New Brunswickers continued to earn their livelihood from mixed farming. The province was noticeably agrarian, with more than two-thirds of the population living in rural areas.[1]

For the second time in his adult life, Rand arrived in a town just as the economy was going bad. Income from the forest industry – one of the key sources of provincial revenue – was way down. During the war and for a few years afterwards, provincial coffers were filled by lumber money. The war had created a temporary artificial demand for New Brunswick timber, one that continued briefly after the war through a short-lived construction boom. Beginning about 1921, however, the demand for New Brunswick lumber sharply dropped, and overall provincial revenues from the stumpage fees followed. Regular forest fires, the lack of investment capital, and insect epidemics, particularly the spruce budworm, were just a few of the factors that left the lumber industry reeling and sent it and the province into a steep economic decline. Sawmills closed, and thousands of men were put out of work.[2]

At the same time, demand dropped for nearly every other commodity New Brunswick produced. Fishers were idle. Farmers watched as drought destroyed their crops and, in due course, reduced their livestock. What little industry existed was hammered hard by post-war inflation and rising freight rates. Although New Brunswick had, in 1920, more train track per person than any other province in Canada, the railway, supposedly its saviour, was a key factor in its declining economy. Development of the Intercolonial and other railways destroyed New Brunswick's regional market and helped to create a national Canadian market against which local industry could not compete.[3] Central Canada was clearly advantaged in having the established infrastructure and population base. New Brunswick's share of the industrial spoils began, proportionately, to diminish. Moreover, the ICR had no monopoly on train transportation to the east coast. Rather, it faced competition from the Canadian Pacific and the Grand Trunk railways – companies that, unlike the ICR, had been constructed to make money, and not deliberately built far from the United States border to avoid a short-lived military threat that had long since ceased to exist. The distance between Montreal and Saint John on the CPR's short line, for example, was 775 kilometres, compared with 1,200 kilometres on the ICR.[4]

Simply put, whatever hopes New Brunswick had in 1867 about the economic benefits of Confederation and the prosperity that would arrive by rail, they were dashed. Population growth slowed, and many of the ablest young people were migrating to other parts of Canada and the United States. Manufacturing was in decline, and the economy was in a free fall. Technological changes favoured large-scale plants in areas of high population density, a trend encouraged by the National Policy, which consolidated industry, including American branch plants, in Montreal and Toronto. In addition, cheap ocean freight rates via the Panama Canal now allowed less-expensive Pacific lumber to flood eastern markets.

New Brunswickers believed that freight rates were largely responsible for the province's economic decline. But were they? Soon after Rand arrived back in town he was presented with this question – and, one way or another, it would preoccupy him for a large part of his career.[5]

For almost fifty years after Confederation, freight rates had been kept low in the Maritime provinces. But that situation began to change after 1912, and, throughout the war years, the rates began a steady move upwards – particularly in New Brunswick. Once the war was over and the movement of troops and supplies came to an end, the ICR began to lose money again. The federal government, which paid the freight-rate subsidy out of general revenue, decided to restore 'fiscal responsibility.' There was less money to go around, yet, at the same time, increased public demands for government spending.[6] Social reformers across the country looked to Ottawa to take on a larger social and economic role. Maritimers in general, and New Brunswickers in particular, had a long list of grievances against the federal government – not just rising freight rates – and they funnelled their discontent into the new Maritime Rights Movement.

For the Rands, however, Moncton was home, and they settled in at 62 Botsford Street, the old McAllister residence. Situated directly opposite Saint Bernard's Church, the house had been built in 1860 in the Italianate style. Compared to the rest of the province, Moncton was faring relatively well. On 5 February 1920, Robert Young Eaton, one of the 'worker Eatons,'[7] turned the key of the firm's new mail-order house, a reinforced concrete and brick building employing hundreds of men and women. The railway, however, was still at the hub of the city's economic life, with a blacksmith shop, machine shop, erecting shop, boiler shop, power house, brass-moulding shop, sheet-metal shop, electrical and battery shop, car paint shop, enamel baking room, upholstering room, and freight-car repair shop. The Stores Department was housed in its own two-storey building, and there was even an apprentice instruction school. A new terminal and roundhouse were under construction. In this community of 17,000 people, many derived their livelihood from the ICR.

But the Intercolonial had never paid its own way and, from the start, it was a money pit. Its early history was marred by extraordinarily excessive patronage, outright corruption, and rampant featherbedding – as with all the government-owned railways. Moreover, instead of joining New Brunswick to the rest of Canada, the ICR's long, out-of-the-way route ensured that it would never be an effective link. Rather, its destiny was to deliver people and goods to local stations. Some sort of governmental response was required, and following the requisite royal commission, which, predictably, recommended more governmental action, a number of money-losing heavily subsidized railways were, in 1919, merged into the new government-owned Canadian National Railways, the CNR. In due course, the ICR was added to the mix.[8]

The CNR was a grab bag of 150 mostly derelict, broken down, bankrupt, indebted, or largely out-of-the-way lines, the product of years of unthinking expansion. Instead of following settlement in new areas of the country, the owners of the predecessor companies had tried to anticipate it. Canada's railway mileage was way out of proportion to population. Making matters worse, Canada had, in addition, an established internal system of water transportation. There was barely enough traffic to support one national railway, much less two. The CNR was now expected to compete against the CPR, which was everything the Crown corporation was not: efficient and profitable. The CNR attracted capital only because its bonds carried a government guarantee and its deficits were routinely added to the national debt. Some sort of drastic action was called for, and that meant new leadership at the top.

Placed in charge of the company in 1922 was the American-born Sir Henry Thornton, a man of large appetites and prodigious business skills who combined impressive British experience and wartime service with American know-how. His new job, paid at the then unheard of rate of $50,000 per year, was to whip the publicly owned CNR into shape. In due course, Rand would work alongside Thornton.

In the meantime, railway reorganization came first. With that accomplished, Moncton was no longer the head office of a railway but the regional office of a much larger enterprise – and one no longer directly controlled by the party in power. All the important management jobs, and many of the clerical ones, soon disappeared, eventually reappearing in Montreal. There were now three divisions: eastern, central, and western. The railway's 35,000 kilometres of track was divided among the three, but, after the reorganization, the eastern division was given about one-tenth of the track, running now only to Rivière-du-Loup instead of all the way to Montreal. Still, Moncton survived the post-war economic downturn better than other New Brunswick communities. It was a relatively busy, lively, although still 'dry' city with an increasingly active Board of Trade and loyal local boosters. For his part, Rand began work in partnership with Clifford Robinson – a decision that would, in due course, see Rand at the centre of the province's political life and in the midst of a political storm.

After graduating from Mount Allison University in 1886, Robinson had trained first as a bookkeeper and had then 'read law' with several prominent members of the New Brunswick bar. He opened a legal practice in Moncton and soon entered politics – first as an alderman, next as mayor, then as a Liberal representing Westmorland County in the New Brunswick legislature, and, briefly, as premier in 1907. When the Conservatives came to power the following year, he held on to his seat and served two years as leader of the opposition before retiring briefly from active politics. Once in power, the Tories gave new meaning in their maladministration of public affairs to the words 'corruption,' 'incompetence,' and 'political scandal,' but the voters were slow to appreciate the damage they had done. The Liberals remained in the political wilderness until the provincial election of 1917, when Walter E. Foster became premier. They, in turn, proved that, in some respects, they behaved no differently in office than their predecessors. Meanwhile, in 1912, Robinson had returned to provincial politics, representing the City of Moncton, and, as an elder statesman of the party, he was given the important portfolio of Lands and Mines in 1920. With this responsibility, Robinson needed another man to look after the office, and Rand's timing was perfect. The two lawyers set up shop as Robinson & Rand.

The practice was primarily small-town fare with, increasingly, some interesting cases and clients at the upper end. Rand practised family law and corporate law, challenged wills and defended them, and represented people sent to jail not just for drinking too much but for drinking at all. He replied promptly to correspondence and tried tenaciously to collect overdue accounts. When difficult legal questions arose, he wrote to Harvard requesting American authorities, because local legal resources were scant. Many of his clients expressed gratitude for his services, but he had the usual share of ingrates too.

In his free time he curled, played tennis, and relaxed at the piano. He joined in community activities, including the local Board of Trade and both the Moncton and the New Brunswick Barristers' Society. Although not seen in church, Rand was often observed walking to his office, his long legs taking huge rapid strides, completely lost in thought. 'The body,' he said, 'was the vehicle which transported the mind.'[9] His first real professional break came when the provincial government, on Robinson's recommendation, asked Rand to lead New Brunswick's fight for fair freight rates.

Freight rates were regulated by the Board of Railway Commissioners (the board), established in 1903. It was Canada's first tribunal charged with overseeing an important part of the nation's economic life, and its primary purpose was to protect the public. Before its creation, rates fluctuated from day to day, and no shipper knew what rate would be charged or what its competitors were paying. Once it was appointed, hearings were held regularly to review rates on all types of commodities and traffic and to approve changes in them, ensuring that they were not 'unreasonable, unjustly discriminatory or unduly preferential or prejudicial.'[10] Unfortunately for New Brunswick, the significant subsidies on its regional rates were gradually eliminated as all of Canada's railways gradually came under the jurisdiction of the board.[11]

Canadian freight rates were among the lowest in the world and rarely came close to reflecting real carrying costs. However, they were never low enough to satisfy regional interests, in both the East and the West. Maritimers argued, not without justification, that because the ICR had been built as part of the original Confederation compact, their preferred rates could not be changed – in other words, that the Maritime provinces were entitled to subsidized freight rates in perpetuity. Aside from this arguable constitutional entitlement, there were also administrative problems in how the system actually worked. As one critic observed, any 'Tom, Dick and Harry down in the Maritimes could make any rate he wanted to make ... the agent had the right to quote his friends any old figure for the transportation of goods.' It was a 'happy partnership' for everyone but the Canadian taxpayer.[12]

In the face of rapidly rising rates, the legislatures of New Brunswick and Nova Scotia passed identical resolutions pointing out that the ICR had been 'constructed to serve a special purpose' and should be 'administered upon principles ... giving such advantages in freight and other rates to the people of the Maritime Provinces as will afford them access to the markets of the Dominion upon such terms as will admit them to fair competition.'[13] The resolutions were ignored. Between 1917 and 1920, there were overall increases between 140 and 216 per cent. Everyone felt the impact. There was simply no way a New Brunswick industrialist could successfully compete with producers in central Canada. Capital had been moving out of the region for years; now smart new money stayed away too.[14]

Public opinion in the Maritime provinces was finally galvanized by a decision of the board in the 'Thirty-Five and Forty Per Cent Case,' effective September 1920. Maritime spokespersons had argued before the commissioners that it was unjust suddenly to apply commercial rates to what was obviously a non-commercial line. The ICR had been built to link the Maritime provinces with the rest of Canada and to compensate, by way of lowered freight rates, for political interference with their established trade links with the United States. That was the agreement reached at Confederation. 'Too bad,' the board replied. Rates could not be lowered to facilitate development or to overcome geography. Moreover, the Confederation bargain was beyond the commissioners' scope. 'We are trying to consider this matter purely from legal and business standpoints,' the chief commissioner, Frank Carvell, announced.[15] Carvell, considered a puppet of the railways, told Maritimers abrasively that they should 'go to the government' if they wanted relief from freight rates.[16] And so, at Clifford Robinson's suggestion, the provincial government retained Ivan Rand to look into, and after, New Brunswick's interests in the dispute.

The Thirty-Five and Forty Per Cent Case was appealed to the Judicial Committee of the Privy Council (JCPC), then Canada's court of last resort. The JCPC was well aware that transportation costs differed from one part of Canada to another. It was more expensive to build and operate railways throughout the Rockies than it was in Ontario. Moreover, there was more competition for freight traffic in the East than in the West. Railways served other purposes too, such as regional development and national unity. Nevertheless, the federal Cabinet made known that it was 'strongly impressed' with the need to equalize rates. In dismissing the appeal in October 1920, the JCPC expressed a preference for equalization of rates and directed the board to convene hearings to consider how best to go about achieving that objective, noting that it was justified because 'conditions have probably changed materially in recent years, tending more and more to make equalization practicable.' It was good theory, but it ignored the Confederation promise and Canadian geography. The result also stood in marked contrast to the situation in the United States, where there were a large number of competing lines, no duopoly, and rates based on varying conditions in different localities.[17]

Rand got right to work preparing for the board hearings ordered by the JCPC. After careful examination of the Confederation debates, communiqués to the Colonial Office in London, and other historical documents, he determined that none of the Founding Fathers had any expectation that the ICR would ever pay its way. Its purpose was political, the price of union, and its cost was to be borne by Canada. 'It will make Halifax and Saint John the Atlantic seaports of half a continent,'

George Brown told the Legislative Assembly on 8 February 1865. Likewise, Henri-Elzéar Taschereau, the representative from Beauce and
one of a long line of Taschereaus in public life (he would later become
chief justice of the Supreme Court of Canada; his son, Louis-Alexandre,
would become premier of Quebec; and his grandson, Robert, would
be chief justice of the Supreme Court of Canada when Rand was on
the court), observed that the ICR was not an attractive investment but
a political necessity: 'It will therefore have to be undertaken and paid
for purely as a national work,' he stated.[18] There was, in short, ample
reason to believe that Canada was not living up to its end of the constitutional deal.[19]

Rand convened meetings to coordinate strategy with counsel retained by the other Maritime provinces and with the 'Maritime division' of the Canadian Manufacturers' Association. On the last day of
1920 he reported to Premier Foster: the situation did not look good. The
board was already on record that it would not consider freight rates in
a political context. Moreover, it had signalled its interest in 'a general
equalization of rates throughout the Dominion,' in accordance with the
observations of the federal Cabinet and the directive of the JCPC. That
being the case, Rand asked, was it really in New Brunswick's interest to
participate in the legal proceeding? That was a decision for the premier
to make, but Rand suggested that, if New Brunswick did participate in
the hearings scheduled for April, it should make it clear that the province was not 'abandoning the political considerations for preference.'[20]

The subject was discussed at a meeting arranged by Rand in Moncton
at the end of April 1921. Angus McLean, the president of the Bathurst
Company, one of the largest lumber concerns in the province, and soon
to be president of the New Brunswick Lumbermen's Association, was
the lead speaker. New Brunswick, he observed, was far from the centre
of the country. To make matters worse, now that the old ICR had been
amalgamated into the CNR, freight rates were so high that lumber and
pulp could no longer be shipped west. We need, he argued, to get back
'to something like former conditions under which the ICR rates were
given special consideration.'[21] Clifford Robinson, who was also at the
meeting, expressed the need for all the Maritime provinces to work
together and avoid sectional feeling. 'All we want at Ottawa,' he said,
'is fair play.' Rand addressed the audience next, having obviously been
instructed to keep up the fight. Were we, he asked, 'going to be admitted to the living-room of Canada or kept always in the vestibule?'[22]
The battle had to be fought on two possible fronts: in the political arena

– a delegation from New Brunswick and Nova Scotia was headed to Ottawa for a meeting with the prime minister – and, should that fail, before the board.

The timing was not good from a political point of view. The controversial Arthur Meighen had succeeded Robert Borden as prime minister in July 1920, and an election was expected. William Lyon Mackenzie King, who had taken over leadership of the Liberal Party from Sir Wilfrid Laurier in 1919, was the front runner. Reducing freight rates for the Maritime provinces was not high on the agenda, although the matter was raised in Cabinet. Meighen's government decided not to get involved, and, in the December 1921 general election, as expected, it was defeated.

Rand worked hard for the Liberals in his area, campaigning alongside local MP and regional Cabinet minister Arthur B. Copp, the member for Westmorland. Copp promised CNR employees in Moncton and elsewhere a 'full dinner pail.' Westmorland included the former ICR headquarters, and local voters enthusiastically responded. It was a regional sweep, as the Maritime provinces gave the Liberals twenty-five of the thirty-one federal seats. Having been promised in the campaign that local interests had attracted the sympathetic interest of Mackenzie King, Maritimers had every expectation that the government would move on rising freight rates and other causes of regional disparity. But these expectations were dashed, as the new prime minister feared defeat in the House. The Liberals, with fewer seats than the Conservatives, could survive only with the support of Prairie Progressives, who were decidedly hostile to special pleading from the Maritimes even as they pursued it with vigour for themselves. Ultimately, the government offered only a few tidbits, including reorganization of the CNR to maintain both regional headquarters and local management. Moncton accordingly benefited, but no one was fooled as Portland, Maine, became the winter terminus of choice. Henceforth, trade would be channelled through Maritime ports only if the government demanded it. In the absence of state coercion, trade will always seek the least expensive route.

Various Maritime delegations continued to make their dissatisfaction known. A special parliamentary committee was appointed to study the issue, and both Thornton and Rand made appearances before it. Addressing leading businessmen in Saint John during his first 'inspection of the Atlantic Region,' Thornton spoke of the city's importance as a winter port, adding, 'there must never be separation of the Maritimes from Canada.' It was essential, he declared, that the Maritimes 'be made comfortable and happy.'[23] Thornton was a 'genius,' according to Copp. When the dust settled, he had clearly done something for Moncton, although centralization of the railway at its new headquarters in Montreal encouraged thousands more Maritimers to migrate to other parts of Canada and the United States.

To reduce the heat on the CNR, Thornton appointed a full-time publicist to take care of 'public relations' and established a Bureau of Economics to provide management with full information about economic conditions in the industry. He also ordered changes to the line itself. The shops at Moncton, and elsewhere, were enlarged and modernized, and harbour and terminal facilities in Saint John were improved. Bridges, trestles, and culverts along the line were strengthened or replaced, and new cars and engines ordered. But even though initial results were encouraging, there was no way in the foreseeable future that the CNR would generate any return on investment.

The Maritime provinces continued their steep economic decline. Although there were many factors at work, one of the important reasons remained the railway's meandering route and the high freight rates. It escaped no Maritimer's attention that western provinces' demands for the restoration of the highly subsidized Crowsnest Pass rates – ridiculously below the actual cost of transporting goods in the West – were largely accommodated while the interests of New Brunswick, Nova Scotia, and Prince Edward Island were not. The betrayal would be avenged when voters next went to the polls.[24] In the meantime, attention returned to the Board of Railway Commissioners.

As promised, it held hearings beginning in the spring of 1921. All the provinces, except Ontario and Quebec, were there with cap in hand. British Columbia wanted its high rates lowered to those applicable in Alberta, Saskatchewan, and Manitoba. The railways argued against this demand, taking the position that building the railway to British Columbia had been particularly expensive and that the geography resulted in higher operational expenses. The three Prairie provinces wanted decreases, staunch in their belief that they were being gouged by the East (which, for them, meant the centre). And the Maritime provinces had their own special grievances. The board first held hearings in the principal cities in the West, from Vancouver to Winnipeg, then, in January 1922, headed east. The opportunity was provided for various interest groups to come and have their say, with the real work being done at hearings held in February and March.

Ivan Rand was there for three days in February and ten days in March, as counsel representing the government of New Brunswick. The case was obvious, he stated: a deal had been made at Confederation, and a 'differential' had been in effect for forty years. 'My principal argument,' he told the commissioners, was that this 'differential is an established economic factor in business ... Businesses have been established because of it.'[25] But that deal had been broken, with terrible consequences for the people of New Brunswick. Rate relief was necessary if New Brunswick and the other Maritime provinces were to compete.

On 30 June 1922 the board issued its decision, reducing rates somewhat west of Fort William and east of Montreal. It was another explicit repudiation of any obligation to maintain rates at a level that would allow Maritime manufacturers and producers to compete in central Canada and the West, and again a rejection of the obligations undertaken at Confederation. It was too little and too late, and certainly not part of any comprehensive plan. Hundreds more Maritime jobs were lost: in all, between 1900 and 1930, some 300,000 Maritimers moved away, many to the United States. Between 1919 and 1921, the total number of New Brunswickers employed in manufacturing dropped by about 42 per cent.[26] After the board's decision, this number declined even further, exacerbated by the post-war recession. As Ernest Forbes, a leading historian of the period, puts it, 'The rate changes were a major factor in both the original collapse of the Maritime economy and its failure to recover after 1923. Not only did they help undermine the competitive position of existing Maritime industry, but they permanently discouraged the location within the region of new industry dependent upon markets elsewhere in the country.'[27]

Ironically, adjustments to the freight rates did little to improve the financial situation of the CNR. The initial increases were, in a buoyant wartime economy, easily absorbed. However, the 'continued leveling up of local rates and an additional 40 per cent increase in 1920 were followed by a decline in traffic on the line of about 40 per cent (compared with 19 per cent nationally) and a drop in total revenue of 17 per cent. The slump in traffic lingered. Despite drastic layoffs, curtailment in services, and centralization of management ... the annual deficits, which had begun just prior to the increases of 1918, rose steadily ... Although hidden from the public ... in the first seven years of centralized control, the net operating deficits on the Atlantic lines were more than triple those of the Intercolonial in its forty-one years of independent operation.'[28] Moreover, the absorption of the ICR into the CNR removed perhaps the major agency for independent regional development and consolidated central Canadian domination of the Maritime economy.

Rand had done the best job possible, all things considered. Between November 1920, when he took the brief, and the board's decision in the summer of 1922, he spent fifty-two days working on the file. With the decision out, it was time to render an account. His fee: $750. He was not going to get rich working for the government of New Brunswick, but there were clearly benefits in becoming a recognized lawyer with good Fredericton and Saint John connections. Indeed, in recognition of his increasing status, Rand was invited on stage with Prime Minister Mackenzie King and the New Brunswick premier at a Liberal nomination meeting in Northumberland in September 1924.

An increasing number of excellent briefs made their way to Robinson & Rand. Reported cases indicate that Rand was regularly in court representing clients of all kinds in varied matters ranging from family to corporate law. He was sufficiently well known to be appointed as a Crown counsel in a number of high-profile cases – a favour generally bestowed at the time on lawyers of the appropriate political stripe. Along with another lawyer, T.T. Goodwin, for instance, Rand prosecuted O. Gaius Steeves, charged in 1921 with murdering his wife and five of his children by setting fire to the family home. 'I was in the barn when it happened,' Steeves claimed, 'and when I realized the house was on fire I could not get in because the smoke was too dense.' Steeves's story was put to the test as the accused was subjected 'to a grueling three hours' cross-examination at the hands of Mr. Ivan C. Rand.' Nevertheless, Steeves stuck to his account. 'When I got to the house,' he testified, 'the fire was far too advanced for me to go inside.' Asked about evidence given by a surviving son that he regularly beat his wife, Steeves denied the assertion: 'My son Curtis told a lot of lies. I did not choke my wife. I am not sure that I hit her. I never said that I would cut her damn throat and see the black blood run. I did not make the vulgar remarks which Curtis swore to.'[29] A surviving daughter agreed, discounting her brother's description of marital disharmony. Complicating the case was the allegation that this daughter's 'relations' with her father – in particular, 'an alleged act' between the two – was a main source of disagreement between husband and wife. The case, front-page news for a week, 'was the most largely attended and most important criminal trial ever heard in Albert County.'[30]

The case went to the jury on Saturday, 14 May. Four hours later they were back. Eight jury members were in favour of convicting Steeves for manslaughter; the remaining four held fast to acquitting him on the charge. None of the jurymen was willing to find the accused guilty of murder as set out in the indictment – an unsurprising result given that the crime could not be directly linked to Steeves and the evidence of discord was equivocal at best. The chief justice, who was presiding, immediately set the case down on the calendar for retrial.

On 12 July Steeves was brought back to court, 'looking bright and cheerful, and apparently in the best of health.' Rand's cross-examination again took three hours, as he attempted to encircle the accused with circumstantial evidence. In his closing address, defence counsel Senator George W. Fowler pointed to the lack of any evidence of any crime. 'Gentlemen,' he addressed the jury, 'you are to decide the fate of your fellow citizen, not by guess work but upon evidence.' There was no evidence of murder and no evidence of manslaughter. The accused sometimes got drunk, but that did not make him a killer. For his part, Rand attempted to poke holes in Steeves's account, pointing out inconsistencies in his evidence and statements which were suggestive of guilt, both before and after the crime took place. It was now time for the judge's jury address.

'Members of the jury,' Chief Justice Harrison A. McKeown began, 'you have a solemn duty' to grant justice to the living as well as the dead. The judge explained the difference between circumstantial and direct evidence, and told the jurors that they could accept either the Crown's or the defence's theory of the case. This time the jury was out for only one hour and returned quickly with a verdict of not guilty. Suspicions, they obviously felt, are not enough.

A great church is more than a pleasing dream. Jesus prayed for it: 'That they all may be one.' And for many years, beginning not long after Confederation, 'church union,' or reunion of the church, was the hope of many Canadians. Geography called, as much as anything else, for a church with larger resources than could be mustered by any single communion. The objective was the formation of an ecclesiastical institution to be known as the United Church of Canada, with a platform of both evangelism and social action.[31] All the Protestant denominations were invited to participate. The Anglicans and Baptists said no. The Congregationalists, most Presbyterians, all the Methodists, and the General Council of Local Union Churches (a smattering of Prairie churches that had come together in anticipation of union) said yes. But the road to union was long and arduous.

Even the longest journey starts with a single step, and the first one was the agreement in principle, in 1904, that 'organic union' was both 'desirable and practicable.' For every step forward, however, there were two back, as seemingly insurmountable questions of doctrine, culture, and politics got in and out of the way. In the end, the Congregationalists, Methodists, and most of the Presbyterians did unite. The accomplishment cannot be overstated. Church union was a remarkable achievement, and all the more extraordinary for occurring long before the ecumenical era. It was a movement whose time had come. In New Brunswick, it required the talents of Ivan Rand.[32]

A number of committees were established to lay the groundwork for union, including one on law and legislation. An act would have to be passed by Parliament incorporating the United Church under federal law and providing for institutions of church government, while provincial legislation was necessary in all the Canadian provinces to confirm the federal law and deal with matters of more local concern. The merger of three denominations, three thousand congregations, and hundreds of thousands of members was an uncommonly difficult and complicated legal task. Property law, trust law, church government, the place of seminaries and educational institutions, not to mention a remarkably generous escape clause for local congregations, ministers, and members going their own way, all had to be addressed. Many of these issues cut across federal-provincial lines. Lyman Duff, a judge of the Supreme Court of Canada, was put in charge of apportioning church properties across the country in cases where the assenting and dissenting congregations could not agree.[33]

The list of legal questions seemed endless. The mastermind placed in overall charge was Newton W. Rowell, the chairman of the Joint Committee on Law and Legislation. Rowell, a Methodist and a Liberal, was one of the most prominent lay people active in the church union movement. As one of Canada's leading lawyers, he appeared regularly before the JCPC – he had, for instance, represented the appellants in the Persons case, the decision that declared women 'persons' and eligible, therefore, to serve in the Senate. Someone was needed to guide the passage of the provincial bill on church union in New Brunswick. Rand was not well known in Toronto, and so, before giving him this important retainer, inquiries were in order. Rand, according to one report, was very well qualified: 'His association with the Hon. Clifford Robinson ... would give him influence both at Fredericton and throughout the province. He has platform ability and is painstaking and thorough.'[34] In January 1924, on the recommendation of the Maritime Church Union Committee, Rand was retained as counsel.

Rand's contact was R.B. Whitehead, the legal secretary of the Joint Committee (he was later succeeded by his brother, A.T. Whitehead). 'It is desirable,' Whitehead wrote, 'that there should be the greatest possible uniformity in the Dominion and Provincial legislation ... In much of the subject matter, it is difficult to determine where the jurisdiction of Parliament ends and the jurisdiction of the Provincial legislatures begins.'[35] It was a sensible process, given the division of powers between the federal government and the provinces, not to mention differences in corporate organization and legal status. The Methodists were incorporated, but the Presbyterians – a voluntary association with no 'legal personality'– were not. Moreover, a large number of provincial and federal corporate bodies had been established for discrete purposes ranging from ownership of a particular church property to management of a seminary to administration of a widows and orphans fund. Rand was provided with a model provincial bill, drafted by Toronto lawyers Gershom W. Mason, an authority on corporate law, and McGregor Young, a former professor of constitutional law. After conducting a thorough review, Rand raised numerous questions and recommended changes proposing draft amendments to accommodate New Brunswick laws relating to trusts and trustees, the holding of property, and the performance of marriage, among other things.

The only real opposition, in New Brunswick and elsewhere, came primarily from breakaway and predominately Scottish Presbyterian congregations.[36] But there were others: 'Some thought that a united Church would be too diffuse to achieve much, others that it would be so tightly organized that it would iron out all diversity. Some feared that it would be too liberal in its theology, others that it would be too conservative. Consumers of alcohol who feared prohibition, politicians who recoiled from a force that might be used against them, serious theologians with reservations about the pragmatic motives of many unionists, and immigrants who clung to memories of home all found their way into the anti-unionist ranks.'[37] This group was bound together not by a common platform but by fear of the new United Church. Depending on individual perspective, church union was either something imposed on the people by church bureaucrats and officials or an inevitable movement willed by God.

After recommending changes to the draft bill, Rand, from behind the scenes, piloted its passage through the New Brunswick legislature in the spring of 1924. The bill sailed through without incident, in contrast to its treatment in other provincial legislatures and the Parliament of Canada. Rand's deft handiwork added to his profile. 'We finished the debate yesterday,' a prominent observer of the New Brunswick proceedings wrote, adding: 'It was a real debate too. The antis put up a better fight than I had ever heard before.' And a pro-union minister who watched from the gallery wrote: Rand 'made a great defence ... He effectively dealt with every point of law. I think [he] made his reputation yesterday.'[38] Indeed, he had.

'All of the arguments ... against church union,' Rand pointed out to the legislative committee studying the draft bill, 'had been heard in 1875, when the Presbyterian Church of Canada was formed ... This Church Union Bill was based on that bill,' yet now those same terms are 'bitterly opposed.' The observation was a good one, but there was more. The anti-unionists appealed to 'tradition,' but did they really think that the Methodists and the Congregationalists had no traditions? Even if they did not, 'must tradition be their guide for eternity?' 'Change,' Rand observed, 'was continually taking place,' and 'enjoyment of tradition could not be allowed to stand in the way of the world's progress.' Church union was all about progress – the progress of man.[39]

Rand's performance left no question unanswered, and everyone in attendance was favourably impressed. 'I was told that Rand considered this Union case the opportunity of his life,' the Reverend George C. Pidgeon (who became the first moderator of the United Church of Canada) reported to union headquarters in Toronto, 'and I assure you that he did not let it slip.'[40] A man like that belonged in politics. But there was one more major matter to be handled before Rand left private practice for public life.

Robinson was one of the commissioners of the Jordan Memorial Sanatorium, an institution in River Glade, New Brunswick, which had been founded and generously supported by Jeanette Jordan. Her estate was worth almost $1 million, and the part designated for the sanatorium was required for long-overdue maintenance and repairs. At the time of her death, however, Jordan lived in California and, under California law, any bequests made to charities within thirty days of the date of death were void. The timing of Jordan's last will was problematic.

The main task for Rand was to repatriate the funds. He went to Boston and did his own legal research at Harvard Law School. There he found cases and law review articles supporting his opinion that the case should be decided by applying the common-law theory of 'dependent relative revocation.' This legal strategy depended on establishing that a section of an earlier will, made five years before Jordan's death, continued in force.

The first California firm Rand consulted demanded a large retainer, so he looked around and found another firm willing to take on the job in return for a contingency fee of 7.5 per cent of the proceeds. Not only did this arrangement allow the action to proceed but it also tied compensation to success.[41] Nevertheless, Rand ran herd on his US counsel and kept the file moving along. In the result, the bequest, which otherwise would have been lost, came New Brunswick's way: $126,475.71, less the contingency fee. What was particularly interesting was Rand's own statement of account: 'I think it but reasonable that I should receive ... two and one-half percent as a commission on the amount collected.'[42] Rand needed the money because he had, the previous month, left the practice of law and entered public life.

The provincial Liberals had lost the election in 1908, but, following their victory in 1917, they quickly made up for lost time. There were some seven hundred permanent jobs in the provincial civil service, ranging from deputy clerk to deputy minister. Within four months of taking over, they dismissed almost six hundred employees. Hundreds of other publicly paid workers, including provincial constables, justices of the peace, licence vendors, and road inspectors, were also provided with pink slips. Foster's government was, however, by and large progressive. It introduced bills creating a Department of Health – the first in the British Empire – and providing for improvements to 'workmen's compensation.' It also spent more on education and increased funding to hospitals. The economy was, initially, good, with full employment. Trains rolled across the province loaded with lumber, produce, and armaments. Saint John was Canada's leading winter port, and, with the war on, it was busier than ever.

It was a time for big and bold ideas and, in 1918, Foster created the Water Power Commission, with Clifford Robinson as the first chairman, to investigate the possibility of publicly owned hydroelectric power for the province. Establishment of the commission gave belated recognition to the fact that electricity was not a local resource but a provincial one. The commission held hearings, the public appeared to approve, and, in 1920, the New Brunswick Electric Power Commission was established to pursue development of publicly owned facilities for the generation, transmission, and distribution of electric power. Government intrusion into this marketplace was something new and, in the private sector, treated with suspicion. But, as Premier Foster, a successful businessman himself, explained, public ownership of electricity was 'different.' He was right. The only way that hydroelectricity could be brought to all the people in the province was for the government to be involved.

It was appropriate, therefore, to seek the people's support. In 1920, after only three and a half years in office, the Liberals decided to return to the polls. The opposition Tories, even with a last-minute leadership switch, were in turmoil as they faced the Liberal record of apparent achievement: 'The government could claim that it now had a public-power policy; it had granted women the franchise; the road-building and public health programmes were impressive; teachers salaries had just been substantially increased; the Workmen's Compensation Act had been liberalized; and there were new agricultural programmes for farmers.'[43] Foster kept reiterating that the sole purpose of the election was to give the people of New Brunswick a future: 'The government has determined upon the development of the tremendous water powers at Grand Falls,' he said. 'Whatever is needed to bring this about will be done.'[44] Remarkably, the government itself had remained virtually scandal free and, after election day on October 10, the Liberals got a working majority by cobbling together a government with the assistance of several independents.

Attention then returned to hydroelectricity. The Musquash dam near Saint John was built first. It would cost only $2 million, the government promised, but it ended up costing $3.5 million. Making matters worse, the site's selection was tarred with allegations of political patronage and government interference. When heavy flooding damaged the power transmission system and part of the dam in April 1923, the public howled with rage. Subsequent investigation revealed that the dam was poorly constructed and built on mud. We made a mistake, the Electric Power Commission conceded, but we learned from it – and immediately announced an even larger project at Grand Falls. International Paper, the huge American-owned industry leader, had earlier been given the development rights to Grand Falls but had done nothing with them. Peter Veniot, who succeeded Foster as premier early in

1923 after Foster returned to Saint John to minister to his struggling business interests, thereupon took the rights back.

Veniot was a phenomenon. The first Acadian to become premier of New Brunswick, he nevertheless spoke English as his mother tongue. As public works minister in the previous government, he had taken charge of a massive road-building program and had borrowed and spent heavily, running up a huge debt for the province. Still, he argued, good roads and a publicly owned hydroelectric system were not just modern conveniences but essential preconditions to a diversified economic and industrial development. Moreover, they provided wonderful opportunities for the party in power to reward its friends – a perk never to ignore in Canada.[45]

It was just that kind of patronage that brought Ivan Rand into public life. Robinson was still serving in the Liberal Cabinet, and he was now Veniot's minister of lands and mines. In 1924, in return for his years of faithful service, Robinson was about to be given his reward: a seat in the Senate in Ottawa. Speculation focused on who would succeed him as one of Moncton's two representatives in Fredericton. 'Ivan C. Rand, law partner of Mr. Robinson,' the *Daily Gleaner* reported, 'said that he was not anxious to get into active politics when it was brought to his attention that he was being mentioned as likely to succeed Mr. Robinson.' That situation soon changed: a by-election was called to fill Robinson's vacant seat, and Rand announced his candidacy.

To give Rand's campaign a boost, even before he entered the legislature, Veniot appointed Rand attorney general, succeeding James P. Byrne, one of the two representatives for Gloucester County, who had conveniently been made a judge by the Liberal government in Ottawa. A judicial vacancy had been created when the chief justice of the Supreme Court of New Brunswick, Harris A. McKeown, was named chairman of the Board of Railway Commissioners, and his position was filled by an existing judge of the court, thereby, in this cascade of patronage appointments, creating a place not only for Byrne but also for Rand.

As their candidate for the Moncton seat, the Conservatives nominated Albert Reilly, a local lawyer who had frequently squared off against Rand in court and who was also a well-known proponent of Maritime rights. Rand had to withdraw from his law practice, and he spent some time transferring files to other lawyers, including the church union file, because the act passed by the New Brunswick legislature had come under renewed attack. Rand gave the brief to the Fredericton lawyer and Roman Catholic Peter Hughes. Rand was, nevertheless, in a good position to serve the interests of his former client. 'Whilst not serving us officially,' the Reverend H.E. Thomas wrote union headquarters in Toronto, 'there is much that he can do unofficially, so I do not think we suffer.'[46] Suffer they did not, for the challenge to Rand's handiwork was readily disposed of. And, right on schedule, the United Church in Canada came into being on 10 June 1925.[47]

Back in New Brunswick, the economic situation had continued to deteriorate, and dissatisfaction with government – all government – was at an all-time high (although it would go higher still). 'Send E.A. Reilly to Fredericton to show Ottawa we mean business,' the *Times*, Moncton's pro-Tory daily newspaper, exclaimed. Another banner headline declared, 'Moncton must not fail to register a protest for herself and the Maritimes.' Only the 'election of Mr. Reilly' would 'serve notice on Ottawa that Moncton is not satisfied with present conditions.'[48] Rand, who had campaigned for the federal Liberals in 1921 and had not spoken out on behalf of Maritime rights, attempted to focus the discussion.

Job losses at the CNR in Moncton were not the issue, he declared. The provincial government had no more to do with that, Rand insisted, than it had with the League of Nations. However, voters were hardly interested in apportioning responsibility according to the *British North America Act* division of powers.[49] Rand may have thought that the railway was a side issue in the campaign, but voters saw it differently. While congenitally hostile to any Liberal, the *Times* could be forgiven for pointing out that, if Rand said the railways did not matter, he 'should not complain if the railway employees decide on Monday next that he is also a side issue and vote for a man who regards the railway as a big factor in our civic life.'[50] That was certainly the opposition's pitch. In his plea to voters, Reilly observed that the policy of the Liberal Party – and he did not specify federal or provincial – had demobilized industry and commerce and crippled and stifled Maritime aspirations, so much so that 'our people are becoming discouraged and leaving for a foreign country to make a livelihood.'[51]

The provincial government was nearing the end of its mandate and left nothing to chance. The premier spent a week in the riding campaigning, and other Cabinet heavyweights were brought in. Victory was confidently predicted. On election day, 1 December 1924, the premier canvassed the polls, personally soliciting votes for Rand as voters trudged through more than a foot of snow. Yet Rand went down to defeat, losing the riding Robinson had held forever by almost one thousand votes. Reilly was gracious to Rand in his victory speech, and other Conservatives went out of their way to speak highly about this 'brilliant young man ... who had to carry the burden of the maladministration of the local government.'[52] But the premier saw things differently.

The result of the by-election was not a vote against his government, Veniot explained, but against the federal government. Its disastrous railway policy – one that, among other things, moved Moncton jobs and families to Montreal – led the workers at CNR in Moncton to send a message to the Liberals in Ottawa. Privately, Veniot predicted and warned Prime Minister King 'that unless some greater effort is made to facilitate transportation at the winter port of Saint John and cut down shipments through the port of Portland ... you will not carry more than two seats in this province's next election.' Something, he warned, 'must be done.'[53]

But laying the electoral defeat entirely at the feet of the federal Liberals was not entirely fair. Voters were also concerned about provincial spending and the mounting debt. Pursuing the Grand Falls project would be risky. Nevertheless, the Conservatives had demonstrated that they could take on a well-known, high-profile, establishment-backed Liberal in a safe seat. The behind-the-scenes work of John Babington Macaulay Baxter did not go unnoticed. He was a former federal Cabinet minister, current member of parliament, and former provincial Cabinet minister and party leader, and he had also been brought in at the last minute to lead the provincial Tories during the 1920 election.

In the wake of Rand's defeat, Premier Veniot was now more determined than ever to make hydroelectricity the provincial election issue – it dominated discussions in Cabinet throughout 1924–25, except when attention focused on matters such as setting the salaries for minor officials and amending regulations governing the licensing of embalmers.[54] While Rand could attend Cabinet meetings from the day he was sworn in, he still had to enter the legislature and could not do so until he won a seat. The premier therefore had to call another by-election, and Rand had to run in it. 'I do not,' Veniot said, 'want to lose the services of a man of his outstanding ability.'[55]

An even safer seat was called for, and the day after Rand lost, one was offered: Gloucester County, a long-standing Liberal stronghold with an overwhelming Acadian base that had deliberately been kept on hold in case Moncton did not go Rand's way. Gloucester sent four representatives to the legislature – and at present the premier was among them. Not surprisingly, Rand was 'certain of an enthusiastic reception from the party's delegates who will gather at Caraquet from all the parishes of the county.'[56] Veniot carefully explained to his constituents the importance of selecting Rand as their candidate for the special by-election.

In the next few weeks, Veniot observed, the New Brunswick legislature would be meeting in one of its 'most important sessions ... since Confederation.' Important international negotiations were now under way in connection with the development of Grand Falls on the St. John River to provide inexpensive electrical power to the province. Hydroelectricity would become the most important factor in the future industrial development and prosperity of New Brunswick – or so the premier claimed.

Other important negotiations would also take place, and we need, Veniot asserted, a 'brilliant legal mind' to come successfully through these negotiations. 'Mr. Rand was an outstanding lawyer' who had the 'qualifications required' to perform this most important job. The fact that Rand had been defeated in Moncton, 'through no fault of his own or of the Provincial Government,' was no reason why 'his valuable services should be lost to the province.' Besides, Veniot promised, if Rand was elected in Gloucester, it was only temporary, for he would run in the general election back in Moncton. The 'opposition' had already begun their 'whispering campaign' against Rand – that he was a 'Protestant'; that he was an 'Orangeman'; that his uncle had led the troops who arrested the so-called Caraquet martyrs when thirteen Acadians were picked up for the murder of two persons during the troubles over the school law in 1871. On and on it went. Rand was a Protestant, Veniot admitted; he was a Methodist, in fact. But the good people of Gloucester, both Acadian and English-speaking Roman Catholics, should demonstrate their resentment of 'these tactics' – tactics that paradoxically also included the dissemination of literature arguing that Veniot had betrayed the Acadians and the French language and should be taught a lesson – and, when they went to the polls on February 5, send this most able of men to Fredericton.

Accordingly, more than eight hundred people were assembled for the selection meeting, and they voted 'unanimously' for Rand to carry the party banner. There was not really a choice, given the circumstances. Awaiting the result at a local hotel, Rand was summoned to the Old College Hall. The audience 'arose en masse and cheered and applauded the brilliant lawyer whose inclusion in the Cabinet has given the Government the benefit of a legal mind completely capable of filling the position which the present Mr. Justice Byrne had graced for the past seven years.' For almost 'five minutes' the delegates applauded and cheered. Rand was 'visibly affected by the manifestation of good will and warmth of the reception.' After thanking the delegates for the honour conferred on him, Rand paid homage to the premier. Veniot, he said, was a 'far-seeing leader ... capable and energetic.'[57]

Hydroelectricity was clearly the issue, and Rand addressed it head on, speaking 'briefly in French.' In fact, Rand never came close to mastering Canada's other official language. 'Big interests,' he warned, were behind the opposition to the Grand Falls project. They wanted hydroelectricity for 'purposes of their own,' regardless of 'the people's interest.'[58] The premier himself again hit the hustings in the constituency of 16,000 voters and took personal charge of directing the campaign in his own riding. There were also promises of future government spending in Gloucester Country. Other bigwigs were brought in, including Rand's law partner, Senator Robinson. And to be even more effective, the speeches were accompanied by 'moving pictures depicting the improvement which the present government has made in the highways of the province.'[59]

'Large majorities' for Rand were predicted in the Liberal press; those papers sympathetic to the opposition dutifully prophesied a rout. 'The people of Gloucester are not taking kindly to having the rejected of Moncton thrust upon them,' was the way the hostile *Times* described the situation just days before the election.[60] Rand was 'an outsider' forced on the people by the premier – someone recently 'rejected at the polls' in his native city.

Polls closed at 4 p.m. on 5 February 1925. When the votes were counted, Rand had won. It was the largest voter turnout in the riding's history, and Rand was elected with a significant majority. As Veniot described it, 'I feel elated to think that the Acadian people in my own county, which is seven-eighths French, responded so nobly to the call for reciprocal feeling towards the English-speaking people of this province and gave the Honourable Rand such a magnificent vote – the largest ever recorded in a provincial election in Gloucester County.'[61]

Behind the hype, however, was a disturbing trend. When the numbers were carefully examined, Rand had won by 1,892 votes. In the last general election, the Liberals had taken the seat with almost three thousand more votes than the opposition. Clearly, the Conservatives had increased their support – their candidate obtained 4,191 votes to Rand's 6,083 – and that was in the safest seat in the province, in a campaign run by the premier in which no expense was spared. By-elections are always a test of the government's strength, and this government, it appeared, was losing its grip.

On 12 March 1925 the legislature reconvened, and both Rand and Reilly were sworn in by the chief justice, Sir Douglas Hazen – a former premier of New Brunswick. In the speech from the throne, the government announced its legislative priorities.

Standing front and centre was the development of hydroelectricity at Grand Falls. In the short legislative session that followed, however, Attorney General Rand was extremely active and progressive, introducing a number of bills soon after the House got back to work. There was an act to facilitate the reciprocal enforcement of judgments and judicial awards, and a bill making uniform the laws respecting the liability of parties in an action for damages stemming from negligence where more than one party was at fault. The first bill made simple sense: a judgment in one Canadian jurisdiction should be enforceable in another. The second bill was particularly important because it removed the barriers to bringing a lawsuit by a plaintiff where he or she was partially at fault. Both pieces of legislation had been recommended by the Joint Committee on Uniformity and were being introduced with the approval of the New Brunswick bar. Likewise, the salary of the Supreme Court reporter was raised from $1,700 to $2,100 per year. The *Judicature Act* was also amended to fix Moncton as the place of residence for one Supreme Court judge.

Other housekeeping items included a grisly motion, though one with the support of all parties, calling on the Liberal government in Ottawa to amend the *Criminal Code* to provide that all executions in the Maritime provinces be carried out at the penitentiary at Dorchester. Local sheriffs, Rand explained to the legislature, 'disliked it' when called upon to officiate at executions in their jails.[62] Rand was also a member of an interprovincial committee that was conferring on the establishment of a prison farm for the Maritime provinces.

Later in the month, Rand introduced more bills, establishing his reputation as a law reformer. An act for the protection of children of unmarried parents, to replace the *Bastardy Act*, primarily provided a detailed scheme to identify the fathers of children born out of wedlock – an 'affiliation order' – and to make them pay for the child and, in some situations, the mother's support. The intestacy law was also amended by the *Widows Relief Act*. Even if so inclined, a husband could no longer deprive his widow of a share of his estate. The new legislation provided for widows to receive, regardless of any provision in a will, what they would have otherwise received had their husbands died without a will. It was hardly a fair share, but it was better than the status quo, which was nothing. The *Motor Vehicle Law* was amended to provide for speed limits on dangerous curves – proof of the growing importance of automobiles in provincial life. In addition, legislation was introduced providing financial aid for the province's pork-packing industry and for free textbooks in the public schools, along with an enactment allowing married women to vote for trustees – indeed, to be trustees. The *Probate Act* was amended to make it easier to prove a will where the witnesses were suffering a disability. Other legislation made it more efficient to collect debts. The list of legislative accomplishment was large and impressive. Not surprisingly, shortly after the election, Rand had quietly been named a King's Counsel, an honour bestowed by the provincial government theoretically on the basis of ability but usually as a minor political reward.

Law reform is always welcomed – particularly by lawyers. But the final legislative session of this government was dominated by one issue: the Grand Falls project. Though the premier had promised to move on Grand Falls, he had also made one other promise the previous year – to call an election first and submit the plan to the people.[63]

Grand Falls was at the heart of Ivan Rand's maiden speech in April 1925. Three hours long, it was, according to the always supportive *Daily Gleaner*, 'the most masterful speech given in the Provincial Legislature in more than a decade.'[64] The electrical revolution, Rand began, would soon equal the industrial revolution. Hydro would have the effect of decentralizing industry and spreading it to undeveloped territories such as New Brunswick. The Grand Falls project would enable the province to compete favourably with Ontario and Quebec, which already had their own hydroelectric supply. New Brunswick had a date with destiny, and it was imperative that the Grand Falls project be given all-party support. Instead, Rand observed, the opposition seemed to be working in concert with private interests to derail the government's plans.

'Not true,' interjected C.D. Richards, the Conservative House leader. Rand effectively dealt with Richards with the observation that, if the

conservatives were not deliberately working with the opponents of the
project, it must be said they were 'unconsciously mounting through
space on a parallel course.' Hydroelectric power at Grand Falls, Rand
remarked more than once, would arouse in the people of the province a
sense of the possibilities of New Brunswick. The opposition, he pointed
out, said time and again that they believed in hydro. The people should
be thankful for that, Rand said, adding, 'No doubt they also believed
in steam and gas.' But were they in favour of public ownership of the
resource? Where exactly did the Tories stand?

Rand had a few other matters on his mind as well, and he turned
to them. Legitimate claims were one thing, he said, illegitimate claims
something else. If the Maritime people want to be heard in Ottawa,
they 'should not make themselves ridiculous.' The ICR was a case in
point. 'Some were asking for the right to fix the freight rates on the Intercolonial Railway, but it must be remembered that the Intercolonial
had never paid a cent on the original investment. How far had they
the right to ask the Dominion of Canada to operate part of the ICR at
a loss for the benefit of New Brunswick?'[65] Freed from the shackle of
presenting a client's point of view, Rand was now able to describe the
freight rate issue as it was, not as so many wished it to be.

Moving on, he continued: 'I support prohibition.' He was a virtual
non-drinker himself, believing that alcohol clouded the mind and impaired judgment. The trouble with prohibition, however, was the essential hypocrisy that accompanied it. The law was unenforceable: 'The
situation was that men in the ordinary ranks of life, in general good
citizens, laugh at this law and conspired to defeat it the day after it
was passed.' Temperance was the goal, and the object was to educate
people to the dangers of drink. Unfortunately, Rand observed, when
people take up the advancement of any moral cause as a profession,
they regularly display a tendency to lose their sense of proportion, ex-
alting that phase of human conduct in which they happen to be interested. The consumption of liquor, he added, was on the borderline
between private and public life. There were certain aspects about liquor
that could and should be legislated, but they did not include the question of use.

But it was the Grand Falls project that mattered above all, Rand continued, and he returned to it at the end of his long and at times rambling
inaugural address. Lower freight rates would not turn things around,
even assuming that federal government policy could be changed. What
mattered was the future, and the future of New Brunswick was hydro-

electricity. If New Brunswick 'was to succeed in holding its own, it was imperative that it should do something, and the most important factor contributing to success was a successful administration and development of the water powers of the province.' The Conservatives, with their 'pernicious political campaign,' had much to answer for.[66]

Opposition representatives tried to intervene, but they could not. 'Bristling with rapier-like thrusts of satire and with full strokes of sarcasm which cut with the keenness of a highly sharpened saber,' the *Gleaner* gushed, 'the Attorney General's speech was also marked by an evidence of analytical ability that was a perfect revelation to those who heard him debate for the first time.' Moreover, 'the masterly manner in which he developed his argument and pressed home his points excited admiration upon the part of his friends and caused consternation in the rank of his opponents.' Even the *Times* was forced to concede that Rand had turned in a masterful performance: 'He showed a wide command of the English language and spoke with great fluency and eloquence. That he is a master of satire and sarcasm, no one who heard him will deny.'[67] It was just like the old days at Mount Allison University when the *Argosy* reported on Rand's performance in Eurhetorian Society debates.

Rand was clearly in the public eye, but even more so when the premier, in his own four-hour address given the following night, proclaimed his new attorney general as his inevitable successor. 'I am over sixty now,' Veniot explained, though still 'full of fight.' But the time had come to consider retiring, and his heir was at hand. 'When I do retire,' he said, 'I make the prediction that the man who will lead this province on will be Ivan C. Rand.'[68] Undoubtedly genuine, the premier's remarks served several purposes, including signalling to that part of the New Brunswick community which could not abide the thought of a French-speaking Roman Catholic in the premier's office that the indignity he presented would soon pass.

On 23 April, just as the legislature was about to rise for the day, Attorney General Rand announced to a stunned House that work on the Grand Falls project would begin immediately. His Grand Falls Hydro bill increased the power of the Hydro Commission to borrow by $9 million. But what of the premier's promise to call an election before the project went ahead? the opposition spluttered. Rand saw no need to consult the people: 'The best expert opinions had been obtained,' he explained, 'and it would be an absurdity to submit that to the judgment of the man on the street.'[69] The 'experts' may have spoken, but they had not been elected to office and had not promised to call an election before proceeding. Veniot was determined to push ahead. The land had been expropriated; the federal and Quebec governments had approved; and the International Waterways Commission was about to give the thumbs up. Although the Grand Falls site was in New Brunswick, almost three-quarters of the dam's upriver storage was located in Maine, almost a quarter in Quebec, and less than 5 per cent in New Brunswick. Potential political limitations posed by the Grand Falls site – requiring interprovincial, national, and international cooperation – had been masterfully overcome. Tenders would be called immediately. 'There will be no betrayal of the people's interests,' Veniot promised the legislature, and he put the Grand Falls bill to second reading.

Rand, who had already become the most important member of the Cabinet after the premier, followed Veniot in speaking on the bill's behalf. He demanded to know the Tories' position on Grand Falls. Were they for it or against it? Did they believe in public power or, as was widely suspected, did they intend to hand the site over to their business friends?[70] There were no immediate answers to these questions, which were good ones. On 30 April 1925 the legislature, with the Liberal's large majority, quickly passed the Grand Falls Hydro bill, and then prorogued. Despite Veniot's and Rand's denial of any need for public consultation, the fact was that the government had but six months left in its five-year mandate. The election call was just a matter of time – and the voters would ultimately decide the hydro project's fate.

J.B.M. Baxter was again persuaded to take charge of the opposition. A Protestant of Loyalist stock, he was well acquainted with the provincial elite. He immediately promised to end the Liberal's 'orgy of extravagance.' With considerable justification, he claimed that the provincial debt had doubled in size over the seven years the Liberals had been in power and now stood at $30 million. Almost half the provincial revenues were used for servicing debt.[71] Baxter's numbers may have been off by a fraction, but what he said rang true.[72] Careful to sidestep their position on Grand Falls, the Conservatives charged that, before any work began, the development should first undergo careful study. More than one provincial boondoggle had left the taxpayers holding the bag, and an appeal for calm deliberation before committing provincial funds was an attractive one. Besides, what possible difference could a few more months of study make?

The rejuvenated Tories were not the only formidable force the Liberals faced as they moved closer to an election. Veniot also had to contend with some very unhappy lumbermen. In only a few years, half the saw-mills in the province had closed. The operators bitterly resented having to pay workmen's compensation dues and insisted that the method of computing stumpage should be changed to follow the Quebec model, so that more wood could be cut at less cost. In early June the lum-bermen met with the premier, who offered some modest concessions, though not enough to bring the business interests on side. Informed that key industry leaders intended to turn against him in the forthcom-ing election, Veniot, even more arrogant than usual, glibly invited them to 'bring on the dogs of war.' The invitation was accepted.

On 17 July the long-expected election call came. Accompanying it was an announcement that Veniot had resigned his Public Works portfolio and named himself chairman of the Power Commission. 'No private corporations will be permitted to lay a finger on our water power re-sources,' Veniot asserted in his campaign manifesto, 'so long as I have the honor of remaining Premier of New Brunswick.'[73] And, within days of the election being called, the premier awarded the first contracts for the construction of the Grand Falls dam to a Montreal firm. Clearly, it was going to be a tough campaign. When one local newspaper editor was offered $10,000 by the Tories for his paper's editorial support, the answer was no: the Liberals had already purchased it two weeks earlier for double the amount.

The Liberals had a record of accomplishment, particularly in the con-struction of roads. But the roads had been paid for with borrowed funds, and dissatisfaction with deficit financing among the hard-working people of New Brunswick was palpable. Moreover, the economy was still in decline, the Maritime Rights Movement had gathered steam, and some of the discontent directed at Ottawa and the federal Liberal Party inevitably spilled over to the provincial scene. Just about everyone was unhappy – the province's dairy farmers, for example, were upset be-cause the minister of health had told them they had to pasteurize their milk and could no longer deliver it in open metal pails. Veniot would also lose some votes because of his stand against prohibition. Though the province's liquor laws were most honoured in the breach, politi-cians who hyped the temperance line did better at the polls. Adding to his woes was the matter of language and culture: French versus English, Roman Catholic versus Protestant.

Veniot was a Roman Catholic Acadian in a province that was di-vided in both language and religion. The divide ran along a diagonal line from the eastern outskirts of Moncton to Grand Falls, in the northwestern part of the province. To the north were the Acadians; to the south, the province's Protestant base. The economy was controlled by the south, and Veniot, facing the polls for the first time as premier, was challenging the status quo. A whispering campaign was clearly under way. In the south it was all about the Acadian and Roman Catholic who had the temerity to think he should be premier. In the north it was about the Protestant who had been brought in only to oppose 'a Frenchman.' A vote for Veniot, one anonymous pamphlet declared, was a 'vote for the Pope.'[74] Another pamphlet contained the 'Oath of Fourth Degree Knight of Columbus.' Widely distributed in predominately Protestant ridings, it asserted that a Knight of Columbus was bound, under this bogus oath, 'to recognize only the will of the Church of Rome in matters political or of state, and shall have no opinion of his own in such matters. He further binds himself to extirpate Protestants from the face of the earth, and to use for such purposes the poisonous cup, the strangulation cord, the steel of the poignard or the leaden envelope.' To make sure the message was not lost, the pamphlet contained the additional information, in bright red printing, that 'Premier Veniot is a fourth-degree Knight of Columbus.' Other literature claimed that the premier planned to introduce separate schools if elected, and even to require Protestants to make the sign of the cross before entering government buildings. The hate campaign was well organized and effective – so much so that a known member of the Ku Klux Klan, J.S. Lord, was elected in Charlotte County.[75]

The lumbermen also played a critical role. It was only because of workmen's compensation dues, industry leaders claimed, that wages had been reduced. The message was clear. The premier was responsible for lowering wages. It was completely ridiculous. 'If the breadwinner of the family was claimed by accident,' Veniot responded, the family should not be 'entirely dependent upon its members for support.' This act alone, he asserted, 'should be sufficient to warrant the electors to return to power the present government.'[76]

A war of words raged in the provincial press. Those for Veniot and the government described him, and the Grand Falls project, in the most flattering terms, focusing on his accomplishments as premier. Those against portrayed a reckless spender who had brought the province to the brink of financial collapse and had no idea how much Grand Falls would cost or what the power would sell for once the project was built. Rand – 'Ivan the Terrible' in some press accounts – was damned as part of the premier's inner ruling clique. The provocation was such that Rand, normally taciturn and reserved, gave the wildest speech of the entire campaign as the election headed into its final week. Before an audience of 1,500 at Saint John's Imperial Theatre, he accused Baxter of deserting the round table of 'Little Arthur' in Ottawa (a reference to federal Conservative leader Arthur Meighen) and coming to New Brunswick in the regalia of an ancient knight of the Round Table, as if to rescue a maiden in distress. But there was no such maiden: the government had served the people well. 'I am proud,' he declared, 'of the records and policies of the present government.' Baxter and the Tories were another matter. Making an unmistakable reference to the whispering campaign, Rand asserted that Baxter's costume had changed: it was now a 'white hood and burning cross,' the unmistakable signs of a Klansman. The Conservatives, working for the lumber companies, did not have the interests of the people at heart. They and their friends were 'a group of men out to kill public ownership of electrical energy ... They are endeavouring to get the water powers in their own clutches.'[77]

It was very simple. These interests, Rand explained, cared about one thing only. They wanted government money, and they wanted to harness the province's natural resources for their benefit alone. They were not opposed to the development of Grand Falls; they just wanted to grab it for themselves. Rand singled out Angus McLean, the president of the Bathurst Company and now head of the Lumbermen's Association, and then went after one of the other 'big interests' who was in the audience: a lifelong Liberal, devout Presbyterian, philanthropist, and temperance advocate named Donald Fraser. This man, Rand said, pointing to Fraser, is not interested in the province's economic welfare but only in its soul. He had a plan to produce pulp in New Brunswick and shoot it across the river through a pipe to be made into fine paper by Maine workmen. Pulp entered the United States duty free, but paper was subject to a tariff, and the whole scheme demonstrated that Fraser and his ilk really cared only about themselves. But what the people of New Brunswick needed desperately was help to make a living and secure food. The crowd loved it and began to cheer, but Rand was not finished yet.

'I am not,' he said to the howling, clapping, and foot-stomping audience, 'going to spend my time telling the people in rags and poverty about temperance.' That was a job left for Tory leader Baxter, who had, improbably, promised to enforce prohibition to the hilt. 'No doubt, Mr. Fraser, when meeting Dr. Baxter, would look up and say, "Oh my

knight in the white hood."' Rand's address was, as one political historian of New Brunswick later put it, 'a wild rambling speech ... the immediate impact was to further inflame political passions.'[78] However,
it all depended on your perspective. The Liberal-leaning *Daily Gleaner*
called it an 'outstanding address,' received with 'hearty applause.'[79]

McLean and Fraser responded to Rand several days later, again at
the Imperial Theatre. 'I charge this government,' McLean said, 'with
proceeding with the Grand Falls work when they do not know definitely what it is going to cost.' A former lifelong Liberal, McLean had
changed sides and now threw his not inconsiderable weight behind
the Conservatives. For his part, Fraser explained that the lumbermen
had not tried to 'hold up' the government. All they wanted was to
be treated fairly, and that meant stumpage fees that were competitive
with those in place in the province next door. With respect to the hydro project, Fraser was in favour of it. But he mightily objected to the
government signing contracts on the eve of an election.[80]

Without a doubt, the election of 1925 was one of New Brunswick's
greatest campaigns. The leaders toured the province by automobile,
attracting huge crowds wherever they went. Baxter attempted to speak
French in Acadia, and, for the first time in his career, Veniot spoke to
audiences in Saint John. The vested interests also played their part: the
Liberals accused the lumbermen of financing the Tory campaign, and
the Conservatives, in turn, charged that the Grand Falls contractors
were financing the Liberal campaign. Each charge had more than a
germ of truth.

As for Rand, he had changed constituencies and was running this
time in Albert County, just outside Moncton. But he was not a natural
politician: in one speech he told the assembled crowd that '25 per cent
of the people do not even know where Grand Falls is.'[81] It was a gra-
tuitous insult not likely to earn any votes. When the booing began, he
tried to explain that he too had to look it up. But it was too late. The locals may not have been able to locate Grand Falls on the map, but they
knew when they were being belittled.[82] 'Aloof,' 'austere,' 'remote,' and
'forbidding' was how he was described. On one occasion he crossed the
street to avoid entering into what he suspected would be a senseless
and time-consuming conversation with one of his constituents. Averse
to compromise, redundant explanations, small talk, shaking hands,
and campaign promises, Rand, for all his smarts, did not impress the
voters.

When the people of New Brunswick headed to the polls on August

10, forty-eight seats were at stake. Voting began at 8 a.m. and, for the first time in New Brunswick's history, automobiles were used to bring out the voters. It was a Conservative landslide: thirty-six Tories were elected. 'The best government which the province has ever had has been defeated,' the *Moncton Transcript* (owned by Clifford Robinson) editorialized in the aftermath of the Liberal's election loss, 'and now the administration will largely be taken over by the same leaders who were responsible for the carnival of graft and corruption which has marked the previous administration.'[83] Veniot bitterly attributed his defeat to the racist whispering campaign directed against him. Baxter may have benefited from this campaign, but there was no direct evidence that he was its architect. Moreover, the Conservatives had run sixteen Roman Catholic candidates, the Liberals only twelve. Along with the deep-seated anger against the federal Liberals for their treatment of Maritime claims and the doubling of the provincial debt, Veniot's ethnic origin was probably a key factor leading to his defeat.[84] More than thirty years would pass before another Acadian premier took power, when Louis Robichaud was elected in 1960.

The election of 1925 was clearly a turning point in New Brunswick history. Veniot was an innovator who got things done, although at high cost. The successful construction of the Grand Falls project, a huge hydroelectric plant owned by and for the benefit of the people of the province, may well have turned New Brunswick's economic tide. Underdevelopment and the decline in industrialization continued, just as the depopulation accelerated. Predictably, after the Conservatives took office, they reported that the fiscal situation was even worse than they had been led to believe. Although the Conservatives were not necessarily opposed to the development of Grand Falls, they asserted that the initiative was best left in private hands, particularly given the state of the provincial finances. Balancing the budget was more important than electrification. We will now never know whether short-term economic pain would have created long-term gain for the people of New Brunswick.

What we do know is that balancing the budget did not bring prosperity to the province. We also know what the Conservatives in power did with Grand Falls: Premier Baxter negotiated a deal with the Saint John Power Company, a subsidiary of International Paper, which gave it development rights to Grand Falls, the Maritimes' largest natural water power, and exempted it from 'all taxes and assessments for a period of 40 years.'[85] The company eventually built a hydroelectric station for the benefit of International Paper, and it stayed that way until the late 1950s, when the power-generating facilities were expropriated and incorporated into the provincial grid.

It was not just International Paper that profited from the change in government. The Bathurst Company, headed by Angus McLean, and the Fraser Company were likewise rewarded by a transfer of Crown land and a grant of generous water-power concessions. According to a *Pulp and Paper Magazine* article published in 1929, New Brunswick was 'the private preserve of the Fraser companies of Plaster Rock ... and International Paper of New York.' What many New Brunswickers did not know was that the Bathurst Company was half owned by International Paper.[86] It was not all bad: pulp and paper took its place as a mainstay of the provincial economy, providing large-scale employment and, for the proprietors, a new source of profits.[87] These benefits aside, however, it would be hard not to draw a connection between electoral support and public policy.

A central publicly owned system of the kind proposed by Veniot and Rand may not have attracted industry to New Brunswick, but it might have changed the direction of development. At the very least, it might have turned it away from the increasing pulp and paper dependency accompanied by overall fragmentation – a state of affairs that left economic life controlled by several families and a number of corporations with a parallel concentration of political power. 'A single corporation' – International Paper – 'achieved a complete monopoly over newsprint in the province, coming to share virtual control of New Brunswick's entire forest economy with only one other corporation' – the Fraser Company.[88] Control of Crown land became even more concentrated, as more than two-thirds of the leased forest lands were in the hands of three companies: International Paper, its partially owned subsidiary the Bathurst Company, and the Fraser Company. Any hope for a diversified economy was dashed as provincial politicians, eager to meet the desires of pulp and paper promoters, inhibited the development of other industries.[89]

Thirty years later the provincial government observed in its brief to the Royal Commission on Canada's Economic Prospects that, during the interwar period, a new factor began to retard the economic growth of the province: 'New Brunswick possessed no sources of energy which were comparable to the great hydro electric power resources which played such an important part in the development of central Canada.' As the result, it said, New Brunswick's relative position within Canada continued to decline, leaving the people powerless at home and the province without real influence on the national stage.[90]

Despite his histrionics at the Imperial Theatre in the last week of the 1925 election campaign, Rand had been on the right side of this fight. Moreover, his attack on McLean and Fraser – the heads of the two biggest lumber corporations in the province – showed some measure of political and personal courage. Regardless, his short political career was over. Rand would soon have a new job: in 1926 he was appointed regional counsel for Canadian National Railways in Moncton.

3

The Railway Counsel at Work and at Home

Ivan Rand's foray into provincial politics had been brief, but his accomplishments as attorney general were highly regarded. He caught the attention of Liberal Party officials in Ottawa – in particular the prime minister, William Lyon Mackenzie King, who was a fine judge of talent. Would he like to throw his hat in the federal ring for the forthcoming federal election? he was asked. He was offered Westmorland County, held by Arthur B. Copp, the region's minister, who had clearly outlived his usefulness. His answer was a polite no. Instead, he went back to work for the railway.

In January 1926 Rand was appointed regional counsel (Atlantic Region) for the CNR, in charge of all the railway's legal business in the Maritimes. He held that job until 1933, when he was named commission counsel: that promotion put him at the head of a large law department, with responsibility for managing the legal affairs of the entire railway. As a lawyer in private practice, Rand had made the case that New Brunswick was deprived of the benefits of its Confederation bargain. It had agreed to union in return for a railway, in order to compete in the central Canadian marketplace. But rising freight rates deprived the people of the province of this opportunity. Now, as a railway lawyer, Rand was called upon to defend even higher freight rates and to close unprofitable branch lines and small stations. Going to work for the CNR turned out to be a good move for him. Had he run in the 1925 federal election, he would almost certainly have lost.

The Liberals had not been listening to Maritime concerns, especially about high freight rates, and the people turned instead to the Maritime Rights Movement.

'What are Maritime Rights?' Prime Minister Mackenzie King asked at an October 1925 campaign stop in Kentville, Nova Scotia. 'Let us know what they are so we may fight for them.' But it was answers, not questions, that the electors were looking for. King, however, had no intention of accepting the blame – he rarely did. In New Brunswick he knew who was responsible: the now hated Copp. 'There is a sort of contempt for him & rightly so,' King recorded in his diary after a particularly unpleasant visit to Moncton, adding, 'He has neglected everything & everybody, let his province go to the dogs ... New Brunswick is in bad shape throughout and I would not be surprised if we got only 4 seats.'[1] That was wishful thinking. The Conservatives proclaimed themselves the champions of Maritime interests and swept the region. They took ten of the eleven New Brunswick seats, and eleven of the fourteen in Nova Scotia. Overall, the Liberals won ninety-nine seats and the Conservatives took 116. But with the support of the western Progressives – and their twenty-four seats – Mackenzie King's government could, for the time being, carry on. Learning from his mistakes, King took a first step to assuage Maritime concerns: early in 1926 he appointed the Royal Commission on Maritime Claims, also called the Duncan Commission after its chair, Sir Andrew Rae Duncan.

Sir Andrew was an extremely capable, hard-working British lawyer with considerable experience in industrial affairs. Joining him on the commission were two distinguished Maritimers with good Liberal credentials: Cyrus Macmillan, a McGill University professor, and W.B. Wallace, a Nova Scotia judge. When the commission came to Saint John, the premier delivered the provincial government's wish list: Canadian trade through Canadian ports; encouragement of immigration to the Maritimes; and, of course, an increase in the dominion subsidy. In addition, New Brunswick wanted the federal government to take over another money-losing railway, negotiate reciprocity with the United States in wood and wood products, provide better rail service for Saint John, and improve overseas marketing of New Brunswick fish. There was also the important matter of freight rates. The increases were unfair, he said, and contrary to the terms on which New Brunswick had entered Confederation.[2]

Unfairness is often in the eye of the beholder, and formal equality is often superficially attractive. Why should Canadians in one part of the country be treated differently from Canadians in another part? As H.J. Symington, the lawyer representing Manitoba and Saskatchewan interests before one of the investigations by the Board of Railway Commissioners into freight rates, observed, 'In my opinion, the equal treatment of unequal things is just as bad as the unequal treatment of equal things.'[3] Maritimers had two points, really. First, there was the Confederation agreement. A railway would be built, and one of its purposes was to overcome geography and open up central Canadian markets to Maritime goods. There was a cost to that, and it should properly be shared by all Canadians. Second, it was hardly right to maintain the National Policy, which discouraged the import of less expensive goods, and then take away from New Brunswickers and others in the region through the imposition of high freight rates the only means by which they could compete in the distant economic hinterland.

The Duncan Commission concluded in its report in September that there was a difference between 'Maritime Rights' and 'Maritime Claims,' the principal claim being that the region had been unfairly treated and was left worse off by Confederation. While Maritime Canada had not prospered, its economic decline was inevitable, Confederation or no Confederation. That did not mean that nothing should be done, however, and the commissioners recommended that Maritime claims receive 'sympathetic consideration and understanding.' It suggested a complete revision of the financial arrangements between Ottawa and the provinces, and, in the meantime, an increase in the dominion subsidy. Transportation was among its bigger concerns: 'We have come very definitely to the conclusion that the rate structure as it has been altered since 1912 has placed upon the trade and commerce of the Maritime Provinces, (a) a burden which, as we have read the pronouncements and obligations undertaken at Confederation, it was never intended it should bear, and (b) a burden which is, in fact, responsible in very considerable measure for depressing abnormally in the Maritimes to-day business and enterprise which had originated and developed before 1912 on the basis and faith of the rate structure as it then stood.'[4] The situation required redress 'drastically and promptly.' That meant immediate reductions in Atlantic Division freight rates all the way to Lévis, opposite Quebec City, with the cost being borne by the dominion government.[5] In addition, the Duncan Commission recommended that rates should be structured in a way that encouraged industrial development in the region.

As opposition leader during the brief Arthur Meighen government in 1926, Mackenzie King had promised that a Liberal government would implement whatever legislation the Duncan Commission recommended. When the report came out, he saw in it the rehabilitation of Liberal fortunes in the Maritimes: 'All I need to do,' he confided to his diary, 'is to stand firm on this report, and count on getting back Maritime support to keep us strong in future years where we may lose a little in Quebec and elsewhere.'[6] Incorporating all the recommendations of the Duncan Commission, however, was out of the question. When costed, Duncan's wide-ranging program was prohibitively expensive and politically unwise. But something had to be done, and, on 1 July 1927, the *Maritime Freight Rates Act* was proclaimed in force.

The reasons for the legislation were set out in its preamble. Reference was made to the Confederation promise and the national need for the Intercolonial Railway with its strategic meandering route, not to mention the recommendations of the Duncan Commission. The clauses then provided that freight rates within the Maritimes, and westward from the Maritimes to Lévis, be reduced by 20 per cent, with the difference paid out of general revenue. The Board of Railway Commissioners was directed to maintain these tariffs and empowered to adjust them from time to time to meet increases or reductions in the cost of operations. The purpose of the act, simply put, was to provide the Maritime provinces with reduced rates – rates that were not based on business principles. A 'fair return' for the railway was not to be the basis on which the rates were set, and 'favoured persons and industries' were to 'enjoy the discrimination.'[7] Significantly, the new legislation did nothing to protect Maritime producers from the centralizing bias in the system which would, in due course, destroy the limited advantage provided by the reduction.[8]

Moreover, on close inspection, the rate reduction was not really 20 per cent. Although the CNR received a 20 per cent subsidy, it was not fully passed on. For instance, the railway applied the subsidy to its Standard Mileage Rates instead of any competitive rates that might be in force. In the summer months, railway rates were reduced to meet direct competition from ocean traffic through the St Lawrence. There were other problems as well. Truck transportation was an emerging and increasingly viable competitor, and later rate increases would, over time, insidiously dissipate the value of the subsidy. The opening of the St Lawrence Seaway, allowing ocean ships to travel all the way to the Lakehead, would further diminish the volume of goods transported by rail. But as any politician knows, and Mackenzie King knew very well, bad news deferred is bad news avoided. Expressing acute concern and promising to implement all the recommendations was one thing; doing it, quite another.

The government also promised that trade would be encouraged on Canadian soil through Canadian ports, but exports continued to make their way through American ports for reasons that are obvious when you look at a map. Parliament may be supreme, but it is hard to suppress market forces and economic laws. Ultimately, New Brunswick's fiscal problems were more easily diagnosed than redressed. There was something for everyone. Nova Scotia's suffering coal and steel industry – centred in Cape Breton – received a boost by passage of the *Canadian Coal Equality Act*, which gave steel producers a payment on coal mined in Canada which was used in the Canadian manufacture of iron and steel. Although nothing could be done to make coal mining in Cape Breton viable over the long term, as Rand would discover later in his career, this subsidy, like the subsidized freight rates, was welcomed. In essence, however, government subsidies are awkward and inefficient tools, incapable of promoting and then maintaining the institutional and other changes that Maritime producers needed if they were to compete effectively. As the Duncan Commission had concluded, regional economic decline was probably inevitable. There was no turning back the clock.

In his new position as regional counsel for the CNR in the Atlantic Region, Rand was engaged at a salary of $9,000 per year, which was soon raised to the incredible sum of $10,000. Moncton was one of three regional headquarters, along with Toronto and Winnipeg, with Montreal as head office. The regional offices were autonomously run, but consultations between regional and head-office counsel were frequent, particularly over matters with system-wide impact. Rand's practice, as for most lawyers in the department, was mixed. There was litigation – CNR lawyers appeared before virtually every Canadian court. There were also arbitration proceedings, applications before regulatory boards, and royal commissions, to name just a few of the forums where CNR lawyers would regularly appear. There was also considerable legal drafting and opinion work. The responsibilities were varied and endless, because the railway almost never admitted fault and litigated everything.

Rand's job required him to defend the company from all sorts of civil actions: in addition to the usual slip-and-fall accident claims by passengers, there were railway derailments, injuries at unguarded rights of way and public crossings, claims for animals that were killed, fires and floods, and automobile, truck, wagon, and bicycle accidents. In the many trials arising out of accidents at level crossings, Rand invariably urged the judge and jury to dismiss the claim because the plaintiff had failed to notice 'the approach of the train.' He also had many commercial matters to address. When PEI and New Brunswick potato farmers sought a freight-rate reduction to match one their Ontario counterparts had obtained, he fought the request all the way to the Supreme Court of Canada. He argued that no Maritime rate should be reduced merely because some local rate outside the Maritimes had been lowered.[9] In another case, also taken to Ottawa, Rand argued that barrels of molasses had been destroyed by the perils of the sea, not because they had been improperly stowed.[10]

There was no end to the disputes. Farmers sought repairs to abandoned crossings, and students demanded cheaper train tickets. Owners of expropriated land for spur lines asserted that the price offered by the railway was not right. Sometimes Rand had to defend cases involving discharge and discipline when employees were dismissed for negligence. There were also disputes with other railways over 'switching charges,' for example, the amount one railway could charge another for carrying some of its freight short distances, or over the railway's right to substitute 'bells and wig wags' for gates and watchmen at shared intersections. These and other cases proceeded first to the Board of Railway Commissioners and then to the Supreme Court. There Rand came to know the judges well as he faced other leading counsel from across the country.

CNR v. Saint John Motor Line Limited was a case in point. A bus and a train had collided in Saint John, and the bus company sued for damages. It was successful, although not entirely, as the jury concluded that there was some contributory negligence on the part of the bus company, and the award – $4,124.11 – was reduced by 10 per cent. The case went to appeal, where the damages were further reduced after the judges determined there was no evidence for part of the loss that the jury had compensated. That decision should have ended the matter, but Rand would not give up and took the case to the Supreme Court. Although the court was generally 'unwilling to disturb the findings of judgment of the Appellate Division,' it decided to do so because 'Mr. Rand for the defendant, raised ingeniously a new and important point, which had not been considered or mentioned at the trial, or upon the provincial appeal.'[11] The CNR included the old ICR, he argued, and so was part and parcel of the Crown. That being the case, New Brunswick's *Contributory Negligence Act* did not apply, and the CNR could not be subject to an apportionment of damages under it. The other side cried foul: it was far too late for the CNR to raise this defence. The Supreme Court sided with Rand, but ameliorated the result by directing a new trial and making the railway pay the bus company's full legal costs at the earlier trial and appeal – cases that were 'lost by reason of the defendant's failure to raise, in the lower courts, the contention upon which it now succeeds.'[12] So Rand won round one.

If cases went against the railway, appeals were invariably filed and clever arguments advanced to avoid liability: one occasional employee, for example, injured while shovelling snow, had, Rand successfully argued, no claim against the CNR because the injury, a collision, was caused by the carelessness of his fellow workers. The doctrine of 'common employment' therefore trumped, even though the worker, through no fault of his own, 'suffered great injury.' Whatever entitlements he had were, therefore, those available under the provincial workers' compensation scheme. That same accident, which left four workers dead and eleven injured, saw the responsible employees taken to task in a grievance arbitration, of a sort, before the Board of Railway Commissioners. Rand again appeared, and the board, exercising jurisdiction over railway accidents, directed the railway to discipline and discharge the employees found negligent in the performance of their duties.[13] The City of Moncton, in one case, claimed it had the power to regulate the speed of trains in the city limits. Not so, said Rand, and, once again, his wily argument prevailed.[14]

The CNR fought with municipalities over just about everything: paying for the repair of roads or unsafe crossings, closing uneconomical stations, replacing an agent with a caretaker, constructing sidings or new routes, and abandoning existing ones. The railway's losses had to be weighed against the public inconvenience that would result from abandonment – and, if abandoned, there was further consideration of the condition the bridges or crossings should be left in and their future maintenance.

According to one sympathetic source, in cases where Rand sought leave before the board to discontinue a branch rail line and the community went unrepresented, his sense of fairness led him to say what he could on behalf of the local interest.[15] A review of all Rand's appearances before the board does not, however, support this contention. In any event, the CNR had almost perfected its method of eliminating unwanted routes: it simply 'demarketed' the line. What that meant was that the railway would deliberately provide such poor service that customers had no option but to use truck transport. Once the demand for rail service declined sufficiently, the line could be abandoned without concern for local protests, should the community try to fight the decision. The approach did not always work, however. When the railway wanted to close the 21-kilometre branch line from Petitcodiac to Havelock and the 22-kilometre line from Petitcodiac to Elgin, for example, residents and shippers howled in protest and filed an appeal with the commission. The petitioners claimed that their properties would be worthless, lumbering interests compromised, local dairy industries destroyed, and back districts isolated during the five months of winter. The CNR had a different slant on the story, as 'Mr. Rand cited financial, technical and operation reports in support of the application.'[16]

The board rejected the railway's request. After noting that forty families had been induced by the provincial government to settle in the area because it was 'handy' to the railway, it ruled that 'suspension of the service would be disastrous to communities which have no other railroad service, and no adequate highways for truck and automobile traffic.' It added that the 'maple sugar industry would be ruined. Farmers would be seriously handicapped in disposing of their products and the handling of supplies. Substantial decreases in the values of real estate would result. Lumber companies would have to close their plants, thereby adding to the list of the unemployed by the dismissal of those now employed in lumbering and milling.' Accordingly, the CNR's application was dismissed.[17] As the board noted in another case in which Rand appeared, 'the mere fact that a branch line of a railway has ceased to show a profit from its operation does not, in every case, justify its abandonment. The issue is clearly, however, whether the loss and inconvenience to the public consequent upon the abandonment outweigh the burden that continued operation of the railway line involved would impose upon the railway company.'[18]

There were also questions that sent Rand back to the law books for answers. Was it possible, he was asked, to split an employee's pay cheque in two and direct one of the parts to the employee's former spouse? The employee and his ex-wife had agreed on the arrangement they referred to as a partial assignment of wages. All they wanted was a little cooperation from the CNR. The answer was no. Without a garnishment order, the employee's salary belonged to him – and if that meant additional, and unnecessary, court proceedings, so be it.[19]

On another occasion, Rand challenged a decision of the New Brunswick Workmen's Compensation Board, which found that a CNR employee had been injured at work and was entitled to compensation.[20] This case was argued before two former Conservative premiers who had been appointed to the bench: Chief Justice Sir Douglas Hazen and Mr Justice John Baxter. Rand also acted for the CNR on an appeal where the railway was held liable for promising to deliver a shipment of potatoes within a certain time and then reneging on its word.[21] Cases like that regularly went all the way to the Supreme Court.[22] And he successfully defended before Canada's Exchequer Court the railway's practice of not paying tax on the seats, berths, and sleeping-car accommodation for employees travelling on business.[23]

At times, Rand's advocacy skills were used outside the courtroom. A bill introduced into the New Brunswick legislature in 1939 expanded the time lines for an estate to claim for loss of expectation of life. On behalf of the CNR, Rand appeared before the legislative committee studying the proposal and argued against it.[24] Obviously, allowing an estate to make a claim on its own behalf for negligence was not in the CNR's interest; Rand's lobbying efforts were directed at limiting the list of potential plaintiffs and the scope of their damages. In another case in 1929, Rand handled the legal negotiations, including meeting with the premier, when the CNR purchased the money-losing Saint John Valley Railway.

Despite his successes before the Board of Railway Commissioners and the Supreme Court of Canada, Rand's record on the other side of the Atlantic before the Judicial Committee of the Privy Council was not as stellar. Of the four cases he argued at the JCPC between 1927 and 1935, the railway's position prevailed only once. Rand first appeared before the Privy Council in 1927, when he was regional counsel, to argue that a statute allowing the City of Halifax to impose a business tax was unconstitutional in certain circumstances.[25] The city imposed either a business tax or a household tax on pieces of property, depending on how the property was used. But if the Crown occupied the property, it was exempt from tax.

In the case at hand, the Fairbanks estate had agreed to lease a building to the minister of railways on condition that it was used solely as a

CNR ticket office. Halfway through 1925, the city assessor delivered a tax bill to the estate. As the lease had specified that the Crown would pay the business tax, the estate appealed the assessment to the courts in Nova Scotia, which were unsympathetic. The Supreme Court proved more agreeable to the plaintiff, holding that the tax was indirect and therefore constitutionally beyond the power of the province and city to levy. Understandably, the city appealed the case to the JCPC. Rand appeared and argued that because a landlord would pass along to the tenant in the form of rent any tax that was levied, the tax must be held to be indirect. The Law Lords disagreed, holding that the framers of the Constitution understood taxes on income and property to be direct taxes, and therefore the provinces were allowed to impose them. Although the case did not come out in Rand's favour, the explanation of direct and indirect taxes is still cited in decisions today.[26]

Rand next journeyed across the ocean in 1931 to argue about something seemingly more mundane than taxes: telegraph poles.[27] But while the subject matter may have been dull, the stakes were high: the Crown was seeking over $700,000 from the Canadian Pacific Railway. The CPR had sought permission from the Crown before the turn of the century to erect a number of telegraph poles on land belonging to the ICR. The permission was denied, but the CPR built a small section of the telegraph line on the land anyway. Over the years the company extended its line along ICR land, sometimes with permission, sometimes without, until the Crown lost patience and began proceedings to have the CPR declared a trespasser on the land and to force the company to remove the poles. The case went to the Supreme Court, which held that the CPR had been trespassing on the land and was liable to pay damages. The CPR appealed the decision. Rand appeared for the respondents. The JCPC disagreed with the Supreme Court's ruling, holding that although the CPR was trespassing when it erected the poles, the fact that the Crown had done nothing about it meant that, by the time the suit was started, the CPR had a licence to occupy the land. Rand did have a small victory, however. The CPR had attempted to convince the JCPC not only that it enjoyed a licence to have its poles on the ICR land but also that the licence could not be revoked by the Crown. Rand persuaded them otherwise, and the JCPC spelled out the conditions under which the licence could be terminated.

In 1934 Rand had his single success before the JCPC in a case between the Canadian Electrical Association and a large group of public

utility companies on one side, and the CNR, the CPR, the Michigan
Central Railroad, and the Railway Association of Canada on the other.[28] As Lord Blanesburgh framed the issue when delivering judgment,
'The contest, indeed, is one between two sets of public utility organizations, Dominion wide in their operations, and it concerns the adjustment of rights and liabilities between them in respect of a matter of
great importance to both'[29] – namely, the transmission wires carrying
electricity and telegraph traffic that were strung along and across the
rail lines.

Any time a utility company wished to build lines and poles on railway land, it had to apply to the board for permission. The board was
then able to decide the conditions under which the construction could
take place. In 1931 the board amended the standard conditions to in-
sert a clause that made the utility companies liable to the railways for
any damage or costs caused by their cables, unless the utilities could
show that the damage was traceable to another cause. Faced with a
clause that forced the companies to accept potentially large and un-
known liabilities, the electrical utilities appealed to the Supreme Court,
arguing that the commissioners were not legally able to impose such a
burden on them. The court disagreed, and the utilities appealed to the
Privy Council. There, they argued that the clause forced them to insure
the entire world against damage resulting from their lines. The JCPC
sided with the railways, finding that the clause was in place to ensure
that, when permission was given to build utility lines, the railways
should be held harmless from damages resulting from their presence.
The provision was not out of the ordinary and would probably be included in any private contract between a utility and a railway. Therefore, the commissioners had the power to impose the condition as they
saw fit.

Finally, on his appointment as CNR commission counsel, Rand took
on responsibility for the appeal of an important contract dispute between the CNR and the CPR.[30] Each company owned a half share in
the Northern Alberta Railway and had signed an agreement in 1929
to ensure that they would both share equally in the freight traffic the
Northern Alberta was sending from the Prairies to different 'competitive points' in British Columbia. In 1933 the CNR persuaded the board
to adopt a clever interpretation of the agreement which would see
certain ports declared 'not competitive.' As a result, grain shipped to
those ports along CNR track would be excluded from any revenue-
sharing calculation. The CPR appealed the decision to the Supreme

Court, which reversed the conclusion of the railway commissioners. The dispute ended up before the JCPC in 1935, the last time Rand would appear overseas. Unfortunately, he was not successful in advancing the CNR's case. In a short decision, the JCPC affirmed the ruling of the Supreme Court.

Rand began his position as regional counsel for the CNR in Moncton just as Sir Henry Thornton, the railway's president, was about to introduce a number of fundamental and radical reforms to the way the company did business. Thornton was an American-born railway man who had been knighted by King George V for his wartime service in Britain. Popular, friendly, and competent, Thornton had distinguished himself by moving supplies and men to the front. He was also named as a Companion of the Legion of Honour of France and as an officer of Belgium's Order of Leopold, and he received the Distinguished Service Medal from the United States. In 1922 he was named chairman of the board and president of the CNR, with instructions to 'make the CNR System pay.'[31] He would never succeed in accomplishing this objective, but he did transform the CNR from primarily a freight carrier into a modern diversified company, offering passenger-friendly service, luxury hotels, an airline, and Canada's first cross-country radio station (the precursor to the CBC) – all but the radio station in direct competition with the CPR. Along the way, Thornton introduced diesel locomotives, which eliminated the largest Canadian market for coal, contributing to the decline of that industry and the jobs that went with it – a matter Rand would be asked to study more than thirty years later. Thornton's most enduring legacy, however, was his common decency and his regard and respect for others.[32] For six years Rand watched Thornton, first from afar in Moncton and later in the executive suite in Montreal. And, indeed, he was someone to behold.

'I believe,' Thornton told a dinner meeting of the Montreal Board of Trade held in his honour several days after he assumed the CNR presidency, 'that every employee of every industry, irrespective of its character, should receive the minimum wage which will enable him to live in decency, in comfort and under proper sanitary conditions, and to educate and bring up his children as self-respecting members of society. Any other policy makes for social unrest.'[33] He had a knack of getting along with everyone. 'The messenger boy,' he liked to say, 'is as important in his sphere as I am in mine.' Thornton took advantage of any opportunity to get together with his staff: the CNR continued to be the nation's largest employer, with more than 100,000 men and women on the payroll. An additional 500,000 men, women, and children – one-twentieth of the country's population at the time – were directly dependent on the CNR for livelihood and support. Under Thornton, the annual report included a section òn the state of relations between management and labour – an issue about which he had strong, well-developed views.

Thornton, who was known for his 'progressive attitude toward organized labour,'[34] realized that relations with the different CNR unions were not what they could – and should – be if the railway was going to be turned around. When union leaders came to see him, he provided them with chairs and invited them to sit down, something many of his contemporaries did not bother to do. He believed in individual effort and teamwork. The first major change he introduced was repeal of a rule prohibiting employees from participating in party politics. Second was an order to all line management: cooperate with the chosen representatives of the recognized railroad labour organizations. And third was his master plan: Union-Management Co-operation.[35] Introduced in 1924 on a trial basis in Moncton, the plan brought together the leaders of the different unions – Machinists, Boilermakers, Electrical Workers, Sheet Metal Workers, Plumbers, Steamfitters, Carmen, Moulders, Patternmakers, Firemen, and Oilers – with members of local management in regularly scheduled meetings to discuss how best to improve working conditions and railway performance. The initial experiment was a huge success. Significantly, in his annual report, Thornton observed that 'the year has been free from labour troubles.'[36] Trade unions, Thornton accurately recognized, 'are here and they are here to stay.' That being the case, it made sense to recognize, as Thornton did, that unions could be 'helpful, necessary and constructive in the conduct of the railway industry.'[37]

There was 'no doubt' that the 'co-operative plan has already reduced maintenance of equipment expenses on the Canadian National by many hundreds of thousands of dollars.' Employees, according to a University of Toronto professor who studied the plan, liked the opportunity to give their suggestions: 'Thus the employee in a co-operative shop becomes rather more than a wage labourer. He is also, in some degree, a consulting manager and his new position gives him an added sense of dignity.'[38] In 1925 Thornton tabled pension proposals before incredulous MPs. Employees who had given their working lives to the railway should get their 'due ... when their working years were over,' he said, and in 1930 he introduced a forty-hour week.[39] Even the prime minister approved: in announcing the renewal of Thornton's contract, Mackenzie King added, 'We have the right man in the right place.'[40]

Initially, it appeared as though Thornton had turned things around. A strong economy, high wheat prices, immigration, and industrialization all led to improved financial results. In 1926, for the first time ever, the CNR was able to pay the interest on its $1.5 billon public debt.[41] And 1928 was another good year. But as the CPR's president, Edward Beatty, pointed out, the CNR had not 'in any year since its creation produced one cent of profit.'[42] Beatty, a staunch capitalist who had led the CPR for a decade, ran a tight and profitable company and had no interest in Thornton's 'mob appeals.'[43] Soon enough, the roaring twenties gave way to the Great Depression. Thornton had spent hundreds of millions of dollars on engines and cars during the good times, and the increased capacity came on stream just as demand all but evaporated. About a third of Canada's gross national income was derived from exports, and, with the international economic collapse, there was no market for Canadian goods, particularly the grain, newsprint, coal, and coke that were shipped to port by train. In the West, crop failures caused by drought conditions, grasshoppers, and early frost limited grain supplies. Normally, scarcity would have increased the price, but, as demand disappeared, prices dropped to their lowest level ever and temporarily destroyed the Prairies' economic base. In the East, the Maritime provinces, which had never recovered from their post-war economic downturn, fared even worse. Only Ontario and Quebec were relatively better off, given their diversified economies. Nationally, unemployment skyrocketed, and it remained above 12 per cent until well after the start of the Second World War. By 1930 the CNR did not earn enough even to pay the interest on its accumulated debt.[44]

Water competition, the Panama Canal, and, increasingly, Canada's own inland sea (the Welland Canal had just been enlarged) took away business from the railways, as did 'commercial motor vehicles.' In 1920 there were only 35,000 licensed trucks in the entire country; ten years later the number had grown to 166,000. And, as more people travelled in private cars or by bus, the number of passengers on Canada's railways dropped between 1926 and 1929 by more than three million.[45] The very basis for the railways' continued existence was in doubt.

The CPR was also a victim of the general economic collapse, but with one difference: it was not publicly owned. The debts of the CNR had to be paid by the public; in contrast, the CPR had to pay its own debts or go out of business. In 1930, for instance, the CNR had an accumulated debt of $2.1 billion, with annual interest expenditures in excess of $50 million. Both railways had, with optimistic recklessness, spent money on ships, hotels, golf courses, and observation cars. Confiding to his diary, Mackenzie King was extremely concerned: 'The whole railway business is one horrible mess – waste, waste so vast that no one can intelligently grasp the whole situation.'[46] The railway also shed thousands of employees, and those who remained on payroll had their salaries reduced. But it was too little and too late.

Thornton, however, was very Canadian in outlook: 'It must be our first endeavour not to operate this publicly-owned railway for profit but to benefit the communities we serve,' he said.[47] His great achievement lay in creating a relatively efficient railway from the piecemeal accumulation of private- and public-sector rejects that no one other than the government would want. But it was at a great cost. Canadian Northern and the Grand Trunk Pacific, two of the predecessor companies, for example, paralleled each other in the West for hundreds of miles. One set of tracks should have been torn up, but Thornton said no. 'People trusted those railroads. They built their homes along them and founded their farms. They have invested their savings and their labours; the roads must stand.'[48] Still, he did agree to abandon some of the less profitable branch lines and to suspend the luxury passenger service.[49] Total debt, more or less, grew to $2.5 billion. Operating and interest deficits were largely met by further borrowing. The CNR's profligacy with public funds could only be cured by Parliament. Finally, in 1931 Thornton asked the Standing Committee on Railways and Shipping to appoint a royal commission to study the whole issue of railway transportation.

Lyman Poore Duff, a judge of the Supreme Court of Canada (and Rand's future colleague and friend), was appointed in November 1931 to head the Royal Commission on Railways and Transportation (the Transportation Commission).[50] Writing in the *Queen's Quarterly*, Ottawa journalist Grattan O'Leary (another future Rand friend) described the situation as a 'crisis' and predicted that 'it will be the most important Royal Commission that Canada has had for many decades.'[51]

The job of the seven-man commission (with requisite regional representation from different parts of Canada, along with Lord Ashfield, the head of the London subway system and an American railway man) was to study 'the whole problem of transportation in Canada ... having regard to present conditions and the probable future developments of the country.' The real focus of the commission, however, was the future and fate of the CPR and the CNR. As the commissioners crossed the country in luxurious private rail cars, speculation ran rampant about what they might recommend. On one side were those who feared the CNR would be abandoned; on the other were those convinced the CPR would be nationalized and merged with the CNR. The commission met *in camera* to hear from Beatty and Thornton, and also heard from A.R. Mosher, the head of the Canadian Brotherhood of Railway Employees, who advocated nationalizing not just the CPR but all other forms of transport as well. After fifty days of hearings, Duff retired to write the report.

When they reported on 21 September 1932, Duff and his colleagues concluded that 'running through' the CNR's 'administrative practices ... has been the red thread of extravagance.' Thornton had 'failed to realize that this country, with the greatest railway mileage in the world in relation to population, could not afford further capital and maintenance expenditures for unwarranted branch lines, for deluxe services, for unnecessary hotels, for the building of ships in competitive service to be shortly abandoned; and generally, for costly adventures in competitive railways out of proportion to the needs of the country.'[52] Thornton had a pretty good idea about what was coming and, six weeks before Sir Lyman submitted his report, with a bit of a push from a group of Tories termed the Wrecking Brigade, he resigned. He had become the centre of controversy when the full extent of his compensation was revealed: it was not just his $50,000 annual salary but tens of thousands more, when the emoluments voted to him by the directors of the CNR's subsidiary companies were taken into account. Moreover, he was not even paying rent: his recently redecorated mansion on Pine Street in Montreal had been acquired for his benefit by the CNR. It was, Thornton believed, a fitting abode for the chairman and president. Taxpayers and opposition critics saw things somewhat differently.

Thornton was an easy target for politicians anxious to distribute the blame for the sorry state of CNR finances. He was criticized as a Liberal hack, mocked for his home life – he had divorced and remarried an attractive younger woman – and mercilessly questioned about his expense accounts. He was, nevertheless, the best friend in management

Canadian working men and women ever had and, at least in one respect, he was a visionary. If the union was here to stay, he held, it was better to work with it than against it. When his resignation from the CNR was announced, the general chairman of all the CNR's unions organized a dinner in his honour for 14 March 1933. Everyone from the world of organized railway labour was expected. The one guest who did not attend, however, was Thornton. He died that day in New York City, broken and riddled with cancer. In response, CNR union members ensured that every member of the Wrecking Brigade went down to defeat, together with their leader, in the next general election. In the end, Thornton had not turned the CNR around, but no one could. He had, however, left in place an organization that, because of the systemic changes he had introduced, was institutionally well equipped to take on the huge tasks presented by the Second World War.

The Transportation Commission's main recommendation was that the CNR and the CPR continue as separate companies. A merger was out of the question, but some machinery should be introduced to allow the two railways to cooperate and improve their financial situation. Accordingly, they recommended the establishment of a board of trustees – of businessmen, not politicians – to replace the CNR directors and to run the line.[53] These trustees should be required by statute to meet with their counterparts at the CPR and to enter into cooperative arrangements with the competition, removing 'unnecessary or wasteful services,' avoiding 'unwarranted duplication,' and sharing property where appropriate. In 1933 Parliament passed the *Canadian National–Canadian Pacific Railway Act*, which directed the two railways to enter into cooperative agreements in the interests of economy and, in addition, mandated compulsory arbitration to settle disputes.

At best, the report was a mild and innocuous document that failed fundamentally to tackle the deep-seated problems facing the publicly owned railway in any meaningful way. Perhaps Duff and the other commissioners recognized that survival of the CNR was the only politically palatable choice. The commissioners undoubtedly realized, as had Thornton, that railways serve a number of purposes, some of which are not easily evaluated by the rate of return. They may lose money on one end but more than pay their way on the other, when the collateral wealth and economic spinoffs are calculated and added to the mix. Marketing western wheat in Europe without a railway would be problematic, just as a remote mine without a branch line would be an obvious non-starter.

In the end, some cooperation did take place. Passenger traffic was pooled in the Montreal-Toronto corridor, and a few duplicating branch lines were abandoned. New economies were put into effect as fifty posts at head office were abolished. Across the system, tens of thousands of employees – about 40 per cent of the 111,389 in the workforce – were let go. Duff has predicted annual savings of about $35 million, but that number turned out to be wildly off the mark. The real savings were less than $2 million per year. As Duff's biographer admits, 'in a practical sense, the Duff Commission accomplished virtually nothing.'[54]

Three trustees were appointed, and they oversaw the operation of the railway from 1 January 1934 until 30 September 1936. Once the government changed and the Liberals returned to power, it was back to business as usual. In due course, Samuel J. Hungerford, a long-time railway man who had risen steadily through the ranks, got the top job.

Rand continued in his post as regional counsel in Moncton but began spending more and more time in Montreal. In 1933 he was appointed commission counsel and began working full time in Montreal. It was a new position, one created especially for Rand to reflect the 'prestige of the duties assigned to him and his personal qualifications.'[55] Although he continued to have his finger in a number of files, he was now responsible for all the CNR's dealings with both the government and the Board of Railway Commissioners. As the CNR continued to be one of the most highly regulated enterprises in Canada, his duties were both important and time-consuming.

By the end of the Depression, the CNR was one of the biggest and most important companies in Canada. It operated one of the largest railway systems in the world, a cross-country commercial telegraph system, a chain of high-class hotels, a steamship service, and Trans-Canada Airlines. All told, in a return to pre-Depression levels, more than 100,000 men and women worked for the company, which was 100 per cent government owned. And, as organized labour itself was the first to admit, 'industrial and labour relations are as harmonious as those existing in any industrial and commercial enterprise on this continent.'[56]

The Second World War brought prosperity back to Moncton, with the railway continuing to occupy centre stage. During the war years, the average number of cars handled in one day rose from 950 to 3,000. Some four million men and women in uniform passed through the city. At the height, one hundred trains were handled every day. The little-used branch lines and duplicate tracks, the source of so much justifiable criticism over many years, finally proved their worth. The CNR's route east now paid dividends, as Canadian troops could not, once war broke out, be transported by the CPR through the neutral United States. Besides, the CPR terminated at Saint John, not Halifax, the departure port for most of Canada's expeditionary force. Much of the CNR's network of track traversed the North Country, where mining revived as the hunt was on to find and extract commodities including chromium, molybdenum, mercury, tin, and tungsten. Freight and passenger traffic broke existing records and reached new heights. Deficits were replaced by surpluses, and operating revenues were able to fund not only interest payments but its huge government debt as well.

Thornton's legacy lived on, and the spirit of cooperation continued throughout the war. As the Board of Directors reported in 1941, 'The relations between management and the employees are excellent.' The cooperative committees not only improved daily workplace life but advanced the interests of organized labour as the various unions at the CNR played a significant role in management. 'Our members,' one union leader told a Harvard University class studying the phenomenon in 1946, 'are no longer mere cogs in the machinery ... The Unions now have an opportunity and an obligation to share responsibility with Management.'[57]

For almost twenty years at the CNR, Rand had been steeped in an institutionalized culture of management-labour cooperation characterized by mutual respect. He learned there that unions had a vital and important role to play in the government of workers' industrial lives and in society more generally. He would have never learned that lesson at the CPR. That spirit of cooperation helped prepare him for one of his most important assignments after he was appointed to the Supreme Court: the resolution of the Ford strike in Windsor, Ontario.

Ivan and Dell had two sons: Robert Nelson Rand was born on 11 July 1914 and Charles Gordon Rand, 'Tig,' two and a half years later, on 9 February 1917. Children are often the best, and worst, judges of their parents and of their parents' marriage, but Robert and Tig agreed about one thing: their father was a stern, judgmental taskmaster and their mother was preoccupied with their father – getting his meals and facilitating his life and career. As a husband, he was nothing like the mild-mannered, somewhat naïve, ardent wooer of Dell. There were periodic muted complaints that she had given up a career in music, but to fill out her social life she regularly worshipped at St John's United Church and became a founding member of the Moncton Community Concert Association and a member of the Imperial Order Daughters of the Empire. In general, though, she spent her days in service of her family, especially the preparation of meals. Ivan liked meat loaf, fish cakes, creamed cod, salmon, oysters, and lobster. Dinner included brown bread with butter, potatoes, canned peas, and, often, creamed vegetables. Dessert was apple pie, tapioca pudding, or junket.

'Anytime we got together at dinner,' Robert recalled, 'you felt like you had to get ready to duck,' as the conversation, and the mood, could quickly turn sour, with Ivan turning on one of the boys.[58] Dell was the talkative one. 'My father,' said Charles, 'was a very private man.'[59] When things got tense, the boys would ask Ivan a question about apples. Ivan adored apples and had one every single night before going to bed. He knew a lot about apple varieties. Ivan would often stop at Laura Secord on the way home but invariably got furious that the clerk would handle both money and confections.[60] Where Ivan was stern, Dell was serene. When he was rigid, she was responsive. 'While his mind was occupied with concepts, theories and applications, Iredell would calmly keep track of their social obligations and the family needs.'[61]

Although the surviving letters from the boys to their father are filled with expressions of warmth and some longing, there was not much love in the house, and what little there was came from Dell. Ivan was often sullen, remote, uncommunicative, detached, and almost totally focused on his work. He told Dell she could not wear earrings. If she did, he threatened, he would 'put a ring in her nose.'[62] He made her record all her expenses in a little book.[63] When the boys were very small, Ivan would take them into the backyard and play catch. He was concerned that they do well at school. Robert was the rebellious son, Charles the more dutiful of the two. Ivan had money, but he was tight. 'I asked him for a loan for our first house,' Charles recalled, 'and the answer was no.' If the boys wanted something, it was up to them to earn it. One way of doing it was by giving their father a massage. 'He'd pay me one cent a minute to massage him, but it would be hard to get past a dime.'[64] The only times they had fun as a family were around the piano, singing, composing doggerel, and laughing. For years, the boys begged their dad to buy a radio. In 1930 he finally did and regularly listened to the Metropolitan Opera broadcast from New York.

Summers were always spent at Shediac, though the boys were encouraged to stay away from the Acadians. Rand did not believe they
'worked hard enough.' When the boys got older – even after they married – there was still a curfew in place: if they were late, Ivan would
put on his boots, get his flashlight, and go looking for them. They were
strictly admonished to stay away from clubs and businesses in the
Acadian enclave of Dieppe. They were also lectured, often in front of
friends, on how to behave appropriately. 'How are you going to make
your contribution,' they were endlessly asked, 'if you don't do – ?'
Rand also made it clear that he did not like rich people, admired so-
cialist playwright George Bernard Shaw, and had no use for American
capitalism. Robert remembered that his father would treat a beggar
like a gentleman but explode at a waitress who did not know her job.
In general, Rand did not attach much importance to women: 'He never
thought they had much to contribute,' Robert said.[65]

Ivan was affectionate with his younger brother Charles, who, like
their father, had a successful career in the railway, but the message
communicated to the sons was less accepting, in part because of Charlie's railway job and also because Charlie spent his free time playing
cards or enjoying a drink. Why, Rand would ask, rhetorically, settle
for the ordinary? Aim higher, he'd counsel his sons, suggesting that
the only difference between him and his younger brother was an ap-
petite for hard work – and neglecting to mention that his brother had
served with distinction overseas in the artillery during the First World
War and been injured in battle. Ivan had stayed home. When Charles
retired from the railway after forty-five years of service, one of the
Moncton papers wrote an editorial about him: 'Mr. Charles W. Rand
has been not only a good operating official but his genial and courteous manner, his great capacity for making friends have gained for him
a particularly high regard.'[66] Ivan could not see that. 'Charlie always
made people smile,' Ruth, the youngest of the brood, born twenty-four
years after Ivan, recalled years later.

Rand had three sisters – Daisy, Minnie, and Baby Ruth – but they
never factored into any equation. It was almost as if they did not exist.
Ivan cast a huge disapproving shadow over all three. For a time, Daisy
ran the Windsor Hotel in Dorchester with her husband. When she suffered the inconvenience of a police raid and was caught with contra-
band liquor, she pleaded to her lawyer brother for help. The answer
was no. You got yourself in trouble, Ivan told her, and you can get
yourself out of it. Likewise with sister Minnie, before she committed

suicide. 'Don't get cross and fly off the handle,' she pleaded with her brother in one letter in which she asked for a favour. But it was Ruth who really bore the brunt of her brother's wrath.

Ruth, the last child at home, looked after their ailing mother for fourteen years before she died. That was understood to be her duty, and she accepted it.(Rand was a faithful visitor in the year before his mother's death. He would quietly sit in the room and keep her company, and every Saturday he sent a bouquet of flowers. After she died in December 1936, Ruth, understandably, wanted a life of her own. She had met a local boy, Omer Hébert, and wanted to get married. The only problem was that Hébert was French Canadian and Roman Catholic. Ivan was furious. Ruth, however, would not be stopped, and they were married soon after Omer enlisted at the beginning of the Second World War. Ivan and Ruth did not see each other until 1966, at Daisy's funeral, and there he met his brother-in-law Omer for the first and only time. Their mother had left Ivan the family home on the condition that he pay Ruth $35 per month as long as she lived. It took Ruth some time after her mother died to gather her things and move out of what was now Ivan's house. Until she did, Ivan charged her rent. After she left, even though he made it clear he did not like the provisions his mother had made for Ruth, he dutifully complied. Senator Robinson offered to try and 'break the will,' but Ruth said she was satisfied with the settlement.[67] Over the years, Dell would write Ruth occasional letters keeping her up to date on family events, so Rand did not entirely cut Ruth off. However, to say that he was not close to his family, including even his own children, is something of an understatement.

Rand did, however, become an active participant in Moncton life, though he and Dell almost never entertained friends or family at the Botsford Street house they owned until his death. His talks to community groups were, in tone and content, substantially about local fare. He complimented a Moncton community group, the Gyros, in late November 1928 on their fine work in establishing a dental clinic in the 'interests of children.' And he heartily approved of another endeavour aimed at fighting tuberculosis: 'The best method of eradicating an evil was to get at the cause and remove it rather than to work on external symptoms,' he said. 'That is, to prevent it by removing the cause.' In this pursuit, friendship and common action were critical. But Rand also sounded a cautionary note. Avoid, he warned, the dangers of a 'group intellect' and focus instead on assertion of 'individualism.' Mob intellect was dangerous. Rather, acquire 'individualism in thought, the

imaginative thinking, and, above all, rationalism.' Did Rand not realize
he was speaking to a service group that was trying to do some good?
In thanking Rand for his stimulating address, the chief Gyro observed
that Rand had given the men 'many great thoughts to ponder over and
from which they would derive considerable benefit.'[68]

There were myriad opportunities for community involvement. In
1928 Rand joined Mount Allison's Board of Regents. In early 1929 he
donated a prize to a local hockey league, impressed, according to the
Moncton *Times*, 'by the importance of the League in fostering good,
clean sport among the boys of school age.'[69] In June 1929 the Moncton Barristers' Society was organized, and Rand was elected president. The following year he took an active part in securing passage
of a resolution calling for a change in the address to New Brunswick
superior court judges from 'Your Honour' to 'My Lord.' Later, under
his leadership, the Barristers' Society passed a motion calling for an
end to the arrest of judgment debtors. In 1930 Rand became president
of the Moncton branch of the Mount Allison Alumni Association and,
for a number of years, played a prominent part at the annual meetings,
which invariably included a 'sing along' of favourite 'college songs.'
In 1933 he was elected president of the New Brunswick Barristers' Society and, two years later, provincial vice-president (New Brunswick)
for the Canadian Bar Association.

All this activity came at a cost. Rand went for a detailed medical in
1935, and the report from his physician, Dr F.J. Scully, was hardly encouraging: 'This patient, due to faulty diet, improper elimination and
severe emotional strain, has depleted his endocrine reserve. Elimination must be accepted in its broader sense, not only the throwing off
of Physical refuse but the complete abolition of mental, emotional and
social worries.' In response, the doctor gave his orders: 'It is suggested
that the enclosed diet be followed strictly for a period of three months,
and then your blood pressure and blood count should be done again.
The abdominal distress will disappear the very moment your diet is
adjusted and you have learned the full meaning of the word *relax*.
Until such time ... walking should be your only exercise. Chew your
foods slowly: remember, if foods were to be masticated in the stom-
ach, the Lord would have put teeth there instead of in the mouth. It
is strongly suggested that you take a cold tub before dinner.'[70] Rand
must have had some doubts about the diagnosis because, six months
later, he booked himself in for another full examination with Allen
Temple, who was also practising in Montreal.[71] Dr Temple found 'evi-

dence of nervous fatigue' and recommended that Rand continue his present diet. However, he chose to emphasize 'Whole grain cereals, Whole Grain Breads, Fibrous and leafy vegetables, all fruits. Avoid: Highly milled cereals, pastry, pies, rich cakes, fried, greasy foods.'

Meanwhile, the work, like the honours, just kept piling on. In 1936 Rand was named honorary president of the Moncton Boy Scouts' Association. He spoke out against changing the spelling of the city's name to Monckton. If that was what the founders intended, he told a citizen's meeting, they would have signalled it one way or another. They had not. Rand regularly attended CNR events, toasting just about every man who retired from the service in New Brunswick, and he refused very few invitations from community groups. Their meetings were invariably held at either the Brunswick Hotel or the Knights of Pythias Hall. Frequently Rand, who hardly ever took a drink, was 'toastmaster.' It was in these toasts, and other public speaking, that Rand set out his views of his world. The December 1929 dinner in honour of Milton Gregg, a First World War hero and winner of the Victoria Cross, is a case in point. Rand's electoral nemesis, E.A. Reilly, now the mayor of Moncton, was there, as was a glittering assortment of local officialdom and society. Rand proposed the toast. 'I do not know that I have ever been accorded a greater pleasure and privilege than to have been asked to participate in this reception to our honoured guest,' Rand began, before moving on to the substance of this toast. Gregg had just returned from a dinner in London hosted by the Prince of Wales in honour of all holders of the Victoria Cross from around the British Empire. Rand approved. 'It is well,' he said, 'that men such as this should have a corner in life's field where they can gather.' Women, he added to general laughter, were heroic too. Why, Rand continued, they were even seeking recognition of their own eligibility for the Victoria Cross. Given that the Privy Council had recently determined that they could enter the Senate, they might need it. 'I will say that the first woman that crosses the threshold of the Red Chamber and sees all the drones there will have sufficient courage to deserve the Victoria Cross. But perhaps those drones are only waiting for the Queen Bee.'

Having warmed up the crowd, Rand moved on to the substance of his remarks: the need for international peace. 'There is still a peacetime battle to be fought, and who should we call on in our civil life for leadership but these men' – Victoria Cross winners who represent the highest in courage and valour – 'of stout hearts and clean minds.' Men must stop killing men, 'and if it is a fact that life has been given for the purpose of destroying life, then it is time that our views are revised. Why should we go through life trailing through slime and slaughter? We have the right to call upon these men to help us establish goodwill on the earth, but it cannot be done overnight and it will not be an easy task.'[72]

For Rand, this call for peace became a recurring theme. Speaking to the Wesley Memorial Men's Association in December 1931, he came out strongly in favour of the work of the League of Nations. Carrying 'his listeners along the paths of history to the present condition from the jungle to the modern condition of progress and enlightenment,' he argued that the old ways of thinking and doing had to be pushed aside. The diplomacy of intrigue had to be replaced with one of openness. There had to be a change in the hearts of men. In the same way that we tolerated the opinions of New Zealanders and Australians, along with our other sister nations in the Empire, we had, he argued, to eradicate inbred prejudices against people of different cultures and race. Only by such 'bigness of outlook' could international peace become possible. While progress was being made, it would be a mistake, Rand cautioned, to leave peacemaking in the hands of the politicians. 'We must not be content, as our fathers were, to leave such problems to our politicians and so-called diplomats. We must think them out ourselves and develop them in others.'[73]

That goal would not be easy, as Rand made clear when he addressed the Model Assembly of the League of Nations at his alma mater later that month. The speech was, the *Argosy* reported, 'a fitting climax to the sessions of the International Relations Club.' The theme of Rand's talk was that radical change was required, along the lines of that imposed by the Bolshevists when they seized power: 'They came into power with a cut and dried philosophy which was immediately opposed by their millions of subjects. There were two ways to regain its footing: 1. By a modification of the existing structure in Russia. 2. The existing structure could be entirely eliminated and a new one set up. The second way was chosen ... Similarly I might say that if the world is to go on, we must get rid of some of things in our conduct internationally that will be as violent in its complete divergence from what has gone on in the past as that change in Russia.'

The fact was, Rand continued, the picture of international relations today is that of 'armed men suspicious of each other.' The new international order promised by the League of Nations and its Covenant, as well as the Kellogg Pact, had not been met. The nations of Europe and Japan were rearming at an alarming rate. Japan had caught the fever, and signs could even be seen in England. There was an explanation, of course – for Rand there always was: 'People interested in selling armaments are behind the war agitation.' Arms dealers had to have customers, and, to destroy their market, Rand proposed a new international order: 'The spirit of arrogance, selfishness, greed, hatred and fear are qualities which civilization ought to root out. They are the springs from which come the inglorious results of war.'[74] Just how to effect this major change in the human condition was, needless to say, a different question for another day.

In 1935, when Rand travelled to London to represent the CNR before the JCPC, he had a first-hand opportunity to soak up the European mood. And what he saw caused concern. Returning to New Brunswick, he sounded a warning bell in an interview with the *Daily Times*. There was, he believed, the possibility of imminent war. 'One senses the apprehension immediately upon entering the country, for it dominates all other topics.' Europe had gone mad. Making matters worse was the fact that Canadians had no idea of the seriousness of the situation overseas: 'The Dominion will have to face the problem sooner or later,' he predicted, 'and decide what Canada will do in the event of another war in Europe.'[75]

In the early 1930s Rand began to spend more and more time at headquarters in Montreal, and he eventually moved into an apartment there in 1933. As commission counsel, he found himself in charge of a huge legal department. There were the usual administrative responsibilities, but that was just the tip of the iceberg. The department was responsible for keeping abreast of any legislative change that might affect the railway, in Canada and the United States. Everything had to be documented, and, in this very large corporation, tens of thousands of legal agreements were entered into every year. There were contracts for the construction of bridges, for purchases of coal, ice, and other supplies, for rights of way, locomotive engines, leases for office premises – the list went on and on. There were, of course, applications for increases in freight rates, and for decreases too.

And there was litigation. There was no end to cases involving the railway, as Rand's experience in Moncton had already demonstrated. Just about every matter, large or small, was contested. In one case that made its way to the country's top court, Rand was pitted against one of the country's top lawyers. He was in Ottawa defending the railway against a claim asserted on behalf of a deceased passenger who, one evening, mistook a cellar door in a rural railway station for the door to the bathroom, fell down the stairs, and died. Louis St Laurent, a highly regarded Quebec City lawyer and future minister of justice and prime minister, appeared for the estate. Rand convinced the court that the lack of any marking on the door was not fatal to the company's case but actually helped it: 'The absence of any notice on the door in question should at least have put the deceased upon inquiry whether he should attempt to open it and (more particularly) to proceed further into a place where he had no business.' The Supreme Court thereupon reversed the judgment of the Quebec Court of Appeal, which, in finding for the plaintiff, had observed that the unlocked door was not only accessible to the public but had been the scene of several earlier accidents.[76]

The legal department's report for 1933 gives some idea of the nature and magnitude of the work. That year, more than 1,000 passengers were injured, or at least claimed they were, and 775 crossing accidents were reported. Animals fared somewhat better than people: 'Canadian laws are particularly severe upon the Railway in the killing of livestock,' internal CNR documents recorded, adding that 'the handling of livestock claims is often simply a matter of negotiation, and this must be undertaken carefully to prevent, if possible, litigation in which the court costs almost equal the small amount of the claim.'[77] In addition, Rand was in charge of a legal department responsible for giving opinions under dozens of federal and provincial acts. Thousands of municipal assessment notices were received each year covering more than 50,000 separate pieces of property from one end of the dominion to the other. They all had to be reviewed. Rand was responsible for instructing and retaining outside counsel, settling cases, and fighting them too.

As commission counsel, Rand regularly presented cases before the Board of Railway Commissioners and, after 1938, the Board of Transport Commissioners, as it then became known. If possible, he became even more of an authority on freight rates. Market forces continued to have little to do with the railway's financial plan, and each year senior officers would estimate the cost of doing business and the adjustments needed in passenger and freight rates. This 'budget' had to be approved by the board. The mundane litigation continued and, if the reported cases are any guide, there was a tremendous amount of it, together with regular appearances before all levels of the courts. In addition, there were negotiations with government and other regulators, along with a host of legal issues, as would arise in any huge national system. Rand was called upon, in a single day, to address issues as diverse as the powers of the railway police, the place of power lines on railway rights of way, entitlements to expropriate, demurrage, derailment, tolls and tariffs, and allegations of discrimination in freight rates. It was not exactly *L.A. Law* or even *Street Legal*, but it was all critical to the railway.

During the Second World War, Rand worked extensively with the Wartime Prices and Trade Board. The railway was highly regulated, and even the most minor change in cost of services had to be approved and properly prescribed. Rand knew the law, but increasingly over the years he was called upon for business advice. He was under no illusions about the money-making potential of the CNR: 'The jerry-built financial structure ... rules out any real commercial basis,' he wrote to a friend.[78]

Rand had his own ideas on how things should be run. And, after Hungerford took over as president, the new boss took the unprecedented step of asking both middle and senior management for their advice on how best to improve the company. Indeed, Hungerford went so far as to assure everyone to 'feel absolutely free to advance any suggestion that may occur to him.'[79] Rand immediately accepted the invitation: 'I would emphasize management personnel,' he wrote. 'A better tone in the service is called for, and this must take its cue from the top. The efficient direction of an army of railway men demands the active exercise of human traits such as interest and appreciation. A machine-like routine can only result in deadening sensibilities and weakening initiative. Nor should we be content to remain a sort of railway plebian; this calls for greater care in selecting men generally and in particular those whose work brings them into public contact, from train crews to ranking officers. There should also,' he continued, 'be a greater disposition to enlarge discretion and responsibility in officers where no vital interest is involved. In following a rigid compliance with formalism, we are too often a penny wise and pound foolish: for example, we antagonize public interests with insistence on what are sometimes properly considered petty or unreasonable attitudes. The actual economy which is the professed end of our method is too frequently insignificant. This tendency is due to a departmentalism associated with Government administration, and so far as possible it should be offset by a greater

freedom of action in individual officers. In other words, my advice is
to build up the officer staff in quality, responsibility and status. The
members must be given a sense of position and standing. With such
leadership good service from the whole organization is bound to
result.'[80]

One of the secretaries in the Law Department had a somewhat different view about who needed to change and how. Rand was 'aloof,'
Edna Kearns recalled years later, adding that he 'had the gift of saying
nothing in many words.'[81] As for the CNR, it was, according to one
of Canada's leading business historians, a 'monument to nationalist
excess ... an ongoing national nightmare, both a parasite on the wealth
of the country and a politicized sacred cow.'[82] It would, eventually,
be privatized and turned around. But that difficult decision was years
away.

For his part, Ivan Rand's work as railway lawyer came to an end
in April 1943, when he received a long-awaited telephone call from
Ottawa.

4

The Framework of Freedom

When Ivan Rand received the call in 1943 asking him whether he would accept an appointment to the Supreme Court of Canada, it was really no surprise. He had been asked eleven years before, he said, when the Maritime seat on the top court became vacant – and he had accepted. But Prime Minister R.B. Bennett's Tory colleagues objected and, in the end, Oswald Smith Crocket, an undistinguished judge on New Brunswick's Court of King's Bench, got the nod.[1] Rand considered him 'the stupidest man in New Brunswick,'[2] and, indeed, as soon as Crocket arrived in Ottawa, his significant limitations became apparent. The chief justice, Sir Lyman Poore Duff, had a very low opinion of Crocket's abilities and treated him like a 'student-at-law.'[3] He believed that Rand should have been chosen instead.[4] On one occasion, the story goes, Crocket, attempting to curry favour with Duff, advised him that he intended to concur with him. 'In that case,' Duff responded, he would 'change his decision.'[5]

Meanwhile, Rand stayed on at the railway. In the years that followed, however, he seems to have been considered for a number of different assignments. In April 1939 the press speculated that he was on the short list for chair of the Tariff Board.[6] In December 1939 rumours flew that he was about to be named chairman of the Board of Transport Commissioners.[7] But Rand stayed put in the CNR executive suite until Crocket retired, again putting the Maritime seat in play. Appointments to the Supreme Court of Canada, then as now, attract attention at the highest levels of government, and, as usual, different

ministers were vying for different candidates, especially since many
believed that this appointment belonged to Nova Scotia.

Prime Minister Mackenzie King blithely recorded the 22 April 1943
discussion and debate in his diary: 'Attended meeting of cabinet and
put through a few appointments ... Mr. Rand ... of the Supreme Court.'[8]
In fact, it was not so simple. The minister of defence, the Nova Scotia lawyer James Layton Ralston, and the minister of finance, another
Nova Scotia lawyer, James Lorimer Ilsley, wanted to appoint Francis
David Smith of Halifax, who was a partner in Burchell, Smith, Parker
and Fogo, Ralston's old firm. Justice Minister Louis St Laurent, the former *batonnier* of the Quebec bar and president of the Canadian Bar
Association, had known Rand for years and strongly supported his
nomination in Cabinet. He was the most scholarly of the candidates
under consideration, St Laurent argued, and, even though Rand had
no judicial experience, he had the foundation that was needed at the
Supreme Court. Moreover, he had a long history of service to the Liberal Party, a point always given considerable weight by King. Ralston,
a First World War battalion commander with a reputation for competence and bravery, was a powerful member of the government and
had to be dealt with carefully. King, however, knew exactly what to
say: 'I told him ... that the day might come when Ralston might wish
to go to the Bench of the Supreme Court, and I thought it might prove,
in Ralston's own interest, not to have an appointment made from his
firm at this time.'[9] On St Laurent's recommendation, therefore, the motion was duly passed appointing Ivan Cleveland Rand of Moncton,
one of His Majesty's Counsel learned in the law, a puisne judge of the
Supreme Court of Canada at the salary of $12,000 per year.[10] The call
came just five days before Rand turned fifty-nine.

Two days later, King and Rand met in Ottawa. 'Had a word with
Mr. Justice Rand for whose appointment to the Bench of the Supreme
Court I am almost immediately responsible. I had once thought of having Rand come into the Federal Govt. to succeed Michaud. He would
have made an excellent War Minister but the Supreme Court today
needs men as much as the Cabinet ... I am greatly pleased,' he confided to his diary that night, adding that 'the Supreme Court has been
strengthened to this extent.'[11] Rand and King already knew each other,
of course, and Rand had taken the appropriate steps to cultivate the
self-absorbed prime minister with regular telegrams and letters salut-
ing King's 'unsurpassed leadership,' not to mention his 'wisdom and
integrity,' reflected in repeated electoral success.[12]

Rand also told the prime minister in the darkest days of the war that he was relieved that the 'national direction' was in King's hands. 'Democratic government is being rationalized at a terrific rate and the concept of an organic structure of principles and laws maintained by the conscious will of the social body, is slowly emerging to a much greater number of the public. To associate the application of the concept with virtually all of the great groups of the human family surely opens the vista of a permanent and glorious Canada.' Although Rand's meaning remained obscure, the sentences were obviously complimentary. Rand also stated that his 'deepest satisfaction at this moment comes from the demonstration of complete worthiness in the leadership of Britain, the United States and Canada. My best wish I can give to this land is that it may continue to have its Cause charted by such intelligence.'[13] King, when he replied, could only agree. In January 1944, at a dinner for the retiring chief justice, the prime minister confided to Rand that he had considered taking him 'into the Cabinet instead of the Bench.' Rand replied that 'he would have liked politics.' But King, being a good judge of men, knew better: 'I sometimes wish I had but I think it is best to have him in the Supreme Court.'[14]

Reaction to the appointment was universally positive. The *Ottawa Journal* observed that 'nothing much better has happened to the Supreme Court in a long time.' Rand, the editorial added, was not well known to the public. But that did not mean he was not respected: 'a limited circle have long known of Ivan Rand, known of his learning, his civilized mind, his breadth of vision, his sense of measure. They know he will take to the Supreme Court intellectual and legal equipment which there should serve Canada well. Upon this appointment, one of the finest he has made in a long time, Prime Minister King is to be commended warmly.'[15] The chief justice wrote to Rand to congratulate him. Rand thanked Duff for his 'generous message,' confiding that his 'highest aspiration has been to sit on a court presided over by you.'[16]

His colleagues at the Moncton CNR shop presented him with a leather travelling bag, while his colleagues in the law, including his former partner, Senator Clifford Robinson, feted him at a reception on the eve of his departure for Ottawa, sending him on his way with a 'handsome Waterman pen and pencil set.' It was a time for celebration – the most extraordinary honour and responsibility to be bestowed on any lawyer – and there was nothing but good cheer. Robinson reminisced about his days of private practice with Rand. He was, he recalled, an 'intimate friend,' a 'citizen of sterling worth,' and 'a good and fine man.' Robinson always knew, he reported, that some day Rand's services would be called for at the Supreme Court. But let there be no mistake, he added; 'no hauling or pulling' was done in connection with the appointment. 'The Dominion wanted him because he was highly qualified and would be an honour to the Bench.'

Rand also got to speak. 'This whole series of events,' he began, 'had taken place so quickly' that he 'felt a sort of nervous pressure from it all.' He was looking forward to the challenge and was humbled by the honour. It was one, he said, that almost never came about. As a young man he had asked Robinson about a career in law, only to be advised to study engineering instead. He had taken Robinson's advice, but eventually got back on track. His only regret was in leaving New Brunswick. He had lived in other parts of the dominion, he told the assembled crowd, but Moncton and New Brunswick were his home.[17]

Congratulatory letters came in from across the country: from the men he worked with at the CNR, from all members of the Railway Commission, and from other judges, politicians, and lawyers. Oswald Crocket also sent his best wishes, adding, 'Still hoping to dispose of red robes to you.'[18] It was a tradition for the retiring judge to sell his robes to his successor, and it was one that Rand would follow sixteen years later too. The other judges of the Supreme Court went out of their way to congratulate and welcome him, and the Moncton Barristers' Society honored Rand at a banquet at the Moncton Club. Roscoe Pound, the retired Harvard Law School dean, wrote: 'You may remember that I prophesied great things for you back in 1912, and this is nothing more than I had expected.'[19] Rand was not the only graduate of the class of 1912 to obtain high judicial office: one of his classmates, Harold H. Burton, a former mayor of Cleveland and a US senator, was appointed to the Supreme Court of the United States on 1 October 1945. Rand quickly put his affairs in order and moved to Ottawa with Dell, establishing residence at 260 Metcalfe Street – the Mayflower, the capital's finest apartment building – just a short stroll from the Supreme Court.

Rand took great delight in the appointment. Writing to his old professor William Morley Tweedie at Mount Allison University on the stationery of a Supreme Court judge, he observed that, as he looked at the red printing, he felt the world had 'gone quite topsey turvey.' Everyone had made him feel at home, and he was looking forward to the work with 'much pleasure.' It was paradise, but he already missed 'the scene and scents of the East.'[20]

Rand joined a seven-person Supreme Court – mostly judicial nonentities – located in the former carpenter's shop of the Department of Public Works. 'If you wish to enter,' Rand later recalled, 'you will find a door over which has been sculpted in the stone the words "Judges Entrance," but which is used by everybody. Then you enter a dingy hall and go up to the first floor by a shaky staircase which leads you into a corridor, on each side of which you have something that might be styled "Monks' Cells," and that is where the Justices of the Supreme Court of Canada elaborate their judgments.' The courtroom, Rand continued, 'has the appearance of a small chapel, with seats very much like church pews.' The judges' chairs were 'Gothic in character.'[21] In fact, the courthouse was a national disgrace: the plumbing was bad; the place smelled; it was poorly lit and ventilated; and rodents and insects resided there. Many of the books and records were decomposing in the damp air. It was also a firetrap, and, in 1935, an inspector's report recommended that the building be condemned. Mackenzie King thereupon hired the famed Montreal architect Ernest Cormier to design a new building. That would take some time and, even after construction was completed, the court could still not move into its fine new quarters because, until after the Second World War, the space was needed for government offices.

Meanwhile, the court was badly in need of a new man. Chief Justice Duff was, in his biographer's words, 'a highly talented expositor of the law, but he was not an original thinker. He was a judicial conservative, a traditionalist. Off the bench, in speeches, he emphasized the law as a living organism responsive to social change, but one sees little evidence of that sentiment in his judgments written over a period of nearly 40 years.'[22] This is not to say that he was not a good judge. His reasoning was both thorough and sound, and he could quickly grasp the essential points of a complicated case. In his decisions, he paid scant attention to the facts, preferring to state the problem and then solve it. He and Rand would serve together on the court for less than a year, as Duff retired in January 1944, his term having already been extended twice. Thibaudeau Rinfret succeeded Duff as chief justice, only the second French Canadian to hold the post since Confederation. Rinfret was a Université Laval and McGill University graduate who had been called to the Quebec bar in 1901. From good Liberal stock, he was first appointed to the court in 1924.

When Rand arrived in Ottawa, the Supreme Court and the Exchequer Court shared space in that musty building at the corner of Bank and Wellington streets. Rand moved into Crocket's old office, but not for long, as the elegant new structure just west of the Parliament Buildings would soon be turned over to the court. Outside the front entrance on the courthouse steps stood two tall statutes, *Truth* to the west, and *Justice* to the east, the work of Walter Allward, the creator and architect of the extraordinary Canadian War Memorial at Vimy Ridge. These statutes flank the main entrance, two bronze oversize doors that open to an impressive grand entrance hall, with walls made of rubané marble, the floors tiled with Verdello and Montanello marble, and four marble columns supporting the deep coffered ceiling. Matching flights of marble stairs lead to the impressive main courtroom, which is used exclusively by the Supreme Court. All the judges had their own private offices, private secretary, and private washroom – but not until the 1960s a legally trained clerk.

The Supreme Court of Canada dates from 1875, when Parliament, using the authority given it under the *British North America Act*, created a 'general court of appeal.' It was not a final court of appeal, as its judgments could be taken overseas to the Judicial Committee of the Privy Council. From its inception until 1927, the court had six judges, and then the number was increased to seven. When all appeals to the JCPC were finally abolished in 1949, two more judges were added. Three of the judges must come from Quebec. Traditionally, three are appointed from Ontario, one from Atlantic Canada (Newfoundland joined Confederation in 1949), and two from the West. 'Normally,' R.G. Robertson, the secretary of the Cabinet, wrote in January 1947, 'the Supreme Court of Canada is composed of four Judges of Protestant faith and three Judges of Roman Catholic faith.'[23] Jews and women would not be added to the mix for a long time to come. So far, no judge from the First Nations or from any visible minority has been appointed. All the judges, when Rand joined the bench, looked more or less like him. The judges appeared in black silk robes, except on judgment days, at the opening of each session and the opening of Parliament, or when hearing appeals in capital cases. Then they donned a different costume – robes of bright scarlet trimmed with ermine – which Rand was convinced was really rabbit fur and made them look like 'Santa Clauses.'[24] No matter what, they daily donned three-corner black hats.

The Supreme Court of Canada was, Professor Bora Laskin famously wrote in 1951, a 'captive court.'[25] There was no independent judicial

tradition – and there never had been. Conservatism reigned. Formalism – a belief that judges should be constrained in their interpretation
of the law, confined to saying what it was rather than what it should
be – governed their deliberations and their decisions. Precedents
were paramount in all judicial activity. The court's decisions, Laskin
observed, were characterized by the 'rigid application of rules,' illus-
trating a 'lack of independent thought.'[26] In part, this rigidity resulted
from Canadian legal education, which taught rules and discouraged
free inquiry, but it was also the product of decades of subservience to
the JCPC.

Instead of developing Canada's law, the Supreme Court exclusively concerned itself with interpreting what the JCPC had decreed and
then, usually without analysis, mechanically applying those rules to
the case at hand.[27] In the 'Persons case,' for example, Canada's Supreme Court held that women were not eligible for appointment to the
Senate. They reached this result in their usual conservative, formulis-
tic, mechanical way: by looking at the BNA Act and concluding that
they could not depart from the original constitutional intent, which,
in 1867, did not contemplate women senators or even women voters.
When the case got to the JCPC, the Privy Council found otherwise.
Purposively interpreted, women were eligible for Senate appointments.
In what has become 'the most powerful and enduring metaphor in
modern Canadian constitutional jurisprudence,' Lord Sankey declared
that Canada's Constitution was 'a living tree capable of growth and
expansion within its natural limits.' The Constitution was, moreover,
in 'a continuous process of evolution.' In a sharp rebuke to Canada's
Supreme Court, Lord Sankey declared that constitutions should not be
treated as ordinary statutes and given narrow and technical construc-
tions – which is what the Supreme Court of Canada had done – but
should be accorded a 'large and liberal interpretation' to meet changing social needs.[28]

Unfortunately, Lord Sankey's admonition immediately became a
'forgotten footnote.'[29] The judges of the Supreme Court that Rand had
just joined continued to behave as though there was a precedent for
everything; the only requirement was to find it and properly apply
it (or engage in tortuous analysis to avoid the 'legally correct' result
where doing so would leave a case wrongly decided). It would have
been much better for the court to exercise reluctance in overruling
previous decisions but, where satisfied that decided authority was no
longer legally or socially sustainable, to declare unequivocally that an

earlier case was no longer dispositive. By and large, the judges themselves were an undistinguished lot. Rand was the first Supreme Court
judge with a Harvard degree, and only the second with an American legal education (the underappreciated David Mills, 1902–3, had
been the first). But Rand at times would be part of the problem. In one
case he declared that 'the authorities in England have pronounced,'
and then went directly to his conclusion without discussing the issues
involved.[30] With exceptions made for Quebec's *Civil Code*, the law of
England was the law of Canada – a view that excited little controversy,
except among a very small academic elite led by Bora Laskin.

The court in the 1940s and 1950s had some very odd practices. In one
1950 case, Chief Justice Rinfret refused to allow counsel to refer to an
article in the *Canadian Bar Review*. The journal was not, the chief justice
declared, 'an authority in this Court.'[31] No one was suggesting that it
was, but simply that it might contain something of assistance to the
court. Supreme Court judges sometimes cited texts and other literature in their judgments, but only when the text was an iconic authority
such as *Wigmore on Evidence*. To his credit, G.V.V. Nicholls, the editor
of the *Canadian Bar Review*, took on Chief Justice Rinfret. 'Law,' Nicholls rejoined, 'cannot be divorced from its social context, and especially
where the court has a choice, where it is playing a creative role, it must
turn wherever it can for assistance and by the discriminating use of
aids supplementary to precedent – one of which is the legal periodi-
cal – strive to make the law serve social ends.' Canadians were entitled
to a 'broad and forward looking' final court of appeal.[32] Nicholls was
speaking to deaf ears. In addition to rejecting law review articles, royal
commission reports, Hansard, and other relevant sources of information, the court made it clear that it had no interest in the Brandeis Brief,
which was a presentation of relevant factual data gathered, organized,
and explained to assist the court in understanding a legal problem in
social context.

Part of the problem was institutional. When he was in charge, Chief
Justice Duff was unable to convince his colleagues that regular meetings and discussions could help clarify the issues in dispute: 'Most of
the judges went about their work in a typically private fashion.'[33] At
the end of a case, instead of meeting to discuss what they had just
heard, the judges retired to their chambers where, alone, they considered the matter at hand and wrote a decision. In contrast, in the United
States, while the court was in session, the judges usually met at the
conclusion of a hearing and regularly on Saturday mornings as well.

The justices expressed their views, and the chief justice would then appoint one of them to draft the majority opinion, following which concurrences and dissents were prepared. That process regularly led to further dialogue and refinement. The inefficiency of the Canadian way was startling, but more serious was the result: multiple opinions, leaving the legal community unsure of the state of the law.

As the court's chief critic, the increasingly high-profile Professor Laskin wrote in 1951: 'Some of the cases reported in 1950 would indicate that from time to time there is a serious effort to arrive at an opinion of the Court in the sense of having one judge speak for all. But there are enough other cases reported in the same year which indicate – if I may so say, with respect – a conspicuous waste of time and an unnecessary cluttering of the reports with separate reasons by individual judges amounting to mere repetition.' A closer examination by Laskin of three cases revealed that, apart from the dissenting judgments, 'the judges of the majority could easily have said once what is set out several times to the same effect. Conservation of judicial energies through some regular method of general consultation would be a greater benefaction to the country and to the legal profession than the present fairly haphazard system of individual and group performances.' It was obvious to Laskin, and just about everyone else except the judges themselves, that 'the advantages of a system of consultation in terms of time for reflection, of preliminary reconciliation of positions, and of clarification of principles, of providing a group opportunity for assessing immediate and long-range consequences – in other words, of enabling the Court to act as an entity – are beyond dispute.'[34] Needless to say, the academy generated many proposals for reform.[35] It was futile. What the JCPC did, or had done, was the law, a state of affairs that all the justices seemed content to accept.

Rand was familiar with the JCPC, having appeared there on several occasions, and he admired the institution. 'The contribution made by the Committee to the structure of Canadian law, constitutional and general, has been immeasurable,' he told a group of law students at the University of New Brunswick in 1950, the first year after the abolition of civil appeals. 'In both fields we have been the beneficiaries of great legal ability ... There is first the thoroughness of oral arguments, of the examination of both fact and law: nothing is left indefinite, there are no dark spots, no point of difficulty is avoided, every authority is consulted, the tangled maze is reduced to order and made ready for adjudication.' There was more, of course: 'The acute analysis, and

subtle distinction, the apt analogy, the exposure of fact and law to every possible aspect, the mastery and competence of it all; by these, the
art of advocacy and of judicial debate, judged by any criterion, is exhibited on the highest level.' He was pleased, nevertheless, when appeals came to an end, that the 'policy' was settled, for it hindered the
development of Canadian courts: 'I have thought almost a conclusive
consideration of the question, namely, that sooner or later this country
must, in the nature of things, have taken over full responsibility in this
field, and that until that responsibility had been accepted, there would
be lacking some degree of that vital sense, inhering in all courts of a
self-contained judiciary, of their own coming of age and of the necessary quality of their administration.'[36]

The truth was, however, that the long-standing subservience to the
JCPC had retarded the evolution of Canadian law. As political scientist Alan C. Cairns pointed out in his respected article 'The Judicial
Committee and Its Critics,' the 'attainment of judicial autonomy was
a prerequisite for a first class jurisprudence ... It is also likely that the
quality of judicial performance by Canadian courts was hampered by
subordination to the Privy Council. The existence of the Privy Council
undermined the credibility of the Supreme Court and inhibited the development of its status and prestige ... In many cases it was bypassed
as litigants appealed directly from a provincial court to the Privy
Council. Finally, the doctrine of *stare decisis* bound the Supreme Court
to the decisions of its superior, the Privy Council. The subject status of
the Supreme Court and other Canadian courts was further exacerbated
by the absence of dissents [at the JCPC] which reduced the potential
for flexibility of lower courts in subsequent cases.' All told, Cairns concluded, 'the inadequate jurisprudence, the legacy of nearly a century of
judicial subordination, which accompanied the attainment of judicial
autonomy in 1949, has harmfully affected the Supreme Court.'[37]

The Persons case should have changed everything. It was a strong
signal to the court that it was time to grow up. Abolition of Privy
Council appeals presented another opportunity for judicial maturity.
It came in two stages: first, when the JCPC in 1937 validated federal
legislation, passed two years earlier, abolishing appeals in criminal
cases, and, second, when the JCPC in 1947 approved another federal
act passed in 1940 abolishing appeals in all cases. By 1949 Canada's
Supreme Court was the end of the legal line (although any case commenced before the 1949 amendments could still be taken overseas).[38]

On 9 October 1950 the court held a special session to mark the occasion. Chief Justice Rinfret hosted a dinner for seventy guests, including the governor general, Earl Alexander of Tunis; Prime Minister Louis St Laurent; and legal worthies gathered from across the nation. More important, Justice Rand soon set out the significance of the final abolition of all appeals to the JCPC. He understood that Canadian courts, especially the Supreme Court, had been structurally crippled by overseas oversight, and that the new responsibility would necessitate accountability and, ultimately, judicial maturity. Canadian courts would have to find the answers to Canadian problems, within the existing constitutional structure.[39]

Many Canadians embraced this vision of a future in which the Supreme Court of Canada would decide cases itself, free from the shadow of the JCPC. In the words of one commentator, 'I venture to think that the Court, in time, will prove itself to be as free of that ghostly influence in fact as it is in law and that it will re-work its way through the precedents of its predecessor in such a way as gradually to make the Constitution as well adapted to the 20th Century as it was to the conditions which gave it birth.'[40] That was, of course, Rand's view: 'The powers of this Court,' he said in a 1957 case, 'in the exercise of its jurisdiction are no less in scope than those formerly exercised in relation to Canada by the Judicial Committee. From time to time the Committee has modified the language used by it in the attribution of legislation to the various heads of ss. 91 and 92 [of the *BNA Act*], and in its general interpretative formulations; and that incident of judicial power must now, in the same manner and with the same authority, wherever deemed necessary, be exercised in revising or restating those formulations that have come down to us. This is a function inseparable from constitutional decision. It involves no departure from the basic principles of jurisdictional distribution; it is rather a refinement of interpretation in application to the particularized and evolving features and aspects of matters, which the expansion of life of the country inevitably presents.'[41] What Rand was prescribing was a court that reconsidered not only the judgments of the Privy Council but also its own earlier work; in the words of US Supreme Court justice Louis Brandeis, a court that 'bows to the lessons of experience and the force of better reasoning.'[42]

Rand's prescription was potentially powerful medicine, which, had it been filled, could have led to a judicial revolution as Canada's

Supreme Court tackled Canadian problems by considering Canadian solutions. By and large, however, the opportunity was lost, and the court continued to look at new problems in old ways. But there were some exceptions in that exciting decade following abolition of Privy Council appeals, and Rand was invariably part of them.

Dell kept a diary of their life in Ottawa starting in 1946. It catalogued dinners at Government House, the opening of Parliament, evenings out at the Rideau Club, the Country Club, the Ottawa Golf Club, the Chelsea Club, and the Roxborough Apartments, and its famous "French" restaurant, La Touraine, lunches at the Lord Elgin, Murray's, and the Château Laurier, and meals with the Esteys, the Judsons, the Kellocks, and the Kerwins – all judges and their wives at the court. Ivan often returned home for lunch, and what she prepared is carefully recorded: salad and sandwiches, with devilled eggs on Saturdays. After waking in the morning, Dell would make 'Dad's bed,' eat breakfast, do the dishes, and go out grocery shopping at Dominion – then Canada's top grocery store – often travelling by bus. After meals, she did the dishes and the laundry, and then diarized what she made for dinner – roast beef, chicken, vegetables, scalloped potatoes – or salmon and lobster when at Shediac – as well as the comings and goings of her two sons, when they came to visit, and the cleaning lady. She kept careful records of letters written and received, telephone calls, and naps – who had one, when, and for how long.

Every summer the family returned home to Botsford Street in Moncton and then went on to Shediac, where the slow of pace of life became slower still. Dell regularly attended Mothercraft meetings (a great promoter of breast-feeding, among other things) and served Ivan his meals and looked after his clothes. Ivan had three suits – cut from good bolts of cloth – and one morning, when dressing for court, he could not find his grey one. Dell gave him the bad news: she had given it to the Salvation Army. 'I was just becoming comfortable with it,' Rand complained. 'It was like being with an old friend.' Well, Ivan, his wife replied, 'even with an old friend, when he dies, you have to bury him.'[43] While the diary clearly indicates that Dell and Ivan had separate rooms – she suffered from various chronic afflictions – they did share a number of activities: they liked to play cribbage and gin rummy, listen to the opera, and occasionally enjoy a small glass of sweet sherry.

In late August 1947 Dell wrote the ailing Mackenzie King a strange and most uncharacteristic letter. She was writing without Ivan's knowledge, she said, and if he found out he would likely be most 'displeased.' She had heard that he was looking for a successor as prime minister, and she had someone in mind: her pilot son Robert. 'I have a talented but unusual boy who needs help,' she wrote, '... I am not so brash as to suggest that this ... is the person, all I want to say is that he has all the qualities, as I understand them, of a leader.' Mrs Rand wanted the prime minister to put him somewhere where he could earn a living wage and where King could 'study him.' I know 'that he has peculiarities, but so had Lincoln,' she continued. 'Please do not mention this letter to Mr. Justice Rand ... But if you could find it possible to ask him a few questions about his son Bob, I am sure he would appreciate it.' Then came the threat: 'If you cannot help us in this, I feel the loss will be yours and the country's and certainly it will ... change ... our appreciation of your qualities and services to our country.'[44] Clearly, Dell had lost touch with reality, but King was gracious in his reply. He agreed to keep the letter confidential from Ivan, and to watch out for 'such opportunity as may present itself.'[45]

Without a doubt, the social highlight of Ivan's time in Ottawa was his invitation from Sir Lyman Duff to join the Dining Club. Founded in the early 1920s, its members met for dinner the first Tuesday of each month at the Ottawa Country Club or the Rideau Club (which still had a 'restricted membership policy'). One of the group was designated each month as the host, the 'symposiarch.' There were drinks at six, dinner at seven, followed by spirited conversation. It was an eclectic group, including, by the time Rand joined, the journalist and future senator Grattan O'Leary, who later recalled: 'Rand was a social historian; seeing Britain's history through the sufferings, trials and triumphs of the masses, but a loving touch for poetry, music, baseball – and people. Where Duff's heroes of the law were the Currans, the Erskines, the Broughams and the Birkenheads, the legal giants Rand seemed to revere were North Americans – Brandeis and Holmes and Learned Hand. But I must say that Duff and Rand did have one thing in common – both were tainted with the original sin of Liberalism and they never quite escaped from it. Duff would recall pridefully how he had stood on the same platform with Edward Blake; and Rand never quite got over an ideological hangover from the days when he stumped for the Liberal party in New Brunswick. I loved them the more for that. Political parties, like my Church and Communism, *do* leave their marks upon people. And hypocrisy has no place in the make-up of judges, anyway.'[46] All the members would move 'heaven and earth to be present at a meeting.'[47] Duff was the heart and soul of the group and, when he died, the Dining Club went with him.

On 7 January 1955 Duff celebrated his ninetieth birthday. Within days he became quite sick and was admitted to hospital. A decade had passed since he had served on the court, and Rand was the only judge who came to visit. First he asked W. Kenneth Campbell, Duff's private secretary at the court, what he should do. 'I said that the sides of the bed were raised, but I always went to Sir Lyman, took his hand and stroked his forehead. When he entered the room, Justice Rand was a little embarrassed but did exactly as I had been dong. Sir Lyman opened his eyes and looked at his visitor. "Rand," he said, "you are my friend." Rand and I were deeply moved.'[48] They both had great respect and affection for each other. Although they were colleagues for only eight months, lawyers and scholars often speculate what direction the court would have taken had their association been longer. On 26 April 1955 Duff died peacefully but alone.[49] His death, Rand later wrote, 'left a void of sorrow.'[50]

In January 1946 the judges filed in to hear the first case in their new building: the Japanese Deportation case. Although it would be an exaggeration to say that the entire country was watching, this case was, to that point, one of the most important ever to come before the court. After all, the government had asked the court whether it could proceed with its plans to banish thousands of Canadian citizens to Japan.[51] What would the conservative, precedent-bound, deferential, unimaginative, formalistic Supreme Court of Canada do?

December 7, 1941, had changed the world. The unprovoked Japanese attack on Pearl Harbor, followed by Germany's declaration of war against the United States, brought America into the Second World War, thus guaranteeing Japan's eventual defeat. In British Columbia, the quick succession of the attack, the sinking of the British battleship the *Prince of Wales* and, three days later, the battle cruiser the *Repulse*, and the capture of Canadian troops in Hong Kong on Christmas Day unleashed the blatant racism of many residents there against 22,000 mostly naturalized or native-born Canadians of Japanese descent. In the face of public hysteria, fuelled by racism and unfounded fears that their neighbours were fifth columnists working on behalf of the Japanese emperor, the state, garbed in patriotic dress, went to war against its citizenry.

First, fishing boats owned by Japanese Canadians were confiscated. Next, all Japanese – nationals, naturalized Canadians, and native born – were required to register with the authorities. Canadians of German or Italian origin had not been required to register and were, indeed, encouraged to enlist. Japanese Canadians, in contrast, were 'exempted' from military service. Then, on 24 February 1942, an order-in-council passed under the authority of the *War Measures Act* gave the federal government the power to 'intern' all persons of Japanese 'racial origin,' including decorated Canadian veterans from the First World War. It was then only a matter of time before Japanese men were taken from their homes and moved to camps in the interior of British Columbia, where they were put to work building roads; others were sent to sugar-beet projects on the prairies or to prisoner-of-war camps in Ontario. Eventually the internees were joined by their families, who had also been rounded up by the government and shipped east. As Ian Mackenzie, a British Columbia MP who acted as the region's minister in Ottawa, put it, 'It is the government's plan to get these people out of BC as fast as possible. It is my personal intention, as long as I remain in public life, to see they never come back here. Let our slogan be for British Columbia: "No Japs from the Rockies to the seas."'[52]

That objective was facilitated when, beginning in 1943 and without permission, a government-appointed custodian began selling Japanese-Canadian property. Everything was put up for auction – homes, farms, furnishings, clothing. And it was all snapped up by the local citizenry and the government at prices far below market value. When auctioneer and realtor fees, government charges, and storage and handling were deducted from the proceeds, little was left for the owners. Extraordinarily, deprived of their homes, their businesses, their jobs, and forcibly transported to the hinterland with no real way of making a living, many of the internees were still charged for their room and board, depleting further still any remaining proceeds from the fire sale. Government apologists claimed, given the prevailing public mood, that the Japanese had to be 'removed' and 'evacuated' for their own safety. Japan was rightly hated, but, although racism was rampant in British Columbia, there is little persuasive evidence that the entire Japanese community in the province was a risk, or at risk. The authorities should have protected them, while appropriately rounding up the handful of loudmouths espousing the imperial line. The government could have shown leadership by lowering the temperature. Instead, Mackenzie and others did the exact opposite, even though there was little evidence that the vast majority of Japanese nationals and Japanese Canadians living in British Columbia were likely to behave disloyally.

While these events were occurring, it was becoming increasingly clear that Japan would eventually be defeated. The prospect of an invasion had always been low, and, after the Battle of Midway in June 1942, it was nil. Not a single Japanese Canadian was convicted, much less charged, with espionage during the war.[53] However, even after Japan unconditionally surrendered, government policies persisted. Instead of allowing its citizens to return to their home province, even though their actual homes were now owned by others, the federal government offered up a classic no-win Catch 22: removal to Japan or resettlement east of the Rocky Mountains. Three orders-in-council were passed, and one of them, PC 7355, dated 15 December 1945, authorized the minister of labour, Humphrey Mitchell, to expel both naturalized and Canadian-born Japanese, provided certain conditions were met. The justice minister, Louis St Laurent, explained that the 'only ones who are to be forcibly dealt with under these orders are the naturalized Canadians of the Japanese race, or Japanese nationals.' But that is not what PC 7355 said. 'No decision,' St Laurent observed, 'had been made about the Canadian-born who wished to remain in Canada but if any action were taken, Parliament, not the cabinet alone, would legislate.'[54]

In marked contrast to December 1941, when Canadian citizens had been wrongfully imprisoned and robbed, this time around there were enough public protests about the plan to attract the attention of the prime minister. The horrors of the Holocaust were still fresh, and the prospect of removing – banishing, really – Canadian citizens to a country many did not know offended the sensibilities of a sufficient number of Canadians to require some kind of response. Yet, rather than reverse the decision, the government referred it to the Supreme Court of Canada.

The case was heard by the Supreme Court on two days in late January 1946. In less than one month, judgment was delivered. On behalf of the majority, Chief Justice Rinfret held that the orders-in-council were constitutional. The Cabinet, he asserted, 'was the sole judge of the necessity or advisability of these measures.' A majority of the court concurred – meaning, in effect, that the Canadian government could expel some of its own citizens. However, a majority of the judges also drew the line at the deportation of wives, children, and the native born who had not agreed to removal but who were swept in because a husband or father had. Paradoxically, at the same time that a majority of the judges were approving the government's plans, the Parliament of Canada was giving the final touches to Canada's first *Citizenship Act*, which would come into force on 1 January 1947. Only one judge addressed the real issue in this Japanese Deportation case: Mr Justice Rand.

'Serious questions,' Rand wrote, arise in relation to 'natural born British subjects resident in Canada.' What were they? 'The process and effects of deportation of natural born British subjects under the Order seem to be these: a physical compulsion to leave Canadian shores; a *de facto* but not *de jure* entry upon Japanese territory: no citizenship rights in Japan and a retention of the rights of Canadian citizenship.' 'Now,' Rand continued, 'I must deal with this case as if, instead of a Canadian national of Japanese origin, I were dealing with that of a natural born Canadian of English extraction who sympathized with Mosley or a French Canadian national who thought de Valera's course of action justified. I am asked to hold that, without a convention with these countries, the Government may, under the War Measures Act, and without affecting the national status or citizenship rights of these persons, issue an order for their deportation, on those foreign shores. I am unable to agree with that contention.'[55] Rand made it clear in these comments that the action the federal government proposed to take was racist. No one used that word in those days, but it was racism that Rand was describing, pure and simple. While the federal government could deport aliens and naturalized citizens, it could not, if Rand had his way, banish native-born Canadians just because they were Japanese. Rand's analogy was not exactly apt, of course. Few, if any, of the Japanese Canadians had expressed any enemy sympathies.

The majority decision guaranteed an appeal to the JCPC, still the court of last resort. Pending its outcome, the government wisely decided to proceed only with voluntary deportations, although it continued with its 'dispersal' program encouraging the settlement of Japanese Canadians outside British Columbia. In the meantime, a royal commission had been appointed to examine whether there should be 'further' compensation for expropriated property. Led by Justice Henry Bird, the commission awarded $1.3 million to almost fifteen hundred Japanese Canadians. This sum did not even come close to redressing real economic losses and did nothing to provide compensation for all the other damage inflicted on these Canadian citizens, including the

4,000 or so Japanese Canadians who had left the country instead of waiting to see if the government's orders-in-council would be upheld. The accounting firm Price Waterhouse later estimated the real direct economic losses suffered were $443 million in 1986 dollars.

On 2 December 1946 the JCPC held that the orders-in-council were valid in all respects, even though the targets – thousands of men, women, and children – had done nothing wrong. According to the Privy Council, which included the former chief justice Lyman Duff sitting on the appeal of a Canadian Supreme Court case for the first and only time, the Canadian government was entitled to deport anyone it wished, 'whatever be his nationality.'[56] By then, however, passions had begun to cool. In January 1947, notwithstanding the Supreme Court's ruling or that of the JCPC, the government abandoned its banishment plans. Persons of Japanese origin still required a 'permit' from the minister of labour to change their residence, a requirement obviously directed at discouraging resettlement in British Columbia. That stayed on the books until 1 April 1949, when Japanese Canadians regained their entitlement to live anywhere in Canada they wished.

In the Japanese Deportation case, Rand stood out. His reasons made no great contribution to the law. More important, he made it clear that he was independent, not, like many of his colleagues, a judicial rubber stamp. He announced how he intended to approach his task as a judge: by probing deeply into the cases that came before him, and not just deciding them in a formulaic way. Rand's humanity shone through carefully chosen words that anyone could understand, even if one of his principal assumptions, that the Japanese Canadians were disloyal, was not founded in fact. Although not clearly expressed, Rand might also have been making the point that a disloyal Italian Canadian or German Canadian would not be banished; in that case, banishing loyal Japanese Canadians was even worse. Whatever the government was trying to do was racist and wrong. People began to pay attention to the court – and to one of its newest members, Mr Justice Rand.

After five years in Ottawa, however, Rand was restless, homesick, and obviously unhappy at the Supreme Court of Canada. Coincidentally, Justice Minister Ilsley had decided to leave politics and was looking for a Supreme Court appointment for himself. He approached Rand about becoming chief justice of New Brunswick and discovered that he was interested. The prime minister was also agreeable: 'I was quite willing to make that change,' King wrote in his diary on 28 May 1948.[57] But the premier, John B. McNair, was not – he wanted the job filled with a warm body, one 'not likely to live very long,' who could be eased out in case he decided he wanted the post for himself. So Rand stayed in Ottawa, and, in 1955, McNair became chief justice of New Brunswick.

If Rand had moved to Fredericton, he would have been known as the author of his famous formula, and somewhat less so for his role in the creation of the state of Israel. But that would have been his legacy. Instead, he remained on the court as it was about to enter its critical decade and, in a handful of cases, Rand moved the law forward. Although nothing in his background presaged this contribution, over the next decade he established a reputation as Canada's greatest civil libertarian judge. This accomplishment cannot be overstated, because, when certain key cases came before him, the civil liberties he proclaimed were invented out of whole cloth. Most of the cases involved a dispute over the division of powers. Who was entitled to legislate: the federal Parliament or the provincial legislatures? By and large, judicial assignment of legislative jurisdiction was a routine task. Even cases that cried out for judicial intervention, such as the Persons case or the Japanese Deportation case, were approached by most Supreme Court judges in exactly the same way as a minor commercial dispute – by applying precedent and determining whether it was Parliament or a province, or sometimes both, that had been assigned legislative authority. Because there was no Bill of Rights, as in the United States, or anything like the *Charter of Rights and Freedoms*, which was more than a generation away, there were no judicial tools at hand. Rand was left with little choice but to imply a Bill of Rights. The opportunity was provided by the premier of Quebec and his 'War without Mercy' against the Witnesses of Jehovah – the religious group that figures front and centre in most of the important civil liberties cases in the 1950s.

Jehovah's Witnesses believe that the world will be destroyed at Armageddon, as predicted in the Bible. They used to believe that would happen in 1925, then in 1975, and now they believe it will come within the lifetime of persons who were alive in 1914. The impending destruction of the world is part of the reason why Jehovah's Witnesses are so insistent about spreading their message – as many people as possible must be shown the truth before the world as we know it comes to an end. Once the world is destroyed, 144,000 chosen ones will dwell with God in Heaven, assisting him in ruling a reconstituted world. Everyone else – the 'real Christians,' a group that includes only Jehovah's Witnesses – will live forever in a paradise on earth, just as it was in the days of Adam and Eve. While awaiting fulfillment of God's plan, Jehovah's Witnesses must live in the world as it currently exists – Satan's world. They pay taxes, but they will not stand for the national anthem or vote. Their obligation is to follow the Bible and spread God's word.[58]

Throughout human history, they believe, Satan has been locked in a battle with God, from the instigation of Adam's eating of the forbidden fruit to the murder of Jesus Christ. The battle continues. What other explanation could there be for the tremendous increase in crime, disease, debauchery, juvenile delinquency, and immorality? Satan's main earthly instrument for this activity is the Church of Rome. Simply put, Roman Catholics are not Christians. The Witnesses are the only real followers of Christ. By bringing this message to Roman Catholics and other non-Christians, Witnesses claim to be demonstrating 'true Christianity.' After all, what could be more Christian than letting false Christians know that they have been deceived and introducing them to real Christians?

Witnesses believe that a period of 'pure religion' followed the death of Jesus Christ. Satan was left powerless to confront it, at first. He seized his opportunity, however, by planting fake Christians among the 'real' ones: 'ambitious men ... who had a desire to shine amongst themselves ... and in due time there was established a clergy class, as distinguished from the common people.' Theological schools followed, then priests, bishops, cardinals, and the Pope. False doctrines were introduced, including the Trinity, the immortality of souls, eternal torture of the wicked, and the deification of Mary. Instead of worshipping Jehovah, Satan saw to it that the people were turned away from God, preoccupied instead with praying to the crucifix and playing with holy beads. 'Gradually, seductively, subtly and wickedly, the Devil, through willing instruments, corrupted those who called themselves Christians.'[59] Accordingly, while Roman Catholics believed that they were Christians, in fact, the Devil had turned them into Satanists. It was the duty of Jehovah's Witnesses to set them straight.

There are two main ways of bringing the message to the people: first, by relentless door-to-door canvassing, in the manner of the early apostolic Christians; and, second, through the printed word. Jehovah's Witnesses first appeared in Canada in the early 1880s, and their numbers slowly but steadily grew. Nowhere in Canada, they believed, was their message more urgently required than in the province of Quebec. But Roman Catholic Quebeckers did not like being stopped on the way to mass and informed that they were on the Devil's team. The Witnesses persistence in getting their message across, together with the message itself, regularly attracted the attention of the authorities. During the First World War, some of their literature was outlawed, and their re-fusal to serve in the military won them few friends. After the war, with their numbers increasing, Jehovah's Witnesses expanded their efforts to spread the word. They took to the airwaves as a new way to reach the masses. In 1928 the federal government cancelled their broad-casts in response to public requests. As the minister in charge told the House of Commons, 'Evidence would appear to show that the tone of the preaching seems to be that all organized churches are corrupt and in alliance with unrighteous forces, that the entire system of society is wrong and that all governments are to be condemned.'[60] This justifica-tion for action was rather weak, but even after the Jehovah's Witnesses petitioned Parliament to rescind the decision, somehow convincing 450,000 Canadians to sign in support, the decision stood.

Radio broadcasting might have been stopped, but preaching contin-ued. Sound cars, trucks, even boats to reach remote communities along the St Lawrence River were used to get the message out. Resistance proved to them that they were doing God's work and that Satan was fighting back. During the Depression, some Canadians sought solace in radical political philosophies of the right and left; others turned to God. From almost no members in Canada at the turn of the centu-ry, the Jehovah's Witnesses had approximately six thousand by Sep-tember 1939, all duty bound to spread the good word. As they did, complaints about them flooded in to local authorities, particularly in Quebec, and they were regularly arrested. In the 1920s and 1930s they were often charged with 'blasphemous libel,' an offence set out in the *Criminal Code*. That was a hard charge to win because Witness litera-ture attacked organized religion, not God. Seditious libel, another *Code* offence, was deployed more successfully.

Canada's *Criminal Code* did not define sedition, so recourse was had to the common law that gave the term a wide meaning: 'acts, words or writings intended or calculated to disturb the tranquility of the State, by creating ill-will, discontent, disaffection, hatred or contempt towards ... the established institutions of the country or by exciting ill-will between different classes of the King's subjects.' While the *Code* also provided a statutory defence in section 133A – allowing for good-faith criticism – it was never difficult to convince a Quebec jury that the accused had committed the crime. The Quebec Court of Appeal had the opportunity in 1938 to balance interests but declined the invitation. Leave to appeal to the Supreme Court of Canada was refused.[61]

Without a doubt, Jehovah's Witnesses intended to provoke the people and the authorities in Quebec. In 1933, for example, deliberately timing their arrival to coincide with the plenary session of the Canadian episcopacy which had attracted almost fifty bishops and archbishops to Quebec City, a caravan of Jehovah's Witnesses arrived in town determined, as they confessed in their own literature, 'to swoop down ... like a plague of evangelistic locusts.'[62] Roman Catholics could not help but see the Jehovah's Witnesses as enemies of their faith. As more and more Witnesses were arrested and imprisoned in Quebec during the 1930s, their literature became even more intemperate: *Consolation*, a new magazine, contained cartoons depicting priests as fat pigs and the Pope as a whore. The arrival of the Second World War gave the federal government an opportunity to react.

The minister of justice was Ernest Lapointe, the MP from Quebec East and an impressive debater in both French and English. As the leading French-Canadian member of the Liberal Party and a staunch, observant, and pious Roman Catholic, he believed that it was his duty to advance French-Canadian interests in Ottawa, and especially those of the church.[63] Once the Liberals were returned to power after the 1935 election, Prime Minister Mackenzie King gave his loyal lieutenant Lapointe a very difficult task – to repeal section 98 of the *Criminal Code*, as King had promised to do in the election campaign. Section 98, which had come into force during the First World War, declared that it was an offence to be a member of an unlawful organization – one that advocated governmental, industrial, or economic change by use of force, violence, or physical injury to persons or property. This definition had been tailored to meet the platform of the International, the worldwide communist organization based in Moscow charged with directing revolutionary movements overseas. There was no question about the target: the Communist Party of Canada. But the wording was just too broad, many citizens thought, and the provision inconsistent with Canadian justice.

Lapointe hated communism. He strongly disapproved of communist atheism and anti-clericalism, and considered the subservience of Canadian communists to the Soviet Union and its policies a threat to the fragile balance of unity and prosperity that the Liberal Party was seeking to bring about. 'But,' as he told the House of Commons in a classical expression of Canadian liberalism, 'I want to fight [the communists] in a successful way, and I believe the way to fight them successfully is by argument, by attempting to have social justice everywhere.'[64] Peace, prosperity, decent living conditions, and religious and moral ideals were far stronger weapons in the fight against communism than arbitrary imprisonment and oppressive laws. Lapointe's stirring words suggested a deep-seated commitment not just to liberalism but to the even-handed principles of British justice and the rule of law. Section 98 was, as promised, repealed. But there was still a problem in Quebec.

In no part of Canada was communism more feared than in Quebec. It was received wisdom there that communists were intent on destroying not only the traditional French-Canadian way of life but Catholicism itself. The fact that most communist activists in Quebec were not of French-Canadian descent served to further emphasize the alien character of the movement. Accordingly, while the federal government was willing to repeal an illiberal law used to suppress communists, provincial authorities went in the opposite direction. In August 1936, when Maurice Duplessis became premier and attorney general, he introduced the *Act Respecting Communistic Propaganda*, popularly known as the Padlock Act. The statute authorized the attorney general to close for twelve months any building used for the composition or dissemination of 'communist' or 'Bolshevik' propaganda. There was no provision for judicial or other review of the decision, leaving owners of padlocked premises with limited means of redress. They could go to the superior court and, if the owner could prove innocence, the court might order the premises unlocked. However, even when successful, the owner was required by the legislation to post a bond, which would be forfeited should the attorney general order the premises closed again. The statute further empowered the attorney general to seize, confiscate, and destroy 'communistic' papers or documents. No warrant was necessary.

Duplessis was a populist lawyer from Trois-Rivières, first elected to office in 1927. Passage of the Padlock Act led directly to the formation of the first Canadian civil liberties organization, but the protests against its use by socialists, English-speaking academics, and mostly Jewish lawyers went unheeded. In just three months, from November 1937 to January 1938, the Padlock Act was applied fifty times.

Communists, socialists, and radicals of indeterminate leftist hue were all among its early victims as the Quebec police launched an aggressive campaign to suppress real or imagined communist activists. But there were serious problems in challenging the law. The Quebec rules of civil procedure, the rules that regulate the operation of the courts, provided that legal proceedings could not be instituted against any officer of the administration or of the police over action taken in enforcing the law. There was, therefore, no one to sue. The law could only be challenged on constitutional grounds: Was the legislation within the proper scope of provincial legislative authority? Or was it something that only the federal government could pass? The Padlock Act was attacked as unconstitutional, a law that went beyond the scope of provincial legislative powers. But the Quebec superior court and, later, Quebec's court of appeal upheld the provision. And so the federal government, and particularly Lapointe, came under heavy pressure to disallow the law.

While communists and principled civil libertarians deluged the justice minister's office with disallowance appeals, the preponderance of correspondence suggests that most of his constituents supported the legislation. The fact that the statute regularly resulted in families being locked out of their own homes should have attracted Lapointe's interest, but it did not. Duplessis wrote to the minister and informed him that 'our law has rendered eminent services and contributed powerfully to ridding us of odious and intolerable communists with whom compromise was out of the question.'[65] As the standard one-year deadline for disallowance by the governor-general approached (transmission of the legislation to Ottawa had been deliberately delayed), Lapointe came under increasing pressure. In Cabinet, the English-speaking ministers were largely in favour of disallowance, seeing the statute as an infringement of Parliament's exclusive jurisdiction over criminal law, not to mention an unlawful attempt to regulate freedom of speech and the press. The French-Canadian Cabinet members, however, saw things somewhat differently.

The Padlock Act stood for everything Lapointe claimed to be against. Held up to the light of day, communism would surely disappear. Driven underground by the Padlock Act and other repressive legislation, it was certain to flourish. Even though Lapointe knew better, on 6 July 1938 he announced that the statute would stand. It did not affect the rights of citizens outside Quebec, but there it was popular. Privately, King realized that Lapointe's position meant accepting 'what really should not in the name of Liberalism, be tolerated for one moment.'[66]

However, to accommodate Lapointe, he let matters be. Lapointe justified his decision in the Commons by claiming that the disallowance power was an extraordinary remedy only to be used in the clearest of cases. Moreover, he suggested, the constitutionality of the provision was a matter best left for the courts. As Lapointe knew, the Quebec rules of civil procedure effectively precluded such judicial review.

The truth is that Lapointe believed more in law and order than in justice, and there is evidence that his conception of the former was dictated by his religious faith. 'In Lapointe's mind, no freedom of expression which challenged the basis of the Roman Catholic conception of society could be tolerated ... his Catholicism took precedence over his liberalism.'[67] While opinions differed on what that conception of society entailed, as the international situation deteriorated, Lapointe's conservatism became entrenched and he became determined to protect what he believed to be the interests of Roman Catholic Quebec. The rights and liberties of some communist agitators were secondary to the preservation of harmony and unity – a position that would soon be confirmed by his treatment of the Jehovah's Witnesses.

There were other reasons for supporting the Padlock Act. It was certainly a crowd pleaser in Quebec, and the federal Liberals needed Quebec seats to stay in power. Disallowing the legislation would assist the Liberals' opponents, who regularly charged that the Liberals were anti-clerical and soft on communists. It would annoy Quebec nationalists, who resented any intrusion into provincial autonomy. And it might have given Duplessis an excuse to return to the polls for a renewed and larger mandate – one that he was sure to use in his never-ending war against Mackenzie King and the federal government. The Cabinet, King later privately explained, accepted the opinion of the minister of justice that the Padlock Act did not fall within the disallowable class of legislation. This explanation gave King a convenient way out, notwithstanding his genuinely liberal beliefs. In this way, King harmonized his own highly tuned political instincts with those of Lapointe.[68] In the result, minority political, and later religious, dissent in Quebec suffered. But the civil rights of some marginal groups did not matter much, especially during the Second World War.

It was, and always will be, the duty of the prime minister of Canada to keep the country united. On 3 September 1939 England and France declared war on Germany. The Parliament of Canada was summoned to meet four days later. Canada would go to war too, not over Poland, but at Britain's side. Preserving national unity meant reconciling the irreconcilable views of English and French Canada. There was no question about how English Canada saw participation in the war. Canada was part of the British Empire, and its place was to support Britain. French Canada, while not opposed to the war, was dead set against conscription. For the country to stay united, the government had no choice but to commit itself fully to the war effort while at the same time pledging not to introduce compulsory military service. Only this contradictory compromise could keep Canada at peace in the midst of the war. That meant achieving an understanding with the Roman Catholic hierarchy – and with Jean-Marie-Rodrigue Cardinal Villeneuve, the archbishop of Quebec and primate of Canada.

Villeneuve was no ecclesiastical lightweight. He was a brilliant, complex, and dedicated prince of the church who, at a critical moment in the life of Quebec and Canada, occupied a position of power and influence perhaps second to none in the province. During the tumultuous Depression decade, he practised the politics of episcopal survival, helping to find solutions acceptable to both the Catholic hierarchy and the governmental authorities. He believed it was his right and duty to speak out on matters of public importance, and, when Duplessis announced in the National Assembly the introduction of the Padlock Act, he broadly hinted that the bill was being introduced at the express wish of the cardinal. Villeneuve was suspicious of attempts to compromise Roman Catholicism with modern thought, and he demanded the supremacy of religious over civil society. He wanted Quebec to remain a church-dominated, self-contained society, and in that way ensure that Quebeckers were not swallowed up in the North American sea. It was not only the communists who threatened this vision but also the Jehovah's Witnesses.

In a January 1938 speech to a non–Roman Catholic audience later published in *Le Devoir*, Villeneuve explained how the universe was ordered: 'I tolerate you ... so that you may admire at once the splendour of my religion and the delicacy of my charity,' he proclaimed. '... I tolerate you in order to have your collaboration. In the common good, and when such collaboration stops, when you preach corrosive doctrines and spread everywhere poisoned seeds, then I can no longer tolerate you. Such, gentlemen,' he concluded, 'is Catholic liberalism, the true liberalism.'[69] This view of society was embraced by the large majority of people in Quebec, other than those who were even more extreme. The Roman Catholic Church in Quebec controlled almost all the hospitals, most of the schools, and many of the charitable organizations. The cardinal had a throne on the floor of the National Assembly. One way or another, Quebec was under church control, and would remain so for many years. The cardinal's support was indispensable to national unity and, when war broke out, Prime Minister King immediately sent an emissary to Villeneuve to gauge his views.

Naturally, Villeneuve did not support Germany. But he also would not publicly support the war or the government, at least not yet. The situation changed in April 1940, when Germany invaded Denmark and Norway and, one month later, moved into Belgium and the Netherlands and then carried on to Flanders and France. It took almost no time for the German army to smash through the French front, forcing British and French troops to retreat to Dunkirk. Most of Western Europe was now in Nazi hands, and the situation looked grave for Great Britain. The British Parliament passed the *Treachery Act*, and British authorities rounded up some of the country's most prominent fascists. In Canada, Mackenzie King had gone to the people for a renewed mandate the previous month, emerging with a huge victory for the Liberal Party. Canada also passed a *Treachery Act* of its own, and it had earlier promulgated some regulations – the Defence of Canada Regulations – under the authority of the *War Measures Act*. The regulations were, in general, sensible and acceptable in scope and in object. They were intended to prevent espionage and sabotage by fifth columnists at home and by enemy agents sent from abroad. Two of the regulations, numbers 21 and 39, were problematic. The first authorized internment, and the second gave the authorities considerable power to impose restrictions on what Canadians could say. Some of the enforcement provisions of the regulations were worrisome. As initially promulgated, the police could search without warrants, and trials could be held in secret, although sentencing always had to take place in public.

Hundreds of Canadian Nazis and communists were taken away to internment camps at the start of the war. By November 1939 Justice Minister Lapointe had become concerned that the regulations did not allow him to take enough action against subversive groups, particularly after Canadian communists came out, publicly, denouncing the 'imperialist' war. Lapointe instructed his officials to draft new regulations providing for the outlawing of groups and associations and the seizure of their property. The draft regulations came before the Cabinet at a meeting held on November 21. While Lapointe was adamant that the regulations be passed, King managed to defuse the situation by convincing his Quebec lieutenant that consideration be deferred until

Parliament had another chance to meet. By May 1940, domestic security concerns, given events in Europe, had moved to the front burn-
er. Meetings on internal security began to be held almost around the
clock. Then, on June 4, the regulations were amended, just as Lapointe
wanted. A new one was passed making the Communist Party and other affiliated groups illegal organizations and continued membership in
them a crime. The government now had the power to ban any group
or association merely by publishing a notice in the *Canada Gazette*. The
international situation, it seemed, would get worse before it got better. On June 10 the Commonwealth lost an ally and gained an enemy:
France fell and Italy declared war on the United Kingdom. The collapse
of the free world appeared imminent. The government responded by
adding to the list of the banned: the various fascist and communist
organizations came first; the Jehovah's Witnesses were next.

There were many reasons to dislike the Jehovah's Witnesses: they
would not enlist; they would not rise for 'God Save the King'; and they
were causing trouble in Quebec. They were regularly arrested and sent
to jail, and many opted not to pay fines because they viewed imprisonment as one more opportunity to spread their message. In Ottawa,
Lapointe, deluged with complaints, inquired whether their literature
could be censored. After reviewing it thoroughly, the press censors reported that, while clearly undesirable, there was no basis to suppress
the pamphlets under the regulations. In fact, the censors reported that
the tracts were generally anti-Nazi in tone. Meanwhile, appeals for action against the group continued and increased. In June 1940 Cardinal Villeneuve instructed the faithful to register, as required, under
the *National Resources Mobilization Act* (the *NRM Act*), legislation that
clearly indicated there would be no conscription, though it was looked
on with great suspicion in Quebec. Later that month, on June 20, the
extremely influential *L'Action Catholique* editorialized against the Jehovah's Witnesses, declaring the group more dangerous than any other.
Monsignor Paul Bernier, the chancellor to the cardinal, sent Lapointe
a copy. Even though the Jehovah's Witnesses requested an opportunity to make representations before any actions against them were
taken, Lapointe said no. On July 4, the Jehovah's Witnesses were declared an illegal organization and continued membership with them
a crime. Monsignor Bernier was informed before the news was made
public. The next day another editorial appeared in *L'Action Catholique*.
Now that the sect had been declared illegal, the paper said, repression
would be easier, quicker, and more effective.[70]

Within the week, a visibly upset Lapointe came to see the prime minister. He told King that he was afraid he was suffering from a complete nervous breakdown. 'Thereupon, he began to cry like a child,' King recorded in his diary. 'I went over and sat beside him.' The prime minister consoled his minister of justice, saying he was not surprised. Lapointe moaned. He told King he could not sleep: 'I hope I am not leaving too much to you and that you will be able to get along without me.' King said he should get away for a nice long rest and get his strength back. Lapointe undoubtedly knew that what he had done was illiberal and plain wrong, but he believed, in his heart, that it was necessary, and he then collapsed from the strain. Cardinal Villeneuve, made of much sterner stuff and completely unconcerned about the entitlements of enemies of the faith, faced no such qualms. He understood what was expected from him in return. He became one of the staunchest supporters of the war effort. Such was his zeal that some Quebeckers began calling him 'le brigadier Villeneuve.' When registration under the *NRM Act* began in August 1940, Villeneuve sent a communiqué to parish priests instructing them to do all they could to facilitate national registration. He stood shoulder to shoulder with politicians at ecclesiastical events, directed his priests to read a prayer for victory and peace every Sunday, and encouraged the faithful to buy war bonds. If the price for all this cooperation was the outlawing of an unpleasant group, so be it.[71]

The Jehovah's Witnesses were, of course, left in great turmoil by the ban. Their church property was seized. But there was no question about them not carrying on with their important work. They went underground. The war and the ban were just two more signs of the world's imminent end. Over the course of the war, they continued publishing and preaching and getting arrested and sent to jail. Just walking door to door carrying a Bible could lead to arrest. One night in November 1940, more than one thousand Jehovah's Witnesses, in a carefully planned operation, delivered a small booklet to hundreds of thousands of Canadian homes: *The End of Nazism: Its Fall Is Certain. Read the Proof Herein*. More than thirty pages long, the text was dense and somewhat hard to understand, but there was no mistaking the attacks on the Roman Catholic Church. The booklet caused a sensation, and the police scrambled, mostly unsuccessfully, to find the perpetrators. Repression worked, but not in the way the authorities had intended. At the end of the war, the Jehovah's Witnesses had more than 10,000 members. Once again, they turned their attention to Quebec.

Maurice Duplessis had gone down to defeat in the October 1939 provincial election that brought the Liberals and their leader, Adélard Godbout, to power. As the war progressed, both he and his government suffered because of their association with the federal government. Godbout sealed his fate by supporting the Yes side during the national plebiscite called to release the King government from its promise not to introduce conscription. Duplessis announced that he was voting No, a more popular and politically expedient decision. When Quebeckers went to the polls on 8 August 1944 they returned the Union Nationale to power, and Duplessis began a personal political epoch in Quebec that would not end until his death on 7 September 1959.

French-Canadian attitudes towards communism did not soften between 1939 and 1945, as they had in much of English Canada after the Soviet Union was attacked and then joined the Allied side. Back in office, with the Padlock Act still on the books, Duplessis set out to eradicate communist influence in Quebec life. His main target was the Communist Party, renamed for some time the Labour Progressive Party. LPP premises were searched, the literature seized, the doors padlocked. A parallel campaign was also begun against the Jehovah's Witnesses. Duplessis called it his 'War without Mercy.'[72]

For their part, the Jehovah's Witnesses were convinced the people of Quebec were 'sitting in darkness.' They were, obviously, in urgent need of attention. The authorities fought back. Before the war, about one hundred Witnesses were arrested annually in Quebec. In 1946 more than 800 charges were laid. The sedition provisions of the *Criminal Code* continued to be put to good use. Municipalities began passing bylaws making it an offence to distribute literature without a licence. The greater the repression, the harder the Jehovah's Witnesses worked to get their message out. In the fall of 1946 they published *Quebec's Burning Hate for God and Christ and Freedom Is the Shame of All Canada* in an edition of 1.5 million copies, 500,000 of which were in French. It was distributed across the country, and it painted a sordid and disturbing tableau of the persecution inflicted on Jehovah's Witnesses. A new wave of arrests followed, more than 260 in the Montreal area alone in the sixteen days following distribution. Duplessis described the tract as 'intolerable and seditious.'

Quebec's Burning Hate was deliberately calculated to inflame, describing Quebec as a priest-ridden state where the clergy and the politicians were in cahoots, together encouraging mob rule and Gestapo tactics against the real Christians, the Jehovah's Witnesses. The Quebec courts were also attacked: 'What of her judges that impose heavy fines and prison sentences against them, heap abusive language upon them and deliberately follow a malicious policy of again and again postponing cases to tie up thousands of dollars in exorbitant bail and keep hundreds of cases pending?' The courts were, the booklet declared, 'under priestly thumbs.' Between 1946 and 1953 Quebec authorities instigated 1,665 prosecutions against individual Jehovah's Witnesses. The police frequently invaded private meetings where men, women, and children were reading from the Bible.[73] The charges ranged from trivial disturbances of the peace to arrests and trials for sedition. The Jehovah's Witnesses continued to fight back, and they took their battle to the courts. Three cases, *Boucher, Saumur,* and *Roncarelli,* would go all the way to the Supreme Court of Canada, where one judge would understand the issues involved and, in his reasons for decision in those cases and several others, principally *Winner, Smith and Rhuland,* and *Switzman,* he would cement his reputation as Canada's greatest civil libertarian judge. His name was Ivan Rand.

Aimé Boucher, one of Jehovah's Witnesses, was arrested in December 1946. A farmer in St-Germain Parish, he was charged with sedition for distributing copies of *Quebec's Burning Hate.* At trial, Boucher relied on the defence open to him and testified that he distributed the literature in good faith and in the hope that it would convince Quebeckers to stop persecuting Jehovah's Witnesses. Conviction was a foregone conclusion when the trial judge neglected to instruct the jury that it should freely decide whether Boucher had acted in good faith and was entitled to rely on the statutory defence. Instead, the judge gave the following instruction to the jurors: 'If you believe that a document of this nature can influence our English-speaking Canadians to believe that in the Province of Quebec, justice is not observed, that the clergy has control of the courts, and finally, that there is in the Province of Quebec a burning hate for Christ, for God and for freedom, in that case you must convict Boucher.' In these words the judge actually proved the Jehovah's Witness point as he reviewed the pamphlet with the jury, saying over and over again, 'That is another falsehood.'

The decision was appealed, but the jury verdict was sustained on the basis that the matter was one for the jury to decide. Moreover, a majority of the court of appeal concluded that the accused had not only received 'substantial justice' but had got what he deserved. Witnesses were, Justice Surveyer wrote for the majority, 'incorrigible.' A dissent – 'the judge's charge was not what it ought to have been,' one of the two dissenting judges wrote – gave Boucher an entrée to the Supreme Court of Canada, by then the final court of appeal in criminal cases.[74]

The *Boucher* case was actually heard twice by the Supreme Court, and the appeal raised important questions about the scope of freedom of religion and freedom of speech. The first time only five judges were assembled, indicating that the chief justice considered the matter routine. Reasons for judgment were released on 5 December 1949. Three of the judges directed a new trial, while the other two would have directed an acquittal. Rand was joined in dissent by one of the court's new men, another former Liberal attorney general (from Saskatchewan) and fellow Harvard Law School graduate (1915), James Wilfred Estey. Taken together, the various judgments gave conflicting views about the state of the law, making it almost impossible for a trial judge to give a good direction to the jury on retrial. Accordingly, an application was filed requesting re-argument before the full court. It was an extraordinary application, and even more unusual that it was granted. This time the case was heard by the full court. All the judges agreed that the trial judge had misdirected the jury, but after that, they split. Five of the nine judges directed Boucher's acquittal, while the minority – all the Quebec judges and Justice John Cartwright – would have directed a new trial with a jury properly instructed. The decision was significant because of the division it revealed in judicial ranks on the proper definition of sedition. It also set the pattern for the Quebec judges to vote in lockstep to uphold Quebec laws.

Although eight of the nine judges wrote reasons, it is fair to say that, on second hearing, the court found that an intent to create hostility and ill will among different classes of subjects was not enough to constitute the crime of sedition. It was an ingredient, but also necessary was an intention to incite to violence or resistance to, or defiance of, constituted authority and the governing of society. In and of itself, the narrowing of the definition constituted an important victory, for the earlier broad definition of sedition had proved to be an effective tool – not in preventing sedition, but in preventing Witness speech. There were still limits on free speech, but the broadly worded 'sedition' definition could no longer be one of them.

In the *Boucher* case, Rand made one of his great contributions to the law. He began by considering the facts in issue, and, clearly, he was well acquainted with the broader context:

The incidents, as described, are of peaceable Canadians who seem not to be lacking in meekness, but who, for distributing, apparently without permits, bibles and tracts on Christian doctrine; for conducting religious services in private homes or on private lands in Christian fellowship; for holding public lecture meetings to teach religious truth as they believe it of the Christian religion; who, for this exercise of what has been taken for granted to be the unchallengeable rights of Canadians, have been assaulted and beaten and their bibles and publications torn up and destroyed, by individuals and by mobs; who have had their homes invaded and their property taken; and in hundreds have been charged with public offences and held to exorbitant bail. The police are declared to have exhibited an attitude of animosity toward them and to have treated them as the criminals in provoking by their action of Christian profession and teaching, the violence to which they have been subjected; and public officials and members of the Roman Catholic Clergy are said not only to have witnessed these outrages but to have been privy to some of the prosecutions. The document charged that the Roman Catholic Church in Quebec was in some objectionable relation to the administration of justice and the force behind the prosecutions was that of the priests of that Church.[75]

Rand considered next the conduct of Aimé Boucher. He had, Rand wrote, done nothing wrong. He was 'an exemplary citizen.' Moreover, he was 'at least sympathetic to doctrines of the Christian religion which are, evidently, different from either the Protestant or the Roman Catholic versions: but the foundation in all is the same, Christ and his relation to God and humanity.' It did not matter to Rand that Boucher, as a Jehovah's Witness, had different beliefs. What mattered was Boucher's right to his expression of his Christian faith.

All that was left to determine was whether the pamphlet that Boucher distributed met the definition of sedition. In turning to that task, Rand began by placing the definition of sedition in its historical context. It was, Rand said, an expression of eighteenth-century social assumptions, one of which was that governors of society were beyond public criticism. The nineteenth century brought with it new views, including the idea that administrators of government were servants of, and owed a duty to, the public. As a result, English sedition cases after the eighteenth century began to emphasize that incitement to violence must be part of the offence, not just criticism, whether intended or not to cause disaffection among the people. In England the common law had evolved to the point where criticism was no longer enough to constitute the sedition offence. And, in his reasons for judgment, in his most quoted passage of all, Rand explained why:

Freedom in thought and speech and disagreement in ideas and beliefs, on

every conceivable subject, are the essence of our life. The clash of critical discussion on political, social and religious subjects has too deeply become the
stuff of daily experience to suggest that mere ill-will as a product of controversy can strike down the latter with illegality. A superficial examination of
the word shows its insufficiency: what is the degree necessary to criminality?
Can it ever, as mere subjective condition, be so? Controversial fury is aroused
constantly by differences in abstract conceptions; heresy in some fields is again
a mortal sin ... but our compact of free society accepts and absorbs these differences and they are exercised at large within the framework of freedom and
order on broader and deeper uniformities as bases of social stability. Similarly
in discontent, disaffection and hostility: as subjective incidents of controversy,
they and the ideas which arouse them are part of our living which ultimately
serves us in stimulation, in the clarification of thought and, as we believe, in
the search for the constitution of things generally.

   Quebec's Burning Hate was, Rand wrote, part and parcel of the democratic give and take:

The writing was undoubtedly made under an aroused sense of wrong to the
Witnesses; but it is beyond dispute that its end and object was the removal of
what they considered iniquitous treatment. Here are conscientious professing
followers of Christ who claim to have been denied the right to worship in their
own homes and their own manner and to have been jailed for obeying the
injunction to 'teach all nations.' They are said to have been called 'a bunch of
crazy nuts' by one of the magistrates. Whatever that means, it may from his
standpoint be a correct description; I do not know; but it is not challenged that,
as they allege, whatever they did was done peaceably, and, as they saw it, in
the way of bringing the light and peace of the Christian religion to the souls of
men and women. To say that is to say that their acts were lawful ... The courts
below have not, as, with the greatest respect, I think they should have, viewed
the document as primarily a burning protest and as a result have lost sight of
the fact that, expressive as it is of a deep indignation, its conclusion is an ear-
nest petition to the public opinion of the province to extend to the Witnesses of
Jehovah, as a minority, the protection of impartial laws. No one would suggest
that the document is intended to arouse French-speaking Roman Catholics to
disordering conduct against their own government, and to treat it as directed,
with the same purpose, towards the Witnesses themselves in the province,
would be quite absurd ... That some of the expressions, divorced from their
context, may be extravagant and may arouse resentment, is not, in the circumstances, sufficient to take the intention of the writing as a whole beyond what
is recognized by section 133A as lawful.

Rand was not opposed to placing limits on freedom of expression. What he was against was the interpretation of the sedition provision, which had, through the complicity of the government, the police, and the courts, enabled the suppression of freedom of speech – in his words, 'the unchallengeable rights of Canadians.' There were, in Rand's judgment, limits to free expression and dissent. They were not, however, at the point where the speakers and dissenters merely caused some ill will, but at the point where the words themselves incited violence against the state. The fact that Roman Catholics in Quebec were insulted by what the Jehovah's Witnesses had to say, or by the literature they produced, was not enough for Rand, or for the majority of the court. Boucher was acquitted. Rand's judgment not only sang out, it drowned out everyone else.

The *Boucher* case took years to get to the Supreme Court of Canada and, in the meantime, state action against the Jehovah's Witnesses continued. Even when the sedition law was placed out of reach, authorities in Quebec used other means to curtail Witness work. One of those means was local bylaws and ordinances requiring permits as a precondition of distributing literature in the streets. Persons charged with violating these bylaws usually found themselves in lower-level courts. When convicted, as they usually were, they enjoyed extremely limited rights of appeal. However, lawyers for Laurier Saumur, a Jehovah's Witness, found a way to challenge one of the ordinances.[76]

Quebec City Council had passed a bylaw forbidding the distribution of any book, pamphlet, circular, or tract without a permit from the chief of police. There was no appeal from the police chief's decision, and it was an incontrovertible fact that the bylaw was passed with one group in mind and directed solely against that group: the Jehovah's Witnesses. Saumur claimed that the Province of Quebec had no right to confer on a municipality the power to pass laws restricting the distribution of literature without a licence. He argued that he had a legal right to preach on the streets and pointed to a pre-Confederation statute, the *Freedom of Worship Act*. This long-forgotten law, passed one hundred years earlier, guaranteed religious freedom. It provided: 'Whereas the recognition of legal equality among all Religious Denominations is an admitted principle of Colonial Legislation ... be it therefore declared ... That the free exercise and enjoyment of Religious Profession and Worship, without discrimination or preference, so as the same be not made an excuse of acts of licentiousness, or a justification of practices inconsistent with the peace and safety of the Provinces, is by the constitution and laws of this Province allowed to all Her Majesty's subjects.'[77]

Not so, said lawyers representing the Province of Quebec. They argued that the *Freedom of Worship Act* did not apply, as the Jehovah's Witnesses were not a religious denomination. They took the position that if it did apply, Jehovah's Witness publications constituted acts of licentiousness and so were not protected under the act. Moreover, the Quebec government lawyers claimed that the refusal of the Jehovah's Witnesses to follow the law was inconsistent with the peace and safety of the province. In the further alternative, they argued that the bylaw was a proper and constitutional exercise of provincial powers. There was no infringement of religious freedom. All that the bylaw did was provide for traffic control.

With the *Boucher* victory in hand, the Jehovah's Witnesses were optimistic about their chances with *Saumur*. The only problem was that Rand was seriously sick and on leave from the court. Spare yourself and take the time you need to get well, Ontario Court of Appeal justice Robert Laidlaw wrote Rand in September 1952, 'not only for yourself and friends, but because of your great strength in the Court of last resort.'[78] Sending his best wishes, University of Toronto law school dean Cecil Wright wrote: 'We all miss you when you are not sitting, and we have come to look forward to your judgments, even though we may not always agree with them.'[79]

Rand was, however, a key man in a key case, and Jehovah's Witness lawyer Glen How wrote to him in Shediac in October. 'I have pending,' he wrote, 'an outstanding case on a question of civil liberty which I believe will eclipse the *Boucher* decision. It involves the power of the provinces to censor literature before it can be distributed.' The case was, How continued, number 6 on the Quebec list. That meant it was likely to proceed at the end of November or early December. It was important that Rand get back in time to participate on the panel because he 'would have some valuable opinion to express and it may be in the best interest both of the case and of the Court to fix the argument at a time when you could be present.' How wished Rand well, of course, but what he really wanted was for Rand to let him know the approximate date of his return 'so the argument could be fixed accordingly.'[80] By any measure, this was an extraordinary letter from counsel in a case proceeding before a court to one of the presiding judges. It would, undoubtedly, have been of interest to Rand's colleagues and to the other lawyers, principally those representing the province of Quebec. At the very best, the communication was improper. In any event, Rand's health improved and he joined the panel that heard the case over seven days in December 1952.

Glen How asked for three declarations: first, that the Jehovah's Witnesses were a religious denomination; second, that Saumur, as a result of his training, was a minister; and third, that his manner of preaching through the distribution of pamphlets was lawful. Just like Roman Catholics and Protestants, How told the court, Jehovah's Witnesses were entitled to freedom of religion – and that meant freedom from civil laws that interfered with their rights to worship. Obviously not liking the direction of these submissions, Chief Justice Rinfret interrupted: 'How,' he asked, 'can a country be administered if all religions took the view that they did not have to obey the law?' Why, someone could merely 'pretend' a law was against their religion and then refuse to follow it. Before How got an opportunity to answer, Rand spoke up. 'That is not what Mr. How is saying,' he interjected. What How was trying to do was demonstrate that a breach of a civil law did not necessarily constitute licentiousness. Rinfret ignored Rand and asked the Jehovah's Witness lawyer if he believed that laws could be broken on religious grounds. Again Rand interjected, but before he could say more than a word or two, Rinfret administered a rare public rebuke. 'I want to hear from Mr. How,' he said heatedly, 'not from another member of the bench.' Rand sat smouldering while Rinfret, off on his tangent, continued by observing that if everyone broke laws on religious grounds, there would be 'anarchy.' That simply was not true, How responded, pointing out that the Roman Catholic Encyclopedia stated that Roman Catholics were duty bound to obey divine law when it conflicted with civil law. That was another matter, apparently. 'We are not here,' Rinfret responded, 'to administer ecclesiastical law.'[81]

Rinfret disliked the fact that the Jehovah's Witnesses attacked other religions. He nodded disapprovingly when Ernest Godbout, the lawyer for Quebec City who was defending the bylaw, pointed to Jehovah's Witness literature that described other religions as satanic and to one book in particular, *Roman Catholic Inquisition*, which portrayed a naked woman being tortured in front of monks and nuns.[82] The Jehovah's Witnesses were not, Godbout argued, a religion, and their acts were incompatible with peace and order. The bylaw had nothing to do with freedom of religion. Rather, Godbout alleged, it was simply a police regulation prohibiting distribution in the streets.

How disagreed and left no stone unturned. As he reviewed legal milestones in religious liberty from earliest times to the present, and with a heavy emphasis on American authorities, he obviously strained the patience of some members of the court. 'You have wasted four days of our time,' the chief justice told him. How was not dissuaded, arguing it was essential to go back through history to demonstrate how various freedoms had been obtained. 'Let's get down to the present century,' Rinfret responded, adding that if he did not speed things up, the court intended to invoke one of its rarely used rules – the judicial equivalent of closure.

A lawsuit, Rand pointed out several years later in *Ross v. Lamport*,[83] was not a tea party. 'Except where there has been a clear and objectionable excess, we should hesitate to put shackles on the traditional scope allowed counsel in his plea to the tribunal of his clients' countrymen. The attempt to divest a trial of any feeling would not only be futile, but might defeat its object which is to ascertain the reality of past events.' There were limits, of course, especially in the conduct of the Crown. Not surprisingly, the limits were set out in one of the Jehovah's Witnesses cases, *Boucher v. The Queen*.[84] 'It cannot be over emphasized that the purpose of a criminal prosecution is not to obtain a conviction; it is to lay before a jury what the Crown considers to be credible evidence relevant to what is alleged to be a crime. Counsel have a duty to see that all available legal proof of the facts is presented: it should be done firmly and pressed to its legitimate strength, but it must also be done fairly. The role of the prosecutor excludes any notion of winning or losing; his function is a matter of public duty than which in civil life there can be none charged with greater personal responsibility. It is to be efficiently performed with an ingrained sense of dignity, the seriousness and the justness of judicial proceedings.' In *Saumur*, Rand strongly objected to the chief justice interfering with How's submissions. The pool of lawyers willing to represent unpopular defendants was very small, and the number of judges willing to listen intently to their arguments was smaller still.

Reasons for judgment in *Saumur* were released on 6 October 1953. Chief Justice Rinfret was exceptionally and/or deliberately obtuse. He could not 'understand' Saumur's contention that the 'by-law had been passed specially for the purpose of limiting the activities of the plaintiff and of Jehovah's Witnesses.' It was to be noted, he pointed out, 'that the by-law itself says nothing of that kind; it is applicable to all, whatever might be their nationality, their doctrine or their religion.'[85] In any event, he thought that the municipality had done the right thing. Who could blame the local government? It not only had 'the right but the duty to prevent the dissemination of such infamies.' Five of the judges, however, held that Saumur's rights had been infringed. Seven of the nine members of the court who heard the case gave reasons for judgment. Four of these judges, with Rand as the lead, held that the bylaw was legislation in relation to freedom of religion and freedom of the press. These two freedoms were not provincial matters. They did not fall within the property and civil rights grant of power given to the provinces by the *BNA Act* and so were beyond provincial legislative purview. A fifth member of the court, Justice Kerwin, held that religious rights did fall within provincial powers, but that the *Freedom of Worship Act* prohibited legislation interfering with the Jehovah's Witnesses' religious rights.

And so Saumur won his case. The court's English-speaking judges had come very close to saying that a provincial legislature (and by extension a municipality) had no right to interfere with fundamental freedoms, such as those of speech and religion. To have said that would have been to logically extend the decision of the court in a pre-war reference on the constitutionality of certain Alberta legislation.[86] In that case, the federal government asked the Supreme Court to decide whether two pieces of Alberta legislation – the *Bank Taxation Act* and *An Act to Ensure the Publication of Accurate News and Information* (the Press Act as it was commonly known) – compelling newspapers in the province to publish a provincial government reply to any criticism of its policies exceeded provincial legislative jurisdiction. Under the Press Act, newspapers could also be required to disclose the source of their information, with contravention of the act punishable by prohibition of future publication. While the Press Act provoked considerable moral outrage, it was difficult to challenge constitutionally.

There were two possible arguments: that the act dealt with an area that only Parliament could legislate in, or that some previously unrecognized constitutional principle protected freedom of the press. While it appears that the lawyers arguing the case before the Supreme Court confined themselves to the first argument, the judges seemed to adopt elements of the second. Chief Justice Duff held, in his 'most celebrated judicial statement,'[87] that free political discussion 'from every point of view' was a matter of national importance and could not, therefore, be subordinated to other legislative objects, or be regarded as a local or private matter within a province or, indeed, as a civil right as set out in the *BNA Act*. The court, in effect, found that freedom of speech was a fundamental right that could not be interfered with by a province. The question Duff left unanswered was whether Parliament could take away this right. Another judge, Arthur Cannon, was even more un-equivocal: 'Democracy cannot be maintained without its foundation: free public opinion and free discussion throughout the nation of all matters affecting the State within the limits set by the Criminal Code. Every inhabitant of Alberta is also a citizen of the Dominion. The province may deal with his property and civil rights ... but the province cannot interfere with his status as a Canadian citizen and his fundamental right to express freely his untrammeled opinion about government policies and discuss matters of public concern.'[88] The principles laid down by the Chief Justice in the *Alberta Reference* came to be known as the 'Duff Doctrine,' and later as the 'Implied Bill of Rights' theory. Many lawyers and academics considered Duff and Cannon's judgments 'radical.' Some fifteen years would pass before the court picked up where the duo left off, primarily in the judgments of Justice Rand.[89]

Two years before the *Saumur* case was heard and decided, Justice Rand, in another case, *Winner v. S.M.T. Eastern Ltd.*, made it clear that citizens enjoyed certain constitutional rights: '[A] Province cannot, by depriving a Canadian of the means of working, force him to leave it; it cannot divest him of his right or capacity to remain and to engage in work there: that capacity inhering as a constitutional element of his citizenship status is beyond nullification by provincial action ... It follows ... that a Province cannot prevent a Canadian from entering it except, conceivably, in temporary circumstances, for some local reason as, for example, health.'[90] 'Highways,' Rand continued, 'are a condition of the existence of any organized state: without them its life could not be carried on. To deny their use is to destroy the fundamental liberty of action of the individual, to proscribe his participation in that life: under such a ban, the exercise of citizenship would be at an end ... These considerations are, I think, sufficient to demonstrate that the privilege of using the highway is likewise an essential attribute of Canadian citizenship.' This entitlement was part and parcel of 'national status embodying certain inherent or constitutive characteristics, of members of the Canadian public, and it can be modified, defeated or destroyed, as for instance by outlawry, only by Parliament.' Accordingly, Rand declared that Canadian citizenship conferred rights.

The *Saumur* case now presented an excellent opportunity to entrench the view that Canadians enjoyed certain fundamental freedoms, or at least that there were some rights the provinces could not impede. Instead, when Justice Kerwin's opinion was added to the four dissents, a majority of the court had held that freedom of religion, along presumably with the right to place limits on it, was a matter of provincial concern. The decision was not a victory, if that term was defined as recognition that Canadians, as Rand described it, enjoyed freedom of religion as an 'unchallengeable right.'

Unfortunately, the *Saumur* case revealed the Supreme Court at its worst. 'The awkward result of the case was that, while six justices denied provincial competence at least in some circumstances, five justices affirmed provincial competence at least in some circumstances, and while four justices affirmed federal competence in some circumstances, five justices denied federal competence at least in some circumstances; and yet only three justices denied any federal power while four justices denied any provincial power.'[91] As another commentator put it, 'seven of the Supreme Court judges went through legalistic contortions to determine whether this was a "civil right" or "local matter" within the province and thus within the latter's jurisdiction.'[92] Nevertheless, the reasons of the four judges who did find that freedom of religion and of the press were beyond provincial powers would prove, in the end, to be more influential than the opinions of the five who placed these rights in the provincial camp. The minority opinions, on this point, none more so than Rand's, established a philosophical and jurisprudential basis for the recognition in law that Canadians do enjoy certain fundamental freedoms, a recognition ultimately given effect in the *Charter of Rights and Freedoms*.

In his ruling, Justice Rand began by looking at the Quebec City by-law. When a licence was sought, the practice was for the chief of police, or some other senior police officer, to peruse the literature. If nothing objectionable was found, a permit was issued. This practice, Rand ruled, was censorship and was wrong. 'From its inception, printing has been recognized as an agency of tremendous possibilities, and virtually upon its introduction into Western Europe it was brought under the control and licence of government. At that time, as now in despotisms, authority viewed with fear and wrath the uncensored printed word: it is and has been the bête noire of dogmatists in every field of thought; and the seat of its legislative control in this country becomes a matter of the highest moment.'[93] Having said that, it was fairly clear where Rand would go next.

Quebec had argued that the term 'civil rights' set out in the *BNA*

Act encompassed civil liberties such as the freedoms of religion and speech. As it was a 'provincial power,' the argument went, the Quebec government was free to pass what legislation it liked. Rand, however, disagreed, concluding that there was no basis to give 'civil rights' an interpretation of that kind. He declared that the term meant matters of private law, the negotiation of a contract, or the right to sue in tort. Provincial legislation in relation to religion was not a local matter. It was of concern not only at a provincial but at a national level: '[I]t appertains to a boundless field of ideas, beliefs and faiths with the deepest roots and loyalties; a religious incident reverberates from one end of the country to the other, and there is nothing to which the "body politic of the Dominion" is more sensitive.' The same was equally true about freedom of speech: 'Under [our] constitution, government is by parliamentary institutions, including popular assemblies elected by the people at large in both provinces and Dominion: government resting ultimately on public opinion reached by discussion and the interplay of ideas. If that discussion is placed under licence, its basic condition is destroyed: the government, as licensor, becomes disjoined from the citizenry. The only security is steadily advancing enlightenment, for which the widest range of controversy is the *sine qua non*.' The way Rand saw it, no province could legislate in regard to a fundamental freedom. Freedom of speech, religion, and the inviolability of the person were, he said, 'original freedoms which are at once the necessary attributes and modes of self-expression of human beings and the primary conditions of their community life within a legal order.' Rand was a path-breaking judge identifying something essential about the nature of Canada's Constitution – namely, that certain rights are inherent in our constitutional order. It would be some time before this principle achieved constitutional protection, but, in the *Saumur* case, the jurisprudential building block was laid.

The decision in *Saumur* did little to improve the lot of Jehovah's Witnesses in Quebec. The National Assembly immediately identified the loophole and amended the *Freedom of Worship Act* so as to make it inapplicable to the Jehovah's Witnesses: it gave the government the power to outlaw any religious group that published abusive and insulting attacks on established religions. The effect of this amendment was to make the majority decision in the *Saumur* case a minority one, for the deciding vote on Saumur's behalf had been based on the freedoms set out in the *Freedom of Worship Act*. Although the decision had been earlier applauded as a great social advance, Premier Duplessis

ensured otherwise. With a legislature at his beck and call, his government introduced and got passed, with no real opposition, a religious
Padlock Act. Duplessis would not relent in his campaign until the final disposition of an action filed against him by a Jehovah's Witness
named Frank Roncarelli.

Roncarelli was the owner of the Quaff Café in Montreal's west end.
Disturbed by the treatment other Jehovah's Witnesses were receiving, Roncarelli arranged bail for some four hundred Witnesses arrested during the first phase of Duplessis's War without Mercy. When
Duplessis was told what Roncarelli was up to, he became enraged. In
late November 1946 he issued a public warning: stop posting bail or
else. Roncarelli failed to heed. In early December Duplessis, in a conversation with the chairman of the Quebec Liquor Commission, Judge
Edouard Archambault, instructed him to cancel Roncarelli's liquor licence *'définitivement et pour toujours.'* The judge did as he was told. The
police thereupon attended at the restaurant and seized Roncarelli's
stock, his establishment now being unlicensed and his possession of
liquor an offence.

On 5 December Duplessis was quoted in the *Montreal Gazette*, explaining what had taken place. 'A certain Mr Roncarelli has supplied
bail for hundreds of Witnesses of Jehovah. The sympathy which this
man has shown for the Witnesses in such an evident, repeated and au-
dacious manner, is a provocation to public order, to the administration
of justice and is definitely contrary to the aims of justice. He does not
act, in this case, as a person posting bail for another person, but as a
mass supplier of bails, whose great number by itself is most reprehen
sible.' Roncarelli was getting only his just deserts: 'The Communists,
the Nazis as well as those who are the propagandists for the Witnesses
of Jehovah, have been treated and will continue to be treated by the
Union Nationale government as they deserve for trying to infiltrate
themselves and their seditious ideas in the Province of Quebce.'[94] Roncarelli was put out of business because he had exercised a legal right to
post bail for others.

When the Jehovah's Witnesses were distributing provocative tracts,
the public only slowly became engaged with their plight. In certain
quarters, the opposite was the case. But the closing of a business because the proprietor merely bailed out his coreligionists was an issue
with much wider public appeal. Members of the public could relate to

it. After all, if the premier could do that to Roncarelli, he could do it
to anyone. Civil liberties organizations, left-wing groups, academics,
and some members, mostly Jewish, of the legal profession were galvanized. There were protests, demonstrations, and meetings. Duplessis
offered a further explanation: Roncarelli had been given a privilege in
receiving a liquor licence. Not only had he abused that privilege but,
by providing bail, he was furthering the spread of sedition in the province and the violation of municipal bylaws. Therefore, the privilege
had to be taken away. Roncarelli decided to fight back.

On 1 February 1947 he launched an action against Judge Archambault in his capacity as head of the Quebec Liquor Commission. That
action, and another one, failed because the Quebec rules of civil procedure continued to preclude claims of this kind. Then Roncarelli's
lawyer, A.L. Stein, made a bold move. He sued Duplessis personally,
demanding more than $100,000 in damages. The immediate result of
the legal move was a new round of state repression, as hundreds of Witnesses were rounded up and taken into custody, some dragged from
their homes in the middle of the night. Even worse, prayer meetings
in private homes were broken up by the police. Jehovah's Witnesses
were regularly attacked by screaming mobs while the police stood idly
by. Witness literature was burned. It was, in all, the most extensive
campaign of state-sponsored religious persecution ever undertaken in
Canada (except, perhaps, the outlawing of the potlatch ceremony in
1885 and the abduction of Sons of Freedom Doukhobor children, taken
into state custody from their arsonist/nudist parents).[95]

In the meantime, Stein proceeded with the case. He had no personal
brief for the Jehovah's Witnesses or their beliefs, but he was offended
by the action Duplessis had taken against Roncarelli. He needed help
and tried to get a French Canadian to sign on as co-counsel. When no
one would, F.R. 'Frank' Scott, a professor at the McGill Law School, a
well-known Canadian poet, and co-founder of the League for Social
Reconstruction (the 'brain trust' for the emerging Cooperative Commonwealth Federation), agreed to join Stein.[96] Together they fought
a case they would take to the Supreme Court of Canada – a case that
is rightly regarded as a shining, enduring, and inspiring paean to the
rule of law.

Duplessis did what he could to delay the proceedings, but finally,
in May 1950, the premier and former restaurateur faced each other
in a Montreal court. Duplessis bustled into the room and made his
way to the bench. After conferring privately with the presiding judge,

he took his seat. The judge, C. Gordon MacKinnon, then announced that Duplessis would give his evidence first because he had pressing business requiring his immediate return to Quebec City. As soon as Duplessis took the stand, he started to lie. He told the court that it was Judge Archambault who called him in November 1946, recommending that action be taken against Roncarelli, not the reverse. The premier concluded his testimony by asserting that he conscientiously applied the law. The rest of the evidence tendered at the six-day trial demonstrated otherwise. At the conclusion, Justice MacKinnon reserved. He did not release his reasons for judgment for almost a year.

The 'War without Mercy' continued, although with diminished vigour. On 2 May 1951 Justice MacKinnon finally ruled. It was a stunning, and totally unexpected, indictment of Duplessis. The judge found, in effect, that the premier had perjured himself and acted without authority in ordering the cancellation of Roncarelli's liquor licence. Roncarelli was awarded just over $8,000 in damages. The award, relative to the actual loss, was paltry, perhaps a judicial sop to the premier. However, the money meant nothing to Duplessis – the Union Nationale had plenty of discretionary funds. What bothered him was the challenge to his authority. A Jehovah's Witness had received justice in a Quebec court. Stein advised Roncarelli not to appeal the damages award but to take the money and try to rebuild his life. Roncarelli agreed – until Duplessis blundered and filed an appeal. Had he just paid the damages, the case would have faded from view. At best, the judgment of the trial court would have become a minor footnote to history. Duplessis's appeal left Roncarelli with no choice but to cross-appeal. Duplessis probably knew that he would lose this legal battle in the end – any good lawyer could have figured that out, as the premier had clearly exceeded his authority. But, as one of his biographers observed, 'Politics is a matter of immediate concern; the final judgments of the law lie somewhere in the distant future.'[97] In the event, Duplessis determined that it was in his political interest to remain at war with the Jehovah's Witnesses.

The court of appeal took until 1956 to hear the case. When the decision was released later that year, neither side could declare victory. Once again, Duplessis decided to take the case further, to the Supreme Court. Stein and Scott got back to work and prepared to fight *Roncarelli v. Duplessis*.[98] By the time the Supreme Court of Canada handed down its judgment in 1959, the Quaff Café had long been closed down, and Roncarelli was working elsewhere. He won at the Supreme Court, but the decision did not restore his restaurant or his livelihood, both of which he lost for exercising his legal rights. The case stands, however, as the pre-eminent expression in Canadian law of the rule of law – the notion that all men and women are subject to, and equal under, the law. And here, too, Justice Rand led the way in setting a framework by which the rule of law could be understood.

Roncarelli was, Justice Rand wrote, nothing more than a private citizen who furnished funds to enable arrested persons to be released on bail pending the determination of the charges against them. There was no other legally relevant consideration to take into account. The issue was the exercise of administrative discretion. It is a matter of vital importance that a public administration that can refuse to allow a person to enter or continue a calling, which, in the absence of regulation, would be free and legitimate, should be conducted with complete impartiality and integrity; and that the grounds for refusing or cancelling a permit should unquestionably be such, and such only, as are incompatible with the purposes envisaged by the statute. The duty of a commission, then, is to serve those purposes, and those only. A decision to deny or cancel a privilege lies within the 'discretion' of the commission; but that means that the decision must be based on a weighing of considerations pertinent to the object of the administration.

In public regulation of this sort, Rand continued, there is no such thing as absolute or untrammelled 'discretion' – that is, that action can be taken on any ground or for any reason that can be suggested to the mind of the administrator; no legislative act can, without express language, be taken to contemplate an unlimited arbitrary power exercisable for any purpose, however capricious or irrelevant, regardless of the nature or purpose of the statute. Fraud and corruption in the commission may not be mentioned in such statutes, but they are always implied as exceptions. 'Discretion' necessarily implies good faith in discharging public duty; there is always a perspective within which a statute is intended to operate; and any clear departure from its lines or objects is just as objectionable as fraud or corruption. Could an applicant be refused a permit because he had been born in another province or because of the colour of his hair? Rand asked. No, the ordinary language of the legislature cannot be so distorted.

To deny or revoke a permit because a citizen exercises an unchallengeable right totally irrelevant to the sale of liquor in a restaurant is equally beyond the scope of the discretion conferred, Rand continued. There was, in this case, not only revocation of the existing permit but a declaration of a future, definitive disqualification of the appellant to obtain one: it was to be 'forever.'[99] The Quebec Liquor Commission was obliged to act in a 'judicial manner,' but it had behaved maliciously, punishing Roncarelli in perpetuity for doing what he had 'an absolute right to do.' It was a gross abuse of legal power, for it had one objective – the destruction of Roncarelli's 'economic life as a restaurant keeper within the province.'

In all these proceedings, Duplessis could not claim immunity from prosecution; his persecution of Roncarelli was not an official act. 'Whatever may be the immunity of the Commission or its members from an action for damages, there is none to the respondent.' Regulation of economic activity was expanding, and there could be no immunity for injury caused by unwarranted intrusion into the activities of a regulatory agency. '[I]n the presence of expanding administrative regulation of economic activities,' Rand declared, there is no reason why 'such a step and its consequences are to be suffered by the victim without recourse or remedy,' or why 'an administration according to the law is to be superseded by action dictated by and according to the arbitrary likes, dislikes and irrelevant purposes of public officers acting beyond their duty.' To condone such action 'would signalize the beginning of disintegration of the rule of law as a fundamental postulate of our constitutional structure.' Duplessis had finally been brought to justice.

The *Boucher, Saumur,* and *Roncarelli* cases were not the only important civil liberties cases to come before the Supreme Court of Canada in the 1950s. In cases dealing with private disputes between citizens, however, Rand was not as prone to the expansive statements that made those decisions so memorable. *Noble et al. v. Alley*[100] provides a notable example. Annie Noble had agreed to sell a cottage property she owned on Lake Huron, in the Beach O'Pines development, to a Jew named Bernard Wolf. The property was part of a cottage community, and the deed contained a restrictive covenant that prevented the lands from being sold, rented to, or occupied by 'any person of the Jewish, Hebrew, Semitic, Negro, or coloured race or blood.' Wolf was concerned that the covenant would be a problem for the sale, but lawyers for both vendor and purchaser agreed that, in light of a 1945 Ontario court decision, *Re Drummond Wren,*[101] the covenant would be unenforceable. In that case a similarly restrictive condition was held to be void, primarily on the grounds that it was against public policy. Justice Mackay of the Ontario High Court looked to the province's recently passed *Racial Discrimination Act*, international documents like the San Francisco Charter (establishing the United Nations), and statements made by world leaders to support his conclusion.

In spite of the result in *Drummond Wren*, Wolf's lawyer insisted on a binding declaration that the covenant was void. Noble made an application to the court, which was opposed by more than forty members of the community. The issue at trial, and before the Ontario Court of Appeal, was whether *Drummond Wren* applied to the facts and, if it did, whether that case had been rightly decided. The five judges hearing the appeal issued four separate opinions but were unanimous in the result – the restrictive covenant was valid and enforceable. The Supreme Court then overturned the Court of Appeal's ruling six to one. As it was being argued, Rand interrupted respondent's counsel while he was seriously submitting that property values would decline if Jews were allowed in the community: 'If Albert Einstein and Arthur Rubenstein purchased cottages there,' he suggested, 'the property values would increase, and the association should be honoured to have them as neighbours.'[102] But instead of deciding the case on the basis of public policy, as Justice Mackay had done, or addressing the merits of the *Drummond Wren* decision, the judges, including Rand, confined themselves to technical arguments about whether the covenant was related to the use of the land.

Rand wrote a short concurring judgment. In just six paragraphs he held that the covenant, properly interpreted, was a restraint on the free transferability of the land and was therefore invalid according to long-standing precedent. He also found that it was void for uncertainty, adopting a decision from the House of Lords dealing with a similar issue and holding that 'it is impossible to set such limits to the lines of race or blood as would enable a court to say in all cases whether a proposed purchaser is or is not within the ban.' Although the result was clearly the right one, Rand's opinion hardly rises to the level of his spirited defence of fundamental freedoms. Perhaps Rand felt restrained by the fact that he was a long-standing member of the restricted Rideau Club.[103]

Rand and his colleagues also resorted to a strict technical approach when interpreting the rights given to First Nations peoples by treaties. In *Francis*, the court was called on to decide whether the Jay Treaty applied to the case of a First Nations man who had been charged duties when he imported several items from the United States into Canada.[104] A portion of the treaty, which was signed by the United States and

Britain in 1794, specified that no duties would be levied on Indians crossing the border with their goods. Louis Francis challenged the customs assessment and petitioned for his money to be returned. He was rebuffed in the Exchequer Court, and seven judges at the Supreme Court unanimously rejected his appeal.

Rand's judgment echoed that of the chief justice. He focused on the fact that the Jay Treaty was not a 'treaty of peace' setting out conditions for the cessation of a war, but, rather, affected matters within the scope of 'municipal law.' Any treaty that claimed to change existing law or to restrict future action by the legislature 'must be supplemented by statutory action.' In this case, there had been a statutory provision in Lower Canada giving effect to the section of the treaty Francis relied on, but it had long since lapsed. As there was no legislation implementing the customs exemption, it was of no effect. The underlying motivation for Rand's opinion might be found in the concurring judgment of Justice Kellock: the *Indian Act* was a complete code governing the rights of First Nations, and unless there were specific exemptions in that act, the terms of the *Customs Act* applied 'to Indians equally with other citizens of Canada.' Rand could not contemplate a conception of equality that involved discrimination among differently situated Canadians. First Nations' special status was a generation away.

A number of other important cases made their way before the court, especially *Switzman v. Elbing*.[105] John Switzman sublet a flat in Quebec belonging to a landlord, Freda Elbing. According to the authorities, Switzman was using the flat to 'propagate communism.' There was no doubt about that. Under the terms of the Padlock Law, they locked the premises and ordered that the flat remain closed for one year. Elbing wanted Switzman to pay her one year's rent and, when he refused, she went to court. Switzman than challenged the constitutionality of the law. The Quebec authorities intervened and attempted to justify the Padlock Act on the basis that the dispute was a local matter, within provincial jurisdiction, and that they needed to protect a backward populace that was, in 1957, 'intellectually ill-equipped to deal with the theories of Marx and Lenin.'[106] Rand disagreed. 'The aim of this statute is, by means of penalties, to prevent what is considered a poisoning of men's minds, to shield the individual from exposure to dangerous ideas, to protect him, in short, from his own thinking propensities. There is nothing of civil rights in this ...'[107] While the object of the legislation was to suppress communism, it could have as easily been directed at suppression of any other ideology, doctrine, or theory. This law could not stand:

Canadian government is in substance the will of the majority expressed directly or indirectly through popular assemblies. This means ultimately government by the free public opinion of an open society, the effectiveness of which, as events have not infrequently demonstrated, is undoubted.

But public opinion, in order to meet such a responsibility, demands the condition of a virtually unobstructed access to and diffusion of ideas. Parliamentary government postulates a capacity in men, acting freely and under self-restraints, to govern themselves; and that advance is best served in the degree achieved of individual liberation from subjective as well as objective shackles. Under that government, the freedom of discussion in Canada, as a subject-matter of legislation, has a unity of interest and significance extending equally to every part of the Dominion. With such dimensions it is *ipso facto* excluded from head 16 as a local matter.

This constitutional fact is the political expression of the primary condition of social life, thought and its communication by language. Liberty in this is little less vital to man's mind and spirit than breathing is to his physical existence. As such an inherence in the individual, it is embodied in his status of citizenship.[108]

The Supreme Court declared that the Padlock Act, as had been long claimed by its opponents, impinged on the federal power to legislate in matters of criminal law. 'It is declared,' the court said in an eight-to-one decision, 'that "An Act to Protect the Province against Communist Propaganda" is *ultra vires* of the Legislature of the Province of Quebec *in toto*.'[109] Ironically, the only dissenter in this case was Justice Robert Taschereau, the son of the former premier of Quebec whom Duplessis had defeated in the 1936 Quebec election. The law that Duplessis had promised more than two decades before would destroy communism had been set aside in a lawsuit initiated by a communist. Not that it mattered any more to Maurice Duplessis. The law had served him well in the 1930s, and it continued to serve him well on his return to power in 1944. The same was equally true about his War without Mercy against the Jehovah's Witnesses. It was useful on the hustings, and it contributed to continued electoral success. But, as Quebec society changed, state action against the Jehovah's Witnesses began to lose widespread public appeal.

With the beginning of the Quiet Revolution and the industrialization and urbanization of Quebec, the Union Nationale's hold on power, like the great influence of the Roman Catholic Church, was coming to an end.[110] Another reason why the campaign against the Jehovah's Witnesses might have lost its momentum was the death, in January 1947, of Cardinal Villeneuve. The torch passed, but to a new generation of Catholic leaders who quickly became more threatened by a rising tide of anti-clericalism than they ever were by the activities of the Jehovah's Witnesses. Public attacks against the sect gained little political mileage. Indeed, none of Villeneuve's successors had the supremacy to unite the bishops or influence the political agenda in an issue of this kind. For their part, the Jehovah's Witnesses had also changed, not in substance but in style, and their literature lost some of its immoderate edge. Perhaps they realized that this was the compromise they needed to make in order to get state protection of their freedom of speech. They remained active in Quebec, but they softened their attacks on the Roman Catholic hierarchy. The midnight raids and disruption of prayer meetings stopped. The courts were no longer, as they had been, agents of the state. Repression of communists, however, still had some life left. But, here too, Rand would draw some important lines.

'With the court's indulgence I will now proceed,' some counsel used to say when they got up to address the judges of the Supreme Court of Canada. 'You need no indulgence from the court,' Rand would always reply, 'It is as much our duty to listen as it is yours to speak.'[111] Rand would then pepper counsel with questions. These questions, Rand's colleague John Cartwright observed, 'were never intended to deter or discourage counsel but only to assist in the quest for the right answer. If, on occasion, his manner was a little terrifying, it only momentarily concealed his essential kindness.'[112] In his sixteen years on the bench, Rand participated in more than six hundred cases and delivered written reasons in over four hundred. He was infrequently in the dissent, and even less frequently the author of the majority opinion – just twenty-three times in sixteen years. 'In strictly qualitative terms,' one commentator said, 'his presence on the court appears to have had little effect.'[113] While Rand got along with the other members of the bench, he did not create alliances or occupy a position of leadership. He was a one-man band. Yet, while the statistics are interesting and revealing, they are ultimately immaterial. Rand made an *impression* – a big and enduring one.

The abolition of appeals to the JCPC shifted attention to Ottawa, at the exact moment when the court was called upon to deal with matters of significant concern to ordinary citizens. Banishing Canadian citizens, arresting men and women for going door to door and talking about God, or taking away a man's livelihood for posting bail were plainly wrong, and when the public learned about them, they demanded that they be stopped. Most Canadians wanted nothing to do with the communists, but they did not want to see people evicted from their homes for reading about Karl Marx or getting together with other like-minded people and dreaming out loud about how a managed economy would bring about social justice. When Premier Duplessis declared, in effect, 'I am the law,' he thought he could get away with using the police, the prosecutors, and many of the judges as his own army, deployed to crush anyone who presented a challenge to the social fabric, and for a long time he did. But the Supreme Court of Canada eventually decided otherwise – and the province had no choice but to obey. A collateral benefit, of course, was the demonstration of federal resolve and the sharp message delivered to Quebec nationalists that they meddled with individual rights and fundamental freedoms at their peril.

These were 'les années noires' in Quebec, and something had to give. The ragtag band of civil libertarians, university professors, leftists, and mostly Jewish lawyers helped create a climate where others could dissent against the oppressive traditionalism and conservatism of Quebec society. The Quiet Revolution brought Quebec into the modern world, its people overwhelmingly rejecting past values in favour of secularism – the one exception being the continued allegiance, in many quarters, to nationalism. Modernity was given a huge boost by a handful of judges at the Supreme Court led by Rand: 'The court's consistently activist approach to constitutional questions during the 1950's produced a rich legacy of landmark decisions which brought about profound changes in two key areas of Canadian constitutional law: the scope of federal jurisdiction and the protection of fundamental freedoms.' 'Even more striking was a monumental series of civil liberties decisions establishing such fundamental principles as the freedom to express one's religious and political opinions without governmental harassment, and the citizen's right to sue even the most high-ranking government officials for unlawful conduct. Although most of these decisions were based on rather technical grounds, the reasons for judgment left little doubt that the court's chief concern was for the civil liberties issues that lay in the background.'[114]

There was only so much the court could do. It was, at the time, generally accepted that so long as the federal and provincial legislatures were acting within their assigned spheres, their enactments could not be invalidated by the courts. What that meant, when faced with social injustice, was that the courts had to find a way to set things right. Making matters even more difficult, the Supreme Court paid rigid adherence to the doctrine of *stare decisis*, having declared that it was bound by its own previous decisions. Obviously, courts should be reluctant to depart from established authority, but no court should adopt a rule binding itself to its previous decisions when those decisions may have been appropriate in one time and place but not in another. However, the *BNA Act* said almost nothing about civil liberties, so, to correct an entire series of egregious wrongs, a Bill of Rights had to be implied. What was so unexpected was that Rand was the judge who did it.

Appointment as a judge can and should be liberating for a lawyer: the foundation of our entire legal system is judicial independence guaranteed by security of tenure. Our judges have the right, the obligation, and the duty to do the right thing free from fear or favour. There was no reason to believe that Rand would, in some cases, become a judicial maverick. There was nothing in his background or experience that presaged his civil libertarian streak. Sometimes, however, there are judicial surprises. US Chief Justice Earl Warren is probably the best-known example; Rand was another.

In the Japanese Deportation case, Rand bravely exposed the rank racism of the Canadian state. He thought the case was so important that he listed it on his curriculum vitae: 'Wrote a dissent against the Court's approval of orders-in-council authorizing the federal government to deport more than 7000 Japanese Canadians.'[115] Rand later said that discrimination based on place of birth or racial origin 'would be in derogation of constituent elements of citizenship.'[116] In *Winner* Rand clearly concluded that citizenship status brought with it certain rights, and they were, at the very least, beyond the scope of provincial restraint. In *Boucher* he referred to 'the unchallengeable rights of Canadians.' In *Saumur* he referred to 'original freedoms.'

There were other cases too. One of the more important was *Smith and Rhuland*. J.K. Bell was the secretary treasurer of a Nova Scotia union, the Maritime Workers Federation. A 'dominating presence,' he was also a communist, a card-carrying member of the Labour Progressive Party. When his union applied for certification by the Nova Scotia Labour Relations Board, under the chairmanship of Dalhousie law school dean Horace Read, the request was denied on the grounds that Bell was committed to the overthrow of the government and the establishment of a Soviet-style dictatorship. It did not matter to the board that the union had signed up a majority of the employees in the bargaining unit and otherwise met the requirements for certification. The board justified its decision: '[T]o certify as bargaining agent a Union while its dominant leadership and direction is provided by a member of the Communist party would be incompatible with promotion of good faith bargaining,' it held, 'and would confer legal powers to affect vital interests of employees and employer upon persons who would inevitably use those powers primarily to advance Communist aims and policies rather than for the benefit of the employees.'[117] The union sought judicial review, and the case eventually made its way to the Supreme Court of Canada. There veteran labour lawyer Maurice Wright, one of the most elegant men ever to emerge from north Winnipeg, took on the legendary and suave J.J. Robinette. Justice Rand wrote the majority opinion.

There were, he began, 'certain facts which must be faced.' There was 'no law in this country against holding such views nor of being a member of a group or party supporting them. This man is eligible for election or appointment to the highest political offices in the Province: on what ground can it be said that the Legislature of which he might be a member has empowered the Board, in effect, to exclude him from a labour union? or to exclude a labour union from the benefits of the statute because it avails itself, in legitimate activities, of his abilities? ... The [Labour Relations Act] deals with the rights and interests of citizens of the Province generally, and, notwithstanding their private views on any subject, assumes them to be entitled to the freedoms of citizenship until it is shown that under the law they have forfeited them.'[118] In this case, Rand pointed out, there was no evidence that anyone had done anything wrong. The members of a union had simply elected a communist to union office.

'To treat that ... as a ground for refusing certification is to evince a want of faith in the intelligence and loyalty of the membership of both the Local and the federation. The dangers from the propagation of the Communist dogmas lie essentially in the receptivity of the environment. The Canadian social order rests on the enlightened opinion and the reasonable satisfaction of the wants and desires of the people as a whole: but how can that state of things be advanced by the action of a local tribunal otherwise than on the footing of trust and confidence in those with whose interest the tribunal deals? Employees of every rank and description throughout the Dominion furnish the substance of the national life and the security of the state itself resides in their solidarity as loyal subjects. To them, as to all citizens, we must look for the protection and defence of that security within the governmental structure, and in these days on them rests an immediate responsibility for keeping under scrutiny the motives and actions of their leaders. These are the considerations that have shaped the legislative policy of this country to the present time and they underlie the statute before us.'

Accordingly, Rand argued, mere membership in the Communist Party was insufficient to deprive a person of his or her entitlement to participate in a labour organization, or to deny the labour organization the participation of a person. Before doing either, evidence of wrongdoing was required.

'I am unable to agree,' he concluded, 'that the Board has been empowered to act upon the view that official association with an individual holding political views considered to be dangerous by the Board proscribes a labour organization. Regardless of the strength and character of the influence of such a person, there must be some evidence that, with the acquiescence of the members, it has been directed to ends destructive of the legitimate purposes of the union, before that association can justify the exclusion of employees from the rights and privileges of a statute designed primarily for their benefit.'

Rand's decision, delivered at the height of McCarthyism in the United States and a somewhat more muted 'Red Scare' at home, showed no lack of judicial courage. What was odd about the ruling was that, in reaching it, Rand, and indeed the entire court, accepted the findings of fact made by the Nova Scotia Labour Relations Board, including the point that 'the Communist party is a highly disciplined organization, the actions of whose members are rigidly controlled by its leaders who require policies and aims laid down by them to be slavishly followed by party members.' Moreover, the board found, and the Supreme Court accepted, that communist policy was 'designed to weaken the economic and political structure of the country as a means of ultimately destroying the established form of government.' The board further found that Bell would use the powers conferred by certification 'primarily to advance Communist aims and policies rather than for the benefit of the employees.' Assuming all that to be true (which it was), which is what the Supreme Court did, how could Mr Bell ever be said to be acting in the interests of the local? He was always acting in the interests of the LPP. If the local union benefited, that was collateral and incidental to his primary objectives. Yet surely union members, like the public, are entitled to choose whoever they want as their leaders, even communists with deeply revolutionary hopes?[119]

In another important case, Rand made it clear that Canadians had a right to protest. That was *Aristocratic Restaurants*. Employees at one of a chain of five restaurants organized a union, which was certified in British Columbia. The union could not, however, reach a collective agreement with the employer. It lost its members at the certified restaurant and decided to bring pressure on the employer by engaging picketers, who paraded in front of the certified restaurant and several others. Except for statements made to prospective patrons and passersby which were ultimately found to be of no legal significance, there was no trespass or obstruction. The employer brought an action for damages and an injunction restraining further picketing.

In his decision Rand held:

There was clearly a trade dispute as well as a grievance in this case and the information conveyed by the placards ... was relevant to the patronage of the restaurants by consumers. The question, then, is whether the mode of persuasion followed was authorized. How could information be effectively communicated to a prospective customer of such a business otherwise than by such means? ... The persons to be persuaded can, with any degree of certainty, be reached only in the immediate locality ... What was attempted was to persuade rationally rather than to coerce by insolence; there was no nuisance of a public nature, and the only annoyance would be the resentment felt by almost any act in the competitive conflict by the person whose interest is assailed. That those within the restaurant, either employees or patrons, were likely to be disturbed by the degree of apprehensive disquiet already mentioned, could not be seriously urged. Through long familiarity, these words and actions in labour controversy have ceased to have an intimidating effect on the average individual and are now taken in the stride of ordinary experience; but the information may be effective to persuade and it is such an appeal that the statute is designed to encourage.[120]

The public, Rand wrote, was 'obviously and substantially interested in the fair settlement of such contests.' It did not concern him that no vote was taken before the picketing; there were, in any event, no employees left to vote. Moreover, the fact that some of the restaurants being picketed had never been organized was, likewise, immaterial. 'The owner's economic strength is derived from his total business; and it is against that that the influence of information is being exerted.' There was a difference, Rand continued, between 'argumentative and rancorous badgering or importunity, and unexpressed, sinister suggestiveness' and 'attending to communicate information for the purpose of persuasion by the force of rational appeal.'[121] Applying these types of distinctions was no easy task, especially in the context of strikes and lockouts.

Aristocratic was yet another in the long line of Supreme Court cases with multiple opinions making 'rather uncertain what actually is the *ratio decidendi* of the case.'[122] Moreover, as we shall see, in the aftermath of this decision, Canadian courts became *more* hostile, not less, to picketing – even peaceful informational picketing. As one commentator observed, '[T]he court majority seemed to adopt the task of taking positive steps in the law in favour of the Union, but doing so in order that the end results might be a pretty good policy of legal and judicial neutrality in the economic contest between union and management. It is fair to say, though, that the doctrinal basis for the adoption of this policy was not carefully laid.'[123] However, the important point was that Rand insisted that Canadians had the right to protest peacefully.

In other cases, such as *Henry Birks & Sons (Montreal) Ltd. and Others v. City of Montreal*,[124] while Rand's rhetoric remained uplifting, the decisions were reached on the basis of the division of powers, principally what was meant by 'civil rights,' and who enjoyed exclusive authority over criminal law. In *Switzman*, Rand picked up where Chief Justice Duff had left off and considered the possibility that neither the provincial legislatures nor Parliament were competent to curtail political speech. Justice Douglas Charles Abbott would have gone even further, saying that 'Parliament itself could not abrogate this right of discussion and debate.' This statement, according to Peter Hogg, the dean of constitutional law scholars, was 'the only unequivocal expression of the implied Bill of Rights theory in the Supreme Court of Canada.'[125]

Rand knew exactly what he was doing. Referring to the *Saumur* case, he observed that, although 'other judicial considerations were involved, the final judgment seems to indicate that neither religious nor political discussion, as such, can be brought under provincial control. This last determination concerns primarily the delineation of power between the two legislative jurisdictions, and, since there is no specific allocation of these subjects, resort must be had not only to the scheme of the statute but also to its *implied* conditions, and to the significant features of the constitutional progress of Canada to its present coordinate status with Great Britain within the Commonwealth. From this it can be seen that in relation to these freedoms we are in the early stages of constitutional interpretation.'[126] Rand later elaborated on the implied Bill of Rights, guaranteeing freedom of speech and religion. 'These exemptions, as I take them to be, from provincial regulation are seen to be *deductions* from the language of the constitutional instrument: the definitions of the fixed institutions of parliament and legislature postulate them as corollaries. It is well to remind ourselves that the freedoms constitute at the same time essential attributes of man, his modes of self-expression; without the world of ideas, feelings, instincts and will with their communications, human beings would be of another order in the animal kingdom; and it is the aggregate of visible and invisible environment, including the manifestations of all man's faculties, that constitutes not only the milieu in which we live but the condition of our being what we are. Around such a being societal laws are drawn; and the freedoms serve the necessities of individual realization as well as of the political economy.'[127] They were fundamental freedoms, but they had to be *implied* and *deduced*. This was a job for the brave.

In 1951 Rand spoke about the 'role of an independent judiciary in preserving freedom' and set out, in part, his conception of an independent judiciary.[128] There was, to start with, more than one freedom, and 'they could,' he wrote, only be 'preserved through a judicial administration which, by intelligence, courage, and unremitting vigilance, maintains their standards inviolate.' But this objective required that the 'judicial mind itself be free.' Judges had to recognize that they were, 'as all other men ... bound by their own mental and emotional organisms: they are exposed to the dominant thought of the day ... There are alien factors that unconsciously may disturb the neutral freedom of judgment and distort the process of adjudication: bias favourable or hostile, a sense of obligation, fear of disapprobation, a weakness for applause; there is the loyalty to class or church or party, the personal preference or dislike, the impulsive reaction of set notions.' Sissies and scaredy-cats with 'tender minds' should step aside, he said. '[I]t is not a question of honesty in intellect or morality; it is of the quality of judicial disinterestedness. One's individual views undoubtedly reflect that general thought of the community; but they can present obstacles to true understanding of what is being examined.'

All citizens looked to the courts for 'security in life, liberty and the pursuit of happiness, security against any attempts by the most powerful to invade his sanctities,' he stated. This expectation imposed a special duty on judges: They were, 'in the ascertainment of truth and the application of laws ... the special guardians of the freedoms of unpopular causes, of minority groups and interests, of the individual against the mass, of the weak against the powerful, of the unique, of the nonconformist – our liberties are largely the accomplishments of such men ... In the defence of this group ... courage in a judge is as necessary as in a general ... the courts must shield the individual with all the safe-guards the centuries have accumulated.' There can be no question but that Rand, deliberately, quoted the most famous phrase in the American Declaration of Independence: 'Life, liberty, and the pursuit of happiness.'

Although Rand identified something intrinsic about our constitutional order, the concept of an implied Bill of Rights was always dubious. If it was based on Canada having a constitution similar in principle to that of the United Kingdom, the theory held no water because, under that constitution, Parliament could, at any time, abolish any existing civil liberty. If the doctrine was based on the *BNA Act* providing for representative parliamentary institutions, that theory was also problematic because Canada's Parliament presumably was established with exactly the same limitation on its legislative powers as the one in the United Kingdom, and there was no restriction on what it could do (although, presumably, it could not abolish itself). So that left civil liberties a matter of the division of powers. The Supreme Court subsequently acknowledged as much when it held years later that not one of the fundamental freedoms inherited from the United Kingdom 'is so enshrined in the Constitution as to be beyond the reach of competent legislation.'[129] The implied Bill of Rights eventually failed. Even though Rand's judgments are among the most remarkable in the history of the Supreme Court of Canada, an implied Bill of Rights could not be constitutionally sustained.

'His judgments were more intimations of what might be.'[130] At best, it could only be argued that the broad foundations of the preamble to the *BNA Act* supported recognition of certain fundamental freedoms. However, Rand's key cases made an enormous impact. They demonstrated, as did so much of our history, that Canada could not rely on its legislators or its judges and courts to protect fundamental freedoms; they had to be enshrined. 'A constitution understood to give no primacy to these principles proved unacceptable to the people of Canada.'[131] In 1949 the Jehovah's Witnesses, interested primarily in protecting their own rights, began their campaign for a Canadian Bill of Rights.

Eight years later they presented a petition to Parliament with more than 600,000 signatures calling for a Canadian Bill of Rights. It came in 1960. The Canadian Bill of Rights, like its author, John Diefenbaker, was a fraud[132] – a paper tiger that perhaps earned some political points but left the citizenry no better off than before its passage. Rand was not fooled. No serious person was. It was, he wrote, 'an ordinary statute' easily overridden by 'a specific enactment of Parliament subsequent in time.'[133] Still, the Jehovah's Witnesses cases were a prelude both to Quebec's Quiet Revolution and to the eventual entrenchment of a constitutional Bill of Rights. Moreover, these cases, together with *Switzman*, provided the substantive juridical foundation for an entire generation concerned about state power and the rights of the individual.

Supreme Court judges continue regularly to refer to some of Rand's other decisions, in a diverse array of cases spanning the legal spectrum from torts to criminal law to tax law.

Rand's decision in *Cook v. Lewis*, relating to factual causation, is among his most controversial.[134] The case turned on a strange set of facts. On the first day of the hunting season, Robert Lewis was injured while out with his brother John and their friend Dennis Fitzgerald near Quinsam Lake on Vancouver Island. David Cook, his friend Mr Akenhead, and another friend, John Wagstaff, were in a separate group hunting blue grouse, heavily built game birds with legs feathered to the toes. Cook's group was using a dog, which had wandered a short distance ahead of them. As they were walking, Fitzgerald suddenly came into view, shouted something at Cook's group, and pointed in the direction of the dog. Fitzgerald was actually trying to warn the other hunting party that his friend Lewis was out of view behind a clump of trees, but Cook thought he was pointing to the grouse that had just appeared near the dog. Cook and Akenhead quickly took aim and fired into the trees, where Lewis was standing. Some of the bird shot hit Lewis in the face and caused him to lose one eye. He sued Cook and Akenhead for negligence.

At trial, Lewis argued that either Cook or Akenhead, or both, had shot him, and that each was liable in damages, even if only one of them had fired the shot that struck him. Cook replied that he had not fired anywhere near where Lewis had been standing and claimed that a third, unidentified, shooter had caused the injury. Akenhead made a similar argument. The jury decided that the defendants had shot

Lewis, but, not being able to determine which one had fired the shot, found that neither was negligent. According to basic principles of tort law, since the plaintiff had not established that one of the defendants had caused the damage, his action could not succeed. Accordingly, the trial judge dismissed the case. Lewis appealed.

At the British Columbia Court of Appeal, Justices Robertson, Smith, and Bird were unanimous in ruling that the jury had acted 'perversely' in not finding one of the defendants negligent. Justice Sydney Smith wrote the short judgment of the court. According to him, the evidence was stronger against one shooter than the other, and a properly instructed jury should not have had much trouble deciding which man was liable. Therefore, a new trial was necessary. Cook appealed the ruling to the Supreme Court, where four of five justices hearing the case agreed with the Court of Appeal.

Justices Cartwright and Rand wrote separate concurring judgments, with Estey and Fauteux signing on to Cartwright's opinion. The problem that each of them had to contend with was a traditional rule from criminal law which said that, if it was certain that one of two people had committed an offence but uncertain which was guilty, neither person could be convicted in the absence of special circumstances. Cartwright held that the same was true in civil cases.[135] Lewis tried to convince the judges that Cook and Akenhead were in a joint venture when hunting, and so fell under the 'special circumstances' exception. Justice Cartwright did not accept that argument. Instead, he reasoned that if the jury was not able to decide which defendant had shot Lewis, but felt both had acted negligently in shooting in his direction, then both should have been found liable. To achieve this result he shoehorned the case into an English line of authority dealing with trespass, which held that where 'a plaintiff is injured by force applied directly to him by the defendant' and can prove this to be true, the onus falls on the defendant to prove that the trespass was 'utterly without his fault.'[136]

Rand's judgment, which none of the other judges concurred with, staked out a much clearer conception of factual causation. Rand's reasoning began from the position that plaintiffs had a remedial right to the proof required to establish their cases. In this particular case, both defendants' actions had 'impaired the [victim's] remedial right of establishing liability' and 'destroyed the victim's power of proof.' Accordingly, Rand ruled, 'the onus is then shifted to the wrongdoer to exculpate himself; it becomes in fact a question of proof between him and the other and innocent member of the alternatives, the burden of which he must bear. The onus attaches to culpability, and if both acts bear that taint, the onus or prima facie transmission of responsibility attaches to both, and the question of the sole responsibility of one is a matter between them.'

In Rand's view, and stated somewhat more simply, actions should have legal consequences. In this type of situation, he wrote, where the plaintiff could not specifically prove which defendant was at fault, the onus of proof should shift to the defendants to prove that they did *not* cause the injury. If neither defendant could demonstrate they were not the cause, then both should be held liable. The fact was, Rand observed, that the woods were 'full' of hunters. In these circumstances, a 'stringent regard to conduct' seemed 'obvious.' It was unthinkable that an injured person should be denied redress. Rand's reasoning was highly controversial among tort scholars.[137] Many have pointed out that his ruling was unfair to the 'innocent party,' since it would be possible for such a person to be made to pay damages when he had not actually contributed to the injury and had no way of disproving liability. In Rand's view, however, this person was not innocent: his actions had contributed to the plaintiff's inability to prove the liable party and he had, in fact, been negligent. Cook and Akenhead should have been more careful. When they were not, Lewis was injured – and it was only right that someone be called to account.[138]

Over the years, plaintiffs have attempted to extend Rand's reasoning to cover situations where defendants were contributorily negligent. Courts have rejected these arguments.[139] On occasion, plaintiffs have attempted to rely on Rand's reasoning in *Cook* at the Supreme Court, and, invariably, the point is made that his judgment was not that of the court. Nevertheless, Rand's judgment in *Cook* remains one of Rand's best-known, and still applied, private law decisions.

Rand also wrote a significant decision in contract law where the court adopted, for the first time, the unjust enrichment theory of compensation into Canadian law. In *Deglman v. Guaranty Trust Co*[140] Laura Constantineau Brunet owned two pieces of property in Ottawa, which were side by side. She agreed with her nephew that if he was good to her and would do chores and other services that she might require from time to time, she would leave him one of the houses when she died. The problem was an ancient English law known as the Statute of Frauds, which required, among other things, that any agreement respecting the transfer of land be in writing. The nephew and his aunt had only made an oral agreement, and when the aunt died, her nephew sued her estate to try to enforce the promise.

The case went up to the Supreme Court on a question of "part performance" – how much was the nephew required to do to demonstrate that a contract did in fact exist? Rand chose to disregard this argument. Instead of engaging in legal acrobatics Rand focused on what he described as the real issue: how to compensate the nephew, who had clearly performed services for free in expectation of eventually receiving the house. Perhaps drawing on his experiences at Harvard, Rand adopted a principle from the American Law Institute's *Restatement of the Law of Contracts,* which he quoted, and held that the nephew was entitled to recover for his services what his aunt would have had to pay for them 'on a purely business basis.'[141] This was the fair result, he said: it would be inequitable to allow the aunt (or her estate) to keep both the land and the money she would have paid for someone else to do the chores. Justice Cartwright authored the majority judgment but wrote that he agreed with Rand's conclusion that the nephew was entitled to recover money. 'This right appears to me to be based,' Cartwright said, 'not on the contract, but on an obligation imposed by law.'[142]

Rand also made lasting contributions to the criminal law. Section 91(27) of the *BNA Act* gave the federal Parliament sole jurisdiction over the criminal law. From the early days of Confederation, the question that had to be answered was what that power entailed. In 1922 the JCPC answered with a strict interpretation, laying down a 'domain of criminal jurisprudence' test that restricted the scope of criminal law to its traditional content existing at Confederation.[143] Lord Atkin at the Privy Council rejected this narrow definition just nine years later in the *PATA* case,[144] in favour of the view that criminal law included any act that was prohibited with penal sanctions. This interpretation was problematic for the opposite reason: under this definition, there was almost no limit to the areas in which Parliament could legislate, as long as the laws had a criminal form.

The problem landed before Rand in 1948, in the clumsily named *Reference re Validity of Section 5(a) of the Dairy Industry Act.*[145] Rand's answer to the question in the Margarine Reference, as the case is known, is one of his most cited decisions, and it is still used by judges to define the scope of Parliament's criminal law power.

Section 5 of the *Dairy Industry Act* provided that 'no person shall manufacture, import into Canada, or offer, sell or have in his possession for sale, any oleomargarine, margarine, butterine, or other substitute for butter, manufactured wholly or in part from any fat other than that of milk or cream.' The section's forerunner was enacted in 1886, on the grounds that certain substitutes for butter were 'injurious to health.' By 1939 Canada was the only major country prohibiting the importation or sale of margarine. The question to come before the court in 1948 was whether Parliament could prohibit the manufacture and importation of margarine.

The attorney general for Canada argued that the prohibition was an exercise of Parliament's criminal law power. Five of the seven justices disagreed. Characteristically, each judge wrote a separate opinion, but Rand's is the only one quoted with any frequency. He got straight to the point. The issue, he said, depended on whether the attorney general's argument was correct. If the prohibition on producing margarine was criminal law, it could clearly be upheld. What, then, was the proper scope of criminal law? Rand started with Lord Atkin's formulation of a prohibition coupled with a penalty. He recognized that prohibitions are not enacted in a vacuum, and therefore the court could 'properly look for some evil or injurious or undesirable effect upon the public against which the law is directed.' He then added a third branch of the test: Was there a public purpose for the prohibition? Acceptable purposes included the protection of 'public peace, order, security, health, morality,'[146] though Rand allowed that his list was not exhaustive. In 1948 the ban on the production of margarine served none of these purposes and, therefore, could not be upheld under the criminal law power. The judgment was appealed to the Privy Council, where it was affirmed.[147]

Rand made other important criminal law contributions.[148] In *Boudreau*[149] and *Fitton*,[150] he developed and refined tests for determining whether a confession was voluntary. In *Boudreau* a convicted murderer challenged the admissibility of statements he had made to the authorities. The common law had established a rule by which confessions made in the absence of a warning or caution by the authorities were inadmissible at trial. Rand explained that the rule is 'directed against the danger of improperly instigated or induced or coerced admissions.' However, he rejected the rigid conception of the rule, holding: 'It would be a serious error to place the ordinary modes of investigation of crime in a strait jacket of artificial rules; and the true protection against improper interrogation or any kind of pressure or inducement is to leave the broad question to the court.' Rigid formulas, he observed, could be both 'meaningless to the weakling and absurd to the sophisticated or hardened criminal.'

Rand gave some guidance on how courts should interpret this 'broad question' in *Fitton*. Again the appeal dealt with the admissibility of a confession and whether it was voluntary. Rand wrote that '[t] he strength of mind and will of the accused, the influence of custody or its surroundings, the effect of questions or of conversation, all call for delicacy in appreciation of the part they have played behind the admission, and to enable a Court to decide whether what was said was freely and voluntarily said, that is, was free from the influence of hope or fear aroused by them.'[151] The trial judge was in the best position to judge these factors, and therefore an appeal court should disturb a finding on the issue only if it was 'evident or probable' that the judge had misapplied the rule.

In *Hepton v. Maat*, Rand laid down what Chief Justice Antonio Lamer referred to more than three decades later as the 'classic statement of the principle in Canadian law' that the state can step in to relieve a parent of custody of a child, when necessary to protect the child's health and safety.[152] 'That view cannot be less than this,' Rand wrote: a child's natural parents are entitled to custody 'unless by reason of some act, condition or circumstance affecting them it is evident that the welfare of the child requires that that fundamental natural relation be severed.' When those circumstances arise, 'the community, represented by the Sovereign, is, on the broadest social and national grounds, justified in displacing the parents and assuming their duties.'[153]

In the tax field, a few of Rand's decisions continue to be relevant. His formulation of the accounting principle of realization and his test for whether a tax is to be considered indirect[154] are both still regularly cited, along with his decision in *Canada Safeway Ltd v. Minister of National Revenue*. There, Safeway had gone into debt in order to purchase a controlling share in its profitable distribution company. The dividends, which were tax-free, more than covered the interest Safeway paid on its debt. Nevertheless, Safeway tried to deduct the interest from its income for tax purposes, an attempt that was challenged by the minister of national revenue. The court ruled four to one that the deduction was not allowed. 'It is important to remember,' Rand held, 'that in the absence of an express statutory allowance, interest payable on capital indebtedness is not deductible as an income expense.'[155]

All cases considered, what was Rand's impact? On administrative law, according to David Mullan, Canada's pre-eminent administrative law scholar,[156] Rand was, 'on the one hand,' someone who 'expected rectitude of those holding public office and, in particular, respect for the civil liberties of individuals. However, at the same time, he was always cognizant of the reasons for the creation of administrative tribunals and of the necessity for recognizing their expertise and role in working out their own policies as well as their desire to function efficiently and effectively.' Rand set out 'broad legal principles in the course of individual cases,' making his decisions 'useful in guiding lower court judges.'[157] He was suspicious of persons administering the apparatus of the administrative state, concerned about checking arbitrary action and abuse of discretion, yet sensitive to the legitimate objects of the administrative process. In criminal law, Rand showed a 'deep-seated concern for fairness, for personal liberty and for the essential rights of an accused person.' He had an eye for 'fair play,' little interest in 'technicalities,' and believed that any infringement of the liberty of the subject must be carefully and expressly delineated, although he also made it clear that the state had the right to enact laws for its protection and for that of society.[158]

In general, in his private law decisions, Rand demonstrated a commitment to order, certainty, and our English law heritage. What stands out, however, are those civil liberties cases. It is on this basis that Rand built his reputation. His other work as a judge in all the other areas of the law was, with a few exceptions, unremarkable.[159] However, few Supreme Court cases from this period have stood the test of time. Very little of legal significance was bequeathed to future generations from this court, concerned as it was with criminal appeals, relatively small commercial matters, and the division of powers. In addition, because the Supreme Court was required at the time to hear a host of cases as a 'right,' many run-of-the-mill judgments in every area of law ended up there – from banking, bankruptcy, intellectual property, and libel to mines and minerals, shipping, taxation disputes, and wills and trusts. The Jehovah's Witnesses case, together with *Smith and Rhuland*, *Aristocratic*, and *Switzman*, make a huge contribution to the development of Canadian law, especially when compared to the usual fodder.

'The first decade after the court became the final court of appeal for Canada could very well be called the "Rand years." All that talk, however, did not lead to much, as the court continued to behave in much the same way as it had before the abolition of JCPC appeals. The conservatism was bone deep. Most of the judges were judicial zombies, without soul or character.'[160] In these circumstances, Rand was a key figure on an institutionally dysfunctional court, one also divided by ethnicity and religion. No francophone judge ever came close to embracing Rand's view that Canadians enjoyed certain fundamental freedoms. Moreover, while Rand's reasons for judgment were not generally accessible and often quite obtuse, he rarely wrote for the majority. His style was idiosyncratic, but his judgments embodied, more than those of his colleagues, the zeitgeist of the era. His judgments were the ones that people would quote. With some exceptions, most of the other judges remained enmeshed in formal legal reasoning – one that leads the reader through a parsing of the facts, a detailed review of the law, and the application of the latter to the former, all under the rubric of *stare decisis* – combined, in Canada, with the doctrine of legislative supremacy. It is a formula that produces, its adherents claim, 'correct' results grounded in a belief that the law is neutral and impartial, which most people agree it is not.

Rand, in his civil liberties cases, rejected this approach. His writing style, however, could cause problems. To be sure, it stood far apart from the stark formalism of his colleagues: there was no logical parsing of legal minutiae for him. Instead, he attempted to deal with larger legal principles and appropriate public policy. His judgments, often convoluted and difficult to understand, were, at their best, like a dry sponge in need of water. When watered, they increased exponentially in size and weight. And, occasionally, they sang. Rand was imaginative and creative, but the court was rule bound. In the result, while his decisions interested law professors, they did not compel his colleagues.

Almost uniquely among the Supreme Court judges, Rand was well aware of the international struggle between tyranny and freedom, and the responsibility of free courts and independent judges to preserve freedom at home. In the United States the Supreme Court had risen to the challenge in a series of important decisions, with the most celebrated, *Brown v. Board of Education*,[161] at the apex. Rand's old Harvard classmate Harold H. Burton was influential in bringing about the court's unanimity in that case, paving the way for integration and the civil rights movement. Desegregation in the United States was a moral imperative;[162] civil liberties at home were equally important. A majority of Rand's colleagues fundamentally misunderstood what the common law was about, failing to see it as a dynamic living thing capable of growth and adjustment as society and its expectations changed and grew. In marked contrast, Rand believed that the judicial process was a creative imaginative function, one involving an examination of the law concerning events similar to those under question, a look at all the facts in perspective and context, and a decision based on those laws and an interpretation of those facts.

This protection and promotion of civil liberties owed nothing to either a *Charter of Rights and Freedoms* or a real Bill of Rights, neither of which existed at the time, but to the happenstance of an independent judge outraged at the transgressions of a provincial government acting hand in hand with ecclesiastical authorities determined to protect the faith at just about any cost. Rand proved his courage and guts from his first important Supreme Court case to his last.

Thomas Berger, another serious civil libertarian judge, observed that Rand's judgments were 'the Canadian judiciary's greatest monument.'[163] That was true. They inspired an entire generation of judges, lawyers, and law students about what the law could be and what it could do if properly harnessed and sent into battle. Of all the judgments from the Supreme Court during his years there, the only ones that stand out and have endured, at least until the modern era of the *Charter of Rights and Freedoms,* are those of Ivan Rand. He was ahead of his time and completely confident in his conclusions. That radiated throughout his decisions. Freedom of speech and religion in the context of the *Boucher* and *Saumur* cases took a step forward, and so did the Supreme Court of Canada. These judgments, Andrew Brewin wrote in the *Canadian Bar Review*, 'inspire pride and confidence in the court that is now in all matters Canada's final court of appeal.' They represent 'the judicial process at its best.' Brewin was the lawyer who fought hard, long, and ultimately unsuccessfully on behalf of the Japanese Canadians who had been robbed of their property and detained during the war.[164]

In any evaluation, of course, much depends on personal opinion about the policy choices that were made. 'How,' one critic asked, referring to *Winner*, 'can Rand discover what no other Canadian jurists had hitherto recognized: a constitutional right to work and to enter a province?'[165] In *Smith and Rhuland,* for example, Rand was undoubtedly correct that people should be judged by what they do, but sometimes, surely, they should be judged by their associations? Was Communist

Party membership not a bar to some things – for example, certain high-ranking positions in government? Members of the Communist Party were, at the time, part of a disciplined, authoritarian organization that was subservient to a foreign state, and their actions could well be assumed to be in conformity with it.[166] Membership in the Communist Party does tell us a lot about a person. However, in *Smith and Rhuland*, the Supreme Court was simply not prepared to approve of guilt by association, particularly where the association, with communism and the Communist Party, was lawful.

As Rand said in *Boucher*, *Saumur*, and *Roncarelli*, citizens have certain rights, and no one is above the law. In his view, freedom of expression and freedom of religion were beyond the scope of the government's authority.[167] 'What is so important about Rand J.'s judgment in *Roncarelli*, is that it articulates the idea that the rule of law is a constitutional concept that operates whether or not there is a written constitution in place.'[168] Rand was, Bora Laskin wrote in his searing indictment of Diefenbaker's 'Bill of Rights,' the 'greatest expositor of a democratic public law which Canada has ever known.'[169] He deliberately breached the convention that required him to decide cases on the most narrow of grounds. In the result, he created an 'impressive degree of judicial protection of fundamental freedoms.'[170] 'To some extent,' Laskin's biographer concluded, 'the Supreme Court fulfilled Laskin's aspirations in the 1950s under the intellectual leadership of Ivan Rand, but Laskin himself did little to assist the Court in fleshing out how Canadian conditions might be invoked to develop Canadian law ... Laskin never ceased to urge the relevance of Canadian conditions upon the judiciary, but never showed them how to incorporate such considerations in their judgments.'[171] In this light, Rand's accomplishments become all the more impressive. As Rand himself observed, although not in relation to Laskin, 'criticism lacking suggestions for improvement in what is condemned can be mere petulant protest against something not fully apprehended.'[172]

It seemed, for a time, that Canada's Supreme Court was a serious institution staffed with high-minded, intellectually equipped, and technically able jurists up to the task of resolving social problems in a modern context. But 'the "golden moments" of the civil liberties decade ended,' the impressive Maxwell Cohen lamented, 'with Mr. Justice Rand's departure from the bench.'[173] His period there was, according to the author of the first really serious study of the Supreme Court of Canada, Paul Weiler, 'a golden age.'[174] The Supreme Court, in the decade that followed, beat a hasty retreat: 'The rampant activism on behalf of fundamental freedoms that had marked the fifties came to an abrupt halt during the sixties,' another critic said. While the court in the 1960s ruled that *Lady Chatterley's Lover* was not obscene, held that federal election advertising was immune from municipal and federal regulation, and concluded that Indians could hunt at night with lights, 'the Supreme Court of Canada was very unsympathetic to civil liberties claims.'[175] Almost always, arguments based on the new Bill of Rights were rejected, but that probably had more to do with the bill's inherent limitations than anything else. Numbers can be misleading, but one leading scholar calculated that, in the 1950s, the court upheld civil libertarian claims 94 per cent of the time. Ten years later, it did so in less than 25 per cent of cases.[176] Clearly, the times and the people had changed.

Rand's great judgments foreshadowed the *Charter of Rights and Freedoms*.[177] What made it especially impressive was that it was done without constitutional, statutory, or judicial authority; there was no written Bill of Rights, no laws to enforce, no precedents to apply. There were no indigenous texts to consult, and there was no tradition to follow. But done it was, either by pigeonholing civil liberties within existing exclusive categories or by distributing them to the appropriate legislative jurisdiction.[178] In *Winner*, for instance, Rand could have simply assigned the right to regulate the highway to Parliament, but he wanted to say something about citizenship – and, within that decision, he created a new and separate citizenship status. However, was it really any accident, given Rand's own views about French Canadians and Quebec, that all his key cases, except *Smith and Rhuland* and *Winner*, arose out of that province?[179]

One of Rand's future colleagues at the University of Western Ontario Law School later provided a partial explanation: 'Rand had to decide who he hated less, French Roman Catholics or the Jehovah's Witnesses.'[180] And constitutional expert Peter Russell wrote: 'It cannot be denied that the three French-speaking judges constituted the indispensable nucleus of that group of judges who rejected the attempt to establish constitutional guarantees of basic civil liberties by judicial construction.'[181] Believing, as they did, that they were untouchable, the authorities eagerly deployed repressive measures when more moderate ones would have likely accomplished their objectives and probably passed constitutional muster. The Jehovah's Witnesses strategy was clear. They carefully selected test cases – those with favourable pros-

pects of success, given the questionable alliance between the province
and its police – and took them all the way to the Supreme Court. 'We
asserted that there was a bill of rights in Canadian law,' Jehovah's Witness lawyer Glen How explained years later, 'and it was the obligation
of the court to give effect to it.'[182] With assistance from Hayden Cov-
ington, an American lawyer and, like How, a Jehovah's Witness, How
deliberately set about to convince Rand and the rest of the court that
Canadians would also enjoy the benefit of a Bill of Rights. Rand agreed,
and their relationship continued long after Rand left the court.[183] Years
later as they reminisced about earlier times, Rand remarked: 'Those
were stirring days, never to be repeated.' 'The wolves fight in packs,'
he continued, 'but the lion fights alone.'[184] Rand made no secret of his
admiration for the Jehovah's Witness lawyer: 'I was always struck by
your quiet determination,' he wrote; '... a great debt of gratitude is
owed to you.'

Roland Ritchie of Halifax was chosen to replace Rand. He was appointed on Friday, 8 May 1959, and, in time-honoured tradition,
bought Rand's gown. On Rand's last day in court, Kenneth Campbell,
the secretary to the chief justice, presented Rand with bound volumes
of all of his decisions. 'We had never done that before for anyone,'
he said.[185] On his last days on the Supreme Court bench, Rand was
asked what made a good judge. The answer, he replied, had little to
do with technical skills in reading, interpreting, and applying a statute,
but everything to do with imagination, an open mind, and a capacity
for analysis. A good knowledge of the law, he added, was also useful.
Rand was not pleased about having to leave the court and, while he
would never criticize that institution, he could not help but point out
that, in the United States, judges could, and often were, kept on past
the age of seventy five. 'I was just getting a grasp of the law,' he would
tell people, 'when they made me retire.'[186]

In May 1959, Rand received an invitation from Dean Erwin Griswold
to deliver the prestigious Holmes Lecture at Harvard Law School. Established by a bequest left to the school by Oliver Wendell Holmes,
the lecture was a high point in the academic calendar and always drew
a good crowd. Proposing Rand to his faculty colleagues, Griswold
noted that he would soon retire and 'that his judicial service has been
notable for the development of an essential bill of rights from the federal structure of the Canadian constitution and the presuppositions of

representative government.' It would be an appropriate occasion on which to ask him to speak at his alma mater, 'freed from the inhibitions of judicial office.'[187] Rand was pleased to accept. 'What I have in mind is an examination of what I think are features of the Canadian constitutional situation which lend themselves to new resources of interpretation,' he replied, 'and I have thought appropriate to describe it as "Some Aspects of Canadian Constitutionalism."'[188] Both Rand and his wife, Dell, were excited about the occasion, and about the opportunity to visit their old haunts.

The lecture was held at Harvard Law School's Austin Hall. Before the lecture, Griswold hosted an informal dinner in the John J. Burns Room of the International Legal Studies Building. The Canadian consul general was there, along with a number of Canadians, including Robert Bourassa and Ivan Head, who were studying law at Harvard. Wisely, Rand had asked Bora Laskin to look over his draft, and the learned professor subjected the work to a thorough critique.[189] Rand knew exactly what he was doing when he played that important role in creating the implied Bill of Rights, and he admitted as much at Harvard. '[W]e have been able to draw implicit judicial support for some part at least of those fundamental rules and principles that with you are constitutionally explicit. We are at an early stage in the formulation of answers to questions which today in a legal aspect reach to the conditions of social cohesion, to the solidarity of free men under the Rule of Law.'[190] When Rand's lecture was submitted for publication to the *Harvard Law Review*, the piece was, to Griswold's embarrassment, rejected. Rand took it in good stride, however, and Griswold arranged for its publication as a pamphlet. The less demanding *Canadian Bar Review* was pleased to publish the piece.

5

Rand's Formula

Windsor 1945: the Second World War was finally over, but a different fight was shaping up on the home front. Almost ten thousand men employed at the Ford plant in the city were embroiled in a battle with their employer. The causes were many, but at the heart of the dispute was management's refusal to acknowledge and contractually recognize the legitimate role of the United Auto Workers – the union freely chosen by Ford's employees. Union and employee discontent had been simmering for years, punctuated by the occasional wildcat strike. With the end of the war, the uneasy labour-management truce could no longer be contained. In September 1945 the first major Canadian post-war strike was called, shutting down the Ford plant and, soon enough, most of the city of Windsor. It lasted for more than three months, until a resolution was brokered which sent the union's unresolved collective bargaining demands to Mr Justice Ivan Rand of the Supreme Court. His formula for resolving the ninety-nine-day strike soon became a standard feature of Canadian collective agreements and one of the defining characteristics of Canadian labour law. How did this come about? And what was Rand's role in it?

At war's end, the more than 100,000 men, women, and children who called Windsor home had every reason to take great pride in their contribution to the Allied victory. Thousands from Essex County had enlisted and served in the army, navy, and air force. More than 1,600 men had taken their basic pilot training on Windsor's airfields. Those who had been unable to go overseas had done their part by taking in British evacuee children, participating in the federal government's Victory Loan campaigns, contributing to the Red Cross, and even organizing the Essex Scottish Overseas Smokes Fund to keep their brave fighting men well supplied with cigarettes. But if one contribution to the war stood out, it was the hundreds of thousands of vehicles the city's industrial plants had churned out during the six long years of war.[1]

With the victory won, Windsor's soldiers were coming home. By the second week of September, hundreds of veterans had already returned in triumph, and thousands more were on their way back to a city very different from the one they had left behind. The population had grown, and many new factories and industrial plants had been built. Economic changes are always accompanied by social ones, and, as in the rest of the country, the transformation to Windsor society was profound. Women were working outside the home, and many had no intention of giving up their jobs to the veterans – or anyone else for that matter. In many ways, the people of Ontario still lived in the dark ages: the provincial government's plan to license 'cocktail bars' as early as 1946 was causing quite the commotion. Allowing beer and wine with restaurant meals was even more revolutionary and required considerable study and thought. Financial forecasts were bleak and, as war orders quickly dried up, thousands of workers were being laid off. Where would all the returning veterans find jobs?

In 1945 the average Windsor worker took home $38.74 a week, when employed. Although there were price controls, the cost of living had increased, and everything seemed expensive. Two loaves of bread sold for 15 cents. A jar of French's prepared mustard cost 10 cents. A pound of Maxwell House coffee rang in at 41 cents (although for 10 cents less you could buy the A & P house brand). For special occasions, prime rib roast was available at the butcher for only 40 cents a pound. Everyday blade roast was more affordable at 24 cents. When meat rationing was reinstituted in mid-September, tongue, kidney, liver, baloney, and wieners were, for the first time, placed on the restricted list along with the more choice cuts. But there was always Kraft Dinner, and two boxes for 33 cents could feed a family of four. At Adelman's department store, boys' 'heavy wool and wool mixed sweaters in pullover style, V and round neck' ranged from 98 cents to $2.98. For that special night out, D'orsay pumps, 'lovely to look at – wonderful to wear,' were available at a 'special price' of $6.50. A return ticket between Windsor and Montreal on one of Greyhound's 'modern coaches' cost $9.20. Rental housing was scarce, although for 'gentlemen doing clean day work,' a room could be found for $4 a week. You could always buy a house; that ran anywhere from $1,750 for five rooms with a bath on a concrete-block foundation in a working-class neighborhood to as much as $15,000 for a four-bedroom, two-bathroom, brick house off Riverside Drive in the more tony part of town.

One thing that had not changed during the war was that the city continued to be dominated by the automotive sector. While local boosters always claimed that there was more to Windsor than cars, automobiles were the lifeblood of the city. According to the 1941 census, more than 14,000 of Windsor's 36,400 wage earners worked in the auto industry – at Ford, Chrysler, and General Motors and at dozens of feeder plants scattered around the city. That trend had only increased and, by the fall of 1945, many Windsor residents, one way or another, depended on automobile manufacturing for their livelihood. In effect, that really meant Ford.

Established in 1904, the Ford Motor Company of Canada was Windsor's largest employer, and its 97-hectare plant on the banks of the Detroit River was about to be hit by a layoff. The assembly line, which during the war had churned out more than forty-five different types of trucks, ambulances, and anti-aircraft gun carriers – 400,000 in all – now needed to retool to meet the peacetime market. Although there was clearly a pent-up domestic demand for cars, the post-war economic forecast was uncertain. Would Canada and the United States maintain wartime economic growth, or would the North American economy, as widely expected, slip into recession, or possibly worse? Moreover, with the national emergency over, the federal government was sure to vacate the labour-relations field, leaving the regulation of most industrial activity to the provinces. What would happen to all the workers employed in the munitions, aircraft, and shipbuilding industries? What was to become of the hard-won wartime labour gains as hundreds of thousands of returning servicemen and women sought re-employment in peacetime Ontario? Would it be open season on unions and their members and leaders, or would the trade union movement be able to maintain, if not build, on its wartime gains? Having helped win the war, organized labour was determined to win the peace. Despite the uncertainty, the 10,000 or so men (and a few women) employed at Windsor's Ford plant were represented by a large and powerful trade union with more than 1 million members – the International Union of United Automobile, Aircraft and Agricultural Implement Workers of America, the UAW.

The battle for union representation at Ford was first fought in 1941, when the UAW took the company on, successfully striking the Rouge Plant in Dearborn, Michigan. After resoundingly winning a supervised election at the biggest automobile plant in the world, Henry Ford II accepted not only the union shop (where everyone had to join the union as a condition of employment) but also the union checkoff (where management would deduct union dues from every employee and forward them to the union). Now the UAW wanted to achieve these exact same terms at the Ford plant in Windsor. That was its number one priority.

Union security provisions – and the more comprehensive the better – are important to unions for many obvious reasons. They provide the union with membership support and financial stability, leaving it free to focus its efforts on collective bargaining and the representation of employees, not on collecting dues. Moreover, the argument goes, it is equitable to require everyone, union member and non-member alike, to pay dues, because everyone benefits from the activities of the union. At the same time, management naturally reacts negatively to any restrictions, real or imagined, on its rights, especially its ability to exercise discretion in the running of the enterprise. The existence of a union and of a collective agreement are two of the main fetters on management's rights to administer the business. In addition, there are principled reasons for opposing the union shop: no one should be forced to join a union (or any other organization for that matter) in order to remain employed. Even more important, there are practical self-interested reasons for employers to be against the union shop and the checkoff: stronger unions are better able to achieve gains for their members, some of which might be in the short-term interests of employees but, over the long term, contrary to the best interests of the business and its shareholders.

At war's end, of the twenty-five automobile manufacturing plants operating in Canada which held union agreements, only two provided for the union shop, and only one provided for the checkoff. These three plants employed about three hundred workers. Approximately eighteen thousand other automobile workers were not required to be union members.[2] In the much larger iron and steel industry – 240,000 men and women employed in 336 plants – only 2.1 per cent worked in a union shop, and .01 per cent in a closed shop (where only union members can be hired). Approximately sixty plants had some form of checkoff arrangements: most of them were voluntary. Other industries were similar. In labour-relations language, the UAW was trying to achieve a breakthrough. But there was an important precedent: Ford's 1941 agreement at its Michigan plant and company headquarters to recognize the union and to institute a checkoff.

In fact, that agreement spurred Canadian Ford employees to organize a union of their own – UAW Local 200. Not surprisingly, it took only a few weeks to sign up a majority of workers: 'Unskilled auto workers laboured on monotonous assembly lines, and the turnover in manpower was high. It was difficult for older workers to retain their jobs: many men were fired after fifteen to twenty years in a plant, and faithful service did not guarantee keeping a job. Discharges were frequently given without notice ... If a man was thirty seconds late, a minimum of a half-hour was deducted from his pay.'[3] Ford responded to the union challenge by offering an employee association – often code for an organization dominated and controlled by management. Choose the company union, Ford of Canada president Wallace R. Campbell promised employees, and you will obtain a collective agreement, grievance procedure, and health and welfare benefits. Fed up with industry conditions – no smoking and talking were allowed on the line, not to mention long periods of layoff and rampant favouritism in deciding which employees were the first to be recalled – Ford employees, two to one, chose the UAW instead in a November 1941 vote supervised by the government. Working men and women were not, in the phrase just coming into vogue, to be treated as a commodity. The following January, Ford signed a collective agreement with the union, recognizing it as the exclusive bargaining agent for its employees.

The new collective agreement provided that employees were free to join a union of their choice, but equally free not to do so. No one would be discriminated against for joining a union or for deciding not to. Union stewards were recognized, and a grievance procedure of sorts was introduced. A number of other bread-and-butter benefits were agreed on. The union had demanded a union shop and check-off. When the employer said no, refusing to follow the pattern it had set across the river, the union could have gone out on strike. Instead, it decided to consolidate its position within the plant. The collective agreement would soon be up for renewal, and when it was, other gains could be achieved.

In the meantime, the UAW extended its reach across Windsor. Chrysler came next, and so did numerous automotive suppliers, aided in large part by the federal government's intervention. If the union could establish that the majority of employees working in a company fell under federal jurisdiction (as just about every industrial plant did during the war), the government would order a supervised vote. Success in the ballot then translated directly into recognition and a collective agreement. In just about every collective agreement, the union was recognized as the exclusive bargaining agent for the employees, and the employer was, again because of the federal government's intervention, required to bargain in good faith with its union.

When the war began, the *Criminal Code* made it an offence for an employer to refuse to hire someone simply because he or she was a union member. It was also unlawful to discourage union membership through intimidation or by threatening loss of position or employment. Another federal statute, the *Industrial Disputes Investigation Act* (the *IDIA*), had, in one form or another, been on the books for years, promoting a system of investigation, conciliation, and, ultimately, delay in labour-relations disputes. Nevertheless, organized labour had few real legal rights. The war changed everything.

The *IDIA* was extended to cover war industries across the country. In 1940 Privy Council Order 2685 signalled a new direction: 'Employees should be free to organize in trade unions free from control by their employer or their agents.' As a recommendation, like the *IDIA*, it lacked teeth, but still indicated a new, more balanced approach. More practical steps were taken in Ontario with the passage of the *Collective Bargaining Act*; then, in February 1944, PC 1003 was promulgated – providing, for the first time, and uniformly across the country, free collective bargaining and establishing a legal process for ensuring compliance. The new regulation established a mechanism for certifying a bargaining agent – for putting a process into place to ensure that the union represented the majority of the employees in the bargaining unit. Employers were legally obliged to bargain with unions, and a conciliation mechanism was created if the parties were unable to reach an agreement. Finally, the new regulation prohibited certain unfair labour practices. PC 1003 was, in a word, revolutionary.

Wartime labour policy had, in general, been favourable to organized labour. At war's end, union membership had reached previously unsurpassed levels. Moreover, unions had grown beyond the traditional crafts and had extended their reach into the new mass industrial plants. They were seen as a good thing, and the contribution of the union movement to the successful prosecution of the war was reflected in widespread public support. Union leaders, headquartered in Ottawa, were an important part of the political conversation.

Union security was not among the issues that were subject to third-party resolution, although the parties were free to come to their own agreement. Rather, if the parties were unable to agree on a union security provision, it became a subject for conciliation. Union security could not be imposed – it could only form part of a recommendation – but it was not something that could easily be sawed off. Wartime experience indicated that, even where conciliation boards suggested union security arrangements, they were ignored.[4] That led to demands that Parliament intervene and impose union security as a matter of public policy and law.

Parliament, however, had other pressing items on its agenda. Given that organized labour had agreed during the duration of the war not to strike, there was little political will to impose a union shop by statute. Neither was there much public support for mandatory union membership. According to an April 1943 Gallup poll, the average Canadian believed that unions were 'necessary and desirable.' However, 37 per cent thought that labour did not have wise leadership. Exactly one-third of the respondents disagreed, while the rest were undecided. Nevertheless, as a result of wartime developments, the most union-friendly legal structure ever was in place at war's end.

Organized labour had taken a great leap forward. The new legal regime, together with organized labour's wartime 'no-strike' pledge, conferred social legitimacy. As a result, union membership, on the rise since the start of the war, continued to grow dramatically. It doubled between 1940 and 1944, even though the promise not to strike was often ignored.[5]

Ford was hit a number of times during the war by labour disputes. As Canada's largest producer of military vehicles, it had been declared an 'essential service.' Accordingly, all these walkouts were unlawful. The first 'wildcat strike,' as they are known in the vernacular, occurred in November 1942, when the union wrongly claimed that Ford had hired women to do work previously done by men and was paying them less. An arbitrator and future superior court judge, C.P. McTague, investigated and, while he upheld the union's claim for equal pay for equal work, he also determined that the work in question was not work previously performed by men and, therefore, could be done by women. There was another walkout in April 1943. The local leadership was not on side, the RCMP reported to Ottawa, noting that private arrangements had been made with the union leadership to end the strike. That report, signalling the importance of even a small labour disruption at Ford, was raised at the highest political levels.[6] A much larger dispute broke out one year later when management suspended some union stewards, leading to a walkout. When the causes of the dispute were examined by a neutral third party, it was hard to determine who was responsible for what. In the end, no one won, but work ground to a halt as other Ford workers laid down their tools in solidarity.

Another walkout, the largest so far, and again interrupting critical war production, occurred later in the spring of 1944. Management now demanded that all grievances be in writing. The union objected and appealed to the National War Labour Board. The employer then suspended six stewards who failed to obey its orders. Matters worsened when employees stopped working to 'discuss' the situation. Ford then announced that, as far as it was concerned, its contract with the union was terminated. Eventually, with the assistance of the National War Labour Board, an umpire proposed a grievance procedure closely resembling that suggested by the employer. However, instead of accepting the result, many union members – thousands, in fact – walked out.

The strike was illegal but lasted less than two weeks, as local union officials, including Roy England, the president of Local 200, under instructions from the Communist Party, brought the workers back in order to ensure no disruption in production. Ever since the Soviet Union had been attacked, the 'imperialist war' had become a 'just anti-fascist crusade.' Communist Party policy was to increase production and prevent strikes. Loyal communists such as England dutifully infiltrated themselves into leadership positions in unions and did what they could – which was often considerable – to ensure that nothing curtailed wartime production. As it turned out, the spring 1944 labour disputes, not to mention sabotage and other unlawful work stoppages, and the important part played behind the scenes by communists, foreshadowed future union-management confrontation.[7] That became clear when the parties sat down the following month to negotiate a new collective agreement.[8]

The union demanded a union shop, the union checkoff, a new grievance procedure, weekly payment of wages, participation in a reconversion committee, recognition of seniority in the case of layoffs, two weeks' vacation with pay, and overtime for weekend work, among other new terms and conditions. The employer's offer, when it came, was concessionary – it expected the union to give up some of its hard-won gains and rejected outright any improvements to the status quo.

(In the vocabulary of industrial relations, the terms 'union demands' and 'management offers' were used.) The National War Labour Board directed that the contract be extended until after conciliation. It also addressed one of the key outstanding issues – the arbitration of disputes – a source of real frustration in union ranks because the employer took the position that it, alone, would decide whether a dispute involved the interpretation of the collective agreement and was, therefore, arbitrable. That question, one of jurisdiction, was not for one party or the other to answer; rather, it was a matter to be put before the arbitrator. The board attempted to right this wrong, setting up a procedure for the settlement of grievances. Louis Fine, an experienced labour-relations officer in Ontario's Department of Labour, was appointed 'umpire' and given the mandate to resolve the backlog of outstanding grievances.

In the meantime, collective bargaining, after a fashion and in compliance with the labour board's order, continued, but relations between the parties only worsened. By early 1945 Ford was claiming, as the negotiations had evidently failed, that it was entitled to terminate the collective agreement. Before that happened, the law required that an attempt be made to reach conciliation, and Fine moved into the role of conciliation officer between the parties. Uncharacteristically, he was not successful. Mr. Justice S.E. Richards of Winnipeg was then appointed as a one-person Industrial Disputes Commission. Regarded as one of the ablest mediators, he was asked to find a middle ground. Ford offered improvements to the grievance procedure and 'fair' rules for determining the seniority of 'employee-veterans,' together with the status quo, 'because the present collective agreement has worked out fairly well.'[9]

The UAW saw things differently, and management's proposal was a clear non-starter. It was time for catch-up, not concessions. The first thing to go as the conciliation went from week to week was the no-strike pledge made at the beginning of the war. Next the union presented a comprehensive nine-pronged package for a new and improved collective agreement. There was no apparent middle ground – one of the union's key demands was for a union shop together with a union checkoff – and, within a matter of weeks, Justice Richards quit, pointing to 'a distinct absence of goodwill and cooperation.' In his report to Humphrey Mitchell, the minister of labour, submitted on 3 August 1945, the judge recommended that the collective agreement continue until the end of the year and that, following a cooling-off period, the parties resume negotiations. When Mitchell released the report in the middle of August, the union rejected it, pointing out that it had been 'cooling off' for several months since the judge left town. In a demonstration of their resolve, more than seven thousand Ford employees attended a meeting and voted in favour of calling for a strike vote. Four days were set aside at the end of August and beginning of September for the balloting. A two-thirds majority was required before the union could take the members out. Mitchell, a former unionist himself, had no intention of letting the workers walk, at least not until he had to. As the strike vote balloting got under way, he announced that he would appoint a conciliation board.

The union reacted badly to the news, pointing out that negotiations had been going on for seventeen months and that, when Justice Richards was appointed as a commissioner, the union understood that his investigation would eliminate the need for subsequent conciliation. Six conciliation boards had made recommendations on contracts in automotive plants in the previous year, yet none of the recommendations had been accepted by any of the automotive employers. In addition, since Richards was first appointed, more than three thousand Ford workers had received layoff notices and, Ford now announced, more pink slips were in the mail. There was a real concern that surplus labour would be used to depress wages. The union described the latest layoff notices as 'a provocative act.'

Sometimes, both sides need a strike, and, on Labour Day, Roy England, who was still president of the Ford local, announced to almost four thousand of his members assembled for the annual parade that 100 per cent of the members had voted in favour of a strike. 'We will,' England promised, 'take action.'[10] The unanimous strike vote was dubious, but there was clearly significant support for industrial action. UAW Local 195, an amalgamated local that held bargaining rights for approximately twelve thousand employees at more than thirty Windsor-area automotive industries, including Ford's competitor Chrysler, had also voted overwhelmingly in favour of a strike. But directed against whom? That UAW local had no dispute with its various employers. What it did have, however, was a local president, Alex Parent, the MPP for Essex North, who was a well-known communist anxiously awaiting an opportunity to lead the class struggle.

The situation at Ford was a little different. There, before the union could take the Ford assembly-line employees out, it had, under the legal regime in place, to await the report of the conciliation board. On 29

August the board was directed 'to endeavour to effect an agreement.' Stanley Springsteen, KC, a Windsor lawyer, was Ford's nominee to the board, and the UAW was represented by law professor Bora Laskin. When the nominees could not agree on a chair, Mitchell appointed another westerner, Edmonton judge G.B. O'Connor, the head of the National War Labour Relations Board. All three had attempted unsuccessfully to conciliate at least one dispute between Ford and its unionized workers in the past, and they quickly determined that, this time around, there was no middle ground.

The commissioners soon identified the main issue separating the parties – union security, 'the root of all difficulties between the company and the union'[11] – but they did not agree over the solution to the problem. The company nominee, naturally, wanted no union security provision. They all rejected the union's demand for a closed shop with a compulsory checkoff, but two of them recommended a voluntary checkoff, irrevocable for the life of the collective agreement.[12] In such an arrangement, employees who chose to participate would direct their employer to deduct dues from their paycheques and remit them to the union. The union, however, regarded it as a weak form of union security and, because it required union members to self-identify in an anti-union environment, completely unacceptable.

Laskin understood the stakes involved. From study and experience, he knew that the 'vast majority' of conciliation boards appointed during the war were concerned with one main issue: union security. On the one hand there were employers, habituated to simple union recognition, but not yet ready to have fixed upon them 'responsibility for guaranteeing the permanence of unions which have not yet achieved an inner stability through their own efforts.' On the other hand, he wrote, 'the very fact that the claim for security is made, is an indication that a union is not only a bargaining agent for employees but that it itself, considered as an entity, has a role to play in industry. If this be true, its desire for a guarantee of its integrity and of its continued existence becomes understandable. But, whether the employer should cooperate in making this possible is not an altogether easy question to answer in terms of a general principle.' If an answer was going to come, Laskin predicted, it would 'more properly come from government.'[13] Organized labour, however, had no intention of putting its fate in Ottawa's hands, realizing, as H.D. Woods, a young professor of industrial relations at McGill University, pointed out, that 'the security drive represents a determination to recast the structure of collective bargaining ... to establish an altered framework within which bargaining is to take place.'[14]

Although union security was the important issue, it was not the only one on the table. The union also wanted a guaranteed minimum wage of $1,800 per year, job security (in effect), as well as wage increases, a shorter work week, a better grievance procedure, overtime pay for weekend work, two weeks' vacation instead of one, better medical benefits (a key term and condition of employment before the introduction of universal medicare), and protections against and during layoffs (the union feared that there would be substantial shutdowns so the company could reorient itself to a peacetime economy). The conciliation board concluded that some of these issues were beyond its jurisdiction, being more properly the subject matter of proceedings before the National War Labour Board, but that none of the demands were insoluble: 'In our view, once the question of union security is settled, the parties should have no difficulty in solving the remaining issues.'[15] There was some truth in this assessment. Even though the parties were at loggerheads, they had established a good working relationship in the plant, and the vast majority of grievances were quickly settled. The few grievances that did proceed before an umpire were usually dealt with in less than half a day, and a dozen or more matters were disposed of in a single sitting.

The conciliation board's report was an advance over the status quo and presented a possible public relations coup. The union had won its certification vote with an ample majority, and since then it had demonstrated that it enjoyed the widespread confidence and support of the members of the bargaining unit. Now, with post-war reconversion about to begin, accepting the recommendations was an option worth considering. Moreover, if there was going to be a fight about the report, it was in the union's interest to allow the employer, as it was likely to do, to reject the recommendations. Public opinion was obviously critical, and the union had the opportunity to take the high road – in the national interest. Instead, the union rejected the report and began a strike. 'Ford workers,' Roy England answered, 'want a real collective bargaining agreement for the post-war,'[16] and he promptly proceeded to tear up the conciliation board report in front of reporters – or at least a document he theatrically claimed was the report.

Ford of Canada was not alone in facing labour unrest. In the United States, Ford had laid off more than 50,000 employees, and the number was growing daily because of disputes at automotive parts suppliers in Detroit and at manufacturing facilities across America. Henry Ford II knew whom to blame – communists, deliberately impeding the progress of reconversion. Communists were a convenient target, and at the time in North America, they were a force to be reckoned with. In the 1940s many communists were active in the labour movement, and especially in the leadership of the UAW and its Ford local – facts that did not escape the attention of the RCMP's Security Service.[17] Vladimir Lenin, the main leader of Russia's October Revolution, had identified trade unions as 'instruments for advancing the proletarian revolution under the close supervision of the party.'[18] Not only was George Burt, the Canadian UAW director, soft on party members but the executive of Local 200 was under communist control, its president, Roy England, a secret party member.[19] Burt's support was most unfortunate, but, given his background, not surprising.

A union man, Burt had helped organize Local 222, the union at Ford of Canada, and he was elected as Canadian regional director, the top position in the UAW in Canada in 1939, with the help of communists, Canadian nationalists, militant trade unionists, and left-wing social democrats. Although not a communist himself, he followed the communist line in much of his dealings, except when they threatened his personal and professional survival.[20] 'Most people,' he claimed, 'didn't know communism from rheumatism. We needed everybody's help. I would have taken help from the Salvation Army, the Methodist church or anybody else.'[21] In 1945 it was often unclear whose goals communist union members and their leaders put first, those of organized labour or of Moscow. What better way to renew the class struggle than by taking ten thousand men and women out on strike, thereby precipitating a crisis in capitalism? At the same time, though, the UAW and its members were well within their rights to withdraw their labour from Ford in pursuit of legitimate collective bargaining demands. Most UAW members were not communists and, like most Canadians, wanted nothing to do with them. They did, however, want to preserve wartime gains. And, after more than a year of negotiations and a democratic election, the union and its members decided to pull the plug.

At ten in the morning on Wednesday, 12 September 1945, when the whistle blew to signal the start of the mid-morning break, ten thousand workers walked out. The assembly line, manufacturing trucks for UNRRA, the United Nations Relief and Rehabilitation Association, came to a halt. The timing, just weeks after Japan's surrender, was not unusual. Conversion from a war to a peace economy requires adjustments, as the 1919 Winnipeg General Strike after the First World War had already shown. Now, if the UAW won at Ford, the gains would be enjoyed at General Motors and Chrysler, and at hundreds of other unionized workplaces throughout the country. But if it lost, the loss to union power and prestige would, likewise, extend far beyond Ford. Only a handful of Canadian industrial unions had so far achieved the union shop, or union security provisions with teeth, and, if the union did not succeed in this dispute, the future of large industrial unions, and their ability to represent employees effectively, would be put in question.

The dispute was important for other reasons too. Organized labour was then divided between old-style trade or craft unions and the new industrial unions, such as the UAW, a member of the Congress of Industrial Organizations. The dividing line was deep, but it was not just the older established unions and their leaders in the rival Trades and Labour Congress who were concerned about the upstarts and their growing numbers. The democratic union leaders on both sides of the fence were extremely troubled by segments of the UAW and some of the other industrial unions with their ties to the Communist Party, operating in Canada as the Labour Progressive Party (LPP). Pursuit of communist goals, they correctly understood, could only harm the democratic trade union movement. A full appreciation of the dark forces lurking in the background would not emerge until later. In the meantime, the walkout, the first major labour dispute since the end of the war, was widely believed by the labour movement to be a critical test of its strength. In the beginning, all organized labour was behind it, and R.J. Thomas, the UAW's international president, promised the strikers the union's unlimited support. Ford's Canadian president, Wallace Campbell, Thomas predicted, would be given a spanking: 'I don't know how long this strike will last; you don't know how long it will last, but Campbell must be shown that he is not the Emperor of Windsor.'[22]

Reverberations were quickly felt. Ford's union payroll was huge, and the 10,000 striking autoworkers were, on the second day of the strike, joined by 1,200 more Ford employees – office workers who, though they belonged to a different UAW local, were prevented by the picketers from going to work (except for a handful of employees

from the finance department who were allowed in to process the outstanding payroll). Although not required to do so, Ford continued to
pay the office workers during the dispute. The strikers were a different
matter, however, and they were not even eligible for unemployment
insurance. Only people actively looking for work can get the benefit,
so strikers are automatically disqualified (ironically, 700 assembly-
line workers laid off before the strike were deemed eligible). Making
matters worse, under the regulated wartime economy, work permits
were required to obtain jobs, and the federal government refused to
give them to striking Ford workers because they already had jobs. The
UAW established a soup kitchen for strikers, provided they presented
an up-to-date union card proving time served on the picket line, but
the union was ill-equipped to maintain the strikers and their families.
Only about 8,000 of the 10,000 men and women on strike could even
ask for union assistance, restricted as it was to members only. There
was no strike pay. Instead, grocery vouchers were handed out – $3 a
week for single men, $5 a week for a couple, and $1 to $2 for each addi-
tional child. There was nothing for the thousands of men and women
sent home when Ford feeder plants began to close down, which they
did within days of the start of the strike.

Most of the action, and excitement, was at the Ford plant. Pickets
were established at all sixteen gates – 1,000 men assigned to duty at all
times. When company president Campbell arrived at work on the second day of the strike, he was not allowed in. He immediately retreated
to his gracious suite on the fifth floor of the Prince Edward Hotel, the
home and headquarters for senior members of management during
the labour dispute. He also called on the police and its chief constable,
Claude Renaud, to enforce the law. The law was clear: picketers are
not entitled to prevent non-striking employees from crossing the line.
They can slow them down or talk them out of going to work, but they
cannot lawfully keep them out. Nevertheless, in the words of the local
Crown attorney, Renaud 'had taken a somewhat vacillating attitude
as to the duty of the police to enforce the law.'[23] One member of the
public shared that view: Angus Gillan was so enraged at the union
that he attacked one of its members, James Speal, who was manning
the picket line, and chewed off part of his ear. Alcohol was said to be
involved. The police arrested Gillan, but on orders from the Windsor
Police Commission, following a highly politicized debate, the officers
assigned to the Ford plant were instructed, whenever possible, to keep
their hands off. Even Ford's request that beverage rooms in the strike

area be temporarily closed was rejected. Union towns are often like that. Mayor Art Reaume was not 'aware' of any problems. Writing to Attorney General Leslie Blackwell in mid-September, he reported that the picketing was peaceful, with only 'a few minor instances of friction.'[24] Blackwell was far from impressed and, in an end run around the mayor, empowered the local Crown attorney, E.C. Awrey, to requisition the services of the active militia if required. The occasional charge was laid, and J.L. Cohen, the Communist Party's favourite lawyer, was always dispatched to conduct the defence.

Within hours of the start of the strike, Bernard Wilson, a mediator from the federal Department of Labour, arrived in town, but it was too early for him to act. The parties, stewing now for seventeen months, needed a strike. One day dragged into the next and a month went by. Labour Minister Mitchell was working diligently to keep the lines of communication open, while the duke of Windsor, MP Paul Martin, tried to do the same thing behind the scenes, keeping in contact with the highest levels of UAW leadership and briefing his Cabinet colleagues in Ottawa.[25] The parties, however, were clearly dug in. For his part, Ford president Campbell insisted that there was nothing to talk about with anyone until the union stopped its illegal picketing and allowed non-striking employees to report to work. Something had to break the logjam, and on October 7, the union made its next move.[26]

More than one hundred union men who maintained the power generation plant had been allowed by the union leadership to continue reporting to work to keep the powerhouse going. Ford generated all its own electricity, but now, on union orders, these men were withdrawn. Immediately, the lights went out, the heat turned off, the water stopped running. There was no auxiliary hook-up to the municipal line, and, with strikers barring access to the plant, it was too late to add one. 'It was getting cooler now,' Burt recalled years later, 'and we decided to close the powerhouse down. We froze the plant right up ... The plant was dead.'[27] This tactical move was designed to get Ford back to the bargaining table, but it was particularly unthoughtful. In all previous strikes, a skeleton powerhouse crew had been kept in place. At the end of the day, closing the powerhouse would only prolong union pain, for once the strike was settled it would take weeks to fully restore services and therefore extend unnecessarily the time spent without work – and wages. It was even worse than that, however. There was a real risk, in the event of a cold snap, that the hundreds of miles of pipe carrying water would freeze. Burst pipes would take months more to repair. Untended machinery would seize and rust and might have to be junked. Burt knew exactly what he was doing: 'It was really cold. The radiators in the plant were all froze up. Machines were heaved off their bases with the frost. The company claimed we were damaging the plant.'[28] It was not just a claim but a fact. The source of everyone's livelihood was at serious risk. With no lights, no heat, no electricity, and no water, what would happen if there was a fire?

The strike was regularly discussed in the House of Commons, where M.J. Coldwell, the leader of the Commonwealth Cooperative Federation (CCF), the social democratic precursor to the New Democratic Party, predictably called on the government to send in a controller to negotiate a new collective agreement containing appropriate union security provisions. During the war and for some time thereafter, the government had, on occasion, in the midst of intractable labour disputes, sent in controllers to run particular industries and plants, justifiably sacrificing property rights to the national interest. C.D. Howe, the minister of reconstruction, rejected the request. Instead, he blasted both the union and management for failing to settle their differences. An unproductive step in that direction was taken when Mitchell unwisely signalled to the employer some support for its position.

The labour minister had earlier revealed himself as an old-fashioned former unionist and rejected outright any legislating of union security. 'I take the British view. I am frank about that,' Mitchell told the House of Commons, adding: 'I was raised in the school in which the union officers collected the dues. They had the contact between the officers or the stewards and the men. I think that is the proper way.'[29] The Liberal government, Mitchell pointed out on October 9, had set in motion a labour code recognizing the rights of unions. Mitchell, obviously, took considerable pride in that achievement, but he did not see imposing the checkoff by statute as the natural next step. Legislating the checkoff would be an unwanted intrusion by the state and, he warned, would lead to totalitarianism, as had happened in Germany, where Hitler had destroyed free trade unions: 'Things move along from one stage to another until freedom has disappeared – freedom as we understand it.'[30] It was all ludicrous, of course. Mitchell was entitled to his views, but so long as he was acting as a mediator he should have kept his opinion about the merits of the dispute to himself, particularly in its early stages. Later, with the power of the Liberals' majority in Parliament, he could, if need be, wield a heavy stick. He belatedly realized as much, and his next step was to get the parties talking.

On 15 October, union leaders and company officials accepted Ottawa's invitation to meet in Toronto. The discussions immediately bogged down, however, over a dispute with the provincial attorney general about jurisdiction. Leslie Blackwell, a loose cannon with obvious limitations, argued that the Ford strike was a federal responsibility, thereby precipitating an extended and unproductive discussion about who was in charge of what. When the parties finally got around to talking about the issues, they quickly reached an impasse. The law-breaking, Campbell asserted, must stop, and he referred to the union leadership as 'criminals.' That was not his call to make, though he did have a score of legitimate complaints. Company executives and non-striking employees had been prevented by union pickets from going to work, and the powerhouse had been closed, endangering the physical plant. Eventually, he stated, the strike would settle, and it was in everyone's interest that there be a company to return to. In the meantime, the police had done nothing to enforce the law or to keep the plant secure. Until the illegality stopped, Campbell declared, until the powerhouse reopened, there was nothing to talk about. And one final point, Campbell lectured the labour minister: Ford will never force a man to join a union. If union security provisions are such a good idea, pass a law requiring it, and Ford will, he promised, obey it. Unless it was the law, Ford would not force anyone to remain a member of a union as a condition of employment. It was not, he concluded, the Canadian way.

Mitchell could, in response, have usefully observed that the union shop and checkoff were not the law in the United States either, but that had not stopped Ford from agreeing to both in free collective bargaining negotiations with the same union. He did not. However, mediators are always looking for a deal and, building on the conciliation board report, Mitchell now recommended a revocable checkoff. Under this plan, employees would be allowed to change their mind. It would also allow the employer, the union responded, to identify union members and establish a blacklist. The union asked Ford of Canada to give it the same thing it had agreed to in the United States. We cannot, Campbell claimed, adding, implausibly, that Ford of Canada was not controlled by Ford of the United States. On 18 October, Mitchell reported to the House of Commons that he was unable to broker a deal – at least not yet. Union leaders now switched gear, and a delegation headed by Burt and England travelled to Ottawa to lobby the government to pass legislation imposing the union shop and checkoff. Their mission also failed.

At the end of October, Mitchell, having gone back to the drawing board, presented a new four-point plan. Dismantle the pickets and re-open the powerhouse, call the men back to work in order of seniority, send the non-monetary issues to an arbitrator, and let the National War Labour Board set the wage rate. Mitchell's proposal, like the union's counterproposal issued a few days later, was rejected by Ford, angered again by the union's latest move: the UAW was now refusing to allow non-union watchmen to cross the line. The physical plant was huge and needed to be patrolled, strike or no strike. Shutting down the powerhouse was a mistake. Keeping the watchmen out was nei-ther strategic nor shrewd. The company now decided to go on the offensive.

Calling on Police Chief Claude Renaud, the Ford president demand-ed immediate action. On the one hand, the chief and his force, standing idly by in the face of increasing picket-line lawlessness, were a national embarrassment. On the other, there was nothing stopping Ford from seeking an injunction limiting the picketing and requiring the picket-ers to stand aside and allow watchmen and non-striking employees to get to work. Moreover, the company, if it had truly been anxious to avoid a confrontation, could easily have arranged for its watch-men and others to be delivered by boat to any one of the company's docks, free from interference. Whatever the failings of the police, then, it seems that a confrontation was just what Campbell and Ford had in mind. When Renaud proved uncooperative, and the attorney general failed to respond to a stream of telegrams demanding action, the Po-lice Commission, guided by the local Crown attorney, finally gave the necessary orders.

After a closed-door meeting and over the strenuous objections of Mayor Reaume, who publicly and privately left no doubt about his sympathies, Renaud was ordered to take action – personally.[31] On 2 November he tried to lead a contingent of officers across the picket line, opening the way for security guards and office workers to return to their duties. But the UAW had been tipped off about where and when to expect the authorities, and the 'flying wedge' was turned back by strikers – the picket lines had swollen in anticipation of Ren-aud's arrival. Renaud and his dishevelled officers were pushed across the street to the tune of laughter, catcalls, and loud boos while union picketers followed instructions given in a continuous stream from the union's sound truck. It did not escape the attention of more careful observers that the police had not made much of an effort.[32]

For the strikers, it was terrific fun and morale was high. The carnival atmosphere got even better the next day with the arrival of a brass band. Roy England promised the men that any further outside interference would be met with a city-wide strike. He then led them in singing 'Solidarity Forever.' The mayor also joined in to show his support. Groups of young girls began to arrive for the party, which now included street dancing. J.B. Salsberg, a communist member of the provincial legislature, denounced Ford at Queen's Park before taking up residence in Windsor, where he began marching with the picketers and mugging for the cameras. From the union's point of view, the company had been dealt a major blow. The timing was right to escalate matters further. Leaders of the UAW's amalgamated Local 195 decided to show the UAW's power in a 'solidarity strike': they took out approximately eight thousand men and women mostly employed in the automotive parts industry, even though they had nothing to do with Ford and at least one-third of them were not union members. The international union objected, but, as Burt explained, 'I closed all the plants then in Local 195 ... I closed them down and broke their contracts. To hell with it.'[33] Eighteen thousand UAW members were now on strike.

All this activity played right into Ford's hands, giving the authorities an excuse to consider other ways of dealing with the dispute. In due course, hundreds of OPP officers began arriving in town by chartered bus, along with RCMP officers and a large contingent of 'special constables' brought in by Dakota air transport. An army unit in nearby Chatham was placed on standby.[34] The Police Commission requested this action, supported by Ontario's premier, George Drew, and the acting prime minister, J.L. Ilsley. Mayor Reaume registered his dissent. Attorney General Blackwell announced that all the police were under provincial control: they would maintain order and ensure that the Ford plant was protected. According to Blackwell, the UAW's failure to allow protection and maintenance personnel to enter the plant put it, and the people of Windsor, at risk. It was, he said, a 'state of emergency.'[35] He could be forgiven for overstating this situation, for, as the Windsor Star correctly pointed out in an editorial, 'law and order' was at stake.[36]

The arrival of massive police reinforcements should have been sobering. The last thing the union needed was a major confrontation with the police. Canadians would not support any threat to peace, order, and good government. Yet, instead of de-escalating the situation, the union leadership decided to provoke a major confrontation. On 5 November UAW members, widely believed to have been imported from Detroit especially for this purpose, stole more than one thousand cars and buses from the streets of Windsor and abandoned them around the perimeter of the Ford plant, completely blocking all sidewalks and streets. Uncooperative drivers were beaten into submission with lengths of rubber hose carried by the members charged with this task. It was a defensive action, some unionists claimed, in anticipation of a police attack. The *Windsor Star* reported that at least six thousand picketers were assembled outside the Ford plant, and noted that a truck was parked at a strategic intersection, piled high with bricks. Stealing other people's property and then blockading the streets had nothing to do with the union's legitimate aims. The union was demanding its rights, but what about the rights of others – to their cars, to use the city streets, to providing the means for fire trucks and ambulances to render assistance where necessary? Union president England expressed regret that some private vehicles had got caught up in the melee. He was, he added with crocodile tears, 'extremely sorry.'[37]

This tactic was another union blunder, one promoted by communists within the local union but resisted by the international union leadership in the United States. Closing Ford and some of its suppliers was one thing; attacking the police, stealing cars and buses, and blockading the streets around the plant another. Threatening the established order by shutting down the city would, as strikers had learned in Winnipeg a generation earlier, leave the government with no choice but to act forcefully – and that likely meant destroying the UAW. Oblivious to the high stakes and to the fact that public support, even in a union town, had began to decline, England and others started musing out loud about a general strike. On 10 November, England and Parent sent telegrams to unions across the country, asking them to join in a one-day 'solidarity strike.' The duo was quickly disappointed.[38] Aside from these safety issues in Windsor, union leaders elsewhere knew that a general strike would never advance the union's goals. What about the collective agreements UAW Local 195 had breached by calling illegal strikes? If unions could ignore their contracts, so too could employers. Slowly but surely it was becoming clear that communists had infiltrated the UAW and hijacked the strike. The vast majority of the strikers had no idea, however, that they were being misled and used. Down at City Hall, increasing numbers of families were applying to the city for welfare.

Exacerbating the situation further, the union continued to break the law, refusing to allow members of management, non-striking employees, and watchmen to cross the picket lines. Local politics played a part, and the mayor publicly insisted that the rights of the strikers deserved as much respect as those of the employer. That was true, so far as *legal* rights were concerned. Reaume began to speculate publicly about city council imposing new taxes to raise funds to feed the strikers and their families. From a political perspective – and politicians are always looking ahead to the next election – Reaume's approach made sense: there were more employees than managers. However, when the city did not enforce the law, it gave the union the upper hand and emboldened its leaders. Ford was left with little choice but to refuse to return to the bargaining table until its legal rights were recognized. Feelings of frustration among the strikers were palpable. Out of work now since the beginning of September, the strikers, their families, and the entire community were suffering.

The labour minister decided to try to break the stalemate and flew to Windsor in a special Department of Transport plane. 'I think we can settle it,' Mitchell told reporters, although the mob scene at the Ford plant could not have been encouraging. Wallace Campbell was ill, a timely coincidence that gave Mitchell the pretext to go right to the top. From his suite at the Prince Edward Hotel, he called Henry Ford II across the river in Detroit and invited him over for a chat. Ford arrived that night at 9 for a three-hour meeting. He explained that he had no control over Ford of Canada, but told Mitchell bluntly that nothing would change until the union removed the blockade, allowed the powerhouse to be reopened, and permitted non-striking workers to get back to work. It was a matter of safety and sanity. The plant was entirely without fire protection, and there was no light or power. The electrical fire alarms were not working. The fire pumps were out of commission, the gravity tank feeding firehoses had been drained, and the sprinkler system and fire hydrants were inoperable. The forty men per shift usually charged with maintaining the physical plant had been reduced to five. There were some chemical fire extinguishers, but if the weather turned cold, their contents would freeze and the canisters might explode. Water still in the sprinkler system would do the same thing, rupturing it, probably beyond repair. A fire would spread quickly – the plant was well beyond the reach of the Windsor Fire Brigade – and likely destroy the entire physical plant, along with the strikers' jobs and the city's economic base. Simply put, the company and the community were facing a multimillion-dollar disaster. If Mitchell had any doubt about that, all he had to do was drive over to the Ford plant, where he would see stockpiled coal visibly smouldering. It was also, Henry Ford lectured the labour minister, a matter of legality. The strikers had no legal right to prevent watchmen from crossing the line, and no legal right to keep the non-striking workers out.

Ford's claim that the Canadian branch plant was run independently was nonsense. The company bore considerable responsibility for the dispute. Its delaying tactics were notorious, and refusing to yield in Canada on a matter already settled in the United States was bad business and bad labour relations. C.D. Howe had now been briefed fully about the dispute and, in the House of Commons, he 'severely condemned' the company.[39] Henry Ford II was always in the driver's seat, but he had earlier identified what he believed to be the real cause of the problem: 'irresponsible labour groups impeding the progress of reconversion.'[40] It was a polite way of referring to communists, most of whom would have liked nothing better than to destroy this particular means of production. The claims of the *Windsor Star* that 2,400 local communists 'report directly to world headquarters,' located in Moscow, was patently not accurate, but the motives of key union leaders were, at best, mixed. Mitchell, an experienced labour minister, had been wise to come to Windsor. 'I never give up in labour disputes,' he told reporters.[41] Eventually, everything in disputes between management and labour does get resolved.

A small step in that direction was taken when Mitchell, after days of talks, persuaded the union leadership to dismantle the barricade in return for an understanding that the government would encourage the employer to resume negotiations and, should the negotiations fail, to proceed to arbitration on any outstanding issues.[42] A major showdown was averted, thanks to Mitchell's quiet diplomacy. As Burt belatedly realized – after having the point hammered home by UAW officials in the United States, the labour minister in Canada, and even Mayor Reaume – if the union did not return the cars to their owners, the troops would be called in and the union would be destroyed.[43] He had to first, however, convince the members, and that required his personal appearance on the picket line. Even after 'pleading almost desperately'[44] for members to follow orders, the answer from Henry Howarth, chief spokesman of the picketers and the man in charge of the sound truck, was no. Eventually, Burt prevailed, but the union leaders had come close to losing control of the rank and file. The need for a settlement was urgent.

Someone always has to make the first move and, on Mitchell's private urging and following a visit to Ford headquarters in Dearborn, the company proposed on November 9 that the strike end, the powerhouse reopen, and the plant prepare for resumption of work; that employees return to work as quickly as possible 'without discrimination'; and that all issues in dispute (other than those properly before the National War Labour Board) be referred to an arbitrator chosen by Mitchell. It was the same old plan – the furniture just slightly rearranged – and it was the plan that would form the basis for the eventual settlement of the strike.

Debating the proposal among themselves, the union leaders were not entirely displeased. The men would get back to work, and there was some reason to believe that union security, having twice been identified as the major cause of discontent in company-union relations by conciliation boards headed by judges, would be addressed at arbitration. Besides, the proposal offered a way out of what could now be seen as a losing situation, one that would likely deteriorate further if left unaddressed. But the union leadership continued to be ahead of the rank and file: when given the opportunity, members resoundingly rejected the proposal and called on all unions in Canada to go out on strike. Disgusted, Mitchell packed his bags and left for Ottawa, after telling reporters he had 'no plans for returning to Windsor.'[45] He had put the power and prestige of his position on the line, had interceded directly with Henry Ford II, and had succeeded, for the first time, in obtaining a commitment from Ford for the arbitration of the key outstanding issues. It was a significant accomplishment, and the union's refusal made clear that it was now the obstacle preventing resolution of the dispute. Obviously, union members needed more time on the picket line. An accordionist was brought in to entertain the strikers – with Strauss waltzes and swing – but the numbers of picketers, on what was now day sixty of the strike, began noticeably to thin.

Behind the scenes, union radicals led by England, working hard at building momentum for a general strike, were successful in attracting more than ten thousand men and women to a raucous meeting at the municipal Market Hall, where Ford was resoundingly denounced and a pretty picture painted of future victories. The local leadership was supported, predictably, by communist politicians such as Fred Rose, the communist MP later convicted of espionage and deported to his native Poland; Joe Salsberg, who was making something of a career out of the dispute; A.A. MacLeod, the other communist mem-

ber of the provincial legislature; and Tim Buck, the leader of Canada's
Communist Party, along with his provincial Stalinist sidekick, Leslie
Morris. Various communist-controlled unions, such as the Canadian
Seamen's Union (CSU) and the United Electrical Workers, immediately announced that they would heed any call for a sympathy strike.
CSU leaders promised to tie up hundreds of deep-sea vessels and lake
ships, and, in due course, they called a strike that paralyzed shipping.
The UAW international leadership was becoming increasingly dubious about the wisdom of the local leaders, but it was not yet ready to
take a public position and even denied the existence of any rift. Others,
like A.R. Mosher, the president of the Canadian Congress of Labour,
pointed out that a national strike would be illegal and unproductive.
If we treat our collective agreements like 'mere scraps of paper,' he observed, why wouldn't employers do the same? In Ottawa, Percy Ben-
gough of the rival Trades and Labour Congress described the call for
a general strike as both 'stupid and dangerous.'[46] Fighting for union
security was just and good, but fighting for communists was absurd.
To the best of its limited abilities, the RCMP kept tabs on some of the
more prominent communist unionists; its file, 'Subversive Activity in
the UAW-CIO – Generally,' began to expand.[47]

Although unhappy about the union's position, Mitchell continued to
work hard at resolving the dispute. The strike began to dominate debate in the House of Commons, much of it far from informed. Patrick
Ashby, a Social Credit MP from Edmonton, compared striking Ford
employees to farm animals. They are, he explained, like hogs that have
broken out of their pen and are now rooting around in the garden. The
thing to do, he continued, was to learn to think like a hog, determine
what hogs need and want, fix up their pens, and then herd them back
inside.[48] More productively, Windsor's former mayor, Colonel David
Croll, now representing Toronto-Spadina in the House of Commons
on his return from distinguished overseas duty, tried to place the issue in context: there was no reason, he argued, that Ford and other
employers could not check off union dues just as they had checked off
war bonds. Administratively, these tasks are all the same. The conclusion was inescapable that management would not do anything to assist a union unless it was left with no other choice. The debate raged
on from one day to the next.

It was time for some frank talk. Mitchell summoned the UAW
leadership to the capital on 13 November, where, after giving them
his view of the likelihood of success should the union remain on its

present course, he sensed, for the first time, 'a conciliatory attitude.' The leaders had accepted the reality that the union was not winning the strike. They also began to appreciate that any escalation of the dispute beyond Windsor would trigger a forceful governmental response. They therefore agreed to recommend to the membership that the powerhouse be reopened and that non-union employees no longer be prevented from going to work. To allow the union to save face, the Police Commission announced that there would be no further need for outside police forces in Windsor if the powerhouse was reopened and security personnel allowed unhampered access to the plant. Proclaiming victory, the union leaders urged the members to approve the proposal. At a meeting on 15 November they did.

Ford announced that these terms were not good enough – all the pickets must be removed. The company's position presented a problem. For weeks, it had claimed that life and property were in jeopardy and that the powerhouse had to be reopened to preserve not only the plant but also public safety. Now the union had agreed to remove all its powerhouse pickets and to authorize powerhouse employees to report to work. 'If the emergency was so great,' the *Windsor Star* pointed out in an editorial, 'the powerhouse should be put into operation without delay.'[49] Ford had an answer to the criticism: once reopened, the powerhouse must not be shut down a second time. If the powerhouse equipment was put back in operation and then suddenly shut down again, the damage would be greater because winter had now arrived in Windsor. There may have been some truth in this argument, but Ford may also have been posturing and trying to gain maximum advantage. Whatever the case, however, the union's softened position opened the door for a resumption in negotiations.

On 19 November the parties met – for the second time since the strike began. Although the mood around the table was good, the discussions were unproductive. The employer had no intention of negotiating anything, other than some minor issues and a return-to-work protocol. The union wanted to talk about all the issues in dispute. The only thing both sides could now, privately, agree on was that negotiations were unlikely to resolve the outstanding issues and that arbitration was the only answer. This realization was extremely important, for it provided the basis for resolution. However, it was still too soon to get an agreement. Everyone knew what the deal was, but it was not yet possible to get both sides to make the move towards the middle. After several days of intermittent discussion, D.B. Greig, Ford's treasurer, announced, 'Well, there's nothing else we can do' and, along with the other company representatives, walked out of the room.[50] The strike now entered its eleventh week, but the parties were at the beginning of the end. As Mitchell had earlier observed, 'I would like to think that the company and the union are about to shake hands, but they have not reached out yet.'[51]

Ford's strategy was working. Within days of this meeting, the union announced an about-face: it gave management its word that, once reopened, the powerhouse would not be closed. Management accepted the offer, and, on 23 November, powerhouse workers returned to their jobs. The strategy was twofold: show good faith in an effort to build on success, and ensure that, with winter at hand, there was no damage in the plant. Momentum was building towards settlement, but, for good or ill, Attorney General Blackwell now decided to bash the union by delivering an inflamed radio address that very evening. In it, he laid the blame for the strike, the blockade, and the future decline of Windsor as a centre of industry squarely on the shoulders of communists who were out to foment revolution. Blackwell's message was classic red-baiting, for it unfairly obscured the legitimate issues in dispute and recast them entirely as a fight between good and evil. The address was not entirely unhelpful, however. As intended, it forced striking workers to reassess the strike, and it also served as a reality check to unionists who needed to know that whatever else they were fighting for, they were also being used to advance Communist Party fortunes. While the union demanded and received equal radio time from the CBC, the damage was already done.

In the meantime, Mitchell continued to work at keeping lines of communication open and, on 27 November, he announced that an agreement had been reached in Ottawa. At its heart, his plan had not fundamentally changed. It provided that, until a new collective agreement was attained, an umpire would be appointed to deal with any issues that arose; further collective bargaining would take place under the supervision of an arbitrator; and all unresolved issues (except those matters under the jurisdiction of the National War Labour Board) would be referred for final decision to that arbitrator – who, signalling the importance of the matter, would be a judge of the Supreme Court of Canada. The next day, Ford informed Mitchell that it accepted the proposal. So too, finally, did union leaders, who were now desperate to reach a settlement, realizing that there would be no general strike and that Ford would not cave in. Once again, however, the union leadership could not deliver the rank and file, who narrowly rejected the proposal after a raucous and most irregular ratification meeting.[52] Fifty-two per cent of the members present – and only about half the union members showed up, in part because the meeting was held at a new location – voted to continue their strike, now well into its twelfth week. That was not the result the government wanted or the union leaders recommended.

One week later, the union leadership presented Mitchell with a modified proposal. The old plan, if resurrected, would require a two-thirds majority to pass; the new plan required only a straight majority. Department of Labour officials studied the proposal, but there was no point. Ford insisted that the earlier deal was the deal, and that it was time for the union leadership to deliver. Once again, Mitchell devised an exit strategy – all strikes and lockouts have to have one – and he provided the union leaders with a way out: he recommended a new secret and supervised ballot. In the meantime, finally facing up to the inevitable, leaders of UAW Local 195, expressing 'sincere regret' that the 'entire Canadian labour movement' had not joined their solidarity strike, announced that their members would return to work.[53] It was far from clear what these employees got out of the exercise, other than the pleasure of being misled and used by local UAW leaders. The closing of approximately thirty other Windsor manufacturing plants did nothing to shorten the Ford strike. It deprived thousands of working people of their weekly wages, adversely affected key industries that supported the community, and unnecessarily and uselessly delayed reconversion. About all that could be said was that it served as a cautionary tale for those who understood its lessons. In support of a larger political objective, certain trade union leaders would, in the increasingly polarized post-war world, abdicate their responsibilities to their electorate and follow the instructions of their Communist Party masters. Attorney General Blackwell's rhetoric may have been overheated, but he was right on the money.

Back at the Ford plant, the economic misery was extended, quite possibly deliberately, for Ford employees. The only good thing about the delay was that the UAW and the Labour Progressive Party persuaded the magnificent but politically misguided singer Paul Robeson to come to Windsor to give a benefit concert at the Capitol Theatre. Eventually arrangements for the supervised balloting at four different locations across the city were completed, and the vote took place on two days in mid-December. This time, absent the shenanigans of the previous election, 72 per cent of the electorate – and only union members were eligible to participate – voted in favour of ending the strike. After ninety-nine days, the strike was over on the basis of a settlement that had, more or less, been available for months. Since 1942, Ford employees had lost, because of strikes, 138 working days, and this number did not even include the days lost on account of periodic layoffs because of maintenance and retooling. More than $6 million in wages disappeared in this strike alone – real money at any time, but serious money in 1945.

The strike ended on 20 December, but it was weeks before all the damage was repaired and operations fully resumed. Machinery had not been maintained for months, countless radiators had burst, pipes were leaking, many of the wood floors had buckled because of the frost, and the plant was filthy. While progress had been made in putting out the coal fires, the pile of fuel was still smouldering. Ford employees had not only lost their wages during the dispute but would stay unemployed while the clean-up and repairs were under way. The men and women who worked at the feeder plants stayed out of work too. It was an unmitigated economic disaster. But the decision to strike is rarely only an economic one. Notwithstanding the underlying motivations of the local union leadership, Ford employees obviously felt that they had to take a stand and were willing to do so, even though that stand, and this strike, came with an economic cost. Ford employees had chosen a union to represent them and, when the company refused to give that union the same respect for its legitimate role that it had done in the United States, Ford left it no choice but to stand up and fight back. The checkoff was worth fighting for.[54]

Speculation quickly began to focus on who was to arbitrate the outstanding issues in dispute. Supreme Court of Canada judges J.W. Estey and Ivan C. Rand were the two leading contenders for the appointment, according to the *Windsor Star*.[55] James Wilfred Estey was, like Rand, a New Brunswicker and a Harvard Law School graduate who also began his legal career in Saskatchewan. He stayed on there and, in 1934, was elected to the Saskatchewan legislature as a Liberal and, again like Rand, served as attorney general. Estey joined the Supreme Court in 1944, one year after Rand, though he, unlike his colleague, went out of his way to write his judgments in plain language. There were, therefore, two good men to choose from.

Paul Martin, the Windsor MP and secretary of state, lobbied behind the scenes to get Rand assigned to the Ford dispute. Hard working, ambitious, and well educated, the left-leaning Martin always had his eye on the ball and the bandwagon, and, with many elections in the future, that meant retaining UAW support. As Martin observed in his memoirs, 'it was fairly obvious that the executives of the car plants could influence only a tiny number of voters.'[56] Rand, Martin later recalled, 'was a man who knew the evolution that was taking place in social thinking ... and it just happened that I was in a position to help bring about his appointment.'[57] Martin never understated his contribution to local, national, and international events, but his opinion about how to handle a legal and political problem in his own backyard was not taken lightly in Ottawa. There was opposition in Cabinet, as some ministers, such as J.L. Ilsley, the acting prime minister, and C.D. Howe, the influential 'minister of everything,' believed that the parties should work out their problems without the intervention of the government. But appointment of a Supreme Court judge to arbitrate the dispute was an essential feature of the agreement ending the strike. It had gone on far too long, Martin told Cabinet, and only the appointment of an eminent jurist as arbitrator would end it. Meanwhile, Martin privately assured the union leadership that Rand had 'progressive ideas.'[58]

It did not take long for the labour minister to announce that Rand was the government choice. For umpire, Mitchell selected Horace R. Pettigrove, a New Brunswicker and industrial relations officer from the federal Department of Labour. Before leaving for Windsor, Rand met privately with Arthur MacNamara, the deputy minister of labour. The deputy soon followed up, writing Rand a 'secret' letter just before Christmas in which he made the government's position clear. There should not be something for nothing, he advised. Union security, if it came, would arrive with a cost.[59] Once Rand arrived in Windsor on 27 December, the last of the auxiliary provincial police and RCMP officers were pulled out. Pettigrove showed up on the 29th and, for the first time, met Ivan Rand.

Pettigrove had started working at the local mill in the summer of 1910, when he was eleven years old, and, three years later, with his grade eight diploma in hand, he signed on full time. For the next eighteen years, he toiled in that crowded and unsafe mill – and, at six foot seven, grew to be a giant of a man. A radical, he enjoyed challenging authority and developed a reputation as someone who stood up for the working man. In 1936 he was appointed one of New Brunswick's fair-wage officers before going on to the provincial Department of Health and Labour. An expert mediator, Pettigrove played a key role in drafting much of New Brunswick's early labour law. In 1942 the federal Department of Labour made him an attractive offer – as industrial relations officer, with jurisdiction throughout the Maritime provinces. Pettigrove knew from his own bitter experience what a determined employer could do, in the absence of real legal protections, to prevent employees from choosing a union to represent them in their relations with management and in the government of their industrial lives.[60]

In Windsor, Pettigrove's task was to facilitate the reopening of the Ford plant and the return to work of the striking employees. He was also given the responsibility, as umpire, of dealing with any disputes that arose until the new collective agreement was settled, by either negotiations or arbitration. Rand's mandate was to supervise those negotiations and, only if they were unsuccessful, to impose a collective agreement by arbitration. The two men had two distinct but interrelated jobs – and they got off to a bad start.

'I met Mr. Justice Rand,' Pettigrove later recalled, 'and we didn't click off at all.' Convinced that Rand, the former Canadian National Railways lawyer, would never be able 'to see the other side of it,' Pettigrove explained to him that he 'didn't want to get involved in his work, and he [Rand] shouldn't get involved in mine.' Rand moved quickly to change Pettigrove's mind: 'I don't mind telling you that I would like to have you act as an advisor to me, as a consultant,' the judge told his umpire in the final days of 1945. The answer was no: 'I thought that we had the understanding that you do your work, and that I would do mine,' Pettigrove replied. 'Don't you think,' Rand responded, 'that you are a little unbending?' 'No, no more than you, Sir,' Pettigrove answered. When Pettigrove reported the conversation to his boss, M.M. McLean, the director of industrial relations, McLean properly put Pettigrove in his place. 'My God, Horace, a member of the Supreme Court of Canada asks you to act as an advisor to him. Why, you can't refuse.' That should have been obvious – and the two men got to work.[61]

The supervised talks began at the end of December and lasted until 8 January 1946. A number of outstanding issues were immediately resolved through mediation. No one had ever believed that there was any realistic prospect of reaching a complete settlement, however. That meant a hearing, and it began at 2 p.m. on 9 January, with John B. Aylesworth, KC, one of the best corporate lawyers in the province and a future judge of the Ontario Court of Appeal, representing Ford. George Burt was there on behalf of the union, together with a committee that included local president Roy England. The first order of business was to deal with a request that Rand had received for representation by a group of employees who did not believe that the union was acting on their behalf. Within minutes, Rand had to face one of the principled issues before him: reconciling majoritarianism, as reflected in the vote by a majority of employees that the UAW represent them in negotiating the terms and conditions of employment with the employer, with the assertion by a minority of employees that they had the right to be heard independently of their elected representatives. Without hearing any representations on point, Rand gave his answer.

'I have,' he stated at the outset, 'always been habituated to the principle that nobody should have compulsion placed upon him without his being heard. On the other hand, this is an arbitration between two recognized parties.' The employees were not a party to the proceeding. Perhaps their specific interests should be taken into account, but that was a decision for the parties to make: 'This arbitration is yours and I am in your hands.'[62] That was the right call to make. The union was one of two parties to the collective agreement: the other was the employer. There was no place at the table for employees acting in opposition to their legally recognized bargaining unit. The dispute was solely between the union and the employer.

It did not take these parties long to agree that the issue which had to be dealt with first was union security. There was no ambiguity about what the union sought. Everyone presently working at Ford who was not a union member had to become one, and anyone hired to work at Ford had to join the union. Continued membership was to be a condition of employment, and the employer would, as directed by the union, deduct union dues from everyone's pay and remit these funds to the union. What the UAW wanted was a classic union shop.

Rand had no difficulty understanding the concept. It was obvious why the union wanted a union shop with checkoff. But did that mean it should have one? 'You have,' he told Burt, 'asserted the desirability of a union shop, but you are not making it clear just what objectives will be served by it which cannot be served by a powerful union which attracts membership by its own qualities and other inducements.'[63] Put another way, why, if the union was any good, could it not succeed on its own? The question was a fair one, and Burt had his answer. Don't forget, he told the judge, that the automobile industry in Canada has been uniformly hostile to unionization for years. Surely, Rand interjected, that would stiffen the backbone of the men and strengthen the union? That was true in some cases, Burt replied, but, while some unions were strong, others were weak, and a union shop would give employees confidence in collective bargaining. They then went on to an extended and meandering discussion about Canadian labour law, one that left Rand announcing, to Burt's obvious pleasure and Aylesworth's noticeable discomfort, that he would be 'proceeding on the basis of the desirability of the social policy of the maintenance of unionism among employees.'[64] That was the old CNR lawyer talking, the one steeped in the progressive labour-relations attitudes of Sir Henry Thornton. Given, as Thornton had put it, 'that unions were here to stay,'[65] and given the desirability of trade unionism, a way had to be found to make it work. Rand, in the first hour of the proceeding, had a suggestion: Why not let employees refrain from joining the union but require them to pay dues? What do you think of that? he asked Burt.

The answer was, predictably, not much. But when asked to explain why, the union official floundered. Rand moved on, temporarily, coming back to the question later in the afternoon. Why would you not be satisfied with a rule that required everyone to pay dues but left it up to each employee to decide whether to join the union? 'I just do not get what you mean,' Burt replied. Rand explained the idea in other words. Now Burt understood and answered Rand's question with yet another question. 'If,' he replied, 'it is recognized that collective bargaining is a matter of public policy, that is accepted by the government and they have passed laws about it, then what is the best way to make sure that collective bargaining works?'[66] What about the power of the group over the individual? Rand asked. Don't get carried away, Burt replied. There was power, but it was nothing to worry about – and, besides, any employee with a complaint about the union had a mechanism for redress. The redress was an internal appeal, ultimately to the international convention – something not dissimilar to the rights of Canadian citizens to have their case ultimately heard at the JCPC. Safeguards were not only appropriate but present. This retort opened up a new can of worms.

Rand was being asked to issue an award forcing every Ford employee to join the union, and requiring the employer to deduct union dues from wages earned by every employee and to turn that money over to the union. He was understandably interested in the relationship between the union and its members and non-members. What position, Rand inquired, did the union now take with respect to non-members? They were, Burt explained, entitled to the benefits of the collective agreement, but if they had a dispute or difference with the employer, they were on their own. If a man was fired and he was not a union member, he was out of luck. Even if he ran to the union hall and joined up, he would not get any official assistance. Union rules demanded that, before the union would take up a particular grievance, an employee had to be a member in good standing for three months. This was, Rand suggested, outlandish. If the collective agreement confers benefits on all employees, how can you deny them representation when they need to have their complaints brought to the attention of management? The answer was simple. It was not good policy to provide this type of assistance; doing so would discourage employees from joining the union. Rand still had trouble understanding this argument. The union, he pointed out, bargained with management on behalf of everyone. The collective agreement was for the benefit of the collective. If the collective agreement provided for a grievance procedure, that agreement, bargained in the interests of everyone, should surely apply to everyone. No, Burt explained, if you are not a member, if you are not paying dues, you are not entitled to representation. What happened to these employees was not the union's concern.

Individual welfare was, however, one of Rand's concerns. 'I confess that I have a very great regard for that individual,' he replied, 'because I picture myself as that individual.'[67] Still, no one 'should get something for nothing,' and the parties got into a lengthy dialogue about that point. When the hearing reconvened the next day, Rand was back at it: What was the basis for unions disciplining members? he asked. For 'conduct unbecoming,' Burt replied. Just what was that? Rand wanted to know, and off they went again, with Rand struggling to understand the protections afforded to individuals who were in conflict with the union. Where loss of union membership meant loss of employment, employees could, he observed, be at 'the mercy of the union.'[68] While the employer also possessed the power to terminate employment, that power, Rand observed, was checked by the protection of the union. Be serious, Burt told Rand. Just because we have the power doesn't mean we are going to use it. 'You have to give us some leeway as far as authority is concerned.'[69] But Rand was concerned – prophetically so.[70]

What if a man spoke out against his union, and the union determined that his protest was conduct unbecoming and terminated his membership – thereby ending his employment in a closed shop. What then?[71] Burt attempted to draw a parallel between the trial the UAW would offer to dissenters, with ultimate appeal to the union's international convention, and the appellate review available from an independent judiciary. Rand cut him off. But before he could move on to another subject, Patrick Conroy, the secretary-treasurer of the Canadian Congress of Labour (CCL), the central labour body to which the UAW was affiliated, jumped in with an extended epistle debunking all the company's arguments in advance – and, as Rand's highlights on the transcript suggest, using language the Supreme Court judge found appealing.

Conroy, a Scot, began working in the coal mines when he was thirteen and, six years later, moved to Drumheller, Alberta, where he worked in the mines again. By 1940 he was vice-president of the United Mine Workers in western Canada and, the following year, he became secretary-treasurer of the CCL, its chief administrator. 'Domineering and intransigent,' Conroy was also a fierce democrat and generally 'thought to be the most accomplished trade unionist in Canada; he was certainly the best informed.' It took him a while to catch on to the communist threat to trade unions and free collective bargaining, but when he did, long after Rand's work in Windsor was done, he became its ardent enemy, in Canada and internationally.[72]

Don't lose sight of the ball, Conroy told Rand. The collective agreement was no ordinary commercial agreement: 'The contract is an instrument, it is a mechanism of relationship, good, bad or indifferent, that in the larger and broader sense is an obligation to the community, to the citizens of Canada, to run the business in a civilized manner. By civilized I mean in an intelligent, decent and restrained fashion.'[73] This approach would earn the respect of the community, but there had to be self-respect as well. 'That self-respect is conditioned by the degree of responsibility that we exercise in living up to our obligation.' Those were 'the requirements of good citizenship.'

'If one is going to make his contribution to the welfare of an industry, his first responsibility is to be a good industrial citizen of that industry,' Conroy continued. And that 'means something fundamentally more than standing aloof in our own pride and our own ego and our own prejudice from the true dominating agency that runs the industry. By dominating agency I mean the invested capital, on the one hand, and invested labour, on the other hand. The one makes up the company, and the other makes up the union.'[74] No industry, Conroy argued,

could succeed if the relationship between the two parties was bad, or
if there was an imbalance of power between the two parties. Minority
groups had no place in this formulation, and, when Rand attempted
to interrupt to ask why, Conroy respectfully insisted on being allowed
to continue. Minority groups could not be tolerated, he suggested, because they sought the benefits of the agreement but would not support
the group that had given them better terms and conditions of employment. That situation would be 'absurd,' and 'no industry can function
on that basis.'[75] Moreover, no community could function if some of its
members stood aside, apart from its accepted laws, and proclaimed
themselves a law outside the law. It was simply wrong that a man
could say, 'I will take the higher wages. I will take my seniority. I will
take the grievance procedure. But I will not pay a penny for any of it.'
No one, Conroy urged in language sure to appeal to Rand, 'should be
above the law.'[76] Economic progress demanded no less than the union
shop. Reason demanded no less: 'To admit futility, to throw up our
hands and say, "What has gone before must continue unless there is a
more rigid application," would be sheer retrogression, an admission of
bankruptcy ... We must bring reason to bear on this question. If we are
going to seek nothing but more laws to apply to these human relationships and neglect the laws of self-government, or self-experience and
of self-examination, then we will not be doing much to find a solution
of this particular question.'[77]

Speaking of human and economic progress and the role of legitimate
trade unions in promoting it, what role, Rand wanted to know, did
the Communist Party play in the dispute? Conroy began his response
by asserting that he, personally, was not a communist, but he did not
'condemn the whole communistic credo'; he thought there were 'some
good elements in it.' Although the trade union official claimed to be
against communists, he could understand how the Communist Party
would go about bringing 'its attractions' to the attention of 'the mass
of the people.' That was very interesting, said Rand, but what he really
wanted to know was whether the Reds were behind the strike. Conroy
refused to give a direct response, but the answer to his question was
clearly yes: 'Frankly,' he said, referring to communist control of the
strike, 'I cannot prove that. I might have my opinions on it, but those
opinions would be related to hearsay. Reading through the papers and
drawing my own conclusions ... I may say to myself that the communists have an objective in controlling the union in the Ford strike.'[78] In
that case, responded Rand, did that not suggest that the union leader-

ship might have been motivated by other than legitimate industrial objectives? Conroy was in no position to answer: he had been in Windsor when the strike was called, in Europe on business for the next six weeks, and only then returned to the border city to help out. He had attended many meetings, and only legitimate trade union issues were discussed there. Rand thereupon decided to get at the issue another way, by interrogating various members of the union committee.

Where were you born? he asked one of them. Scotland. Do you believe in free enterprise or communism? The man refused to answer. Rand moved on to the next man, another of the local delegates. Scotland, he replied, and another refusal. Then England, and a refusal. Then to the next man. Canada was the answer to the first question. 'You ought to be pretty safe,' Rand observed out loud, but, instead of posing the same second question, he asked whether Conroy had got it right when he said that only legitimate union objectives were behind the strike. The answer was yes, though Rand realized that his question was ridiculous 'because if there were other motives, they would not be revealed.'[79] Finally, late in the afternoon on the second day of hearings, it was the company's turn to speak to the main issue separating the parties.

Unions were an important part of our economic system, Ford lawyer John Aylesworth conceded at the outset. But they possessed significant powers that imposed considerable responsibility on them. There was, however, no reason to conclude that the relationship of members to their union was anything like the relationship of a citizen to the state. To be sure, citizens had no choice about paying taxes, but no matter who was elected to office, citizens had freedom within the state. That could not be said about compulsory union membership, where the union could deprive employees of their livelihood. It was apples and oranges. Make no mistake, the management lawyer warned, union security gave the union financial security, it protected the union against membership raids from other unions, and, most important, most objectionable of all, it gave the union undisputed control over the lives, destinies, and right to work of individual employees.[80]

The employer did not have any current objection to the union – although Aylesworth candidly admitted that, in the beginning, management went out of its way to frustrate collective bargaining. Nor was Ford at all interested in assisting a rival trade union. It was satisfied that Local 200 represented a majority of its employees. These matters were established once and for all, and a union security provision was not therefore necessary to ensure either of them. What remained to be decided was union security: the company was completely opposed to it because the union did not require it to bargain, and bargain well, on behalf of the Ford employees. If the union had the power to deprive men and women of their jobs, it would do so. At that point Aylesworth provided Rand with a recent example from across the river where twelve employees were terminated at a union's behest when they had the temerity to disagree with some internal policy of their local.

The company forecast other problems as well. If the union had enhanced security, the next time around the damage to plant and equipment would be greater, more men and women not involved in the labour dispute would be prevented from entering the workplace, and episodes like the near revolt on November 5 would start earlier, last longer, and cause greater destruction. Aylesworth, as though peering into a crystal ball, told Rand that all these events could be predicted with near certainty unless there was an adequate system of checks and balances, no union shop, and substantial and judicially enforceable fetters on the union's exercise of its naked power, including the right to sue and be sued for breach of its contractual obligations, and unless individuals had access to an impartial tribunal when they come into conflict with their union. Aylesworth did not believe these safeguards needed to be set in stone: 'If it were demonstrated that the counter checks were too extensive or not extensive enough, or that in this particular or that particular a substitution ought to be made ... well and good; those are matters of progress and are matters that are not necessarily static but which can be changed as progress demands it.'[81]

What about making everyone pay union dues and, at the same time, Rand suggested, allowing everyone, whether member or not, an equal vote on the question of going out on strike? Here Aylesworth got excited: 'This is a new idea to me, and I must confess that I am somewhat struck with it. I am rather inclined to kick myself because I did not perceive it myself.'[82] Ford would support such a scheme, he indicated: '[T]o approach it in that way will be going quite a measure along the lines of setting up regulations and counterchecks such as we have been talking about.'[83] There was more, of course, and after the lunch recess, Aylesworth told Rand what he required. A method had to be introduced in law in which the union could be held liable for a contractual breach that caused damages. Aylesworth had a perfect example. In the Ford dispute, Local 200 had lawfully gone on strike. The same could not be said of Local 195. That amalgamated local had collective agreements with dozens of employers but no collective bargaining disputes with any of them. Yet, in solidarity with Local 200, it had pulled more than eight thousand men and women from their jobs and kept them away from work for a month. In each case, the collective agreement had contained a covenant not to strike during the life of the collective agreement. And, in each case, the union had ignored that covenant. If Rand was giving any thought to any type of checkoff, it was incumbent on him, Aylesworth argued, to ensure that any growth in union strength resulting from the checkoff be accompanied by a growth in enforceable union responsibility. Just like anyone else, the lawyer submitted, unions must be responsible for breach of contract.

That was a good point, Burt piped up; everyone should be liable for breach of contract. And, after reviewing the tremendous opposition Ford had raised to unionization in the early years, and after agreeing with Aylesworth that matters had improved substantially in recent years – the fall strike being the exception – the UAW director observed that Ford had refused to implement certain awards that went against it, even though the company was bound by custom and agreement to arbitrate disputes and then accept arbitral results. The union also needed a legal mechanism to enforce its legal rights.

Not so, the company retorted. Burt had got it all wrong. Refusing to implement an award was one thing; raising a jurisdictional objection and then defending oneself from an application to prosecute before the Labour Board was quite another. More to the point, there had never been any lockouts when the employer did not get its way. In marked contrast, the union had condoned several wildcat strikes.

Union security was the focus of the arbitration, but the parties touched on a number of other issues as well – picketing, for instance, an issue of particular interest to Rand. How was it done? What were its legal limits? What were its purposes? And what about the practice of 'taking motor cars?' What did the union leaders think of that? Rand could not conceive of a circumstance where it would be justified – and, he was informed, the union did not officially disagree. But the union had done nothing to prevent the thefts and nothing immediately to remedy that wrong, he replied. What about shutting down the powerhouse – did that not hurt the union too? When Burt gave a wily and political answer – that it was only through the union's efforts that the powerhouse was put back into operation – Rand was not impressed. These acts were 'not only idiotic, but illegal.'[84]

When the submissions on the big issue were completed, the parties

shifted gear and began to consider, clause by clause, the other outstanding matters in dispute. Here Rand was quite effective, gently
prodding one party or the either into agreement on actual contractual
language. 'It seems to me,' the union representative would begin. Moments later the company representative would respond by saying, 'It
seems to me,' and then it would be Rand's turn, and he would attempt
to compromise the positions.[85] On other occasions, as new topics were
introduced, Rand would inquire whether the parties wished him to
express a view at the outset or whether they wanted to make representations first. Invariably, it was the latter. What was the point in having
an arbitrator if one could not persuade him to find for your side? The
process was an education for Rand in how the union went about its
work and management ran the plant. Rand knew something about the
railway unions, but a modern assembly line with ten thousand employees was completely beyond his experience. He was a fast learner,
and he quickly absorbed the details of modern industrial life – to the
evident satisfaction of the parties.

Rand's views on some matters were conservative: it was, he said,
up to management to decide what industrial penalty fit what industrial crime. On other issues his take was quite progressive. Don't you
think, he suggested, it would be best if management called in a union
representative before dismissing a man – a representative who might
suggest something that the company had overlooked? 'Why can't you
agree on this?' he asked, referring to one intractable question that was
occupying too much attention, adding, 'You have agreed on nearly everything else.' The answer was obvious: the parties had been able to
agree on much, in Burt's words, 'because you are here.'[86] The parties
actually engaged and turned to important issues such as employing
and re-employing veterans, the need for the union to repudiate unlawful strikes, the necessity of maintaining the powerhouse in the event
of a future labour dispute, and bread-and-butter clauses dealing with
the daily administration of a collective agreement covering, in a good
North American market, as many as 16,000 employees. They were all
important matters, but also detailed, complex ones requiring careful
attention. To a remarkable degree the outstanding issues were settled,
or, if not, were refined as Rand was instructed about what was really
important and why.

Despite Horace Pettigrove's earlier misgivings, Rand could see the
other side of it. And Ford made it easy for him to do so. The company,
based on information that Pettigrove was 'pro-labour,' made life mis-

erable for Rand's increasingly trusted aide, mistaking his success in settling strikes for a partisan attachment to the labour side. In truth, if Pettigrove was in favour of anything, it was collective bargaining.

After almost six days of evidence, the hearing came to an end, and it was up to Rand to write the award. Not surprisingly, the matter of union security had to be dealt with first. 'What do you think,' he asked Pettigrove one day, 'of an associate membership?' Well, Pettigrove replied, what's that? 'For example, if you belong to a club and you have an associate membership, you would not have any right to vote or anything like that, but you would pay your dues and you would have the facilities of the club.' The same could be true with associate union membership, Rand explained. Pettigrove liked the idea: 'I remember distinctly, I said: "That's a mighty rare bird – original thinking."' Discussion then turned to how the formula would work. Rand had been giving that matter some thought. How much are union dues? he asked Pettigrove. Somewhere around $1.00 per month, he thought. So what about associate members paying 60 cents? Rand suggested. Absolutely not, Pettigrove replied, 'that's union busting tactics.' Rand glowered at Pettigrove: 'I am not here to bust unions,' he told the umpire. He then agreed to think about what Pettigrove had said.[87]

The next day the discussion resumed. 'I've been thinking about what you said,' Rand announced. 'About this checkoff thing, I think that if they pay anything, they pay it all. Now they won't have to pay any initiation fees or that sort of thing, but they will pay the dues, the regular dues, they will pay the same as the others.' That was fine with Pettigrove. That left the question of how the money would be collected. Requiring the company to deduct the funds from the employees and remit them to the union was the only practicable method. Not only could there be no free riders, Pettigrove explained, but this method would avoid problems with collection. If a man fell behind on his dues, that was one thing, but if he refused to pay, that was another: 'something would fall on his head, or a truck would run into him.' That's the way voluntary checkoffs were enforced, Pettigrove told Rand. 'Well, they can't do that,' Rand asserted. 'They do do it,' Pettigrove replied.[88] Obviously, the responsibility for collecting dues had to be placed on the employer. There would, however, be no union shop, Rand confided to Pettigrove – that would give the union too much power over its members.[89]

The 'Rand Formula' was announced at the end of January 1946 at
Toronto's Royal York Hotel. 'I have every hope,' Rand said, smiling
as he handed out his six-thousand-word award, that 'this may prove
to be the beginning of cooperation ... that will be to the benefit of the
entire industry.' The negotiations, he added, 'were on a most pleasant plane,' and there were 'good tempers, good manners and a good
spirit.'[90] Balancing the respective interests of the parties was Rand's
objective: 'I do not want anybody here to look upon anything as a victory. We are trying to arrive at a rationalization of arrangements that
are essential to the industry. I do not want anybody to consider that
one side or the other side has anything in the matter of a win or a loss.
We are just settling controversies and that is all there is to it.' Or, as one
of the union representatives correctly put it, they were simply 'getting
down to business.'[91]

At the outset of his award, Rand noted that his assignment was not
a conventional arbitration, in the sense of a right under a contract or
some other legal relationship. No legal right was being claimed; no
legal entitlement was violated. Instead, what was at stake was the
resolution of a series of competing interests arising out of modern industrial life: 'Here is a highly congested and articulated undertaking;
the work generally is the repetition of limited operations; the psycho-
logical effects, or in another aspect, the employee psychology, under
the best conditions would require a sympathetic handling; in a hostile
atmosphere they could be deplorable.' There were 'strains and frictions' arising out of the 'anomaly of a magnificent engineering plant,
machines and functions coexisting with a human engineering.' It was
these strains and frictions that had to be addressed, within the context
of private enterprise, where capital would always have more power.
'Against the consequence of that, as the history of the past century
has demonstrated, the power of organized labour, the necessary co-
partner of capital, must be available to redress the balance of what
is called social justice: the just protection of all interests in an activity
which the social order approves of and encourages.'

'The organization of labour must in a civilized manner be elaborated
and strengthened for its essential function in an economy of private
enterprise. For this there must be enlightened leadership at the top and
democratic control at the bottom.' Capital, a term Rand regularly used
to describe management, had to face similar constraints: 'The absolut-

ist notion of property, like national sovereignty, must be modified and the social involvement of industry must be the setting in which reconciliation with the interests of labour and public takes place.' Conflict between these interests was inevitable, but 'it ought not to be necessary that the inevitable loss to every interest should be actually suffered in labour strike,' given 'their real mutuality of interest in this enterprise.'

That was not, of course, the approach to date: 'Certain actions which took place during the strike appeared to the public mind as extraordinary ... Beyond doubt picketing was carried on in an illegal manner. The resistance to preservation of plant property was from the standpoint of the strikers a supreme stupidity. The filling of the street alongside the plant with vehicles and the interference with innocent members of the public was an insolent flouting of civil order. But beyond doubt too, there was exasperation and provocation, and these actions seem to indicate the intensity of conviction on the part of the men that fair demands were being met only by stolid negativism ... [A] strike is not a tea party and when passions are deeply aroused, civilized restraint goes by the board unless the powers of order are summoned to vindicate them. Illegal action is for the civil authority to deal with.'

That is exactly what did happen during the ninety-nine-day strike. But Rand, like the union and the employer, was 'desirous of avoiding futile recriminations' and positioning the parties to provide for 'the future protection of the industry as a whole.' Were they up to it? 'An irresponsible labour organization has no claim to be clothed with authority over persons or interests,' Rand continued. 'But I am dealing with a body recognized as the bargaining agent for approximately 9,500 employees and, while their abuse of striking power cannot be excused, much less justified, we cannot disregard the complex of hostile attitudes and resulting exasperations from which that abuse in fact arose.' So the union was justified, after all. But that was, as Rand saw it, a matter of historical interest. Not only could Ford employees change their bargaining agent if it continued to act irresponsibly but he was satisfied, having looked George Burt and others in the eye, that they had the best interests of the employees at heart. Union leaders conducted themselves in negotiation 'with intelligence and reasonableness.' Rand had no doubt that their objective was 'to attain for those employees and their families a secure and self-respecting living, which seem to be the object of most Canadians.'

There was, in fact, no need to worry about excessive union power: 'It has been suggested that the union officers, as other labour leaders, are primarily concerned with the maintenance of their positions and power, and no doubt some of them have experienced stirrings of that nature. But union organization is admittedly necessary in the present set-up of our society, and we cannot expect these men who have gifts of leadership – and it is by such leaders that movements against wrongs are initiated – to be quite free of those human frailties from which only a few saints escape. The only effective remedy for abuse of this nature is a greater democratization of the union.' But first the communist threat had to be dealt with.

That threat, Rand wrote, was overstated: 'It is intimated also that they are merely the instruments of a communistic group which seeks not the realization of private enterprise but its subversion.' There was certainly considerable evidence of that, as the calls for a general strike illustrated. Moreover, it had been clear to Rand, when questioning some of the union delegates, that they were party members. Those were the facts, and Rand could not back away from them. 'There may be such a group among the automobile workers in and about Windsor. There may be some degree of organization and leadership. But the employees who would be susceptible to one-sided teachings of that sort would not in general have the remotest understanding of communist ideology and would grasp at its promise an escape from what is vaguely felt to be a dictatorship of capital.' But that did not stop the eight thousand members of Local 195 from following their communist union leaders and going out on a solidarity strike, even though their collective agreements committed them to work and they had no dispute whatsoever with their employers or with Ford.

Rather than assigning importance to the communists and their goals, Rand cleverly buttressed the other side: 'I should say on principle that a leadership which is opposed to communistic ends and methods, as I think this is, should be supported in a democratic economy; it is the failure of that leadership that furnishes the opportunity for strengthening the position of its opponents. I have no doubt that in the situation of Windsor today, a city so immediately exposed to the pressure of labour action in the United States, an unreasoning denial of some effective form of union security would throw the controversy into a cauldron of deepening animosities ruinous to the interests of men, industry and the public. Nor is it sufficient to say that these men must recognize their responsibilities. Responsibilities are the correlatives of rights, and where the latter are unreasonably denied it is somewhat of a mockery to be told that you must discipline your title to justice.' Rights must accompany responsibilities. That was the governing assumption underlying the resolution of the key issue in dispute.

The UAW wanted a union shop with a union checkoff. This union, however, did not need it: '[T]he negotiating union is unchallenged in the organization of workers of automobile and affiliated industries.' Moreover, awarding a union shop was inconsistent with 'the principles which I think the large majority of Canadians accept ... and it would deny the individual Canadian the right to seek work and to work independently of personal associations with any organized group.' It was not the Canadian way. 'On the other hand, the employees as a whole become the beneficiaries of union action, and I doubt if any circumstance provokes more resentment in a plant than this sharing of the fruits of unionist work and courage by the non-member.' Ford was on record that 'substantial benefits for the employees have been obtained by the union, some in negotiation and some over the opposition of the Company. It would not then as a general proposition be inequitable to require of all employees a contribution towards the expense of maintaining the administration of employee interests, of administering the law of their employment.' That was the compromise of union security – Rand's singular, inventive, and creative solution to the dispute. It was brilliant: he brought the union inside the tent. Everyone would pay his or her fair share, but no one, in contrast to the union-shop arrangement agreed to by Ford and the UAW in Michigan in 1941, would be required to join the union.

Rand believed that this solution was particularly suited to mass industry. In his view, making the checkoff mandatory would promote union membership and encourage union democracy. 'It may be argued that it is unjust to compel non-members of a union to contribute to funds over the expenditure of which they have no direct voice; and even that it is dangerous to place such money power in the control of an unregulated union. But the dues are only those which members are satisfied to pay for substantially the same benefits, and as any employee can join the union and still retain his independence in employment, I see no serious objection in this circumstance ... Much more important to the employee will be the right which is being secured to him in the conditions to be attached to the check off, to have a voice in that of which he is now a victim, the decision to strike. Whether the constitution of the union is sufficiently democratic in securing the powers of the members or such money power is dangerous are matters which concern the members and the public. The remedy lies essentially in the greater effectiveness of control in the members; but outside interference with that internal management is obviously a matter of policy for the legislature. Apart from the strengthening of the union ... I see no special interest of the employer as such in these possible dangers and in the present state of things, those who control capital are scarcely in a position to complain of the power of money in the hands of labour.' Rand therefore ordered the checkoff of union dues from all employees, whether members or not, during the term of the collective agreement.

The UAW did not, however, get something for nothing. Rand ordered that all strike votes be supervised by Labour Department officials and that all employees, whether union members or not, be entitled to vote. Illegal strikes were prohibited, and illegal strikers would be fined. If the union was involved in any illegal strike, or if it failed immediately to repudiate an illegal strike commenced without its involvement, the checkoff would be suspended. Rand also introduced an 'open period.' Ten to twelve months after the date of the agreement, the Department of Labour would, if requested by one-quarter of all employees, hold a vote where the employees could, if they wished, vote the UAW out or some other union in.

Pettigrove, on instructions from Ottawa, took special steps to ensure that the award was intelligible.[92] For the most part he was unsuccessful, given that Rand's turn of phrase was often difficult to follow. Still, the government wholeheartedly approved. M.M. McLean, the director of industrial relations for the federal Department of Labour, told Pettigrove that the award was 'a masterly document of historical and social significance.'[93]

Although the award was clearly intended to apply only to Ford, McLean predicted that it 'would become a state document of lasting importance in the history of labour jurisprudence.' He clearly understood the balancing involved: 'Am impressed with Justice Rand's profound understanding of the forces which operate in our private enterprise economy, especially the predominance of power which resides in the control exercised by Capital,' he noted. 'Rand's observation that responsibilities are co-relatives of rights points up a blind spot in the vision of the average employer. The employer expects the union to enforce the provisions of the collective agreement and discipline its refractory members but does not accord it the means by which that can be done; in fact ... the employer ... regards this as quite appropriate if [it] can render the Union impotent to carry out its responsibilities.'[94] Rand believed that the formula would have a positive effect on unions and would, indeed, promote internal democracy by encouraging membership participation. Whether he intended it or not, by making unions a partner with management in the government of the business, Rand drove a stake right through the heart of the class consciousness that the communists hoped to build in this, and so many other, labour disputes.

Rand's award also institutionalized the existing trend in conciliation board reports that had, in the years before the Ford strike, generally recommended some form of union security.[95] Where Rand went one step further was in satisfying both union and employer concerns with his particular 'formula,' and he did so by imposing important responsibilities on the union in return for union security.[96]

It was all part of a piece, one set into place several years earlier in PC 1003 and the regulatory prohibition of industrial action during the life of a collective agreement. Illegal work stoppages would still be a matter for the courts and the labour board, but there was now a new power to hit the unions where it hurt – in the pocketbook. As a number of post-war arbitration and judicial decisions soon established, unions would be held responsible for illegal work stoppages during the term of a collective agreement. The contract would be respected, or the union would be punished. In addition to bargaining for employees, unions would also exercise control over those employees within a contractual context. The Rand Formula can, and should, be seen as part of the federal government's post-war settlement – its accommodation with organized labour – an important element of which was institutionalized collective bargaining, statutory recognition, and financial security for unions in exchange for organized labour's continued commitment to free enterprise and, to a considerable extent, the Liberal Party.[97]

The beauty of the formula was its simplicity. It avoided the union shop but provided the union with financial security. The checkoff gave the union real financial security – at $1 per employee per month, the union would have more than sufficient funds to administer and enforce the collective agreement.

Of all the issues facing the union, the potential loss of seniority was particularly significant. More than five thousand Ford employees had enlisted and served in the Canadian forces, and they had continued to accrue Ford seniority while in uniform. Ford had treated these men well – most of them received allowances and other payments from the company while overseas; over $1 million was paid out in all – and, for obvious reasons, Ford was anxious to hire as many of them as possible when they came back. In fact, on their return, many of them had displacement rights over newer hires with less seniority. Any truncation of seniority would have a direct impact on job security as more men with displacement rights came back to work and during the inevitable layoffs that would accompany reconversion. If the market for cars declined, seniority would be even more important. Moreover, other provisions, buried deep in the award, cemented the union's position in the workplace. Plant 'committee men and negotiating committee men,' notwithstanding their seniority status, were, in the case of layoff, to be kept at work as long as there was work in their classification. Fifty years from the date of Rand's award, many Canadian unions remain unsuccessful in negotiating 'super seniority' for stewards and other local officials.

For the parties, the Rand Formula signalled the end of one era, characterized by confrontation, and the start of another, marked by negotiation. Both parties, it seemed, needed the strike: the union, to obtain the security measures it required to represent its members; and the employer, to drive home the point that unions were here to stay and that the UAW was the legitimate representative of its industrial workers. In the aftermath of the strike, grievances – often a useful barometer about the state of the world – declined. Rand was privately pleased, in the honeymoon period following the release of his award, to be told by both labour and management that relations between the two were 'a sort of heavenly harmony.'[98] Peace prevailed until 1954, when the union again went on strike; it was another bitterly fought but ultimately successful battle for company-paid health and welfare benefits.

Soon enough, the obdurate Wallace Campbell was named chairman of Ford of Canada, capping his forty-two-year career with the company. D.B. Greig took over as president of an extremely profitable enterprise and immediately introduced a less paramilitary management approach.[99] Average annual net profit during the war was, after taxes, just over 2 per cent. Even in 1945, with a long strike, the company posted a profit of $1.7 million. Undistributed profits or earned surplus went from $29,948,416 in 1944 to $30,535,481 in 1945, a period that included the strike.[100] Shareholders had been regularly rewarded with handsome dividends. The company's challenge was to continue that tradition.

Windsor's mayor, the UAW's firm friend, was made an honorary life member of the UAW-CIO at its Atlantic City convention in March 1946, in recognition of his 'liberal outlook' during the Ford strike. Roy England held on to his post in the next set of local union elections, easily beating two opponents who promised a more conservative leadership style. England's campaign literature touted the Rand Formula as one of his major successes. Indeed, it is inconceivable that union security would have been achieved without the long strike. It would take a while, however, for public acceptance to grow. Gallup reported in late 1946 that only a slim majority – 52 per cent of Canadians – supported the Rand Formula. There was much stronger support for the 'right' of Canadians to join or not join a trade union. The 'checkoff' was a 'harsh-sounding word. It sounds almost Russian,' one MP noted, explaining its continuing unpopularity in some quarters.[101]

The 1945 Ford strike, like some of the other celebrated post-war disputes, never seriously threatened the social order. Unlike the situation in 1919, when state action successfully crushed labour unrest during the Winnipeg General Strike, the landscape had profoundly changed. Disputes were now about the checkoff and wages, and they were confined to single industries, preceded by lengthy negotiations under a legal umbrella, and monitored and mediated by government officials. In the post-war world, industrial conflict would be carefully managed, with the communist threat dealt with first.[102] The first thing communists did when they came to power was to destroy organized labour (although the same was true about US-backed Latin American dictators, who showed little compunction in ordering the murder of union activists and suppressing independent labour movements by both official and semi-official state violence of the most appalling kind). As Maxwell Cohen, the future dean of McGill Law School, correctly observed, 'the time may not be far off when Canadian legal and political thinking will have to accept the premise that the Communist Party and Communists are not in fact "political" entitles in any traditional sense of the term, but represent truly conspiratorial agencies bent upon the ultimate destruction of the social and political rules within which they now safely operate and carry out their policies.'[103] Slowly but surely real unionists, together with social democrats, aided by union lawyers like the young David Lewis, identified the real enemy. It is 'extremely desirable,' Lewis wrote to one of his union clients, 'to oust communist control from Canadian trade unions.'[104]

Badly stung by communist activities during the strike, the UAW

International moved forcefully to eradicate communist elements – a precursor to organized labour's attitude and actions throughout the late 1940s and early 1950s as the real objectives of communist activists, within and outside the union movement, became known. The communist leadership in UAW Locals 195 and 200 was on borrowed time, and most of them were, sooner or later, sent packing.[105] The final showdown came just a few years after the Ford strike, when organized labour loaned support to American-born gangster Hal Banks and the Seafarers' International Union in its campaign to oust the thoroughly communist-dominated Canadian Seamen's Union. In that case, it was far from clear whether the cure was better or worse than the disease. There was no doubt about the real objectives of communist unionists or, as Igor Gouzenko established when he defected in September 1945, international communism. Finally, even the true believers had to concede defeat after Nikita Khruschev's 1956 'secret speech' on 'The Personality Cult and Its Consequences,' which detailed the many crimes against humanity by communist dictator and mass murderer Joseph Stalin.

In the meantime, Ford employees and managers seemed happy to get back to work and to the peacetime prosperity which, against all expectations, kept them and other workers across Canada gainfully employed. On 15 February, Ford and the UAW signed their new collective agreement, incorporating all the elements of Rand's award. It was the first collective agreement between the parties since 1944, when Ford 'terminated' the existing agreement after the union launched a wildcat strike. Rand had obviously done something right, for the next time the parties had a serious dispute – over layoffs in October 1950 – they asked Rand for his help. He could not be persuaded, however. Judges, he told the parties, should stick to judging, and acting as the arbitrator in the 1946 Ford strike was an exception to this rule. It was a bad idea to leave the bench, because, first, the courts were overburdened and judges were needed to deal with the backlog. Second, in taking on appointments such as this one, a judge lost the immunity from public criticism that went along with the exercise of judicial functions. It did not do the judiciary any good to have judges criticized for the conduct of their extra-judicial functions and, especially, their fees (though this was not the case with judges of the Supreme Court, who were statute-barred from receiving extra-judicial compensation).[106]

It did not take long for the Rand Formula to spread. On 20 February, Border Cities Dairy signed a deal with the Windsor Milk Drivers

Union incorporating the Rand Formula. By the end of 1946, twenty-three UAW plants in Windsor had the Rand Formula, and it quickly caught on across the province and the country, the result of both voluntary settlements and, increasingly, legislation.[107] Conciliation boards that were reviewing disputes in companies big and small frequently recommended to the parties that the settlement of their collective agreement include the Rand Formula. Indeed, many collective agreements adopted the exact wording awarded by Rand.

Company lawyer John Aylesworth said Rand's union security provision 'went quite a way to meeting his objections for a union shop.'[108] But it did much more than that, as Aylesworth well knew. In fact, as early as 1943, two years before the strike, Aylesworth had testified before the Select Committee of the Ontario Legislative Assembly holding hearings into proposed collective bargaining legislation. If there was going to be legislation, the canny corporate lawyer told the elected officials, it was necessary to ensure that it actually improved industrial relations, and one way of doing that was by imposing greater responsibility on the 'bargaining agencies.'[109] As Rand himself had observed when he first toured the Ford plant, 'there seems to be a lot of mechanical engineering around here but not much *human* engineering.'[110] Rand and his formula fixed that. The formula put the brakes on union militancy by legalizing the rights and obligations of the parties, ultimately putting into place a regime of industrial legality in which all disputes were channelled to arbitration – the labour boards or the courts. It is no accident that a new professional class of labour and management lawyers arose in the aftermath of the Rand Formula.

Not everyone was enamored with the award. The Rand Formula, some unionists believed, was at best a mixed blessing: 'Previous to Rand, the stewards had to go round every payday and collect the dues. The union and the stewards had to be doing a good job to get those dues. Not so today. The Rand Formula turned the unions into big businesses.'[111] To the extent that union militancy was truly an expression from the rank and file or reflected some kind of class consciousness that might one day lead to a general strike and social change, which is what the communists wanted, the Rand Formula put an end to that. Simply put, unions and their leaders became the guarantors of industrial peace. There would still be strikes, but they would usually be lawful, and they would mostly be about money.

Of course, on more careful examination, there were unanswered questions about Rand's overall enterprise. Rand expressed a need for 'some sort of law or convention' regarding industrial relations. He may have been right, but was it his job to provide it? He thought so, and that, in large part, was the objective of his formula. Others, minority voices in the hoopla surrounding the award, were concerned that, assuming a need for a law or convention, it should be Parliament that provided it, not an arbitrator assigned to adjudicate an ad hoc dispute.[112] Public policy, traditionalists claimed, should be set by Parliament. At the root of the concern was this question: Was Rand, in deciding a case between Ford and the UAW, entitled to direct the employer to deduct wages from third parties without their consent and to direct those wages to a union they did not belong to or support? On the other side of the argument, democracy is also based on majoritarianism, and the union had already demonstrated that it enjoyed the support of the majority of Ford employees. What was the difference between taking employee money and taking taxpayer money as directed by the majority, at least as represented by its elected representatives? The difference is that unions, supported by the majority of employees, are exclusive and speak for all employees on all matters related to the terms and conditions of employment, whereas in our multi-party, first-past-the-post system, few governments are elected by majorities, and electors always have a choice. To participate in the government of their industrial life, employees must join the union chosen by the majority of employees.

Rand knew that his award on union security might be far-reaching: 'A great many people are looking to the issue of this arbitration as indicating some basis or principle upon which controversies of this sort may be settled,' he said.[113] George Burt declared satisfaction: 'It is a work of literary craftsmanship as well as a legal document that will have repercussions affecting all future relations between employee and employer in the auto industry, if not in other fields.'[114] Praise was welcomed, but Rand was irritated by any 'ill-informed criticism.' The award's critics had not 'read the award,' were 'incapable of understanding' or just plain 'stupid,' he said.[115] His real contribution, he believed, was to 'have broken through the hide-bound thinking into which the whole question had become solidified.' On reflection, Rand told Pettigrove that there was only one way to solve problems like this one: with flexibility and resilience, 'to see the setting and implications of the problem in all its aspects – like looking at an object at the centre of a globe from every quarter of the surface – to range freely about the whole field: that is the method I think best and that is what we did.'[116] Yet, as Rand wrote in a totally different context, in his fourth decision sitting as a judge of the Supreme Court, 'there is, too, a striking illustration of the fact that simple solutions are sometimes most invisible.'[117]

On Rand's part, there was no pretence of revolution: 'I do not for a moment suggest that this is a device of general applicability,' he said. 'Its object is primarily to enable the union to function properly. In other cases it might defeat that object by lessening the necessity for self-development. In dealing with each labour situation we must pay regard to its special features and circumstances.'[118] Modesty aside, Rand surely understood that his award, following a lengthy strike, blessed with his stamp of approval as a judge of the Supreme Court of Canada, was not likely to be ignored. Most important of all from Rand's perspective, his formula promoted the rule of law. 'That was,' Pettigrove later observed, 'his constant harping, the rule of law.' If there was a contract, a deal, it had to be honoured. Although the various penalty provisions quickly evaporated as the parties negotiated them out of successive collective agreements, the formula itself has endured and become one of the fundamental and defining features of Canadian labour law. The strike itself took on mythological status as a shining example of 'solidarity, courage and action.'[119] It became, according to received wisdom, 'one of the most important strikes in Canadian working-class history' and 'the most important strike in Canada's postwar labour history.'[120] Ideological cant aside, the strike's importance can be judged by its results: the Rand Formula, as it became known, soon became the default provision of Canadian labour law, although it would take time for Parliament and the provincial legislatures to catch up.

In 1948, for the first time since the war, Parliament turned its attention to a new federal labour code. The rights first set out in PC 1003 were now enshrined in statute. The Committee on Industrial Relations, when examining the government bill, considered and approved an amendment providing for the inclusion in the new law of a revocable checkoff. Entirely voluntarily, employees could, under the provision, if they were union members, direct the employer to remit union dues to the union. They could also amend the direction. When the new measure was being debated in the House, one of its promoters, the former mayor of Windsor David Croll (who had resigned from the Ontario government of Mitch Hepburn in 1937 over its handling of the Oshawa strike, famously saying at the time that he 'would rather walk with the workers than ride with GM'), pointed out that Rand's formula 'has brought us peace in the automobile industry.'[121] He believed that the Rand Formula was fair and just: 'What Mr. Justice Rand has done is obvious,' he said. 'He has taken management-labour disputes out of the brick-and-tear-gas stage. His decision has delivered potential members to the union and given it union security. And to the company he has given a measure of security as well, protection from wildcat strikes.'[122]

Not everyone agreed. Labour Minister Mitchell remained opposed, not to the checkoff itself but to giving it statutory effect. He therefore arranged for the provision to be defeated when the bill was brought back before the House. If the parties want measures such as this, he told the MPs, they should sit across from each other at the bargaining table and negotiate them. That was not exactly what Rand had done. 'In essence,' Mitchell said, Rand's report 'was straight collective bargaining.' Actually, it was an arbitrator's award. Union security was not, he believed, a matter for Parliament. It was not even good for unions: they should collect the dues themselves. That was, the labour minister told the House, the better way, the one in the long-term interests of the trade union movement.[123]

Mitchell's remarks were rooted in a different time and place, not a modern mass industry with thousands, sometimes tens of thousands, of employees working around the clock. Moreover, Mitchell was a unionist of the old school and suspicious of the modern industrial unions. He could not understand that, without the checkoff, unions would be unable to administer and advance the affairs of their members, for they would be continuously engaged in collecting dues. He also completely failed to appreciate what the checkoff would do to entrench the union movement in Canadian society. Employers, H.D. Woods accurately predicted, would soon find that all 'their labour problems will become involved in union relationships. The power of the unions will be enhanced very considerably. There will probably be a gradual increase in union influence, and management may of necessity have to concede larger functions to the unions and to share some management functions with them.'[124] A strengthened, secure union movement also had an opportunity to coordinate its activities and use its power to bargain not just wages and working conditions but broader issues of social and economic policy as well. For a variety of reasons, however, that opportunity was lost.

It was not until the late 1970s that the Rand Formula was finally passed into law in Ontario, in large part as a result of another highly politicized labour dispute.[125] Fleck Manufacturing Company made

electrical wiring for the automotive industry. It was a dirty, dusty, un-
sanitary plant with a predominately female workforce. Located about
40 kilometres north of London, Fleck was organized by the UAW.
The 1978 dispute, as in so many first collective agreements, was about
union security and improvements to wages and working conditions.
When management said no to all three, union members walked out.
What was especially interesting about this strike was that Fleck was 50
per cent owned by Margaret Fleck and her children. Her husband, the
company's founder, although not a shareholder, was James Fleck, at
the time the deputy minister for industry and tourism and, previously,
the chief executive officer in the Ontario Premier's Office. Mr Fleck
claimed to have no involvement in the management of the company,
but the optics did not look good. They got worse as further facts were
revealed – that the factory was built on land leased from the Ontario
Development Corporation, a body that Fleck was in charge of as deputy minister. When, on the first day of the strike, the company bused
in strikebreakers and the police arrived en masse, the stage was set for
a huge confrontation, exacerbated by the arrival of other union members, groups such as the New Democratic Party's Women's Caucus,
the Canadian Postal Workers, and out-of-work actors from Toronto
Workshop Productions.

   More than one violent exchange broke out, and the police took the
brunt of much of the criticism for treating the picketing and protesting
'as if it were a veritable insurrection.'[126] At times, police outnumbered
the picketers two to one. It was one dispute organized labour could
not lose if it was going to have any success in organizing women – a
new pool of potential union recruits. Often dressed in full riot regalia
– black shiny helmets, visors, clubs – the police were there more to
intimidate the picketers than maintain order. At first the government
took a hard line: the attorney general said the police 'had handled the
situation well'; the minister of labour, contradicting her own inspectors, claimed that the accident rate at the facility was 'not high'; and
the minister of industry and tourism defended his deputy in his assertion that there was 'no conflict of interest.' Nevertheless, public criticism began to grow, and the government realized it was on the wrong
side of this fight. Eventually, Fleck Manufacturing signed a deal with
the local. Back at Queen's Park, anxious to wash its hands of the whole
episode, the legislature made the Rand Formula the law. By 1983,
when the Rand Formula was introduced into the *Canada Labour Code*,
the successor to the *Industrial Disputes Investigation Act*, legislation was

in place in just about every jurisdiction in Canada that required an employer, on receipt of a request from its union, to deduct union dues from all employees and remit them to the union.

The formula easily survived the enactment of the *Bill of Rights*. The advent of the *Charter of Rights and Freedoms* was a different matter, however. Did freedom of association, one of the *Charter* guarantees, include freedom from association? Under the Rand Formula, no one was forced to join a union, but everyone, with limited statutory exceptions for persons asserting a religious objection to unions, was required to pay his or her share of the freight. What was really at issue, of course, was how the money was being spent. Were mandatory union dues inconsistent with the *Charter*?

At first, a judge said yes, accepting the argument of community college teacher Francis Edmund Mervyn Lavigne, who, with the backing of the National Citizens' Coalition, challenged the constitutionality of the Rand Formula. Lavigne was required to pay union dues to the Ontario Public Service Employees Union. Under the OPSEU constitution, money collected could be used towards the advancement of the membership's 'common interests, economic, social and political.' Lavigne was not a union member and he objected, among other things, to the union directing a fraction of his annual payment – $2 of his $338 total – to causes with which he disagreed, most particularly abortion rights, a union of healthcare workers in Nicaragua, disarmament campaigns such as Operation Dismantle, and the New Democratic Party. Simply put, Lavigne claimed that he had a right not to be forced into association with socialists and fellow travellers. He argued that the money should be exclusively spent for collective bargaining. He claimed that his *Charter* right to associate also gave him the right not to associate, and that compulsory union dues interfered with his rights. When the case finally got to the Supreme Court of Canada, the Rand Formula was, in a 1991 decision, upheld.[127] Although two of the judges concluded that Lavigne's *Charter* freedom of association rights had been infringed, they went on to hold that the violation was justified under section 1 of the *Charter*. That meant that the infringement was a reasonable limit, prescribed by law and demonstrably justified in a free and democratic society. The rest of the court, for different reasons, concluded that there was no violation at all. Decades after the Ford strike was settled by Rand's formula, that compromise, that settlement, was confirmed by the Supreme Court as the defining feature of Canadian labour law.

6

Rand Tackles the Palestine Problem

In 1947 Palestine was an armed camp, and 100,000 British soldiers were attempting, unsuccessfully, to keep the peace. There were four key rival groups. The Haganah was the military arm of the Jewish Agency, the organization created by the World Zionist Organization to represent the Jewish community in Palestine. It focused its immediate attention on defying the British ban on further Jewish immigration to Palestine by running ships bursting with homeless Jews past the Royal Navy's blockade. The Irgun Zvai Leumi, the military arm of Zionist revisionists, was composed of extreme nationalists who believed that every Jew had the right to enter Palestine, if necessary by force. They fought the British by attacking their men and bases – the previous July, they had blown up the King David Hotel in Jerusalem, the British headquarters, killing ninety-one people in all. The Stern Gang was a small, fanatical organization, specializing in assassination and terror. And, finally, there were the Arabs, 1.2 million men, women, and children who were implacably hostile to the 650,000 Jewish settlers already in Palestine and the plan for a Jewish state in *their* country, on *their* land.

Palestine had come under British care following the First World War, when the victorious Western powers divided up the Ottoman Empire and gave the Holy Land to Britain, a 'mandate' later formalized by the League of Nations. Under the 1917 Balfour Declaration and the 1920 Palestine Mandate incorporating that declaration and approved by the League of Nations in 1922, the British government undertook to 'secure' and 'reconstitute' 'a National Home' for the 'Jewish people' in Palestine. Great Britain was not only responsible for Palestinian development, then, but bound also to act in accordance with this commitment to help re-establish a home for Jews. This formula was problematic from the start: Was the Jewish 'home' meant to be a 'state'? Moreover, how was it to be achieved without prejudice to the 'civil and religious rights of existing non-Jewish communities'? The commitment made to Jews for a home and to Arabs to respect their rights was irreconcilable. In addition, while the British government was formally committed to the Balfour Declaration, the local administration in Palestine was decidedly ambivalent about facilitating Zionist goals. As Arab opposition and violence increased, there were waves of rioting in 1921 and 1929. In 1936 the general unrest escalated into a full-scale Arab revolt, leading to three years of disturbances.

Britain derived little benefit from its role in Palestine, economically, diplomatically, militarily, or strategically, so was anxious to divest itself of its responsibility there. In 1936 a commission led by Lord Peel, the former secretary of state for India, came to investigate the situation, the members arriving in the Holy Land wearing top hats and tails. They concluded that peace between Jews and Arabs was impossible and proposed, instead, independent Jewish and Arab states, with the British exercising a permanent mandate over Jerusalem, Bethlehem, Nazareth, and a corridor to the sea. The proposal was promptly declared 'impractical' by the British government. Like other earlier plans proposing partition, it was dropped the following year. An alternative policy had to be devised, and the task fell to Malcolm MacDonald. His 1939 White Paper imposed strict limits on Jewish immigration (a death sentence, as it turned out, for millions of Jews seeking refuge from the impending Holocaust in Europe) and even more severe restrictions on land ownership for the Jews already in Palestine, and suggested some sort of sovereignty for the area within a decade. No one, other than the British, endorsed the scheme, and it was denounced as illegal by just about everyone else. It was a non-starter for the Jews: Whatever had happened to the Jewish home? they asked. And the proposal did not even come close to satisfying the Arabs.[1]

In the course of the Second World War, the Arab Higher Committee, the umbrella organization for Palestinian Arabs who were bitterly opposed to the Jewish occupiers, was dissolved when its leader, Haj Amin el Husseini, the Mufti of Jerusalem and a notorious Nazi collaborator, was exiled to Cairo. After the war, Zionists, devastated by the Holocaust, were more committed than ever to the establishment of a Jewish state as a refuge for the thousands of homeless survivors. That meant creating a Jewish state in Palestine – an objective that became increasingly urgent as none of the other likely receiving countries, including Canada and the United States, took any steps to welcome displaced Jews. Inevitably, violence between Arabs and Jews in Palestine accelerated, and fighting between the Jews and the British became ferocious, particularly as British forces mounted a blockade against Jewish immigration. The British White Paper limited Jewish entry to Palestine to 1,500 a month. Making matters even worse, the British forcibly transported would-be refugees apprehended en route to Palestine, largely concentration camp survivors, to internment camps in Cyprus and elsewhere. For the Jews, there was only one possible solution: the end of the British mandate and the creation of a Jewish state.

The British, who alternated between pro-Arab sentiments and disdain for both Arabs and Jews, continued to look for a solution, as did the United States, an emerging Zionist hotbed with 4.5 million Jews among its citizens. In October 1945 the Anglo-American Committee of Inquiry was established with a double-barrelled mandate: to investigate both the condition of Jewish refugees in Europe ('deplorable' by any measure) and the situation in Palestine.[2] In its unanimous report six months later, it recommended the creation of a federation in Palestine: a single state of Jews, Arabs, and others, all subject to continuing British rule until the United Nations could implement a trusteeship agreement. Again, the plan failed to attract either interest or support; it pleased no one except Jewish and Arab extremists, who used it as an excuse to expand their activities. Britain was obviously losing its grip on administration in the area, yet its navy continued to divert the slow, unarmed, and overloaded refugee ships. As the occupying force, it could not keep the peace in the region between Jews and Arabs, Arabs and Arabs (always a rich source of internecine conflict), and the British and everyone else.

Bowing to the inevitable, and desperately in need of a way out, Britain placed the future of Palestine before the United Nations. The Special Session on Palestine opened on 28 April 1947. It was obvious to everyone that there was a need for speedy and effective action: 'Not only does the situation in Palestine demand it,' Lester Pearson observed, 'but the prestige and the reputation of the United Nations itself demand it. This is,' he continued, 'the first time a problem of this magnitude and complexity has ever been submitted by the General Assembly to one of its committees. If we do not deal with it quickly and effectively, the reputation and prestige of the United Nations will suffer.'[3] Pearson, the distinguished Canadian diplomat and future prime minister, was now serving as chair of the First Committee, the body responsible for drafting the terms of reference for the Special Committee on Palestine. What was required was a fresh approach directed at finding a fair, equitable, and practical solution. The committee's mandate was straightforward: to prepare a report to the General Assembly containing proposals 'appropriate for the solution of the problem of Palestine.' Member states were directed to 'appoint persons of high moral character and of recognized competence in international affairs.' Those appointed were given the task of acting 'impartially and conscientiously, in accordance with the purposes and principles of the charter of the United Nations.'

After considerable discussion at the United Nations, a committee of eleven members, mostly 'middle powers,' all without vital interests in the Middle East and with no large and active Jewish community at home, was struck: Australia, Canada, Czechoslovakia, Guatemala, India, Iran, the Netherlands, Peru, Sweden, Uruguay, and Yugoslavia. Significantly, there was no member from the 'big five' – the permanent members of the Security Council – China, France, the USSR, the United Kingdom, and the United States. Obviously, Canada, Australia, and India represented the British Commonwealth; Sweden and the Netherlands, Western Europe; Czechoslovakia and Yugoslavia, the Soviet Union; Guatemala, Uruguay, and Peru, South America; and Iran, Islam. India played triple duty as a member of the Commonwealth and as a second representative of the Muslim world and Asia.

Canada was not at all anxious to participate in the work of the committee, but, after being repeatedly pressed by its American neighbour, it let the United States know that, if nominated, it would serve. There was a catch, however. The Canadian government intended to appoint a prominent Canadian 'whom we would expect to act in an independent capacity.'[4] Any Canadian serving on the committee would be given free rein – a neat diplomatic trick that would allow the government, if it wished, to disavow both the committee and its work.

On 16 May, the day after the UN resolution establishing the Special Committee was passed, External Affairs Minister Louis St Laurent presented the Prime Minister's Office with a shortlist of names: one judge of the Supreme Court of Canada, two provincial chief justices, two senators, a serving ambassador, and the chancellor of a Canadian university. Appointing Ivan Rand as a commissioner had been considered before. In October 1944, when the Cabinet met to choose the head of a proposed Commission on Cooperatives, Rand, as well as Sir Lyman Duff, had been suggested. But the new chief justice, Thibaudeau Rinfret, felt 'it was not in the interests of the Supreme Court for its members to be on a Commission.' That night, King recorded in his diary, 'I agree.'[5] But events would soon make him change his mind – in particular, that long strike at Windsor's Ford plant. Rand had solved that dispute to general kudos. Now there was an even more important one on the international agenda.

Reviewing the shortlist for the UN position, Mackenzie King put the Supreme Court judge at the top. 'Rand,' he noted in his diary, 'was easily the best.' The assignment was 'important to the world and to the future success of the United Nations.' And, in short order, King convinced Rand that he should take it on. In the circumstances, Rinfret agreed to let Rand go, and, after expressing some misgivings about missing the summer at Shediac, Rand agreed to accept.[6] On 22 May the order-in-council was passed appointing Rand to be Canada's representative, with, as his deputy, Léon Mayrand – an experienced External Affairs officer who had served at Canada House during the Second World War and then at Canada's embassy in Moscow. The appointment was announced to applause in the House of Commons. Rand was, Prime Minister King said, 'the best possible choice.'[7] Even the *Ottawa Journal*, which could be relied on to criticize anything the Liberal government did, was impressed: 'Somebody in our Department of External Affairs has a sharp eye for good men in tough jobs,' it observed on its editorial pages.

Ivan Rand was a reluctant participant, and it was not just because he would be away from his summer home. He was, after all, a judge and he was concerned about the impact of the assignment on his judicial function. As he told St Laurent, who, as minister of justice, had recommended his appointment to the Supreme Court and would soon succeed Mackenzie King as prime minister, participation on the United Nations Special Committee on Palestine (UNSCOP) was contingent on continuing governmental recognition of his independence. The government's agreement was quickly put to the test. Soon after the appointment was announced, Pearson cabled Rand and requested a meeting so he could give him direction. They eventually met, but Rand made it clear from the outset: 'I take no instructions.'[8]

Rand was, as the Department of External Affairs noted in a dispatch to London, 'fresh' to the Palestine problem and needed to be brought up to speed. He was therefore provided with a lengthy memorandum from Elizabeth MacCallum, Canada's pro-Arab Mid-East expert. The daughter of missionaries, she had spent her formative years in Turkey and was fluent in Turkish and Arabic. Before joining the Department of External Affairs in 1942 – one of the few female employees with a senior rank – MacCallum had worked at both the League of Nations Society in Ottawa and the Foreign Policy Association in New York. Extremely knowledgeable about Mid-East issues, her sympathies, as her superior Norman Robertson described them, 'rather obviously incline towards the Arabs.' Indeed, 'for every persuasive, well-written brief the Zionists presented to officials in External Affairs, she prepared a detailed, convincing counter-balancing memorandum on the subject.'[9] This was, she believed, her 'special duty.'[10]

'In Palestine,' MacCallum stated in her first brief to Rand on the 'Historical Background of the Palestine Problem,' 'our generation is dealing with the consequences of two great historical tragedies. One befell the Arabs seven hundred years ago and kept them isolated and submerged until the close of the 19th century. The other befell the Jews even earlier, causing their forced or voluntary dispersion and leading through a great variety of experience … to the extinction in our own day of one-third of the Jewish people and the consequent revolt of a certain proportion of the remainder against continued dispersion and the lack of a territory in which the Jews as Jews may exercise sovereignty.'

'It is futile,' she continued, ' to ask which was the greater catastrophe – the dispersion of the Jews through Europe of the Middle Ages or the conquest of the Arab lands by the Turks – the destruction of one-third of the Jewish race by Hitler or the obliteration of Arab civilization by the Mongols.'[11] MacCallum not unreasonably equated the genocide of six million Jews by Nazis with the murder of 800,000 Arabs by Mongols in Baghdad in 1258. 'Both peoples,' she continued, 'have been the victims of a savage, cataclysmic fate. For both the period of suffering has been counted in centuries not decades. At the same moment in the world's history both have recovered hope. Both feel themselves destined to recreate today conditions in which a national culture of their own may flower again, unhampered by the dominance of others. For each it has been a source of bitterness that the other should advance

claims whose fulfillment would make their own hopes unreliazable
... Two potent forces, both stemming from injustices suffered over an
extended period of time, are at work in Palestine. The strength and
the nature of both must be understood fully by the United Nations if
each is to be given a direction which will neither provoke not intensify
destructive tendencies in the other.'

It was important, MacCallum pointed out, that the members of the
committee appreciate 'the new problem created by the deliberate use
of anti-Semitism as an instrument of national policy in our own generation.' It was equally important that the members of the committee
'balance' what knowledge they have about the history of the Jews with
the history of the Arab peoples: 'For three hundred years the Arabs
were guardians of arts, of learning, of the spirit of inquiry and research.
Their contributions were momentous in the sciences of medicine, mathematics, astronomy and navigation and rich in the fields of poetry and
philosophy ... Their willingness to base belief on experiment and independent discovery was one of the living forces which gradually freed
Christendom from the bonds of authoritarian tradition.' The committee
should not, she concluded, be swayed by the greater experience of the
Jewish leaders in the ways of the Western world and their commitment
to democracy. Above all, she did not believe that it was appropriate to
solve the problem of one people (the Jews) at the expense of another
(the Arabs). There was a lot to that: Why should the Jewish home problem be solved on the backs of the Palestinians who had nothing to do
with the cataclysm in Europe? MacCallum then began showering Rand
with dubious materials and foolish propaganda, such as the utopian
and self-evidently unrealistic proposals of philosopher Martin Buber –
he gave new meaning to Lenin's term 'useful idiot' – for the creation of
a bi-national Palestinian state.

Summoned to New York in May 1947 and travelling with his new
diplomatic passport, Rand met most of the other ten committee members there. Dr Nicolass Blom of the Netherlands was a legally trained
civil servant with a passion for detail and obvious sympathies for British difficulties in administering the Mandate. Dr Jose Brilej, the director of the Political Department of the Yugoslav Ministry of Foreign
Affairs, was a former journalist and lawyer with impressive wartime
service with the Yugoslav partisans. He was Yugoslavia's 'alternate
delegate,' serving until Vladimir Simic, the president of the Yugoslav Senate, took over in Palestine. Nasrollah Entezam was a cultured
linguist from Iran with extensive Western diplomatic experience. A

polished, elegant, and courteous man, the pinnacle of his career came in his election, in 1950, as president of the UN General Assembly.

Professor Enrique Rodriguez Fabregat, a former minister of education from Uruguay, had been imprisoned for his political beliefs, as had Jorge García-Granados, Guatemala's delegate. García-Granados was the grandson of a former president of Guatemala and, in his own right, a fearless fighter for democracy at home. When a more friendly government came to power, he was appointed as ambassador to the United States before being appointed to UNSCOP. His anti-British, pro-Israel bias became immediately apparent and, once he arrived in the Promised Land, he was quickly converted to the Jewish settlers' point of view (aided in part, according to American intelligence reports, by the 'beautiful friendship' he developed with 'a Jewess named "Emma" in Tel Aviv').[12] Left-leaning already, García-Granados was enthralled by the kibbutz movement: 'the most successful achievement in socialism today,' he gushed in his memoirs.[13]

John D.L. Hood, the Australian delegate, a Rhodes Scholar and senior counsellor of Australia's Department of External Affairs, soon revealed his pro-British point of view. Dr Karel Lisicky, minister plenipotentiary in the Czech Foreign Service, was a well-known Social Democrat and close friend of Jan Masaryk – already on record as a Zionist supporter. Sir Abdur Rahman, a high court judge from Lahore, was the Indian representative. Highly excitable, with a hair-trigger temper, Sir Abdur shouted and screamed, unfortunately with a stutter, when he did not get his way – which was most of the time. A Muslim and one of the few who followed Nehru's leadership, he made his opposition to the Jewish case clear from the beginning, even before the committee had started its work. Partition in India, only months earlier, had provoked extensive religious strife, incredible civil dislocation, and tremendous loss of life, largely the result of a cycle of gruesome communal riots. Sir Abdur was understandably reluctant to recommend it in Palestine. The Indians tended to see Zionism as a European colonial project, and, when it could, India's Congress Party generally tilted towards Muslim positions to bolster its secular credentials and retain the support of the Muslim population. Dr Arturo Garcia Salazar, Peru's ambassador to the Vatican, sat grimly unemotional throughout the proceedings, never giving any inkling of his attitudes and views. Finally, Emil Sandstrom, a former justice of the Supreme Court of Switzerland and his country's representative on the International Court of Arbitration at The Hague, was reticent and reserved, a gentleman of the old school. He was elected chairman of the committee and, like Rand, had received no official instructions or direction.

From north and south, east and west, Anglo-Saxon and Latin, Catholic, Muslim, and Protestant, the committee was at once restrained and careful, temperamental and unpredictable: eleven different nationalities, eleven very different personalities, and eleven men accustomed to deference. All told, UNSCOP was a travelling circus of fifty: delegates, deputies, aides, secretaries, translators, and administrative clerks. The committee had the 'widest powers to ascertain and record facts, and to investigate all questions and issues relevant to the problem of Palestine.' It would be a challenge, UN secretary general Trygve Lie told the delegates when they first assembled in New York, one 'fraught with so much emotion and passion, surrounded by so many appeals for humanity and for justice.'[14]

The Jews claimed Palestine largely on the basis that, two thousand years earlier, they had a kingdom in part of it. According to these Jews and all Zionists, Jews were in the majority within and around Israel from 1200 BCE until the second century CE. During roughly half that time, they enjoyed religious autonomy while under foreign domination. For the rest of that time, they exercised political sovereignty, first as a tribal confederacy, then as a kingdom, and then as two kingdoms. Just before the Common Era they were a kingdom again. The actual scope of territorial control varied over time. Under Kings David and Solomon, Jewish authority encompassed the entire modern state and extended to western Jordan, Syria, and southern Lebanon. So the Jewish claim was largely based on history, with some modern-day guilt thrown in about Jewish suffering during the Holocaust and the moral weight that carried in support of a Jewish state. Besides, the Jewish accomplishments in Palestine were regularly showcased to UNSCOP members, who could not help but note the contrast with those of the indigenous population. Palestine should, for all of these reasons and others, the Jews said, be given to them.

This was all ancient history, the current occupants responded. The Jewish population in the Holy Land had been negligible for some two thousand years, increasing to minority status only in the late nineteenth century. Palestine should be for Palestinians, not Zionists from around the world and concentration camp survivors and other displaced persons from Europe. The fact that the desert now bloomed had nothing to do with who was entitled to what. What Palestinians could not endorse was 'that after a lapse of 2000 years, contemporary

Jews anywhere have an overriding political right in Palestine which negates, supersedes, and annuls the political rights of Palestinians in their own homeland.'[15]

Getting their messages across was critical for both sides, and an opportunity was provided when the committee, before departing from New York for Jerusalem, decided to invite liaison officers from the British Mandate, the Arab Higher Committee, and the Jewish Agency to supply 'information' and 'assistance.' The British appointed Donald C. MacGillivray, a relatively even-handed colonial administrator with Palestine experience. The Jewish Agency selected David Horowitz, an economist with good political skills, and Aubrey (later 'Abba') Eban, a distinguished Cambridge graduate with an appointment as Israeli foreign minister in his future. Horowitz and Eban divided up the committee members between them, and Horowitz got Rand. The Arabs declined to participate, not their first or their last big blunder as the committee began its work.

From his refuge in Cairo, the Mufti of Jerusalem made clear the Arab position: The committee was a 'conspiracy' and all its members were 'pro-Zionist,' 'deciding only what the Jews of New York and Palestine want ... against the national interests of the Arabs of Palestine.' When it was explained to the Mufti (a term denoting an Islamic scholar who is an interpreter or expounder of Islamic law and qualified to issue fatawa, religious edicts or rulings) that the committee was not a Zionist plot, he remained obdurate, observing that he had 'no wish to lend legitimacy to a committee which was going to betray the Arabs.' Accordingly, he ordered a 'boycott' of the committee, even though, as he was warned, that meant that the Jews would take advantage of the committee's ignorance of the Palestinian cause. 'No use, no use,' he kept repeating to one of his emissaries, adding, 'How do you expect me to allow a Swedish second-rate diplomat to decide my fate or my country's fate for me? ... His other colleagues are only secondary judges from Canada and Holland, and so on. Would Holland accept that an Arab Palestinian judge ... decide the fate of the Dutch nation?' Even though the committee also included two 'second-rate' Muslim members, that was not enough to attract the Mufti's confidence. Anyone, he ordered, who appeared before the committee was a 'traitor' and 'those we consider as traitors will deserve our punishment.'[16]

The boycott decision turned out to be a grave mistake. 'The Palestinians,' the eminent historian Walid Khalidi observed, 'failed to see why they should be made to pay for the Holocaust (the ultimate crime against humanity, committed in Europe by Europeans).'[17] 'The justice of the Arab cause may have been perfectly apparent to the Arab Higher Committee,' was the assessment of one historian of the Special Committee, 'but few of the UNSCOP members, with the obvious exception of Sir Abdur Rahman, were ready to accept anything on an *a priori* basis.'[18] Rand simply could not believe that the Arabs would not come before the committee to make their case. It was not, he recalled, 'rational.'[19] To be fair, there was a risk that, by participating in the process, the Arabs would bestow legitimacy on it. But by their not participating, committee members were denied the opportunity to hear a different and legitimate point of view – a problem that got worse when they arrived in Palestine and black flags were raised in all the cities and villages the commissioners visited. In the meantime, the Jews exploited the opportunity, and the Arabs' absence, to the hilt. As Eban recollected in his autobiography, 'Between tours, conversation and hearings, the liaison officers were required to fill the minds of Committee members with some ideas on a future solution ... the Palestinian Arabs contemptuously refused to nominate their liaison officers. We benefited greatly from Arab errors in those days.'[20]

After general familiarization at the UN in New York, on 11 June the committee members and staff boarded a UN plane for their long flight to Jerusalem. Before leaving the United States, Rand wrote to Prime Minister King. 'So far as I can judge the committee is open minded and aware of the urgency and importance of its task,' he began. 'Our object seems to me to be quite clear: to satisfy, not the Jew nor the Arab, but the enlightened and intelligent conscience of mankind as represented by the United Nations. The appeal on both sides is really moral and is peculiarly complemented by such a geographical locale as Palestine. That seems to me to furnish a clue to the solution; I am disposed to think that ... the highest morality will ultimately prove to be the highest strategy. At any rate, one may see.'[21] Indeed.

Eban and Horowitz were on board the UN plane, and they were not impressed: 'As we analyzed the eleven members on whose vote so much would depend, we reached the conclusion that none of the governments had sent first-rank representatives. They were men of competence rather than inspiration ... Not one of them had been involved in any decisions as momentous as that in which he would now have to participate.' Their task would clearly be a difficult one, as there was no evidence that any of them had studied either 'Jewish history or the Palestine problem.' It was, Eban later recalled, 'a strange assortment.'[22]

Rand, Guatemala's representative, Jorge García-Granados, confided to his diary, was a 'large man in his sixties, with a bald pate and baby-blue eyes behind thick lenses. He carried himself with an almost melancholy air, a bit stooped, as if always meditating an abstruse point of the law.'[23]

When the delegates, alternatives, and assorted assistants arrived at Jerusalem's Kadimah House, they were welcomed to the country not just by the Arab boycott of the committee but by a general Arab strike, called on instructions of the Mufti to press the point that the entire exercise was unlawful. Arab spokespersons, including those representing the Arab League, had earlier warned UNSCOP that there was only one solution to the Palestine problem – recognition of Palestine as an Arab state. Hatred between Arabs and Jews was palpable. Sir Henry Gurney, the chief secretary of the mandatory government, told the committee about his failure to mediate the differences – 'irreconcilable aspirations' was the way he described them. The committee could see for itself the means the British used to maintain their rule: road blocks, barbed-wire barricades, machine-gun posts, and armoured car patrols were among the most visible manifestations of the British presence. Less obvious were the laws the British had passed, regulations empowering British authorities to detain persons for 'unlimited periods,' to place persons under 'police supervision' for up to one year, jail with no warrant, charge or trial, and deportation – many to Kenya – whenever the high commissioner considered it 'justified.' Virtually none of these actions could be appealed, and they were, almost exclusively, directed against Jews. While the Arabs went out of their way to be unpleasant – the Palestinians, Abba Eban liked to say, never missed an opportunity to miss an opportunity – and the British were acting like the unwelcome colonial occupier they had become, the Jews took a different approach: they laid on the charm, making committee members feel welcome and important. Just as MacCallum predicted, the Jews made full use of their experience in the 'ways of the Western world.'

As the committee commenced its work, a British court sentenced to death three Irgun members who had been captured in the aftermath of a daring attack on the government prison at Acre in which more than a hundred Jewish and Arab political prisoners had been 'liberated.' No one was killed during the escapade, but a British military tribunal imposed the death penalty nevertheless. The parents of the condemned men – barely out of their teens – appealed to the committee for assistance. First, however, the matter of jurisdiction had to be addressed. 'Justice Rand,' García-Granados recollected in his memoirs, 'said he could not see how the administration of the laws of Palestine would impede our work. The executions were part of the general question of the workability of the Mandate. We could take note of them,' Rand added, 'but we had no right to intervene.' This was all music to Sir Abdur's ears: How could he disagree with the distinguished Canadian Supreme Court judge? 'It is preposterous,' Sir Abdur said, echoing Rand, 'for us to interfere in the internal administration of a country which we have been sent to for certain purposes only!'[24]

Rand's attitude was legalistic in the extreme, as more than one committee member pointed out in a hastily called session in Chairman Sandstrom's rooms at Kadimah House. The General Assembly had appealed to Arabs, Jews, and the British to refrain from any acts of violence while the committee was carrying out its work. Hanging three boys for what was, arguably, a political act, and one in which no one had died, was excessive. More than one committee member made that point, urging the others to seek commutation of the death sentences. Agendas were mixed. The Yugoslavs, Soviet surrogates, intent on embarrassing the British, urged that the committee take a political stand and pass a resolution against the executions. Other delegates took a more principled position, both for and against getting involved. After five 'secret' and bitterly contested meetings, a diplomatic compromise of sorts was reached. A resolution was passed, with Rand, Blom, and Rahman voting against it, expressing concern about the 'unfavorable repercussions' any hangings would have 'upon the fulfillment of the Committee's task.' The British were unmoved, but the Jews, learning about the dissension in the committee's ranks, accelerated their lobbying. Early on, the Zionists identified Rand as a key delegate, and, given his vote, turning him around became a priority.

Rand later recalled that although he had come to Palestine with a 'limited and one-sided acquaintance' of the problem, he was determined to do his job, 'freed so far as possible from the vapors of partisanship' and any 'personal engagement' with the issues in dispute. It was an appropriate approach for a man sitting on the bench, though its utility was more questionable when it came to deciding a matter so far beyond the letter of the law. An important step in getting Rand on track was taken during a dinner, soon after he arrived in Palestine, with a Canadian minister, William L. Hull, an evangelical Christian whose 'mission' to Palestine dated back to 1935. 'Somewhat to my surprise,' Rand wrote years later, 'I listened to words of high admiration for the Jewish people, their standards of life and the tremendous work they had done since returning to their ancient homeland.' This 'sympathetic attitude' liberated Rand from 'irrelevancies and shadowy prejudices': 'The controversy at once ... became one for decision in light of subtle appreciations and comprehensive understandings,' he wrote.[25] It was a seismic shift, and whether Hull knew it or not, he broke the ground that the Jews immediately tilled – and with great success. The committee was about to embark on an extended tour of Palestine, to learn about the country and its peoples. Invited by Rand to join him and Mayrand in their official car on one of their early outings, Horowitz established an immediate rapport with Rand. Rand told Horowitz about himself and his progressive ideas, 'founded on the belief that a transformation of the social structure and of world polity was imperative.' Thereafter, Horowitz knew how to pitch the Jewish case.

Rand, Horowitz later recalled, 'showed his understanding of the relationship between the events of the Second World War and our political orientation, especially our position regarding immigration. He wanted to know the origins of the terrorist movement, and I explained the growth of this phenomenon in the fertile soil of desperation, frustration, and inequities. When I outlined the various possible solutions, Rand displayed particular interest in partition. I told him candidly that while the Jewish Agency and the Zionist movement had not finally decided on their attitude, I thought that in existing conditions the proposal offered the sole possibility of extricating the country from its political dilemma.' In fact, partition was the Jewish objective, Jewish Agency officials having long privately conceded that there was no prospect of the United Nations agreeing that Palestine should become a Jewish state. Partition was the best that could be hoped for.

How exactly, Rand asked, did the Jews intend to set up their new state? Horowtiz delivered a welcome response: 'I said that peace and tranquil construction without involvement in international adventures were consonant with the spirit and idealism of our movement and people, who were tired of being the fuel for other nations' fires. Moreover, we wanted to become an integral part of the constructive effort in the part of the world in which we lived, in close and friendly concert with our Arab neighbours.'

When Rand expressed admiration for this attitude, Horowitz was delighted. 'I sensed that the idea of partition was coalescing in his mind as the only means to an objective solution,' he wrote. 'We went on talking of the historical aspects of the Jewish problem, with which his mind was actively occupied. It was evident that the reservations concerning our movement which he had brought to the country were rapidly disappearing and being replaced by a deep understanding that was inspired by his humanity and human conscience, joined to a vigorous political philosophy of far-sighted perception.'[26] This humanity was offended, early in the tour, when an Arab factory owner refused to admit the Jews accompanying the committee. Rand could not believe it. He was appalled and made his disgust apparent. Rand was not alone. The initial Arab decision to boycott the committee and launch a national strike was a major mistake. Arab hatred and racism aggravated a situation that was already close to intolerable. But the sour taste only got worse as Rand and the others saw child labour and other harsh working conditions. At a tobacco factory in Haifa, Rand viewed 'with horror' the plight of the Arab children working in the blazing heat. [27] The Jews looked good on their own, and even better in comparison. In the meantime, Rand's education at Horowitz's hands continued. Rand was, Eban later recalled, Horowitz's 'special preoccupation.'[28]

Horowitz showed Rand the rusting hulks of the 'refugee fleet' and instructed him on the meaning and significance of refugee immigration. Hundreds of thousands of Holocaust victims were confined to displaced persons camps in Europe. Canada would not take them, nor would the United States. They were wanted in Palestine, but the British would not let them in. Horowtiz told Rand about the internment in Palestine of key Jewish leaders, detailed the excesses of the British occupiers, and described, in heroic terms, the Jewish struggle for statehood. Rand was an enthusiastic student, especially after seeing for himself actual evidence of the Arab attitude towards Jews. 'He had listened to my explanations and recital for eleven hours,' Horowitz wrote in his memoirs about the first day the two men spent together, '... and had been able to grasp the full scope and significance of our position. These impressions, scenes, ideas, and personal experiences had combined into a vivid picture, and I knew that the sympathy which had been engendered within him was bound to become more pronounced as UNSCOP's work proceeded. All he said as we parted was: "I fully appreciate that you're fighting with your backs to the wall." The way he said it was encouraging and offered some future hope from a quarter in which we had expected very little sympathy in our struggle.'[29]

The committee members travelled from place to place, alternating between Jewish and Arab areas, but, given the Arab boycott, spending most of their time during their two-week tour in Jewish areas within a day's drive of Jerusalem. In Tel Aviv they received an enthusiastic welcome and their motorcade was cheered as it drove around the city. Jewish progress was presented along with Jewish suffering. They were taken to homes of European orphans and introduced to workers with concentration camp numbers tattooed on their arms. The message being conveyed was not exactly subtle, but the impression it made was compelling. The Jews had endured a great tragedy, and it was within the committee's power to help these Jews make things right. Of all the people Rand met in Palestine, the concentration camp victims had the most impact. They convinced him of the need for a Jewish homeland.[30]

With a crowded agenda, the committee travelled in a caravan of cars – Haifa one day, Beersheba the next. Sandstrom's car went first, and those of the other delegates followed, arranged in alphabetical order. There was no shortage of ceremonial events and visits to schools, farms, and factories. There were also the inevitable moving pilgrimages to various holy sites: the Wailing Wall, where Jews prayed at the last remnant of the Second Temple; the Dome of the Rock, from where Mohammed, Moslems believe, ascended to heaven; and the Holy Sepulchre, which, many Christians claim, holds the tomb of Jesus Christ. The Holy Sepulchre was itself beset by the rivalry of the different Christian sects: Greek Orthodox, Roman Catholic, Copts, Armenians – a rivalry resolved only by entrusting the key to a Moslem family.

There were the formal occasions, such as the luncheon for UNSCOP members in Tel Aviv on 25 June – Iced Melon American, Vol au Vent Montglas Champignon Sauce, Beef Tongue, Roast Duckling, Fresh Asparagus, Peach Melba, Turkish Coffee, and Assorted Fruits made up the menu – and many informal lunches and dinners as well. The Palestine Philharmonic performed for the committee at Jerusalem's Edison Hall on 10 July, and, six days later, Rina Nikova presented her 'Biblical Ballet' at the Hebrew University. Rand met David Ben Gurion, Dr Chaim Weizmann, the past president of the World Zionist Organization, and an American Zionist and future Israeli prime minister named Golda Myerson, later known as Golda Meir. At receptions and cocktail parties, leading questions were floated and everyone's response was carefully gauged. What would the Jewish reaction be to partition accompanied by economic union? Rand asked Ben Gurion. A full and frank discussion ensued, though no one committed to anything. At a dinner party at the Rehovoth home of Dr Weizmann, Zionism's elder statesman, Rand was spellbound as his host, obviously in decline and ousted from his position of leadership, but still a formidable advocate, spoke about Jewish history and destiny, interweaving his personal quest with that of the Jewish people. The issue, Weizmann explained, was not between right or wrong, but between the greater and the lesser injustice. Arabs and Jews, he explained, could co-exist, but only on a basis of sovereign equality. Driving back to Jerusalem, Rand 'sat silent and meditative, and only murmured: "Well, that's really a great man."'[31]

The committee travelled in suffocating heat to the Negev desert, where, seemingly out of nowhere, a lush Jewish settlement, Revivim, appeared, demonstrating the capacity of Jewish settlers to make things grow in what was undoubtedly one of the harshest climates in the world. 'Here,' Rand observed to a Jewish escort, 'you have a very strong argument on your behalf.'[32] It was not just Revivim: there were lush green gardens everywhere, including places like the Dead Sea, where nothing had ever grown before. The kibbutzniks were, evidently, a different type of Jew from any whom the committee had ever encountered: self-sufficient farmers and citizen soldiers. There were trips to Arab villages and Jewish settlements, along the coast, in the north, and along the Jordan River. Everywhere the committee members went, they were feted by the Jews. But they were barely welcomed by the Arabs, who maintained their general boycott even though they brought an end to their strike. In community after community the Jews described their economic and social accomplishments – at Dan, along the Jordan River, Rand and the other members were told that malaria would have been eliminated entirely but for the lack of interest and cooperation from the Arabs. As they travelled about, committee members were assured that, small as Palestine was, there was room for hundreds of thousands of homeless Jews. The orchards, gardens, artificial fish ponds, factories, and other emblems of a generation of effort seemed to bear this claim out. The tour ended on 3 July, and, the next day, the committee began to hear evidence in Jerusalem.

There Ben Gurion testified about the historic claims of the people of Israel to all of Palestine, including Transjordan, the Golan Heights, and southern Lebanon (while making it privately known that the Zionists would accept partition as part of a political settlement).[33] His history lesson spanned the centuries. He argued that the Balfour Declaration, incorporated into the Mandate, constituted international commitments made to the Jewish people and that the time was long overdue for these 'pledges,' as he called them, to be given effect. His evidence ended with some current events, including an alarming recital of some of the excesses of British rule. There were only four choices: a Jewish state, an Arab state, a bi-national state, or partition. And of these, only the last had a fighting chance – it was the only option that attempted to accommodate the divergent interests of Arabs and Jews. From the outset, the understood objective of the Jewish Agency was straightforward: partition and the creation of a Jewish state in a suitable part of Palestine. Ben Gurion, like Weizmann, personalized his address with an account of his own struggle to build a Jewish home. Rand was particularly impressed as he heard how Ben Gurion ploughed the land with a rifle on his back. This, Rand later confided to Horowitz, required 'real toughness and character.'[34]

Other Jewish witnesses described the advances that had been achieved in Palestine and the plans for the future, particularly for turning the deserts into gardens. A rabbi testified – to considerable laughter – that only in Palestine could a Jew fulfill himself fully, adding that the Bible promised Palestine to the Jews. Rand was curious about the biblical basis to the Jewish claim, but was perturbed by the levity with which the audience received the rabbi's remarks. The Zionists wanted a Jewish state, not a *Jewish* state. While a handful of witnesses – Jewish communists and fellow travellers – came before the committee and advocated a federation of equals, Arabs and Jews, with international supervision, it was obvious to almost everyone that these proposals were naïve at best. Relations between Arabs and Jews were such that cooperation was impossible. Moreover, the Jews would never agree to any limits on immigration – restrictions the Arabs would insist on to preserve their numerical superiority. All things considered, it made more sense to focus on real solutions. Golda Meir later described the strategy: realizing that the committee members knew little or nothing about the history of the Jews and the basis of their claims, the Jews decided to provide them with the necessary instruction. 'Since it was essential,' she recollected in her memoirs, that they learn quickly, 'we began to explain and expound as we had done so often before, and eventually they started to grasp what all the fuss was about and why we were not prepared to give up our right to bring the survivors of the Holocaust to Palestine.'[35]

Several committee members also travelled to Beirut, where the Arab League was given an opportunity to make its case. All Jews who had arrived in Palestine since the Balfour Declaration were, they were informed, illegal and must be expelled. There was only one solution:

majority Arab rule and immediate deportation of the illegal aliens – about 400,000 of approximately 700,000 Jews. No Jewish state would be tolerated and, were one to be established, that would be considered an act of war against the Arab people. Transjordan's King Abdullah was, relatively speaking, more moderate and, as usual, self-interested. He told a group of committee members, including Rand, who flew to Amman to meet him, that any Jews in Palestine should be allowed to remain with full citizenship rights, but that no new ones should be allowed to join them.[36] Rand and the other committee members – aware of the hundreds of thousands of Jewish refugees clamouring to come to Palestine – could only be disturbed by what they heard. The urgent need for a workable solution was obvious, and it became even more so when, just before the committee left Palestine for Geneva, the British Labour government flexed its muscle and attracted international sympathy for the plight of the Jews.

The *Exodus*, a 98-metre steamer built for 700, but carrying 4,500 mostly Holocaust survivors heading for Palestine, was rammed, attacked with tear gas, and boarded by the Royal Navy on the open sea. 'All night long, a vicious hand-to-hand battle ensued, relayed to the outside world, blow by blow, by Haganah transmitters.' At one point it looked as though the boarding party might retreat, but disagreement then broke out among the Jewish leaders on board. The ship's captain believed he could beach the ship, allowing many would-be immigrants to escape. The Haganah decided otherwise. Its main goal was to 'show how poor and weak and helpless we were, and how cruel the British were.' The immediate welfare of the 4,500 passengers was secondary.[37] The ship was then towed to Haifa, where the refugees, instead of being sent to Cyprus, were dragged kicking and screaming on to British prison ships and returned to Europe. Even when confronted with an eyewitness account of the British assault, Rand initially demonstrated great difficulty in accepting that the *Exodus* was not, as the British conveniently claimed, armed to the teeth: 'You are sure there were no guns on the ship?' he asked.[38]

There were no guns (except those misused by the British), and the plight of the refugees landing in Haifa was witnessed first-hand by Sandstrom and other committee members, who immediately described the disgraceful spectacle to their colleagues. The fate of the *Exodus* passengers could leave no one unmoved, particularly when they got to France and refused to leave their prison ships – ships that nevertheless sailed on to Germany, forcibly returning Hitler's victims to the scene of the crime. The episode drove home the significance of the committee's task. The fate of an entire people was in their hands, and the world was watching.

That something needed to be done was proved by what the British did next: they executed the three members of the Irgun Gang. Its leader, the future prime minister Menachim Begin, made good on his earlier threat, and two captured British soldiers were promptly strung up. The cycle of violence was escalating, and it was not hard to identify at least one of the culprits – something that, paradoxically, pushed Rand into the partitionists' camp. 'As long as the mandate continued, or in the event Palestine became a unitary Arab state, or even a bi-national state, the killings, the retaliations, the illegal immigration, the political and military resistance of the Jews would continue.' The committee had an opportunity, an obligation, and a duty to recommend a real and lasting solution.[39]

Arriving in Geneva on the last day of July, accompanied by his deputy, Léon Mayrand, Rand and his committee members had exactly one month to issue a report for the General Assembly of the United Nations, scheduled to convene in mid-September. The Jewish Agency liaison officers came with them, and Horowitz continued to focus on his assigned charge. The agency knew what it wanted: an unequivocal report from the committee calling for the termination of the British mandate and the creation of a Jewish state. Following the murder of the two army sergeants, public opinion in Britain had hardened against the Jews and their request for a state. The British would leave, but they insisted that they would not do so until they were fully satisfied that there was a workable plan that had Jewish, Arab, and international support. This ultimatum made it all the more vital that any report issued have the support of a strong majority of UNSCOP members and that Canada be in that majority.

One of the first issues to be decided after arriving in Geneva was whether a subcommittee should visit displaced persons camps. From the Jewish perspective, the link between the Holocaust and the present pressing demand for a Jewish homeland was obvious. India, Iran, and Yugoslavia were opposed. 'You take my land ... I kill you!' was the way Sir Abdur Rahman generally understood the problem – an understanding informed by the belief that the Jews had no intention of staying put in Palestine but intended to use the country as a beachhead for their vast territorial ambitions, aided by strategically placed Jews in England and the United States.[40] Sir Abdur had never previously travelled outside India, and he was susceptible to conspiracy theories of an anti-Semitic sort. The majority disagreed with him and, in a harbinger of votes to come, a subcommittee headed by John Hood went to visit a camp. There they observed conditions of squalor, overcrowding, and misery. Hood reported that there was no doubt about the readiness and ferocious determination of the vast majority of the homeless Jews to make their way to Palestine. Under no circumstances would they repatriate to their countries of origin, where they would be haunted by their memories and subjected to the horrors of a revitalized and active post-war anti-Semitism.

Some kind of solution was obviously required. Rand said as much to Horowitz, who continued his lobbying efforts in Geneva. Reiterating his 'admiration of our people's ardor and vigor,' Rand 'asked probing questions in a low, controlled voice. He questioned, listened, meditated, and weighed what he heard in what appeared to be a spiritual turmoil within his being. His was the most thorny path of grappling with personal conscience.'[41] As it turned out, he was about to play a key role.

When the committee began its formal deliberations, the issue of whether representatives of the mandatory government would be given a final opportunity to make representations was still unresolved. To general surprise, Rand now entered the debate. 'The Mandatory Government,' he argued, 'is a party in this dispute, and any invitation issued to it for official consultation at this stage of the proceedings will impair the Committee's independence and neutrality.'[42] He was right. Representatives of this government had had their chance to testify when the committee was in Israel. Rand's intercession was widely viewed as significant.

Undoubtedly part of the Palestine problem, the British and their instruments of government were not going to be part of the solution (although they might be called on for assistance in carrying it out), and, by making this point clear at the outset of the committee's deliberations, Rand liberated the committee from the British shadow by enabling it to devise its own solution. 'England always delays doing the right thing,' Rand privately confided, 'and when it finally gets around to it, far too late, finds that the opportunity has been lost. It was late in South Africa and was saddled with the Boer War; it was late in Ireland, and now it's losing the chance in Palestine.'[43] Rand's time in

Palestine convinced him that the British had lost their right to govern: the 100,000 soldiers and strict security measures – a 'police state' was the way Rand referred to it in his private notes – were ample evidence of that.[44] The British had been given a legal mandate by the League of Nations to facilitate a Jewish national home that they themselves had earlier promised. Instead, they had abdicated their responsibilities and made matters worse. Rand was acutely aware that UNSCOP had to come up with a solution. Flying over Palestine, he was struck by 'the serpentine windings of the Jordan River and thought,' he confided, not very originally, to one of his Jewish Agency minders, 'these are the wanderings of the Jews.' Rand resolved to find a solution that did not lead these Jews to 'the Dead Sea.'[45]

Rand made these views known when the committee got down to its serious work. The British mandate, he believed, had failed and it must be terminated. On this issue, there was a consensus. Again taking the lead, Rand argued against either a single Arab or Jewish state. An Arab state, he asserted, would violate international agreements – the Balfour Declaration and the Mandate to start, and would, moreover, be a betrayal of the Jewish people. The committee's tour of Palestine left little doubt that, despite the diversity in the origins of Jewish Palestine, the Jewish people in Palestine were united by a common purpose – they shared a single hope. They were, in other words, a nation. Still, to constitute all of Palestine as a Jewish state would be a betrayal of the Arab people. Again, there was a consensus. Palestine could be neither wholly Jewish nor wholly Arab. Jews could not rule Arabs, and Arabs could not rule Jews. What about bi-nationalism, he asked, a federation?

Here Rand again led the discussion. It was not, he argued, the answer, for it would, as David Ben Gurion had testified, lead to political deadlock. It would not give effect to the nationalist aspirations of either the Jews or the Arabs. At best, given the numerical strength of the Arabs, it would be an Arab state with valueless guarantees of Jewish minority rights. Among the most pressing of problems was the British ban on further Jewish immigration. There could be no agreement on any plan that imposed fetters on additional Jewish settlement. 'The idea of a holy land in which both Jews and Arabs will live together peacefully is,' Rand explained, 'a possibility beyond the masses of Arabs and Jews. The ideal itself is not sufficient to make the masses live together peacefully.'[46] The Yugoslav delegate, Vladimir Simic, in what appeared to be deference to Moscow, promoted bi-nationalism, with the Jewish minority subject, then and forever, to an Arab majority. He was joined by Iran's Entezam and India's Rahman. Everyone else was opposed.

That left only one other option (as doing nothing was not considered): partition, exactly what the Peel Commission had recommended ten years earlier. Interestingly, the visit to Beirut and Amman had convinced a majority of the delegates that the Arabs would never accept the Jews, and that it would be pointless to come up with a plan predicated on their doing so. Invited by Chairman Sandstrom to come up with a proposal, Rand developed a wholly impractical scheme – one that attempted to establish a synthesis between political autonomy and economic cooperation, that recognized the legitimate claims of both peoples, and that created a framework for long-term regional stability.

'Palestine is a land which,' Rand wrote in a confidential memorandum to his fellow commissioners, 'because of the religious conceptions and social sentiments to which its culture has given rise through nearly three thousand years, the hundreds of millions of adherents to the three great monotheistic religions whose spiritual interests are localized in its scenes and historical events, and the centuries of contests over its possession, is set apart irrevocably from the rest of the world, and recognition of that fact ought now to be formally declared by the nations. It is the uniqueness of this land, as well as that of the Jewish people and their relation to it, that in large measure justifies the Balfour declaration and the Mandate of 1922.' 'My suggestion then,' he continued, 'for a scheme of partition of Palestine which preserves its economic and social integrity is this: There would be three independent states: one which we may (for present purposes) call the Jewish state, the second, the Arab state, and the third, the State of Jerusalem. In each there would be vested full powers of political sovereignty except so far as they may be specifically modified by the constituting instrument.'[47]

Without a doubt, Rand identified in broad strokes the only solution to the problem, but his eleven-page plan, while undoubtedly well intentioned, was unworkable, inconsistent, and unfair. Among other things, it called for the creation of a new bi-national institution – 'the Central Authority' – with jurisdiction over transportation and communications, customs, currency, trade and commerce, and other matters too numerous to list. There were curious aspects: the Jews could not tax Arabs residing in the Jewish state, but there could be no discrimination against Arabs residing in that same state in the distribution of unemployment relief. In his proposal, Rand suggested that the Arab state could require resident Jews to surrender their land and leave, on payment of 'fair and reasonable compensation.' The Jewish state could not, however, expropriate Arab lands unless those lands remained 'uncultivated and unused' for a minimum of five years and, in any event, expropriation was limited to 'public purposes.' Neither state could maintain an army, but home guards were permissible, together with 'auxiliary air units.' Each state would have authority over immigration within its territory, but no Jew would be allowed to take up residence in the Arab state.

Realizing that the extensive governmental and other institutions he proposed would be unable 'to function free from deficit,' not to mention relative rates of economic progress, current and anticipated, in the proposed Arab and Jewish states, Rand even introduced the concept of transfer payments, with the Jewish state permanently subsidizing 'the deficit of the Arab state' (one proposal the Iranian and Indian delegates fell over themselves to endorse). And Britain, Rand recommended, should be put in charge of the new arrangement, pending its complete implementation when general supervisory authority was assumed by the United Nations, or some other 'international force.' It was, Rand believed, Great Britain's duty to participate because, 'after all, she did get herself into the mess by issuing the Balfour Declaration and it would be immoral for her to withdraw now without seeing the thing through.'[48]

'The primary objectives sought in the foregoing scheme,' Rand wrote in a parallel 'Commentary on Partition,' 'are, in short, political division and economic unity: to confer upon each group, Arab and Jew, in its own territory, the power to make its own laws, while preserving to both, throughout Palestine, a single integrated economy, admittedly essential to the well-being of each, and the same territorial freedom of movement to individuals as is enjoyed today. The former necessitate a territorial partition; the latter, the maintenance of unrestricted commercial relations between the States, together with a common administration of functions in which the interests of both are in fact inextricably bound together.' Rand believed that the machinery of government he proposed could, by creating a common ground, transcend the conflicts between Arabs and Jews.

Idealistic and high-minded perhaps, not to mention guided by the Canadian experience, predisposing him towards some form of the division of powers that maintained the centre – in this case, Jerusalem, no longer 'the arena of human strife' – Rand's proposal was, nevertheless, impractical. Canada confederated by agreement, but there could be no agreement in Palestine, neither by federation nor by sovereignty association. As Dr Ralph Bunche, a senior UN bureaucrat (and future Nobel Peace Prize winner) assisting UNSCOP, pointed out to Horowitz and Eban, Rand's 'confederation mechanisms were very confusing and ... would discredit partition at the United Nations Assembly.'[49] If the Palestinian tour should have taught Rand anything, it was the absolute impossibility of Arabs and Jews cooperating about anything, much less complicated and lopsided institutions of government or half-baked fiscal schemes divorced from existing economic realities – realities that Rand and the other committee members had seen in spades in Palestine.

Rand was not the only committee member to propose a plan, and two full weeks were spent, with no evidence of success, in discussing the various proposals and solutions. Eventually the committee members realized as much, and they began to focus their attention on a partition option that provided for separate states – one recognizing that Jews and Arabs lived side by side, but not together; that provided the Jews with enough land to create a country; and that avoided complicated, unworkable, supra-governmental institutions, predicated as they were on wishful thinking and erroneous assumptions. The objective was, in short, to generate a realistic proposal, but the task was not an easy one. By the third week of August the committee's work ground to a halt and the prospect of failure loomed high as the deadline for submission quickly approached. There was less than two weeks left to complete the report. It did not take long for word of the impending failure to leak out.

Jewish Agency officials assigned to the talks decided to make one last attempt to ensure a strong, unassailable report recommending a Jewish state with viable boundaries. The alternative would be worse than useless, for it would confirm what the British had been saying for years – that the situation was hopeless. Horowitz went to see Rand in his room. 'I know it isn't proper to intrude on you at this time and in this way,' he said, 'but I remembered our first talk at Haifa. You then said: "You're fighting with your backs to the wall." If one is fighting with one's back to the wall, one does not observe the proprieties of the situation.' Horowitz stopped to gauge his host's reaction, and, when Rand smiled in return, he continued to make his case. Any proposal reducing a Jewish state to a mere sham would fail. It would deprive the Jews of their entitlement to a real state. It would fail at the United Nations. Only the Arabs would be happy and, instead of the committee

solving the Palestine problem, it would make matters worse. 'I won't
allow you to be placed in a territorial ghetto,' Rand replied, evidently
appreciating that UNSCOP had to come up not only with a solution
but with one that had a fighting chance of success. The two men shook
hands, and Horowitz left. 'I knew the purport of his words,' Horowitz recalled. 'I knew, too, the personal, moral, and political authority
behind them, and that was enough for me.'[50] He became an uncritical
fan of the Canadian judge: 'This obstinate, fiery, and explosive liberal,
of broad outlook and deep intellectual and moral caliber, sought truth,
morality, justice and humanity in the tangled skein of the problem. He
showed little patience with ephemeral political considerations; he was
animated by a warm humanitarianism, unassailable moral principles,
and a deep perception. In accepting the task, he had made it clear to
those who commissioned him that he would obey no directives save
those of his own conscience, and he behaved in that spirit throughout.'[51] Rand had been brought on side. His status and prestige would
now, and in the future, be deployed to advance the Zionist cause.

Rand was true to his word. 'The pledge concerning a Jewish national
home has never been fulfilled,' he told the committee when it reconvened later that day. 'For the past ten years, immigration and land
purchases have been artificially restricted, and the Jewish community
has had to remain static. It's clear that were it not for the White Paper and the land legislation, the Jews would have had far larger areas
then they hold today.'[52] Rand was persuasive. All committee members
agreed that the British mandate had to be brought to an end. Where
they disagreed was about what should happen next. On 31 August, the
deadline, the committee completed its work, issuing a majority as well
as a minority report. The majority report, following a section titled
'Justification,' set out its recommendations.

The outlines of 'The Plan of Partition with Economic Union' were
straightforward. Two states, one Arab and one Jewish, would be created, linked by an 'economic union.' Initially it would be a sovereignty
association, with full independence after a two-year transition period.
Immigration of Jews would be strictly limited during the interregnum,
with those allowed in restricted to the Jewish side of town. After independence, Arabs and Jews would become citizens of the states in
which they resided, with the privilege of seeking citizenship, after one
year, in the other state. Independence was contingent on both states
adopting democratic constitutions and signing a ten-year treaty of
economic union. There would be a common currency and a customs

union, among other bi-national economic arrangements, even though the committee had recognized earlier in its work that two parallel economies operated in Palestine – 'economic separateness' was the way it was officially referred to – with only limited interaction between them. However, if those links could be made to work, the idea for a federation could be revisited in the future. The majority plan was almost as unrealistic as Rand's first draft had been, but it left the door open to build on success. As expected, the national boundaries were less easy to resolve.

In committee, Rand worked hard to ensure the maximum geographic area possible for the new Jewish state. The whole of the Beeersheba subdistrict, which included the Negev, the Esdraelon plain, most of the coastal plain, and eastern Galilee, went to the Jews; the hill country of Samaria and Judea, the coastal plain from Isdud to the Egyptian frontier, and western Galilee went to the Arabs. 'Kissing points' served as junctions between corridors that linked otherwise unconnected Jewish and Arab lands. Jerusalem was a major problem, and the majority report called for it to be put under international trusteeship. There were myriad other details, and many of them incorporated elements of Rand's earlier scheme. In language clearly drafted by Rand, the majority report observed: 'The Jews bring to the land the social dynamism and scientific method of the West; the Arabs confront them with individualism and intuitive understanding of life. Here then, in this close association, through the natural emulation of each other, can be evolved a synthesis of the two civilizations, preserving, at the same time, their fundamental characteristics. In each State, the native genus will have a scope and opportunity to evolve into its highest cultural forms and to attain its greatest reaches of mind and spirit.'[53]

For all of its faults, the majority report compared favourably against the minority report (India, Iran, and Yugoslavia), which recommended the creation of one federal state of Palestine with Jewish and Arab parts. Immigration to the Jewish part would be controlled by an international commission, which would determine how many Jews, if any, would be allowed in. The capital of the new state was to be Jerusalem, the home of a new federal legislature. Federation might be an ideal solution for a country like Canada or Switzerland, but in Palestine, where Arabs and Jews were at loggerheads, it would never work.

In fact, UNSCOP's partition plan would never be implemented (and no serious person ever believed it would). The borders were contorted and incapable of defence. Large pockets of Jews remained in the proposed Arab state, and the new Jewish state would, at least initially, have more Arabs than Jews. But the impracticability of the plan did not matter. From the Jewish point of view, the 'report of Mr. Justice Rand,' as the Canadian Jewish Congress referred to it – a conceit deliberately designed to legitimize Jewish rule in Palestine with the Canadian people – served its key purpose: the establishment of an internationally recognized Jewish state.[54]

The partition recommendation was the first major Zionist victory since the Balfour Declaration. Although the UNSCOP report left a lot to be desired – international control of Jerusalem, for example, was not then viable – the overall achievement was monumental. A UN committee had approved the creation of a new Jewish state: 'Only by means of partition can these conflicting national aspirations find substantial expression and qualify both peoples to take places as independent nations in the international community and in the United Nations,' the report asserted. Horowitz and Eban made their way to the formal signing ceremony, but Horowitz stopped first at Rand's room: 'I shook hands with him in mute emotion,' he remembered.[55] That night, at the Palais de Justice, the eleven committee members signed the report. Rand and his deputy left Geneva the next day for home. 'The "conversion" of this old man was of the utmost importance,' according to Moshe Shertok, the head of the Jewish Agency and Israel's second prime minister. That mission was accomplished. Rand was Horowitz's 'greatest conquest.'[56] The Jews had played Rand perfectly, and the Arabs had made it all possible, even inevitable, by their boycott.

Mayrand reported to External Affairs Minister St Laurent that Rand was 'by far the main contributor to the partition scheme.'[57] 'Everyone surmised correctly that Rand had turned the scales,'[58] was the way Horowitz described it. Clearly, he did make a contribution, although his major initiative, even in its muted articulation, was stillborn. His scheme was elaborate, imaginative, and principled, but unrealistic. He was sympathetic to the Jewish dream, but had no intention of denying the Arabs their rights. Nevertheless, his plan was out of touch with reality and fundamentally flawed. It is possible that Rand larded his scheme with details he knew would never work in order to obtain majority support for his main objective: partition. Ralph Bunche thought little of Rand – 'an elderly, crotchety gentleman who had apparently never been outside of Canada ... and who talked incessantly without contributing anything.' Rand was, he reported to the American government, 'the greatest disappointment.' But Bunche thought little of the committee as a whole: 'the weakest ... in which he had ever participated.'[59]

Rand clearly played a critical role at an important time, even if some of his stated ideas were naïve and half-baked. We can also measure his contribution by considering the alternatives. What would have happened had Rand, like the Australian delegate, abstained? Canada was Britain's most important Commonwealth ally, and Canada's vote meant something. Even worse, what would have happened had Canada joined the federationists and signed the minority report? While the underlying motivations were undoubtedly different, Rand's original conception could easily have put him in that camp. Once Rand signed the majority report, the Canadian government could hardly disavow it. 'Despite St Laurent's disclaimer that Rand would not bind the Canadian government, the policy-makers and political leaders in Ottawa could not totally ignore the considered views of the respected jurist they themselves had picked as the best man for the job.'[60]

'The one who tipped the scales,' Israeli historian Uri Milstein concluded, 'was the Canadian representative, Judge Ivan Rand.'[61] In Canada, Zionists embraced the report and repeatedly stressed Rand's contribution to it. 'Canadian Jewish Congress hails with gratification the report of Mr. Justice Rand,' Samuel Bronfman, the president of the Canadian Jewish Congress telegraphed St Laurent, adding, 'the forthright attitude which Mr. Justice Rand has taken is a tribute to his acumen and prescience and we trust that the official action of the Canadian government will follow these recommendations.'[62] 'This is most satisfactory!' wrote Shertok. 'We should by all means play up Rand with the Canadians, so as to strengthen their noblesse oblige complex.'[63] As a strategy it was too clever by half, but it worked.

The British were happy to end their mandate – or at least said as much – but reiterated the position that Her Majesty would only implement a plan on which the Jews and the Arabs had agreed. If experience taught anyone anything, the British should have known that, where the future of Palestine was concerned, there could be no agreement between Arabs and Jews. Were the British trying to sabotage the plan? The Mufti immediately rejected the majority report, and the surrounding Arab states began to prepare for war. However, as the biographer of the prominent Palestinian Musa Alami wrote, the committee could have done nothing to affect the ultimate resolution of the General Assembly, which, 'in the face of so baffling a problem as Palestine obviously presented, was almost bound in the end to adopt some form of partition as the only possible solution.'[64] The Jews agreed, 'reluctantly,' to accept the partition recommendation, but they had no intention of implementing any of its terms except for one: the creation of a Jewish state.

When consideration of the report moved to New York, Lester Pearson took up where Rand had left off. Canada's Palestine policy was not fixed, but the delegation was instructed to take into account the fact that 'a distinguished member of the Supreme Court of Canada had arrived at certain conclusions after careful consideration of the issues involved.'[65] In the end, and with serious misgivings, Canada supported partition, rightly convinced that there was no other alternative. Prime Minister King later regretted Canada's ever becoming involved. It would have been wiser, he confided to his diary, not to have sent Rand, 'better for us to keep out.'[66] King always believed in conciliation as the way to resolve disputes, but he also wanted to keep above the fray and, whenever possible, postpone difficult decisions for another day. Nevertheless, Canada's cautious but ultimately constructive role at the United Nations in the Palestine settlement demonstrated the contribution a middle power with no direct interests in an international dispute could make – a positive harbinger for the future of the United Nations and Canada's role in it.

Rand would have understood how important it was that the UN not only work effectively but be seen to do so. The Palestine problem was its first real challenge, and failure there would have undermined its ability to render any future service. As Abba Eban observed in his memoirs, Rand was a 'key figure,' part of an important task: 'The United Nations seemed to matter very much to the world in those days. It was still regarded as the central arena in which the destiny of mankind would be determined.'[67]

There was considerable manoeuvring at the United Nations as the outlines of a UN resolution adopting UNSCOP's majority report were refined, giving the Jews, constituting approximately 35 per cent of the country's population and owning less than 7 per cent of the land, 55 per cent of Palestinian territory, while the Palestinians, who made up two-thirds of the population and who had lived continuously in Palestine for centuries, ended up with less than half of the country. Typically, 'in the run-up to the UN vote,' the Zionists engaged in 'frenzied lobbying,' while the Arabs 'lackadaisically looked on, sure of an effortless victory.'[68] In late November 1947 the General Assembly voted – with Canada among the majority – in favour of the report's partition recommendation. Canada ultimately decided to support partition, despite serious misgivings – diplomatic, moral, legal, and practical – in part because of Rand's involvement, but mainly because a less than desirable solution, Pearson and others believed, was better than no solution. Simply put, there was no other alternative – or, as Weizmann had put it, it was a matter of choosing between the greater and the lesser injustice. The legitimacy of partition was greatly advanced first by UNSCOP and then by the United Nations.[69]

In addition to partition, the UN resolution called for the establishment of a commission to oversee Palestine and to work with the British in winding down the mandate. Nevertheless, as hostilities between Arabs and Jews accelerated, the British refused to cooperate, leaving the UN commission unable to intervene. Although British forces did little but protect British lives and property, the UN could not act to stop the fighting so long as the British remained in charge. The British would not even allow the UN commission to take basic preparatory steps, such as the demarcation of boundaries. Until its mandate ended in the middle of May, the British were determined to maintain their rule, such as it was.

Instead of economic integration, the bloodshed not only continued but escalated. When the new Jewish state declared independence on 14 May 1948, both the United States and the Soviet Union announced their recognition of it – a remarkable but unrepeated example of American-Soviet agreement at the dawn of the Cold War.[70] Israel's successful War of Independence followed immediately. Rand's work in Palestine was long done, and he had returned to the Supreme Court. Both at the time and in the future, Rand reaped much of the credit for being the handmaiden to the birth of Israel, but he was characteristically modest when it came time to accept the accolades. 'Not for a moment,' he wrote years later to one student asking questions, 'did I nurse the idea that I was directing the course of things! I was working hard – that is all.'[71] For Israel, the majority UNSCOP report was simply the end of the beginning. For the Palestinians, it was the beginning of the end; the Arab states' violent rejection of partition precipitated the *nakba*, or catastrophe, an unmitigated national disaster.

7

King Coal

By the early nineteenth century a major coal industry had developed in Cape Breton, in the Sydney area, and in mainland Nova Scotia in Pictou County, in the Stellarton-Westville area, and in Cumberland County, in the Springhill-Joggins area. The reserves were huge, particularly in the Sydney field. Over time, a people and a culture grew up around the mines. Even though many of the miners and their families lived in company houses in company towns, and even though their jobs were among the most hazardous in the country – many miners died in industrial accidents while others were felled much later from years of inhaling poisonous coal dust – generation after generation of Cape Breton men went to work underground and at the steel mill in Sydney, built on the back of the coal industry. It was part of the Cape Breton way of life. However, the abundant Canadian deposits were located far from commercial centres, making coal expensive to transport. And, by the mid-1950s, other cheaper and more efficient energy choices were readily available. It seemed that the continued operation of the collieries, and the economy of most of the island, was about to come crashing down – and there was nothing to replace it.

Cape Breton coal mining had never been a major money earner. From the start the industry was supported with public funds because production costs incurred from extracting the coal were extremely high. The island's submarine mines extended miles under the ocean, and it took time for miners to travel to the coal face and bring the coal back to the pithead. Ventilation in the huge underground mines was difficult and expensive. The 960-kilometre strip between Montreal and Windsor accounted for three-quarters of Canadian iron and steel manufacturing, and two-thirds of the country's coal consumption. Yet the eastern end of this area was 1,600 kilometres away from Nova Scotia's mines. American coal was closer, less expensive, and of higher quality. The only way Canadian coal could ever compete was if market forces were not allowed to govern. That meant government money.

Tariffs were in place to keep the cheaper American coal out, and preferential freight rates allowed Cape Breton coal to compete in Ontario and Quebec. But these special subsidies were never enough.[1] Between the beginning and the end of the Second World War, the federal government spent more than $50 million supporting the Canadian coal industry. The wartime economy increased demand, and the Emergency Coal Production Board was established to assist existing companies, in Cape Breton and elsewhere, to boost production with the assistance of government funds, loans, subsidies, and outright handouts – to buy machinery and equipment, fund wage increases, and subsidize operating costs. The industry's appetite for tax dollars was insatiable. After the war, demand began to drop and costs rose. Without continued government assistance, many Canadian coal mines would close, throwing thousands out of work. In Canada, governments usually react to a problem of such social magnitude with one response: a commission of inquiry.[2] And so the Royal Commission on Coal was appointed in 1946.

Government funding had, over the years, created a dependency in the coal industry, bringing with it labour unrest and gross inefficiency in production. The commissioners might have been expected, then, to conclude that the old model had not worked and that it was time for a change, perhaps even reorganization on a commercial basis. For their part, the mine workers, through their union, District 26 of the United Mine Workers (UMW), urged 'nationalization' as the solution. But the commissioners rejected all such proposals in their 663-page report and ensured perpetual inefficiency by recommending that the tariffs, transportation subventions, and subsidies be continued indefinitely. The exact amounts were left flexible, so that assistance could 'vary from time to time with changes in the competitive situation.'[3]

Post-war Canada was remarkably prosperous, and many Canadians believed that the government should intervene in the marketplace, and that social problems could and should be solved by passing a law or writing a cheque. Moreover, Canada was not alone in subsidizing the coal industry: Germany, France, and the United Kingdom, among others, did too. The United States, in contrast, had stopped all subsidies, direct and indirect, including tariff protection, well before the Second World War. As it happened, American coal was not only less expensive to produce but of a higher quality, and it could be shipped to Canada at market transportation rates and still be sold for less.

In 1947 just over 12,000 men were employed in Nova Scotia's mines, producing almost 6 million tons of coal a year, unfortunately with the second lowest productivity in the country (and dropping steadily).[4] That same year many Cape Breton miners decided to go on strike. Many of their customers accordingly decided to switch suppliers and fuel – and they never came back. Still, some customers remained: the Sydney Steel Mill, the pulp and paper industry, the Province of Nova Scotia for the production of thermally generated electricity, and also central Canada, particularly Ontario Hydro. For the most part, those markets existed courtesy of 'production subsidies' provided by Canadian taxpayers. Transportation costs were a big part of the problem. In 1956, for instance, American coal cost $8.33 per ton delivered to Toronto; Nova Scotia coal cost $15.24. Without the subvention and the artificial subsidized freight rates, there would be no market for East Coast coal.

At the same time, a revolution was taking place in energy supplies as consumers everywhere switched from coal to oil and natural gas; futurists even talked of nuclear power one day replacing oil.[5] In contrast to coal, oil and natural gas were easy to extract and inexpensive to transport. Canadian coal mining's prospects were limited at best, as anyone who looked at the problem could see – except, of course, the coal miners, their unions and employers, and the regulator, the Dominion Coal Board (DCB).[6] In 1956 the government appointed another commission to inquire into the economy generally – the Royal Commission on Canada's Economic Prospects, chaired by Walter Gordon, a left-leaning Toronto blueblood associated with the prestigious family accounting firm, Clarkson Gordon & Company. In short order, Gordon assembled a team of academic specialists to investigate 'the probable economic development of Canada and the problems to which such development appears likely to give rise,'[7] and published thirty-three comprehensive volumes outlining their research and conclusions. It was an unprecedented undertaking.

The preliminary report accurately predicted increasing Canadian demands for energy, but it was petroleum, natural gas, hydro power, and nuclear fuels that had a future, not coal. As a result of the new trans-Canada pipeline, coal sales would drop further as major industries along the pipeline's route built spur lines to assure themselves of a year-round energy supply at competitive prices. From coal's supplying 69 per cent of Canada's total energy source in 1926, the number dropped to 39 per cent in 1953 and would, the commission forecast, fall to 16 per cent by 1980. The Nova Scotia coal industry was a particular problem because of the lack of alternative employment in the mining towns. Since 1930, Cape Breton's large coal mines had been owned by the Dominion Steel and Coal Corporation (Dosco), a private holding company and one of the largest employers in Canada until well into the 1950s. It controlled about 90 per cent of Nova Scotia's coal mining, and was responsible for about 30 per cent of all the coal produced in Canada. It had 13,000 employees, mining coal and iron ore, producing coke, making steel, building ships, bridges, and railway cars, and manufacturing pipe, nails, wire, and screws.

To meet industry challenges, Dosco developed and produced a machine – the mechanical miner – that cut coal from the face and loaded it directly onto a conveyor system, eliminating most of the hand labour. With just seven men to service it, the machine replaced forty men using their sweat, pan shovels, and dynamite to extract the coal. Productivity improved – by 1956 it was up 47 per cent over 1945 rates, while output per miner per day had gone from 1.58 tons to 2.33[8] – but it was not nearly enough to make Cape Breton coal competitive. Still, the company lost only $400,000 in 1954 compared with more than $3 million the previous year. However, the initial attempts to mechanize were greeted with hostility by the miners, and the program took so long to implement that, when it was finally in place, rising wage and material costs cancelled out production savings.[9] Dosco had received a $7.5 million 'loan' for its mechanization initiatives, and that was just a small part of the continuing governmental support as the hodgepodge of financial aid programs remained in place. At best, mechanization, considered in context, merely delayed the day of reckoning.[10]

Economic studies indicated that the industry could not survive without increasing the existing transportation subventions and other subsidies.[11] In its preliminary report, the Royal Commission accordingly recommended increasing coal consumption locally, particularly to generate thermal power, and acknowledging that 'there must be some limit to the amount of assistance which should reasonably be given to any one industry, no matter how important it may be.'[12] It also recommended that 'generous assistance' be provided to displaced workers. But it was the 'special measures' that the commission recommended for Cape Breton miners that attracted the most attention: 'We suggest that on economic grounds alone, having regard to the amount of the present subsidy, there would be every justification for paying the full amount of the transportation costs of all the members of any families who may be willing to move to other parts of Nova Scotia or elsewhere in Canada; for assistance in the provision of housing; and for training for other occupations, possibly in co-operation with industry.'[13] The recommendation unleashed a barrage of criticism of the central Canadians who did not appreciate the need to protect an established and treasured taxpayer-subsidized way of life.

When the commission issued its final report in 1957, the commissioners reiterated their view that the time for tinkering had long past. Mines had to close and miners had to move.[14] They accurately and wisely assessed the state of the Canadian coal industry, and they made courageous sensible recommendations to address the problem (in contrast to their draconian suggestions about limiting foreign investment). But the pro-business St Laurent Liberal government, enjoying the benefits of Canada's post-war economic boom, was not interested in what Gordon had to say. When Conservative party leader John Diefenbaker came to power in time to receive the final report in the fall of 1957, he paid even less attention, and it was only with the return of the Liberals in 1963, under Lester Pearson, that many of Gordon's main recommendations became government policy.

Meanwhile, Canadian coal production continued to decline, and consumption reached its lowest levels since the height of the Great Depression. Mild winters, high water levels (increasing hydroelectric power production), completion of the railways' dieselization campaign, and the increased reliance on fossil fuels were all factors that threatened the very existence of the coal industry, which, if not yet dead, was on life support in dire need of the last rites. In addition, natural gas was on its way east, and the St Lawrence Seaway was nearing completion. When it opened in 1959, the cost of moving already competitive American coal to Montreal and Toronto would drop by an estimated $1.00 per ton. The residential market had completely collapsed as consumers switched from coal to oil and then natural gas to heat their homes.

Then tragedy struck, not once but twice. The Springhill Coal Field in Cumberland County, Nova Scotia, was one of the oldest and most dangerous mines in the province. In 1891, 125 miners had been killed there in an underground fire. In 1956 another explosion left thirty-nine dead. Two years later, a 'bump,' or underground earthquake, in the No. 2 colliery, thousands of feet below the surface, left more than seventy men dead as the floor of the tunnels at the bottom of the mine slammed into the ceiling. The community and the country were devastated. Dosco shut the mine down and left town, throwing nine hundred miners out of work, most of them over forty-five years of age.[15]

Things would only get worse. 'In Nova Scotia,' the Dominion Coal Board wrote in its 1959 annual report, 'the crisis in the industry continued to deepen and the outlook for much improvement, without basic readjustments, was grave indeed.'[16] Dosco posted a $2 million loss on its mining operations and suspended operation in some of its mines for more than forty days to reduce stockpiles and lower costs. Why the mines were stockpiling product no one wanted was not immediately apparent. Major Ontario steel producers such as Stelco, Dofasco, and Algoma Steel did not want the Nova Scotia coal – it was, they said, unsuitable for their needs. American coal was cheaper, burned better, and was easier on the furnace. The Ontario mills were not government subsidized and, therefore, could not defy economic laws. Ontario Hydro expressed some continued interest in Nova Scotia coal, but its high moisture content was a disadvantage. By the end of the decade, the federal government was paying at least $12 million per year to keep the industry going. The old sources of support continued, and new ones were introduced: federal government buildings, for instance, were directed to burn Canadian coal, provided the cost was no more than 20 per cent higher than the competition.

Tough decisions needed to be taken – and were, in the United States. Americans aggressively mechanized and closed unprofitable and uneconomical mines. They also enjoyed the benefits of geography, in that their coal was not only of a higher quality and cost less to extract but was closer to market. The UMW and its pragmatic leader, John L. Lewis, decided, rather than fight to preserve marginal jobs, to preserve the industry and focus on good jobs with substantially improved wages and working conditions for the men and women who worked in it. In just ten years, as mechanization cut the workforce in West Virginia mines from 117,000 to 40,000, more coal was produced and sold than ever before. In 1958 the average cost at pithead of Nova Scotia coal was $10.72 a ton, while American coal cost between $3.60 and $5.33 a ton.

By early February 1959, even though Dosco had completed much of its mechanization campaign, the price per ton of coal was increasing and would keep on rising. On the financial side, the company was in 'technical default' of its huge government loan. It was also indebted to the bank for $9 million, and it owed its parent company an additional $5.3 million. Government officials were informed that the company needed a $6 million infusion and was looking to Ottawa to provide it. Finally acknowledging that fundamental reforms needed to be introduced, the Dominion Coal Board recommended that the government undertake an investigation, by an 'outstanding coal mining authority,' into Dosco's 'structure, organization and business methods.'[17]

Robert 'Bob' Bryce, the Cambridge- and Harvard-educated secretary to the Cabinet and a distinguished public servant, thereupon advised Prime Minister Diefenbaker that they had come to a 'turning point.'[18] The continuation of the status quo in the coal industry was neither reasonable nor good public policy. The fact was that 'progressive increases in subventions, without any attack on the underlying problem, would mean rising expense and demoralization for all concerned.' The only real solution was a 'long-term solution.'[19] A meeting of senior officials from Finance, the Privy Council Office, the Department of Trade and Commerce, and the Dominion Coal Board the previous month had agreed that 'a fundamental solution should be sought rather than to merely pay additional millions into subventions on the present basis to maintain an inefficient operation.'[20]

The government was desperate for solutions, but moving miners and their families was at the bottom of the list of preferred outcomes. 'The cabinet had reservations about taking any initiative of this kind,' Bryce reminded the prime minister on the eve of a scheduled appointment with Nova Scotia's premier Robert Stanfield in April 1959. 'If, however, some such agreement should be suggested by the Province of Nova Scotia as an immediate measure to cope with the present labour surplus in Cape Breton, it is presumed that the Ministers would give sympathetic consideration to the proposal.'[21] However, recommending redeployment was, in Canada, playing with political fire. The suggestion was sure to be seen as an attack on an inviolable way of life, an entitlement, something sacred. Besides, it was not just a question of moving miners; an entire society had grown up around them – secondary businesses, schools, hospitals, churches. Understandably, Stanfield made no such suggestion. Rather, he recalled, 'Our policy was to dig in and hold on. Closure of a mine would have a catastrophic effect on a mining community and a terrible effect on the men involved, especially the older men.'[22] He knew there was no politically acceptable solution to the problem, so he left it to the federal government take charge.[23]

The coal industry remained Nova Scotia's number one employer, accounting for about 12 per cent of the workforce, and many communities relied entirely on the mines. By 1955 there were 11,337 miners, 93 per cent of them employed by Dosco, while tens of thousands more directly and indirectly depended on Dosco fortunes. If four thousand miners were displaced, at least 30,000 would be directly 'affected': as one study put it, 'the multiplying effect of unemployed miners on the economy of the province would be ... severe.'[24] Unemployment was already high, mining skills were not transferable to anything else, and living standards in the Atlantic provinces were already lower than in the rest of Canada – and would have been lower still without federal transfer payments.

The stakes were raised when Dosco announced another round of major layoffs. Having sold $900 million worth of coal in the past twenty years without earning a penny of profit, and having drained the federal treasury of millions more, the company was, belatedly, interested in achieving economies. These layoffs, if allowed by the government to proceed, would throw thousands out of work. They were, as Diefenbaker immediately appreciated, a stop-gap and would do nothing to change the fundamentals. So, in Canadian fashion, in mid-March 1959 Diefenbaker announced in the House of Commons 'a thorough study' of the problem 'as expeditiously as possible.'[25] When New Brunswick's Conservative Party premier Hugh John Flemming heard about the study, he insisted, having a good nose for federal funds, that the small coal-mining industry in New Brunswick also be examined. The scope of the inquiry was then expanded to include the 'problems' faced by the industry in western Canada too. Diefenbaker typically dithered and dallied, but, after a summer of reflection, realized that he could not postpone taking action forever. Accordingly, he telephoned Ivan Rand.

'We must,' Diefenbaker told Rand, 'do something,' and he added that he knew 'of no more important work to be done.'[26] Rand was not exactly keen. He had just started a new job as the founding dean of the new Law School at the University of Western Ontario. How could he possibly say yes? Yet, even though he understandably had a dim view of Diefenbaker,[27] he could not bring himself to say no because national duty called. 'I don't relish the idea of undertaking this job,' Rand confided to his Ford-formula colleague Horace Pettigrove, 'but it is virtually impossible to refuse, point blank, a request ... from the P.M.'[28] The prime minister made it clear that 'whatever the consequences,' he wanted 'the best report that could be made.'[29]

The 20 August press release began, 'The Prime Minister announced today that a Royal Commission will be appointed to enquire fully into the serious problems relating to the production and marketing of coal both in the Maritimes and in Western Canada.' Reaction to Rand's appointment was good. Thank goodness 'one of the best minds in Canada' would be applied to the problem, the *Ottawa Citizen* editorialized. The newspaper could not help but observe that coal was 'actually unwanted' and could only compete if sold well below cost, and even then its future and use were dubious. Still, it was looking forward to Rand's recommendations 'with considerable anxiety as well as curiosity.'[30] Down east, the Halifax *Chronicle-Herald* declared Rand the perfect choice: 'The ills of coal in Nova Scotia constitute not only an economic problem of great magnitude, but a complex social one. Sales charts, production graphs, federal subventions are important; even more so, however, are the miners, their families and all those who, directly, or indirectly, depend upon this declining industry.'[31] This view probably reflected the prevailing Nova Scotia consensus that some way had to be found to maintain the status quo. It was not going to be easy.

One of Rand's first calls was to Horace Pettigrove, inviting him to come on board as labour adviser. He agreed, and Rand instructed him to research and report on the 'benefits – federal, provincial and municipal – which are or will be available to miners and their families who are or will be affected by mine production curtailments or mine closures.'[32] W.A.D. 'Bill' Gunn, QC, a lawyer from Sydney, Nova Scotia, was hired as commission counsel, while W. Keith Buck, the head of the mineral and resources division of the federal Department of Mines, was appointed as secretary. Rand also brought in a number of experts. Dr Alan E. Cameron, a former professor at the University of Alberta and then Nova Scotia's deputy minister of mines, was named as technical adviser to the commission; and W.V. Sheppard, the United Kingdom's director general of reconstruction – the man in charge of dealing with similar coal problems there – came to Canada as a consultant. Diefenbaker immediately expressed concern about the appointment of an overseas adviser in this 'sensitive matter.' Pridefully meddling in small matters as usual,[33] he was also unhappy about the per diem agreed to by Rand: $150 a day. No more appointments, Rand was instructed, unless the prime minister has consented in advance.[34]

The commission's mandate was straightforward: to inquire into and make recommendations on the present and future markets for coal in Canada, and the steps that could reasonably be taken to reduce the cost of production and distribution of coal, the changes that the industry could make to secure as large a market as possible for coal while operating on an economical basis, and the measures that could be taken by governments to support the economic production, distribution, and sale of Canadian coal. The commission visited thirty-one coal-mining communities by car, train, and plane, went underground five times, and held twelve days of public hearings – in Victoria, Calgary, Regina, Toronto, Montreal, Halifax, Sydney, and Fredericton – beginning on 2 February and ending on 19 April 1960. By any measure, it was a gruelling schedule of travel, hearings, meetings, and tours. In the process, Rand consulted with government officials, mine operators, union officials, and community leaders. He also commissioned several studies and received many briefs.[35]

Rand heard about the problems, but never any practical solutions. In central Canada, where there was still a vestige of a market, the commodity was in free fall. Ontario Hydro told the commissioner that it preferred American coal – and it was not just a question of price, though that differential was determinative. Simply put, Nova Scotia coal was not as efficient or as inexpensive as the US competition. Representing American interests at the commission was Dr C.J. Potter of the National Coal Association. He told Rand that old assumptions should be set aside in favour of a new approach: free trade in energy. Even though various levels of government had subsidized the Canadian coal industry for years, Canadian coal producers had been unable to increase their share of the market. For at least twenty years, American producers had been supplying more than half of Canada's coal needs. Despite the tariff, better American coal could still be delivered to markets in Ontario and Quebec for less than it cost to produce the coal in Nova Scotia. Federal government financial support to the industry was a barrier to trade. The American government took this same position: 'The subsidization of comparatively uneconomic production of a basic material readily available on advantageous terms from other sources

raises serious questions of the effective use of natural resources. A reduction of costly subventions that now bar American coal from parts
of Canada would, in the opinion of the United States Government, be
preferable as economic policy in the use of energy resources in one
continent.'[36]

Two of the largest private-sector operators, Stelco of Hamilton and
Algoma Steel of Sault Ste Marie, reinforced this message that the tariff
on American imports, combined with the transportation subventions
and other subsidies, hurt Canadian producers and consumers. They
explained to Rand that there was no realistic prospect of switching to
Nova Scotia coal because its high sulphur content made it less than
optimal for their blast furnaces. We have been 'compelled,' Stelco told
Rand, 'to use coal imported from the United States' because there was
no 'adequate supply of Canadian coal with the requisite qualities for
metallurgical coke.'[37] Indeed, Stelco's American mines produced high-
quality coking coal at a price that allowed the company to prosper in
a highly competitive market (they had also invested in iron mines and
limestone quarries). Their coal properties in Pennsylvania and West
Virginia were, the company told Rand, completely mechanized – output per man per shift was 14 tons – and the product was perfect for
making steel. They would, the company added, prefer to buy Canadian, but that was not an option. Price and quality always win out.

The other historically important buyers of Canadian coal were the
railways. The Canadian Pacific Railway made it clear to Rand that it
was no longer a customer for coal. Canadian National Railways informed the commissioner that, although its coal-fired steam engines
had already been retired, its coal consumption for powerhouse operations would continue, but would not increase. Sometimes Rand
listened quietly as the presentations were made. On other occasions,
obviously engaged and animated, he posed question after question.
To what extent, he asked when the commission opened its hearings in
Fredericton in early March, can the government be expected to subsidize an industry that is not capable of looking after itself? Was there
a rational conception of subsidization? About six thousand people in
New Brunswick depended on the coal industry for their livelihoods,
and Premier Flemming urged Rand to recommend continued financial assistance for the province's coal mines. Indeed, government funds
should, he suggested, be increased during a transitional phase as some
of the producers moved from surface strip mining to underground
mechanized mining. Any losses incurred during the transition should

be borne by Ottawa. Neither the problem nor the solution, Rand wryly observed, had changed in forty years.

In Halifax, the Nova Scotia government likewise argued that the subsidies should be continued, if not increased, until expanded energy needs created new coal demands. There were the expected calls for more government money to diversify the province's industrial base, and for more federal funds to support research into new methods of cutting production costs.

Rand's scope was national – there were coal mines in British Columbia and Alberta, too, and issues there that had to be addressed. But there was no doubt about his real mandate: to come up with a solution for Cape Breton. 'I want to cover the Nova Scotia situation with the utmost care,' Rand told reporters.[38] Nova Scotians, and Cape Bretoners in particular, held that something could be, should be, and must be done to preserve the industry and their way of life. It was, accordingly, in Sydney, Cape Breton, where Rand expected to come face to face with the problem and, he hoped, to begin devising a long-term solution.

Dosco was already on record as wanting to close three 'money-losing mines' – the collieries at Florence, New Waterford (No. 16 colliery), and Glace Bay. We have no choice, the company told Rand, but to close these mines and reduce production at our remaining facilities. 'If the industry is to be saved from bankruptcy, some action must be taken to bring production more closely in line with disposals.'[39] But these closures would throw almost three thousand men out of work, and that specific threat had provoked the government into appointing Rand in the first place. Dosco's Alabama-born president, Albert Fairley Jr, told Rand that the decision would not be changed unless a market could be found for the coal. Dosco had agreed to keep the mines open only until Rand finished his work – a decision aided, it turned out, by a special federal subsidy of $3.5 million.

Dosco's 20,000-word brief, presented in mid-March, took a whole day to deliver, setting out, in excruciating detail, the production, freight-rate, and marketing problems besetting the industry. The situation was grim: Dosco was losing about $2 million a year in its coal-mining operations. There were no profits and no expectation even of breaking even. The company, understandably, wanted to focus its attention on its more economical pits and close the rest. This 'drastic measure,' Premier Stanfield announced, will be accepted 'only as a last resort.' Such comments always played well in the newspapers but did nothing to advance the conversation.

The United Mine Workers union agreed with the premier. On behalf of its nine thousand members, it criticized Dosco and the way it ran the business. Describing the situation as a 'national emergency,' the union demanded increases to the federal tariff and higher provincial taxes on oil imports. Instead of closing mines, the UMW suggested that new mines be opened and existing mines 'modernized and mechanized.' Other union proposals included outright prohibitions on the importation of US coal until Canadian coal was 'fully utilized,' and legislated requirements that federal and provincial institutions use and burn only Canadian coal. After listening to the union case in a meeting held in Ottawa, the prime minister 'expressed a sympathetic understanding.'[40]

In fact, the UMW and its leader, the bushy-browed William 'Bull' Marsh, could see only one side of the story. Personable and popular, Marsh, who first went into the 'deeps' when he was sixteen in New Waterford, now warned the government either to allocate more funds to the industry or face the consequences of massive labour unrest. 'The mine workers are not going to peacefully witness the deterioration of their churches, schools, hospitals ... which they have built over a long number of years because a single corporation which exists partly on public funds decides to displace approximately 3000 miners.' Further closures, he predicted, would be met 'by forceful action.'[41] Of course, Marsh was playing right into Dosco's hands: the company was desperate to rid itself of its collieries and the obligations that went with them, and a general strike would provide it with the opportunity to close the mines at much lower cost than if it had to negotiate a shutdown. As Pettigrove privately observed to Rand, the situation was comparable to what Herbert Agar once said about labour relations in the United States: 'red with spilled blood, black with ill will, and gray with stupidity.'[42]

The commission coincided with an era of industrial and social planning, and the experts, blind to history, testified that any subsidies would be temporary. The Canadian economy, they explained, was growing. By 1965 the demand for 'economical fuels' would be enormous. 'Atomic power' might not yet be available, and coal would come back into its own. The industry had, therefore, to be kept alive for the national good for a need just around the corner. Rand was repeatedly told that it was his mission to figure out how to make that happen.

Rand had his own ideas. Excoriated in the Cape Breton press for suggesting that some miners and their dependants might have to leave the island to find work, Rand continued to think out loud. On the last

day of his ten-day Maritime tour he met with the deputy mayor and
other worthies in Westville, New Glasgow, a mainland community
hard hit by the industry's decline. While Westville's largest mine once
employed eight hundred men, only ninety were working underground
now, and for as little as three days a week. Dosco was to blame, Rand
was told. The community could not collect taxes because of the unemployment, and when it seized the homes of owners who fell into
arrears, they sat empty because no one wanted to buy them. There
were more than 80 kilometres of municipal roads to keep in repair, a
water-main system on its last legs, and an overcrowded, inadequate
school. Rand acknowledged that the townspeople were not to blame,
'that the coal market was lost.' However, he also pointed out that part
of the problem was that 'people don't look ahead.' If they had, they
would have seen that the 'mine won't last forever.'[43]

There was also the matter of living beyond one's means. People in
the province, Rand, observed, may be living at too high a level: 'Why,
you can hardly get through New Glasgow there are so many automobiles. Why don't you attract some new industry?' Rand asked. We've
tried, was the response, and part of the problem was that new companies did not want to train men who were mostly over forty-five years
of age. That was nonsense, Rand replied, and he suggested that a trade
school might be built. We had one, the deputy mayor replied, but it
was moved out. Rand was not impressed: 'You will have to get down
to work and try to help yourselves,' he told the men. 'If you cannot
find the money to repair your streets, then you will have to let them
go. Urge the residents of the town to put in gardens to supplement
whatever income they have.' Stating the obvious, Rand observed that
it was not 'well to depend on only one industry, because when it goes,
all is lost.' 'I wish I could give you something that would give you
hope,' he concluded, 'but I can't.'[44]

The story was a familiar one. In New Waterford, the workforce in
the soon-to-be-closed mine was primarily made up of married men
with wives and children depending on them for support. On average, the miners had a grade seven education. 'There is not a provincial
training scheme we know of in Canada set to train people with grade
seven education,' a brief prepared by Father Andrew Hogan of the St
Francis Xavier University extension department observed. Still, he told
Rand, people took precedence. The Anglican Deanery of Cape Breton
agreed: in areas such as ours, 'where activity or inactivity in the coal
industry affects the whole community economically, socially, morally

and psychologically, we believe that the approaches to the problems should be primarily on the basis of human values rather than economic value.'[45] It would be 'unthinkable' if their mine was closed, the town of Florence told Rand, an attitude echoed by Glace Bay. All told, if Dosco went ahead with its plans to close three mines, thousands of men would lose their jobs and, together with their families, their homes and their way of life.

Anyone who had the temerity to suggest some hard-headed economic thinking on the problem was singled out for abuse. Dr W.J. Woodfine, an associate professor of economics at St Francis Xavier University, told the annual meeting of the Antigonish Board of Trade in early 1960 that, while assistance had to be provided to miners, their families, and their communities, ongoing coal subsidies and subventions were just bad business. For his trouble, the professor was bitterly attacked for his 'economic theories, *as such*.'[46]

Out west, the coal industry was also taking a beating. In the immediate aftermath of the Second World War, coal miners in Alberta and British Columbia had been confident of their future. Alberta's collieries produced more than 8.5 million tons per year of high-quality coke – a fraction of the 47 billion tons of proven reserves. Likewise, in British Columbia, the industry was, for a time, on a sound footing. There were flourishing coal communities in the Crowsnest Pass through the Rocky Mountains, along and around the foothills, and over the plains. But almost overnight, the hard times – and ghost towns – arrived because of the discoveries of oil at Leduc. Consumers switched to less expensive, more versatile petroleum and natural gas. As in the east, the railways dieselized and industries switched from coal to oil, propane, or natural gas. The coal market collapsed, along with the communities built on and around it.

Drumheller, Alberta, for example, was a one-industry coal town – and now it demanded subsidies to keep it operating. Rand asked the mayor, E.A. Toschach, what percentage of the city's residents had switched from coal to the locally abundant and inexpensive natural gas. 'I must admit,' the mayor replied, 'that I am the only one still using coal' – and that, probably, was 'the reason I was elected as mayor.'[47] As Rand travelled west, he was constantly asked to tide the mining communities over until the price of petroleum peaked, and then the market for coal would come back. How long would that take? he asked. The Coal Operators Association of Western Alberta estimated that natural gas production would pass its peak around 1980, but Alberta's deputy minister of mines and minerals suggested sixty years into the future. To be sure, there were huge proven reserves – British Columbia and Alberta shared about 75 per cent of all the known coal in Canada – but no one wanted it any more. That did not stop appeals for subventions and the promotion of ideas that had clearly not been thought through. Some western producers suggested opening up central Canadian markets to their coal by transporting it in a pipeline – by suspending fine coal particles in oil, pushing the mixture through the pipeline, and extracting the particles at the destination point.

In Edmonton, the deputy minister of mines called for federal cash to support the industry. Would the province contribute? Rand asked, noting that Alberta was extending very favourable terms to the blossoming oil and gas industry. No, that was different, the bureaucrat responded – and, in any case, why should one province pick up the check while, in all the others, the federal government would treat? There was something to that.

In Estevan, Saskatchewan, a community that had once depended almost entirely on coal, oil and gas now occupied primacy of place. Saskatchewan coal producers, nevertheless, called on Rand to recommend help for the coal industry despite the fact that not a single provincial government building used coal as fuel, and the province itself did nothing to succour the industry. On what ground, Rand asked C.M. Thomson, the vice-president of the Manitoba and Saskatchewan Coal Company, would government intervention in the coal industry be justified? But before he could reply, Rand supplied the answer: 'It would probably depend on the economic disturbance that might result in the community.'[48] But, if a provincial government with the means did nothing to alleviate the suffering, why should the federal authority?

Western coal, like that in the East, was already subsidized, but, again, the federal subventions were not sufficient to prop the industry up as the domestic markets disappeared. There was one difference, however: western coal had a potential overseas market in Japan. Japanese coal had to be blended with superior coke for its blast furnaces, and much of that now came from the United States. If high-quality western Canadian coking coal could be subsidized to make it competitive with existing suppliers, it might find a market. And that meant a federal subvention of $4.50 a ton.

To put it simply, Canadian taxpayers would have to subsidize Canadian coal for the benefit of the Japanese, who would then make things with it that were sold back to the people who had contributed to its cost. Complicating matters further was the fact that, in this high-tariff era, the Japanese found it difficult to sell their goods in Canada, so had trouble coming up with the Canadian dollars to buy the Canadian coal. It probably all made sense to the politicians, civil servants, and economists in Ottawa: as federal Finance Minister Flemming, the former premier of New Brunswick who had joined the Diefenbaker government, told the House of Commons, without the subsidy, the Japanese 'would not buy.'[49] That meant the Canadian people would have to pay.

By the middle of April 1960, the commission had completed its hearings and was no closer to arriving at a long-term solution than when it began its work. Grasping at straws, Rand made a plea for 'new ideas.' It was just more of the same everywhere he went: pleas by the producers, their employees, and their unions for additional federal cash to support an industry and a way of life. 'There certainly is a dearth of ideas on this subject,' he complained to a Halifax audience.[50]

For months, Rand and his colleagues had crisscrossed the country, visiting communities, listening to testimony, and talking to people, searching for an answer to an insoluble problem. Now it was time for him to write his report, and he settled in at his cottage in Shediac to do just that. It took more than four months, working eighteen-hour days, to write the 127-page report.[51] Dr Cameron provided Rand with the costings he needed as he reconceived the subsidies, and Pettigrove was always ready to discuss direction and approach. One day when they were eating lunch, the telephone rang. 'Mrs Rand answered the phone, turned to I.C., and said, "That is a long-distance call for Mr. Justice Rand,"' Pettigrove recalled. 'While Rand was on the phone, I told Mrs Rand about the various witnesses calling him Honourable Justice, My Lord, Your Honour, etc. etc., and that I had asked him if he would mind if I called him God. Mrs Rand replied rather pointedly, "Well, Horace, to tell the truth, I think that is what he would like to be called in his own home." At that stage, I think Mrs Rand was getting a bit fed up with his eighteen hours a day on his report.'[52] By the end of August, the work was done.

Not only was the coal industry in 'dire straits,' Rand observed at the outset, 'it has, in fact, been in that condition for some years.' Without a doubt, the 'simplest and most effective mode of dealing with the problem' was to allow market forces to govern: the 'weaker competitor ...

left to his fate.' That was the American model. But it was not the Canadian way. Economics must be 'harmonized' with national unity. The well was not unlimited, but it had not yet run dry, for the price paid to date was merely a 'small item in the general national ledger.'[53]

Without federal aid, all Cape Breton's mines would close – leading to a predictable outcome. 'Should we then allow disaster to take its course or should we resort to efforts to try to salvage, in part at least, existing social and political values? In the latter case, what are the considerations on the basis of which action can be taken and to what extent can that action be fairly justified?'[54] Put another way, if 'ruthlessness, a relatively easy solution, is not to be followed, what measures are legitimately available?' That was the fundamental question that preoccupied Rand in his report.

The centres of supply were far from market, and the costs of production made the supply uneconomic. 'These are the elements in the Canadian situation which have given rise to the coal "problem" and have led to such extravagances in assistance. They demonstrate the futility of crying for a "National Coal Policy," in the sense of rational measures founded on ordinary business considerations.' The discovery of oil in the West, and its increasing import from overseas in the East, had fundamentally changed patterns of energy consumption. Eastern coal was so threatened by overseas oil that Maritime coal producers could not only expect to lose the limited central Canadian market they had managed to retain but were about to lose their local, natural market too. The 'conclusion to which the Commission is driven is that, to avoid a grave social disruption, assistance must be continued, and its nature and justification become the principal purpose of the enquiry.'[55] In expanding on this finding, Rand set out a comprehensive and well-argued justification for the transfer-payment state.

Assistance was, he believed, a national obligation: The Fathers of Confederation had envisioned a 'Canadian nation of free men and women with all sections of its land and people bound together by a community of interest and sacrifice ... evolving a wholesome ethos and enjoying, so far as reasonable measures could effect it, a substantially uniform level of material prosperity.' True, he continued, the provinces possessed jurisdiction over natural resources, but they obtained that jurisdiction from Canada for the benefit of all Canadians: 'The great iron deposits in Northern Quebec, by whom were they conferred on that Province? By the rest of Canada under whose absolute jurisdiction they remained until 1912; and Ontario's northern extension? and the carving out of the new provinces of Alberta and Saskatchewan extending northerly to the 60th degree of north latitude, embracing within that area the wealth a part of which is now embarrassing the Eastern coal operators and threatening to send its miners to walk the street? ... They, as all the others, are to be administered as wealth vested ultimately in a single Crown for the welfare and progress of the Canadian nation. That basic assumption, even though not at all times clearly articulated or even appreciated, has determined the broad measures of parliamentary policy of the past and has been the vital factor in creating a sense of national identity and solidarity.'

Nova Scotia and New Brunswick had no territorial ambitions, but their role in creating Canada was decisive; 'without them there could not have been the Canada we now know; and although plagued ... with geographical and economic trammels, they are not now to be relegated to the status of poor relations.' The cheque was not blank, however. Rand knew there were limits: 'What is called for must satisfy the sense of rational measure and balance. So far as possible each province must bring its capabilities into action and restrict national action to measures which it is not itself able alone to undertake.' Where, then, to draw the line? 'If assistance to any interest can be applied to a more permanent or effective purpose than one proposed, good sense dictates a change; and good sense will detect equally well when the boundary of acceptable policy has been reached.' Rand was now ready to apply that good sense. 'A minimum of difficulty attends the reaching of conclusions on the Western coal situation; the serious condition is that of the East and, in particular, the Sydney district.'

Saving established communities was one thing. However, it would be 'absurd,' Rand wrote, to maintain, without other action, a subsidy of over $13 million a year. That was obvious when one considered what that money could bring about if put to different purposes. 'What is there now of permanent sources of new productive wealth from the $100 million paid out over the last 30 years?' The answer was nothing. According to Rand's report, over $200 million had been funnelled from the federal treasury over the years to support the Canadian coal industry – $135 million in transportation subventions alone, mostly to the benefit of Cape Breton. No one on the island could justifiably 'complain of a lack of sympathetic appreciation on the part of the Dominion government,'[56] he wrote. One could, however, question whether the money had been spent wisely.

There were some unusual observations – at least for a royal commission report. 'Personalities' were described, with cameo snapshots of the leading figures, replete with Rand's assessment of their character. Harold M. Gordon, Dosco's vice-president of mining, was 'strong-minded and able,' but some of his 'judgments and attitudes' were not 'sound.' Frank Doxey, the Dosco general manager, was of 'a liberal and flexible intelligence.' Union leader Bull Marsh was 'neither arrogant, insolent, supercilious nor cynical.'[57] About the miners, however, Rand pulled no punches. There was a history of labour strife, passed down through the generations, the emotional embers of which were fanned by 'ignorant' albeit 'influential persons.' It was time for the miners to realize that they needed Dosco more than Dosco needed them. There were annual deficits in the millions and huge loans to repay. Moreover, no dividend had been paid on preferred shares since 1952, and no dividend on common shares since 1922. 'To hand down as an heirloom this mental complex of bitterness and suspicion is to defeat the means of succoring the mining communities now facing formidable difficulties.' With the constant apprehension of mine closings, Cape Breton suffered from 'an ingrown outlook and a degree of social blight which, if not arrested, will steadily grow into social decay.'

The union clearly had a job to do – and Rand accepted that some but not all of its criticisms were fair. 'One complaint, that the operating costs of individual collieries are never made public, appears to be justified.' The company's response that making the information public would undermine its competitive position was laughable. 'The annual statements of the Dominion Coal Company, read with the annual reports of the Dominion Coal Board setting forth the total subventions paid to provincial groups, are sufficient to give, today, the most dull-witted competitor most of whatever information he might desire.' The union must, however, radically change its approach. Union politicians, used to taking a tough line with management to secure electoral success, had to appreciate that this attitude was not true leadership. 'The hope for betterment in these relations is pursuit of the course of extending trust, of co-operating in mining direction, and in meeting operational issues as matters to be adjusted by rational discussion, not by infuriating exclusiveness. By this means, controversies will be aired around a table, and the mining policies will cease to furnish the material of uninformed public clamour.' The union, Rand continued, 'had to concede "that management is vital." Consultations of the kind he recommended should eliminate general community criticism in which vociferous denunciation becomes effective only as pablum for headlines.'

Reorienting labour-management relations was part of the cure, but there was more that had to be done to replace the prevailing 'atmosphere of gloom and apprehension with one of hope and aspiration.' Canada must, Rand wrote, working with Nova Scotia, provide conditions to allow Cape Breton to regain its confidence and affirm its will to a 'new vitality' – and he went on to outline the practical steps to be taken. 'Direct assistance to the mining works is the first and obvious one: what has been done for the past 32 years must, in some degree, be continued, for how long, however, no one can say.' It was clear to Rand, however, having carefully reviewed the decades of transportation subventions – at times providing as much as $9 per ton to support the movement of Maritime coal to central Canada, where it could 'compete' with American imports – that they had not worked. 'I am unable to agree that this method has been successful or should be followed in the future.' Instead, he proposed something new: time-limited basic and social subsidies.

Continuing federal expenditure was justified for a number of reasons. There were 'international tensions' – the Cold War was well under way, with no end in sight – and closing mines could put Canada at risk. There was a continuing domestic demand for coal for making steel – and it would only increase. These reasons alone supported maintaining 'at least skeletal operations.' For these purposes, Rand recommended a 'basic subsidy' to be paid for each ton of coal produced. The amounts would vary, depending on what kind of coal and where it was mined.

Rand's justification for supporting the industry in Atlantic Canada went well beyond contingency planning in the case of another war or the even less likely scenario of export restrictions on American coke. The risks involved in mining were obvious, Rand acknowledged – to those who put up their capital and their labour. 'It may be urged that in these extractive industries from the beginning, the parties see a limited working life ahead of them; that the risks involved are patent and that all concerned should be held to their natural consequences.' Rand, however, rejected that view: 'When the conditions are such that indefiniteness in time, reaching virtually to permanence, is attributed to the working of such resources, the element of temporariness disappears and the foundations [are] laid as if for good.' Government aid had gone on for so long that it just would not be right to change the rules of the game. A 'social subsidy' was therefore proposed to conserve 'for future use the economic values of the local population which have grown up dependent on the mining industry.' Wholesale unemployment and the abandonment of homes, businesses, and public buildings was, Rand said, too 'tragic to contemplate.'

'Nothing has been found to be more difficult than to attempt a large-scale uprooting of long-settled home life. Younger men may heed the call of distant scenes, and are adaptable to new surroundings; and in communities where family roots are not deep, movement and change are normal.' The conditions in Cape Breton and the other mining communities of Nova Scotia, however, were exceptional. 'How can it be looked upon as acceptable to see men of all ranks easily abandon the slow and modest accumulation of years? How can they contemplate the disappearance of all those values and, with nothing but a past experience, set out to re-establish themselves within the rigidities of settled interests and relations?' How, Rand asked, could a country with the wealth of Canada 'tolerate, as a normal fixture of our industrial life, the conditions now publicly described as existing in parts of West Virginia?' Nova Scotia miners were awaiting work: 'the merchants, professional men and skilled and unskilled workers ... are awaiting and hoping.' It was the government's job to look after all these men, women, and children, and the communities they had built, a least for a while longer. If there was to be disruption, it had to be graduated.

'It is scarcely arguable, assuming that society may be under an obligation to furnish opportunity to work, that the individual worker is entitled to dictate the place, kind and terms of work: the beneficiary of social decency as a principle of action, is primarily obligated to make the fullest effort of which he is capable toward adjustment in situations for which the underlying and operating forces of our civilization are alone responsible.' Under different forms of government, the state, Rand observed, compelled action and obedience: 'workers are told what they are to do and where, and that is the end of it.' Canada was different. 'Steadily permeating our society ... is the conception of reasonableness, and it is appropriate to the socio-economic field as to the political ... arbitrary dictation will not be accepted whether attempted by so-called "capital" or "labour," nor between government and individual. In this interim difficulty of an industry, then, we cannot do better than attempt to apply a rule which can be brought empirically within general application' – the social subsidy.

It was expensive, and it came with a series of complicated rules: $2 per ton on all Nova Scotia sales for consumption in the Atlantic provinces and the eastern part of Quebec, and larger amounts for coal shipped to the rest of Quebec and Ontario. (A substantially smaller social subsidy was recommended for New Brunswick coal.) As the subsidies for coal sold out of region were less than currently available under the transportation subvention regime, Rand expected that those sales, and those subsidies, would dry up and the industry would focus on the local market. He recommended that both subsidies be put into place for ten years and that expenditures, in the overall, not exceed existing allocations. More than $135 million had been spent supporting the industry with transportation subventions since 1929 – $15 million in the last year alone. That money would now be given to the collieries to defray the cost of business, to support the local industry and the communities dependent on it – businesses that, without the handout, would fail.

'The main object is to assist coal production to a better competitive position in its own market.' Rand's idea was that, by eliminating the transportation subvention, the main source of public money, and paying the collieries directly, they would concentrate on local and regional markets instead of on uncompetitive declining markets half a continent away.[58] Moreover, Rand believed, his plan would give affected communities a 'breathing space to examine their position.' There was no hope that the mines would ever operate at a profit, and Rand warned the unions to keep that in mind and to moderate their wage demands.[59] 'To send fuel, at the general government's expense, a thousand miles for consumption for purposes which are present locally but are served by foreign fuel, appears to be an ultimate in absurdity.' That was true, but it was not clear how giving collieries money to offset production costs would create, or even maintain, local markets in the face of a global shift in the industrial world to oil and gas. Rand knew that American coal could be landed anywhere in Atlantic Canada for less than the home-grown variety, and his report was replete with the numbers demonstrating the huge difference in output per miner per day achieved in the United States compared to Canada. Rand understood that consumers everywhere preferred oil and gas.

Social subsidy expenditures were justified in the Maritimes – in part, Rand concluded, because governmental action was the cause of much of the suffering. Accordingly, 'the repair of that injury must, in special situations, be made a general charge.' The government had been subsidizing the industry for decades, and it should not be allowed suddenly to change course. Moreover, Cape Bretoners were the victims of government action: 'To put it concretely, the building of a necessary link in a gas pipeline across Northern Ontario has made miners in Cape Breton and other sections idle, for which compensating action should be taken. Although this consideration can easily be carried too far ... it cannot be refused any recognition whatever.' Which industry, Rand asked, was deserving of protection? 'The industry that has run wild in the urgency of immediate exploitation' – the oil and gas industry – 'or the existing industry acting within legitimate functions?' Obviously, the existing industry was deserving of 'counterbalancing action' to 'preserve in some degree existing structures.' Rand therefore decided that money for Nova Scotia and New Brunswick was justified, but not for the West.

British Columbia, Alberta, and Saskatchewan were, he said, the main sources of Canadian oil and gas. 'It is these new fuels which are now responsible in greatest measure for the difficulties of their own coal reserves ... In this situation, should the Dominion then undertake to succour, in the interests of possible minor social dislocations, a provincial resource the difficulties of which are the direct and foreseen results of provincial action?' Astutely, Rand appreciated a difference in outlook. In the West, coal was viewed like any other fuel. 'Its position must be left to its inherent strength, and if that is not sufficient to enable it to continue competitively, then it must go the way of all weaklings and yield to its competitors.' There was some unemployment in the West – and in Alberta, provincial aid was provided to enable displaced miners to move to places where there were jobs. The same was not true in British Columbia, a province with an increasing population of 'persons seeking livelihood in an inviting and salubrious climate.'[60] Besides, Rand observed, 'it is of no force to object to it on the score of interference with the "natural workings" of private enterprise; the latter has become the beneficiary of special governmental action injurious to others.'[61] Accordingly, Rand recommended that the existing subventions on the export of coal to Japan be terminated.

Rand was reluctant to predict the future, although the subsidies he suggested were to have a shelf life of only ten years before they were re-examined. It was possible, he conceded, that sooner rather than later, existing markets for coal – such as they were – might disappear. 'It is because of that possibility that the need exists, especially in Cape Breton, to build up alternative means of productive wealth.' While the

subsidies would maintain the industry, they were only part of the solution. 'A single extractive industry, by its nature, is not a desirable
economic base for a community, and in coal there are incidental ac-
companiments that render it more undesirable than others. For the
Sydney–Glace Bay–Louisbourg district, alternative and supporting
economic and cultural activities must be considered, a scheme adequate to introduce new wealth into Cape Breton and bring fresh and
heightened scenes and an elevation of mind and spirit to its people.'
On this score, Rand had some ideas.

To begin, tourism. 'The Island, without excessive cost, can be so exhibited and revealed as to bring to its people that new outlook and
spirit, as well as economic betterment.' Cape Breton is a beautiful
place, and the island's natural beauty should be exploited. 'Carefully
planned, and with money carefully spent, Cape Breton could become
not just the "western heath of the Scottish people," but a national treasure to be shared among Canadians and with the world.' Equally impressive, and ripe for exploitation, were the historical relics of man's
work. 'Mouldering on the southeastern coast of the island is a mute
reminder of the wastage of time. Here is the scene of one of the striking
events in the historical course of things that has led to the Canada of
today. In the early part of the 18th century began the work of building
the strongest fortification then existing on the Atlantic Coast of North
America and of establishing a community bringing to the New World
the architecture, traditions and culture of the French people at the direction of the most polished court of continental Europe … the Fortress
of Louisbourg.' It should, Rand recommended, be reconstructed. To
round out the picture, Rand called for the establishment of a vocational school in Cape Breton. The sons and daughters of Cape Breton
might never be able to find good jobs at home, he acknowledged, but
with proper training, they would have the opportunity to 'expand
their roles throughout the land.' Of all the recommendations in the
report, these last two, given very little elaboration, were prescient.

Rand handed his report in at the end of August 1960. Diefenbaker announced that his government intended to study it before releasing it to
the public. There were significant expectations. Three mines with thousands of jobs stood in the immediate balance, while a community and
an entire industry were looking to Rand for salvation. At least, that is
the way the newspapers made it appear: 'The report,' the *Cape Breton*

Post wrote, 'which has been anxiously awaited by the industry, union and government, is expected to offer some proposals aimed at putting the faltering coal mines on a better financial footing.'[62]

While Rand was working on his report, Bathurst Pulp & Paper, New Brunswick's second-largest coal consumer, quietly announced that it would be switching to oil in the interests of 'more efficient production.' The company had used about 100,000 tons of coal a year – 90 per cent from New Brunswick's Minto fields – but its new energy source was the Irving oil refinery in Saint John, to the tune of just under 18 million gallons annually. And there was more bad news on the horizon. New Brunswick's largest coal purchaser, the New Brunswick Electric Power Commission, would soon announce that it, too, had signed up with Irving Oil for its new $10 million thermal plant in East Saint John, conveniently located close to the Irving refinery. The utility estimated that it would save $250,000 a year by making the change.[63] Overnight, the two biggest markets for coal in the province were gone – but that did not stop the provincial government from giving $1 million to one New Brunswick coal producer to purchase a giant coal-digging machine.[64] In Montreal, Canada Cement, the city's biggest coal consumer, announced its switch to gas. Meanwhile, Dosco mothballed two of its coal carriers because there were no customers for their cargo.

In early August 1960 Stelco in Hamilton announced it was studying the introduction of natural gas. Its findings were conclusive, and coal shipments soon stopped. Later that month, its arch-rival, Dofasco, opened a new $10 million furnace, the first blast furnace in the world equipped to use oil or natural gas in addition to coke. The trend was international and irreversible. In West Germany, for instance, mine closures had, in just a few years, cost 96,000 jobs – but the coal industry was located in the heavily industrialized Ruhr area, and most of the miners were able to obtain alternative employment. (Rand had wanted to send Horace Pettigrove to the Ruhr Valley and Wales to see what he could find out, but he had refused. 'Justice Rand,' he replied, 'I am not going.' The coal commission staff could not believe that anyone had the temerity to say no.)[65] Cape Breton had no such alternative to offer, but expectations there were unrealistically high about what could and should be done to save the industry. When the report was released in late September, reaction on the island was harsh.

It was a 'sell-out,' according to the partisan left-wing *Atlantic Advocate*. Cape Breton miners supported Ontario and Quebec manufacturers by buying their goods instead of less expensive American products kept out of the country by higher customs tariffs. Central Canadians, the *Advocate* argued, should subsidize Cape Breton miners. Dosco, seeing things differently, announced that it planned to go ahead and close the three previously targeted uneconomical mines. 'They can't do it,' Bull Marsh responded, calling for the government to 'nationalize' the money pits and expressing outrage that jobs and lives would be sacrificed on 'the altar of a high production and low cost operation.' Marsh was representing his members, and they had elected him for that job. However, he had clearly not taken heed of Rand's admonition that Dosco would be better off without its coal operations. Any suggestion that Dosco management had not struggled to preserve its collieries was, Rand wrote, 'contrary to the facts.' Dosco had a duty to its shareholders and, having kept uneconomical mines open longer than they should have been, it closed them now. That left only five Dosco mines operating on the island and one on the mainland.[66]

Nowhere was Rand more heavily criticized than in his native New Brunswick. Even though, by at least one costing, the subsidies he proposed for New Brunswick coal would have almost doubled the return to Minto producers, the New Brunswick Coal Producers Association denounced Rand and his report for giving Nova Scotia too much – so much, in fact, that New Brunswick's coal would, it claimed, no longer be able to compete on price in New Brunswick or anywhere else. 'Rand report threatens existence of industry,' ran the headlines in the *Fredericton Gleaner*, adding that Rand's report was a 'deadly threat.' Miners and coal operators, the paper argued, should 'band themselves together to fight with all their might against the most irresponsible and dangerous proposals that were ever advanced in a Royal Commission Report.'[67]

When D.W. Gallagher, New Brunswick's economic adviser, wrote to Rand purportedly to demonstrate that the subsidy differential would detrimentally affect New Brunswick's producers, Rand invited him to Western's law school, where, 'in confidence,' he would show him 'some aspects of this matter which are not generally known.'[68] New Brunswick coal was strip-mined and, as such, it could be extracted at a fraction of the cost of Nova Scotia's coal. 'As you will understand,' Rand wrote, 'these subsidies are not for the purpose of enabling coal-mining companies to maintain normal profits. This money is being contributed to keep alive both the industry and the social organizations that have accompanied it, which in New Brunswick are not very extensive.'[69] Rand also provided a principled explanation for ending transportation subventions: 'A flat subsidy has this merit, that it tends to induce sale in the nearest market. This, as you see, is supplemented by a similar subsidy on production. On the other hand, there is no variation of profit in the case of transportation subsidy, the subvention goes to the carrier and the market is stretched out farther and farther in the area of its sale to the sole benefit of the carriers.'[70]

This point was critical in assessing the different subsidy rates recommended for Nova Scotia and New Brunswick. Special pleading aside, New Brunswick had not been ignored: its producers were in line for cash grants of 70 cents for stripped coal and $1 per ton for underground-mine coal. Together with a transportation advantage of nearly 500 kilometres, it was hard to see how New Brunswick was being discriminated against. 'The amounts fixed by me were considered to be ample to meet any coal competition and any local oil competition,' Rand responded.[71] Indeed, if the subsidies were not 'sufficient to enable a coal competition within New Brunswick of New Brunswick production, there must be something wrong with the Sales Department of the New Brunswick mines.'[72] Rand was extremely annoyed at the rejection of his recommendations by the Minto operators. It demonstrated, he wrote to Pettigrove, their 'level of intelligence.' They were, he concluded, 'idiotic.'[73]

At the other end of the spectrum, the *Financial Post* described the report as 'a heroically realistic view of a complex problem.'[74] The *Globe and Mail* was generally approving, even endorsing Rand's proposal for social subsidies: 'If such a subsidy is needed it must, of course, be paid. Canada cannot sit by while men go without work, and their families without food, through no fault of their own. However, it should be borne in mind that a subsidy of the kind which develops nothing, which builds nothing, is only a temporary expedient. It is neither prophylactic nor therapeutic; it prevents nothing, neither does it cure.'[75] That was not quite right: subsidies and subventions are like narcotics and, as the Cape Breton experience established, they are highly addictive. There was simply no point in building an export industry significantly dependent on federal funds. Cape Breton proved that years of government subsidies and subventions, even if well meaning, were evil. They created a dependency that was, over time, transformed into an entitlement. There was nothing to show for the investment of hundreds of millions of dollars – no new sources of wealth, no bright future for Cape Bretoners and their children, nothing but a kind of welfare that corrupted the soul. Governments play an important role in regional economic expansion, but that does not mean prolonging industries and activities that are economically unjustifiable, particularly when the government resources themselves are limited and priorities have to be chosen.

There was something very Canadian and admirable about Rand's approach: it was a targeted expression of an essential Canadian characteristic expressed years earlier in the 1940 Report of the Royal Commission on Dominion-Provincial Relations. In the preamble to its recommendations, that report had observed that the economies of all the provinces had been interlinked and mutually dependent since Confederation, but that a large part of the surplus was concentrated in a few specially favoured areas. However, Canada was founded on the principle of provincial interdependence. Accordingly, no part of the country could detach itself and prosper in isolation from the rest. It was, therefore, axiomatic that if one part of the country was in trouble – and Cape Breton had been for years – the other parts would help.[76]

What Rand sought through the basic subsidy was to maintain the coal industry, at least skeletally, in the national interest. The objectives of the social subsidy were broader: to make it possible for a good number of miners to remain on their jobs and live out their lives in their established communities. Life would go on as it always had, but with new sources of livelihood evolving to replace old ones, which would be reduced on a graduated and humane scale. Diversification was a key part of the answer to the problem. New industries had to be established, burning home-mined coal. But, as Rand wrote in a private letter to Father Hogan, that particular goal would be difficult to achieve, given 'the innate situation of the island: its distance from large markets, the absence of a variety of natural resources and, among other things, the unfortunate reputation for labour which Sydney district seems to have acquired.'[77] The real solution was reflected in Rand's call for increased vocational training, including establishing a school where the children of miners could learn real skills for real jobs – jobs with a future.

Arguably, Rand's report was the first break between the old regime and a new one. The measures he proposed were not drastic but moderate and digestible. They opened a window to a different way of looking at the problem. Rand rejected the simple solution of letting market forces take their natural course. Rather, he recommended time-limited and focused intervention to ease the pain of transition. While subsidies continued as the main medicine, for the first time a plan was attached to the money. The number of miners would be reduced by attrition. Production would meet local demand and, possibly, spur local development. As a result, displacement, disorder, and disaster would be avoided. Implicit in Rand's proposal was the orderly decommissioning of certain mines – Rand knew that three Dosco mines would soon be shut, throwing thousands out of work – along with appropriate transitional arrangements for displaced workers and their communities.

The social subsidy recommendation stood in marked contrast to that earlier, more controversial recommendation by the Royal Commission on Canada's Economic Prospects that miners be encouraged, through subsidized transportation and other means, to leave town. Now Walter Gordon approved of Rand's solution. 'You have come up with an imaginative set of proposals,' he wrote to Rand. 'It is a courageous report and an honest one ... I really do think you have made a great contribution towards some sort of settlement, or at least alleviation, of this perplexing situation.'[78] Rand's recommendations for social subsidies by the federal government in support of depressed provincial areas, *Saturday Night* magazine observed, 'represent a new concept of social planning for national unity in Canada.'[79]

Wholesale unemployment, abandonment of homes, stores, schools, churches, offices, hospitals, businesses – the organized apparatus, such as it was, of a society and civilization – were too tragic to contemplate for someone like Rand, who was not a businessman more attuned to the bottom line. If disruption was inevitable, it should be gradual, and that is exactly what he suggested. Some mines would be kept open and, he hoped, be profitable through measures designed to improve coal's competitive position in its natural markets. Parallel measures – improving tourism, restoring Louisbourg, encouraging industry, establishing a vocational and technical school – would begin to reorient Cape Bretoners from their established way of life to a new way of living. Rand could have called for federal money to build and attract new industries to Cape Breton. Wisely, he did not. What industries could realistically be established in Cape Breton and other Maritime coal-mining regions, given their limited resources and distance from the central Canadian markets?

Rand also displayed a keen understanding of the role that the federal government could and should play in promoting national unity. After all, Ottawa did what had to be done to facilitate construction of a trans-Canada pipeline, bringing natural gas to the country's industrial heartland. The clock could not be turned back, and many miners had lost their livelihoods because of this pipeline sooner than would otherwise have happened. Surely, Rand argued, the building of this pipeline bolstered the case for 'compensating action.' Everyone who needed it got money as part of the Confederation compact.

The 'literary quality' of the report presented some challenges. It had no real organization and no headings, and many sentences and turns of phrase required careful reading. It jumped from one idea to another and was marred by many typographical errors. As the Dominion Coal Board pointed out, 'Various of the Report's sentences and paragraphs required the most intensive kind of study.'[80] Overall, though, the Halifax *Chronicle-Herald* editorialized that Rand 'displayed special considerations for human values in a changing society,'[81] and the prime minister called it 'the best report that could be made.' That did not mean, of course, that Diefenbaker would do anything about it.

The Rand Report was a 'complex document,' Minister of Mines Paul Comtois told the House of Commons in November, adding that it 'required the most serious study.'[82] Accordingly, an interdepartmental committee on coal was put in charge of that task. True, the government had a lot on its plate, but it was clearly trying to buy some time as it figured out what, if anything, to do with Rand's recommendations. Rand and Pettigrove recognized the delay for what it was.[83]

The interdepartmental committee agreed with Rand that coal was likely to continue to decline and that, in these circumstances, there was no economic justification for supporting the Maritime coal industry. It also had no difficulty in concluding that 'the large expenditures have accomplished little except the temporary maintenance of incomes.' Indeed, instead of being part of the solution, federal funds were part of the problem, leading to 'the creation of amenities, such as schools, hospitals, and homes, which has increased the problem of social immobility.' Accordingly, the committee concluded 'that to continue the present policy would be ... both futile and harmful. The continuance of this aid combined with the inevitable decline of the industry would aggravate the very difficult problems of social readjustment.'[84] So far, so good.

The committee decided that Rand's key recommendations – a basic subsidy for all producers and, in the Maritimes, a per ton social subsidy – while undoubtedly well intentioned, would not deal with the problem in any lasting way. More drastic measures were required.[85]

It recommended, therefore, that the subsidies, which it agreed should be directed to producers, be reduced annually and terminated within a decade. Market conditions would dictate the amount of coal production that remained when the subsidies came to an end. On the other side of the ledger, plans had to be put in place for the 'rehabilitation' of workers released from the mines. Here, too, the committee distanced itself from Rand's report: 'To absorb the workers in other occupations, and to alleviate the resultant social disruption, well-conceived measures, going beyond the proposals of the Royal Commission, must be implemented.' This conclusion was correct. The only problem was that the committee members had no new ideas, so they reverted to age-old platitudes about early retirements, retraining, and tourist development.

On the western coal industry, the committee took an even stronger line. There was, it asserted, no economic justification for any federal aid for any western producer. The western coal industry – including the shipments of metallurgical coal to Japan – was neither vital nor necessary to the economy. With one big exception, western Canadian miners could be and were being absorbed into other occupations with little or no disruption. In the Crowsnest Pass – the mountainous region between Alberta and British Columbia – alternative employment was less accessible. If public money was to be spent, it was much better to spend it on relocation and other forms of social assistance than on maintaining an uneconomic industry, particularly where there was accessible alternative employment elsewhere in the province.

Rand, like the good social scientist he had become, had recommended 'research' into new uses and applications for coal. That recommendation was considered by the interdepartmental committee in a special report. Desirable though it might be – and the committee had some ideas about where money could be spent – solving 'the problem' required direct and urgent schemes, not 'increases in competitive ability effected by engineering research.'[86] That decision was short-sighted, given the minuscule results Canada had to show for the hundreds of millions of dollars spent to that point.

Economic laws do not operate according to the parliamentary calendar, and imports of residual oil not only continued but increased, rising from 2.7 million barrels in 1958 to 7.4 million in 1960, the year Rand issued his report. The numbers were heading in one direction and, as was reported to the Cabinet Committee on Coal in February 1962, the immediate impact was further erosion of the remaining coal market. Among the options the committee considered was extending federal financial assistance to make coal competitive, not just with American imports but also with fossil fuels. When the full Cabinet discussed the issue in late February 1962, Jacques Flynn, the minister of mines and technical surveys (and chair of the Cabinet Committee on Coal), recommended that 'something be done.' He meant money, of course, and Hugh Flemming observed that it would be ironic to 'subsidize Maritimers to buy their own coal.'[87] That had never been his public position when, as premier of New Brunswick, he held his hand out for federal largesse with as much enthusiasm as the rest of the Maritime premiers.

The interdepartmental committee took its time to make its views known, and the Cabinet committee took longer still to consider them and decide what to do. In the House of Commons, opposition MPs regularly demanded to know when the government was going to take action and implement Rand's recommendations. The answer, when Diefenbaker finally gave it, appeared to be never. Apart from Rand's bold suggestion to restore the fortress at Louisbourg – and that particular recommendation would be implemented at great cost but to universal acclaim, with many ex-miners employed to assist – the other recommendations were non-starters. All Diefenbaker would say was that the problems of the coal industry were continuing to receive careful study. 'I think I would not be transgressing,' he told the House, 'if I said that examination of the recommendations did not convince the government that they would meet the overall problem over a period of years.'[88] What that meant, of course, was maintaining the status quo, as Cape Breton mine closures were delayed and ever-increasing funds allocated for both eastern and western coal. Eventually, the mines minister admitted that Rand's report had been relegated to the dustbin, explaining politely that the government had decided against following his recommendations so as to reserve to itself the flexibility necessary to respond to a fluid market situation.[89]

Would the reprieve for Cape Breton miners continue? Not if Dosco were allowed to have its way. Glace Bay, the company announced in November 1960, was to close first, on 14 January 1961, and Florence and New Waterford at 'a later date.' 'Frankly,' Glace Bay's mayor, Dan MacDonald, said on hearing the news, 'I am shocked.' The union announced it would fight the closure, and in January 1961 Mines Minister Comtois announced yet another reprieve – until the end of May for Glace Bay and until the summer for Florence and New Waterford. 'The Government of Canada,' he said, 'has agreed to pay a subsidy to the Corporation to be applied against the losses which the Company reports as due to the operation of these mines.' The provincial government also agreed to assume part of the cost. That was fine for the short term. For the long term, miners 'must be provided with work at industrial plants located at the pitheads,' H.J. Robichaud, the MP for Gloucester, New Brunswick, demanded in the House of Commons. In the meantime, the government should cover company losses – whatever they were – to the break-even point rather than close down any mines.[90] It took until 1963 for the last of the three mines first scheduled for closure before Rand finished his report to be boarded up.

So it was business as usual, more or less. The Dominion Coal Board encouraged Dosco to seek new markets for its annual production of 4 million tons. Market forces played no part, however, for the operations were unprofitable and the coal had to be sold at a loss – a loss made good, year after year, with public funds. As W.V. Sheppard, the British mining expert, had concluded, even if new money was spent and labour relations and productivity greatly improved, 'coal from the Sydney coalfield can never hope to compete.'[91] Nothing changed. The communities, the company, the employees, and their unions remained conditioned to the status quo instead of facing up to economic reality. But who could blame them? If the people of Canada were willing indefinitely to fund an industry and way of life rather than make hard decisions and take unpopular steps, why stand in the way?

The 1962 federal election reduced Diefenbaker's government to a minority, but this time around the Liberals demonstrated that they had learned some lessons about the way to win Nova Scotia votes. Leader Lester Pearson told Cape Bretoners that coal had a future, supplying power for thermal plants. That was true – but not Cape Breton coal. The election promise was dubious, although there were some signs of regional economic diversification: establishment of a Volvo assembly plant in Halifax was seen as a step in a new direction. Public money was behind it, as it was behind the move of the Clairtone Sound Corporation from Rexdale, Ontario, to Stellarton; a $9 million railway-car order given to a Dosco subsidiary; and a $50 million pulp mill in Abercrombie. Over the years, more industries would follow, but the lure was always the same – public money. In the 1963 general election that brought him to power with a minority government, Pearson called for a 'new agency' to assist disadvantaged areas. Diefenbaker also had his own plan to 'raise living standards.' Both Liberals and Conservatives were promising the same thing: federal funds. Maritime voters responded appropriately, dividing the popular vote and giving the

Conservatives seven and the Liberals five federal seats. Either way, more money from Ottawa was on its way.

In the mid-1960s, coal consumption increased – so much for the economic prognosticators – and both domestic and American coal producers benefited. Ironically, at the same time that demand went up, Cape Breton's ability to meet marketplace requirements went down. Incredibly, in 1964–5, Nova Scotia experienced a coal shortage because of 'operational problems' – old mines with extensive undersea workings in desperate need of rehabilitation and repair.[92] Moreover, the Cape Breton mines were proceeding to ever greater depths, meaning longer distances to haul the coal from the face to the surface, and no money to offset these physical disadvantages with modern machinery. The federal government announced that 'feasibility studies' on the 'rehabilitation of the industry' would be carried out, with 'the possible benefits of such expenditures upon the welfare of the industry and its associated communities ... carefully evaluated.'[93] The private sector had no intention of forwarding the funds, and that meant public money as the only alternative. Dosco was willing to hand over its coal interests to any takers. Its antiquated Sydney steel interests were no prize either: market forces demanded that, to be successful, steel mills must be located close to their customer base.

Productivity had increased through mechanization, but the savings were quickly eaten away by rising operating costs. Besides, there was only so much that could be done. Nova Scotia mines were generally unsuited to the room-and-pillar method used in mining the large seams common in the United States. While Nova Scotia mine operators were trying and, to a considerable extent, succeeding in reducing production costs, so too were their competitors to the south. As a result, the differential between Canadian and American coal continued to expand. In the mid-1960s it cost twice as much, on average, to mine coal that no one wanted in Nova Scotia. By and large, industrial users continued to meet their energy needs much less expensively, even with the various subsidies, with oil and natural gas, or with low-volatility, low-sulphur, inexpensive coal from the United States.[94]

Whatever the solution for Cape Breton was, it was not welfare payments propping up a people and a way of life on the back of an industry that had long been surpassed. The mines had to be phased out in an orderly fashion. Instead, new workers continued to be recruited: up to three hundred a year in the mid-1960s. If Cape Breton had an economic future, it was in the development of a diversified economy, focusing

on tourism – one able to stand on its own feet. There could have been
a difficult but manageable transition process had the miners and their
union leaders faced up to reality. But the various subsidies remained
in place and new ones were introduced, such as an oil equalization
payment that artificially decreased the cost of coal in the Maritimes
to make it competitive with imported oil. By 1965, just five years after
Rand issued his report, the cost to the Canadian public was about $24
million per year, or $3,000 per job. And the numbers were rapidly ris-
ing; in 1966 the federal government threw $31 million at the problem,
and it was still no closer to being fixed. That worked out to $3,500 per
year per miner, in jobs where earnings averaged $5,000.[95] The follow-
ing year, the cost had grown to $3,700.[96] In 1950, by comparison, the
cost to maintain a miner had been just over $100 per year.[97]

By 1965 Dosco wanted out of the business. It announced that its remaining mines had fifteen years of life left. There would be no further
capital expenditures, and the mines would, in a matter of months, be
permanently closed. There was really only one solution – to discontinue Nova Scotia's coal industry. At a Cabinet meeting in June 1963,
the point was repeatedly made by several ministers that subventions
on coal sales to Ontario should be stopped, and money paid only 'to
encourage the use of coal in the Atlantic region.'[98] The one realistic
market for Nova Scotia coal was in Nova Scotia. But Prime Minister·
Pearson was concerned about his earlier election promise and aware
of the 'political difficulties involved.'[99] The government therefore did
what it often does when it has a problem with no easy solution: it appointed yet another commission, headed by James Richardson Donald,
a chemical engineer with extensive private- and public-sector experience. Hearings were held in 1965 and 1966. The problem, Donald
wrote in his report, 'is essentially, the dependence on the Cape Breton
economy and ... that of Nova Scotia on the coal mining industry and
the costs to the federal government of sustaining these operations.'[100]
This conclusion had a familiar ring. But it was even worse than that.

Donald concurred, 'in general,' with what Rand had found and
what he had recommended. It was, he continued, 'regrettable' that
'more positive action' did not follow from Rand's report. 'Through the
Dominion Coal Board, Dosco was encouraged to seek markets to absorb
an annual production of 4 million tons and was assured of the necessary
financial support. The communities, the Company and the employees
had become conditioned to the receipt of federal government support, despite the continued unprofitable nature of the operations. No

incentive existed for either Dosco or the union to take the constructive but drastic approach which the situation demanded.'[101] Donald noted that, had the subsidies not been continued and new ones introduced, the industry would have shut down because 'there would be virtually no market for Nova Scotia coal.'[102] The federal cash was accomplishing one objective: postponing the inevitable.

There were now some seven thousand miners on the island who, according to one Cabinet document, 'could not be placed in employ- ment elsewhere in Cape Breton' should the industry be 'closed out.'[103]. The steelworkers at the Sydney mill would likely face a similar fate. Accordingly, the Cabinet decided to continue investing in the Cape Breton coal industry through indefinite subsidies and subventions, and it even put in its long-term plan the opening a new mine at Lin- gan, where it was believed the coal was readily accessible and could be efficiently mined. These plans were converted to political promises in the 1965 campaign and hailed by Cape Bretoners as a symbol of hope for the long-term survival of their livelihoods and way of life. Unfortu- nately, the promises also sent exactly the wrong message. Almost $100 million had been spent propping up the industry in the five years since Rand issued his report, even though the economic prospects for Cape Breton coal had worsened.

As the Cabinet was informed in April 1966, Cape Breton coal ac- counted for about 3 per cent of the total Canadian reserves. Dosco was in default of loans more than a decade old which it had taken to mechanize and rehabilitate its unprofitable mines. Coal was cur- rently being extracted from workings up to 6.4 kilometres out to sea, at depths approaching 900 metres from the sea bottom. Even with the best mining techniques, the coal was too far out, too expensive, and too unsafe and difficult to extract, particularly when there were attractive, less expensive alternatives. The only thing keeping the industry alive was federal cash spent by politicians who lacked the will to prescribe and then administer bitter medicine. Dosco was suffering on the coal front – badly – and its Sydney Steel Mill was hardly doing any better (ironically, since 1962, it had been using imported American coking coal almost exclusively).

As the Dominion Coal Board noted in its 1967–8 report, Nova Sco- tia's coal-mining industry had continued 'to deteriorate and became even less competitive in the energy markets of the Atlantic Provinces and Central Canada.'[104] The situation was grave and, sadly, familiar. Coal production was down; subvention aid was up. The collieries were old and obsolete. The operators could not make money – only lose it. By 1968, federal funds – never intended to subsidize the entire production and regional economy – were required in the marketing of 86 per cent of Nova Scotia's coal. The industry was in a deep coma. 'In response to this expanding problem,' and following through on one of the recommendations of the Donald Commission, the federal government announced that it had 'taken the logical next step – beyond the subvention policy – by deciding to assume on-site control of the largest mines in Nova Scotia through the establishment of the Cape Breton Development Corporation.'[105] A Crown corporation, almost everyone agreed, especially Dosco, was the logical next step.

The preamble to the legislation said it all: The Sydney coal field had a limited life and, for forty years, had been kept alive thanks to federal financial support. Because no one in the private sector wanted the company, the government decided to buy it – a decision justified in part because Cape Bretoners depended on the mines for their livelihood. But no one should get the wrong idea, the preamble continued. The mines would be reorganized and rationalized, and the Crown corporation, having achieved what the private sector could not, would then withdraw from the field in accordance with 'a plan.' That plan envisaged broadening the island's industrial base.[106] The Cape Breton Development Corporation, Devco, never achieved its stated objectives successfully. As Pettigrove had observed to Rand years earlier, in February 1961, when the Nova Scotia legislature was debating the possible nationalization of the coal mines, it would be an exercise 'in utter futility.'[107]

And so it was that Dosco went out and Devco and a provincial Crown corporation, Sysco, the Sydney Steel Corporation, came in. Devco took over Dosco mines, while Sysco took over the Sydney Steel Mill. Devco had the opportunity to rationalize the industry by eliminating inefficiencies – in lay terms, closing down all the uneconomic mines. It also had the obligation to put into place a realistic plan, one that did not involve perpetual subsidies of an industry whose time had long passed. If the status quo were continued, one Cabinet document predicted, total expenditures over the next fifteen years would amount to $400 million: 'Moreover, the coal problem and the fundamental difficulties of the Cape Breton economy would still remain. Massive new assistance would be required near the end of the period.'[108]

Devco was given the mandate to diversify the Cape Breton econo-

my, and a number of industries were attracted – not by the presence
of either markets or materials but by financing that was not available
anywhere else. Business failures followed. In 1969 the federal government gave Devco another $21 million to cover losses arising out of
the operation of its coal division. Meanwhile, out west, the tough love
worked. With relatively limited and annually declining government
assistance, western coal producers had developed a profitable and
growing market in Japan. The duty on imported coal was removed in
1969. In 1970 the *Coal Production Assistance Act* and the *Canadian Coal
Equality Act* were terminated. The Dominion Coal Board was incorporated into the Department of Energy, Mines and Resources. But more
money was ploughed by Canadian taxpayers via the politicians into
Devco and Sysco. Some of the old mines were modernized, while new
ones were established at Lingan and Phalen, even though the Donald Commission had strongly recommended against opening any new
mines at all. No matter what was tried, however, nothing could be
done to turn the situation around in any long-term meaningful way.

It was not completely irrational. The new mines were opened to
meet renewed demand resulting from the OPEC embargo after the
October 1973 Yom Kippur war. There were actually a few good years
in the deeps. Another generation of Cape Bretoners was promised a
future and enticed back underground. How long will these jobs last?
they all wanted to know. The answer, they were told, was forever.
'Your *kids* will get a pension here. There's unlimited coal.'[109] There was
abundant coal, but there were few pensions, and soon enough these
miners would be left unemployed, in their middle age, beaten up from
years of hard and dangerous work, with little education, limited skills,
nowhere to go, and nothing to do. Devco's 'coal division' lost money –
tens of millions each year right from the start. It had all been predicted,
right down to the last detail. As the Donald Commission reported, 'It
is ethically wrong and economically unsound to be introducing young
people into the mining force where there is no assurance of future employment; where operations are basically unprofitable, and where no
skills useful in other fields of industry except mining are acquired.'[110]

Ultimately, Walter Gordon had got it right. 'It was a realistic recommendation,' Robert Stanfield admitted years later about Gordon's
proposal that miners follow jobs, but it was just not politically feasible:
'There was no political motivation to tell the people the truth.'[111] Rand
was philosophical about it all. Writing privately to Keith Buck, he lamented not just the continuation of the subvention regime but its ex-

pansion. 'This is part of the elaborate welfare state, and no doubt the beneficiaries will be very grateful.'[112] But the real situation was grave. 'Here we are,' he said, 'ten years later, the public treasury millions of dollars poorer through the continuance of subventions, the mines of Nova Scotia thousands of feet deeper, the men who work those mines ten years older, and a whole new generation of young Nova Scotians now entrapped within the industry.' Rand resolved, next time he was appointed a commissioner, to leave the government with little choice but to implement his recommendations: 'In order to be effective he would have to develop more of an advocacy role and in essence argue that effectiveness in a manner which could not be eclipsed by other priorities.'[113] Part of the problem was that Rand's plan was a half-measure when something much more dramatic was required. It was well intentioned and humane, but it allowed Ottawa to vacillate and administer to the people of Cape Breton a death of one thousand cuts.

In 2000 the Nova Scotia government finally washed its hands of the idle and abandoned Sydney Steel Mill. It had cost the taxpayers about $3 billion since 1967.[114] One year later, the last coal mine on Cape Breton Island, the Prince colliery in Point Aconi, 40 kilometres north of Sydney, was closed, throwing the last three hundred coal miners on the island out of work and onto the unemployment rolls. It was, one of the miners told *Maclean's* magazine, 'the worst hellhole anyone could ever work in.' Almost every single miner was scared by it: 'Missing fingers, ruined backs, worn-out knees – few seem to have emerged from the mines entirely in one piece. Everyone, even the nonsmokers, constantly hack and cough, their lungs ravaged by decades of inhaling coal dust.'[115] 'We are shocked and disappointed,' the administrator of the United Mine Workers announced, adding, 'We thought this day might come, but we didn't expect it to come with so little warning.'[116] Devco began the process of winding up.

Supporting Cape Breton's coal mines had, since 1967, cost $1.6 billion and resulted, for the most part, in myriad lost opportunities to productively develop the regional economy if only difficult decisions been taken and money wisely spent.[117] Another legacy was the massive environmental despoliation and degradation, especially the polluted Sydney Tar Ponds – North America's largest toxic waste dump. More than thirty times the size of the Love Canal in New York State, the Tar Ponds contain more than a million tons of deadly dioxins, PCBs, lead, arsenic, benzene, and heavy metals. It will cost hundreds of millions of dollars, and take a decade or more, to clean it all up. They are yet another liability bestowed on Canadians by leaders who were afraid to do the right thing.

'The truth is,' historian Margaret Conrad wrote, 'that most Canadians know little about Atlantic Canada.'[118] 'There are,' Rex Murphy, another Canadian commentator and diatribist, observed, 'a basket of easy clichés and prefabricated pseudo-thoughts about the Atlantic provinces that some people cherish in place of any real acquaintance with the facts, the people or the region.' The view from the mainland, he continued, was 'shallow and condescending,' with lots of jokes about unemployment insurance, a dependency culture, and happy, friendly easterners – observations that were never made when it was Windsor auto workers who needed help, or some other cataclysm at the centre.[119] There is much to that. But the coal industry in Cape Breton, once ennobling, had become imprisoning, with Canadian taxpayers left on the hook for a way of life with no future.

How bad would the upheaval of closing the mines and the mill really have been? What targeted, forward-thinking adjustment programs might have been put in place to generously fund, train, and move people to real jobs? The economy is always changing, and people adapt. The government should have done what was right instead of what was easy, though the union, the local newspapers, and the parish priests were also complicit.

Public money should always be intelligently spent to ensure a future, not perpetuate the past, whether it is assistance to a coal mine or to an automotive-parts manufacturing plant that is under consideration. When he announced the closure of the last working mine, Natural Resources Minister Ralph Goodale said the whole situation was unfortunate: 'The decisions taken in the 1960s were taken with the very best intentions and hopes and expectations.'[120] A grade eleven Cape Breton student named Jackie Smith understood something the politicians never did. At a rally in Glace Bay protesting the final mine closure, he explained how things really worked: 'If there are no jobs around, we're just going to move away, get our education somewhere else and work somewhere else.'[121] In total, almost $5 billion had been blown since 1967, with little to show for it. Coal was no longer king. In fact, it never had been.

8

A Founding Dean of Law

In 1957, after years of insisting that all future Ontario lawyers receive their legal education at Osgoode Hall, the Law Society of Upper Canada reluctantly changed course and approved the establishment of new law faculties in Ottawa, Kingston, and London. Two years later, on 1 May 1959, having earlier reached the age of mandatory retirement at the Supreme Court of Canada, Ivan Rand became the founding dean of the Faculty of Law at the University of Western Ontario.

The Law Society was, and is, an institution established by statute. Its mandate is to govern Ontario lawyers, and, most agree, to do so in the public interest. Every four years, Ontario lawyers elect benchers. These benchers meet in convocation and run the affairs of the society, including, until mid century, the recruitment, education, and qualification of Ontario lawyers. For years, hidebound, stubborn benchers rejected the revolution in legal education that had already taken place in the United States and other parts of Canada. They refused to change the way in which lawyers were trained in Ontario – a combination of classes at Osgoode Hall and 'office work,' punctuated intermittently by examinations. Indeed, as late as 1949, the denizens of Osgoode Hall adopted a report that emphasized practical training in law over academic study.[1] Even the casebook method, the one used by Harvard Law School when Rand was a student there from 1909 to 1912, came in for criticism by benchers who declared that 'the advantage of a study of authoritative text books and the orderly arrangement of general principles of law

should not be unduly minimized.'[2] Although there were some valid
criticisms of the casebook method and some compelling proposals for
reform, the benchers were oblivious to the former and not interested,
assuming they even knew about them, in the latter.[3] They refused to
give up their monopoly over legal education: they had complete control of who got in (high school graduates with an average of 'at least
60%' were welcomed) and what they learned – rules and how to fill
out forms. It was a vocational education, and almost totally applied.[4]

For all its faults, however, the system generated many excellent
lawyers, including at times someone (they were almost all men) who
began with only a high school diploma. But the relatively open admissions policy was not without cost. Osgoode Hall Law School opened
its doors to 'all technically qualified students who desire to proceed to
the bar,' the 'good, bad and indifferent, of every grade of intelligence,
and with widely differing educational equipment.'[5] Not surprisingly,
at the end of first year, many students were asked to leave, their results disclosing that they should never have been admitted in the first
place.

The Osgoode program took five years to complete and involved a
total of 900 hours of lectures. To gain the practical experience so prized
by the benchers, the high school graduates, together with a growing
number of students with university degrees, attended law school at
Osgoode Hall in year one. For most of these law students, lectures
were held at 9 a.m. and 4:40 p.m., and often on Saturday morning as
well. In years two and three, they articled, and then they returned to
Osgoode Hall for two more years of study. There were few academic
courses, as those with a practical orientation were favoured. Cecil A.
'Caesar' Wright, a University of Western Ontario and Osgoode Hall
graduate who had received his doctorate in law from Harvard Law
School, complained about the stupidity of it all. He had been on the
Osgoode faculty since 1926, and in August 1938 he gave his opinion
to the Law Society in his usual abrasive style. He was not opposed to
practical training, he said, but lawyers in a modern society had functions other than filling out forms. 'To master the technical and practical
aspects of the law, the lawyer must be aware of the conflicting interests
at stake. The lawyer must be practical; he must know and appreciate
the relevant facts of the case at bar, but this required going beyond the
narrow technicalities of the law. To know the law meant more than
"finding" it in ironclad rules and principles inherited from the past.
It was foolhardy to present a static picture of the law without provid-

ing a means by which the student could come to terms with changes in social realities and political structures. The student-at-law, in short, must be trained as a professional and equipped with a sense of public responsibility. The concurrent school-and-office scheme in operation in Ontario,' Wright believed, 'failed to provide either adequate practical training or an academic education.'[6]

In 1939 the benchers implemented a system of oral examinations on 'practical' matters for students in the first and third years of their articling term. Most of the students barely passed. The whole point of the program was proficiency in office work, and these results showed that the central objective was not being met. Meanwhile, up the street at the University of Toronto, W.P.M. Kennedy had a different approach to legal education. A historian with a degree from Trinity College, Dublin, he had joined the university in 1914, written a textbook on Canadian constitutional law, and manipulated his way to become head of a law department, separate from history, even though he had no legal education.[7] 'Kennedy's school,' as the program became known, did not aspire to train lawyers. 'We have no professional ends to serve,' Kennedy declared.[8] His honours undergraduate program in law emphasized the casebook method and reflected a broader conception of lawyers in a modern world: 'The course is ... specially designed not merely for those who propose to practice law – and for them it is of first class importance – but also for those who might look forward to public administration, to the Dominion and Provincial Services, and to commercial life. It forms the finest training for a student whether he looks forward to practising law or to these other activities.'[9] The faculty was first-rate – but the graduates who wanted to practise law were still required to attend Osgoode Hall Law School.[10]

When the brilliant Sydney Smith, a lawyer, law professor, and former dean of law at Dalhousie University, became president of the University of Toronto in 1945, he formed a behind-the-scenes alliance with Caesar Wright to change the way in which lawyers were taught. Hopes therefore ran high in March 1948, when Wright was appointed dean of Osgoode Hall Law School. But still the majority of the benchers remained committed to the status quo. They took pride in the fact that Ontario was the only place in North America that placed university legal education second to office work.[11] They met in secret and cancelled the modest reforms that Wright had been able to extract. Wright went public with the story, resigned, and, in January 1949, accompanied by the school's leading faculty members, Bora Laskin and

John Willis, moved over to 'Kennedy's school,' though Kennedy had by this time faded largely from the scene.

Wright's ambition was to turn the University of Toronto's law school into a first-class institution, one that delivered a liberal education and trained lawyers. He followed the Harvard model, but also recognized the value of some practical training. University of Toronto law graduates continued to face barriers to Law Society admission, and they still had to attend Osgoode Hall Law School for an extra year to qualify for their call to the bar. Every other common-law province in the country accepted the University of Toronto degree with no further studies required. Meeting in secret to replace their lost faculty, the benchers reached out to a Canadian expatriate named Charles Ernest Smalley-Baker, a man with excellent paper credentials but not much else going for him. His best-before date had long expired, but he was a charming, affable buffoon, a caricature of a law dean sent down from central casting. He was able, however, to attract some good teachers.

The numbers of future lawyers presenting themselves at Osgoode Hall's relatively open door kept going up, reflecting Canada's growing population, the general rise in national income, and the economic enterprise fuelling demands for legal services. Many lawyers were preoccupied with matters such as wills, partnerships, and real estate transactions, but lawyers and law firms were increasingly involved in complex corporate financings, sophisticated securities transactions, and other mandates that went well beyond the abilities of high school graduates trained in office work. There was an urgent need to train new lawyers for these tasks. Modern law students, McGill law professor Maxwell Cohen wrote in 1950, must understand law in society: 'The work of a lawyer stands always on the line between private claims and public policy, for every claim involves underneath the expression of some kind of social value.' The modern lawyer, he continued, 'is there to make the balance, to ease the frictions of an increasingly organized society. He is both technician and counselor and he must above all other men be interested in the formulation and reformulation of the rules of the game that make our society function with a minimum of collision in individual or group interests and a maximum of social equilibrium.'[12]

Cohen was a big man and a big thinker. He had a plan: 'More rigorous admission requirements; adequate buildings and libraries; larger teaching staffs, with leisure for scholarship and funds for research and post-graduate students; the production of texts and case-books

Rand with his father. Rand family
photo

Rand (left) with his younger brother,
Charles. Rand family photo

Rand with his sisters and brother: Daisy, Charles, Ivan, and Minnie. 'Baby Ruth' followed many years later. Rand family photo

Minnie and Nelson Rand with 'Baby Ruth,' 1911. Rand family photo

The Valedictorian: Rand graduated from Mount Allison University in 1909.
Rand family photo

Wedding day: Iredell and Ivan were devoted to each other.
Rand family photos

Rand's sons, Robert and Charles, 1926.
Rand family photo

Rand with his sons. Rand family photo

Rand made several appearances at the Judicial Committee of the Privy
Council. Rand family photo

Donald Spence, Glen How, and A.L. Stein, KC, in the Supreme Court of Canada robing room for the first hearing of the *Boucher* case. Watchtower Bible & Tract Society photo

Frustrated by their lack of progress, in early November 1946 striking Ford employees stole more than a thousand cars and abandoned them around the perimeter of the Ford plant. *Windsor Star* photo in Walter P. Reuther Library, Wayne State University

Mr Justice Ivan C. Rand enters the Foreign Ministry in Beirut for a meeting with Arab leaders. AP Photo / Tom Fitzsimmons

UNSCOP members visit one of the oldest synagogues in Jerusalem. Sitting on Rand's left is Justice Emil Sandstrom, the chair of the Special Committee on Palestine. AP Photo

Rand visits 'his' forest in Jerusalem: Jewish and Zionist leaders regularly feted
Rand for his role in the creation of the state of Israel. Rand family photo

Rand in the classroom at the University of Western Ontario, where he was a beloved dean. Rand family photo

The opening of the new law building: left to right, Western president G. Edward Hall, Ivan C. Rand, Josephine Spencer Niblett, and John J. Robinette. University of Western Ontario photo

'Pleading for my honour' before Parliament: left to right, Terry Donnelly, student at law, Leo Landreville, and chief legal counsel, the legendary David Humphrey. Leo A. Landreville photo

Mr and Mrs Rand being piped into an event. Rand family photo

Rand at his beloved Shediac: Dell's death left him bereft. Rand family photo

required for effective teaching and more efficient practice; full co-operation between teacher and practitioner in resolving the problems of practical training; the recognition of the role of the full-time teacher and of scholarship in the creation of an educated and technically sound Bar; and finally the sense that the lawyer's function is something more than merely vocational. That he is the servant and the leader of the community in a very special way and must, therefore, have much insight into the social order, its values and rules; all this is necessary to ensure that legal education in Canada will move progressively toward higher professional competence and social usefulness, and at a pace matching the needs of a people now quickly becoming in its own right a nation and a power.'[13] It was all so obvious. Cohen wrote a few years later: 'The law is both philosophy and social engineering. The law is art and analysis. The law is history and logic. The law is form and substance – and all these qualities must be communicated to the student, as an essential part of learning about contracts and torts, crimes, property and procedure.' Under this broader view, legal education was not just about teaching law but understanding and re-examining law. 'What kind of rules will make for better criminal justice, for greater fairness and modernity in domestic relations, for a more practical resolution of business disputes?' he asked.[14] Part of the job of law students was to think about the rules as a whole, how the law was developing, and how it should be reformed. Underlying this kind of education was a broad purposive view of the role of law and lawyers in society.

Years passed. In their carpeted dining room at Osgoode Hall the benchers continued to behave as if time stood still. And for many them it had. Little changed at Osgoode Hall Law School after the Second World War. Meanwhile, the University of Toronto Law School was top-heavy with professors and light on students, as many prospective applicants concluded that a university education in law was not worth the extra year of studies to qualify for admission to the bar. Eventually, the fiscal realities of running a law school for an increasing number of qualified applicants forced the benchers to reconsider their role in legal education. The physical plant was, by the mid-1950s, completely inadequate to accommodate the student body. It was not just renovations that were required but considerable new space. Osgoode Hall Law School was a private institution, run without government funds. The Law Society faced not only massive capital expenditures to accommodate its law students but huge and ever larger operating costs. When Law Society members realized that they would have to pay, they

suddenly saw the benefits of publicly funded university legal education: 'Pushed finally by the fiscal realities of modern mass education,
the benchers decided that it was time to assess the possible roles of
universities in legal education in Ontario.'[15] From that moment on, it
was only a matter of time before the Law Society exited the field of
training lawyers and the universities moved in. The Law Society still
set the rules, however: three years of full-time study, including eleven
compulsory courses, followed by one year of articling and the Bar Admission Course examinations.[16]

The University of Western Ontario was one of the universities that applied to have its own law school – something it had tried to do once
before and been refused.[17] In 1957, when it received approval, it turned
to selecting the first dean. Attention soon focused on Mr Justice Ivan
Rand, who faced mandatory retirement from the Supreme Court on 27
April 1959.[18]

Rand was curious about Canadian legal education, unusually so for
a judge at this time. In 1950 he had asked McGill Law School professor
Frank Scott if he could attend the annual meeting of the Association
of Canadian Law Teachers. He was interested in knowing more about
'the question which has agitated the two groups in Toronto: the question of what part the law school should play, in mode and degree, in
introducing the student to initial familiarity with law in operation.'[19]
Four years later, as the war between the benchers at Osgoode Hall and
Caesar Wright at the University of Toronto raged on, he set his views
out in a long article in the *Canadian Bar Review*. Written at the request of
the Canadian Bar Association as part of its survey of the legal profession
in Canada, it left little doubt about where Rand stood.[20]

The fact was, he wrote, most Canadian lawyers left a great deal to
be desired. 'The lack of economy and clarity; the repetitious legalisms
that deface draftsmanship; the cumbersome formulations and the poverty of vocabulary in advocacy; the slovenly enunciations as well as
mispronunciations – they indicate a lamentable absence of individual
self-discipline in its use.'[21] In part, that was the result of the explosion
in law: 'One hundred and fifty years ago a library of two hundred volumes was an extensive collection even for what then passed as a place
of instruction in law. Today, in the common law jurisdictions, the volumes of reports … are numbered in the thousands and are increasing

in the rate of production each year: and the multiplication of statutes has ceased to astonish us.'[22]

The sorry state of the professional landscape was largely the result of tension between theory and practice. If lawyers were 'to become only polished adepts in legal technique, as for example in the vast mechanics of corporate elaboration or, as one critic put it, in the job of "keeping the business man out of trouble," then association with the centres of scholarship will have little appeal or advantage.'[23] That was, of course, the ambition of the majority of the benchers at Osgoode Hall. Although not original in his opinion, Rand had a larger forward-looking vision.[24] A lawyer, he held, was 'a member of a profession which has become part of the constitutional structure of the nation: a ministrant of justice, to whom law is a branch of government; whose equipment embraces the rules as well as the skills of the craft but in a setting of broad understanding of the social organization which gives rise to their nature and necessity; to whom the just government of human beings in society, in all its aspects, is a fundamental concern of men. He is of a class to which the community will look for much of its political and community leadership, and, in a democracy, for the organization of freedom and its cognate institutions, for the reconciliation of its conflicts, and for the vindication of government by law. In emergencies, he becomes the challenger of tyranny or despotic power in any form and barters his independence to no group or interest.'[25]

It was clear to Rand that the craftsmanship model had led to the complete commercialization of the American bar: the big firms could not handle cases of importance to individuals – cases without financial significance – while the small firms, struggling to remain afloat, had a vested interested in prolonging proceedings. In Ontario, 'a special situation exists.'[26] That special situation was the Law Society's effective monopoly and the priority given to 'practical' instruction. 'In stressing the "practical," meaning the preparation of documents, the giving of advice, representing the interests of another, we tend to overlook the fact that behind every external act of a lawyer lies a body of knowledge bound together by ideas called theories. ... Who, for instance, appreciates much of the language of a deed of land at common law without first having acquired some knowledge by the study of "theory" expressed in writings of the nature and modes of tenure? Certain words of art or limitation are essential for the conveyance of certain interests in land: would the proper method of teaching be to use a

standard form of deed, select the significant expressions, give a superficial gloss to them, and then rest satisfied that the tyro[27] can thereafter rely on the printing houses to keep him out of trouble? I agree that
method in legal education is a subject for close scrutiny, but I dissent
from the view that the background knowledge to draftsmanship can be
furnished by instructions in phrases, through familiarity with forms, or
that statutes can be interpreted otherwise than through a knowledge
of the underlying legal aspects of the matters with which they deal.'[28]
Rand, like Caesar Wright, understood that practical legal education
mattered. He just wanted to reverse the emphasis: 'Tangible aids, such
as sample documents, are undoubtedly of value in strengthening the
realistic appreciation of the ideas being communicated. But the great
teachers have always recognized that the mastery of traditional law,
consisting of rules and principles evidenced by records, but operative
only when applied by the mind to concrete situations, involves primarily a conquest in varying degrees of abstract thought; and I am sufficiently conservative to hold that no form of exposure to such aids in a
school can do more than, in a strictly limited degree, give strength and
coherence to ideas aroused in a purely intellectual milieu. I agree that
such aids should accompany discussion, but I consider them to be of
minor importance.'

Rand turned next to who should teach and how law should be
taught. Experience in private practice was not, Rand asserted, a prerequisite for a faculty appointment. It depended on the individual. 'Some,
undoubtedly, are endowed not only with superior minds but with an
instinctive and imaginative sense of realism. Others, with equal reasoning or analytical skills, would benefit, undoubtedly, from a substantial period of practice.' There was a place for part-time teaching in
law schools, but it was a small one: 'Part-time teaching by practitioners
has weaknesses: the subject is too often mastered only in sectors; there
is wanting pedagogical skill; the regularity of lectures is at the mercy
of professional necessities.' On the other hand, 'a core of permanent
and full-time teachers ensures the essential workings of the school: the
strictest regard to punctuality, availability of instructors for discussion with students, the development of traditions of thoroughness and
standards, the opening up of the horizons of law, and the recognition
by both faculty and students of the mutual obligations owed to each
other. These are best served in an atmosphere of intimacy, of respect
for scholarship in the teachers, and serious purpose in the students.'

Achieving these goals was easier said than done. The Law Society's effective monopoly over legal education was standing in the way of progress: 'We are lacking in a strong, liberal and artistically uncompromising tradition of scholarship and creative thinking, which can best be achieved only through the freest competition of educational facilities.' Educational monopoly was an 'enemy': rivalry and competition were called for. 'Our law schools, and law teachers, need the spur of emulation. What great jurists has Canada produced? They can be counted on the fingers of one hand. What outstanding legal scholars? Who, of them, have been recognized by the world centers of jurisprudence or admitted to columns of legal publications of world standing? Not many.'

The elephant in the room was, of course, the fight between Caesar Wright and the benchers. 'Considerable heat,' Rand observed, had been generated, but not much light. In a clear swipe at Wright, he wrote that some professors 'do at times appear to be somewhat arrogant, intellectually, toward those who man the front lines of law in action.' However, it went both ways, as successful lawyers exhibited 'a similar attitude' towards teachers. The solution was 'a little broader, more liberal and intelligent understanding, on both sides, of the essential functions of each, and a recognition that, although we are all fallible in judgment, we do, together, serve the cause of rational order and freedom in our society.' What was needed was a recognition that while both the academy and the Law Society had important intertwined roles to play, some jurisdictional lines had to be drawn. Rand acknowledged the importance of 'consultations' with the practising bar, meetings with 'advisory committees,' where curriculum was discussed 'by men of intelligence in good manners,' but he made it clear that he could not 'look with confidence upon any body of practitioners as a school for instruction in pedagogy.' While 'practicing lawyers know the specific problems the days bring,' law-school teaching, 'apart from the special gift of evoking the interest and curiosity of the student, calls for mastery of a subject as a rationalized whole. Through his absorption in the unfolding of a subject, the teacher comes to see it in aspects and relations that no mere practice, except over many years, can reveal.'

The Law Society's insistence that university law graduates attend at Osgoode Hall for additional training was, Rand wrote, contrary to the public interest. He did not object to a year of 'office work' following completion of a university law degree. It was the Law Society's demand for a fourth year of lectures, given by it, that he rejected: '[T]he fourth year's course, so far as it includes lectures, has more than been covered by the university school and, with the additional office attendance, rules out, except for a few whose time and means are not matters of concern to them, a legal education at any other, even the finest, of the world's law schools.' What mattered, Rand argued, was fitness. That was for the Law Society to determine. However, exercising as it did a 'public trust,' it could not make that determination by 'arbitrary rule or ritual or circumstance, but by the ascertainment of its reality.' Weed out the incompetents to be sure, but rejecting a lawyer or making him jump through meaningless hoops made no sense. This was 'discrimination,' and it 'ought to be utterly foreign to our institutions.'

What, then, was the primary task of law schools? Rand asked. To 'produce a professional class able to meet the needs of a greatly diverse community.' To do that, students must be trained to think like lawyers. That training *must* take place in a university; it could not come from office work. Trained in this way, students would be 'able to grasp and appreciate ordinary instruments, procedures and the like much more swiftly, thoroughly and accurately than through any other process of education. Specific rules and formulations are securely embalmed in the numberless volumes of our libraries, whence they can be disinterred by students or librarians; but their significance to the concrete situation presented will be gauged by minds so trained.' That was a very good point, and Rand expanded on it: '[T]he tempo of affairs has stepped up immeasurably; and the typewriter and the typist have dispensed with the office drudgery of drafting in handwriting that familiarized the apprentice with the technical language of all forms of conveyancing. In the common law provinces the forms of action have been dispensed with and we have the modern rules ... to enable any one with effective training in principles to make his way in the simpler procedures of court. We now have excellent encyclopedias of forms and precedents and conveyances which have kept the examples remarkably in step with decisions and statutes. There are finally the statutory forms, as in leases, the memorandum and articles of incorporation in company law, and the multiplicity of forms found in administrative legislation. Form has lost the importance it held years ago, and we can now look with comparative safety to the precedents so furnished us ... Law has ceased to bear the character of mystery and appears in its true nature of clear thinking and accurate expression; but this means the necessity for deeper theoretical understanding of its guiding rules and principles.'

Accordingly, while office work before law school, during the summers, and after completion of law school made sense, combining that work with study did not. 'Concentration exclusively on the subject-matter of study is of the highest importance. The object of intense application is to saturate the mind with the matter, to establish intricate association in depth; and talking shop should be the rule among students. Only in this manner does the mind rise to the peaks from which new aspects appear. The unremitting absorption in this broadening process of working and understanding by reason and logic, and of assimilating its products, anchors concepts which afterwards become instruments at hand for any use.' But creating the proper environment for this kind of scholarly pursuit required a reallocation of society's resources.

At a minimum, Canadian law schools needed an immediate infusion of resources. First, the libraries must be brought up to a satisfactory level and well maintained. Second, there was an urgent and pressing need for faculty renewal – not with part-time professors drawn from the practicing ranks, but with 'first class minds,' properly paid, 'to furnish the instruction which we agree is essential.' Nothing less than the future of the country was at stake, and the public purse should be opened: 'What in this we must look to is the life of Canada fifty years hence; and our capacity to meet the demands of high responsibility in national and international life at that time will depend on the foundations we lay today.' Finally, it was time for Canada to build a national law school: 'The national school should be in a centre where the arts and sciences flourish, each fertilizing the other; and it should have behind it resources that are capable of supporting adequately the work for which it is designed ... With our vigorous population, our wealth and our enterprising spirit, we must accept the responsibilities of our world position ... We have yet to produce our Maitland, Pollock and Dicey, but the obligation is inescapable; and it would be a sorry conclusion to the possibilities of this country and its people that we should have attained only to a bleak and barren materialism.'

By and large, the reaction to Rand's article was positive. Harvard's law dean, Erwin Griswold, wrote to Rand in September 1954 telling him that he had read his report with great interest. 'Your views on the Ontario situation seem so obviously right that I cannot believe that they won't eventually be accepted.' Ontario, he added, should be one of North America's great sources of strength in legal education. 'But,' he pessimistically concluded, 'as things now stand, that was unlikely to become the case.'[29] Although the logic of Rand's approach was not original, as a judge of the Supreme Court of Canada he commanded respect, and the benchers could not afford to dismiss or ignore him. His article was, undoubtedly, another factor contributing to the Law Society's decision to give up its monopoly – or so the *Globe and Mail* thought.[30]

Realizing that Rand would soon be available – and having canvassed the idea of a new school with the Middlesex Law Association, received approval from the Board of Governors, and obtained authorization from the Law Society (which set minimum standards for admission, curriculum, teaching hours, and faculty strength) – Western president Dr G. Edward Hall inquired whether Rand might like to come to London as the founding dean of the Law School. In fact, Rand was Western's second choice.[31]

The first choice was Canada's pre-eminent barrister, John J. Robinette – but Robinette said no. In early November 1958, with Rand's retirement from the Supreme Court just six months away, Dr Hall went to Ottawa to see the respected judge. By Remembrance Day, the two men had reached the basic outlines of their deal, there being no need, in those days, to set up a committee, establish criteria, and conduct a search. In due course, Hall made a formal offer that incorporated Rand's condition that he be allowed to spend the summers in Shediac. Rand visited the campus before Christmas and accepted the appointment early in the following year. Rand was big game, reflecting the university's desire to 'launch the School on the highest plane possible.'[32] The university also believed, incorrectly, that Rand would be only seventy years old when he accepted the appointment, not understanding that mandatory retirement at the Supreme Court was at seventy-five. Nevertheless, Hall assured the Board of Governors, who were called upon to approve Rand's appointment, that the new dean was of 'vigorous health and mind.'[33] His salary was a rich $18,000 per year. No one on the board questioned the president's choice or the stipend.

The appointment was clearly made without a thorough consideration of the options. What kind of law school did Western want to create? What kind of dean could make that vision a reality? Was an old man at the end of his career the best choice? The University of Ottawa had selected a *sitting* Supreme Court of Canada judge – Gérald

Fauteux – as one of its founding deans. Was this just another case of choosing sizzle, not steak?

Lieutenant-Colonel D.B. Weldon, chairman of the university's Board of Governors, beamed with pleasure when he reported the news: 'His Honour is one the really great jurists of our time. He is a lawyer of experience, a judge of distinction and a profound scholar. We are most fortunate that Mr Justice Rand will join our faculty.' After announcing the appointments of Professors Ronald St John Macdonald, Robert Mackay, and Douglas M. Johnston, President Hall predicted that Rand's 'younger staff will follow him with enthusiasm.'[34] Congratulations flowed in, from the minister of justice, the prime minister, and the academy: 'We have always considered that you belonged to us in a most special way, and you have occupied a position in our personal and intellectual affections not shared by any other judge in Canada,' Professor Bora Laskin wrote from the University of Toronto. Being dean, he continued, would provide Rand with an opportunity to continue his life's work: 'The only difference perhaps is that you will no longer have the last word. The students will see to that.'[35]

The school's mission was ambitious: 'The principal objective of the Faculty of Law is the thorough preparation of its students for the practice of law and for careers in government service and commercial enterprises, national and international. The courses are designed to develop high competence in legal analysis, synthesis and research; to relate law to the social and economic contexts in which it operates; to present an awareness of the values and procedures of the law, and to impart a sense of the lawyer's responsibilities to society for improving the legal system in form and substance. The Faculty is committed to the policy of keeping the classes small so that rewarding classroom discussion will be possible and students may have the benefit of individual attention from their instructors.'[36]

Surprisingly contemporary sounding, this mission statement was changed after Rand arrived. He replaced it with a 'General Statement of Policy' – one that lasted at the law school as long as its first dean:

Among other things, it may be said that the object of the law school in The University of Western Ontario is to develop, in the minds of its students, the habit of thinking in terms of the tradition, in the broadest sense, of our law; of thinking, in other words, as one who has attained some degree of intellectual mastery of legal ideas and their application to life, accompanied by an imaginative sense of reality, relevance and logic. The purpose, in short, is to start minds on the way to do their own thinking on matters with which the law is concerned. Education in law in particular calls for an intimacy between teacher and student in the appreciation of analysis, relevance, analogy and evaluation which is limited in its reaches to students in large group instruction. The Faculty is inclined to the view that the best effects of education are attained indirectly as well as directly by the practice of full and argumentative discussion which a medium sized class permits. In this way, the conception of legal precepts, principles and standards, as objectified in the life of the community, and the understanding that they must be sensed to the point of realized responses to given situations become more deeply implanted in the thinking of students. With such a training law is seen as the vital part of the apparatus inhering in human regulation and the objective of this school is to play its part in the cultivation of minds with such attitude and training. The purpose of the school then is to strive constantly towards the attainment of excellence in that task. The programme of instruction covers the traditional topics essential to the work of the law, and affords, in addition, in second and third years, an opportunity for modest specialization.[37]

Students were required to have at least two years of university studies – that was now a Law Society requirement – and selection was based on 'the applicant's record' and the faculty's 'assessment of his fitness for legal studies,' no thought being given, the times being what they were, that women might apply to the new school. There were female students, but Rand was no modern man. Asked about women lawyers, he conceded they had a place: doing solicitors' and office jobs. A woman, Rand explained, did not possess 'the natural toughness required for criminal work,' adding, 'man, by his very function in society, gets better prepared for the certain hardness necessary in human relations than a woman could.' Rand admitted, however, 'there are exceptions to this.'[38]

In some cases, applicants were interviewed by the dean or 'by persons designated by him.' Students interested in becoming lawyers were advised to 'seek a well-rounded programme with emphasis upon philosophy, history, economics, political science, literature and mathematics.' Pre-law courses of study would be evaluated in 'light of their appropriateness to the study of law and the lawyer's usual roles in practice, government and business.' Accordingly, 'non-theory courses in domestic arts, teaching techniques, advertising and such like are considered generally inappropriate.'[39]

The challenge of law students, Rand asserted, was 'to become artists in thinking.' That meant using imagination to 'carry facts and situations backward or forward ... to look at a problem not only in one or two dimensions, but as if it were a centre within the dimensions of a globe, in which it presents an aspect from every point on the surface.'[40] 'You will come to understand,' Rand told law students at the University of New Brunswick in 1950, 'that no fact exists in isolation.' Imagination, disciplined imagination, 'allied with reasoning faculty, by summoning up all pertinent factors, and ranging about their circumference, enables you to effect that global appreciation with clearness and conviction; and its long-continued practice will furnish you with a power of great facility and of incalculable benefit.' The exercise of imagination led to the capacity for pictorial representation. 'It is essential to a lawyer that he be able to reproduce rapidly in his mind the factual scene or event with which he is dealing; and again that accomplishment may become largely the product of the conscious effort of the imagination.' Using imagination had other benefits as well: 'By that use, also, you will be enabled to enter into the minds of others, to recreate the thoughts, passions, intentions and volitions as they operated in the unseen portion of the external situation which you are examining.' Lawyers had to look below the surface. 'The reconstruction of matters of objective fact alone – in the ordinary sense – is difficult enough, but that of these states and processes of mind and feeling is far more so; but that invisible world will ever be of vital significance to your problems; and you must equip yourselves, figuratively, to be skilled and courageous explorers of depths.'[41]

Becoming an 'artist in thinking' was only half the battle. Lawyers must, Rand argued, deal with the facts as they found them, to deploy them to maximum legal advantage. 'Your task,' he told the future lawyers, 'will be to bring them within an attractive mould or picture, an intellectual conception. It will be of advantage that it bear features similar to those of some known formulation to which the law has already attached an effect. You thus make use of the old but always influential means of analogy to extend legal decision.' Rand clearly understood the limitations of the casebook method. 'Intellectual self-reliance and the capacity for the formulation of opinion represent the maturity of a lawyer and neither can be attained by mere patch work use of decided cases. Excessive initial dependence on authority weakens the ability to cope with the reasoning behind it.'[42] This was all extremely good advice. But how should these students and skills then be taught?

Rand's stated ambition was that Western's law school be 'second to none.' In fact, his privately expressed objective was quite different from either this lofty goal or the prospectus he had set out for Canadian legal education some years earlier in the *Canadian Bar Review*. In a private memorandum to faculty, Rand clearly outlined what he really intended to accomplish:

Law students will come to this or any other law school because, in the main, they intend to become lawyers and engage in practice. As they have several institutions from which to choose, their choice, in the main, will be directed to those institutions which offer them the best legal education and training in relation to the realities of practice and the problems which will *normally* confront them in the course of earning a livelihood and serving their clients. Our primary, indeed almost exclusive, obligation is to prepare law students so that they will become good lawyers in the 'typical' sense of that word. In my opinion it would be, in the final analysis, a grave disservice to our students to embark on projects which over-emphasize our own particular interests and personal preferences and give undue attention to remote or, at best, peripheral matters at the expense of basic essentials. The Law Society has demanded approximately 20 subjects as imperative and as constituting these basic essentials. These, in their great variety, are the matters that we must concentrate on and, if they are to be done well, they are quite enough to tax most of our time and talents and the energies of our students. Naturally, having pride in our own faculty, we should aim for some sense of special identity and not content ourselves with being carbon copies of other law schools or slavishly conform to unimaginative orthodoxy. But the best way to establish a name for our school is to establish a standard of excellence in teaching the basic materials. They afford perfect vehicles for the development of disciplined reasoning and, if properly taught, will inculcate the critical faculties and other virtues which are so necessary for the 'well-rounded' lawyer to have.[43]

It was not as though deviation from the standard required curriculum was prohibited. Rand made clear that other courses could be offered, provided they served a functional purpose – that the students were interested and, more important, that they fit within the university's overall academic goals. 'Particular attention might, for example, be directed to special and general problems of corporations, combines and restraint of trade,' he said.[44] When some of his colleagues suggested otherwise, Rand said no.[45] 'Colloquially, the student must be given a solid meal of meat and potatoes, not thin gruel, which can offer nourishment for a long time and maintain them through a wide variety of day to day legal crises. Fancy pastries should only come at the end of the meal, as luxuries, but only when they can be afforded and only in digestible quantities.'[46]

Notwithstanding what Rand had written in his 1954 article, he actually had a narrow conception of the role of the law teacher: 'There is no doubt a role for the teacher in the rationalization of rules or applications by means of articles and instruction to exert in some degree influence toward change. But I doubt the desirability of his active participation in public affairs except by way of addresses as from an impartial observer, the influence of which will gain from the detachment. This would not, of course, prevent their appearance before a body such as a committee of parliament on proposed legislation. In this I have assumed participation in public affairs as a candidate or member of a political party.'[47] The job of the law teacher, simply put, was to teach the rules.

The new law school needed faculty, and Ronald St John Macdonald, a full professor at the age of thirty-two from Osgoode Hall, was the first recruit. 'Will you come with me to London,' Rand had asked the eager young academic shortly after assuming the dean's post, and Macdonald agreed. Being a somewhat affected individual, he taught at times wearing his academic gown.[48] However, he was the best teacher in the place, and the only one with substantial legal teaching experience. Joining him on the full-time faculty for the first year of operation was Robert S. Mackay, a professor from the University of Toronto with a Columbia LLM who was contemplating a job offer from McGill Law School. Douglas M. Johnston, a Scot who had won the gold medal at St Andrews Law School and then studied at Yale University, came next, while Abraham Siskind, a local lawyer and president of the Middlesex Bar Association, was recruited as a part-time sessional lecturer. They were all filled with great enthusiasm about their new law school.

'It will,' Professor Macdonald told reporters, 'be *avant garde*. We hope to give a new direction to legal education. We hope to turn out leaders not just for the law profession but for society. We haven't taken our law schools seriously enough in Canada ... where is the great Canadian law school? It's time we had one.' Professor Johnston agreed. 'We're declaring war on the more parochial aspects of legal education. This is a changing country, and law training can't stand still. Dean Rand is the living example of the type of man we want to produce – not narrowly legal or technical, but with a broad humanitarianism.'[49] Macdonald and Johnston were in for a shock. Rand had taken over the curriculum committee in May 1959, and the curriculum he directed differed in no material way from the one he had followed at Harvard almost half a century before. When colleagues asked him to recommend teaching materials, he referred them to his old casebooks. The key principles were still there, he argued, even though Harvard no longer used these texts.[50] The professors were scandalized but said nothing. Even the students soon cottoned on to the fact that their materials were long out of date.[51]

When the new faculty arrived in August 1959, the law school was in chaos, in part the result of Rand's having spent the summer at Shediac. Matters immediately worsened when Rand accepted the appointment to head the Royal Commission on Coal. That was a shocking abdication of his primary responsibility to build a new law school. Rand was not the only person in Canada qualified to head the coal commission. He should have said no – and the fact he agreed illustrated a complete lack of understanding of his role and duties as the head of an academic institution. Nevertheless, Rand disappeared within weeks of classes beginning and did not return until the end of the school year. 'I regret the separation for the next few months,' he wrote to President Hall, 'but the institution will not suffer, and I'll be back at the earliest possible moment.'[52] In effect, Johnston, Macdonald, and Mackay were left to run the school, although Hall made all the important decisions in a process shrouded in secrecy.[53] Rand had earlier provided the law school's first librarian, Miss Shanne Lush, a history graduate from Cambridge University, with a list of texts, reports, and statutes that had to be acquired. Remarkably, 7,500 volumes filled the shelves by the end of the first academic term. Another important hire, and among the best in the school's history, was Margaret McNulty, a secretary from the Physics Department. Rand hated administrative work, so that burden fell to Ms McNulty – an especially difficult job that first year, when Rand was rarely on campus. The dean, she recalled years later, was always courteous, polite, and formal. In the five years they worked together, he always called her 'McNulty.'[54]

Thirty-five students, paying an annual fee of $450, were accepted for the first-year classes, held on the second floor in the west wing of the Engineering Sciences Building. Two failed to appear for registration when classes began on September 17. The remaining students formed a law society and elected William Jarvis, a future member of parliament and federal Cabinet minister, as their president. Students were 'expected to dress and conduct themselves in keeping with the standards of the profession they are preparing to enter.' At the end of first year, once the exams had been graded, only twenty-three students had passed.

The faculty grew in second year with the additions of Earl Palmer and Arghyrios A. Fatouros. Palmer, from Guelph, had attended William and Mary University on a football scholarship and then Yale Law School, followed by an LLM at the University of Toronto. Fatouros was a Greek national who would soon defend his doctoral dissertation at Columbia University, and his doctoral supervisor, the famous Wolfgang Friedman, had recommended him. In its third year, Earl A. Cherniak, Osgoode Hall Law School's gold medallist, a former clerk to the chief justice of the High Court, and a new addition to London's legal landscape, was appointed a sessional lecturer. The range of course offerings steadily increased, as did the number of scholarships and awards. J.J. Gow joined the full-time ranks in 1962, as did R.E. Scane. The next year, Julian Payne, a competent British family law scholar, signed on, along with J.F.W. Weatherill, soon to be an expert in labour law. In 1961 Margaret Banks, having earned a PhD in history but unable to secure an academic appointment, replaced Miss Lush as law librarian. She would become known to many generations of law students as the author of the definitive guide to using a law library.

In 1960 the *Western Law Review* was launched. Even more innovative, however, than the standard law journal was the ambitious *Current Law and Social Problems*. The object of the series was to promote collaboration between lawyers, social scientists, philosophers, and others interested in exploring social values, processes, and institutions. Macdonald edited the first two volumes, while Palmer, a brilliant and wickedly funny young scholar, edited the third – the first of the volumes in the series to be devoted mainly to a single topic, in this case labour law. It was also the last of the volumes to be published, the initiative proving too ambitious for a small faculty. Rand was not sad to see it go. Writing privately, he described 'public policy' as 'a very much limited contractual gimmick today.'[55] He was not overly impressed with the new 'academic vocabulary,' including phrases such as 'policy oriented,' which found its genesis in American law schools and which his faculty were attempting, unsuccessfully, to import into Western classrooms: 'My criticism goes to the point that I don't think these present men are sufficiently impregnated by nature or by education with philology or more possessed of sensitivities of euphony as well as the sense of words, to impose such a vocabulary upon the innocent groups who present a blank mind upon which the imprint is to be made. I had an experience of this at Western University with a Yale graduate on the faculty and, belonging to the past century, there was unfortunately generated a hostility that still remains.'[56]

Local, regional, national, and international worthies stopped at Western to pay their respects. In the first year of operation, Caesar Wright, still dean of law at the University of Toronto, gave 'an arresting talk.'[57] E. Davie Fulton, Diefenbaker's minister of justice, 'delivered an able address on aspects of our constitution.'[58] Over the years of his deanship, many celebrated visitors came to speak at this small new school, drawn no doubt because of Rand's prestige as a former judge of the Supreme Court of Canada. The visitors included US Supreme Court justice William O. Douglas, who took time out to address the students in the school's second year of operation, and Rand arranged for Harvard Law School dean Erwin Griswold to receive an honorary degree. Meanwhile, in his report to the president, Rand declared the first year an unqualified success.

The second year of operations got off to a rocky start. Fifty-one students signed up for the first-year class, and there were the twenty-three survivors of the inaugural class. Rand did not like what he saw. In his 1960–1 Annual Report he wrote: 'In these days of multiple distractions, too few Canadian students are committing themselves to that absorption in the subjects of instruction which characterize the foremost professional schools of both Europe and the United States; too many fail to appreciate the intensity of work done [there].' To succeed at law school, Rand believed, required complete dedication. It was not a picnic: 'For all persons except a sprinkling of the most gifted, a certain degree of treadmill application in initial training, pleasant or unpleasant ... is inescapable from any substantial achievement. ...'[59] No one had it easy: 'I do not believe it possible for the vast majority of those who enter the profession to attain a minimum mastery in knowledge and technical competency without long and exacting toil. The production of a lawyer fit to take on responsibility to clients cannot be brought about by easy or pleasant stages or methods; intense and tenacious efforts are inescapable; and rugged grappling for intellectual and artistic conquest in the realities of legal and human relations must mark his whole professional life.'[60]

Rand loved teaching and working with his students. He revelled in their adoration and consistently demonstrated a real interest in their progress and plans.[61] Ms McNulty would often have to go looking for him when he was late for an appointment, and she usually found him in the corridor surrounded by students. He was eager to pass on what he had learned, to discuss the law, and also to talk baseball – about which he was extremely knowledgeable.[62] Rand was so eager to teach that, on at least one occasion, he entered the wrong classroom and started lecturing. No one had the nerve to tell him he was in the wrong place, including the professor properly assigned to the course, who looked in from outside.[63]

Many professors consider students a necessary evil. Rand courted them, accepting all their invitations and giving generously of his time. When asked to speak to the 'law school wives,' the spouses of married male students, for instance, he immediately said yes. He told the young women that it was their duty to ensure that their husbands balanced their work with a social life. He suggested that several hours be set aside every Sunday afternoon to listen to the opera. 'The wives were mostly thunderstruck,' Palmer later recalled, 'being well aware, as Rand was not, that their husbands were "drunken louts."'[64] That was an obvious exaggeration, but that Rand seriously believed that young couples would gather round the radio on Sunday afternoons to listen to the opera showed how out of touch he was about what interested the younger generation and how most of them actually lived. On another occasion a group of male students asked Rand if the rule he had promulgated – that only law students could study in the law library – could be stretched to allow their wives and girlfriends to use the library too. No, he replied, the library was for 'serious work.' Rand later told Palmer that the male students 'wanted him to say no.' In fact, they were furious.[65] Still, Western Law School was a fun place to be: there were drinks every Thursday night at the old CPR Hotel – 'Ceeps' everyone called it – though that was one invitation Rand declined. There was a tremendous *esprit de corps* and community spirit, and, long after Rand stepped down as dean, he happily responded to reference requests from former students seeking to pursue graduate studies in law.

It was his classes in constitutional law that really impressed the students. Standing at the front of the room, with his hands placed squarely on the lectern, Rand spoke with great authority and tremendous recall. His lectures, compared to his writing, were also remarkably clear, although generally dry. He wore the same three-piece grey suit nearly every day of the week, together with his brown shoes. Watching him at the front of the classroom, students felt they were actually in the

Supreme Court as he discussed the facts, the law, and the players.[66] 'We were very conservative. We had respect for people in authority,' Al Osterhoff, a student in the third year of operation and later a professor at the school observed.'[67] Another student, Roger Yachetti, the gold medallist in his year, was more voluble, speaking with 'pride and self-satisfaction in the realization that we had been in the presence of greatness for a brief moment of time.'[68]

Rand made it clear that he adored Sir Lyman Duff, but occasionally he had to criticize his hero. 'Sir Lyman,' he told the students with a smile on his face, 'had some very bad habits and was not himself that day.'[69] (Some confidences were, however, only for his colleagues. One day he leaned over to Palmer and said, in the strictest of confidence, 'Sir Lyman had a dark streak in his character. Every six months of so he'd leave the bench, drink gin, and read poetry for a week.')[70] Rand always encouraged his students to let their minds roam freely and even to criticize, provided it was well thought out. He could not understand why the students objected to his scheduling all five 100 per cent examinations on five consecutive days, though he was capable of real empathy and understanding. Once he spied a student, Robert Daudlin, a small-town boy from Port Crewe on Lake Erie, looking particularly morose, and he asked him what was wrong. 'Dean, I don't think I am cut out for this,' the young man replied. Rand invited him to his office and explained that it was difficult to study law, but that the best lawyers were often not the best students. 'I think,' he told the future Liberal MP and judge, 'that you will be a good lawyer.'[71] When other students needed a jolt, he would call them in and tell them to pull up their socks. If a student came to his office with a legal problem, he would listen and then, pulling down a volume of the *All England Law Reports*, point out the answer. And he gave every student an extremely useful piece of professional advice: 'In court, emphasize the facts if the law is weak, and the law if the facts are weak.'[72]

The law school needed its own space, and a handsome new neo-Gothic law building was opened on 27 October 1961. It was named after Josephine Spencer Niblett, one of the university's most generous benefactors. A plaque was to be unveiled during the ceremony and, just before the crowd assembled, it was discovered that someone had attached a *Playboy* centrefold on top of the plaque under the veil. It was removed before the dignitaries arrived.[73]

Western Law School was a strange place in the early 1960s. The dean had graduated from law school before the First World War, and

most of the faculty had graduated at least ten years after the Second
World War. The grand old man, who had been deferred to for years,
was thrown together with a bunch of young men, all anxious to reinvent the world, eager to experiment with new ways, new courses, new
approaches. Rand was reasonably respectful of the upstarts but determined to have his way. When one professor expressed an opinion
about some matter under discussion, Rand replied that his opinions
were interesting, but his own 'were the law.'[74] There were long faculty
meetings, but, increasingly, matters were categorized as administrative and left to the dean to decide – reinforcing the culture of secrecy
that began in that first year when Rand was away on the coal commission. Rand, an academic outsider, had no idea how universities
really worked. 'His judicial temperament, in particular, his restraint
in applying pressure or being demanding of the powers that be at the
University, was at times a handicap, in terms of his defence of the interests of the Faculty and of faculty members,' Fatouros recalled years
later. 'He seemed to consider the kind of infighting for a larger share
of university funds, for faculty positions or promotions that is common in universities, as beneath his dignity, as the kind of self-serving
conduct no respectable person, and especially no judge, should engage in.'[75]

This attitude drove the faculty crazy. The honeymoon was being
squandered by an old man with no idea how to take advantage of an
open purse and, as yet, unsullied goodwill. Rand would turn down
money from the university, thwart legitimate requests for pay increases, and reject applications for travel and research funds. After their first
year of teaching, Rand advised Palmer and Fatouros that they were
being promoted from lecturer to assistant professor and would be getting a salary increase to boot. When the official letters arrived, there
was no mention of any promotion or salary increase. Palmer went to
see the dean: 'It's Macdonald's fault,' Rand explained. 'He made too
many long-distance calls and I can't ask the university for any more
money.'[76] Rand, meanwhile, was drawing a salary three times higher
than his best-paid faculty member, as well as his Supreme Court and
CNR pensions. On another occasion, the men were sitting around discussing faculty recruitment. Mackay asked, 'What about appointing
Earl Cherniak to the faculty?' He would 'be an ornament.' The answer
was no. 'This is a small town,' Rand replied, and they could not hire
too many Jews. 'We already have a Jew,' he continued, referring to
Abe Siskind. 'Of course I don't feel that way,' he added, 'but they do.'[77]

Not only did the faculty no longer have a Jew – Siskind had died – but who 'they' were was left unstated.

In February 1961 Rand was named national co-chairman of Brotherhood Week by the Canadian Council of Christians and Jews. 'The human race,' he told more than 130 members of the London Junior Chamber of Commerce, including twenty university students from various countries, 'has advanced a great deal in the past century and man should be able to properly judge qualities of other people rather than exercise prejudice. Instead of looking at apparent peculiarities of various races,' he continued, 'people should look at the contributions of these races to the community as a whole.' Only by doing that could 'countries be rid of their notions of superiority.'[78] Later that year, Rand was named honorary president of the London chapter of the African Students Foundation. In March 1962 he was awarded the Beth Shalom Brotherhood award for the 'brilliance of mind, depth of compassion and the humanity of his philosophy.'[79] Just three years earlier, the Ivan Rand Forest in Israel, with 10,000 planted trees, had been dedicated, and Rand was there for the occasion. All this public activity was totally at odds with what Mackay and the others had heard in the meeting – and on several other occasions.[80] Reeling as he absorbed what Rand had just said, Mackay could not help but wonder whether the Jews knew the man behind the trees.[81]

Rand's observation, however, was not at odds with his worldview. When serving on the United Nations Special Committee on Palestine, Rand had met early on with William Hull, an evangelical Christian whose 'mission' to Palestine began well before the Second World War, and he had been surprised to hear the minister speak in admiring terms about the Jewish people.[82] Rand could not change his general opinion about Jews, though he would make individual exceptions. He also saw the citizen-soldier Israelis somewhat differently. After all, they were building a 'civilization.' However, to be fair, in the 1960s, London was a conservative, self-satisfied place in the heartland of southwestern Ontario, run by a family compact and not particularly welcoming to perceived outsiders like Jews. Besides, as far as recruiting faculty was concerned, he was certain that Harvard was the place to go.

'My dear Dean,' Rand wrote Harvard's Griswold in February 1962, could you please tell me the names of Canadians studying at Harvard and what you think of them. There were six Canadians at Harvard, Griswold wrote back, and three of them – Pierre Fournier, R.C.B. Risk, and Barry Strayer – were the most interested in teaching. While it was too early to tell, it seemed to Griswold that Risk and Strayer were the most able of the group.[83] Neither man, apparently, was interested in moving to southwestern Ontario. And the one qualified man in London – Cherniak – had been considered and rejected, without even knowing that his name was in play.

If a faculty member was sick, Rand would approach another one and say, 'Go and fill in.' 'He would just assume that you could do it,' Palmer said; there was no question about whether you should.[84] He also believed that a man's handwriting revealed his character. One day Rand called Palmer into his office, showed him a letter from Harvard's Austin Scott, and asked him to read it. It was a thank-you letter for something Rand had sent. Palmer had no idea what was going on. Look at the signature, Rand directed; 'fine, bold, handwriting,' he observed. He then showed him a letter from Roscoe Pound. 'Vigorous handwriting,' he exclaimed. Then he leaned back in his swivel chair and said, 'Poor Williston,' referring to well-known Toronto lawyer Walter Williston, 'I understand that his handwriting has been reduced to palsy scribble.' Palmer was appalled but said nothing.[85]

It sometimes seemed to the faculty that Rand's main objective as dean was to return money to the university. He simply did not understand how universities worked – that the objective was never to return money at year-end to the central administration but to figure out how to extract more money to raise salaries, fund research and travel, and direct whatever was left over to the school and the students. As a result, Western Law School did not grow as quickly as it might have. In part, that was because Rand was always opposed to excessive consumption and counselled his faculty to make do.[86] He could never comprehend why some of the faculty behaved as they did: they avoided exercise and they smoked and drank – often to excess. Go to bed earlier, he would always say. Another part of the problem was that Rand had no tolerance for hypocrisy and deviousness: he would not believe that the world had its share of cutthroats, knaves, and scoundrels and assumed that everyone was just like him.[87]

Rand was a workhorse and, other than the year away studying coal, he took on more than his fair share of teaching. He taught constitutional law, creditors' rights, equity, mortgages, trusts, and the legal system. He turned down arbitration appointments after becoming dean – he just did not have the time, even when one union nominee, A.A. Borovoy, implored him to reconsider. There were non-stop calls for his advice and assistance. Horace Pettigrove was often on the line, and

Rand, through his old friend, would advise Deputy Minister of Labour George Haythorne and the Government of Canada how best to resolve the increasingly frequent labour disputes that broke out across Canada in the 1960s. In his frequent absences, 'McNulty' kept things on track and Rand up to date on faculty goings-on. Kenneth Campbell, the secretary to the chief justice, updated Rand fully on developments at the court, supplying him with judgments as they were released, along with the current court gossip. Justice Ritchie, Rand's successor, Campbell reported, 'seems a little nervous about the prospect of having to write reasons. I suggested he cultivate the friendship and confidence of Judson J. and he would have nothing to worry about.'[88]

Faculty meetings were held in the dean's office. One of the professors, Douglas Johnston, was, like many new law teachers, overeager and anxious for change. He would write long memoranda on improvements and reforms he thought were called for and distribute them on onion-skin paper to other faculty members. One classic Johnston memorandum complained, in turn, about the laziness, lack of intellectual curiosity, mediocre intelligence, unresponsiveness, and complacency of the students. If something was not done, he warned, 'the consequences for our new law school might be serious indeed.' Rand, who could not abide arrogance in others, decided at this point that Johnston had to go. At the next faculty meeting, Rand pulled out one of Johnston's missives, one that was complaining more generally about the low level of intellectual engagement at the law school. Rand said, 'Let's turn to Professor Johnston's memorandum.' He read the first sentence, calling for faculty self-improvement or some such thing. He asked: 'Professor Johnston, what have I done wrong and how should I improve?' He then proceeded to tear Johnston apart through a sustained unrelenting critique of his missive. Later he called Palmer and Fatouros in for a private chat and suggested that Johnston be fired. 'If I told you,' Rand said, 'that the presence of a person or persons endangered the existence of an institution, would I be justified in firing that person?' Johnston was apparently not popular with the students, who found his courses too theoretical, Rand explained, adding that his teaching left a lot to be desired. The two men pointed out that Johnston was a new teacher and that his wife was expecting a baby. Rand agreed to defer the decision, while Johnston, oblivious to his close call, continued to appear at the school in his cricket whites, whistling as he made his way through the halls.[89]

Being a great man in a small city led to all sorts of invitations from community groups, and Rand accepted them all. When something else came up, as was often the case, he would deploy one of his staff members to speak in his stead. On other occasions, he would simply commandeer their services as chauffeur. Even though Rand had a CNR pass that entitled him to free travel anywhere in Canada serviced by the railway, he would call Mackay or Palmer and ask them to drive him to whatever event he had agreed to address. If either man drove too fast, Rand would object. Once he obliged Mackay to drive him to an event in Sarnia. When they got there, Rand ignored him and did not introduce him to anyone. Then, when they sat down for dinner, they were invited to order whatever they wanted. Mackay fancied the steak, but, as he began his request, Rand interrupted: 'I will have a poached egg on spinach, and so will Mackay.'[90] After a while, faculty began hiding from the dean, not opening their door if they thought he was outside.

The Rands had a small apartment and occasionally they invited faculty members over for dinner, followed by the obligatory session listening to opera records. One glass of sherry would be served – a thimbleful – that the professors soon learned had to be nursed all night. Occasionally the Rands would invite only the married couples to dinner at London's posh Hunt Club, where he had been given a membership by the university. Fortunately, there were no full-time married Jewish professors, as the club had a 'restricted' membership (this policy did not change until the 1970s, more than twenty years after Rand participated in the majority decision in *Noble et al. v. Alley*).[91] He allowed only one drink at the start of dinner. Once the meal was over, the band would begin to play. 'Go dance,' Rand would say, and the couples would oblige. He then had the chairs removed from the table, except for his and Dell's, so the dancers would not sit down and order another drink – or so Palmer, Mackay, and the others were convinced. However, once a year, Rand would order several crates of lobster from Shediac – the 'chickens,' or one-pounders, known for their sweet meat – and deliver them to the Mackay household, where there would be a big spread for all the faculty members. At these social events he liked to reminisce about his experiences in Moncton, at Harvard, in Medicine Hat. He never discussed his sons or any other member of his family, nor did he ask questions about anyone else – the talk always revolved around him. His favourite descriptive adjective was 'first-rate,' and he would describe witnessing a first-rate accident, eating a first-rate piece of cod, or being caught in a first-rate blizzard.

When the evening was over, the Mackays, the Palmers, and whoever else had been invited would immediately head to the local pub to quench their thirst.[92]

The faculty often ate lunch together, invariably at Stevenson Hall. Rand enjoyed the company of his colleagues while he talked about himself and, inevitably, ordered Jell-O for dessert. The only question was yellow, green, or red. When it arrived, Rand would remove the dollop of whipped cream on the top and, placing it off to the side, devour what was left. Much of his social life revolved around the university – such as cocktail parties at the homes of the Iveys and other prominent families. The faculty wives often got together. The Rands attended the occasional concert, and the flow of speaking invitations for Rand never stopped. Organized Jewry also never lost interest in him – and more honours and speeches followed. At the end of every school year, however, the Rands immediately disappeared to their cottage at Shediac. They never put down any roots in London, even though one of their sons, Charles, lived there – a professor at the medical school.

There was a huge turnover in staff at the law faculty. In Rand's last year as dean, Johnston, finally reading the writing on the wall, resigned to teach in Louisiana; Scane left to join private practice in Toronto; Weatherill went to the Ontario Labour Relations Board; and Mackay took a leave to work for the McRuer Commission. Earlier, Macdonald (with a push from Rand), Gow, and Fatouros had given notice and accepted better opportunities. It was more than a little ironic that Macdonald and Johnston went on to become academics with truly international reputations – but they did not make them at Western Law School. Macdonald's work on the European Court of Human Rights (he was the only non-European judge) and his founding of the *Journal of the History of International Law* inspired an entire generation of academics in Canada and around the world. Johnston's work on fisheries and the law of the sea – he published more than thirty books and ninety articles – also brought him international acclaim. The two best scholars ever to work at Western's faculty decided to make their careers elsewhere.

Rand could never understand how a man could give notice and leave for another assignment, or why the university would allow it (conveniently forgetting that he skedaddled in his first year to serve on the coal commission). Although he was quite prepared to fire a professor without due process or much notice, he could not comprehend how one of his professors could put his own interests first. He was furious when Fatouros announced his departure – and he immediately contacted the dean in Illinois and charged that he was 'a buccaneer boarding his ship.' Incredibly, Rand actually called Chief Justice McRuer in an unsuccessful effort to get him to withdraw his offer to Mackay. These professors were just trying to make their way in the world and Rand's conduct was nothing short of outrageous. 'Slight attention,' the dean wrote in his final annual report for the year 1963–4, 'seems to be given to the effect upon the school of voluntary withdrawals.' Such behaviour was wrong and disloyal: 'It seems to be assumed that the teacher is at liberty to leave the service at the end of the school year regardless of notice; and this circumstance presents a problem for newly established schools in the course of building up their faculties.' This problem even showed up on one of Rand's examinations in his equity course: 'A agrees to play football with the Argonauts for the season. After playing two games, he enters into an agreement with Montreal to play for the Alouettes in the remaining games. Both teams belong to a league of 8 member teams with the games fixed by a schedule. What considerations must be taken into account in an action for injunction to restrain A from playing for the Alouettes, and from the facts given what would be the result?'

Rand made it more difficult for faculty than he had to. Unpaid leaves of absence were 'out of the question.'[93] Although he did not see it that way, a big part of the problem was Rand's standing in the path of the staff's professional development. While the library continued to grow – by the end of Rand's term it had more than 20,000 volumes – more money was needed across the board. Rand believed that the faculty members, like so many young people, were motivated by greed. He did not understand that they needed money. They needed promotions and the raises that came with them. Money was essential to counter the call of practice, public life, institutional rivalry, and the free market, and to provide better salaries, research, and travel.

As good men left, other good men applied – but not every applicant was well treated. When one potential faculty recruit was brought in for a meeting with the dean and he unwisely mentioned some Supreme Court decision of Rand's, he was met with a barrage of questions. It soon became apparent that he did not really understand the case, at least not the way Rand saw it. After Rand picked up a book and started reading it, the reject realized, after an embarrassed silence, that the game was up, and he slunk from the room.[94] Another candidate, liked by the staff but burdened with a German-sounding name, was

similarly turned down. 'I've had enough of Germans,' Rand said. He
felt the same way about Ukrainians, French Canadians, Roman Catholics, and Jews. Experiences with individuals in any of these groups did
not change the stereotype: rather, they simply led to Rand's creating
individual exceptions to an otherwise governing rule. At Mount Allison's 1961 summer institute, 'French Canada Today,' Rand, on behalf
of his alma mater, had welcomed his old sparring partner Louis St
Laurent to Sackville with his own plea for unity: 'We must discuss explicitly and frankly those points of difference or controversy that may
arise. And we must not yield to the temptation to suspect or attribute
wrong motives.'[95] Unfortunately, in his personal life, Rand did not follow his own advice.

A significant number of students left every spring when the first-
year results were posted. Attrition was less significant in second year,
and negligible by third year. In May 1962 the faculty's first class of
seventeen, including one woman, received their LLB degree (four others, following supplementals, received their degrees in the fall). The
library continued to grow, and professors began to write book reviews
and articles, even though the rate of academic production was low and
no sustained work ethic was established. Western graduates had no
difficulty in obtaining articling positions, as there was an insatiable
demand for lawyers. Over time, course offerings expanded, albeit in
the limited way proposed by Rand. The school's reputation for excellence in business, however, depended more on its perceived association with Western's business school than with anything it offered or
accomplished on its own.

Students seemed to like the way things were organized – they had
no interest in learning how their professors thought society should be
organized. All they wanted, just like the benchers, was to learn tangible skills they could use. Following complaints from the students
that there were too many theoretical courses and not enough practical
courses, Rand, without consulting anyone, placed a notice on the bulletin board stating that the course on international law was cancelled.
It was replaced with new courses on equity and creditors' rights. Rand
listened to what the students said, apparently agreed, and paid little
attention to what the faculty thought.[96] But what about Rand's stated
objective of legal education – to instill a 'habitual vision of greatness'?
Rand was institutionally hobbled by the Law Society's prescription
of a large mandatory core curriculum, which remained in place until 1969. Still, he did have room to manoeuvre. It was difficult to see

how Western's curriculum was fulfilling Rand's stated ideal for a law school: to create lawyers who were 'ministrants of justice.'

'I think it was during the 1960–1 academic year,' Fatouros recalled thirty years later, 'that the students insisted on the addition of more "practical" courses, which were of no interest to most faculty members. Symbolic of such courses was one in mortgages which the students wanted and which no faculty member would accept to teach. Dean Rand was on the students' side, partly because, like all deans, he wanted to avoid conflict with them (and with the profession, which appeared to support them). Confronted with the refusal of faculty members to teach the course, he gracefully took an original way out: he undertook to teach it himself. What then happened is quite typical of his approach and personality. He taught the course out of a turn-of-the-century casebook, by Dean Ames I seem to recall, containing few, if any, twentieth-century cases. We had to borrow the single existing copy of the book from Harvard's Law School Library and reproduce it for student use.'[97]

In his goodbye letter to the dean, W.H. Jarvis, who was studying law as a mature student, with a successful career in business already behind him, insisted that the school must focus on the basics: there was too much pastry and not enough meat and potatoes, he complained. 'The purpose of the faculty,' he wrote, 'is not to develop statesmen, government leaders, and outstanding jurists. This is not to say, however, that the school should not be prepared and equipped to encourage highly gifted students who will eventually pursue these ends, but not to such a degree as will endanger the basic purpose. This purpose dictates the faculty's role, which is to offer a logical combination of the theoretic and the practical where a student's ability to recognize the ordinary legal problem is not distorted by such advanced philosophical concepts as will tend to confuse the simple, but important practicalities of the practice of law.'[98] In fact, Rand's real objective for his law school had already been accomplished: a traditional legal education with an emphasis on practical business-oriented courses.

By the end of the 1963–4 academic year, Rand's five-year term was coming to an end – and, besides, he was turning eighty. On 26 March 1964 a testimonial dinner was held for him at the old Hotel London. More than 360 colleagues, students, and friends were there, including Chief Justice Robert Taschereau; two other judges of the Supreme Court, J.R. Cartwright and Wilfred Judson; and Dana Porter, the chief Justice of Ontario. There was also a contingent of Superior Court judges from Osgoode Hall, including one particularly flamboyant, fun-loving member of the bench named Leo A. Landreville – whom Rand would get to know much better soon enough. An assortment of law-school deans rounded out the guests of honour. In proposing a toast to Rand, Cartwright commented that his greatest attribute as a judge was his 'deep and abiding sense of justice. He never lost sight of the importance of every case to those concerned in it, or of the fact that the primary duty of the court is simply to do justice between the parties who come before it, and that we are bound to the performance of that duty to the best of our ability not by a contract but by a vow.'[99] Cart-wright was given a standing ovation.

When it was Rand's turn to speak, he warned of the danger of Ca-nadian society's becoming 'fanatical' about individual rights. It would be far better, he said, if the newspapers were filled with articles on 'the responsibilities of men.' There were choices to be made: 'We must accept the rules of reason or the rule of passion, of hatreds.' The es-sence of democracy was 'self-restraint.' The first priority was 'a rec-onciliation of clashing demands and ideas. When we achieve this, then we are making headway, but we mustn't be in too much a hurry. Advances are slow to become part of tradition.'[100] What exactly this meant was, for most of the audience, unclear. Tributes flowed in from all quarters, including the prime minister and the Israeli ambassador. A portrait of Rand painted by Clare Bice, now hanging halfway up the law school's main stairway, was presented, and the Dean Ivan C. Rand Honour Society inaugurated, with David Crawford Smith, Don-ald Taliano, and Roger Yachetti the inaugural members. Each year, no more than three graduating students were to be named as members, with selection based on academic achievement and contribution to stu-dent life. In May, along with the graduating class, Rand was granted an honorary degree of Doctor of Civil Law, in recognition of his service to the faculty and the university. Rand was also presented with a pair of white gloves. In court, that meant no capital cases on the docket. At this convocation, every student had passed. Rand was a man who rarely showed emotion, but he did that day.[101]

Rand hand-picked his successor, A.W.R. 'Fred' Carrothers, an im-pressive and youthful scholar who had graduated in law from the Uni-versity of British Columbia in 1948 and from Harvard in 1951 with an LLM, and had won the Viscount Bennett Scholarship, the Ford Foundation Fellowship in Law Teaching, and the Royal Society Senior Fellowship, to name just three awards. After a year as assistant profes-

sor at Dalhousie in 1951, Carrothers returned to Vancouver, joined the
law faculty, and was appointed a full professor in 1960. Rand came
to see him at Harvard, where he was on sabbatical completing one of
Canada's first textbooks on labour law. Rand offered him the dean's
job, without consulting any of the faculty, and Carrothers accepted.
Afterwards, Rand inquired whether he was a Roman Catholic. He was
curious about things like that, Carrothers recalled, adding that they
became great friends.[102] Carrothers faced no shortage of problems, personal and professional, as he took the academic helm. Most important
were his academic ambitions, which charitably can only be described
as pedestrian.[103] He had no imagination. All the original professors
had gone, although Mackay would eventually come back and become
dean. Fortunately for the others, Carrothers and his wife threw a good
party, where there was always plenty to drink, and he proved to be
expert at extracting money from the administration. Under Carrothers,
faculty members got their own telephones as well as promotions and
salary increases. There were also funds for travel and research.

Many of the things that Rand had called for in Canadian legal education in 1954, while not particularly original to him, did come to pass
both in law schools across Canada and in the Faculty of Law at the
University of Western Ontario.[104] The full-time university law school
gained acceptance as the place for education, and no one seriously believed anymore that the legal profession was only the bench and the
bar. It was now understood to include a third branch, the academy.
Osgoode Hall Law School carried on after a fashion. Caesar Wright had
beaten the benchers into submission and Osgoode Hall remodelled its
program so that it was, by and large, identical to the curriculum in
place up the street. But Osgoode Hall could not shake off its reputation
as a trade school – it took some kind of perverse pride in the fact that
its admission standards were *lower* than those of the universities.[105]
It eventually bowed to the inevitable and joined York University in
far-off Downsview. Across Canada, new buildings were constructed,
libraries filled with books, graduate programs inaugurated, and law
professors with postgraduate degrees from serious schools recruited,
and these men – and, increasingly, women – began compiling case-
books and writing articles for the law journal attached to every law
school. Teaching loads were lowered, admission standards were
raised, and the case method gained priority over almost everything

else. That was the most unfortunate part of the pendulum swing. Lost in the transition was what was, or could be, good and salvageable about applied teaching and learning.

The library was at the centre of the casebook method. It always has been and always will be. The case method, obviously, has a lot going for it. It teaches students how to read, distinguish, and reason. But it is not and never will be the be-all and end-all. Textbooks and lectures provide vital information and perspective. However, no legal education can be complete without first-hand knowledge of what went on in the courts and the law offices. The benchers had wanted to produce legal technicians. Rand and others had postulated a higher calling for modern lawyers, and time proved them right. But in his design of his law school, Rand quickly forgot about his earlier high-minded aspirations and slipped into prevailing norms and the status quo. Like so many deans, he became fixated on pleasing students, recruiting faculty with good degrees, and the number of volumes in his law library and the variety of articles published in top journals, but he forgot that government, administrative tribunals, clients, witnesses, judges, juries, and ordinary men, women, children, Aboriginals, minorities, and the poor were equally important.[106] Rand paid no attention to the lessons being taught and learned by legal realists who were examining the actual operation of law in society: What impact does law have? Should it promote the public interest? Should it serve higher goals or merely provide a mechanism for the controlled regulation of social and commercial conflict?

Law can be dirty and messy and contingent and contextual and rigid and purposive, sometimes just and sometimes unfair. Although Rand had dismissed moot and mock trials in his 1954 report as 'make believe,' echoing the official Harvard view that they provided little benefit to students other than 'amusement ... and ... a relief to the tedium of serious work,' he completely changed course as dean and ensured that the new law-school building had an impressive moot courtroom. That was a start. But then he made no provision in the curriculum for the careful observation of real trials or the representation of real clients. Few of the faculty members he hired had any experience in legal practice. He also ignored legal ethics, believing that, by the time students arrived at law school, they were ethically formed: 'at such an age, the attitudes, habits, ideals and discipline that manifest moral integrity in the home, the community, the schools, the colleges would long since have been moulded and ingrained.'[107] And he asserted, 'without hesitation, that the law schools have no special responsibility for building up moral character.'[108] But law is often complicated, ethical dilemmas are highly nuanced, and, in every law school, legal ethics should be taught.

In his writings, Rand clearly understood the expanded role of lawyers in government, but in the curriculum he designed he settled for the status quo, the ordinary. He did not even try to establish a middle ground between the office work of the benchers and the idealized role for lawyers that he had so persuasively set out in his article. For someone with his imagination, this decision is inexplicable. On the other hand, Rand was a seventy-five-year-old thinking like a seventy-five-year-old. What Western president Hall was thinking is the better question. Hall obviously wanted cachet and prestige.

Rand knew exactly how lawyers should be trained. In his previous experience as a lawyer and a judge, he had always said the 'most important tools of the advocate's trade were an active imagination and a flexible mind.' Lawyers must be able to reconstruct the realities of their clients' situation if they were to separate the relevant from the irrelevant facts and serve the clients' best interest.[109] Why, then, was there not a single course at Western's Law School to teach this indispensable skill?

The first-year curriculum Rand put into place at Western was just like the first-year curriculum of every other North American law school. It will probably never change. Over time, more and more optional offerings became available in second and third year, at Western and everywhere else. Year after year, greater opportunities have arisen for supplementary clinical work. Today, after that long and bitter fight between the benchers and the academics, a man or woman can graduate from law school without ever having met a client or seen the inside of a courthouse. Consider for a moment a medical school staffed by professors who had never treated a patient. Many full-time faculty at law schools have never ever dealt with a client, except, of course, in high-paid consultancies and occasional *pro bono* work. The general trajectory for legal faculty is academic success at law school, often a Supreme Court of Canada clerkship, and then graduate work at an elite institution, with little connection to the real world. There are real problems with clinical legal education. However, it is, as the authors of the 1983 report *Law and Learning* conceded, the way in which students 'develop the ability to apply analytical skills and intellectual insight as the practising lawyer must apply them.' Like everything valuable, it comes with a cost. 'It is labour intensive and requires special subsidy ... close supervision of students and quality control.'[110] One wonders what someone with courage, drive, imagination, willpower, and a budget could accomplish in legal education if given half a chance.

There were challenges ahead at Western, for all Rand's successors as dean – women and the law, critical legal studies, political correctness – while the law school also had to be made accessible to the poor and disabled, First Nations and other racialized minorities, and to gays, lesbians, and the transgendered. The challenges were especially complicated at Western because Western, was, well, Western, where inappropriate, juvenile, sexually laden, alcohol fuelled behaviour in the law school was, at worst, encouraged and, at best, condoned for a very long time.

A law school often reflects the strengths and weaknesses of its dean, and early decisions have a way of influencing future events. Rand founded a school that centralized decision-making and institutionalized conservatism in outlook, curriculum, and recruitment of faculty and students. These choices were reflected in the decisions to keep to the basics and to limit options to Western's key strengths in business and commerce. Even this decision turned out, over time, to be self-serving puffery and exaggeration, as other law schools had stronger faculty in law and commerce. In the early days, some of the law professors taught their classes while well lubricated in the Faculty Club. Western's great strength lay in creating a school with camaraderie and small-town collegiality – and that seemed to be what the students wanted. By and large, they were not intellectuals and dreamers. They intended to make their living practising law, and they insisted on a curriculum that enabled them to do so. That was nothing to scoff at, but hardly an institution that was 'second to none.' Rand did not attempt to reconcile the practical and theoretical divide, a legacy that was embraced by his early successors and one that haunted the later deans.[111] Not surprisingly, when the pedal finally hit the metal, Western, as one law dean put it, 'adopted a conservative approach; it sought changes at the margin, not at the core.'[112] Faculty members and new faculty recruits, for a long time, always seemed to look pretty much the same. To be fair, Western Law School was not alone in facing the gender wars that broke out in law faculties across the country in the 1980s, but it was among the hardest hit.[113] From Rand's day forward, disrespecting and destabilizing the dean became the number one faculty sport in the law school.

Rand was now, for the second time, officially retired. Back at the house on Botsford Street in Moncton and the cottage at Shediac, Dell could not have been happier. 'He needs the rest,' she wrote to Rand's sister Ruth, 'and life will be simpler for us both. I'll just have two places instead of three to manage!'[114] Within a matter of months, however, at the end of September 1964, Rand's world came crashing down when Dell died of a heart attack. 'It was very sudden and unexpected,' he confided to Ruth. Dell was gone 'in the space of minutes. We had no sign that any such condition existed.'[115]

The service was at St John United Church, where the organist played 'Unto the Hills' and 'The Lord Is My Shepherd.' The Reverend Frank Archibald presided. Dozens of flower arrangements arrived for Rand, and countless letters and cards of condolence from students he had taught at Western, judges he had served with on the Supreme Court, lawyers, family members, friends, politicians, the prime minister, the minister of justice, the premier of New Brunswick, the president of Israel, Israel's foreign minister and future prime minister Golda Meir, the Israeli ambassador to Canada, the crackpot mayor of Moncton Leonard Jones – on and on it went. Rand quickly tackled and completed what must have been a dreaded job as he replied to every one of them, thanking them for their kindness and good wishes. He was particularly consoled by the words of the local minister: 'We can never forget, but as the years go by, we find it easier to remember.'[116] The *Moncton Transcript* wrote an editorial in Dell's honour: 'Those who knew Mrs. Ivan C. Rand, and she enjoyed many warm friendships not only in her native Moncton but in other parts of Canada, will have been deeply shocked and saddened by her sudden demise. And it will be difficult to realize that such a charming and gracious personality is no longer with them.'[117]

It was especially difficult for Rand. Dell had kept her heart condition a secret and continued to devote herself to her husband, particularly in getting him his meals.[118] Rand, though always acutely aware of his own emotional state, was totally detached from the emotional needs of others. After a quarrel, for instance, one of his sons remembered, he would become quiet and later wonder out loud why the other person had got so upset with him.[119] Now, writing to his old friend Horace Pettigrove three weeks after his wife died, he expressed disbelief about what had happened – 'life swept away. Only acceptance remains.'[120]

When Pettigrove encouraged him to socialize with his Moncton friends, he responded, 'Horace, life's not the same since Dell died.'[121] He was even bitter at her in a way, one colleague recalled, for dying on him just as he was finally ready to retire.[122] No one dared tell the grand old man, however, that he could have retired in 1959 when he left the Supreme Court.

Although Rand was inconsolable after Dell died and would never be the same again, he did, fortunately, have a new venture to engage his attention: the demolition of the career and reputation of another judge.

9

Canadian Gothic Meets the
Mambo King

Room 182 at Osgoode Hall was no ordinary judge's chambers, and its occupant, Leo A. Landreville, was no ordinary judge. Franco-Ontario's representative on the Supreme Court bench, Landreville was a small, well-dressed man who had made it big in northern Ontario. His Sudbury law office had been the busiest in town, and the income from it had been handsomely supplemented by his many investments. A lifelong Liberal and successful local politician, Landreville had been elected mayor in December 1954. His two-year term was interrupted, however, by a telephone call from Ottawa. Would he accept a judicial appointment? Yes, he decided, after much soul-searching and thought. On 13 September 1956 Landreville, at forty-six, became the youngest judge at Osgoode Hall.

He had a second home, Landra Villa, in Cuernavaca, and he decorated his Osgoode Hall office in a Mexican motif. He worked at a large kidney-shaped walnut desk with leather inlay. The carpet was vivid red, and the walls were covered with straw. A coffee table inlaid with ceramic tiles, sofa, bar, hi-fi, and several occasional chairs completed the furnishings. Outside, Landreville parked his Cadillac Brougham. He and his wife lived at fashionable Benvenuto Place and joined the elite Granite Club. Landreville had no worries in the world – except for one little secret.

This story is, in many ways, a northern one.[1] By the 1950s northern Ontario had a distinctive identity within Canada's most populous

province, one that stemmed above all from the land. The Canadian
Shield's 'rugged, hilly, lake-pocked plateau'[2] created a natural border
with the south, while the Hudson Bay lowlands to the north boasted
one of the most forbidding climates in the world.[3] Copper and nickel had been discovered near Sudbury in the 1880s, silver at Cobalt in
1903, and gold near Timmins in 1909. Northern Ontario, or 'New Ontario' as it was briefly known, became firmly fixed in the public mind
as a provincial treasure chest. Its rapidly developing mines, its apparently endless forests, and its rivers, which held the promise of unlimited and inexpensive electricity, all made northern Ontario a land
of opportunity.

Despite this economic potential, most of the hundreds of thousands
of immigrants who flowed into Canada in the nineteenth and twentieth centuries made their way south and settled in the cities or the
rich agricultural lands there. Taming the north was a job for a hardy
few. Still, increasing numbers of newcomers, finding opportunities in
mines and forests, headed north and joined a society that was mark-
edly different from that of the south. Finns, Ukrainians, Italians, Germans, Poles, and a few other 'foreign' groups made up about a quarter
of northern Ontario's population by the 1920s. French Canadians, migrating most often from overcrowded farms in Quebec, formed another quarter. Aboriginal peoples and Canadians from British stock
completed the picture. Northern Ontario, which had a population of
just over half a million in 1951, was a very different place from the
rest of the province, which remained, until the 1950s and 1960s, overwhelmingly British in outlook and stock. In sharp contrast, northern
Ontario was bilingual and multicultural before politicians in the rest of
the country had even heard of the concepts or discovered ways to use
them to garner votes.

To be sure, the social mix made for some problems, resulting in
cultural conflict in northern Ontario's unions, churches, and politics.
Overall, there was a sense of otherness in Ontario's north – a sense that
deci-sions and disbursements were made in the south for the south.
Franco-Ontarians in the north like Leo Landreville knew this feeling
well. Along with French-speakers in Ontario's eastern counties, they
were the victims of successive anti-French policies of the provincial
government. Regulation 17, passed by the legislature at Queen's Park
in 1912, had severely restricted French-language education rights. The
intent of the provision was obvious, and fortunately it was most often
honoured in the breach. Though eliminated in 1927, it symbolized a

widespread sense that French Canadians were not truly welcome in Ontario. A legacy of bitterness about the infamous law remains to this day.[4]

Still, northern Ontario was a land of opportunity, a frontier that was exciting, risk-laden, and filled with potential. John Diefenbaker's 'Northern Vision' campaign during the 1958 general election struck a popular and timely chord with Canadians and promised massive investment in transportation and communication to create a 'new soul for Canada' that would 'safeguard our independence' and 'restore our unity.'[5] The actual attempt to reorient Canada northward was less successful, though investment did increase and roads made many northern communities less remote. In the 1950s and 1960s scientific exploration was funded as never before, and the budget of the Department of Northern Affairs increased annually. Northern resource industries boomed and, fuelled by post-war military and consumer goods markets, Ontario's mineral, timber, and power production exploded. Places like Kenora grew rapidly, other communities were built from scratch, and the population of northern Ontario expanded at a record rate during the 1950s.[6] But the new northerners were serving the same function as those of the previous generation: getting resources out of the north for delivery and consumption in the south and elsewhere. Still, the north was a place where business could be done and fortunes made by men with savvy, guts, and an eye for opportunity. The building of a trans-Canada natural gas pipeline provided one such opportunity.

In the early 1950s the market for natural gas was minuscule, outside of a few small centres in Alberta. More Canadians burned wood than natural gas for fuel, while oil and coal were still fuels of choice in most Canadian cities and towns. All that changed by the middle of the decade. Natural gas was inexpensive and efficient, and, because of advances in technology, it could be transported long distances by pipe. Gas pipelines were being planned and built all over the world: a giant pipeline, 15 metres in diameter, was on the drawing board to take gas from the Caspian Sea to Moscow, while another network of pipelines was beginning to tap both North Sea and Sahara Desert reserves.[7] Western Canada had huge proven reserves. Ontario, which had suffered a critical coal shortage during and immediately after the Second World War, was an obvious market for the natural gas, but the real market was the energy-starved United States. All that was needed was a pipeline to transport the gas to eastern markets.

Accordingly, by 1950, several groups of businessmen were seeking permission to build natural gas pipelines out of Alberta. It was widely assumed that the millions of dollars needed for financing would largely come from the United States and be contingent on the pipeline's bringing gas south. Alberta gas producers, characteristically indifferent to Ontario's needs, favoured a north–south route. They wanted to get the gas to America's industrial heartland as quickly and as inexpensively as possible. That meant exporting it to the United States via Emerson in Manitoba, down to Minneapolis and Milwaukee, and then over to Chicago and Detroit. This route also left open the possibility of re-importing any leftover gas across the Niagara River, about 5 kilometres north of the Lewiston Bridge. Southern Ontario and Quebec would have service, but not northern and northwestern Ontario.

Conventional wisdom held that there were no markets for natural gas in Ontario's north. The population and the industrial base were insufficient to justify the large capital cost of building a pipeline across the Canadian Shield. But building the natural gas pipeline involved more than dollars and cents. It was to become another chapter in the continuing Canadian dream: resistance to continental pressure from the United States through establishing strong east–west links.

C.D. Howe, Canada's 'Minister of Everything,' supported the idea that there should always be 'at least one great national enterprise under way and something stirring to get it done.'[8] A trans-Canada pipeline was such a project. It was, Howe and other like-minded Liberals in Ottawa believed, a national undertaking rivalling the building of the Canadian Pacific Railway. Once completed, it would be the longest pipeline in the world, and its construction would create thousands of jobs and bring western energy to the industrial East. On 13 March 1953 Howe announced in the House of Commons that the building of an all-Canadian natural gas pipeline was government policy. There would, he said, be one pipeline, and it would be built entirely on Canadian soil.[9] A new company, Trans-Canada Pipe Lines Limited, was incorporated to build, own, and operate the business. But by the fall of 1954 the company was in trouble.[10]

Trans-Canada Pipe Lines, which planned to bring gas to Winnipeg by 1955 and to begin constructing a pipeline across Ontario the following year, had invested heavily in personnel and engineering plans. It now needed more money to finance its expansion plans, but the largely American-owned Alberta energy companies would not cooperate. They refused to sign supply contracts. Eastern utilities, such as Consumers Gas of Toronto, declined to sign purchase contracts, preferring instead to maintain established, and American, sources of supply.

Without these agreements in hand, the prospect of Trans-Canada Pipe Lines raising capital on Wall Street was remote. American money was required because Canadian capital markets were believed incapable of generating the required funds. It was obvious that many in the gas business were waiting for Trans-Canada Pipe Lines' plan to collapse and be replaced with a more logical, less expensive, and more profitable north–south route.

An all-Canadian route was a pipedream, not a pipeline, the critics claimed. But to the nation-building federal Liberals, the pipeline was another important national link akin not just to the railway but to Trans-Canada Airlines and the Canadian Broadcasting Corporation. Successful prime ministers from John A. Macdonald forward have understood that national unity depends, in part, on national projects that span the huge distances separating Canadians. The trans-Canada pipeline was one such project, and, in an era of rising concern about the American domination of the Canadian economy, it possessed considerable symbolic appeal.

Even though an all-Canadian route was government policy and Trans-Canada Pipe Lines was committed to that route, it was hardly a done deal in the mid-1950s. Nevertheless, on 24 July 1954 the Board of Transport Commissioners, the successor to the Board of Railway Commissioners with which Ivan Rand was so familiar and the regulatory agency responsible for railways, airlines, and interprovincial pipelines, released a decision granting Trans-Canada Pipe Lines preliminary approval to build a 3,500-kilometre-long pipeline. It was to start about 2 kilometres west of the Alberta-Saskatchewan border and generally follow the main line of the CPR from Alberta to Port Arthur and Fort William, past Nipigon, and across to Marathon, Sudbury, and North Bay, then south to Toronto. There one branch would head west to Oakville and another east, this time tracing the route of Canadian National Railways along the St Lawrence River to Montreal. Before reaching Montreal, however, a branch line would head north to service Ottawa-Hull. A lateral branch would be built from Winnipeg to Emerson, to serve Minneapolis, St Paul, and other localities in the United States.

In granting preliminary approval to this 'southern route,' the board prevailed over objections from representatives of Ontario's north. They had proposed that the main line should follow a northern route and go from Nipigon to Geraldton and Hearst, following Highway 11 through Kapuskasing, Smooth Rock Falls, Cochrane, Iroquois Falls (with a lateral to Timmins), Kirkland Lake, Englehart, and Cobalt, then south to

North Bay, with a lateral travelling west from North Bay to Sudbury. Trans-Canada Pipe Lines opposed this plan, arguing that it did not make economic sense, and the board agreed. However, the board left open the possibility that the route could be changed if evidence was put before it that the 'northern route' was financially feasible.[11] The northern municipalities and mayors could ignore this possibility only at their peril. If they wanted natural gas, and the jobs and industries that this low-cost, versatile fuel was sure to provide, they would have to prove to Trans-Canada Pipe Lines, the Board of Transport Commissioners, and federal and provincial politicians that there was a market for natural gas in the north. To create and service that market, a new company was born: Northern Ontario Natural Gas Limited (NONG).

Ralph K. Farris, a Vancouver businessman, sportsman, oil man, and stock promoter, was the main force behind NONG. A striking man, wiry and athletic, with a patrician nose and a full head of hair, Farris was the son of a prominent British Columbia politician and past president of the Canadian Bar Association, John Wallace deBeque Farris. The senior Farris, a New Brunswick native, had served as attorney general and labour minister in Liberal provincial governments between 1917 and 1922, and he subsequently became the party's key organizational man in British Columbia. In 1937 he was summoned to the Senate by Mackenzie King, his reward for service rendered. The Rands, after moving to Ottawa in 1943, regularly socialized with Farris and his wife, meeting often for dinner at the Rideau Club. Farris's mother, Evelyn, was the founder of the University Women's Club in Vancouver and the first woman to sit on the governing board of a Canadian university. His uncle was the chief justice of British Columbia, and his brother, John, would also go on to become the province's chief justice. The family was about as 'establishment' as one could find in British Columbia.

Ralph Farris had been educated at the University of British Columbia and at the Harvard Business School. After Harvard he worked for two years in New York, married a Northwestern University co-ed, and, in 1934, returned to Vancouver and began work as a stock-broker. Five years later, he had his own seat on the Vancouver Stock Exchange.[12] When the post-war oil boom erupted in Alberta, he began to commute to Calgary, learned the oil business, and established the Charter Oil Company, an Alberta gas producer. He invested widely and knew everyone in the industry. In 1953 a middle-aged file clerk, Gordon Kelly McLean, suggested to Farris that they create a company to distribute gas in northern Ontario. As McLean explained it, Trans-Canada Pipe Lines had decided to follow the southern route, basically hugging the shore of Lake Superior, and would bypass the major communities of northern Ontario. The southern route was shorter, but, to lay the pipe, the company would have to blast a trench through the world's oldest and hardest rock, the Precambrian Shield.[13] In contrast, a pipeline following the northern route could service a large number of communities and might even be less expensive to build, since it would require digging through soft clay most of the way. Moreover, the advantage of the northern route from a gas distributor's point of view was that it could service all the northern communities through short laterals attached to the line. Trans-Canada Pipe Lines was a primary carrier that would make its money by transporting and then selling gas to local and secondary distributors. From NONG's perspective, this arrangement was perfect. Someone else, in effect, would pay the huge cost of building the pipeline.[14] All NONG would have to do was sell and deliver the gas.

Farris was immediately attracted to the idea,[15] though he did not know much about the geography of northern Ontario. McLean was not a close Farris associate or even a reputable businessman, having served time in jail for fraud,[16] but he had one indisputable advantage: his uncle, Philip 'Phil' Kelly, was Ontario's minister of mines. Kelly, an accountant who represented Smooth Rock Falls and adjacent areas in the Ontario legislature, knew all about the north: the industries, the cost of West Virginia coal and fuel oil, and the potential market there for natural gas. Kelly was the mastermind of the deal. He saw the opportunity, developed the idea, and made an agreement with his nephew to split any profit that resulted.[17] Obviously, given his public portfolio, Kelly's involvement had to be kept quiet. What the project really needed, however, was an established oil man with a proven track record – and Farris was that man. NONG was formed the following year as a limited company with a handful of investors to bring gas to the north and profits to its promoters – though not necessarily in that order.

Lower construction costs aside, the northern route had a number of other advantages. Northern Ontario was the centre of Ontario's pulp and paper industry and the heart of mining in Canada; it supplied 85 per cent of the free world's supply of nickel,[18] as well as copper, gold, iron ore, and uranium. If companies like Ontario-Minnesota Pulp and Paper in Kenora, Spruce Falls Power and Paper in Kapuskasing,

International Nickel and Falconbridge in Sudbury, Du Pont in North
Bay, and Abitibi Power & Paper in Iroquois Falls, Smooth Rock Falls,
and Sturgeon Falls could be persuaded to switch to gas, there was vast
potential for growth and profit. The north was a high-cost-fuel area.
Natural gas, less expensive and more efficient, could easily compete.

But first, Trans-Canada Pipe Lines would have to choose the northern route. If it did not, NONG would have to build a lateral of its own,
travelling north from North Bay, and it would be responsible for all
the construction costs, estimated at $40–50 million. This would make
the venture financially questionable, to say the least. However, even
assuming that Trans-Canada Pipe Lines was willing to follow the
northern route and the board agreed, financial success was not assured
unless the northern municipalities granted NONG exclusive franchise
agreements. Only through obtaining agreements with most, if not all,
of the northern communities could the necessary economies of scale be
achieved. Without them, the scheme could not work.

Farris tackled the job with his customary enthusiasm and, by the end
of April 1955, NONG had signed distribution deals with sixteen northern Ontario municipalities from North Bay to Hearst. The excitement
was palpable. 'The impact and influence of natural gas in Northern
Ontario,' Farris later told the North Bay and District Chamber of Commerce, 'will trigger a great development.'[19]

There were, however, two holdouts: Sudbury and the Lakehead. In
the Lakehead another company, Twin City Gas, obtained franchises
for both Port Arthur and Fort William. Twin City also secured the
franchise rights for a number of other northwestern municipalities, including Dryden and Kenora. NONG later overcame this problem by
buying an interest in Twin City and soon acquired control.[20] That left
the Sudbury franchise.

Sudbury, 500 kilometres from Toronto, got its start as a CPR town
and endured because of the huge copper and nickel deposits found in
the nearby basin.[21] By the 1950s the mines and mills of Sudbury were
operating at near capacity and, like much of the country, the city was
experiencing a boom.[22] The new Sudbury shopping centre was under
construction, three banks were opening new branches downtown, and,
by 1956, 107,889 people called Sudbury home, a 34 per cent increase
in just five years.[23] As long as business was good – and INCO's first-
quarter profits and Falconbridge's continued growth proved it was –
the future was bright.[24] At City Hall, business activity was reflected
in the Council agenda. Economic development preoccupied municipal

politicians like Leo Landreville, followed by new problems such as municipal plans, traffic congestion, and the new city arena.[25] The outlook was bright and, with the arrival of natural gas, it would become brighter still – once the franchise was awarded.

NONG's projections indicated that Sudbury was the largest potential market for its product. The company expected to attract almost 5,300 residential customers in its first year of operation in Sudbury. Timmins, the next largest market, had an anticipated customer base of 3,300. There were parallel projections for industrial use: Sudbury was expected to have 144 commercial consumers in the first year, followed by 105 for Timmins. In terms of actual volume, the NONG study stated that Sudbury would be the largest overall consumer by far. INCO, a nickel-producing facility located in the adjoining community of Copper Cliff, accounted for most of the anticipated volume.[26] By the end of 1955, however, Sudbury was the only community, and INCO the only industry of any significant size, that had not yet signed up with NONG. And so Farris made the trek to Sudbury to take personal charge of negotiating the deals. There, for the first time, he met the ebullient mayor, Leo A. Landreville.

Landreville, born in Ottawa in 1910, was the only son among six children of an illiterate merchant father. He was educated in good separate schools and at the University of Ottawa, where academic success always eluded him though he excelled in acting and debates. His family expected him to become a lawyer, so he enrolled at Osgoode Hall, failed first year, but was then accepted into Dalhousie Law School. Nearly all his marks were between 50 and 60 per cent, but he scraped through, and in 1937 received his law degree.[27] Admitted to the Ontario bar the following year, Landreville moved to Sudbury, worked in the law chambers of J.A.S. Plouffe, a prominent criminal and civil litigation lawyer, and by 1950 had opened his own firm, Landreville, Hawkins and Gratton.

Landreville was one of five French-speaking lawyers in town, and he soon established a reputation as one of the best. He insisted that his office be staffed with multilingual clerks – Finnish, Polish, Italian, and Ukrainian – and he attempted to provide service to all Sudbury's varied clientele. Appointed a provincial QC in 1956, Landreville specialized in civil and criminal litigation. 'Leo the Lip,' as some people called him, defended clients in twenty-nine manslaughter cases, and not one was convicted. His record in murder trials was equally impressive: of the twelve clients he defended, five were convicted of lesser crimes, six were acquitted, and one was sent to the gallows. He was a courtroom natural with his smooth manner and well-modulated actor's voice. Landreville also founded and operated a business school and was an able investor, where he made considerable money in real estate.[28]

An indefatigable Sudbury booster, Landreville became the city's goodwill ambassador to the world. He clearly enjoyed meeting people, travelling, and the good life, even learning to fly a seaplane and using it for hunting and fishing trips to his fully equipped hunting camp in the far north.[29] He also had a taste for politics, running first as a school trustee and then as an alderman on Sudbury's City Council. Like many Franco-Ontarians, he was a fervent Liberal, and he became friends with Lester Pearson, the MP for neighbouring Algoma East. After the 1953 election, Pearson thanked Landreville for his help during the campaign. 'In return,' Pearson wrote, 'one day I will stand beside you and in front of a sign which will read, not "We Like Mike" but "We Love Leo!"'[30]

In January 1955 Landreville became mayor of Sudbury. 'I believe,' he told City Council, 'that a mayor is not only a chairman at meetings. His prime duty is to know, inform, and give guidance to the members of his council – he must disclose fairly and entirely all aspects of a problem for his members to discuss, to weigh the merits and demerits and decide by majority rule. He must lead fearlessly and not follow sheepishly the proceedings.'[31] The biggest issue on the new mayor's plate was NONG's application for the natural gas franchise.

By early 1956 NONG was the only company actively seeking the Sudbury franchise, and Sudbury was the only community of consequence that had not yet signed up. In February, Farris travelled north and, for the first time, met the mayor. Fortunately, Farris and Landreville hit it off, and their business relationship soon turned into a social one as well: there were dinner parties at Landreville's home and visits to his camp on the lake. By the end of April, NONG and INCO had reached a tentative agreement. Landreville had earlier made it clear that, as soon as INCO was on board, City Council would follow suit. Even better news came from the Board of Transport Commissioners, which announced that it had changed its mind and now approved the northern route. The only problem was money: the capital markets could not raise sufficient funds to pay for part of the trans-Canada pipeline. When the opposition refused to play ball, the Liberals invoked closure and voted the necessary funds. All that remained, from NONG's point of view, was for Sudbury to sign on.

When City Council met in May, the result was preordained that NONG would get the franchise. C.D. Howe even urged council to move final passage and grant the franchise without any further delay. Farris wrote that he would return to Sudbury soon and, referring to some earlier correspondence from Landreville, added, 'as you say, we have important things to discuss.'[32] First and second reading on the bylaw took place on 22 May. When the city solicitor raised some concerns about the bylaw and the contractual agreement with NONG, third reading was delayed, but not for long, as Landreville and others pointed out that passage of the bylaw had become a matter of some urgency. This message was repeated, publicly and privately, by the chair of the Ontario Fuel Board, who made it clear to Sudbury councillors that their dallying threatened the entire project. Finally, after some negotiations with NONG which made a good deal even better, City Council, on 17 July, granted the franchise to NONG.

Landreville took no part in council's formal vote. NONG was, after all, the natural choice. That evening Farris and Landreville went out for a late supper. They had much to celebrate and to discuss. As Farris later recalled,

He was most impressed with our company and its future. I think he advised me his term of office was shortly expiring and he would not be standing for office again. I think he initiated it but I wouldn't be too sure of that, of the desirability, from his point of view, of being associated with a new utility such as ours and my agreeing we would need a lot of people in our organization, each with certain talents, each able to contribute something to a company that, up to now, had practically no employees and ... we were just at that time changing the capital of the company and going to make a rights offering on the new company of $2.50 a share and it is quite logical ... in response to his inquiry as to his ability to participate in the stock of the company, that I would tell him, yes, when that association took place that he could and would be allowed to buy shares at this price.[33]

The next day Farris returned to Toronto, and a NONG directors' meeting was purportedly held. Among the issues said to be discussed was the future relationship with Landreville. Three days after Sudbury finally approved the deal, Farris wrote to the mayor:

You have recently expressed an interest in our company indicating that when free to do so, you would like to assist us in some capacity, particularly with reference to representing us as we face the many problems ahead in the Sudbury area and Northern Ontario generally. You have indicated your faith and interest in us by expressing also a desire to purchase stock in our company. We greatly appreciate this twofold approbation of us by you.

At a directors' meeting held the 18th of July ... your participation in our company was discussed. The shareholders' meeting had approved a change in capital whereby the authorized capital was increased to 2,000,000 shares and the outstanding shares split five for one to bring the total issued shares to approximately 660,000. The directors resolved to offer existing shareholders the right to subscribe for 40,000 additional shares of the 'new' stock at a price of $2.50 per share.

At the same time it was resolved to offer you 10,000 shares at the same price of $2.50 per share. This offer is firm until July 18th, 1957. Should you wish to purchase portions of these shares at different times that will be in order.

At your convenience and when you are free to do so we would welcome the opportunity to discuss our relationship for the future in greater detail.[34]

Landreville responded at the end of the month:

I have your very kind letter of July 20th at hand.

I fully appreciate the advantages of the offer you outlined to me and I fully intend to exercise this option before July 18th, 1957.

There is the additional question of the personal interest I will devote to your Company in Northern Ontario. While all the management questions may be at a problematic stage in your Company, I would like to assure you of my interest in promoting the welfare of your Company in the time to come.

My present Office, as Mayor, does not permit me to a definite committal but in the course of the months following January next, I feel sure we may sit down and see if your Company and I have something which we could exchange to our mutual benefit.[35]

In the summer of 1956, the sum of $2.50 might have been a fair price for the NONG shares. That quickly began to change and, by December, there was active public interest in the shares, now valued at around $10 each (the price rose to a high of $28 just before the public issue in June 1957). By the end of February 1957 the future and profitability of NONG was assured, and this success was reflected in its share price. On 27 February the Metropolitan Life Insurance Company agreed to buy $90 million of Trans-Canada Pipe Lines' mortgage bonds. The private and public (mostly from the federal and Ontario governments) financing for the trans-Canada route was completely in place. That meant that NONG was no longer a speculative venture with paper assets, but had become a company with a tangible commodity to sell.

Landreville was not the only politician to benefit from NONG's largesse. A number of other northern mayors were given outright gifts of NONG shares. In accordance with its stated policy, NONG also made an early offer to residents of franchise areas. Farris approached Landreville's successor as mayor, Joseph Fabbro, and asked him to provide NONG with the names of persons who might be interested in participating in the public offering, which consisted of one debenture and one share with an initial price of $30. Fabbro, happy to comply, presented Farris with a list of preferred customers. Although demand was in excess of supply, Fabbro allocated the largest number of the units – 1,650 – to himself. Various other members of City Council and the clerk-comptroller were allotted much smaller amounts, ranging between 100 and 150 units each. After these arrangements were made, the units were offered to the public, and the offering was an unqualified success. Unit holders who immediately sold took easy profits, as the units rapidly reached a market price substantially above the offering price.[36] Similar arrangements were made with other northern mayors, who also drew up subscription lists that were forwarded to NONG.

Altogether, 400,000 common shares were offered for sale, which netted NONG more than $11 million. A further $8 million in subordinate debentures was also sold, and commitments were obtained from both Canadian and American institutional lenders for $12 million of mortgage bonds. A majority of NONG shares were held by Canadians. By the spring of 1958 Farris's dream was almost realized. The construction program was ahead of schedule and below budget. The basic industrial sales program was complete and, more important, the projections indicated greater potential revenue than originally forecast.

NONG began preparations for an aggressive sales campaign once the gas lines were installed. Local dealers were trained in the sale, service, and proper installation of gas appliances and gas-fired equipment. A NONG information bus equipped with demonstration material began travelling from one community to the next, staging informational meetings for the public. A company-sponsored finance plan was expected to bolster residential sales. Appliance dealers who wished to avail themselves of the plan, and who conformed to company and regulatory requirements, were designated as 'Authorized Blue Flame Dealers.' A twenty-four-hour service department was in preparation. Standards exceeding legal requirements were established to ensure the safety of all service lines, installations, and appliances. Other promotional activities such as the 'Gasarama,' a fair with the arrival of natural gas as its theme, were planned for the larger centres.

Gas was coming to the north, and so was prosperity. An army of construction crews arrived with money to spend – some five thousand workers at one time. Hotel and restaurant owners profited, and so did local building- and cement-supply companies. In more than half the communities it crossed, Trans-Canada Pipe Lines became the largest taxpayer. 'The arrival of this low-cost, versatile fuel, available for the first time to energy-hungry industries and communities,' NONG's annual report observed, 'and at a price significantly lower than in Southern Ontario, promises to initiate an era of growth the extent of which time alone can fully assess.'[37] For the first time, compared with competitors in the south, northern industries operated at an energy-price advantage. Instead of simply being a colony of Toronto, there was every reason to believe that the north would become an economic power in its own right.

All the signs pointed in this direction. The population of the north was growing. New industries were being established, and it was expected that the market for established ones, such as pulp and paper, would continue to increase. NONG might also expand: the uranium mines at Blind River and Elliot Lake, the Steep Rock–Atikokan iron ore development, and the gold and copper mining areas of Rouyn, Noranda, and Val d'Or in northern Quebec all held out the promise of much new business. NONG was sponsoring research in the use of natural gas, and new applications and possibilities were being discovered every day. By the end of 1958, NONG would be delivering gas to thirty-four communities located between the Manitoba-Ontario border and Orillia, with a population of more than 300,000.[38] The future was extremely bright – for the north and for Leo Landreville.

Landreville was at the pinnacle of his professional life. He was planning to retire from municipal politics and to begin a promising and rewarding future with NONG. However, on 13 September 1956 he was appointed to the Supreme Court of Ontario, one of the last judicial appointments Louis St Laurent's government would make before its defeat in the general election the next year. An appointment to the bench is the dream of many lawyers, for service as a judge brings with it status and prestige. Judicial appointments are highly sought, and supplicants usually take many steps to make their desire known. Political connections used to help, and, notwithstanding all the reforms to the appointment process, they still do. Landreville's elevation had been rumoured for weeks, and he was sworn in early the following month.[39]

He had to tell Farris, of course, and an opportunity arose at a Chamber of Commerce dinner in North Bay where Landreville was one of the guests of honour. After breaking the news, Landreville reminded Farris that he had promised to join NONG – that was the whole basis on which the stock option had been granted – but Farris urged him to accept the judicial appointment. The stock option was his no matter what decision he made.[40] 'After the dilemma of whether to have my appendix out or not, the dilemma of remaining a bachelor and happy or get married – this was the biggest dilemma!' Landreville wrote to Farris. 'I feel that given three or four years and with my ambition, I would have squeezed you out of the Presidency of your Company – now I have chosen to be put on the shelf of this all-inspiring, unapproachable, staid class of people called Judges – what a decision! However, right or wrong, I will stick to it and do the best I can ... I want to assure you,' he continued, 'that my interest in your Company, outwardly aloof, will, nevertheless, remain active. I am keeping your letter of July 20th carefully in my file.'[41] Farris sent a gracious reply. 'I know that your decision was not an easy one,' he wrote, 'and those of us who have learned to appreciate your many facets will understand what a difficult decision it was. There can be no question as to the wisdom of the appointment and I hope that time will show that there was equal wisdom in its acceptance.'[42] Landreville reconfirmed that he wished to retain the NONG option, and Farris, ever generous, again indicated his agreement.[43]

Landreville was Franco-Ontario's new representative on the bench. The tradition of a French-speaking superior court judge at Osgoode Hall began in October 1935, when E.R.E. Chevrier, a well-known and highly regarded Ottawa lawyer, was appointed. The reaction of the *Fortnightly Law Journal* was typical. 'We shall watch with interest,' it announced, 'the experiment of appointing a French-Canadian to the Ontario Bench. We note that in the recent Benchers' election, another French-Canadian did not make much of a showing, which would seem to indicate that

the profession is not enamoured of such an encroachment in a traditional Anglo-Saxon Province.'[44] Chevrier was eventually promoted to the
Court of Appeal in 1953, the 'experiment' having proved a success.

It took Landreville some time to settle his affairs, and there was also
the matter of the stock option. It was complicated but turned out quite
well for him. In early 1957, at Farris's request, the Continental Investment Company, a well-known Vancouver brokerage firm known as
Convesto, 'purchased' 14,000 shares from NONG for $2.50 each 'on
behalf of clients.'[45] Convesto sent NONG a cheque for $35,000. The
shares were then, on Farris's instructions, allotted to various persons,
including Landreville, who received 10,000 shares in February 1957 at
the agreed-on option price of $2.50 each. 'Some time ago,' a 12 Febru-
ary 1957 letter to Landreville from John McGraw, the head of Convesto, reported, 'we were instructed by Mr. Ralph K. Farris to purchase
for your account 10,000 shares of NONG at $2.50 per share. We have as
of this date sold 2,500 shares for your account at $10 per share which
clears off the debit balance of your account. You will find enclosed
7,500 shares of NONG with stock receipt attached, which we ask you
to sign and return to this office at your convenience.'[46]

Normally in a transaction of this kind, Landreville would have been
required to purchase the stock himself by making a payment directly
to NONG. The option had been granted by the corporation, and the
payment should have been made to its treasury. Landreville had the
financial means to buy his shares outright and could easily have done
so if asked. However, there are many ways of organizing corporate
affairs, and there was nothing necessarily wrong with this one. As a
result, Landreville ended up with 7,500 NONG shares without laying
out a dime. The transaction was not recorded in the usual way. Convesto atypically made its handsome commission by keeping the difference between its purchase price of 2,500 of Landreville's shares at
$10 a share and the selling price on the open market, which was then
upwards of $13 a share.

The sale was also interesting for a number of other reasons. It was
recorded by journal voucher and, other than a single ledger entry in
Convesto's records, nothing in NONG's books indicated that Landreville was the beneficiary of the transaction. It was not unheard of to
structure a transaction this way, but why had Farris not followed the
usual course? It was almost as if the sale and the profits were being
deliberately concealed.

In any event, the remaining shares were sent to Landreville in 'street form' – his name did not appear on the certificates. Beginning in February 1957, Landreville sold the stock in a rapidly rising market. Ultimately, he pocketed $117,000. He had reason to be grateful, and he wrote to Convesto on his Supreme Court of Ontario stationery expressing his thanks and adding, for good measure: 'Should I be of any assistance to your firm for the promotion or betterment of this company in Ontario, please do not hesitate to contact me.'[47]

Landreville put the money to good use. He improved his Mexican home, bought his wife some jewellery, and increased his real estate investments. In February 1957 Landreville and Farris met in New York and a grateful Landreville thanked his friend for the delivery of the shares.[48] He welcomed the supplement to his salary now that he was a judge. The annual stipend of $18,000 a year was only about a third of what he had earned from the private practice of law.

Although Landreville was not the only northern mayor to receive free NONG shares, he made by far the most money on them. That fact, and the manner in which the transaction was recorded on the Convesto books, would raise suspicions about exactly what services Landreville had performed to merit such generous treatment from Farris and NONG. Farris also arranged for three other northern mayors and one city solicitor to receive free shares, but on a much reduced scale. These transactions were also handled in a slightly different way. An account was opened in Convesto in the name of Gordon Kelly McLean, who was now employed by Farris as his executive assistant, and 800 NONG shares were deposited into that account. Immediately, 200 shares were sold to clear the account. Convesto then mailed the remaining shares to Toronto, again in street form, where McLean gave lots of 150 shares each to Gravenhurst mayor Wanda Miller, Bracebridge mayor Glen Coates, Orillia mayor Wilbur Cramp, and Orillia city solicitor W.L. Moore.[49]

Landreville enjoyed his new career. He did not, as a judge, develop any area of jurisprudence or gain any particular expertise, but, unlike some Supreme Court judges of the day, he was not automatically biased against plaintiffs whose last names ended with a vowel. He ran a surprisingly orderly court, and lawyers felt they received a full and fair hearing, whether they won or lost.[50] In addition, Landreville did not suffer from 'judgeitis': he remembered what it was like to be a counsel, and when he travelled to the county towns on the Ontario Supreme Court circuit, he understood that the administration of justice was important everywhere in the province.

Landreville was, in short, a decent man and an all around good judge who quickly grasped the facts. He carried a heavy workload and did a good job. Still, many of his colleagues at Osgoode Hall resented what they saw as his flamboyant manner and extravagant lifestyle, and some could not tolerate the fact that he had a crucifix in his office. There was nobody else like him at Osgoode Hall – certainly, no one else had decorated his office and installed a sofa, hi-fi, and bar. But Landreville loved life and, whenever he could, he got away to enjoy Landra Villa. Everything was going well for him, until the police came calling.

Money was being made. Mines minister Phil Kelly's initial $5,000 investment had, by early 1957, grown to half a million dollars. His nephew did almost as well. Two of Kelly's Cabinet colleagues were included on the gravy train, and Kelly even reached across party lines and ensured that future Liberal leader John Wintermeyer was cut in for a share of the spoils. The only problem for the minister, and his Cabinet colleagues, was that Premier Leslie Frost had ordered all members of his government not to invest in any pipeline stocks. After all, the Ontario government had joined with Ottawa in providing some necessary financial guarantees and other contributions to ensure the success of the project. Eventually Kelly's profiteering came to the attention of Frost, who accepted his resignation. CCF leader Donald C. MacDonald soon found out what had happened, and in March 1958, raised it in the legislature. It was a true political scandal, and the press latched on to the story. An enterprising *Toronto Star* reporter named Blaik Kirby bought one share of NONG stock and exercised his right to examine the shareholders' list. All hell then broke loose. The Ontario legislature had approved a $35 million contribution to the financing of the pipeline, and Cabinet ministers had bought and held on to shares in brazen defiance of the premier. Frost initially tried to deal with the crisis by stonewalling, but public demands for an inquiry escalated, and in May, the attorney general announced an Ontario Securities Commission (OSC) investigation of NONG stock sales. More Cabinet resignations followed. Ralph Farris was charged with some technical breaches of the securities regulations and fined $500. But lurking in the background was a bomb waiting to go off. Why had NONG provided 14,000 shares to Convesto at a wildly discounted rate, and who had benefited from that sale of shares?

During the OSC investigation, Farris was, while under oath, asked that question. 'Are you aware of the disposition of those 14,000 shares issued and allotted to Convesto under date of January 17, 1957?' No, he lied, he was not. He went on to claim that he never, directly or indirectly, sold or gave any shares to any provincial Cabinet minister, MP, or MPP, or any member of any municipal council with which NONG had done business. In fact, Landreville had been given an 'option,' and the mayors of Bracebridge, Gravenhurst, and Orillia were all given gifts of shares. As CCF leader MacDonald kept on the case, he became especially interested in the fate of those 14,000 shares. In the legislature he pointed out that the Sudbury franchise was of particular importance to NONG, so much so that Farris had personally handled the negotiations. The authorities insisted that everything was above board, even though 14,000 shares had disappeared into a nominee account. Landreville, holed up in his Osgoode Hall office, kept a deliberately low profile, with his fingers crossed that the scandal would blow over. For a long time, it looked as though it might.

Four years passed. There were rumours, but not much else. A leading official in Sudbury was said to be involved. 'Who is the mystery man of gas scandal?' the *Toronto Star* asked. In 1962 the situation changed. Acting on a tip, the RCMP began investigating the activities of a dubious British Columbia stockbroker who had fled to New Zealand. Next they found the name of Mr Justice Leo A. Landreville, and a paper trail that raised more questions than answers. When the police interviewed Landreville in his Toronto chambers, he lied. He told the Mounties that he ordered the shares through a Sudbury broker. The press found out that Landreville was at the centre of the renewed probe, and the scandal was back on the front page. Farris was charged with perjury arising out of his evidence during the 1957 OSC investigation. Landreville testified at both the preliminary inquiry and the trial, but Farris was convicted, and sent to jail. A second OSC investigation commenced and attention focused on Landreville. As the details leaked out, it became increasingly clear that something was fishy. In the summer of 1964 Landreville was criminally charged with municipal corruption and conspiracy. At that moment his usefulness and career as a judge were over. A preliminary hearing was held in Sudbury before Magistrate Albert Marck, where Landreville was represented by the skilful John J. Robinette.

As Canada's most accomplished lawyer, Robinette was already a legal legend for his role in the defence of accused murderer Evelyn

Dick and in the Gouzenko spy trials. He specialized in appellate advocacy, appearing frequently before the Ontario Court of Appeal and the Supreme Court of Canada. A bencher and former treasurer of the Law Society, Robinette knew everyone and was widely admired. He was the lawyer to go to if you were in trouble. The hearing lasted six days, and the Crown adduced considerable evidence about NONG and its dealings with Sudbury City Council. After hearing all the evidence, Marck concluded there was insufficient evidence that Landreville had committed any crime – certainly not enough to forward the case for trial, where the legal standard is proof beyond a reasonable doubt. The decision was dubious, but it was the magistrate's call to make. The stock option was a problem for sure. Marck accepted Landreville's explanation that it was a gift made out of friendship, not the result of corruption. The charges were dismissed, even though it was difficult to understand how giving money to Landreville could be in the interests of the shareholders of a public company.

Privately, Prime Minister Pearson sent Landreville a message that it was time for him to step down. The instructions were clear: resume your duties for the current session and then tender your resignation. In those circumstances, the government would give favourable consideration to a pension request. That was good advice – but Landreville, increasingly erratic under the stress of fighting off a criminal charge, rejected it. Then the Law Society, in one of its most egregious acts, assembled a small kangaroo court of elected benchers, held hearings behind closed doors, 'convicted' Landreville of being unfit to serve as a judge, and imposed that report on a docile convocation of all the elected benchers, which duly passed it and sent a copy on to the justice minister in Ottawa. From start to finish, the entire process was beyond the jurisdiction of the Law Society, and it was conducted in flagrant breach of basic rules of fairness and procedural justice. The first Landreville heard of it was when the verdict was delivered to the minister. Cornered, he went on to make the most self-destructive decision of his life – he wrote to the federal minister of justice and asked for a formal inquiry. Landreville did have something to hide, and in these circumstances only a madman would ask the government to establish an investigatory commission. The minister quickly agreed.

It was a logical first step to appoint a commission of inquiry to consider whether Landreville had done anything that rendered him unfit to continue as a judge. At the time, individual lawyers could not complain about a sitting judge – the bench was sufficiently small and inbred to raise a real fear of judicial reprisals. Provincial chief justices did not have any authority to deal with errant judges (although they did have, and used, considerable moral authority over their judges to correct some misbehaviour and get an errant judge back on course), nor did the chief justice of Canada or any of the provincial attorneys general. There were, in short, no mechanisms in place to receive complaints and determine whether a recommendation should be made to Parliament for the removal of a judge.

Accordingly, a royal commission was needed to examine Landreville's dealings with NONG and to report whether anything done by Landreville in the course of such dealings constituted misbehaviour in his official capacity as a judge or unfit conduct to continue on the bench. Once that report was in, depending on what it said, the government could take the next step, which was either to leave him alone or to ask Parliament to remove him. Landreville announced that he was ready for the inquiry to begin so he could 'vindicate his name.'[51] Robinette was consulted privately about the choice of commissioner. How about Rand? Robinette, to his everlasting regret, agreed. An order-in-council was duly passed, and Rand got to work.[52]

As commission counsel, Rand selected Edmonton lawyer and future Alberta appellate judge William George Morrow. The two men got off to a rocky start. One day, Morrow tried to help Rand on with his coat, but the commissioner did not appreciate the gesture: 'When I need that kind of help,' he said, 'pack me off.' Morrow received the same reaction when he opened the door for Rand. As they travelled from one city to the next, they ate modest meals in small hotel rooms and flew economy class everywhere they went. Finally, Morrow suggested to Rand that they have a glass of sherry before dinner to 'aid the digestive process.' Rand agreed. They also shared a love of apples. 'One evening,' Morrow recalled in his memoirs, 'as I indulged myself, Rand popped in with a question. He noticed my apple and, as he exclaimed, it was his passion too, I offered him one of mine. He went to his room and then returned with a small knife that he carried solely for the purpose of paring apples; the apple-a-night routine crept into our inquiry. Each evening, after our work was accomplished, the great man would begin to reminisce and tell stories of the Maritimes, of his earlier life in Alberta as a lawyer, of the intrigues of politics, and of the Supreme Court of Canada.'[53]

The commission first met in Vancouver on 14 March 1966. The star witness was Ralph Farris, who had been released on parole on Canada Day, 1965, after serving five months in jail. Farris provided a convoluted explanation of his dealings with Landreville which made no sense. He told the Rand Commission that, when Landreville bought shares in January 1957, the purchase was not connected to the July 1956 option arrangement. That deal was based on his coming to work for NONG and, when he failed to do so, the option was effectively cancelled. After Landreville became a judge, he indicated to Farris that he was still interested in buying shares. Farris insisted that the $2.50 price was, at that time, a fair one.[54] What made the transaction appear questionable, he acknowledged, was the explosion in the share price that began in the last days of 1956 and the first month of 1957, when, as it coincidentally happened, Landreville and the others finally got the opportunity to execute their earlier purchase agreements.

The only problem with this explanation was that it was at complete odds with the truth. As Farris knew, Convesto was trading NONG shares in early December for $10 each, and he could find no record of any sale from that period for any lesser amount. There was no way of getting around it: selling 14,000 shares for $2.50 each anytime after October 1956 was, in effect, giving away money – NONG's money. The recipient could immediately cash out with a huge tax-free capital gain. The explanation that NONG needed the money was bogus – if the company was truly cash starved, it would have sold the shares at the market price.

NONG's corporate records were a mess. On 17 July 1956 Sudbury City Council had finally approved the NONG franchise agreement. A NONG directors meeting was purportedly held on the 18th, at which time Landreville's stock option was approved. NONG's minute books did not record this meeting. Farris did not deny that NONG's record keeping was lax. He did, however, point out to Rand that NONG was a young company, and, while there were a number of directors, he basically ran the show. Sometimes, Farris admitted, directors meetings were never formally held, though they were recorded as if they were. 'We might all have been in New York on some business and the lawyer says: "Where were you all together so we can constitute a meeting?"' It was difficult getting people together, and NONG once held a directors meeting 'in the elevator of the Ritz Hotel in Montreal.'[55] Rand found these goings-on hard to understand. He was far removed from the realities of business life, and when he practised law, it was largely for a publicly owned company that was subject to constant scrutiny and regulation. His understanding of business had little in common with the practices that were now being described. Farris's testimony that the share option, when offered, was completely legitimate was of some significance, although it was ultimately unbelievable and entirely self-serving. Farris insisted that the option was not for the purpose of inducing Landreville to betray his office or his duty to the people of Sudbury. Rand made it clear from the start that he saw things differently: he was extremely sceptical about Landreville's relationship with Farris.

Rand also signalled that Landreville's character was one of his chief concerns. Over Robinette's objections, he let Morrow lead evidence about the distribution of free shares to Mayors Miller, Coates, and Cramp. Those transactions, Robinette pointed out, had nothing to do with Landreville and Rand's terms of reference. Rand disagreed: 'The character of these men' made the evidence relevant, he stated. Robinette was incredulous: 'Well, I hope you aren't going to decide Mr. Landreville's case on the character of other mayors; I would take very strong objection to that.' Rand quickly recovered. 'I don't mean their character; I mean, the character of the position. They were all mayors, and they all had shares distributed from this same vote of 14,000.'[56] He let the evidence in, prejudicial and irrelevant though it was to the issue of whether Landreville had done anything that made him unfit to serve as a judge. That Landreville was in for a rough ride became obvious when the commission reconvened in Sudbury on 21 March.

Every living member of the Sudbury City Council of 1955 and 1956 was called to give evidence, though it was all largely the same. Sudbury wanted natural gas, NONG was the only company in the running, and, by the spring and summer of 1956, there was some urgency, communicated in large part by C.D. Howe and others, to sign the deal. Landreville, the evidence established, took virtually no part, public or otherwise, in the decision. He did not press anyone to vote for NONG. A majority of council members were satisfied not only that it was a good deal but that Sudbury had got the best deal.

While everyone knew that Sudbury would sign with NONG, no one knew at the time the franchise agreement was before council that Landreville had asked for an opportunity to buy NONG shares. Most of the council members were later given a chance to buy shares, and they did. They insisted in their testimony before the commission that there was nothing wrong with any of these purchases. When Robinette asked

Joseph Fabbro, who had voted to delay the passing of the franchise by-law, whether he viewed the shares he received as a reward, he smiled and said, 'Hardly.'[57] NONG was a generous company. This was not the evidence the commission counsel was looking for, and he made a direct appeal to the people of Sudbury through the press: 'May I say this to any member of the local press who are reporting these proceedings, will they please put this: Should anyone here have any information or wish to give me any information that they think might help me in these proceedings, I am at the President Motel, if they would contact me.'[58] No one did – at least, no new witnesses were called as a result.

If Landreville had been on trial, the case for the prosecution would have been going badly. Rand, obviously and increasingly frustrated, could not resist interjecting himself into the proceedings, and he relentlessly pursued every allegation of misconduct. When one former Sudbury City Council member testified, for example, that he felt compelled to approve the NONG deal, Rand spent considerable time trying to find out what and who caused the witness to feel that way. And when this same city councillor reported a disagreement with Landreville on matters entirely unrelated to NONG, the commissioner, without hearing Landreville's version of events, suggested out loud that Landreville was somehow to blame. On another occasion, Sudbury's engineer testified that Landreville, in the weeks leading to the final vote, accused him, in a meeting held in the mayor's office, of being 'obstructionist' in his demands for further contract modifications as a condition for NONG's being awarded the franchise. In cross-examination, Robinette established that the witness was obstructionist. He was making demands that were both unrealistic and unlikely to be approved by the Ontario Fuel Board. However, when Rand got his chance to ask questions, he wanted to know if 'that was the only occasion on which you were subject to that sort of address.' He also wanted to know if Landreville 'had gone beyond the realm of politeness' in expressing his views. Later, he asked another witness whether Landreville was a 'dominating personality.' The questions were ridiculous, and witness after witness, including Sudbury's former city solicitor, indicated as much in their answers.[59]

Rand made no secret of the fact that he despised Landreville. While Landreville's judgment and behaviour clearly left a lot to be desired, so too did Rand's, both in public and behind the scenes. Rand's *ex parte* approach to the Law Society was a case in point. The society had been largely responsible for the Rand Commission's being struck. It had reported to the minister of justice that Landreville was not fit to continue as a judge and asked that he be removed. When Rand was appointed, he was provided with a copy of the Law Society report. While it is quite ordinary for commission counsel, in preparing a case, to interview prospective witnesses to determine if they have anything useful to contribute to the proceedings, commissioners themselves usually stay above the fray, in order to maintain at least a semblance of impartiality in studying the matter under review. For some reason, Rand did not understand that there is a difference between an inquiry and an inquisition.

In February 1966 Rand asked for a private meeting with the treasurer of the Law Society. He wanted to know why the society's report was considered confidential. Over lunch at the University Club, John Arnup set him straight. The report was sent to the minister of justice, but the Law Society at no time took the position that it was confidential. Once received by the minister, it was 'his communication,' and he 'was free to do what he liked with it.'[60] Rand invited the Law Society to appear before his commission to present its views. Arnup took the matter under advisement.

Arthur Pattillo, the chairman of the kangaroo court that 'convicted' Landreville without going through the formality of hearing his side of the story, insisted that the Law Society appear. 'Having been the responsible party for initiating this inquiry,' Pattillo wrote, 'we owe a duty to make representations to the Commission.'[61] This view did not prevail, and Rand's invitation was declined. 'Having in mind the material that you ... are obtaining for consideration by the Commission,' Arnup wrote Morrow, 'and in view of the fact that it is Mr. Rand who is Commissioner, the Law Society does not desire to make any representations during the hearings.'[62] The society had every confidence in Rand's grasp of the 'ethics which ought to govern a judge.'[63] After Arnup's account of his luncheon discussion, the Law Society could be satisfied that there was no need for it to air its views publicly and be cross-examined about its activities.

Rand also contacted the RCMP in February 1966 and asked them to provide him with the transcripts of the interviews taken with Landreville in 1962, when the judge claimed to have bought NONG shares from a Sudbury broker. After considering the matter, the commissioner agreed that Rand could be shown the materials, though he would not be given a copy.[64] Landreville had no idea that Rand was personally conducting his own investigation.

For his part, Attorney General Arthur Wishart told Rand that the Government of Ontario had no interest in becoming involved: 'Having ordered and seen to the prosecution of Mr Justice Landreville, I feel that my duty as Attorney General in the matter has been completed.' Wishart went on to say that 'all of the facts which were available to us were, I believe, presented in a hearing lasting some six days. Anything which I might now add would be merely an expression of opinion, and it would be presumptuous of me to trespass on the area where you have been commissioned to render judgment.'[65]

Landreville began to give evidence on 25 April, in a practically empty courtroom located in the Supreme Court of Canada in Ottawa. Rand's mind was already made up, but Landreville was still given the opportunity to present his version of events, which he did over the course of two long days. At times he was confident, but at others his voice would become thick with emotion and his eyes fill with tears. 'If I had stayed in Sudbury,' he told Rand, 'I would have peace of mind and my health.'[66] If Landreville was searching for sympathy, however, he was looking in the wrong place. Without any basis for doing so, Rand suggested, midway through Landreville's first day of testimony, that he had a 'good imagination.' Landreville, apparently, could see 'what was under way,' and the real reason he ran for mayor in 1954 was in order to 'play a part ... in the carrying out of this rather astonishing enterprise.'[67] Incredibly, Rand was suggesting that Landreville ran for mayor in December 1954 having determined that gas was on its way and that he would cash in on the development. When Landreville suggested otherwise, and pointed out that he had campaigned on a platform of municipal amalgamation, Rand, clearly annoyed, directed him to change the subject.

Virtually all the events under review had taken place a decade earlier. Yet Rand had difficulty in accepting Landreville's assertion that his memory was not perfect and that, as he heard and read about the evidence of different witnesses in different proceedings, his memory was refreshed. Although this explanation might account for relatively minor variations in his overall account, it *was* disturbing that Landreville gave conflicting accounts over the course of his evidence in these proceedings on when exactly it was that he first approached Farris about acquiring shares in NONG.

When Landreville testified before the OSC, he said that he approached Farris some time between 1 June and 15 July 1956, after the first and second readings on the Sudbury franchise had taken place.

By the time Landreville appeared before Rand, he had changed his account. He recalled that the approach was made late on the evening of 17 July, after the bylaw received final reading. Well, which one was it? Rand wanted to know. All Landreville could do was repeat his explanation that his memory had been refreshed and assert that he now believed the discussion took place later than he had thought originally. It was marginally better, from Landreville's point of view, to situate it after the franchise bylaw had passed rather than before it received third and final reading. If it took place before the franchise was granted, there would be more reason to believe that the shares had been offered as an inducement to ensure speedy passage. Rand was clearly troubled by Landreville's shifting accounts: 'Well, all I have to say to you, Mr. Landreville,' he said, 'is that you impress me as a person of a bright mind with a good memory.'[68] Rand had formed the view that Landreville was modifying his evidence to suit the circumstances, although the distinction between an inducement and a reward was really not that great. Also noteworthy was the fact that Landreville and Farris had each testified to a somewhat different version of events. It was truly amazing that these guys never got their stories straight.

On 27 April, commission counsel began his final argument by referring to the order-in-council. 'You are charged,' Morrow told Rand, 'with deciding whether anything done by Mr. Justice Landreville in the course of his dealings with NONG constituted misbehaviour in his official capacity as a judge or whether Landreville had by such dealings proved himself unfit for the proper exercise of his judicial duties.'[69] In Morrow's view, it was appropriate, in answering these questions, to consider Landreville's conduct both before and after he was appointed a judge.

Turning to Landreville's conduct as mayor, Morrow suggested that in discharging his mandate, Rand had to answer a number of questions. First, was Landreville's 'energy and drive' directed at facilitating the passage of the franchise bylaw 'prompted by the hope or expectation of a later benefit?' Second, did the share option 'reflect the possibility of an arrangement or reward for the passing of the franchise?' Third, was the exercise of the option arranged in such a way as 'to keep secret the transaction and to keep Landreville's name off the share registry?' It was up to Rand, in answering these questions, Morrow argued, to determine whether there was evidence 'of a degree of moral turpitude, or lack of ethics that may affect this man's usefulness as a Judge.'

In Morrow's submission, there were also a number of problems with Landreville's conduct after he was appointed to the bench, and Rand would have to confront them as well. Had Landreville lied when he told the Mounties in September 1962 that he had bought the NONG shares through a Sudbury broker? If Rand found that he had, rejecting Landreville's explanation that he had merely expressed the view that it was likely he had purchased the shares in this way, then the commissioner would have to draw some conclusions about the propriety of a judge telling falsehoods to the RCMP. Rand must also, Morrow argued, review all Landreville's sworn testimony before the 1962 OSC investigation, the Farris preliminary inquiry, the Farris trial, and his own preliminary inquiry, in order to decide whether Landreville had told the truth. In doing so, it was important to recognize that some discrepancies could be the result of the passage of time. However, Morrow added, there was always the possibility that the confusion 'may show a callousness or carelessness in giving serious testimony, and a disregard for the consequences which may arise … it may be … an abrogation of one's normal duty as a judicial officer.' Characterized in this way, the callousness or carelessness was arguably 'contempt of court.'

Robinette saw things differently and, when he made his final submissions, he explained why. Referring to the order-in-council, he pointed out that there was no evidence suggesting any misconduct or misbehaviour by Landreville in relation to his official capacity as a judge. There was nothing to suggest neglect of duties, bad manners, corruption, or any action that would indicate 'bad behaviour.' He pointed out that the *Act of Settlement*, together with section 99 of the *BNA Act*, guaranteed security of tenure for judges 'during good behaviour.' That being the case, Robinette suggested to Rand, the sole issue before him was whether Landreville had, in his dealings with NONG, proved himself unfit for the proper exercise of his judicial duties. Here, too, Robinette argued that all the evidence indicated he had not.

'Fitness,' like 'beauty,' is in the eye of the beholder, and to assist Rand in focusing on the issue before him, Robinette suggested a test: 'Has he so conducted himself that reasonable litigants, knowing the true facts, would not desire or permit their cases to be tried before him? Put slightly differently, has he so conducted himself that reasonable litigants, knowing the true facts, would justifiably lack confidence in his keenness of perception, his sense of fairness, his objectivity, his ability to distinguish between right and wrong?' Given the constitutional guarantee of security of tenure for superior court judges, Robinette took the position that unfitness must be proven according to the strictest of standards, and with the clearest of evidence, before a 'Superior Court judge could properly be destroyed and not only destroyed as a judge, but destroyed as a man.'

There was, on the contrary, considerable proof of Landreville's good character. 'It must also be remembered,' Robinette continued, 'that Landreville was prepared to sacrifice the monetary advantages of continuing in a busy practice for the position on the bench. It seems to me reasonably clear from what occurred that he deemed it to be his duty to his profession and also to his racial origin as a representative of the French-Canadian group, and as I know, one of the few leading French-Canadian lawyers then practising in Ontario, he felt it his duty to accede to Mr. St. Laurent's perfectly legitimate and proper persuasion that he should accept the post in the Supreme Court of Ontario in succession to the late Mr. Justice Chevrier.'

Robinette pointed out that no Sudbury City Council member felt cajoled by Landreville to support NONG. All the testimony was to the opposite effect and established that he had done nothing wrong in his capacity as mayor. To be sure, there was, by the spring of 1956, a sense of urgency in approving the franchise arrangements, but that haste was communicated by C.D. Howe, the chair of the Ontario Fuel Board, and others, not by Landreville. Not only was NONG the sole contender but Landreville did not even participate in the vote. The selection of NONG was a *fait accompli*. That decision had been effectively made the previous year. When Sudbury finally approved the deal, it was bowing to the inevitable, but was doing so having achieved the best overall franchise agreement. These facts, Robinette argued, hardly suggested that Landreville, years later, was somehow unfit to serve as a judge. There was no evidence that Landreville 'improperly exercised his powers as Mayor or put any undue or improper pressure on anyone, or that he, in any respect, betrayed his municipality or disregarded his duties to the municipality and to his ratepayers, in his capacity as Mayor.'

It was true enough that Landreville and Farris had contradicted themselves and each other about some of the key factual circumstances leading to the request for and the granting of the stock option. Many years had passed since those conversations had taken place, and Robinette urged Rand not to draw any inferences from discrepancies that were explainable given the passage of time. All that mattered was whether Landreville had subordinated official business to his personal interests, and the evidence clearly indicated that he had not. Interrupting, Rand made it clear to Robinette that he thought Landreville was an outright liar. In February 1957, Rand pointed out, Landreville had sent a telegram to Convesto's McGraw reporting that he had sold all his NONG shares, when he had not. Rand now suggested to Robinette that this telegram provided sufficient proof to conclude that Landreville had lied. Robinette rejoined that Landreville may not have told the truth on this occasion, but his transgression was only a 'white lie,' and was hardly the basis on which a finding of credibility could be made.

Frustrated by Rand's constant interruptions, Robinette continued in his attempt to justify Landreville to the commissioner. Landreville should not, he argued, be attributed with responsibility for Farris's 'cloak and dagger activities in connection with Convesto.' Landreville knew nothing about the operation of the Convesto account and had nothing to do with the gifts of shares to the other mayors. Landreville could hardly be found guilty by association. Rand, however, would have none of it and continued to break in with caustic remarks. 'I couldn't get over it,' Robinette later recalled. 'Rand just hated the guy.'[70]

As Robinette was concluding his remarks, there was one final interruption. What did he have to say, Rand asked, about the Law Society report? Until that point, the report and the resolution that followed had not once been raised in evidence. Robinette was clearly taken aback. What possible relevance did that report have on these proceedings and the discharge of Rand's mandate? The answer, at this stage, was none. If the report was relevant, it should have been properly introduced. Witnesses should have been called and subjected to cross-examination. How was the report prepared? What facts were considered? What was the nature of convocation's debate? Only if the report was properly tested could it be relevant. It had never been proved. It was simply a document filled with hearsay. The report was useless, and Robinette attempted to explain why. 'Well, sir, I would say this. First of all, now one thing I want to make plain is that I am a bencher of the Law Society and a former treasurer and I took no part in the deliberations with respect to that report, for obvious reasons, because I was counsel and had been counsel for Mr. Landreville.' Robinette knew a conflict of interest when he saw one. He went on, however, to outline the deficiencies in the report:

The fact of the matter is that the Committee didn't give Mr. Landreville any opportunity to be heard. It purported to make a decision. It refers in the body of the document to speculation and then, from this speculation, the Committee draws certain inferences. Now, I don't like to be critical of my brethren on the bench, but it is sufficient to say that is something that ought to be investigated. Now if it had gone just that far, there would be no objection to it ... but when a Committee purports to make a decision affecting an individual, the first rule of natural justice, the elementary rule of natural justice, is to permit that person to be heard.[71]

That was all very interesting, Rand responded, but he wanted to know whether Robinette had any objection to his making public a copy of the report and the resolution convocation had passed calling for Landreville to be removed. 'I have it on vested authority,' Rand advised Robinette, that, 'so far as the Law Society is concerned, it is a matter of indifference whether the Minister or whether this Commission should make it available, as you might say, as an attachment to its proceedings.' Personally, he did not think it made any difference. What did Robinette think? 'No,' Robinette replied, 'I wouldn't think it made any difference at all.'[72] Rand now had what he wanted, and Robinette, distracted by the discussion, continued with his summation.

It was important to remember, he told Rand, that when a judge went on the bench, he abandoned a great deal. He gave up his practice. He lost his earning capacity. Accordingly, it was proper and consistent with legal principles that had survived the test of time that only in the clearest cases should a judge be impeached. He asked Rand, as he went about considering the evidence and writing his report, to keep these principles in mind. The inquiry was not, however, formally over. It was only adjourned, Rand announced, *sine die*. Those words mean something to lawyers: that the hearing was adjourned with no date set for its resumption.

Over the course of the proceedings, Landreville had become understandably concerned that Rand was moving away from an inquiry into the facts and towards an inquisition into his morals. Morrow's concluding remarks convinced him that Rand was clearly heading in that direction. Landreville therefore urged Robinette to be 'bold' and to write to Rand, reiterating that the inquiry was not about ethics and that it would be wrong for Rand to impose his own moral code on Landreville. After all, as Landreville observed, Rand was not 'born in my century.'[73] Robinette suggested that it might offend Rand to make an

intervention of this kind, and so the matter was dropped. As it turned
out, Landreville's fears were justified.

Rand's report started out normally enough. It sketched the history
of the discovery of natural gas and the efforts to bring that gas east.
Various developments were discussed and, by and large, Rand got
the chronology right. By the spring of 1956, Sudbury alone among the
major northern municipalities had not yet signed with NONG. Rand
found that something extraordinary had occurred at the end of April
1956. Farris travelled to Sudbury and had dinner at Landreville's
home. According to Rand, Farris was 'a business executive with a re-
ceptive mind ... a man of sensitive imagination which seems to have
been set aflame with the prospect of a unified gas distribution from
Manitoba east.'[74] It was from this point forward that Rand characterized every event, insofar as they related to Landreville, in the most
negative light.

   Rand concluded that Farris and Landreville, when they met, cooked
up a deal, not dinner. Landreville then rammed a resolution through
the Board of Control recommending that City Council give the franchise bylaw first and second reading. The only explanation for this
outcome was that an agreement had been reached between Farris and
Landreville: support at City Council in exchange for NONG shares.
Standing in the way of that conclusion, however, was the judgment of
Magistrate Marck. His judgment must, Rand found, 'be accorded a respectful recognition.' However, even if the facts establishing municipal
corruption and conspiracy did not satisfy the requirements of the criminal law by constituting the elements necessary to establish an offence,
that did not mean Landreville was necessarily fit to serve as a judge.

   According to Rand, Landreville's personal history suggested concern. He was a man of 'roving mind.' He had a 'sharp eye for business
and is now of considerable wealth.' He invested in real estate. Once,
Rand observed, Landreville bought a property with his law partner, a
future judge, and they sold it a few years later for a profit. Landreville
was 'plausible in statement and his resourcefulness, superficially, is
considerable. His emotions are active and he can be highly expansive;
he is fascinated by the glitter of success and material well-being. His
outlook is indicated by a residence in Mexico, as well as a lodge some
miles from Sudbury.' He was also 'capable of being disingenuous'
and had been caught making more than one 'utterly false statement.'

In short, Rand concluded, 'he presents the somewhat versatile character of a modern hedonist of vitality whose philosophy is expressed in terms of pragmatic opportunism for public prominence, financial and social success, tinctured with arrogance towards subordinates and confidence in his ability to move around.'[75] Rand continued his amateur psychology exposition by saying that a man like Landreville was likely to settle in the north:

That section of Canada, for the past sixty years, has been nurtured in speculation; beneath ironized masses of rock lay the substance of colossal wealth; fortunes shot up over night; and the response to the proposed gas developments exhibited the inherited trait of its people. Everybody, as it was said, wanted to 'get in on the ground floor.' Such a land with such a spirit was a magnet to the young lawyer fresh from law school and itching for action. It is not surprising that he should have been caught up even in 1955 by the vision of the bold project and it may be that from the first he viewed it as presenting a rare opportunity for public and personal profit. In Farris he met a kindred spirit, between whom there would be mutual loyalty serving personal interest, the determinant of the short-sighted and disastrous course of action which has been somewhat detailed.

Farris, a man in his early 50's born and brought up in Vancouver, with a mind sharpened by the keenness of the struggle for fortune, of a driving energy, who viewed the petty morality of the middle class as no more than a hindrance to the public and private interest of large-scale enterprise, found a congenial associate in Justice Landreville. In both, the titillating speculative prospects were irresistible and in the northland of Ontario an unsurpassable locus presented itself. For the past sixty years it had furnished foundation wealth to many sections of Canada and the United States: gold, silver, cobalt and other metals and minerals drew adventurers to what was otherwise a wilderness; and in the course of those years there has been built up a spirit for speculative fortune that in 1956, in a somewhat minor degree, broke out anew.

After only four months of mutual acquaintance, Farris and Landreville developed, according to Rand, a 'mutuality of understanding ... an instinctive recognition apparently by each of an identity of outlook, attitude and interest, an "affinity,"' so much so that Landreville felt comfortable in approaching Farris for shares. If any more evidence of impropriety was required, Rand declared it could be found in the correspondence between the two men. The night after Farris dined at Landreville's home, he sent Mrs Landreville some flowers. Landreville then wrote Farris a letter: 'Do come back soon as I note any delay in your return – I shall purposely sabotage this contract to compel a return visit. Further, you and I have a few important things to discuss – re co.' Landreville testified that the important business to be discussed was the passage of the bylaw. Rand concluded that no legitimate business would be mentioned in such 'occult language.' The letter was of interest to Rand for another reason as well: the use of 'what is called the "first name" relation.' Rand was convinced, notwithstanding the lack of evidence proving this to be the case, that the whole transaction involved the sale of influence, and that it was artfully designed to keep Landreville's identity off NONG's books. Farris, Rand added, was a 'denizen of the market place,' and his actions were hardly appropriate for the nephew of the former chief justice of British Columbia.

There was no doubt that the timing of the letters offering and accepting the stock option raised cause for concern, as did many of the words used. But the letters did not prove anything. The evidence against Landreville was entirely circumstantial, and, as circumstantial evidence goes, it left much more than a reasonable doubt. Rand saw things differently. 'It must be apparent,' he wrote, 'that those circumstances though short of a sufficiency for the purpose of a criminal proceeding, do raise a deep suspicion of a secret understanding. Suspicion is not sufficient in itself to establish criminality nor is this Commission a Court. But for the purpose here, the question arises why has there been so much obvious concealment about the share acquisition?' No one corroborated Landreville's evidence that he made his purchase option known, and his failure to come forward at the first opportunity to reveal the truth – Rand was referring to the first OSC investigation in 1958, when Landreville kept a low profile – was, 'considering his public office, extraordinary behaviour, and its implication serious.'

Also extraordinary, according to Rand, and equally, if not more, serious, was Landreville's behaviour on the witness stand. His evidence in all the proceedings in which he testified was 'vague, indefinite, qualified, non-committal, replete with half-truths, overstressed accounts of indifferent or non-significant facts, irrelevant digressions, emphasis on the obvious, indignant assertion in the nature of shadow-boxing, protestations of anxiety to vindicate himself, and airy looseness with truth in small matters: all bringing about an essentially misleading picture of governing facts.' Likewise, Landreville's memory left a lot to be desired: 'His remark on that faculty that for some matters it was good and for others bad, can, without reserve, be accepted; but the classifi-

cation becomes extremely simple: on the vital items where the probing touches the nerve there is failure; on the unimportant, a quick and
clear recollection.' In short, Landreville was not a man to be believed.
He was not fit to be a judge:

Some observations of Justice Landreville in the letter of September 19 are here
relevant; his description of judges: 'an all-inspiring [sic] unapproachable, staid
class of people'; his concern for the future: 'I want to assure you that my interest in your company, *outwardly aloof*, will, nevertheless, remain active'; his
keenness for the promise of shares, 'I am keeping your letter of July 20 carefully in my file.' This letter was addressed to 'Ralph' and signed 'Leo.' Making
all allowances for a tendency to display cleverness and for the speech and
thought of one familiar with the market place, these are strange remarks from
a person just about to enter into membership of a Supreme Court; it demon-
strates an astonishing insensitiveness to the plenary importance of that public
office. The one absolute condition required of a Judge is a free mind, untrammelled in judicial action by foreign or irrelevant interest, relations or matters
which might colour or distort judgment.

Rand had concluded that Landreville lacked the qualities necessary
to serve as a judge. As he elaborated,

... the facts show an astonishing departure from what is dictated by an elementary conception of a judge's personal behaviour. By a course of presenting a confused picture of facts before judicial and administrative tribunals, the
purpose of discovering the truth of certain matters sought by both an important agency of government and by the courts of the province, has been or has
attempted to be frustrated. That conduct was to prevent disclosure of facts
touching the administration of regulations relating to shares and securities of
a company incorporated in Ontario; and to protect directly an official of that
company in a prosecution arising out of such matters. The desire of the Justice
in each case was to shield both himself and the other and is quite understandable. But the moral standard for a judge in his private capacity cannot admit
such an interference with the course of government or of the proceedings of
courts of justice. That is the duty of every citizen but it is supremely so for a
judge: he cannot make his conduct an example of tolerated obstruction.
    That such conduct is a breach of the duty which our conception of the judicial
office sets for a judge cannot, in the opinion of the undersigned, admit of any
doubt. He is sworn to the administration of Justice as our evolving ethical intelligence has fashioned it, but that obligation is not limited to the adjudicative

role. He comes under another but equally sensitive duty. To respect the Law which he administers and to promote its processes to their proper ends. For a judge in his private capacity so to impede and defeat those processes is a grave dereliction, a gross infraction of the canons governing him.

Rand then turned to the matter of the independence of the judiciary:

Mr. Robinette properly stressed the independence of judges and, rightly conceived, that principle admits of no limitations. It enables the guarantee of security to the weak against the strong and to the individual against the community; it presents a shield against the tyranny of power and arrogance and against the irresponsibility and irrationality of popular action, whether of opinion or of violence; it enables the voice of sanity to rise above the turbulence of passion; and it is to be preserved inviolate. But what does the independence of judges imply? That can be nothing short of this: that the minister to whom such an authority is committed shall himself be the first to respect what has been entrusted to him, the administration of the rule of justice under Law, including loyalty to its institutions. The public acceptability of character for such a function is of that which exhibits itself in action as beyond influences that tend to taint its discharge with alien factors.

Rand concluded his report with three findings:

I – The stock transaction between Justice Landreville and Ralph K. Farris effecting the acquisition of 7,500 shares in Northern Ontario Natural Gas Company Limited, for which no valid consideration was given, notwithstanding the result of the preliminary inquiry into charges laid against Justice Landreville, justifiably gives rise to grave suspicion of impropriety. In that situation it is the opinion of the undersigned that it was obligatory on Justice Landreville to remove that suspicion and satisfactorily to establish his innocence, which he has not done.

II – That in the subsequent investigation into the stock transaction before the Securities Commission of Ontario in 1962, and the direct and incidental dealing with it in the proceedings brought against Ralph K. Farris for perjury in 1963 and 1964 in which Justice Landreville was a Crown witness, the conduct of Justice Landreville in giving evidence constituted a gross contempt of those tribunals and a serious violation of his personal duty as a Justice of the Supreme court of Ontario, which has permanently impaired his usefulness as a Judge.

III – That a fortiori the conduct of Justice Landreville, from the effective dealing, in the spring of 1956, with the proposal of a franchise for supplying natural
gas to the City of Sudbury to the completion of the share transaction in February 1957, including the proceedings in 1962, 1963 and 1964 mentioned, treated
as a single body of action, the concluding portion of which, trailing odours of
scandal arising from its initiation and consummated while he was a Judge of
the Supreme Court of Ontario, drawing upon himself the onus of establishing
satisfactorily his innocence, which he has failed to do, was a dereliction of both
his duty as a public official and his personal duty as a Judge, a breach of that
standard of conduct obligatory upon him, which has permanently impaired
his usefulness as a Judge.

'In all three respects,' Rand found, 'Justice Landreville has proven himself unfit for the proper exercise of his judicial function.' Landreville's
conduct gave rise to suspicions, and it was up to him to prove his innocence. He had failed to do so. This conclusion led to one of only two
possible results: if Landreville failed to resign, he must be removed.
    Rand was absolutely determined that Landreville and the govern-
ment not be left with any wiggle room to skirt around his conclusions.
After his recommendations in the Coal Commission were ignored,
Rand resolved, according to one of his commission counsel, to draft
future reports 'in such a way as to make his conclusions and the results
that flowed there from inescapable ... He was, since the Coal Inquiry,
no longer content simply to report his findings and make recommendations. He felt obliged to ensure that they were made in such a way as to
compel action. He would not and did not lobby for the enforcement of
his recommendations after the report. That would have been improper.
But he did attempt to argue as effectively as he could within the context
of the report itself, and to that extent he became the advocate of his
own conclusions.'[76] Privately, Rand asked his old Western colleague
Ronald St J. Macdonald, 'What kind of judge puts up a crucifix in his
chambers?' No judge of any court, Rand continued, should display his
religious beliefs.[77] This comment leaves little doubt that Rand's negative views about French Canadians and Roman Catholics had entered
into the mix. When his sons were growing up, Rand had advised them
to stay away from the Acadians because they lacked ambition. When
Rand came face to face with a successful French-Canadian entrepre-
neur, he did not like him much either. In fact, that was even more
unpardonable.
    Rand submitted his report on 11 August 1966, and the Cabinet

considered it at a meeting twelve days later. 'Mr. Rand's conclusions were highly critical of Mr. Justice Landreville's behaviour in the matter,' the minutes recorded, 'to the extent that it would be impossible for Judge Landreville to remain on the bench.'[78] Cabinet decided to forward the report immediately to the governor general, but also to give Landreville an opportunity to meet privately with the minister before the report was released in order to discuss its 'implications.' On 25 August, Cabinet again discussed the matter, deciding to release the report quickly, in part to avoid the impression that the government was unduly favouring Judge Landreville. Before doing so, however, Landreville had to be advised formally of the contents, and he was summoned to Ottawa for an urgent meeting with Justice Minister Lucien Cardin.

Landreville was provided with a copy of the report before his interview with Cardin, but its contents came as no surprise. A summary of the report had been leaked and published in the *Globe and Mail*. Once again, Landreville was headline news: 'Report called devastating to Landreville,' the *Globe* announced, adding that it had learned that Landreville was treated 'roughly' by Rand.[79] The *Toronto Telegram* had better sources, and some of the contents of the report were published on its front page.[80] The next day, the *Globe* stated that the Rand report had enough in it to warrant impeachment proceedings in Parliament.[81]

When Landreville met with Cardin on 25 August, he was prepared for the worst.[82] Cardin told him that the government had no choice but to table the report and move for his dismissal. Landreville was advised to resign, and the government's wish in this matter was again indirectly communicated to Landreville with the assistance of some sympathetic friends.[83]

Once the report was leaked, the government tabled it in the House of Commons before formally releasing copies to the press. That was done on 29 August, and it was a deliberate decision. Ministers, concerned that Landreville might sue Rand for libel, decided to insure against that result by tabling the report in the House, where, because of parliamentary privilege, it would be immune from attack.[84] At the same time as he tabled the report, Cardin told the House that he was giving 'notice that it is my intention to make a motion ... at the first opportunity for an address to His Excellency praying that the judge be removed from office on the grounds set forth in the report.' It was also the government's intention to refer that motion to a joint committee of the House and Senate, 'so that the fullest inquiry can be made by

Parliament itself and so that the judge can be given an opportunity to appear and speak on his own behalf.'[85] Landreville announced that he would fight any impeachment attempt.[86]

Landreville's complaint was simple: he was convicted of a 'crime' of which he had not been charged. As he noted in a letter to the minister of justice, Rand's findings were not based on his dealings with NONG in 1955 and 1956, but on the commissioner's review of events after that date, a review coloured by his negative assessment of Landreville's character. 'Mr. Rand's report,' Landreville added in a statement given to the *Sudbury Star*, 'is based entirely on my manner of giving evidence on several occasions on which I appeared in court and before a commission. It draws a malicious portrait of me in contrast and contradiction to what all witnesses have said about my character.' Landreville insisted that he had engaged in no wrongdoing, legally, morally, or ethically, and he made it clear that he had no intention whatsoever of stepping down because of a 'malicious, iniquitous, unjust and prejudiced' report.[87]

Reaction to the report was mixed. One commentator wrote that it was 'highly significant' because 'for the first time in Canada the qualities required of a judge have been set forth by a high authority in an official publication.' Rand's enumeration of these qualities was 'masterly.'[88] 'The Rand Report on the former Mr. Justice Landreville,' the *Law Society Gazette* stated, editorializing the party line, 'may well be proven to be one of the most important constitutional documents on the judiciary.'[89] Many newspapers demanded immediate action. 'Boot judge off bench' was the way one put it.[90] More careful readers, however, took issue with the presentation of the facts, if not the conclusions and opinions that were reached. The report was rambling and, in places, incoherent.[91] Particularly noteworthy, and questionable, was Rand's repeated use of hearsay to support the findings he made.

Relying on newspaper clippings, Rand reported that Landreville and his former law partner made a nice profit on the sale of some real estate: 'In 1955–56, while the gas development was taking place he was a party in equal interest with a former partner, now a County Court Judge, in the sale of land in Sudbury, acquired by them in 1949 for $173,000 and sold in 1956 for $325,000. That he is not to be taken as an innocent in such dealings is demonstrated by language addressed to the Tax Appeal Board in the course of an appeal from a gift tax arising out of that sale.' Rand either did not know, or did not care, that Landreville and his former partner, J.M. Cooper, bought a vacant shell, gutted by fire, rebuilt it, and, some time later, sold it. That information would put the sale – and the profit – into perspective, but it was exactly that kind of information which Rand either did not seek or ignored. Moreover, there was nothing wrong with buying a building, fixing it up, and selling it for a profit. That transaction, like the fact that Landreville owned a home in Mexico and a camp up north, was completely unrelated to the issue of whether he had committed an improper or illegal act and was, in the result, unfit to serve as a judge. Very simply, there was nothing inconsistent about owning a second home, or having been a successful businessman, and later becoming a judge.

Another strange conclusion was Rand's finding that Landreville was a 'snob.'[92] When asked about his lobbying efforts on NONG's behalf, and, in particular, about a party he was reported to have held to introduce Farris to members of City Council, Landreville testified that he 'was not on a social basis with many of the Aldermen and Controllers; I would not invite them to my home.' And then, 'I am looking over the list of Aldermen, and I can say there would not be more than two with their wives, if at any time I had made an invitation.'[93] In his report, Rand made an extraordinary finding based on this testimony: 'He stated that there could be no social gathering in his home of the City Council of Sudbury for the purpose of promoting NONG's application for a franchise because there were too many members of the Council who were not of his social rank and would not be invited.'[94]

Landreville was anything but a snob. Snobs are not apt to get elected to progressively senior positions in municipal government over a period of twenty years in a multi-ethnic community like Sudbury. Rand read Landreville wrongly, from start to finish. The report's findings about Landreville's personality and wealth, his home in Mexico, and his camp in the north had nothing to do with evidence Rand heard, but everything to do with what he had read in the newspapers, particularly the *Toronto Star*.

Rand also appended to his report a copy of the Law Society's report, thereby giving it authority and respectability, neither of which it deserved. As Donald S. Macdonald, a future justice minister, pointed out in the House of Commons, the Law Society, in investigating Landreville and issuing a report, had exceeded its jurisdiction and acted contrary to established principles of natural justice. The Law Society's report, Macdonald stated, was nothing more than an 'attack ... on a judge.'[95] If he was interested in balance, Rand might have also appended a copy of Magistrate Marck's decision. Significantly, he did not.

There were other problems with the report. Rand found Landreville guilty by association. Farris may have had reasons for hiding the NONG transaction, for example, but Landreville could hardly be faulted for that. He never hid his dealings in NONG shares; he even wrote Convesto on his Supreme Court of Ontario stationery acknowledging receipt of the shares. There was no evidence that Landreville had ever shown contempt for the law, 'gross' or otherwise. Maybe he should have presented himself to the OSC in 1958 when he first heard that an investigation was under way, but he had no legal obligation to do so, and there was absolutely no evidence that he knew, at that time, that Farris might have attempted to conceal the beneficiaries of the sale of the 14,000 shares. Moreover, in finding Landreville guilty of 'gross contempt,' Rand exceeded his mandate by a considerable extent, for even the most liberal interpretation of his terms of reference did not require him to determine whether Landreville had engaged in this misbehaviour. Had the government wanted a general investigation into Landreville, the terms of reference would have indicated as much. Instead, Rand was directed to inquire into Landreville's dealings with NONG and whether anything done 'in the course of such dealings constituted misbehaviour ... or whether Landreville has by such dealings proved himself unfit for the proper exercise of his judicial duties.' The investigation was limited to Landreville's dealings with NONG, and Rand had strayed far off course.

Most important of all, Rand ignored section 13 of the *Inquiries Act*, the statute under which his commission had been constituted. Section 13 provided that before any findings of misconduct were made against someone, that person should be given an opportunity to refute that allegation. Rand had adjourned the inquiry *sine die* and, before concluding the proceeding, he had a legal obligation to advise Landreville of this finding and to provide him with an opportunity to rebut it. These legal concerns aside, and they were important ones, the language Rand used in describing Landreville was intemperate and unnecessary. Ultimately, it was not only unfair but it coloured and discredited the basic conclusions he had reached.

There were more than enough facts on which to find that Landreville had, by his conduct, 'proved himself unfit for the proper exercise of this judicial office.' The share option was highly questionable. Why would a public company give a judge what turned out to be more than $100,000, if Farris's evidence in this inquiry was to be believed? What corporate benefit did that gift serve? The share option, in return for an agreement to later go and work for NONG, to accept another version of events, was not against the law – Marck's judgment established that – but it was a clear conflict of interest. It said something very important about Landreville and about his fitness to serve as a judge, no matter when the option was requested or when it was obtained. Inducement or reward was a distinction without much difference. Rand could have reached some significant conclusions based on this single fact. Moreover, some of the words used by Landreville in his correspondence with Farris and, after he became a judge, on his official stationery with Convesto were highly suggestive of impropriety. They were not, as Rand put it, 'occult,' but they certainly gave cause for concern about both Landreville's behaviour as mayor and his fitness to serve as a judge. Findings could have been made on these points alone, instead of clouding them with conclusions about hedonism and other extraneous observations

Clearly, Landreville's letters, sworn testimony, public statements, and general demeanour in the aftermath of the disclosure of his ownership of NONG shares did not reflect well on his character or on the temperament and disposition the public rightly expected in a Supreme Court of Ontario judge. Many people would consider the option (or if not an option, then the gift) and the circumstances in which it was obtained and exercised inconsistent with the type of behaviour required of a judge. The public does have expectations of the judiciary, and judges should be held to the highest standards. Rand could have set out some useful rules and guiding principles – there were none at the time – about municipal conflict of interest and the conduct of public office holders. That would have made a real contribution. Unfortunately, instead of dispassionately stating the facts, applying the larger principles to Landreville, reaching a reasoned decision, and contributing to an improved public policy, Rand attacked the man in an offensive and demeaning way. Like the Law Society before him, Rand had failed to give Landreville his due by providing him with an opportunity, which he was entitled to by law, to refute the negative findings that Rand was making against him. As Robinette justly complained, Rand never gave Landreville a break.[96] The result might have been right, but the process was a disgrace.

Landreville told the press he would not step down. 'To resign,' he said, 'would be to admit guilt.'[97] This point was reinforced by Landreville's new lawyer, the colourful and controversial David Humphrey of Toronto, who also had a judicial appointment in his future. Robinette was acting as counsel in the Leitch Gold Mines case and could not take on another brief. As it happened, Humphrey, retained to represent Landreville before Parliament – for that is where Landreville's case was now heading – would not be defending him for some months, as various procedural questions had still to be addressed. This was, after all, the first time in Canadian history that the government had moved to impeach a judge.

Landreville found himself before a committee of Parliament 'pleading,' as he put it, 'for my honour.' It did not go well. The hearing began on 20 February 1967 and dragged on from one day to the next, the parliamentary calendar being what it was. Landreville was clearly breaking under the strain, regularly requiring adjournments as he became overcome with tears. He attempted manfully to justify his conduct, but the committee had trouble with most of his explanations. When Sudbury City Council, for example, gave the franchise bylaw third and final reading, a legal relationship between the city and NONG was just beginning, not ending, and how could Landreville, as mayor, accept an option from the company and agree to go and work for it later? There was no satisfactory answer to this and many other questions.

In many respects, Landreville was his own worst enemy. On 9 March he testified, for example, about the 28 February 1957 telegram he sent to Convesto claiming he had sold all his NONG shares. In fact, he had sold only some and was in the process of selling the rest. Faced with the facts, Landreville admitted the truth: 'Well, gentlemen, I did send that telegram and that was a lie.' He added, unnecessarily, 'I can only say to you that ... I lie often. I might say to a woman – she has a beautiful hat or advise my secretary to tell the other party I am not in, even advise others to lie ...'[98] By his own words, Landreville was making it clear to the committee and the Canadian public that he was not fit to serve as a judge. Instead of appearing judicial and a little remorseful, he came across as a man who had learned nothing and had nothing to learn. The committee voted to recommend his removal.

Landreville continued his fight, demanding his 'right' to appear at the bar of the House of Commons before any removal address was put to a vote. The Liberals, for all sorts of reasons, were anxious to avoid that spectacle and dispatched several of their senior statesmen to cut a behind-the-scenes deal. Senator John Connolly, the leader of the government in the Senate, had the Department of Justice run the numbers, and he told Landreville what pension he could expect if he were to resign. He also said that Landreville could have faith in Prime Minister Pearson and Justice Minister Pierre Trudeau. After reviewing this information, and not knowing that his support was growing in the Senate and somewhat less so in the House of Commons, Landreville unconditionally resigned on 7 June 1967. He then applied for his pension, as agreed, but the government refused, even after Senator Connolly reminded his Cabinet colleagues that assurances had been given and relied upon. Landreville, however, made a good decision. He hired the highly respected Ottawa lawyer Gordon Fripp Henderson to take his case. It took Henderson ten years, but Rand's report was eventually largely set aside because he failed to give Landreville notice, as he was required to do, that misconduct findings were going to be made. This was, a Federal Court judge declared, 'with diffidence' to the 'eminent and renowned judge of the Supreme Court of Canada,' an 'error in law.'[99] In due course, Landreville received an *ex gratia* payment from the government of Canada of a quarter of a million dollars.

There are important lessons to be drawn from the Landreville case. The Rand Inquiry and its report illustrated some of the problems with the use of royal commissions to investigate allegations of individual misconduct, and raised, not for the first or last time, some of the problems in appointing judges and retired judges as royal commissioners. Was it really consistent with judicial independence to embroil judges in political and partisan matters? Not only were the legal rules governing these commissions unclear, but the process itself, with commission counsel supervising the investigation and calling the evidence, made the exercise nothing more than a glorified trial of an individual, without the legal safeguards that usually accompany such proceedings. In this case, Rand, despite clear terms of reference, wandered far off topic, and his commission became little more than a fishing expedition desperate to find something to justify the conclusion that Rand reached. The inquiry inevitably became an inquisition, and character assassination a national sport. Few options were available at the time, however, and asking a former judge of the Supreme Court of Canada to head the inquiry was a reasonable thing to do, at least in theory.

A better mechanism was obviously required to receive and respond to complaints about sitting judges. The *Act of Settlement* of 1701 established an independent judiciary, and since that time the separation between the legislature and the judiciary has been a hallmark of democratic life. In order to promote and guarantee this independence, judges are granted security of tenure and remuneration. Without either one, they could easily become pawns of the state, and in totalitarian societies they invariably do. While Parliament is supreme, an active role in the removal of judges is simply inconsistent with established norms of judicial independence. If Parliament can remove a judge for good reasons, it could also do so for questionable ones. As the Landreville case began to unfold, it became clear that a better way had to be found to deal with complaints of judicial misconduct.

It took some time, but in 1971 the Canadian Judicial Council (CJC) was created, and the Landreville case figured prominently in the decision to establish it. The CJC, whose membership is composed of the chief justices and senior associate and associate chief justices of the federal, provincial, and territorial superior courts, with the chief justice of Canada as chair, was empowered to conduct investigations of complaints about the competence of judges, as well as to look into allegations of judicial misconduct. The act establishing the CJC sets out the formal grounds necessary to support a removal recommendation. A formal investigation must have taken place, and the council, as a result of that investigation, must have formed the opinion that the judge has become incapacitated by reason of age or infirmity, misconduct, or failure in the due execution of office.

Having received a report from the CJC recommending removal, the minister of justice may then proceed in one of two ways. The minister may ask Parliament to establish a special committee to consider the CJC's report as well as to conduct its own inquiry, or, somewhat more likely, if a full hearing has already been held by the CJC, the minister may simply and immediately introduce a motion for a joint address of Parliament requesting that the governor general remove the judge. No case has yet gone to Parliament. There are many complaints and quite a few internal investigations, but only rarely a recommendation for removal. This system is an obvious improvement over the ad hoc process used in the Landreville case.

Yet even the creation of the CJC, together with its comprehensive and fair rules for investigation and reporting on complaints of judicial misconduct, fails to answer one of the key questions raised in the Landreville case. What should be done about conduct that occurred before the judge was appointed, but which comes to light only after the appointment has taken effect? Ultimately, one of Rand's questions, buried deep in his report, will have to be answered when the behaviour of a judge, either before or after appointment, is brought into question:

'Would the conduct ... lead such persons to attribute such a defect of moral character that the discharge of the duties of the office thereafter would be suspect?' The test was later rephrased somewhat in the Marshall case. Only this essential question, alone among all the findings set out by Rand in his report, will stand the test of time.[100]

10

Rand's Disastrous Investigation into Labour Disputes

Much had changed since January 1946 when Ivan Rand awarded his now famous formula. Twenty years later, industrial unionism was firmly established in Canada's economy. The legal regime prohibited unfair labour practices and required employers to recognize and bargain collectively with the union selected by a majority of their employees and certified as the bargaining agent. The growth in union density was accompanied by a rise in real wages and the introduction of fringe benefits such as pensions, paid holidays, shorter workweeks, sick pay, and disability insurance. Seniority did not just protect employees from economic downturns ('first in, last out'); it also became the most important factor for distributing other job-related benefits such as overtime and promotions.[1]

Grievance arbitration brought the rule of law to the workplace: any dispute arising during the term of the collective agreement which the parties could not resolve had to be referred to final and binding arbitration. Unions could still strike, and employers could still lock their employees out, but when and how were strictly prescribed by labour-relations statutes in every Canadian jurisdiction. Strikes and lockouts were prohibited during the term of a collective agreement, and that meant that unions were legally required to use all reasonable means at their disposal, including disciplining their members, to ensure that disputes were resolved by arbitration, not by industrial action, especially wildcat strikes. 'Work now, grieve later,' summed up the state of the law. Indeed, in one celebrated case, later upheld by the Supreme Court of Canada, Bora Laskin, who had been intimately involved in the failed conciliation leading to the 1945 Ford strike, ruled, when sitting as an arbitrator, that a union could be required to pay an employer compensation for any economic damages it suffered from a breach of the no-strike ban.[2] This conclusion was an elaboration of the Rand Formula, which tied the union security provision, the checkoff, to a requirement that the union enforce the collective agreement against its own members. As Pat Conroy, the United Automobile Workers leader who played such an important part in bringing the Ford strike to an end, told a House of Commons committee in 1946, 'Make us industrial citizens, and you may expect us to behave accordingly.'[3]

What exactly did that mean? 'In economic terms, it meant that the union and its leadership accepted the legitimacy of private property and free enterprise. Politically, it meant a commitment to constitutionalism and electoral change; strikes for political purposes were simply unacceptable. In the context of industrial relations, it meant that the union accepted the integrity of the collective agreement and would make all reasonable efforts to prevent wildcat strikes.'[4]

The post-war settlement with organized labour brought huge gains to the union movement and the millions of employees who directly and indirectly benefited from it. Canada was no workers' paradise, but, in addition to the labour laws, anti-discrimination laws, health and safety codes, and labour standards legislation setting out minimum conditions of employment all created a floor that would be raised over time.

As the economy expanded in the early 1960s, unemployment rates dropped. Then inflation arrived, and there was a growing gap between government revenues and expenditures as the construction costs of the social welfare state began to skyrocket. Everyone wanted more. In 1966, as a new wave of labour militancy swept the industrialized parts of the country, Canada was second only to Italy in the number of days lost due to strikes and lockouts. Might was not necessarily right, but industrial sanctions, strikes, and lockouts continued to determine the content of collective agreements. Not just industrial workers hit the street; they were joined by hospital employees, railway employees, longshoremen, letter carriers and inside postal workers, steelworkers, lumbermen, and pulp and paper workers. Everyone was seeking the same thing: more money. The militancy from public servants was surprising and disquieting to a citizenry habituated to docility in that quarter. There was also violence – and not just in isolated incidents. Ri-

val seafarers fighting for bargaining rights beat each other up and dis-
rupted shipping along the St Lawrence Seaway. In Toronto, residential
construction workers vying for jobs sometimes took matters in their
own hands while the police generally stood by – the Brandon Union
Group, for instance, used coercion, intimidation, violence, and flying
squads to ensure that its members got the work. Even farmers formed
a 'union' and protested low prices for milk and other commodities by
slowly driving their tractors on provincial highways. They wanted the
same thing as everyone else: money, in the form of 'subsidies.'

Labour strife became an epidemic – or so it seemed to many observers at the time. Picketing expanded to include not only the struck
employer but others, such as retail stores, well down the line. It was
too much for the judiciary, and the courts intervened to declare that
secondary picketing, even if peaceful, was a civil wrong and illegal
per se. This legal ruling came courtesy of J.B. Aylesworth (and two
other judges of the Court of Appeal), Ford's lawyer during the 1945
strike. He had been appointed to the Ontario Court of Appeal in 1946,
and his platform was a 1963 case called *Hersees of Woodstock*.[5] Earlier,
while in practice, Aylesworth had advocated that, if there was to be
compulsory bargaining legislation, labour leaders should be made legally responsible; now he had the opportunity to narrow the scope
for workers' collective action. Without any legal basis and contrary to
established precedent, he declared all secondary picketing unlawful.
Rand, in *Aristocratic Restaurants*, had reached a completely different
conclusion about secondary picketing more than a decade before when
he was sitting as a judge.[6]

Most strikes, however, involved direct picketing of the struck employer. At issue were several competing legal rights: the right to strike
– the right of employees to withdraw their labour; the right to picket
the struck employer; the right of non-striking employees to cross the
picket line and continue working; and the employer's right to continue
operating during a strike, including hiring replacement workers and
their right to work. In these circumstances, conflict during a strike was
inevitable and had to be carefully managed. That was a job for the police – but the police did not like intervening in labour disputes. For that
reason, the regulation of industrial conflict shifted to the courts.

The law, set out in the *Judicature Act*, required that 'a breach of the
peace, injury to persons or damage to property has occurred, or an
interruption of an essential public service has occurred or is likely
to occur' before an injunction could be ordered.[7] Injunctions were

granted on affidavit evidence based on 'information and belief.' Employers could and did say what they wished in their affidavits. They were often drafted in vague terms and sometimes contained half-truths and outright lies. In other cases, they accurately described the factual circumstances that, management claimed, required immediate attention from the courts: some of the picket-line conduct was truly unacceptable, involving property damage and violence or threats of violence to persons trying to cross the line.[8] The rules required that two days' notice be given when an injunction was sought. In a great many cases, the unions were not even notified about an application – there was no time, the employer lawyers always claimed – and so the application would proceed *ex parte*, without the union being there to present its side of the story or to challenge the evidence of the other side.

In practice, the judiciary could be counted on to grant injunctions with few or no questions asked. In addition, the orders were directed at a wide population: the named defendants, their 'servants and agents,' and anyone else 'having knowledge of this order.' Individuals with interests that were different from, albeit aligned with, those of the striking union were bound by the judicial order, without ever having been notified or given the opportunity to make representations about its scope. Contributing to the problem, and the criticism, was the fact that injunction applications were usually heard in weekly court, alongside twenty or thirty other matters set down for hearing. In these circumstances it was not surprising that many judges did not give all the cases that came before them their complete attention.

These *ex parte* injunctions had a set shelf life: four days. The court orders invariably restricted the numbers of picketers at struck premises to symbolic levels. But those few days were often sufficient to break a strike, particularly at smaller workplaces where managers, aided by replacement workers and strikebreaking employees, could keep the concern going. If more time was required, the judges were invariably accommodating, faced as they were with usually uncontradicted evidence of mass picketing, property damage, and violence, or at least the threat of it. While Ontario politicians endlessly debated the use and abuse of injunctions in labour disputes, unionists became increasingly enraged as their strikes, on the basis of the employer's word, were shut down by court orders vastly limiting what they asserted was lawful picketing. There was, the *Globe and Mail* editorialized, 'a curious unease, a mood of rebellion.'[9] The judiciary was seen by organized labour as management's handmaiden. Time after time, the union movement claimed, judges were used to defeat the right to strike, to picket, and to engage in lawful trade union activities.[10] In response, management complained about mass picketing, property damage, and violence, a situation the employers argued was especially untenable because local police forces invariably refused to become involved in labour disputes.

There were some important exceptions. In Metro Toronto, as it was then known, the various municipal police forces had been merged in the late 1950s, creating Canada's largest municipal police force. A 'riot squad' was established which included picketing control in its mandate. At the start of a labour dispute, the police would explain the ground rules to the picketers, management, and the wider community, noting that the police were on hand to enforce the law if need be. As a result, although there was plenty of picketing in Toronto labour disputes, few employers made allegations of property damage or violence. Most of the injunction applications came from outside Toronto, where the police took a hands-off approach and the injunction became an indispensable part of law enforcement, drawing the civil courts into labour disputes. In part, that was not the fault of the police. In 1966 more than 70 per cent of Ontario forces had fewer than six police officers. The Ontario Provincial Police would not get involved, and local law enforcement officials were untrained, ill-equipped, and disinclined to become involved in the communities where they too lived. Employers had little recourse but to obtain an injunction, and that, in turn, infuriated the union movement, even in cases where picketing activities did stray from the legal limits.[11]

Eventually, something had to give. Finally tipping the balance and forcing the Ontario government's hand were two strikes, one in Oshawa and the other in nearby Peterborough. The strike at the *Oshawa Times* came first.

It was late January 1966 when the reporters at the *Oshawa Times* went out on strike. There were two main issues in play: low wages and technological change. The Toronto Newspaper Guild, the union representing the striking employees, wanted more money and a collective agreement provision guaranteeing that no bargaining unit member would be dismissed or demoted as a result of the introduction of new production methods. The union further insisted that the newspaper work with the Guild to develop retraining programs and other options for employees whose jobs were affected as a result of automation. The employer declined both union demands. When management raised the stakes with the announcement that it intended to keep publishing with Guild members who crossed the line (only thirty-six of the fifty employees in the bargaining unit were Guild members), together, possibly, with members of the Printing Pressmen's Union (who had no dispute with the employer), confrontation was inevitable. This time, however, the Guild appealed for assistance: six thousand leaflets were distributed to General Motors workers in Oshawa as they came off the night shift, asking them to report to the UAW hall and get ready to join the Guild's picket line. Many of them did.

On day one of the strike, at the end of January 1966, more than a hundred picketers, most of them UAW members, shut the newspaper down. Day two came and the paper was again prevented from publishing. But lawyers for the *Oshawa Times* were already at Osgoode Hall: they applied for an injunction restraining the picketing, and they sought damages for inducing breach of contract and 'intimidation' of those newspaper employees who had wanted to report for duty.

The union was given notice of the injunction and attended the proceeding. The specific terms of the court order were agreed upon by union and management counsel, John Osler (later a distinguished judge) and Bruce Stewart, respectively. There was going to be an injunction – both sides knew that. From the union perspective, it was better to meet with management in advance and agree on its terms, rather than leave it to the whim of the presiding judge. The union lawyer therefore informed the court that he did not consent to the injunction, nor did he oppose it. The court dutifully complied with management's request, and the hearing came and went with the order issued as requested – the number of picketers limited to four at the front entrance and three at each of the side and back doors. In the normal course, that would have been the end of any effective picketing, and probably the strike too. But this was no normal strike.

Oshawa is a union town. Subscription cancellations to the *Times* began on the first day of the strike and grew from one day to the next. Pressure on local businesses not to advertise was intense. This strike had to be settled by negotiation. However, the employer foolishly attempted to continue operating with its non-striking pressmen, employees who crossed the line, managers brought in from other papers, and replacement workers. Notwithstanding the agreement, the union therefore decided to violate the injunction order. The number of picketers began to swell, mostly UAW members coming to assist.[12] Government mediators were immediately deployed, but neither side was prepared to budge. The employer said its last offer was the final one, and the union made it clear that 'the war is on.'[13] One thousand picketers soon surrounded the *Oshawa Times*, drowning out the local sheriff, who was trying to read the injunction order over a loudspeaker. Nobody dared leave the plant and, needless to say, nobody tried to go in. It got worse. The sheriff was pelted with snowballs, and one brazen picketer ripped the injunction from his hands and tore it to shreds. There was no doubt that the dispute had increasingly less to do with wage rates and technological change at the *Times* and more to do with the use of injunctions in labour-management disputes.

Clifford 'Cliff' Pilkey, the head of the Oshawa and District Labour Council, made his position very clear: 'We will take on ... Lord Thomson [the proprietor] ... and beat him,' he swore.[14] A GM employee who had risen to become president of his UAW local, Pilkey objected to American domination of his Canadian local and so came into conflict with national and US union leaders. He thereupon redirected his energies, became president of the local labour council in 1957, and got himself elected as an Oshawa alderman. Clearly, Pilkey was not afraid of a fight.

The *Globe and Mail* predicted doom for the picketers in an editorial published on 3 February: 'The City of Oshawa does not appear to be satisfied merely to be known as the Cradle of Industrial Unionism in Canada. It seems bent on becoming known also as the Graveyard of Organized Labour's Respect for Law and Order, and the step from cradle to grave in this instance is an alarmingly short one.' The editorial board did not like to see the law defied, but it also understood that there was a real problem: 'The people of Ontario would be well served if other processes were devised to govern the conduct of labour and management in strike conditions. Laws providing right of access to struck premises, laws to provide for picketing for a reasonable number of strikers – these would help to reduce the need for injunctions. These are proper matters for debate and might be expected to be dealt with in the Legislature.'

Back at Queen's Park, both Premier John Robarts and Attorney General Arthur Wishart played dumb. They told reporters that they had not received any complaints that the law was not being enforced in Oshawa. Any suggestions that the local police were not upholding the law, the premier said, have 'not been made to me.'[15] Just as in Windsor in 1945, another union town, the police and the troops might be readied, but no politician was going to order their deployment until left with no other choice. Local police made it clear that their sympathies were with the strikers, while *Oshawa Times* management appeared to be caught completely off guard. They decided again to appeal to the courts.

Bruce Stewart, later to become the pre-eminent management counsel in Ontario, studied the *Judicature Act* and found a section that ordered all law-enforcement officers to aid in carrying out court orders. He had it served on Oshawa's chief of police, members of the local police commission, and the mayor, with argument on what was, in effect, a legal motion scheduled several days hence. When the case got to Osgoode Hall, John J. Robinette had been retained by the *Times*, and he asked the court to direct local and provincial authorities to enforce the injunction restricting picketing with all the 'forces at their disposal.' Any picketer who did not disperse was to be arrested. In fact, more and more people began arriving at the picket line offering support, including twenty members of the Seafarers' International Union, who had substantial experience in throwing their weight around, and Ontario's New Democratic Party (NDP) leader, Donald C. MacDonald, who made it clear that the time had come to stop management from using 'the courts to secure injunctions to break legal strikes.'[16] Even Osgoode Hall law professor Harry Arthurs, already a rising star in the Canadian academic firmament, gave the picketers some limited approval. 'Our society,' he observed, 'is shot through with people who defy laws in order to bring their injustice before the public.'[17] The United Church agreed and called on Lord Thomson to intervene personally to end the strike.

All this activity finally came to the attention of the premier as it became *the* topic of conversation in the legislature and in Ottawa. Behind the scenes, Premier Robarts arranged for the Guild and the employer to meet for the first time since the strike began. Legal skirmishes, at both the Ontario Labour Relations Board and in court, were then put on hold as William H. Dickey, one of the most able mediators and Ontario's chief conciliation officer, shuttled between the parties. Finally, after twenty-eight hours of non-stop mediation, a settlement was announced on 11 February. The Guild achieved major gains in wages and job security. While Cliff Pilkey applauded the outcome, he made it clear that the fight against injunctions was just beginning.

Indeed, organized labour had learned a good lesson. As the president of the Ontario Federation of Labour observed, 'tactics used in the strike against the *Times* cannot be applied in every strike, but where they can be, big labour supporting small labour, they should be.'[18] In fact, organized labour had already identified another target: Tilco Plastics Limited in Peterborough, a small manufacturing firm with mostly female employees making plastic combs and barrettes. The Textile Workers Union of America, which represented these workers, had been out on strike since the middle of December 1965. Thirty-two of the thirty-five strikers were female production workers paid just over the provincial minimum wage (there were sixty employees at the plant, a large number of whom crossed union picket lines). The employer's efforts to keep operating were further aided by an *ex parte* injunction that severely restricted the number of picketers. In the union's view, the employer had engaged in repeated unfair labour practices – as time went on there was more evidence of that – and the union was getting nowhere. Although the earlier-obtained *ex parte* injunction had a four-day shelf life, it gave the company the time it needed to round up some fresh employees and try to break the union. Management certainly saw it that way; one of the Tilco proprietors, Harold Pammett, announced that 'if it was not for the injunction, [the union] would have flattened him, but because of the court order, he could ride it out and would have [the union] decertified.'[19] When the *ex parte* injunction came up for renewal, the union was given notice and its counsel agreed to permanent limits on the number of pickets – twelve – apparently fearing that, without agreement, the presiding judge would allow no pickets at all. At that point it seemed that the strike was lost.

Then, on 12 February, the Oshawa and District Labour Council offered to place its 25,000 members at the disposal of the Tilco strikers. Tilco immediately contacted the attorney general and asked for help.

Wishart did not feign ignorance this time around but sternly warned organized labour of the consequences of non-compliance: 'any ... disobedience to the laws of this country, or the orders of our courts, will be prosecuted in the manner that our community demands. If any person shows contempt for our courts in these matters, he will be brought before our courts to answer for the contempt.'[20] Wishart, a lawyer who was first elected to the legislature in 1963, was actually a reformer, and the Tilco strike was his second major challenge as attorney general. Throughout 1965 and 1966, it occupied much of his attention.

An attempt by Peterborough's mayor to get the parties back to the bargaining table failed when the employer refused to play ball. While there was some picket-line violence, it was not serious and, in any event, mostly management inspired.[21] Nevertheless, on 23 February, hundreds of union supporters defied the injunction order and began picketing Tilco. This time Wishart meant what he said, even though he knew that management had not been bargaining in good faith and that there had been 'no violence.' He had been assured by local authorities that 'the picketing and actions have been orderly.'[22] The next day more than two dozen picketers were served with notice of criminal contempt of court proceedings against them. Wishart made it clear that he was not against lawful assembly, but he opposed the 'contumacious defiance of the order of the supreme court.'[23] The Crown would be looking for jail time, he said, and he instructed the prosecutor assigned to the case to proceed in a process called 'originating notice of motion,' a summary procedure. The Crown could have preferred an indictment. Had it done so, the accused would have had their cases heard by judge and jury instead of by judge alone. The choice may not have been a deliberate decision to deprive the accused of maximum due process, but it appeared that way as the charges began to make their way through Osgoode Hall.[24] Back in Peterborough, William Mulders, the president of the local labour council, called off the picketing. 'We have accomplished what we set out to do, and there is no point in continuing the demonstration,' he said, adding, 'It is now up to the courts.'[25]

All the accused landed in the courtroom of Chief Justice George Alexander 'Bill' Gale, an expert in the rules of civil procedure who had frequently attracted the enmity of organized labour. Perhaps he took carriage of the case as a signal of the seriousness with which he viewed any violation of court orders. Certainly, he did not appreciate any criticism of the judiciary, constructive or not. Even before he heard any evidence, Gale publicly rejected union claims that the courts granted injunctions against picketing as a matter of course. 'I dispute that,' he said.[26] The case went on for days. Wishart dispatched a senior provincial counsel (Frank Callaghan, a future chief justice of the High Court, assisted by a young man recently called to the bar, E. Marshall Pollock), and the strikers were represented by a pantheon of leading labour counsel, notably Edward (Ted) Bigelow Jolliffe, the former leader of Ontario's CCF; Ian Scott, the future Ontario attorney general; and Sydney Robins, a future treasurer of the Law Society and distinguished judge of the Court of Appeal.

In the legislature, Wishart emphasized the significance the government attached to the matter: 'I am sure he is aware of the importance of the decision in this case,'[27] he said on May 18, when asked when the government expected the chief justice to rule. Just over a week later, he again expressed confidence in the entire process as further inqui-

ries were made: 'I think that justice should be swift, as well as sure.'[28]
Both comments were completely improper, as the case was before the
courts. Judges should rule based on the evidence, not to curry favour
with politicians or in fear of them. But the passing of time was not the
only problem. James Renwick, the New Democratic MPP for River-
dale, observed in the legislature that the atmosphere in Gale's courtroom was such that the 'impartiality which is such an important and
vital part of our criminal procedure was lost to the men who were
tried.' Renwick, a Second World War hero and lawyer, knew what he
was talking about: he had attended virtually the entire proceeding.[29]

On 8 June, Chief Justice Gale convicted all but one of the men
charged with criminal contempt for picketing in defiance of the injunction. In a fifty-page decision, he set out the problem as he saw it:

No one should be permitted to express his displeasure at the state of the law
by deliberately flouting it. To follow any other rule would be to tread the road
to anarchy and chaos. There appears to be a misconception among certain
leaders and members of trade unions concerning the respective privileges of
employers and employees. They seem to think that once a strike is called, the
employer must close his doors to await the outcome. At present, that is not
the case. Employees have the right to strike, but by the same token, employers
have a right to continue their operations and to protect their property. With
the enhanced role of the trade unions there must be an increased social responsibility to recognize and promote support for law and order. Any program,
no matter how worthy the ultimate goal, which prescribes willful defiance of
the law can only be regarded as an exercise in irresponsibility. It is more than
a mere coincidence that demonstrations in Peterborough followed closely the
illegal mass picketing at the strike-bound *Oshawa Times* plant. Manifestly, the
lawlessness displayed in either case ought not to be condoned or allowed to
be repeated. If trade unions feel that present legislation is unfair or unrealistic and that they should have unbridled power to use mass picketing, then
they should seek proper channels for bringing about a change. In this respect,
they have no higher right than any citizen of this country and no one should
be permitted to express his displeasure at the state of the law by deliberately
flouting it.[30]

What happened at the *Oshawa Times* was legally irrelevant to activities in Peterborough, and it should never have formed part of the
judge's decision. Reference to that strike indicates that Gale was bothered by general union lawlessness, not just the specific acts of the

accused. Although he went out of his way to pay tribute to the important role played by unions in Canadian society, he sentenced all of the convicted men to jail. 'If there had been an apology tendered to me,' the chief justice told the picketers, 'I might have felt otherwise.'[31] Five of the accused were sentenced to two months each, and the others were incarcerated for fifteen days. Only Sydney Robins got his man off.[32] Gale was 'relentlessly unsympathetic to any appeals concerning men's jobs or their health needs in sentencing,' a historian wrote of the event. 'He told one diabetic who required insulin injections daily that there were medical facilities in jail and that he "should have thought of this before embarking on his irresponsible behaviour." And, indicating a rather contemptuous view of the protestors, he told the part-time firefighter in the group that he would actually like to punish him more stringently because he, of all the men, "appeared to be intelligent and industrious enough" to hold two jobs and should have a greater sense of responsibility.'[33] The result was popular in some quarters, but the union movement reacted with predictable outrage.

Peaceful picketers were going to jail, while managers at Tilco Plastics, who broke the law by bargaining in bad faith, went free. Why was nobody enforcing compliance with section 12 of the Ontario *Labour Relations Act*, which required unions and employers to bargain in good faith? Obviously, something was wrong in the administration of justice in Ontario. George Burt, the director of the Canadian UAW, described the sentence as 'an act of madness,' adding that, if the courts thought that jailing people for picketing was the way to enforce injunctions, 'it had better get a crash building program going on jails, because it is going to run out of space.'[34]

Later, in the summer of 1966, the union asked the Ontario Labour Relations Board for permission to prosecute Tilco for its numerous unfair labour practices. There was no shortage of ammunition, including Pammett's announcement that he would not have 'no-good older women' or 'lesbians' working for him.[35] By then, Tilco had a new lawyer, the future Supreme Court justice John Sopinka, and he knew exactly how to deal with this problem. 'Didn't he [Mr Pammett] have a reputation for making statements he didn't always mean?' Sopinka asked one union witness.[36] Outmatched yet again, the board ruled against the union's request. Then an appeal of Chief Justice Gale's decision failed and, in October, the convicted felons were taken away to jail. One of the most interesting things about the Tilco strike was the way it went 'from being a just struggle of women against their employer to a heroic war of men sent to jail for their principles,' but that is another story.[37]

Organized labour was furious about a lot of things – the injunctions, the jail sentences, the loss of the Tilco strike – and it announced a series of province-wide protests. This approach was in marked contrast to the strategy the union movement, together with other like-minded groups, had earlier pursued in their campaign for fair employment and housing legislation: to create, though education and persuasion, a political climate in favour of racial and social justice, which was soon given effect with remedial legislation. In the same way that politicians and opinion leaders subscribed to these earlier campaigns, their support could have been enlisted in favour of establishing an appropriate legal regime where unions would be free to picket, while any excesses on the picket line would be dealt with at a fair hearing in accordance with established rules. As Harry Arthurs expressed it, 'The use of conferences, rallies, speeches, deputations is a slow and exasperating process, but it is the way in which support is created among the uncommitted.'[38]

Working within the system takes time, and conditions have to be right. In the 1960s the union movement had lost patience, believing that the rules and the courts were stacked against it (and often they were). Still, Ontario was not Selma or Birmingham. Unions and their members were protected by Ontario laws. A legal system was in place that allowed a union to become certified without even a secret ballot vote – a right Ontario's unions have enjoyed since 1944, with one brief interruption during the years when Mike Harris was premier. Nevertheless, positions were polarized and the social fabric threatened. The government had no choice but to take charge, ensuring that the file was carefully managed. Accordingly, the premier called in key labour leaders for a meeting at the end of June 1966. Queen's Park then announced it would study the use of injunctions in labour disputes, hoping to quell social unrest in time-tested fashion by referring the problem off for study. The *Globe and Mail* thought it was probably unnecessary. While the injunction may have occasionally been misused, it editorialized on 2 July, 'the review is also likely to show that the injunction legislation is, on the whole, good legislation.' One thing the people of Ontario would not tolerate, it continued, was 'a system that would determine every labour dispute simply by how much brute force a union could recruit to pack around a plant.'

The *Globe*'s editorial board was on to something. While civil disobedience has a place in democracies, should it not be reserved for those situations where all other avenues have been exhausted? Moreover, for all the legitimate criticisms about the role of the courts in labour disputes, the truth was, as Arthurs put it, 'the labour movement has grown and flourished under the protection of the law and with the assistance of the law.'[39] Besides, it was not just organized labour that wanted changes to the law. Management began forwarding petitions to Queen's Park calling for legal bans against mass picketing. There were, on both sides, some voices of moderation. Warren Winkler, a young management labour lawyer and future Ontario chief justice, told a joint labour-management meeting that 'a mutual agreement could be reached on the injunction question' if the two sides sat down and spoke 'sensibly.'[40]

But how to find that middle ground? The first thing the government did was ask A.W.R. Carrothers, the dean of law at the University of Western Ontario, Rand's successor and the author of the first real labour law text in Canada, to conduct a study on the use of injunctions, to provide some background information for an anticipated larger examination into labour law. On July 8 Premier Robarts announced in the legislature that the government would also, in due course, be appointing a royal commission into labour disputes – exactly what opposition MPPs and organized labour had been demanding for years.

In the meantime, Carrothers got to work and submitted his report in October 1966. It did not include anything in the way of policy prescriptions. Most interesting was a study that Carrothers commissioned from Horace Krever, a professor at the University of Toronto Law School, a future judge of the Ontario Court of Appeal, and the lawyer who, when in private practice, had successfully convinced the Court of Appeal to invent a new tort in the *Hersees* case. While Krever's study was mostly descriptive, the professor was critical of the court's failure to consider the interests of unions when granting injunction requests, as well as the complete reliance on affidavit evidence. Krever was making an important point: any solution had to provide for all-round procedural fairness. For reasons real and sometimes imagined, the reputation of the courts had been seriously undermined by union criticisms. Even thoughtful and disinterested observers such as Harry Arthurs, the author of a 1964 study for the Department of Labour which spelled out some of the problems with the legal regime, were rightly 'critical of the way in which the law of picketing has developed, not because it is bad labour-relations policy – it is not all that bad – but because it is bad judging. Many of us who care about the courts and about the law, who feel that respect for judges and their decisions is critically important, are anxious to find a solution to the present crisis which will restore their damaged prestige.'[41] The Carrothers report was a good first step, but what was really needed was someone to examine not just the use and abuse of injunctions but all the laws regulating strikes, lockouts, and picketing.

Premier Robarts had a perfect judge in mind – Bora Laskin, appointed to the Court of Appeal in 1965. Laskin was an excellent academic who had spent some time in the labour-relations trenches, serving first as a union nominee and later moving over to the centre, where he became one of the most respected arbitrators in Ontario. The problem the government faced was that the entire judiciary had been implicated in the abuse of injunctions, and the premier was concerned that it might not be seemly to appoint a judge to study the activities of other judges. 'Whom should I choose?' Robarts asked H. Carl Goldenberg, an expert in labour relations, the author of the well-received 1962 report *Labour-Management Relations in the Construction Industry*, and one of his own special advisers.[42] 'Rand's your man,' Goldenberg replied. 'But he's ancient,' the premier responded. 'He might be old,' Goldenberg said, but 'take a chance.'[43] For almost thirty years prime ministers and premiers had been relying on Goldenberg's advice and his amazing ability to get things done. Now Robarts, notwithstanding his private misgivings, decided to accept that advice.

On 19 August 1966 the appointment of the eighty-two-year-old Ivan Rand as chair of the Royal Commission on Labour Disputes was announced. His job, Premier Robarts said, was to review and examine all aspects of the processes and procedures currently in effect for dealing with labour disputes after the regular procedures of negotiation, conciliation, and arbitration had been exhausted. In short, Rand's job was to study industrial warfare. The premier added that part of the mandate was to ensure that the rights of the general public, as well as those of employees and employers, were adequately safeguarded.[44] In the strikes at the *Oshawa Times* and at Tilco Plastics, the union had openly defied the law. Without a doubt, without those strikes and that defiance, the government would have been much slower to appoint a commission, if it did anything at all.

After taking up residence first at Toronto's Park Plaza Hotel and then in a spartan room at the University Club to save government money, Rand's first order of business was hiring E. Marshall Pollock. The good-humoured twenty-eight-year-old Pollock was a graduate of the law school at the University of Saskatchewan and a former graduate student of Bora Laskin. After a brief stint in private practice, Pollock joined the attorney general's office. Rand interviewed him for the position of associate counsel, but was so impressed that he offered him the top job.[45] Commission Counsel Pollock would be Rand's aide, assistant, and closest companion – Rand's wife and soulmate had just died – for the next two years as they traversed the province, the country, and the world, always, the frugal Rand insisted, by economy class.

There was no secret about the approach the commissioner intended to take. Rand told reporters that he wanted to find the best way to carve up the total production pie without destroying the pie or preventing anyone at the table from getting his fair share. The problem, he continued, in coming up with solutions was that, 'in some ways, we're still in the jungle.'[46] Rand had long been on record proposing compulsory arbitration as a reasonable alternative to strikes. Take disputes out of the jungle and subject them to the rule of law: choose reason over force, reason enforced by law, is what Rand believed. To be sure, his experience in Windsor in 1945 and 1946 contributed to the formation of that belief. After all, his formula brought an end not just to a specific labour-relations dispute but to the one issue that was behind so much industrial conflict. The arbitration model had clearly worked. But there was more to the project than that, and changing the vocabulary was part of it. Instead of talking about industrial warfare, Rand suggested, the parties should talk about 'social differences.'[47] Robert Sarginson, a United Steelworkers of America official who was sentenced to two months in jail for supporting Tilco strikers, was not impressed. He told Rand that 'those of us who were confined to jail, whose families were so inconvenienced by our serving of those sentences, are more convinced than ever today that our actions in demonstrating were for the good of all citizens of this province.' Rand disagreed: 'We need some methods to have these things resolved in a very civilized manner.'[48]

In fact, Rand had been mulling over the problem of strikes and industrial conflict for years and already had specific solutions in mind. Months after settling the Ford dispute, he made his views known. Speaking at the closing banquet at a conference exploring contemporary policy issues, organized by the Roman Catholic Church and held at Assumption College in Windsor in mid-September 1946, Rand observed: 'The usual accompaniment of strikes, personal violence, destruction of property, obstructions of all kinds, picketing and boycotts, are part of the residue of barbarism waged against entrenched property, analogous to fighting over the division of the spoils.'[49] Only the law could put the barbarians in their place.

'Reason or Force, which will it be?' Rand asked a September 1962 conference, also in Windsor. The fight was 'over the division of the spoils.' Society was suffering from the 'tyranny of shibboleths,' such as the 'right to strike.' Strikes needed to be curtailed and should only be allowed to proceed following a secret ballot. Anything less was an 'insult' to democracy. Better yet, Rand said, strikes should be replaced by compulsory arbitration, 'realized by procedures and tribunals worked out by patient intelligent thinking.' Clearly, years before he was appointed to study and report on reforms to Ontario labour law, Rand had identified the main problems and his specific solutions. The following month, Rand wrote his old friend and aide Horace Pettigrove and tested his idea out on him. What would you think, Rand asked, about a council of wise men 'drawn from every interested group, that is the public, the government ... the industrialists and I would say the class of publicists and academicians who have paid special attention to the workings of the economy as a whole ... determining the issue of the quantum of wages in light of the industry as a whole and its setting in the community?' Adjudication of collective bargaining disputes, Rand suggested, made sense: 'On the view that we never can have compulsory arbitration, it would seem that the people of a modern state are doomed forever to the senseless and wasteful automatic performance which is gone through now ending in a cessation of important public functions. To confess this as a necessary end is really to admit that human intelligence has reached the limits of its expansion. I can't accept that at all.'[50] Pettigrove, a man with real-world experience, was dubious and told Rand as much.[51]

Rand began work by getting to know key players in the labour-relations community, and Pollock got busy gathering background research. Public hearings began on 10 January 1967. 'We want a frank expression of opinion in which we can tear the clothes off ideas and see them in their nakedness,' Rand announced at the outset, and thus work began on the fourth and final inquiry of Rand's career.[52] In fact, Rand's objectives were even wider than bare naked ideas:

How are we going to reconcile the conflicting desires of human beings – desires for freedom and also the desire for goods, the desires for a standard of

living? This clash and this struggle, you might say, between those who have
and those who have not ... For our purposes here we must select only certain
features of that, I won't say 'contest,' because I think it is a mistake to look
upon these questions as solely a matter of internal and civil war. I think that is
ridiculous and reflects upon the intelligence of the men who claim to be democratic that it should be so. But we do have these conflicts and we must here
confine ourselves to such things as the phenomenon of strikes, picket lines,
boycotts.[53]

Two of the main players were present at the very beginning: the
Ontario Federation of Labour, representing a staggering 500,000 union
members (in a province with a population of 7 million), and Ontario's
most important employer organization, the Central Ontario Labour
Relations Institute. They both submitted their briefs on day one, with
testimony following on succeeding days.

Predictably, the OFL's biggest complaint was the use of injunctions.
Citing the Carrothers report, the OFL pointed out that Ontario courts
had, since 1958, issued injunctions in one-quarter of all strikes. More
than two-thirds of those injunctions were issued *ex parte*. The union
was usually not even notified that an injunction was being sought. Although it was valid for only four days, those days were often critical,
with the injunction application clearly timed to exert maximum pressure to break a strike. It was impossible, OFL president David Archer
told Rand, to determine with any certainty how many lawful strikes
had been lost because of injunctions. That situation had to change, beginning with divesting the courts of the authority to issue labour injunctions. That was a job, Archer believed, for the expert tribunal, the
Ontario Labour Relations Board. Injunctions were '18th century law
applied to 20th century conditions.' Why should there be any limits
on the numbers of peaceful picketers? The police could deal with any
picket line excesses that might occur. All injunctions did was give the
public the impression that unions were lawless and lacked membership support: 'No other section of Canadian society is subjected to the
kind of treatment unions are getting with regard to injunctions,' Archer argued. While some strikes and some pickets had gone bad, that
was not justification for banning them both: the pastor who makes off
with the collection plate, or the judge who takes up with a blonde, well,
neither were, in the OFL's view, reason to abolish churches or courts.
In addition to reforming the law of injunctions, the OFL asked Rand to
recommend that the use of strikebreakers be outlawed and mass pick-

eting permitted. For the picket line to work, Archer explained, quoting Marshall McLuhan's dictum 'the medium is the message,' it must have large numbers.

Rand did not like either the medium or the message. He told Archer that anything a union needed to say to its members could be said in the union hall: 'I think your language unconsciously reveals the fact that you do prevent access by intimidation and that you do reach that peak [in collective agreement negotiations] under the menacing shadow of your instrument – the strike and picket line. You are really advocating a picket line,' Rand continued, 'that is exerting an intimidating effect – not only on your own men but on outsiders.' Rand went on to reinforce this point, recalling seeing a newspaper photograph of picketers 'jamming' a sidewalk outside Tilco Plastics: 'No one else could possibly have walked on that sidewalk,' he observed.[54] As far as Rand was concerned, and he was challenged about this view over and over during the course of his commission, the only purpose of picket lines was to intimidate workers and others out of favour with a particular strike.

Rand's musings must have been music to the ears of the Central Ontario Industrial Relations Institute. An employers' organization with almost five hundred members, it proposed that, before being allowed to go out on strike, unions would have to obtain permission from a 'Labour Relations Act administrator.'

The institute had a number of other novel ideas as well. Picketing, general counsel J. Clifford Adams argued, was obsolete. There were many other means of mass communication. If the objective was to inform others of a dispute, then, at most, only a few picketers, presumably armed with leaflets, were necessary to bring the facts to the attention of the general public. Besides, all that mass picketing did was provide a cover for wrongdoers, screening illegal activity of 'malefactors who slash tires, put sugar in gas tanks.'[55] Picketing for informational purposes could be satisfactorily accomplished by the proper placement of some informational posters. Under the institute proposal, the 'administrator' would be in charge of placing 'placards on the plant to communicate the issues of the strike both to the public and potential job seekers.'[56]

The institute also called for the appointment of a special prosecutor to investigate violations of the law arising out of strikes. The total failure of the police to enforce the law during the *Oshawa Times* strike was the most recent example of the authorities keeping their hands off, and then, when the strike was over, even though the union had blatantly and consistently violated the orders of the court, nothing was done to hold the wrongdoers to account. A special prosecutor, Adams suggested, should be appointed (although he neglected to mention that it was management who invariably chose not to proceed with any legal actions after a strike was settled, preferring to focus on the future, not the past). Rand was not opposed to assigning responsibility where it belonged, and he pointed out to the management lobby group that sometimes the employer was at fault, so all aspects of the situation should be investigated.

Rand made clear from the outset that he was considering arbitration as the solution for all problems, with a few other bells and whistles thrown in for good measure. Strikes might be minimized or their duration reduced by restricting the right of employers to hire strikebreakers and the right of strikers to take other jobs. 'You would be giving great power to the workers and taking away management's ability to offer resistance. You would be taking sides,' Adams replied. Well, Rand responded, 'the law always takes sides.'[57] If picketing was banned or curtailed, and if strikers were not allowed to accept alternative employment, then, Rand suggested, strikebreakers should be banned too, in order to create an 'economic balance.'[58]

Did it not make sense, Rand asked, to ban or at least curtail strikes and refer disputes to arbitration, a legal process with the mandate to arrive at an equitable result? Neither the unions nor the employers thought so. All arbitration would accomplish was to relieve the parties from their responsibility to bargain in good faith, Donald Montgomery, the president of the Toronto and District Labour Council, told Rand.[59] Management agreed, and Adams sounded a further cautionary note: neither unions nor management wanted to be told how to settle their disputes. 'Is that intelligent?' Rand asked.[60] The parties certainly thought so.

By and large, what Rand heard was as predictable as it was polarized. Most union submissions reinforced those of the OFL: that the courts were in bed with management, and organized labour was getting the short end of the stick. Management expressed satisfaction with the status quo, although, as the institute submissions made clear, there was room for improvement. Except when Rand expressed his musings, no one ever said anything new, at least not very often. As veteran labour observer Wilf List put it, 'from labour and management the commission is getting the traditional positions of the parties – views that are hoary and self-serving; the extreme positions of two protagonists.'[61]

One day in May 1967 that changed. Labour lawyer Edwin (Ted) Stringer testified on behalf of the Hamilton Construction Association, an employer organization. He had clearly studied the transcript and had paid close attention to Rand's musings. He came with a plan. 'There was no point,' Stringer reflected years later, 'in parroting the party line.'[62] What he wanted to do was introduce some real balance into industrial conflict and reduce violence. No new employees, he began, could be hired during a legal strike, subject to the following conditions. First, no legal strike could be called unless it was approved by a majority of employees in the bargaining unit by secret ballot. Second, during the strike, all employees who wanted to work, including members of the bargaining unit, must have free access to the plant without intimidation, though these employees could not be paid any more than what was offered to the union during negotiations. Third, strikers who wanted to protect their jobs in the plant could not work elsewhere; the employer could hire a replacement, however, for any striker who took another job. Fourth, pickets would be limited to one per gate, since the strikers' jobs would be protected and there would be no need for mass picketing. Fifth, if a majority of striking employees returned to work in the struck plant, the strike would be considered at an end. And sixth, the legislature would pass strong measures against coercion and intimidation.[63]

Rand was visibly excited by Stringer's proposal: for the first time since the commission began work, he exulted, someone had come forward with specific proposals. Moreover, the plan was fully in sync with Rand's own approach of limiting, if not eliminating, picketing by introducing rules that made it unnecessary. Stringer explained that his plan would restore strikes to their original purpose – economic showdowns between the parties – by appropriately limiting the economic opportunities of both employer and employee.[64] Stringer was able to put his finger on Rand's pulse, and, eventually, his plan would form the basis of Rand's own approach. When the lawyer for the Ontario Chamber of Commerce suggested that there was nothing wrong with strikers taking temporary jobs, Rand strongly disagreed: 'Nothing wrong, except it allows the strike to continue.'[65]

On different days, the commission heard complaints about the quality of arbitrators, the impact of technological change, and petitions – the documents circulated during a union organizing campaign in which employees withdrew their earlier union support. Obviously, the temptation for management mischief once it learned that a union was on the scene was often irresistible. Unions cried foul, and the labour-relations board would investigate to ascertain the true desire of employees in the proposed bargaining unit. Petitions introduced delay and, when they originated with management, they often put an end to an organizing effort. Unions, of course, were often exceptionally zealous in 'encouraging' enough employees to sign union cards; if the union signed up more than 55 per cent of the employees in the proposed bargaining unit, it could be certified without a vote.

Concerns were also raised about the introduction of compulsory arbitration in disputes involving some essential services. Why not try arbitration, Rand asked a CUPE representative on the last day of May 1967, as the means of resolving wage disputes in the health-care sector? Arbitrators were biased, the official answered, and issued awards that left low-paid workers subsidizing the hospitals and the public. One arbitrator, the CUPE representative claimed, had even awarded wages below provincial minimum rates.[66] When a second CUPE official had the temerity to disagree, to oppose compulsory arbitration for public sector disputes, Rand let him have it. Public service strikes were neither an inconvenience nor the price to be paid for free collective bargaining – they were intolerable. In his sharpest public statement made during the proceedings, Rand said that he was 'revolted by strikes directed against the public.'[67] When a third CUPE leader, the head of the Ontario Hydro local and its nine thousand members, argued that no one should have to accept an unreasonable settlement, Rand suggested that the real message being communicated by the union to the employer and the public was that, unless union demands were accepted, 'we are going to throttle you.'[68]

The commission heard evidence from a wide spectrum of interests, some on the fringe. The leftist United Electrical Workers called Rand 'a capitalist.'[69] The Communist Party of Canada, amazingly still in business, published a pamphlet entitled *What Is Commissioner Ivan C. Rand Up To?* Nothing good, it appeared: the communists charged that Rand had turned his commission into a sounding board for anti-labour propaganda.[70] Meanwhile, the Ontario Teamsters Union announced it was boycotting the commission: 'It appears that the labor movement has been hoodwinked,' Ray Taggart, the president of 20,000 truck drivers, charged, 'and the commission is merely setting the stage for changes in the labor and other laws that will make it even more difficult for workers to organize and negotiate effectively.'[71]

Taggart had reason to rethink his decision to boycott the proceedings when one of his employer targets showed up at the commission hearing with blood-stained shirts and stones hurled through truck windows, claiming they were evidence of what the Teamsters would do to force an employer to sign a collective agreement. Taggart was furious and sharply criticized the authorities: 'If they have evidence of wrongdoing on the part of Teamsters, then lay criminal charges and bring guilty parties to justice.' In the meantime, Rand, who had heard only one side of the story, suggested that the solution might be the immediate arrest of all pickets: 'If, as you say, the picket line is illegal, proof is not necessary. They have no excuse to be around your gates at all. They could be arrested immediately.'[72]

Throughout the proceedings, Rand did little listening but engaged in a lot of talking, chiding, questioning, and expressing a fair share of politically incorrect remarks, by today's standards. His questions often degenerated into long speeches, to the obvious discomfort of his counsel, who was trying to keep the proceedings on track. Off and on, the hearings continued until early June. All told, the commission sat for forty-one days (with local travel to Toronto, Kingston, Windsor, London, Peterborough, Hamilton, Port Arthur, Sudbury, and Ottawa) and received more than ninety briefs from a wide variety of organizations and interests. Pollock was in charge of the administrative arrangements, and the hearings were usually held in a courtroom. When the commission was not in session, Rand was almost always at work. One weekend in November, Pollock brought his two children to the office, which was well situated for watching the Santa Claus Parade. Rand was at his desk reading briefs, but he gave the children a quarter each for a candy bar. Pollock also worked hard, writing summaries of the briefs and collecting information from other jurisdictions as well as authoring long but interesting background reports.[73] He also took charge of some major social science research. A questionnaire was prepared and liberally distributed to unions and employers involved in recent labour disputes. Detailed and thorough, the questionnaire investigated what had led to the strike or lockout; what remedies were sought, before the courts and the labour board, as the strike continued; and what the outcome of the labour dispute had been.[74]

Out of the public eye, Rand continued privately to consult. He had definite views, but said he wanted them challenged. That was always his stated approach: to begin with a premise and have it tested or corrected through intense discussion with others, all in pursuit of what he saw as a rational, civilized, forward-looking solution. At least that was the operating assumption. On 19 July, for example, he met with Harry Arthurs. The professor was blunt, although perhaps not blunt enough. It would be a huge mistake, he told Rand, to appoint a permanent arbitration board to settle collective agreements. The current system worked in part, Arthurs explained, because it was voluntary. Parties could not complain, at least not as much, when they had agreed on the arbitrator. What would be useful, Arthurs suggested, was the creation of a wider panel of skilled individuals from which the parties could choose an arbitrator. That would reinforce voluntarism but avoid the institutionalization of a panel whose effectiveness was not judged by its consumers.[75] It was good advice.

Rand was convinced, and had been from the outset, that a legal substitute for industrial conflict had to be found. In Australia, he observed in January 1968, arbitration of labour disputes was 'accepted by everyone.' The Australian system had been in place for more than sixty years, 'but there hasn't been a word of amendment by any government, including a Labor government.' Although Rand insisted he was only thinking out loud to test his ideas, his frequent references to the Australian model and his increasingly obvious antipathy to picketing and all forms of industrial conflict – 'more appropriate to the 5th century' than to 1968 – suggested otherwise. 'I think,' he told one labour leader, 'you can have the best kind of settlement when the best men are available.' Compulsory arbitration, Rand continued, might take some getting used to, 'but you will never make any advance if you don't try.' Unions and their members might not like it, but, Rand said, 'sometimes you can't have the government follow the headlines of social change. It must go first. By leadership it must increase the pace.'[76] These statements were all good hints that Rand had already made up his mind, and, according to Marshall Pollock, he had. They left on a research trip to Australia not to get new ideas but to validate the conclusions Rand had already reached.[77] Nevertheless, he took full advantage of the visit by learning for himself how the system actually worked and which of its features might be imported to Canada.

Down under, labour-management wage disputes were ultimately resolved by arbitration. The parties negotiated and, if that failed, there was conciliation. If that failed, depending on the state or whether the matter was subject to federal jurisdiction, the dispute would go to one tribunal or another and a binding award would be issued. This system had, according to one scholar, the 'full acceptance' of the parties.[78] Nevertheless, 'this must not be taken as a statement that industrial relations in Australia are wonderfully harmonious,' Harry Glasbeek, an expatriate Australian teaching at Osgoode Hall Law School, continued.[79] Australians still went on strike – long strikes, short strikes, work-to-rule strikes, one-day wildcat strikes. They even went out on strike to protest arbitration awards. Arbitration was the final destination, but, although the statistics were difficult to compare, getting there appeared to involve at least as much industrial unrest as in Canada. About the best that could be said for the Australian system was that it had a stabilizing effect on wages.[80] In practice, wages became harmonized by the inflexible application of the same pattern to similar workplaces. Employees of prosperous firms obtained the same outcomes as employees of marginal firms, and vice versa. The system discouraged direct bargaining and voluntarism. The feature that impressed Rand the most was that labour disputes were settled rationally based on principles, not through the exercise of power.[81] He realized, however, that the system, even though it had many advantages, did not cure the disease of industrial disputes. An extended meeting with Bob Hawke, soon to be president of the Australian Council of Trade Unions, leader of the Australian Labor Party, and, ultimately, prime minister, exposed some of the myths of the Australian arbitration system. 'Like every other person that I have come in contact with in my life in government, law or business,' Pollock later recalled, 'Rand took from those meetings that which he wanted and ignored the rest.'

Rand and Pollock toured Australia for a month and were treated like visiting royalty. The Canadian high commissioner hosted a reception in their honour in February 1967 to which prominent Australian lawyers and academics were invited. As was expected, Australians were forthcoming with their Canadian visitors, providing them with extensive assistance and information about how things were done. In Canberra, Rand and Pollock were entertained by Governor General Lord Casey, among other members of the Australian elite. There were also trips to Sydney, Adelaide, Perth, and Melbourne, with serious study during the day followed by dinners and cocktail parties at night. Small talk was the one part of the job the abstemious and socially awkward Rand could not stand, especially without Dell at his side. By the end of the tour, however, Rand clearly understood that a 'made in Australia' solution was not the answer, 'except for the rationality involved in the exercise of articulating the annual case for higher national wages to the Conciliation and Arbitration Commission.'[82]

There were also trips to New Zealand, France, Sweden, Switzerland, the United Kingdom, and the United States. Rand and Pollock became quite close. One day, after a meeting in Vancouver with Tom Berger, the NDP hotshot and future judge, Rand turned to his trusted counsel and said, 'Marshall, I am fond of you, so please don't take this the wrong way.' Pollock was alarmed. What had he done? Would he be fired? 'Marshall,' Rand continued, 'it is "between you and me," not "between you and I."'[83]

When the travel was done and the research complete, Rand began, in the fall of 1967, to work on his report. He continued, however, to accept speaking invitations.

Rand was convinced that the law, the rational law, could resolve all human conflict. There was, he said in an Ottawa speech in September 1967 to a group of labour-relations professionals, too much self-dealing and greed in society. 'Obstinate and unreasonable demands or resistance by any group can serve only to weaken the community as a whole. We are no longer in a society of stagnation and poverty; it is distribution within an affluent society with which we are concerned.' It was not just 'labour' and 'capital' who were the culprits. 'Similar attitudes are exhibited by claimants for all sorts of special benefits. The demonstrations for example of farmer organizations against the prices for certain products are of the same genre.' It was all because of money: 'The deepest root of social decay lies in the realm of money.'

Greed, Rand explained, threatened peace at home and abroad because it prevented social justice and the fair distribution of society's riches. Labour and capital, to use these two words as Rand did, were increasingly important in the management not just of the economy but of society. They had a 'duty,' and that duty imposed on them an 'obligation of reasonable attitude toward claims ... they are to bargain in good faith.' There was more, of course. 'Labour and Capital, in the broad view, have been entrusted as primary participants with the task of maintaining the economic life of the country. In that assumption of social trusteeship lies the justification – if any is needed – for the imposition upon them of legislative obligation.' Rand had something in mind, of course, but that would come later, in his report. 'This country with its colossal material resources can be denied greatness only by the failure of its people.'[84] These ideas underlay Rand's approach as he took pen in hand – he wrote everything in longhand – and began drafting his report.

The main problem was picketing, Rand told a select group of academics invited to a series of consultative meetings as the year turned. The solution was to eliminate it. The method, Pollock announced, was to be through 'the Central Trilogy.' One: restrictions would be placed on the right of striking employees to work elsewhere, putting economic pressure on them. If striking employees took another job, they lost any right to return to their original positions. Two: management lost its right to hire replacement workers – except where striking employees had gone to work for someone else. It could use management personnel to perform the struck work, and it could make use of employees who stayed at work or later crossed the picket line, but there would be no fresh employees. Three: strikers would be guaranteed their jobs while on strike (unless they went to work elsewhere). Recognizing, however, that some strikes went on for too long, in those situations employees would be given notice that, if they did not return to their jobs, they would lose any rights to them. This Central Trilogy, which some referred to as 'the trade-off theory,' was really the Stringer plan warmed over with a new name.

The reaction from the hand-picked academics was not good. John Crispo, the young director of the Centre for Industrial Relations at the University of Toronto who had served as Carl Goldenberg's director of research on his Royal Commission into Labour-Management Relations in the Construction Industry, had sound criticism for Rand. Picketing 'is clearly not just a method of conveying information,' he said. 'In a society where labour solidarity does not mean as much as it does in many other countries, the picket line is the major device workers have to convince those who would undermine their cause not to do so. As long as this pressure does not take the form of physical coercion or property damage or manifestly threaten to do so,' he didn't see why 'it should be barred.' That was a good point. 'It must be remembered,' Crispo continued, 'that a picket line serves several purposes from the point of view of those who feel compelled to resort to it. Above all, it is often the rallying ground for those on strike and in this role is just as important to dissuade any of those involved to go back to work as to discourage others from seeking their jobs. In addition, and sometimes equally important, is the fact that a picket line is often the most effective means workers have to bring their cause to the attention of the public and thus to command wider support. For all of these reasons, and perhaps more, loss of the right to picket could be the undoing of many a legitimate strike.'[85]

Crispo was never afraid to express an unpopular view. While his method of delivery sometimes caused controversy, the content of his commentary was often correct. He turned next to the Central Trilogy. There would be obvious difficulties in administering the system, he advised, and it also challenged the fundamental balance of power between unions and employers. Guaranteed employment status removed from the equation the element of risk associated with a strike. Why not consider some alternative solutions that were less radical, less drastic? There had been some 'problem cases,' he argued, but nothing in the record warranted the imposition of 'drastic remedies.'[86] Set out and spell out the legal limits of picketing. Empower an expert tribunal such as the Labour Relations Board with the authority and jurisdiction to regulate the new rules, backed up, if need be, by the police and by court orders, including specific authority to award damages when the rules were broken.

Crispo was proposing a refinement of the current system, not the wholesale invention of something new. He also recommended that strikers be allowed to return to work at any time, so long as suitable work remained available. Strikebreakers could be hired, but they could not, to ensure that no professional strikebreakers were employed, be paid anything other than regular wages and benefits. 'It may well be,' he concluded, 'that the day will come when we have to resort to the measures the Rand Commission is now seriously entertaining, but I don't believe that time has yet come. In the meantime, there are realistic alternatives which can provide us with the means to cope with some of the vexing problems now plaguing our industrial relations system without exposing it to potentially profound changes which might lead to fundamental alterations that could prove its undoing.'[87] Every single one of these points was valid, but they were all ignored as Rand and Pollock got to work drafting their report.

To assist the commissioner, Pollock prepared a document analyzing the most important legal issues that had been raised in the proceedings. Among the priorities he identified were abolishing the *ex parte* injunction, except where the slightest amount of delay might cause irreparable harm; introducing mechanisms for the fair adjudication of injunction requests; establishing a process in which unions could sue and be sued; and codifying the rules respecting picketing. 'I think it is beyond question,' Pollock wrote to Rand, 'that the laws relating to picketing, both as to conduct and scope, ought to be statutorily codified rather than judicially declared.'[88]

Pollock worked diligently behind the scenes to moderate Rand's views favouring more regulation, not less. Establish a new tribunal, he suggested to Rand. Provide a research function or secretariat. Limit it at first to those sectors of the economy – police, firefighters, hospital employees – where there was no right to strike. Add to this list other industries when the government determines there should be no right to strike or that a strike should be stopped. Refer collective bargaining disputes to that tribunal. Begin modestly, he advised, and if the new tribunal gained public acceptance, then expand its jurisdiction.[89]

This limited plan was not what Rand had in mind. Even though the focus of the inquiry was industrial conflict, picketing, and strikes, Rand decided to take an expanded view of his jurisdiction. Both men worked together over the winter, spring, and summer. Rand would draft and then Pollock would comment, attempting to refine Rand's ideas or at least make them clear.[90] As the report began to take shape, Pollock became increasingly concerned, advising the commissioner that some of his ideas were arbitrary while others were utopian. 'I warned him,' Pollock later recalled. 'I said, "You are in control of the fate of two people, yours and mine. They will say that this is the work of a senile old judge and a young man who did not know his ass from a hot rock."'[91] That was not the response Rand wanted to hear, but he agreed to think about it. The next day he asked Pollock whether he really felt that strongly about the matter. Pollock said yes. Rand agreed to take another look at things, but no real changes were made.

When Pollock travelled to Shediac in the summer of 1968 with the page proofs in hand, Rand, obviously lonely and depressed, told him that he would rely on him to check the text. Rand was alone most of the time and was having trouble getting his meals.[92] He missed his wife terribly. He was happy to see Pollock, however. He began to play the accordion that he kept at his summer home, and, as he did, tears streamed from his eyes.[93] Rand's countenance would always 'soften' as the sound of music reminded him of Dell.[94] Premier Robarts should indeed have followed his instincts and gone with a younger man.

Towards the end of August 1968, some two years after his appointment was announced, speculation began to build that Rand's report was imminent. Different commentators weighed in, and the general consensus was that it would be original, independent, and influential. On 5 September the report, replete with a striking red and white cover with gold trim, was released to the press. Rand recommended what amounted to a complete overhaul of the industrial-relations system in Ontario. All hell then broke loose.

The report proposed strict and elaborate regulation of industrial disputes by a new, all-powerful, virtually unreviewable industrial tribunal, responsible only to the legislature and staffed with professional judges drawing huge salaries. The president would be paid the same amount as the chief justice of Ontario ($36,000); his two deputies the same as Supreme Court judges ($32,000); and the commissioners, another eight men, the same as county court judges ($25,000). There would also be advisers, economists, statisticians, labour-relations experts, accountants, clerks, and maintenance employees. The new tribunal, as Rand's recommendations for legislative reform made clear, was designed to the last detail and made responsible for everything involved in industrial relations.

Only primary picketing was to be permitted, and with limitations. The tribunal was in charge of the number of picketers and the information they conveyed. Mass picketing was banned as was secondary picketing, with limited exceptions. Boycotts were banned. The parties could still appeal to the courts for injunctions, but restrictions were to be introduced on *ex parte* injunctions. Strikers had new job security rights, and employers faced certain restrictions on hiring replacement personnel. Mechanisms were to be introduced to end strikes. After forty-five days, any employee, whether striking or not, could apply for a supervised vote about whether the strike should continue. After ninety days, either party could ask the tribunal to issue an award settling the dispute. If one of the parties rejected that award, the tribunal could still impose it if the party had, in its estimation, failed to bargain in good faith or had acted 'clearly unreasonably.' The tribunal would have the authority to terminate any strike after six months. Strikes by public employees were banned. The tribunal would arbitrate disputes in essential industries, business, or services and in other workplaces according to an elaborate set of rules.

The new tribunal could also, at the request of the government, look into any labour-relations matter and make recommendations, or not. It could, on its own initiative, intervene in any labour-relations matter – whether sources of industrial unrest, wages, hours of work, the cost of living and benefits, and, of course, strikes – and endeavour to bring about a settlement. The tribunal would have the power to direct the production of books, accounts, financial statements, and all other corporate and financial records. It could issue cease-and-desist orders and compliance orders and enforce its edicts with heavy fines and imprisonment. Almost one-third of the fifty-six recommendations dealt with fines, penalties (including prison terms), and civil liabilities. A new director of enforcement, responsible only to the legislature, would be in charge of overall compliance. Instead of voluntarism, there would be intervention.

There was a hodgepodge of other recommendations, including some that related to Rand's mandate. For example, he recommended that unions be recognized as legal entities entitled to sue and be sued. Others had nothing to do with his mandate, such as the recommendation that no employees with seven years or more of service could be terminated without just cause until they reached mandatory retirement age.

The report itself began with a survey of labour law from earliest times to the present, with a focus on Great Britain and the United States: 'What that history, beyond serious doubt, establishes is the fact that the government of labour-management relations cannot be left to the uncontrolled action of the immediate parties to them.'[95] The biggest problem that Rand identified was human nature: 'There are ... both the primal demands for food, clothing and shelter, and the secondary but equally insistent demand for greater participation in the ornamentations of life, the luxuries, the products of wealth, the ostentatious display of which creates the standards of acceptance. That is the background against which labour relations of today must be viewed and procedures adopted for their adjustment to societies of order.'[96]

Unions and employers, Rand asserted, 'have attained a *de facto* control of vital elements of the country's life.' It was not necessarily 'villainous or undesirable,' but it did require 'regulation.' Self-regulation and state regulation: 'What that means here is that capital (or management) and labour have in this country reached a stage at which they must accept limitations on the impacts of their ... action.' The public interest had to govern. Accordingly, the parties 'must accept the rule of mutual accommodation, and toward the public, the rule of reasonable restraint.' Unions and employers had a duty to 'be reasonable and straightforward in negotiations. That is essential to the proper attitude toward the public interest.' Their 'co-action' was, Rand said, a 'social partnership.' That was all part of a system he named 'social qualification.'

Free collective bargaining had, therefore, to be seen in this new context. 'There is assumed by those who treat it as an inviolable ritual that its terms affect only the interests of the parties to it ... But that is not so ... it can affect other important interests than those of the parties to it.'[97] What 'free collective bargaining' really meant 'is that the parties want no governmental compulsion: they demand to be let alone to fight it out with their own weapons regardless of the effect on the public or any other interest; "free" means from the rules of society.' Free collective bargaining, Rand believed, was the modern-day equivalent of the ordeal and trial by battle, with only one side leaving the field alive. It was, he said, 'barbarian.' It was definitely not, to borrow one of his favourite words, 'civilized.'

Industrial conflict was, therefore, an anachronism. One way of limiting industrial action was by introducing new rules to govern both the rights of employees to retain their jobs during a strike and the entitlements of employers to hire new employees. If strikers did not have to worry about losing their jobs, Rand reasoned, there would be no reason for picketing. And his objective was to limit picketing. 'If we are not to revert to lawlessness ... clashes of interest must be settled by reason, not by muscle or guns.' That meant strict limits on primary picketing and the virtual abolition of all other forms of picketing. Besides, Rand thought picketing was unnecessary: 'In these days of general sophistication, what effect can such limited, general information produce by way of inducing sympathetic action? The ordinary passer-by knows nothing of the merits of the dispute; all he gathers is an implication that an employer is unfair. If the line affects, say, a retail store, it becomes more of a nuisance than an effective persuasion, although some shoppers may shrink from becoming involved in any manner in any kind of labour dispute; to some extent, depending on the circumstances, it might influence unionists; if a manufactory, the ordinary individual is not interested in it; and a large-scale purchaser would rarely be in need of information or affected by it.'

Much better than strikes was arbitration. Better than fighting it out was going before the tribunal: 'The recommended Tribunal with its Commissioners will furnish a competency for judgment in this field as intelligent, objective and enlightened as the human quality of the province can supply.'[98] It was not going to be easy, but Rand was optimistic: 'persons of high gifts, sound judgment and thorough training are essential; they must possess the imaginative self-awareness and the versatile intellect that are vital to pragmatic adjudication.' The time had come to 'replace the crudely developed bargaining, conciliation and strike ritual.' Only by a 'concentration of first-class abilities in action can we hope to evolve schemes of solution which will modify or eliminate the present disfiguring and wasteful procedures.' Rand knew it would be difficult, given the 'ingenuity in evasion of a regime' that would be quickly employed given 'our present scale of values.'

Rand had someone in mind to head the tribunal. Anticipating a favourable reaction, he had approached County Court Judge J.C. Anderson about becoming the chair of his proposed tribunal. Should I mention your name to the premier? Rand asked the judge. Anderson responded that he would be 'honoured,' but he sounded a prudent cautionary note. Let's wait and see whether your proposed tribunal comes to pass, he suggested, as the actual implementation of the recommendations was likely 'a considerable distance in the future.'[99]

Waiting at his cottage in Shediac, Rand conceded to some apprehension about how the report would be received: 'It's always there when you launch something like this.' He had also been apprehensive about what reception the Rand Formula would receive, 'but I like to think that has proved itself over the years. I think most people take it as a matter of course now.' He predicted the same fate for this report: wide acceptance over time.[100] He thought that the most important of his recommendations was the one that makes a strikebreaker a provisional employee only, subject to displacement when the strikers returned. 'One of the greatest complaints from the unions,' he observed, 'was that strikers were compelled to watch others take their jobs.' He also anticipated criticism from the unions, especially about his recommendation that they become legal entities, capable of suing and being sued. 'But they can't really complain. Now if they cause damage, they are liable.'

In Toronto, officials at the Department of Labour announced that the minister, Dalton Bales, was carefully reading the report. It was obvious that it would require a great deal of thoughtful consideration. When a senior department official was asked about the government's plans, he sighed deeply and said that the unions would not like the 'sue and be sued' recommendation, while it was most unlikely that management would buy into the super-tribunal.[101]

That reaction was mild, compared to most of the commentary. 'On each of the six major subjects which concerned the commission (collective bargaining, picketing, boycotts, injunctions, strikes and lockouts, automation) there are hundreds and hundreds of scholarly studies which were available to it ... There is no evidence in the report that either the commissioner or his counsel read any of it. The evidence indicated,' newspaper columnists Doug Fisher and Harry Crowe observed, 'that they read none of it.'[102]

If there was not much secondary research, a lot of emphasis had clearly been placed on the Australian system. Rand and counsel met with more than one hundred Australians, or least the appendix to the report suggested as much. But what they never understood was that the Australian experience was fundamentally irrelevant. Rand's many trips to other countries left him confused, and his references to the labour-management situation in those places were largely incomprehensible. Had Rand spent more time with unionists and less with diplomats, professors, and business leaders, with the occasional top union bureaucrat thrown in for balance, he might have reached some different conclusions about the real problems that needed to be addressed. There were, records indicate, too many diplomatic receptions, cocktail parties, and private lunches and dinners at the University Club, the Granite Club, and the Park Plaza Hotel with representatives of the business and legal elites. For the most part, these were distractions to Rand, who devoted himself to his work, although some of these encounters must have provided him with an opportunity to find out what some people really thought and to test his ideas, or at least go through the motions of doing so. The record clearly establishes that, on those few occasions when Rand was told something he did not want to hear – by Crispo and Arthurs, for example – he ignored it.

'One afternoon,' Shirley Goldenberg recalled, 'Rand came over to visit Carl.' Shirley Goldenberg was a distinguished industrial-relations professor in her own right and the wife of H. Carl Goldenberg, who had recommended Rand to the premier. Rand arrived early in the afternoon. He sat there talking non-stop about what he thought about various things. 'He told us he didn't like pickets. He told us he didn't like strikes. He told us that he didn't like the attitudes of young people. He was there for most of the afternoon. Around 4:00 p.m., Carl took me aside and said, "He's not leaving!" At that point it became clear that he intended to stay for dinner. Finally, I suggested to Carl that we invite Alan Gold to join us. Alan was not yet a judge but was active as a labour arbitrator in Quebec. Gold came over. Gold would say, after Rand expressed a point of view, just as Carl had all afternoon, "With respect, Judge, I can't agree."' On and on it went, and it became clear to the Goldenbergs that the liberal of the Rand Formula had become a reactionary.[103]

Rand claimed that there must be more regulations because history

required it. In fact, he believed that increased regulation was necessary to counter the attack on the social fabric. Labour unions and mass
picketing were a part of it, but so too were the advent of automation,
the arrival of inflation, the bomb, the Black Panthers, the hippies, the
yippies, the Summer of Love, social unrest in American ghettos, Martin Luther King and Bobby Seale and Jerry Rubin and Abby Hoffman,
Weathermen blowing themselves and others up, rioting students and
communists in France – the list of challenges to the 'establishment' occurring every day was what really motivated Rand.[104] 'The monstrous
repudiation of law and the substitution of disorder and force can lead
only to social chaos which seems just to have been avoided in France,'
Rand observed, although he did not go on to explain what that had to
do with the strikes at the *Oshawa Times* and at Tilco which had led to
his appointment.[105] In 1945 Rand had been concerned about unlawful
union conduct during the Ford strike, but not nearly as much. In the
intervening years, society had become much more messy.

'The destruction of laws begins in the minor infractions,' Rand
warned in his report, a finding that led him to the conclusion that the
power of the state had to be brought to bear 'if we are not to revert to
lawlessness.' Instead of understanding that a strike was not only lawful but a safety valve in a system of voluntary collective bargaining,
Rand saw industrial conflict as 'a residual of the primordial struggle.'
He did not understand that free collective bargaining and the right to
strike were flip sides of the same coin. Unless unions could withdraw
labour (and management could lock out), there could be no free collective bargaining, for there would be no need for employers to bother
bargaining at all. Collective agreement negotiations were successful
most of the time because both union members and management knew
that the alternative was a strike, where no one gets paid and no profits
are made. Collective bargaining had imperfections, as does almost everything, but it was a system that basically worked.

Rand did not have a clue what was meant by free collective bargaining, absurdly comparing it with the ordeal and trial by battle.
Obviously, he wanted to create a mechanism that allowed unions
and employers to settle their differences while reducing violent con-
frontations and limiting collateral damage to the public. That was a
laudable goal. But the plan he prescribed was an overreaction to an
overstated problem. Whatever was good in his approach got lost in the
shuffle. Just about everything in Rand's report ultimately pointed to
arbitration, and many of the recommendations would likely have been

destructive of free collective bargaining. They all had as their effect
reducing the pressures on labour and management to reach an agreement. It all made sense to Rand. 'He called strikes and labour problems,' Pettigrove recalled years later, 'particularly strikes, he called
them the barbarous scrimmage. It was totally foreign to his experience
... he had an orderly mind and he wanted it all in neat little packages,
which just would not work in labour-management relations.'[106]

Free collective bargaining married the collective actions of employees with the demands of employers, the two sides bargaining until
they reached some common ground, and if unable to reach a settlement, the union could withdraw the employees or the employer could
lock them out. Eventually, free market forces would determine the outcome. Rand, ever the rationalist, could not abide the prospect of conflict, when all that was required was some expert tribunal to determine
the matter. But how could that tribunal do a better job than the parties
themselves? How could it know better what outcome the free market
would generate? His tribunal was empowered to set wage rates. Eventually, the judges would not even be able to consider prevailing or nor-
mative rates, because they would set them all. And what about ability
to pay? Or real market forces? Or inflation? Or productivity? It was a
massive interference with capital and its efficient allocation.

Giving an individual employee the right to force a government-
supervised vote forty-five days after a strike began was, self-evidently,
a union-busting tactic, and it was roundly condemned by organized
labour as such. Limiting picketers to employees and union officials meant that there could never be any labour solidarity. In some
cases, the ordinary onus was switched around: guilty unless you could
prove yourself innocent, as the union had to establish that it had no involvement in certain designated unlawful activities of its members. All
sorts of prohibitions were placed on unions and their members, while
management was encouraged to profit share. Picketing allowed only
in limited numbers effectively reduced it to ineffective expression. But
what exactly did Rand mean by 'appropriate placards with legitimate
information?' As determined by whom? The tribunal? Coming from a
real believer in the rule of law and a champion of free expression, this
recommendation was astonishing.

The new tribunal would also have fundamentally changed the role
of labour lawyers. Instead of being problem-solvers, they now would
be confined to a legalistic cocoon in which every aspect of labour-
management relations was highly regulated, with fines and prison

terms the possible consequence of non-compliance. 'Leave it to the tribunal,' would become the predictable response. Part of the problem was that Rand did not have any practical experience. Privately, he confided as much to Horace Pettigrove: 'I haven't got the feel of this thing. I admit it.'[107]

In his heart, Rand was a social engineer. He was convinced that social problems could be solved by 'experts.' It was almost as though he had become a technocrat, willing to hand over government reins to the technical experts. The alternative was 'social anarchy and chaos.' He had no understanding of free enterprise, and he confused 'capital' with 'management.' For some reason, he thought there were two coherent groups and that they enjoyed equal power, thereby demonstrating his high degree of economic illiteracy.[108] The central problem with the report was that it rejected voluntarism, ridiculed free collective bargaining, and proposed expanded state regulation to labour-management conflict through a Big Brother nanny-state tribunal. Moreover, it was a mistake to suggest that the public interest was at stake in every labour dispute. The public interest was rarely involved; it was usually private interests that were in play, and it was in the interest of those parties to resolve them. By and large, they did.

Rand really believed that some all-wise, all-powerful, all-knowing tribunal could solve all our problems, predicated on the belief that the parties themselves could not be trusted to work their problems out and that the public interest demanded an end to all forms of industrial conflict. 'The trouble with his tribunal is that there is no guarantee its omnipotence would be tempered by omniscience,' the *Toronto Star* observed. 'Its members are visualized as men of phenomenal education and wisdom, trained in labor law, economics, political science, philosophy, history, sociology, and industrial relations; but it is doubtful if 11 such paragons exist outside of Mr. Rand's imagination.'[109] 'Are twelve wise men the answer?' the *Labour Gazette* asked.[110] That depended in large part on the question.

Rand should have listened to Professors Arthurs and Crispo. Reform around the edges; recommend rules for limiting injunctions, rules that respond to some of the demonstrated excesses of *ex parte* applications; provide enhanced employment security to strikers, but allow employers to keep operating during a strike – the list of possible reforms was extensive. 'Instead, he ran amuck through the whole realm of collective bargaining, clamping on handcuffs, slamming down bars, and strewing red tape everywhere.'[111] Rand wanted industrial conflict completely regulated, with the experts ruling from above. Industrial pluralists like Arthurs and Crispo wanted the parties to resolve their own problems in a more loosely regulated system staffed by people with expertise at the Ontario Labour Relations Board. Industrial conflict had to be managed, but the way to do it was with largely consensual institutions that had earned community confidence.

Reaction from organized labour was predictable. The labour leaders were furious (although in those days they had a lot to be angry about). The report was 'a travesty of justice harkening back to the days of indentured slavery,' according to Donald MacDonald, the head of the Canadian Labour Congress. Meanwhile, Donald C. MacDonald, the leader of the Ontario NDP, was equally scathing: Rand's tribunal 'would appear to discourage labour and management from settling disputes on their own, and seriously detract from the freedom of the collective bargaining process which our society has come to recognize as a basic right of employees.'[112] David Lewis, the head of the federal NDP and a truly fine labour lawyer, dismissed the report and its central recommendation for a super-tribunal. The powers Rand would assign to the tribunal, he suggested, were 'frighteningly wide and deserve to be described as dictatorial.'[113] Ironically, one of the few recommendations that appeared to favour organized labour, the right of striking employees to return to their jobs within certain time frames, was privately viewed in government as in management's interest. When Ontario's labour laws next came up for reform, Department of Labour officials pointed out in a memorandum to Cabinet that 'it actually is not at all favourable to the striking union ... it favours the individual employee ... gives him support, if he sees that a strike is being lost, in abandoning the union's position and going back to work.' Another memorandum expressed the benefits to the employer even more starkly: 'Employers may not object once they realize that it may affect the power of the union to control its members.'[114]

Louis Laberge, the head of the Quebec Federation of Labour, ignorantly compared Rand to Franco and Castro (not such an odd pairing when you think about it), and added that 'Rand should take his pension and enjoy himself.'[115] Rand was eighty-four when he finished writing the report, and it showed. The language was frequently tortuous, and the syntax often inscrutable. As one civil servant told a colleague, the report was 'too confusing for rational beings to cope with, so I suggest you forget about it.'[116]

'It would be a good investment if it was needed to save the country,'[117] was the way one commentator described Rand's report. But there was the rub. There were real problems in labour-management relations in Ontario in the 1960s, but nothing justified Rand's recommendations considered overall. Keen observers of his inquiry were not taken by surprise. Rand's comments and statements had been widely reported throughout the proceedings, along with specific questions he asked some of the witnesses. 'How would you respond,' he asked several of them, 'if your wife needed hospital care and staff were on strike?' All told, his observations had been correctly described as 'shocking and ominous.'[118] While, in isolation, some of the recommendations had an appearance of reasonableness, taken as a whole they could not wash.

From labour's perspective, Rand ignored reality if he believed that union leaders favoured strikes. According to William Mahoney, the Canadian director of the United Steelworkers, labour leaders spent most of their time trying to avoid strikes. Sometimes there was no alternative to striking. Even though the public may be inconvenienced, that was, lawyer Ian Scott told a conference at the Centre for Industrial Relations, 'tough on the public.' Companies might go out of business and union members might lose their jobs, but that was an appropriate price to pay, unless the public interest was involved.[119] Scott, one of the ablest labour lawyers in the province, and later among its best attorneys general, had little good to say about Rand's recommendation of allowing unions to be sued. 'A trade union is not like a corporation,' he told the conference. 'There is no corporation in this land which is responsible for the wrongful acts of its shareholders. It is responsible only for the wrongful acts of its servants or agents.' Union members were not employees. 'To say that a trade union should be responsible for damages for the acts of a person on a picket line or anywhere else is to require a policing function in a trade union that is virtually impossible.'[120]

In part, the labour movement shared some of the blame. Harry Arthurs warned organized labour in early 1967 that moaning and griping about bad treatment would get them nowhere. Nothing, he predicted, would change until organized labour came up with 'a clearly-stated, defensible and realistically-attainable program of legislation.'[121] The Central Ontario Labour Relations Institute came before Rand with a plan, as did Ted Stringer. Of all the proposals he heard, these two were the most clearly laid out and, more or less, they found their way into his report.

The management organizations and their representatives kept quiet in the days and weeks following publication of the report. It was much better to let the labour movement and its leaders sputter and scream; the more intemperate their remarks, the better. That is what the public would remember long after the Rand Report and its recommendations were put on some shelf to gather dust. At the end of 1968 the Canadian Manufacturers' Association (CMA), a key constituency for the governing Tories, let Labour Minister Bales know that it opposed the creation of a tribunal with power over private-sector disputes.[122] Public-sector disputes were another matter. However, if any money was to be spent, or any new laws passed, the 'effective and highly commendable' Conciliation Branch of the Department of Labour should be assigned additional resources. In its December 1968 brief to the Ontario government, the CMA said that wages and working conditions in the private sector should result from free collective bargaining.[123] Voluntarism had won another round.

At the same time as Rand was going about his work, the federal government announced the appointment of a task force headed by Professor Harry D. Woods, dean of arts and science at McGill University, to study Canada's labour law. Dean Woods, joined by Professors John Crispo and Dean Carrothers and Father Gérard Dion, understood that his job was not to reinvent the wheel (although that did not stop the commissioners from visiting nine countries to get a first-hand look at the situation overseas). Months before his report was formally released, in October 1968, just a month after Rand's report came out, Woods told the Canadian Chamber of Commerce in Calgary that he believed in collective bargaining. It was an essential feature of free enterprise. And he warned against radical changes of the kind recommended by Rand: 'If, under public pressure, governments in Canada introduce compulsion in the settlement of labor-management disputes, it is not merely the industrial relations system that would be radically altered but the enterprise system itself.'[124]

When it reported in December 1968, the Woods Task Force concluded that strikes and lockouts served as both catalyst and catharsis for parties who had to work out their own relationship but were required to do so in a regulated environment. That inevitably meant providing labour-relations boards with greater powers. It took a while, but 'a range of labour-friendly changes were made: preambles declaring that public policy supported collective bargaining were added; the remedial powers of boards, especially with respect to unfair labour practices and breaches of the duty to bargain in good faith, were strengthened; provisions for the imposition of first collective agreements in specified circumstances were introduced; unions gained the right to compulsory dues check off; minimum reinstatement rights for workers who participated in economic strikes were enacted; and permanent replacement workers and professional strike breakers were prohibited.'[125] No one seriously believed anymore that unions were or even could be vehicles for the expression of class power. 'Union leaders who did not control members who defied legal restrictions on their freedom to strike faced incarceration. Collective withdrawal of labour power outside of a tightly restricted economic frame simply was not tolerable. However, the tradeoff was real gains for workers in terms of wages and economic activity.'[126]

The injunction, however, remained an open sore. The only hope for a reasonable compromise was through the political process, where the interests of the parties and the public interest guided the discussion. There was no reason why the courts should not remain involved, provided the rules that applied to labour disputes were clearly set out. In 1970 new restrictions on granting injunctions in picketing were introduced in Ontario when the Conservative majority, with NDP backing, amended the *Judicature Act*. Before any injunction could be granted, the court had to be satisfied that 'reasonable efforts to obtain police assistance, protection and action to prevent or remove any alleged danger of damage to property, injury to persons, obstruction of or interference with lawful entry or exit from the premises in question or breach of the peace have been unsuccessful.' This provision reflected the reality that, when the police enforced the law – the right to strike and picket as well as the right to remain operating during a strike – there was rarely a need to appeal to the courts for assistance. Put another way, many of the problems that led to the abuses of the injunction powers, real and imagined, and that had led to the appointment of the Rand Commission, arose out of the refusal of the police to enforce the law in labour disputes.

The amendments strictly limited *ex parte* applications for an injunction to situations where delay would result in irreparable damage or injury, a breach of the peace, or interruption in an essential public service. Applicants had to prove to the judge that it was a proper case to dispense with notice, and they had to demonstrate what reasonable steps had been taken to notify the other side. Moreover, the evidence no longer could be by affidavit – witnesses had to be called. As a result, *ex parte* labour injunction applications are now largely of historical interest only. What was needed was legislative change, together with a judiciary more representative of society and sensitive to natural justice, along with a mature professional labour bar. Insofar as secondary picketing was concerned, that law changed only after patriation of the Canadian Constitution and entrenchment of the *Charter of Rights and Freedoms*. This time the law changed in favour of the union movement, when the Supreme Court of Canada ruled in January 2002 that 'secondary picketing is generally lawful.'[127] With a stroke of a pen, illegal activity became legal activity.

Rand was not the only person who believed in institutionalizing some industrial conflict. There was no doubt, Harry Arthurs observed, that in some situations employees could not be allowed to strike. The right to strike, he said, did not carry 'the same aura of sanctity as motherhood.'[128] Where the public interest, the public order, and the health and safety of the community were at issue, whatever rights organized labour had should be circumscribed. Arbitration was a last resort and should be employed only after all other attempts at resolving the dispute had failed.[129]

The real solution was more effective collective bargaining and dispute resolution, and more encouragement of voluntarism. Ontario Department of Labour statistics indicated that more days were lost to strikes in 1968 than in any other year. Still, the vast majority of labour disputes were settled without strikes or lockouts. Most strikes did not last very long and affected only those directly involved. 'Out of the total 3,000 bargaining situations,' Labour Minister Bales told the legislature in May 1968, 'I believe it is safe to estimate that no more than 200 will become work stoppages of major proportions.' In those cases, his department would be involved in helping the parties settle their differences. 'Viewed in this way,' he continued, 'one can say that collective bargaining in this province is doing the job expected of it.'[130] A strike was not a social catastrophe or a failure of the imagination, and it did not spell the end of the world.

Fundamentally, Rand did not understand that in a system of free collective bargaining, there had to be, with exceptions for essential services, a right to strike and to lock out, and that those rights had to go hand in hand with the right to lawfully resist strikes and lockouts. He did not understand that, messy as they sometimes were, strikes and lockouts were among the methods to reach a collective agreement. There was a place for government – in setting out an industrial-relations framework and in passing laws providing the rules governing industrial conflict when it could not be avoided – but not, unless absolutely necessary, in compelling outcomes to labour disputes. Collective bargaining, *free* collective bargaining, involved compromise and barter best left to the parties to work out, and it was in the public interest to do so. Greater government intervention and the creation of huge bureaucracies were not the answer. More arbitration was not the answer either. If some tribunal was waiting in the wings to determine the content of a collective agreement, neither party would make any concessions. Why bother if the matters in dispute are ultimately to be determined by a third party? Rand's Central Trilogy was the exact opposite of what was needed to reduce industrial conflict. Instead of adding to the pressure to settle the dispute, the employment security and the limitations on strikebreaker proposals were not only unenforceable administratively but would have reduced the pressure to settle, thereby extending the dispute.

Rand knew that neither of the parties wanted more government intervention in the bargaining process, but he rejected that approach because it was a repudiation of the public interest. The parties wanted the government to provide good mediation and conciliation services, within a legal framework setting out generally applicable rules, but otherwise they wanted the government to stay out of their business.[131] Rand took the polar opposite view, a lesson he learned in the crucible of the Ford arbitration. George Burt and John Aylesworth, he privately told Pollock, were 'Neanderthals,' intent on wanting to be left alone to settle their disputes, by fair means or foul, and 'to the devil with the public interest.'[132] Rand was determined that the public interest come first. But he seemed to be unaware that the public interest rarely arose in labour disputes, and that most cases were settled without conflict or controversy.

Part of the problem was asking a judge to study and report. Judges mostly apply the law to the facts, and their decisions usually bring finality to disputes. When Rand, as a judge of the Supreme Court of Canada, ruled in the majority, his decision was law. But labour relations are not amenable to the imposition of a final solution. Rand's tribunal was meant to solve everything, but in the dynamic world of union-management relations, flexibility and creativity, within a legal structure, are needed, not rules written in stone and imposed from above. Labour-relations disputes arise in a continuum. They can and are decided by labour-relations boards and the courts, but they are also regularly resolved with a nudge, a wink, a handshake, and minutes of settlement brokered by a trusted third party. Settlements that are imposed in labour relations do not survive, and they must be reserved for those few clear cases where the parties have proven incapable of reaching an agreement – and only when a compelling public interest is at stake. Rand thought he could solve problems that had no single solution by creating a tribunal that was nothing more than an authoritarian legal straitjacket, headed by a czar and populated with mythical wise men. It did not matter what he heard during the proceedings or when he was wandering around. It did not matter that voluntarism was working to the satisfaction of the parties.[133]

Rand's tribunal was doomed from day one. At one time he had been a true champion of free speech. For him now to recommend what was effectively the abolition of picketing was a radical departure from his ruling in *Aristocratic Restaurants*, and it showed how reactionary and out of step he had become. Did he really think that picketing was a meaningless 'ritual'? Did he really believe that incipient lawlessness lurked in every picket line, even though the evidence was the exact opposite? 'We are today,' Rand wrote in his report, 'witnessing what a general strike of workers, as in France, can do in paralyzing the functioning life of a nation.'[134] What about Canada? Was there any evidence of paralysis here caused by any picketing? 'Sloppy' would be a kind way to describe the thinking that went into his report. At best it was naïve. In 1946 Rand was completely in tune with the times, reflected in the fact that both labour and management, and then the country, accepted the just-out-of-the-box compromise solution he figured out. In 1968 no one would agree to his plan. Rand was asked to do a difficult job, and he worked hard at it, doing his duty. But he was out of his ken and at the end of his game.

In 1968 the government's Speech from the Throne barely mentioned the Rand Report, but what little it did say signalled where the government was going: 'During the session an opportunity will be afforded honorable members to give serious and responsible attention to the machinery of collective bargaining and related labor and management matters arising out of the Rand Recommendations.'[135] The government could not have made its intentions more obvious: it was most unlikely that any of Rand's recommendations would ever make their way into legislation. As the Tory *Toronto Telegram* observed in an editorial, 'This is probably just as well.'[136] The following February, Dalton Bales gave another hint about the government's plans for the report: it had none. Informed sources at Queen's Park indicated that the government remained committed to free collective bargaining, with compulsory arbitration reserved for special cases.[137] The opposition Liberals and NDP were on side; neither party had anything other than criticism for Rand's report.

Even for the times, when many believed that most, if not all, social problems could be resolved by passing a law or writing a cheque, or both, Rand's report was an extreme and absurd response. Reforming labour law, experience indicates, is best done incrementally. William Lyon Mackenzie King certainly understood that, but, unfortunately, Rand did not.

Where next for the peripatetic judge? To Newfoundland and Labrador, where Rand had, on 26 September 1968, been appointed to the final royal commission of his career. There he had been given the task of reviewing and reporting on labour legislation in Newfoundland.

Conclusion

Rand first met Premier Joey Smallwood in the summer of 1967, when he visited the province during his investigation into labour disputes. Soon after, Smallwood asked him to look at labour law and labour relations in Newfoundland and Labrador, and to make recommendations for both a labour code and a new government department of manpower and industrial relations. As usual when duty called, Rand's answer was an immediate yes.[1] Previously, Rand had harboured a negative view of the premier, but now, he told his friend Horace Pettigrove, Smallwood had 'imagination.' He particularly admired the premier's 'willingness to listen to other views.'[2]

Throughout the fall of 1968, Rand held meetings in Corner Brook and Grand Falls, undertaking 'preliminary inquiries.' He was expected back on 5 January 1969. After spending Christmas with one son, Robert, a civilian administrator with the Department of National Defence in Ottawa, Rand travelled south to London to spend the New Year's period with his other son, Charles, an associate professor of community medicine at the University of Western Ontario. On 2 January, Rand returned to the campus and dropped in on some friends at the law school. He then walked up the hill to his son's office, sat down, turned very pale, and appeared to faint. 'It was over very quickly,' Dr Rand said. Besides his sons and grandchildren, he left his sister Mrs Ruth Hébert of Airway Heights, Washington, and his brother Charles of Moncton. He was buried in his hometown, with the Reverend Frank E. Archibald, the minister of St John's United Church, conducting the brief graveside service at the Elmwood Cemetery, just as he had done for Dell. Moncton's mad-man mayor, Leonard Jones, quoted from *A Pilgrim's Progress*, while the rabbi from the city's small synagogue movingly read from the Old Testament. There were fifteen people there in all. Rand had been looking forward to attending the sixtieth anniversary celebration of his graduation from Mount Allison University, scheduled for 10 May 1969, and he had also made plans for another trip to Israel.

His death at eighty-four, one newspaper editorialized, 'seems strangely premature.' This tall, spare man had always seemed the epitome of indestructability. After Dell died, Rand had become increasingly reclusive and reserved. His neighbours at his Shediac cottage were reluctant to approach him, and, except for his brother and one or two very old acquaintances, he lacked for company – as he had for years. In January 1966, for example, Rand wrote a letter to Pettigrove. After describing how he had spent Christmas – he had gone to Ottawa to visit his children and grandchildren, and was full of pride about their accomplishments, particularly the one who was probably headed into law – he made a revealing comment. He knew people in Ottawa, he said, far more than 'in this spot,' who were interested in 'the important matters of the world,' and he urged his former aide to come to Moncton to 'stir up' some labour dispute.[3] 'I do wish,' he wrote Pettigrove the next Christmas, that you were here, 'that I might have some one to challenge on ideas. Everybody seems to be afraid of getting off the rails no matter how rusty they may be and into the ditch.'[4]

As his birth doctor had prophesied, Rand did have a great and worthwhile life. He pulled himself up by his own bootstraps, with some help, and made his way to Harvard Law School. On graduation, he demonstrated an adventurous spirit by heading west to Medicine Hat. Returning to Moncton, he was a versatile and effective lawyer, responding to the diverse needs of his community and the people in it. But the first time duty called, during the Second World War, he stayed home while encouraging others to enlist: 'The fundamental obligation under law is that when the state is in danger every member should place his services, and if necessary, give his life in its defence. If we enjoy the privileges and liberty, we must also assume our responsibilities in connection with it.' The next time the opportunity for public service arose, Rand said yes, even though few people were less suited to public life than he was. In just a short period in office as attorney general, Rand established a modest reputation as a law reformer. On the central question of his time and place, building a publicly owned hydroelectric generating plant, he was on the right side and fought hard for New Brunswick. One can speculate endlessly what different turn New Brunswick might have taken had Peter Veniot, Rand, and the Liberals won that fateful provincial election.

Becoming regional and then commission counsel for the CNR was, for this son of a railway mechanic, a huge accomplishment. Rand was a very good lawyer, always promoting the interests of the railway and establishing a national reputation. It was because of that reputation, and his earlier achievements in public life, that Mackenzie King turned again to New Brunswick when it came time to replace Oswald Smith Crocket on the Supreme Court of Canada, even though it was Nova Scotia's turn. King was an excellent judge of character and men, and he was quite right when he confided to his diary that the court needed someone like Ivan Rand. It is hard to fathom how the court, without Rand or someone like him, would have responded to those key cases that made their way onto the docket in the 1950s.

Rand was a complex, confounding, and often contradictory man who defies easy characterization. As a politician, he worked hard to establish public power in New Brunswick, an initiative clearly in the interests of the citizenry. As a judge, he became acutely aware of the potential for the misuse of state power: he saw that in case after case, and he did what he could to impose appropriate restraints. His judicial career was marked by an overarching theme of distrust of government, particularly the Quebec government.

Citizens, Rand concluded, had the right not only to use the highways but also to think unpopular thoughts, express unpopular ideas, do unpopular things, belong to unpopular organizations – all with a minimum, if not an absence, of governmental interference. The problem was that Canada's Constitution was based on the supremacy of Parliament and the provincial legislatures. Given this legislative supremacy, the only real question was which level of government had the right to wreak injustice. The Province of Quebec was generally the one intent on restricting freedom, so Rand deprived it of that power by deciding that Quebec legislation was unconstitutional as beyond the scope of provincial powers. When a case could not be decided by determining the appropriate division of powers, Rand reached into his legal arsenal and used two other tools: he applied administrative law principles, most famously in *Roncarelli*, and, when the federal government had to be stopped in the Japanese Deportation case, he interpreted the government orders as narrowly as possible. Despite some of his own less than liberal views, he would not countenance government interference with fundamental freedoms.

Rand had been a good frontier lawyer in Medicine Hat. Back in Moncton, he became more establishment and, through law practice with Senator Robinson, was quickly integrated into the local elite. Although an able attorney general, there was nothing in his brief political career that would have produced liberal or civil libertarian views. Indeed, at one point Rand argued that there was no reason to consult the people about the Grand Falls project because 'the best expert opinions had been obtained and it would be an absurdity to submit that to the judgment of the man on the street.' Absurd perhaps, but that is the way democracy works, particularly when the premier had promised to seek the approval of the people before proceeding. Democracy is messy, chaotic, and irrational, and, clearly, the electorate had Rand's number: he was defeated in the provincial election that followed. He could help solve people's legal problems, but he did not want to engage authentically with their circumstances – he would rather cross the street than speak to a constituent. Rand could not empathize with 'lesser' beings, including his own sons. As he admitted to Dell, he envied other men, carried a small chip on his shoulder, and was, as the years passed, increasingly self-involved. Nevertheless, he always engaged with the world around him and tried hard to devise rational solutions to social problems.

As commission counsel at the CNR, Rand was head of a huge legal department and responsible for protecting the railway's interests, although exposure to Sir Henry Thornton and his truly progressive ideas must have made Rand reconsider some of his assumptions. Working at the CNR, and because of his association with Thornton, Rand learned that unions have a vital role to play in the representation of employees and in the government of a modern industrial enterprise. Moreover, his own experience at the Intercolonial Railway, not to mention that of his father, undoubtedly engendered respect for working people. But what else was it about his background and experiences that turned Rand into such a great civil libertarian judge?

The answer, admittedly speculative, is Harvard Law School. The United States of America, born out of and forged by revolution, was founded in large part on the notion of individual liberty and the pursuit of happiness – that most American term that made its way into Rand's writing. Americans had a Bill of Rights, and that bill and those rights were, and are, front and centre in American legal education. When Rand arrived at Harvard in 1909, he saw the future – and it worked. The American Bill of Rights, Rand wrote in the early 1950s, was 'man's highest attainment in constitutional establishment.'[5] Had Rand been legally trained in New Brunswick, or even educated at Dalhousie, the only constitutional law principles he would have been exposed to were the division of powers. Harvard and America, tempered by instilled Canadian values of peace, order, good government, responsibility, decorum, and duty, undoubtedly made a difference. Rand's particular brand of liberalism – Canadian liberalism – produced both the Rand Formula and the implied Bill of Rights.

Given that many of his most important decisions involved freedom of religion, it is reasonable to ask what role Rand's own religious views might have played in his life and work. While educated at the Methodist Mount Allison University, Rand was not a churchgoer, although his mother and wife were, and there is absolutely no reason to believe that Methodism, the social gospel, or a belief in the divine had any influence whatsoever. Rand was too much of a rationalist for that. There are only a few hints about Rand's religious views. It was noticeable, he observed during the 1925 New Brunswick election campaign, when talking about prohibition, that men, when they took up the advancement of any moral cause as a profession, regularly displayed a tendency to lose their sense of proportion.

Another hint about his religious views comes in his discussion of *Boucher*. Aimé Boucher was, Rand found, one of a number of 'peaceable Canadians,' 'conscientious followers of Christ,' participating in 'Christian fellowship,' and 'bringing the light and peace of the Christian religion to the souls of men and women.' That perspective was not universally shared, particularly by the Roman Catholic hierarchy in Quebec. Indeed, as Rand pointed out, for exercising this 'unchallengeable right of Canadians,' the Jehovah's Witnesses were 'assaulted and beaten and their Bibles and publications torn up and destroyed,' with 'members of the Roman Catholic Clergy' not only witnessing these 'outrages' but 'privy to some of the prosecutions.' Rand left no doubt who the real Christians were. In his judgment, he made another singular contribution to Canadian law. 'Freedom in thought and speech and disagreement in ideas and beliefs, on every conceivable subject, are the essence of our life,' Rand wrote, setting aside the sedition law used to prevent Boucher and other like-minded people from spreading what they believed to be the word of God. But lurking in the background, in this case and others, is the question, What else might have motivated the result?

Admonishing his sons to stay away from the Acadian enclave of Dieppe is one thing, and rejecting his brother-in-law another, but Rand's views also spilled over into his public life. Paradoxically, it seems more likely than not that Rand's great civil liberties judgments were to some degree motivated by a dislike of Roman Catholics and French Canadians. As his University of Western Ontario law school colleague Robert Mackay put it, 'Rand had to decide who he hated less, French Roman Catholics or the Jehovah's Witnesses.'[6] Whatever the underlying motivations, it is hard to quarrel with the outcomes in *Boucher, Saumur,* and *Roncarelli.* But the case of Leo A. Landreville is something quite different. Without any doubt, as J.J. Robinette put it, Rand 'hated' Landreville – not exactly the disinterested detachment one might expect from a former Supreme Court of Canada judge conducting an inquiry. Rand did not just ignore the rules of natural justice, as was subsequently determined on judicial review, but he flouted them by his private meetings with the treasurer of the Law Society and his behind-the-scenes review of Landreville's RCMP file. Rand's public treatment of Landreville as the commission unfolded made it clear that he had determined before all the evidence was in that Landreville was completely unfit to serve as a judge. If Rand had just kept to the facts, that conclusion could have been generously justified. Instead, he larded his report with all sorts of irrelevant and prejudicial findings and observations about Landreville's character, material success, and lifestyle. Rand could not stand this *bon vivant,* financially successful, good-natured judge from the hinterland who had achieved success along with a beautiful wife and fancy car. He made it very clear what he did see: 'What kind of judge,' he asked his old faculty colleague Ronald St J. Macdonald, 'puts up a crucifix in his chambers?' Landreville was not just a stereotype, but to Rand he was also a Roman Catholic and a symbol of everything that was wrong with a money-driven materialistic society.

The attack on Landreville was bad enough, but it made the entire inquiry worse than useless. Rand had the opportunity and the obligation to make findings about Landreville, but also to suggest how best to investigate errant judges. On his first day of classes at Harvard

Law School, Rand was told always to ask: 'What, in principle, do you think the law ought to be?' In a society that places great value on an independent judiciary, what mechanism should be established that recognizes that independence but also allows complaints to be made, and appropriately addressed, about judges and their activities? Moreover, Rand could have developed recommendations about appropriate conflict-of-interest requirements for municipal officials. That would also have been useful. Instead, his prejudice came into play, with predictable, and for Landreville terrible, consequences. In 1951 Rand had addressed the role of an independent judiciary in preserving freedom. He made an excellent case for judicial disinterestedness. 'One's individual views,' he wrote, 'undoubtedly reflect that general thought of the community; but they can present obstacles to true understanding of what is being examined.' Unfortunately for Landreville, Rand failed to take his own advice.

What had happened to the Rand of 1931 who, speaking to the Wesley Memorial Men's Association, called for a change in the hearts of men? We must, he told the church group, eradicate inbred prejudices of different cultures and race. What about the Rand of 1961, speaking at Mount Allison University's Summer Institute on 'French Canada Today'? Rand welcomed his old friend Louis St Laurent to the campus and made a personal plea for national unity: 'We must discuss explicitly and frankly those points of difference or controversy that may arise. And we must not yield to the temptation to suspect or attribute wrong motives.'[7] Not everyone, however, agrees that Rand harboured negative thoughts and feelings about French Canadians and Roman Catholics. J.E. Belliveau, a local New Brunswick historian and the author of *The Monctonians*,[8] wrote a lengthy obituary published in the *Globe and Mail*: 'There were some who looked on Rand as subtly anti-French. I was not among them ... He grew up among Acadian French, as had his parents and grandparents. He had lived his life with French Canadians. His sympathies were strong, his understanding clear and his sense of fair play exceedingly warm.'[9] Unfortunately, the weight of the evidence is otherwise. It is ironic that Rand's single election victory was delivered to him by the Acadians in Gloucester riding.

There was a different Rand, of course – the brave Rand who stood up for the Japanese Canadians in the face of continued state brutalization meted out by the federal government. Even if Rand's underlying assumption was wrong – there was never more than a handful, at best, of actively disloyal Japanese – Rand said no. Without embellishment, and in just a few paragraphs, this junior judge at the Supreme Court of Canada tried to put the brakes on the federal government's removal scheme. His Supreme Court civil liberties decisions, whether about the forced removal of Japanese Canadians, religious rights of the Jehovah's Witnesses, the picketing rights of organized labour, or the rights of communists, can all be considered as part of a piece, the product of a man and a view that was enlightened, progressive, and attuned to the dangers of unfettered state power and the need, therefore, for legal restraint. Without a Bill of Rights, that meant implying fundamental freedoms into our Constitution, a singular albeit unsustainable achievement, but one that pointed the way ahead. Early on, and more or less alone, Rand understood that human rights and fundamental freedoms are innate, not a gift of Parliament or any provincial legislature.

Even so, Rand did not exhibit consistently a broad civil libertarian approach in all matters involving the state, especially in cases concerning disputes among citizens. In *Noble v. Alley*, for example, Rand declined to strike down a racist restrictive covenant on broad policy grounds. The covenant was invalidated on the basis that it was uncertain. Rand's remarks from the bench demonstrated a greater understanding of the stakes involved, but that did not make it into his reasons for decision. Why did Rand not void the covenant because it was so obviously contrary to public policy? Rand was a member of the restricted Rideau Club in Ottawa and joined the restricted Hunt Club in London. Does this explain why he held back? Like many well-educated late Victorians and early Edwardians, Rand drew a bright line between his public and his private lives. Canadian society was divided at the time, and Rand shared many of the prevailing prejudices.

It is interesting to note that on the few occasions when he had the opportunity to consider the unique constitutional entitlements of members of Canada's First Nations, Rand again took a very narrow technical approach. He undoubtedly found it difficult to accept that 'Indians' had rights that other citizens did not enjoy. All citizens enjoyed certain rights, and Rand implied them into the Canadian Constitution when necessary in order to achieve just outcomes. He was also at the heart of the Supreme Court's expansion of federal authority in the 1950s. 'No longer was the federal government the beast to be caged,'[10] once the Supreme Court, thanks in large part to Rand, 'displayed unusual vigour and imagination, and an unprecedented determination to adapt the law to Canadian conditions, even if this meant departing from the paths previously trodden by the Judicial Committee of the Privy Council.'[11] It was the provinces that had to be constrained, as Rand's key cases demonstrated, and doing so made the country stronger.

Even though Rand could be personally self-centred, narrow-minded, intolerant, and bigoted – his first-rate mind accompanied a third-rate temperament – he rose above it all in a handful of key cases that defined not only his career but the court and an age. He deployed legal tools to achieve justice and made a great, enduring, and inspirational contribution to Canadian law. He was also a good problem solver.[12] Of all the judges to have served on the Supreme Court of Canada, Rand is, without question, the most distinctive in substance and in style. Read alongside his colleagues, before, during, and since his time on the court, no one comes close to his poetry, his verve, and his style. At the same time, no other judgments are as convoluted and opaque.

Off the bench, Rand's career was remarkably mixed, and his work was similarly varied in quality. His coal report was passable. He could not, unlike Walter Gordon in his commission on Canada's economic prospects, bring himself to prescribe the strong medicine that was urgently required. Rand was sensitive to the needs and interests of those Cape Breton communities that had become dependent on coal, and, like so many others, he was not prepared to make difficult economic decisions when lives and communities hung in the balance. No one ever is, whether it is coal miners in Cape Breton or automotive workers in Ontario.

When Rand finally got the opportunity to put his legal ideas into action in the new law school at the University of Western Ontario, he stepped back. By 1959 he had lost his spark, and he became yet one more dull, mediocre, traditional dean, ready to accommodate the students while privately complaining about their limitations. The quality he clearly articulated for future lawyers – imagination – was almost completely absent from his curriculum. Rand was a throwback to an earlier age, several generations removed from his faculty and completely oblivious to the real role of a university. That the university turned to a seventy-five-year-old for the position is nothing less than astonishing.

The Royal Commission on Labour Disputes completely missed the mark, about both the problems to be addressed and their solutions. For someone who believed in the rule of law, Rand could not abide strikes, even though, under certain conditions, they were completely lawful. What had happened to the Rand of *Aristocratic Restaurants*? In that case, he clearly acknowledged that 'attending to communicate information for the purpose of persuasion by the force of rational appeal' was entirely appropriate, accepted by members of the public 'in the stride of ordinary experience.' In 1951 Rand did not propose fettering the content of union free speech, yet in 1968 he proposed a scheme in which only 'appropriate placards with legitimate information' would be permitted. It is hard to believe that it was the same man who had put Quebec authorities in their place for interfering with the free speech of Jehovah's Witnesses. Rand not only dreamed up a solution to a problem which was untenable – his tribunal – but he invented the problem and then devised an unworkable response to it.

To be sure, in the 1960s society was divided about the proper scope of the legal regulations governing picketing and injunctions, and there was an urgent and compelling need for law reform, not overhaul. Instead, Rand convinced himself, although he failed to persuade others, including his own commission counsel, that public order was seriously threatened, notwithstanding all the evidence indicating otherwise. 'The monstrous repudiation of law and the substitution of disorder and force can lead only to social chaos which seems just to have been avoided in France,' Rand observed, and then prescribed an authoritarian and potentially repressive legal and regulatory regime to cure all manner of social ills in Ontario, most of them imagined. Rand believed that the labour problem could be solved by 'experts.' But our society is not run by experts or wise men – and it is not surprising that Rand's labour disputes report was put on a shelf to gather dust.

But to dwell on his failures would be to ignore Rand's other important contributions that made his career brilliant, as was predicted by his classmates in 1909 when he graduated as valedictorian. He was called upon to settle the most intractable dispute facing organized labour at the end of the Second World War. Questions of union security and the checkoff were bedevilling not just Ford of Canada and the United Automobile Workers but organized labour and management across the land. At Ford, there was a lengthy strike. There was huge potential for conflict to spread – not the general strike hoped for by communist union officials and fellow travellers, but legitimate disputes about the place of organized labour in post-war Canada. Rand, with Horace Pettigrove's assistance, figured out a compromise, one that was slightly outside the box but close enough to win national acceptance. The Rand Formula, by any measure, was an excellent piece of work – and one consistent with the rest of Rand's legal philosophy, especially the importance of the rule of law. After all, a collective agreement is a sort of law setting out the rules for running a workplace, something that was and is very important in modern industrial plants. Bora Laskin called it the 'the law of the shop.'

It was obviously very difficult for Rand to swallow the idea that someone could be forced to join an organization as the price for continuing in employment. At the same time, equally unacceptable was the idea that a person could benefit from a collective agreement but contribute nothing to its negotiation or administration. He therefore came up with a classic and brilliant compromise. It was not libertarian – no real libertarian would ever legally compel another person to support a cause financially that he or she did not believe in. Rand was a great civil libertarian, but he was not a libertarian, and his formula was an expression of liberal values, values acceptable in his time and place, and today too. It brought unions, their leaders, and their members into the tent, and, whether intended or not, once insiders, they became an institutionalized part of the process with an interest in making the system work. Not surprisingly, the attractions of the Communist Party and its deeply revolutionary goals diminished and then disappeared. Rand could probably see the union leaders for what they really were, but he knew there was no point in calling them to account for the way they had behaved. It was far better to look to the future and realign their interests in a legal framework. The Rand Formula was both innovative and pragmatic.

Management and labour, or to use Rand's terms, capital and labour, were co-partners in an industry or a workplace. Rand got that right. But they have never held equal power in society. Rand got that wrong in Windsor in 1945 and 1946 and, twenty years later, when he was studying labour disputes in Ontario. The organization of economic and political power in society is far more complicated than that. However, no greater testament to his formula can be found than the fact that it became one of the signature characteristics of Canadian labour law – and remains so to this day.

Often there is no right solution. Palestine presented just such a case. The Palestinians made the United Nation's committee's work so much easier by their boycott, but Rand still struggled to find an accommodation between Jewish and Palestinian interests. In doing so, he had to put some of his preconceptions about Jews to one side, while those he held about Arabs were confirmed by what he saw and by the boycott – the committee never really got to hear the other side of the story. Once he made up his mind, however, he became the truest of believers. Rand's colleague at the court, Douglas Abbott, once remarked that Rand regularly described himself as a 'partisan.' What Rand meant by that, Abbott explained, was once he 'developed and held an opinion, it was there for good, and although he would patiently listen to adverse views, he very seldom changed his mind.'[13] 'Once Dad made up his mind,' his son Charles observed, 'he would not change it.'[14] That is not entirely true – on occasion Rand was persuaded by the facts and by reason.

In Palestine, the evidence was overwhelming – the Zionists were making the desert bloom. Undoubtedly played by the Jews, both during and after the commission, Rand came to Palestine with his preconceptions in place and then changed most of them because of what he heard. He was undoubtedly moved by the plight of Holocaust survivors desperately searching for a home. We can only imagine what might have happened had the Arabs bothered to make a case to Rand and the other members of the UN committee about *their* legitimate entitlements. Instead, the committee members saw only violence, boycotts, and medieval conditions on the Arab side of the equation. The Israelis, in sharp contrast, appeared to be building a 'civilization,' a society with rules.[15] 'I knew the Jewish people would make a success of it,' Rand told the *Jerusalem Post* on his 1959 visit. 'I was impressed by their tenacity and exaltation combined with the most exact realism ... I was very sure that the experiment would succeed.'[16] Rand fell for the Israeli line, and who can blame him? He supported Israel to his dying day, even making personal contributions to the Hebrew University. Yet his views on Jews, French Canadians, and people with ethnic-sounding names were another matter. These views never really changed, but he was always ready to make an exception for a particular individual.

It was in the Supreme Court of Canada that Rand made his most enduring mark. Extraordinarily, he did it in just a few cases. In part, Rand's legacy lives on, as the Supreme Court frequently turns to his decisions from the 1950s to 'illuminate, historicize, and legitimate the entrenched rights that define so much of the Canadian constitutional present.'[17] More than any other Supreme Court justice, Rand wrote extensively in reviews and articles on issues outside his judicial responsibilities, and he regularly accepted invitations to speak. He loved Canada, the natural wealth of the land, the capacities and industry of the people. It was always important to Rand that 'we' not let the country down. 'We live,' Rand wrote, 'in what can be fairly described as a country with possibilities of greatness.'[18]

In May 1945 Rand received his first honorary doctorate, from his alma mater, Mount Allison. He then addressed the graduates, setting out, as it happened, the judicial program he would follow at the Supreme Court:

These last six years have witnessed the greatest social cataclysm in history. At this moment a vast community of people is disintegrating. The old Germany is in her death throes. She is dying because she attempted to destroy the dignity of man.

It is that dignity that democracy postulates as its first condition ... How are we to prepare ourselves for the duties that such a state imposes upon us? .... It demands effort, imagination and honesty in a degree that little else does and it is or can be most painful ...

You saw the spectacle of the whole body of German scientists denying their intellectual bases and substituting their own racial lunacies. That is the suicide of intelligence. Our enterprise is government through debate: you may call it clamor; but it is better – we must postulate some propositions, and this is one of them – it is better than tyranny. And it is astonishing how often clamor about ideas leads to clarification. Ventilation is good for more than houses. The fatal mistake is to clothe an unsound idea in mystery through attempted suppression. Great Britain has attained the highest social stability but with the greatest freedom of speech: we have still to learn from the lesson of the man exhorting from his soap box in Hyde Park. It is a matter of growing up.

In this country, questions of great moment are before us: questions of race, creed, and social, political and economic doctrine. It is, on a smaller scale, the problem of the world. We must resolve that solutions shall be reached that will reconcile diverse traditions on the broad basis of mutual respect. Within the framework, the great freedoms of speech and of belief, our social governance, must be worked out. All of us need a pinch of scepticism ... to the composition of most of our opinions. Indeed, fundamental notions and convictions must surely be able to withstand the rigors of examination and criticism. Let us beware of too many absolutes and of the tyranny and dangers of perfect concepts. Free and open discussion, honest and in good manners, but sturdy and virile, not only toughens the mind but reveals the ultimate divergences.[19]

'The unifying theme in Rand's judicial pronouncements, and, indeed, in his life's work,' Marshall Pollock, the commission counsel on the Ontario labour disputes inquiry, wrote, 'is this: We are privileged to be a society of free persons, the hallmark of which is the use of reason in the ordering of its affairs, the continued existence of which depends upon a high degree of individual responsibility. This was his message, first, last, and always; it is the continuous thread visible throughout his judicial and extra-judicial writings, extending from 1909 to 1969.'[20] Rand was impatient of authority unless it could be shown to be founded on reason. Rationality was in his bones, though at a time before its reality or its biases were seriously questioned, much less put in doubt.

'Every man,' Rand once observed, 'must live as if he had a monitor looking over his shoulder.'[21] He had a puritanical approach to duty and responsibility, one that was obvious with Landreville and that continually showed an intolerance for excess, especially where liquor was concerned. But he still numbered among his closest friends drunken characters like Sir Lyman Duff. He had an abiding faith in institutions. He believed in hard work, and although he was rewarded with acclaim and numerous honorary degrees and made a Companion of the Order of Canada, he never slowed down, always accepting invitations to lecture, to teach, and to write. Would he be a visiting professor at the Faculty of Law at the University of New Brunswick delivering a set of special lectures? Would he accept the title of Honorary Professor? The answer to both questions was yes. 'I think you have done a good piece of work with the school,' and for that reason, Rand wrote the dean in April 1964, you 'are entitled to any help that can be given, at least by me.'[22] 'I begged him to fly down,' Dean William Ryan recollected, 'but he insisted on traveling by bus.'[23] 'He neither sought personal acclaim, nor did he back away from any difficult task asked of him by various governments of Canada,' John P. Robarts accurately recalled.[24]

There are a number of constants in Rand's life: a belief in society and community; a commitment to the rule of law – one that not only brought out-of-control premiers to justice but informed the resolution of all manner of disputes by looking at them as a whole and applying rationality. Some differences are irreconcilable, such as Palestine, where there is so little common ground between Arab and Jew. The same applied to labour relations, at least as Rand saw it in his later years, where labour and capital, left unfettered, would act like barbarians and slaughter each other and everyone around them. In those cases, Rand prescribed social engineering. The more detailed the prescription, as both UNSCOP and his inquiry into labour disputes illustrate, the more impractical and unrealistic it all became.

Discipline and determination, together with character, hard work, duty, and thrift, were his hallmarks. Rand made very few real friends, except for Horace Pettigrove. Even when Rand was sitting in court, he was still in motion. He was incapable of letting his hair down and could not unwind. He had a medical history of gastrointestinal upsets and cardiac irregularities, all attributed to constant tension. But he was a man with a mission. The law was his instrument, and he understood the key role it had to play in building this nation – like the railway, the law could knit the country together.

'It is difficult to write fairly about Ivan Rand the man,' one of his successors as dean at Western's Law School has written. 'In our materialistic world, his frugality and austerity can seem faintly ridiculous. His brusqueness and tendency to seem aloof, though couching shyness and genuine warmth, can seem rude. His manner of written expression can seem off-puttingly turgid and archaic. But if we consider him in the light of his own day – if, in other words, we consider him in the only setting in which a person should be judged – what emerges is the picture of a principled man who thought deeply about the best way to enhance the standards of his profession as a means of strengthening, and preserving for future generations, the rule of law. When Rand spoke of things like "duty," "greatness," "artistry," and "imagination," he did so with a view to arming law students with transcendental skills – skills which would stand the test of time, and which would enable them to assume a place alongside the heroes of the common law as the guardians of our constitutional tradition of freedom. Would that we today could be so inspired.'[25]

Rand said much of it in his valedictory address at Mount Allison: 'As we go out, let us take as a working principle, Do the duty that lies nearest you – and let it be done honestly and thoroughly. If we do this, perhaps our living here will not be altogether in vain.' 'I have known no one,' Chief Justice J.R. Cartwright wrote in the *Canadian Bar Review*, 'who possessed a more complete independence of mind than he. He was impatient of authority unless it could be shown to be founded upon reason.'[26] He understood that the courts are the special guardians of the freedoms of the unpopular, of the individual against the mass, the weak against the powerful, but he understood, too, that fanaticism over individual rights posed on equal threat to the social fabric.

In 1950 Rand was invited to give one of the sesquicentennial lectures at the Faculty of Law at the University of New Brunswick. His topic was 'The Student at Law School.' Rand began with the observation that he had never stopped studying the law. He was, he told the future lawyers, as much of a student of the law as he had been when he arrived at Harvard four decades before. He then reached out to the students before him:

We all have different natural investments: but in the end, the question will be, Have we made the best of them? To prepare yourselves for these responsibilities, should they offer, by quiet but indefatigable application to the mastery of your art, ought to be your first ambition; in the jargon of the day, raise your sights.

Here is my second purpose. With independence, with unremitting industry, with high standards and loyalty to public and private duties, we owe it to the people of this country to make the legal profession an instrument of the highest competency in an enlightened administration of justice. The future of Canada will be one of great growth and achievements; her population will double and treble; her wealth will be staggering; her business life will take on tremendous dimensions; she will become a nation of strength and influence. But all that growth will carry corresponding responsibilities: and in this vital function which has been committed to our hands, we cannot permit any failure.[27]

'Each man,' Rand would often say, 'has his own vocation. The talent is the call.'

Notes

A Note on Sources and References

In addition to many public sources, this book has relied heavily on Ivan Rand's papers. The Rand papers are of two kinds. Charles Rand, Ivan's son, generously gave me five boxes of his father's papers, comprising mainly private materials – letters, diaries, etc. They are referred to in the notes as Rand Papers. Other Rand papers dealing more with public matters are housed at Library and Archives Canada, the Public Archives of New Brunswick, and the University of Western Ontario. Each of these collections is referenced to its collection number in these archives.

I also conducted interviews with Rand's family and colleagues. These interviews are referred to in the notes for each chapter as 'interview,' along with the relevant name.

Three people – Rand's sister Ruth Hébert, his colleague Horace Pettigrove, and David Bercuson – also provided me with papers. They are simply referred to here as Hébert Papers, Pettigrove Papers, and Bercuson Papers.

Following the publication of this book, the Rand Papers, the transcripts of the interviews, and the Hébert and Pettigrove papers were donated to the University of Western Ontario Archives, along with the other research materials used here.

Preface

1 G. LeDain, 'Sir Lyman Duff and the Constitution' (1974) 12 *Osgoode Hall Law Journal* 261 at 263.
2 D.R. Williams, *Duff: A Life in the Law* (Vancouver: University of British Columbia Press and Osgoode Society for Canadian Legal History, 1984).
3 D. Gruending, *Emmett Hall: Establishment Radical* (Toronto: Macmillan of Canada, 1985); F. Vaughan, *Aggressive in Pursuit: The Life of Justice Emmett Hall* (Toronto: Osgoode Society for Canadian Legal History and University of Toronto Press, 2004).
4 W.H. McConnell, *William R. McIntrye: Paladin of the Common Law* (Ottawa: Carleton University Press, 2000).
5 E. Anderson, *Judging Bertha Wilson: Law as Large as Life* (Toronto: Osgoode Society for Canadian Legal History and University of Toronto Press, 2001).
6 R.J. Sharpe and K. Roach, *Brian Dickson: A Judge's Journey* (Toronto: Osgoode Society for Canadian Legal History and University of Toronto Press, 2003). For a critical view, see R.W. Kostal, 'Shilling for Judges: Brian Dickson and His Biographers' (2006) 51 *McGill Law Journal* 199.
7 P.V. Girard, *Bora Laskin: Bringing Law to Life* (Toronto: Osgoode Society for Canadian Legal History and University of Toronto Press, 2005). See also P.V. Girard, 'Judging Lives: Judicial Biography from Hale to Holmes' (2003) *Australian Journal of Legal History* 9.

Chapter 1: The Right Start

1 E.M. Pollock, 'Ivan Rand: The Talent Is the Call' (1980) 18 *University of Western Ontario Law Review* 115.
2 A family tree, however, indicates that he was born in 1842. He died in 1912: interview with Ruth Hébert, 27 July 1988.
3 Pollock, 'Ivan Rand,' 116.
4 Ruth Hébert interview.
5 See K. Cruikshank, 'The People's Railway: The Intercolonial and the Canadian Public Enterprise Experience' (1986) 16 *Acadiensis* 78; S. Fleming, *The Intercolonial: An Historical Sketch of the Inception, Location, Construction and Completion of the Line of Railway Uniting the Inland and the Atlantic Provinces of the Dominion* (Montreal: Dawson Brothers Publishing, 1876), 101; G.R. Stevens, *History of the Canadian National Railways* (New York: Macmillan, 1973), 75–105.
6 P.A. Buckner, 'The 1870s: Political Integration,' in E.R. Forbes and D.A Muise, eds., *The Atlantic Provinces in Confederation* (Toronto: University of Toronto Press, 1993), 63.

7 E.R. Forbes, 'Misguided Symmetry: The Destruction of Regional Transportation Policy for the Maritimes,' in D. Bercuson, ed., *Canada and the Burden of Unity* (Toronto: University of Toronto Press, 1977), 65.

8 J.P. Coutrier, 'Prohibition or Regulation? The Enforcement of the Canada Temperance Act in Moncton, 1881–1896,' in C.K. Warsh, ed., *Drink in Canada: Historical Essays* (Montreal: McGill-Queen's University Press, 1993), 146.

9 N. Frye, *The Bush Garden* (Toronto: House of Anansi Press, 1971), v.

10 Pollock, 'Ivan Rand,' 117.

11 The following section is drawn, in large part, from J.G. Reid, *Mount Allison University*, vol. 1: *1843–1914* (Toronto: University of Toronto Press, 1984).

12 Rand Papers, 1905 Diary, Memorandum, n.d.

13 Cited in Reid, *Mount Allison University*, 1, 95.

14 A full report on the debate can be found in the *Argosy*, April 1907.

15 Ibid., April 1908.

16 Ibid., March 1908.

17 Ibid., October 1909.

18 Rand Papers, 1905 Diary, Memorandum, n.d.

19 Rand Papers, Speeches, 15 January 1909.

20 Rand Papers, Scrapbook, Newspaper Obituary, n.d.

21 Reid, *Mount Allison University*, 1, 244.

22 E.M. Pollock, 'Mr. Justice Rand: A Triumph of Principle' (1975) 53 *Canadian Bar Review* 520.

23 *Argosy*, October 1909.

24 D.G. Bell, *Legal Education in New Brunswick: A History* (Fredericton: University of New Brunswick, 1992), 83. See also H.O. McInerney, 'Notes on the Law School History' (1948) 1 *University of New Brunswick Law School Journal* 14, and G.A. McAllister, 'Some Phases of Legal Education in New Brunswick' (1955) 8 *University of New Brunswick Law Journal* 33.

25 P. Girard, 'The Roots of a Professional Renaissance: Lawyers in Nova Scotia 1850–1910,' in D. Gibson, ed., *Glimpses of Canadian Legal History* (Winnipeg: University of Manitoba Legal Research Institute, 1991), 176, 179.

26 Ruth Hébert interview.

27 C.I. Kyer and J.E. Bickenbach, *The Fiercest Debate: Cecil Wright, the Benchers, and Legal Education in Ontario* (Toronto: Osgoode Society for Canadian Legal History and University of Toronto Press, 1987), 9.

28 Rand Papers, Harvard Notebooks. Rand kept all of his Harvard notebooks, and all these quotations are drawn from them.

29 Brief portraits of many of Rand's professors can be found in A.E. Sutherland, *The Law at Harvard: A History of Ideas and Men, 1817–1967* (Cambridge, MA: Harvard University Press, 1967), 206–63.

30 *Official Register of Harvard University, The Law School, 1911–12* (Cambridge, MA: Harvard University, 1911), 6.

31 Sutherland, *The Law at Harvard*, 222.

32 Cited in J.R. Cartwright, 'Ivan Cleveland Rand' (1969) 47 *Canadian Bar Review* 156.

33 Law Society of Alberta, Rand to Secretary of the Law Society, 24 January 1913.

34 Rand Papers, Iredell Baxter to Rand, n.d.

35 Rand Papers, Rand to Iredell Baxter, n.d.

36 Rand Papers, J. Baxter to Rand, 25 May 1913.

37 *Medicine Hat News*, 23 January 1912.

38 W. Kilbourn, *Pipeline* (Toronto: Clarke, Irwin, 1970), 10.

39 *Medicine Hat News*, 9 January 1912.

40 P.M. Sibenik, 'The Doorkeepers: The Governance of Territorial and Alberta Lawyers, 1885–1928,' MA thesis, University of Alberta, 1984, 199.

41 *Fulton v. Randall, Gee & Mitchell Ltd.*, [1918] 3 WWR 331 (Alta. DC).

42 *Rhinard v. Ginther* (1916), 28 DLR 628 (Alta. CA).

43 See *Forster v. City of Medicine Hat*, [1914] 17 DLR 391 (Alta. SC).

44 *Medicine Hat News*, 4 July 1916.

45 'A Conversation with Ivan Rand' (1969) 3 *Law Society of Upper Canada Gazette* 49 at 51.

46 *Medicine Hat News*, 30 October 1914.

47 Ibid., 14 April 1915.

48 Ibid., 27 June and 17 December 1919.

49 Pollock, 'Ivan Rand,' 130.

50 See, for example, *Innis v. Costello et al.* (1916), 27 DLR 711 (Alta. SC).

51 *Innis v. Costello*, [1917] 33 DLR 602 (Alta. CA). See also *Royal Bank v. Nesbitt and Hansen* (1918), 13 ALR 408 (SC).

52 *The Southern Alberta Land Company v. The Rural Municipality of McLean* (1916), 53 SCR 151.

53 D.C. Jones, *The Weather Factory: A Pictorial History of Medicine Hat* (Saskatoon: Western Producer Prairie Books, c. 1988), 15.

54 Ibid., 17.

55 The following section is derived from the report in the *Medicine Hat News*, 17 December 1917.

56 Pollock, 'Ivan Rand,' 127.

57 *Toronto Star*, 17 January 1967.

58 Rand Papers, Daisy Sangster Rand to Rand, 11 June 1919. Emphasis in original.

59 Ruth Hébert interview; Hy Bloom to William Kaplan, 30 November 2008.

60 Rand Papers, C.W. Robinson to Rand, 16 September 1919.

61 Interview with Robert and Margaret Rand, 26 October 1988.
62 *Medicine Hat News*, 15 May 1920.

Chapter 2: The Young Lawyer Tries Politics

1 The key sources used in the following section are K. Cruickshank, *Close Ties: Railways, Government and the Board of Railway Commissioners, 1851– 1933* (Montreal and Kingston: McGill-Queen's University Press, 1991); E.R. Forbes, *The Maritime Rights Movement, 1919–1927: A Study in Canadian Regionalism* (Montreal: McGill-Queen's University Press, 1979); and H.G. Thorburn, *Politics in New Brunswick* (Toronto: University of Toronto Press, 1961), 14.
2 Forbes, *The Maritime Rights Movement*, 57.
3 Thorburn, *Politics in New Brunswick*, 14.
4 K. Cruickshank, 'The Intercolonial Railway, Freight Rates and the Maritime Economy,' in K. Inwood, ed., *Farm, Factory and Fortune* (New Brunswick: Acadiensis Press, 1993), 175.
5 See T.W. Acheson, 'The National Policy and the Industrialization of the Maritimes, 1880–1910' (1972) 2 *Acadiensis* 3.
6 This section is derived in part from J.D. Francisco, 'New Brunswick Finances, 1917–1952,' MA thesis, University of New Brunswick, 1992.
7 http://en.wikipedia.org/wiki/Robert_Young_Eaton.
8 See generally *Report of the Royal Commission to Inquire into Railways and Transportation* (Ottawa: King's Printer, 1917) (The Drayton-Acworth Commission), lxxv: 'With proper economic and politically undisturbed management, the attainment of a satisfactory financial result is only a question of time.'
9 E.M. Pollock, 'Ivan Rand: The Talent Is the Call' (1980) 18 *University of Western Ontario Law Review* 119.
10 *Report of the Royal Commission on Coal* (Ottawa: King's Printer, 1947), 333.
11 Initially independent of the Board, freight rate increases ordered by it were, by and large, passed on to the ICR. Later, the ICR, for rate-setting purposes, came under the jurisdiction of the Board. On the Board, see B. J. Hibbitts, 'A Change of Mind: The Supreme Court and the Board of Railway Commissioners, 1903–1929' (1991) 41 *University of Toronto Law Journal* 60.
12 See Forbes, *The Maritime Rights Movement*, 70, and E.R. Forbes, 'The Origins of the Maritime Rights Movement,' in Forbes, ed., *Challenging the Regional Stereotype: Essays on the 20th Century Maritimes* (Fredericton: Acadiensis Press, 1989), 103.
13 E.R. Forbes, 'Misguided Symmetry: The Destruction of Regional Transpor-

tation Policy for the Maritimes,' in D. Bercuson, ed., *Canada and the Burden of Unity* (Toronto: University of Toronto Press, 1977), 69.

14 J. Frost, 'The Nationalization of the Bank of Nova Scotia, 1880–1910' (1982) 12 *Acadiensis* 3.

15 Forbes, 'Misguided Symmetry,' 68.

16 Hibbitts, 'A Change of Mind,' 96; Forbes, 'Misguided Symmetry,' 68. See also A.W. Currie, 'The Board of Transport Commissioners as a Regulatory Body' (1945) 10 *Canadian Journal of Economics and Political Science* 342.

17 Cruickshank, *Close Ties*, 149.

18 All these quotations are from D.R. Cowan, 'A History of the Intercolonial and Prince Edward Island Railways of Canada,' MA thesis, University of Toronto, 1918, 19–20.

19 For a contrary view, see H. Darling, *The Politics of Freight Rates: The Railway Freight Rate Issue in Canada* (Toronto: McClelland & Stewart, 1980).

20 Rand to W.F. Foster, 31 December 1920, Public Archives of New Brunswick [PANB], Rand Papers, MC603, MS3, Correspondence re Railway Rate Increase, 1920.

21 *Daily Times*, 30 April 1921.

22 Ibid.

23 'Progress Seen at Year's End' (1926) *Canadian National Railways Magazine* 8.

24 Forbes, *The Maritime Rights Movement*, 94. See also E.R. Forbes, 'The Intercolonial Railway and the Decline of the Maritime Provinces Revisited' (1994) 24 *Acadiensis* 3.

25 *Daily Times*, 25 March 1922.

26 The Dominion Bureau of Statistics was narrowing its definition of manufacturing during this period.

27 Forbes, 'Misguided Symmetry,' 69.

28 Ibid., 71–2.

29 *Daily Times*, 14 May 1921.

30 Ibid., 30 April 1921.

31 J.W. Grant, *The Canadian Experience of Church Union* (London: Lutterworth Press, 1967), 54.

32 See, generally, G.W. Mason, *The Legislative Struggle for Church Union* (Toronto: Ryerson Press, 1956).

33 J.G. Snell and F. Vaughan, *The Supreme Court of Canada: History of the Institution* (Toronto: Osgoode Society for Canadian Legal History and University of Toronto Press, 1985), 134.

34 W.H. Barraclough to R.B. Whitehead, n.d., United Church of Canada Archives [UCC Archives], Church Union Papers, Series II, box 25, Property and Legislation.

35 R.B. Whitehead to Rand, 11 January 1924, ibid.

36 Ephraim Scott, *'Church Union' and the Presbyterian Church in Canada, 1925–1926* (Montreal: John Lovell & Son, 1928), 9.

37 Grant, *Canadian Experience of Church Union*, 54.

38 L. Pidgeon to G. Mason, 29 March 1924, UCC Archives, Church Union Collection.

39 *Synoptic Report of the Proceedings of the Legislative Assembly of the Province of New Brunswick, Session of 1924, Appendix, Report of the Proceedings of Committees* (Fredericton: Mail Printing Company, 1924), 16.

40 L. Pidgeon to G. Mason, 29 March 1924, UCC Archives, Church Union Collection.

41 W. Tuller to Rand, 5 July 1923; E. Hughes to Rand, 21 July 1923, PANB, Rand Papers, MSIJ.

42 Rand to Jordan Memorial Sanitarium, 28 December 1925, ibid. The board of the sanatorium obviously thought otherwise; it knocked Rand's commission down to 1 per cent. See also *The Provincial Secretary-Treasurer of the Province of New Brunswick v. Robinson Executor et al.* (1922), 50 NBR 367 (NBAD).

43 A.T. Doyle, *Front Benches & Back Rooms* (Toronto: Green Tree Publishing Company, 1976), 210.

44 (1920) *The Canadian Annual Review* 713.

45 Francisco, 'New Brunswick Finances,' 21.

46 H.E. Thomas to R.B. Whitehead, March 1925, UCC Archives, Church Union Collection, Series II, box 25, Property and Legislation.

47 The bill establishing the church was so well drafted that, more than sixty years later, it prevented congregations unhappy with the direction of the church from withdrawing, together with their 'property.' See *United Church of Canada v. Anderson et al.* (1991), 2 OR (3d) 304 (GD).

48 *Daily Times*, 22 November 1924.

49 Ibid., 28 November 1924.

50 Ibid., 29 November 1924.

51 Ibid., 1 December 1924.

52 Ibid., 2 December 1924.

53 Forbes, *The Maritime Rights Movement*, 140.

54 See, for example, the discussions on 9 December 1924, PANB, RS 9.

55 *Daily Gleaner*, 2 December 1924.

56 Ibid., 20 January 1925.

57 Ibid., 22 January 1925.

58 Ibid., 30 January 1925.

59 Ibid., 3 February 1925.

60 *Moncton Times*, 27 January 1925.

61 *Daily Gleaner*, 6 February 1925.

62 *Synoptic Report*, 91.

63 Ibid., 238.

64 *Daily Gleaner*, 16 April 1925. The following account is derived from that paper's detailed account of the address.

65 *Synoptic Report*, 183.

66 Ibid., 184.

67 *Daily Gleaner*, 16 April 1925; *Daily Times*, 18 April 1925.

68 *Daily Gleaner*, 17 April 1925. See also *Synoptic Report*, 202.

69 Pollock, 'Ivan Rand,' 133.

70 *Synoptic Report*, 250.

71 Thorburn, *Politics in New Brunswick*, 15.

72 Doyle, *Front Benches & Back Rooms*, 244ff.

73 *Daily Gleaner*, 25 July 1925.

74 R. Wilbur, *The Rise of French New Brunswick* (Halifax: Formac Publishing, 1989), 127.

75 Ibid., 117–33.

76 *Daily Gleaner*, 8 January 1925.

77 Ibid., 29 July 1925.

78 Doyle, *Front Benches & Back Rooms*, 252.

79 *Daily Gleaner*, 29 July 1925.

80 *Daily Times*, 31 July 1925.

81 *Moncton Times*, 4 August 1925.

82 *Daily Times*, 4 August 1925.

83 Doyle, *Front Benches & Back Rooms*, 257.

84 Francisco, 'New Brunswick Finances,' 23–4.

85 B. Parenteau, 'The Woods Transformed: The Emergence of the Pulp and Paper Industry in New Brunswick, 1918–1931' (1992) 12 *Acadiensis* 30.

86 Wilbur, *The Rise of French New Brunswick*, 130–2.

87 Parenteau, 'The Woods Transformed,' 6.

88 C.S. Beach, 'Pulpwood Province and Paper State: Corporate Reconstruction, Underdevelopment and Law in New Brunswick and Maine, 1890–1930,' PhD thesis, University of Maine, 1991, 6.

89 Parenteau, 'The Woods Transformed,' 7.

90 C.S. Beach, 'Electrification and Underdevelopment in New Brunswick: The Grand Falls Project, 1896–1930' (1993) 13 *Acadiensis* 60; *The New Brunswick Economy: Past, Present and Future Prospects, A Brief presented by the Government of the Province of New Brunswick to the Royal Commission on Canada's Economic Prospects* (Fredericton, 1955), 21.

Chapter 3: The Railway Counsel at Work and at Home

1 E.R. Forbes, *The Maritime Rights Movement, 1919–1927: A Study in Canadian Regionalism* (Montreal: McGill-Queen's University Press, 1979), 147.
2 For a contrary view, see K. Cruickshank, 'The Intercolonial Railway, Freight Rates and the Maritime Economy,' in K. Inwood, ed., *Farm, Factory and Fortune: New Studies in the Economic History of the Martime Provinces* (Fredericton: Acadiensis Press, 1993).
3 K. Cruickshank, *Close Ties: Railways, Government and the Board of Railway Commissioners, 1851–1933* (Montreal and Kingston: McGill-Queen's University Press, 1991), 159–60.
4 *Royal Commission on Maritime Claims* (Ottawa: F.A. Acland, King's Printer, 1927), 21.
5 Ibid., 22–3.
6 Forbes, *The Maritime Rights Movement*, 171.
7 See *Re The Maritime Freight Rates Act*, [1933] 4 DLR 764 at 773 (SCC).
8 E.R. Forbes, 'Misguided Symmetry: The Destruction of Regional Transportation Policy for the Maritimes,' in D. Bercuson, ed., *Canada and the Burden of Unity* (Toronto: University of Toronto Press, 1977), 68.
9 *Daily Times*, 4 February 1937.
10 *CN Steamships v. Bayliss*, [1937] 1 DLR 545 (SCC).
11 *Canadian National Railway Company v. Saint John Motor Line Limited*, [1930] SCR 482 at 485.
12 Ibid., 485, 493.
13 *Re Accident at M. 66.5 Tignish Sub., C.N.R., Prince Edward Island* (1932), 40 CRC 127 (Board); *Shea v. CNR* (1933), 6 MPR 337 (NBKB).
14 *Daily Times*, 23 September 1929.
15 E.M. Pollock, 'Mr. Justice Rand: A Triumph of Principle' (1975) 53 *Canadian Bar Review* 520.
16 *Daily Gleaner*, 1 and 2 May 1935.
17 *CNR v. Petitcodiac, NB et al.* (1936), 44 CRC 29 at 39–40 (Board).
18 *CNR v. Tweed* (1936), 44 CRC 53 at 58 (Board).
19 *Daily Times*, 24 April 1926 and 26 November 1927; Rand to G.T. Feeney, 8 May 1936, CNR Papers, Moncton.
20 *Daily Gleaner*, 23 November 1933.
21 Ibid., 8 September 1941.
22 *F.W. Pirie Company Ltd. and CNR*, [1943] SCR 275.
23 *The King v. CNR and CPR*, [1938] CLR 147 (Exch.).
24 *New Brunswick Gleaner*, 5 April 1939.
25 *City of Halifax v. Estate of J.P. Fairbanks*, [1928] AC 117 (PC).

26 See, for example, *Ontario Home Builders' Association v. York Region Board of Education,* [1996] 2 SCR 929, and *Hudson's Bay Co. v. Ontario (Attorney General)* (2001), 52 OR (3d) 737 (CA).

27 *Canadian Pacific Railway Company v. The King,* [1931] AC 414 (PC).

28 *Canadian Electrical Association v. Canadian National Railways,* [1934] AC 551 (PC).

29 Ibid.

30 *Canadian National Railway v. Canadian Pacific Railway* (1935), 44 CRC 1 (PC).

31 An Address by Sir Henry Thornton, 11 December 1922, empireclubfoundation.com/details.asp?SpeechID=2069&FT=yes.

32 On Thornton and the CNR in this period, see G.R. Stevens, *History of the Canadian National Railways* (New York: Macmillan, 1973), and D. MacKay, *The People's Railway: A History of Canadian National* (Vancouver: Douglas & McIntyre, 1992).

33 D. Marsh, *The Tragedy of Henry Thornton* (Toronto: Macmillan, 1935), 37.

34 Ibid., 21.

35 *Annual Report of the CNR System, for the Year Ended December 31, 1924,* 10.

36 Ibid., *1925,* 9. On the labour-management committees, see E. Ackerman, 'Union Management Co-operative Movement' (1941) 20 *Canadian Congress Journal* 14; J. Corbett, 'Union-Management Co-operation' (1946) 25 *Trades and Labour Congress Journal* 6; A. Seager, '"A New Labour Era?" Canadian National Railways and the Railway Worker, 1919–1929' (1992) 3 *Journal of the Canadian Historical Association* 172; H.M. Cassidy, 'Labour Co-operation on the Canadian National' (1926) *Canadian Forum* 42; J.A.P. Haydon, 'Industrial Democracy on Canadian National Railways' (1939) *Canadian Congress Journal* 15.

37 Seager, 'A New Labour Era?' 172, and Cassidy, 'Labour Co-operation,' 44. See also Corbett, 'Union-Management Co-operation,' 6–8.

38 Cassidy, 'Labour Co-operation,' 43.

39 Stevens, *History of the Canadian National Railways,* 325.

40 Ibid., 326.

41 The second, and last, time was two years later, in 1928: MacKay, *The People's Railway,* 60, 90.

42 E.W. Beatty, '"Mistaken Enthusiasm" and Where It Has Landed Us,' Speech delivered before the Gyro and other service clubs, Toronto, 9 April 1935, 14.

43 Beatty is quoted in Seager, 'A New Labour Era?' 181.

44 M. Grattan O'Leary, 'Canada's Railway Crisis' (1931) 38 *Queen's Quarterly* 725.

45 Ibid., 728.

46 MacKay, *The People's Railway*, 61.

47 Stevens, *History of the Canadian National Railways*, 338.

48 MacKay, *The People's Railway*, 54.

49 Stevens, *History of the Canadian National Railways*, 348.

50 *Report of the Royal Commission to Inquire into Railways and Transportation* (Ottawa: King's Printer, 1932) [*Railway Royal Commission*].

51 O'Leary, 'Canada's Railway Crisis,' 732.

52 *Railway Royal Commission*, 13.

53 Ibid., 64.

54 D.R. Williams, *Duff: A Life in the Law* (Toronto: Osgoode Society for Canadian Legal History and University of British Columbia Press, 1984), 156. See also A.W. Currie, 'The Senate Committee on Railways' (1939) *Canadian Journal of Economics and Political Science* 56 at 57.

55 Correspondence File, 1943–61, Rand Papers, Library and Archives Canada [LAC], MG 30, E77.

56 Haydon, 'Industrial Democracy,' 15.

57 Corbett, 'Union-Management Co-operation,' 8.

58 Interview with Robert Rand, 1 August 1989.

59 Charles Rand to William Kaplan, 2 July 1987.

60 Interview with Robert and Margaret Rand, 26 October 1988.

61 E.M. Pollock, 'Ivan Rand: The Talent Is the Call' (1980) 18 *University of Western Ontario Law Review* 114 at 125.

62 Interview with Ruth Hébert, 27 July 1988.

63 Robert Rand interview.

64 Interview with Charles Rand, 10 September 1989.

65 Robert and Margaret Rand interview.

66 'First-Class Rail Official Retires,' n.d., in Hebert Papers.

67 Ruth Hébert interview.

68 *Daily Times*, 27 November 1928.

69 Ibid., 20 February 1929.

70 F.J. Scully to Rand, 16 January 1935, Rand Papers, SCC File.

71 Allen Temple to Rand, 24 July 1935, ibid.

72 *Daily Times*, 5 December 1929.

73 Ibid., 10 December 1931.

74 'Ivan C. Rand, K.C., Moncton, Addressed Model Assembly of League of Nations at Mt. A.' *Argosy*, 19 December 1931.

75 *Daily Times*, 29 April 1935.

76 *CNR v. Lepage*, [1927] 3 DLR 1030 (SCC).

77 Legal Department Files, 1933, CNR Papers, Moncton.

78 Rand to Pettigrove, 30 March 1961, Pettigrove Papers.
79 MacKay, *The People's Railway*, 122.
80 Rand to E.E. Fairweather, 26 May 1937, LAC, RG 30, vol. 2190, file (CNR) 1937.
81 Interview with Edna Kearns, 2 February 1991.
82 M. Bliss, 'One Last Spike into a Canadian Myth,' *National Post*, 22 December 1989.

Chapter 4: The Framework of Freedom

1 J.E. Belliveau, 'The Gentle and Generous Side of Ivan C. Rand,' *Globe and Mail*, 6 January 1969. The story is a bit hard to believe. According to Bennett's private secretary, 'Appointments made by the party for party reasons are anathema to him. He wants a man of integrity, of capacity, and if such man happens to be a political enemy, that makes no difference.' See also G. Adams and P.J. Cavalluzzo, 'The Supreme Court of Canada: A Biographical Study' (1969) 7 *Osgoode Hall Law Journal* 61, and J.G. Snell and F. Vaughan, *The Supreme Court of Canada: History of the Institution* (Toronto: Osgoode Society for Canadian Legal History and University of Toronto Press, 1985), 147.
2 Interview with E.M. Pollock, 13 August 1990.
3 W.K. Campbell, 'The Right Honourable Sir Lyman Poore Duff, P.C., G.C.M.G: The Man as I Knew Him' (1974) 12 *Osgoode Hall Law Journal* 243 at 252.
4 D.R. Williams, *Duff: A Life in the Law* (Vancouver: Osgoode Society for Canadian Legal History and University of British Columbia Press, 1984), 247.
5 Snell and Vaughan, *Supreme Court*, 164.
6 *Daily Times*, 17 April 1939. The *Ottawa Journal* had, one week earlier, on 5 April 1939, published an editorial calling on the government to 'recruit or conscript' his services for this task.
7 Ibid., 2 December 1939.
8 William Lyon Mackenzie King Diary, 22 April 1943, 294, Library and Archives Canada [King Diary].
9 Ibid., 24 April 1943, 301.
10 The prime minister also believed that a specialty in organized labour was required: Interview with J.A. Gibson, 14 February 1989.
11 King Diary, 24 April 1943, 301.
12 Rand to King, 22 May 1942, LAC, William Lyon Mackenzie King Papers [King Papers], MG 26, J3, volume 120, General Correspondence.

13 Ibid.
14 King Diary, 6 January 1944, 14.
15 Rand Papers, Scrapbook, n.d.
16 Williams, *Duff*, 276.
17 *Daily Times*, 28 April 1943.
18 Rand Papers, Oswald Crocket to Rand, 24 April 1943.
19 Roscoe Pound to Rand, 25 October 1943, Roscoe Pound Papers, Harvard Law School Library, Folder 22.
20 Rand to W.M. Tweedie, 2 May 1943, William Morley Tweedie Papers, Mount Allison University Archives.
21 Speech, untitled, n.d., Rand Papers, LAC, MG 30, E77, vol. 7, File speeches n.d. 1951–58.
22 D.R. Williams, 'Legal Biography in Canada,' in J.N. Fraser, ed., *Law Libraries in Canada: Essays to Honour Diana M. Priestly* (Toronto: Carswell, 1988), 128.
23 R.G. Robertson to Harry Jackson, 24 January 1947, LAC, MG 26 J2, vol. 436, file J-20, Judgeships 45–46–47.
24 Speech, untitled, n.d., Rand Papers, LAC, MG 30, E77, vol. 7, File speeches n.d., 1951–58.
25 B. Laskin, 'The Supreme Court of Canada: A Final Court of and for Canadians' (1951) 29 *Canadian Bar Review* 1038.
26 I. Bushnell, *The Captive Court: A Study of the Supreme Court of Canada* (Montreal: McGill Queen's University Press, 1992), 344.
27 Arguably, the Supreme Court started off charting a different and more contextual course, but then became enslaved to the Privy Council: see R.C.B. Risk, 'The Scholars and the Constitution: POGG and the Privy Council,' in G.B. Baker and J. Phillips, eds., *R.C.B. Risk: A History of Canadian Legal Thought* (Toronto: Osgoode Society for Canadian Legal History and University of Toronto Press, 2006), 233–70.
28 See R.J. Sharpe and P.I. McMahon, *The Persons Case: The Origins and Legacy of the Fight for Legal Personhood* (Toronto: Osgoode Society for Canadian Legal History and University of Toronto Press, 2007), 6.
29 Ibid., 7.
30 See the discussion in Bushnell, *The Captive Court*, 281–328.
31 G.V.V. Nicholls, 'Legal Periodicals and the Supreme Court of Canada' (1950) 28 *Canadian Bar Review* 422.
32 Ibid., 445.
33 Snell and Vaughan, *Supreme Court*, 162.
34 Laskin, 'The Supreme Court of Canada,' 1047–8.
35 E. McWhinney, 'Judicial Concurrences and Dissents: A Comparative View

of Opinion-Writing in Final Appellate Tribunals' (1953) 31 *Canadian Bar Review* 595.

36 I. Rand, 'The Student at Law School,' *Sesquicentennial Lectures* (Fredericton: University of New Brunswick, 1950), 1, 2.

37 A.C. Cairns, 'The Judicial Committee and Its Critics' (1971) 4 *Canadian Journal of Political Science* 301 at 344–5.

38 *Winner* was the last JCPC decision.

39 *Reference re Farm Products Marketing Act*, [1957] SCR 198 at 212–13.

40 V.C. MacDonald, 'Legislative Power and the Supreme Court in the Fifties,' *Lectures Delivered at the Osgoode Hall Law School* (Toronto: Butterworths, 1961), 27.

41 *Reference re Farm Products Marketing Act*, [1957] SCR 198 at 212. See also J. Saywell, *The Lawmakers: Judicial Power and the Shaping of Canadian Federalism* (Toronto: Osgoode Society for Canadian Legal History and University of Toronto Press, 2002), 238–54.

42 *Burnet v. Coronado Oil & Gas Co.* 285 U.S. 393 (1932).

43 Interview with E.M. Pollock, 2 December 1988.

44 Mrs Rand to King, 24 August 1947, King Papers, MG 26, J3, volume 120, General Correspondence.

45 King to Mrs Rand, 27 August 1947, ibid.

46 I.N. Smith, *The Journal Men: P.D. Ross, E. Norman Smith and Grattan O'Leary of the Ottawa Journal: Three Great Canadian Newspapermen and the Tradition They Created* (Toronto: McClelland & Stewart, 1974), 150–1. See also Williams, *Duff*, 265.

47 Williams, *Duff*, 265. See also J.L. Granatstein, *A Man of Influence: Norman A. Robertson and Canadian Statecraft, 1929–68* (Ottawa: Deneau Publishers, 1981), 112.

48 Campbell, 'Sir Lyman Poore Duff,' 259.

49 Williams, 'Legal Biography in Canada,' 131.

50 Ivan Rand, 'Rt. Hon. Sir Lyman Poore Duff, G.C.M.G., 1865–1955' (1955) 33 *Canadian Bar Review* 1113 at 1114.

51 *Reference re Validity of Orders in Council in Relation to Persons of the Japanese Race*, [1946] SCR 248, aff'd [1947] AC 87 (PC).

52 For a completely different view of all these events, see P.E. Roy, J.L. Granatstein, M. Iino, and H. Takamura, *Mutual Hostages: Canadians and Japanese During the Second World War* (Toronto: University of Toronto Press, 1990).

53 T.R. Berger, *Fragile Freedoms: Human Rights and Dissent in Canada* (Toronto: Clarke, Irwin, 1982), 113.

54 Roy et al., *Mutual Hostages*, 173.

55 *Reference re Validity of Orders in Council in Relation to Persons of the Japanese Race*, [1946] SCR 248 at 290.

56 *Co-operative Committee on Japanese Canadians v. Canada (Attorney General)*, [1947] AC 87 at 106 (PC).

57 King Diary, 28 May 1948.

58 The following section is derived from W. Kaplan, *State and Salvation: The Jehovah's Witnesses and Their Fight for Civil Rights* (Toronto: University of Toronto Press, 1989).

59 H.H. Stroup, 'The Attitude of the Jehovah's Witnesses Toward the Roman Catholic Church' (1942) 2 *Religion in the Making* 151.

60 See M.J. Penton, *Jehovah's Witnesses in Canada* (Toronto: Macmillan, 1976), 97.

61 *Duval v. R.*, [1938] SCR 390. See also 'In Re Jehovah's Witnesses' (1947) 16 *The Fortnightly Law Journal* 221, and J.T. Eyton, 'The Jehovah's Witnesses and the Law in Canada' (1959) 17 *University of Toronto Faculty of Law Review* 96.

62 Penton, *Jehovah's Witnesses in Canada*, 113.

63 L. Betcherman, *Ernest Lapointe: Mackenzie King's Great Quebec Lieutenant* (Toronto: University of Toronto Press, 2002).

64 House of Commons, *Debates* [*Debates*], 19 June 1936, 3899ff.

65 C. Black, *Duplessis* (Toronto: McClelland & Stewart, 1977), 180. See also Memorandum of Law, 4 April 1938, LAC, Lapointe Papers, MG 30, A94, vol. 35, file 18 23, and *Debates*, 30 May 1937, 3377

66 King Diary, 6 July 1938, cited in H. Blair Neatby, 'Mackenzie King and French Canada' (1976) 11 *Journal of Canadian Studies* 9.

67 P. Bychok, '"La Muraille Qui Vous Protégé": Ernest Lapointe and French Canada, 1935–41,' MA thesis, Queen's University 1984, 132.

68 W.L.M. King to L.V. Smith, 23 July 1938, Lapointe Papers, vol. 43, and Kaplan, *State and Salvation*, 25.

69 Translation of passages from a speech by Cardinal Villeneuve to the Cercle Universitaire, Montreal, 'Liberty and Liberties,' 28 January 1938, reported in *Le Devoir*, 31 January 1938. Supplied to author by Eugene Forsey.

70 *L'Action Catholique*, 5 July 1940; see also J.M. Bernier to P. Bernier, 4 July 1940, Lapointe Papers, vol. 34, file 1939–41, Témoins de Jehovah.

71 King Diary, 24 and 25 June 1940. There is a suggestion in the *Debates* that the members of the House of Commons were aware of Lapointe's mental state: *Debates*, 12 June 1940, 714. See also J.W. Pickersgill, *The Mackenzie King Record, 1939–44* (Toronto: University of Toronto Press, 1960), 103, and J.L. Granatstein, *Canada's War* (Toronto: Oxford University Press, 1975), 102.

72 Kaplan, *State and Salvation*, 232.

73 See L. Capelovitch, 'Case and Comment, *Chaput v. Romain et al.*' (1956) 2
   McGill Law Journal 128. Invariably the raid was instigated by the local curé,
   who would tip off the police that the Bible was being read.
74 *Boucher v. The King* (1949), 95 CCC 119.
75 *Boucher v. The King*, [1951] SCR 265 at 285. The quotations below are at 285,
   288, and 291–2.
76 *Saumur v. Quebec (City)*, [1953] 2 SCR 299.
77 1851, 14 & 15 Vict., c. 175 (Province of Canada).
78 Rand Papers, Robert Laidlaw to Rand, 29 September 1952.
79 Rand Papers, Cecil Wright to Rand, 31 October 1952.
80 Rand Papers, SCC file, Glen How to Rand, 28 October 1952.
81 *Montreal Herald*, 12 December 1952, and *Toronto Telegram*, 12 December
   1952.
82 *Globe and Mail*, 16 December 1952.
83 *Ross v. Lamport*, [1956] SCR 366 at 375–6.
84 *Boucher v. The Queen*, [1955] SCR 16 at 23–4.
85 *Saumur v. Quebec (City)*, [1953] 2 SCR 299 at 310 [translation].
86 *Reference Re Alberta Legislation*, [1938] SCR 100. For more on the political
   context and judicial aftermath of the case, see D. Gibson, 'Bible Bill and the
   "Money Barons": The Alberta Origins of Canada's Implied Bill of Rights,'
   in R. Connors and J.M. Law, eds., *Forging Alberta's Constitutional Framework*
   (Edmonton: University of Alberta Press, 2005) 191–236.
87 Gerald Le Dain, 'Sir Lyman Duff and the Constitution' (1974) 12 *Osgoode
   Hall Law Journal* 261 at 319.
88 *Reference Re Alberta Legislation*, [1938] SCR 100 at 136.
89 See also Le Dain, 'Sir Lyman Duff and the Constitution,' at 319.
90 *Winner v. SMT (Eastern) Ltd.*, [1951] SCR 887 at 919–20. The quotations following are at 920 and 918.
91 B. Laskin, 'An Inquiry into the Diefenbaker Bill of Rights' (1959) 37 *Canadian Bar Review* 77 at 116–17.
92 See P. Weiler, 'The Supreme Court and the Law of Canadian Federalism'
   (1973) 23 *University of Toronto Law Journal* 307 at 348.
93 *Saumur v. Quebec (City)*, [1953] SCR 299 at 326. The quotations below are at
   329, 330, and 329, respectively.
94 *Montreal Gazette*, 5 December 1946.
95 See T. Loo, 'Don Cranmer's Potlatch: Law as Coercion, Symbol, and Rhetoric in British Columbia, 1884–1951' (1992) 73 *Canadian Historical Review*
   125; J. McLaren, 'The Doukhobor Belief in Individual Faith and Conscience
   and the Demands of the Secular State,' in J. McLaren and H. Coward, eds.,
   Religious Conscience, the State and the Law (Albany: State University of
   New York Press, 1999); J. McLaren, 'The Seizure and Indoctrination of

Sons of Freedom Children in British Columbia, 1950–1960,' in J. McLaren, R. Menzies, and D.E. Chunn, eds., *Regulating Lives: Historical Essays on the State, Society, the Individual and the Law* (Vancouver: University of British Columbia Press, 2002); G. Woodcock and I. Avakumovic, *The Doukhobors* (Toronto: Oxford University Press, 1968); and S. Holt, *Terror in the Name of God* (Toronto: McClelland & Stewart, 1964).

96 On Scott, see S. Djwa, *The Politics of the Imagination* (Toronto: McClelland & Stewart, 1987). See also S.M. Trofimenkoff, *The Dream of Nation* (Toronto: Gage, 1983), 276–7.

97 L. Roberts, *The Chief* (Toronto: Clarke Irwin, 1963), 126–7.

98 *Roncarelli v. Duplessis*, [1959] SCR 121. For a more favourable interpretation of Duplessis's role in the Roncarelli affair, see Black, *Duplessis*, 385–90.

99 *Roncarelli v. Duplessis*, [1959] SCR 121 at 140–1. The quotations from *Roncarelli* below are found at 141 and 142.

100 *Noble et al. v. Alley*, [1951] SCR 64.

101 *Re Drummond Wren*, [1945] 4 DLR 674 (Ont. HC).

102 See *Canadian Jewish News*, 25 April 2002. On the case itself, see J.W.St.G. Walker, *'Race,' Rights and the Law in the Supreme Court of Canada: Historical Case Studies* (Toronto: Osgoode Society for Canadian Legal History and Wilfrid Laurier University Press, 1997), 182–245.

103 Caroline LePage, Membership Liaison, Rideau Club, to W. Kaplan, 22 April 2009.

104 *Francis v. The Queen*, [1956] SCR 618.

105 *Switzman v. Elbling and Attorney-General of Quebec*, [1957] SCR 285.

106 Berger, *Fragile Freedoms*, 158.

107 *Switzman v. Elbling and Attorney-General of Quebec*, [1957] SCR 285 at 305.

108 Ibid., 306–7.

109 Frank Scott also acted as counsel in this case.

110 But see M. Gauvreau, *The Catholic Origins of Quebec's Quiet Revolution, 1931–1970* (Montreal: McGill-Queen's University Press, 2005).

111 Rand Papers, 'Tribute to Dean I.C. Rand,' by Mr. Justice J.R. Cartwright, 26 March 1964, 2.

112 Ibid.

113 E.M. Pollock, 'Mr. Justice Rand: A Triumph of Principle' (1975) 53 *Canadian Bar Review* 519 at 526.

114 D. Gibson, 'And One Step Backward: The Supreme Court and Constitutional Law in the Sixties' (1975) 53 *Canadian Bar Review* 621 at 622.

115 Rand Papers, Curriculum vitae, n.d.

116 I. Rand, 'Some Aspects of Canadian Constitutionalism,' Harvard Law School, Occasional Pamphlet No. 2, 1960, 25.

117 Berger, *Fragile Freedoms*, 152.

118 *Smith & Rhuland Ltd. v. The Queen*, [1953] 2 SCR 95 at 98–9. The quotations from the case in the paragraphs below are at 99–100, 100, and 104.

119 See M. Cohen, 'Case and Comment, *Re Labour Relations Board of Nova Scotia*' (1952) *Canadian Bar Review* 408–19.

120 *Williams v. Aristocratic Restaurants*, [1951] SCR 762 at 786. The quotations from *Williams* in the following paragraph are at 785–6 and 787.

121 *Williams v. Aristocratic Restaurants*, [1951] SCR 784.

122 E. Palmer, 'The Short, Unhappy Life of the "Aristocratic" Doctrine' (1960) 13 *University of Toronto Law Journal* 166 at 168.

123 P. Weiler, 'The "Slippery Slope" of Judicial Intervention: The SCC and Canadian Labour Relations, 1950–1970' (1971) 9 *Osgoode Hall Law Journal* 1 at 37–8.

124 *Henry Birks & Sons (Montreal) Ltd. and Others v. City of Montreal*, [1955] SCR 799.

125 P.W. Hogg, *Constitutional Law of Canada*, 2nd ed. (Toronto: Carswell, 1985), 636.

126 I. Rand, 'Man's Right to Knowledge and Its Free Use' (1954) 10 *University of Toronto Law Journal* 167 at 168–9.

127 Rand, 'Some Aspects of Canadian Constitutionalism,' 24.

128 I. Rand, 'The Role of an Independent Judiciary in Preserving Freedom' (1951) 9 *University of Toronto Law Journal* 1. The quotations in the following paragraphs are found on pages 5, 6, 7, and 13, respectively.

129 See *A.-G. Canada and Dupond v. Montreal (City)*, [1978] 2 SCR 770 at 796, and *A.-G. Canada v. Law Society of BC*, [1982] 2 SCR 307 at 364.

130 Le Dain, 'Sir Lyman Duff,' 263.

131 L.E. Weinrib, 'The Supreme Court of Canada in the Age of Rights: Constitutional Democracy, the Rule of Law and Fundamental Rights under Canada's Constitution' (2001) *Canadian Bar Review* 720.

132 See, generally, D. Smith, *Rogue Tory: The Life and Legend of John G. Diefenbaker* (Toronto: Macfarlane Walter & Ross, 1995).

133 Rand Papers, Personal File, 1959–60, Rand to Irving Himel, 14 May 1959.

134 *Cook v. Lewis*, [1951] SCR 830.

135 In dissent, Justice Locke held that the action was properly dismissed since liability could not be attached to either defendant.

136 *Cook v. Lewis*, [1951] SCR 830 at 839. The excerpts from Rand's reasoning in the next paragraphs are at 832 through 834.

137 For discussion and criticism of Rand's judgment, see T.B. Hogan, 'Cook v. Lewis Re-examined' (1961) 24 *Modern Law Review* 331.

138 See *Joseph Brant Memorial Hospital v. Koziol*, [1978] 1 SCR 491.

139 See, e.g., *Lange v. Bennett*, [1964] 1 OR 233 (HCJ), where the plaintiff was

hunting with friends and had knelt down to take a shot, then stood up suddenly in the line of fire of the two people standing behind him. The judge declined to extend the rule from *Cook v. Lewis* to a situation where the plaintiff was also negligent.

140 *Deglman v. Guaranty Trust Co. of Canada and Constantineau*, [1954] SCR 725.

141 Ibid. at 729.

142 Ibid. at 734.

143 See *Reference re The Board of Commerce Act*, [1922] 1 AC 191 (PC).

144 *Proprietary Articles Trade Association v. A-G Can.*, [1931] AC 310 (PC).

145 *Reference re Validity of Section 5(a) of the Dairy Industry Act*, [1949] SCR 1.

146 Ibid., 49–50.

147 *Canadian Federation of Agriculture v. AG Quebec*, [1951] AC 179 (PC).

148 In addition to the cases covered here, see *Deacon v. The King*, [1947] SCR 531 (admissibility of a witness's inconsistent statements), and *R. v. O'Brien*, [1954] SCR 666 (definition of conspiracy).

149 *Boudreau v. The King*, [1949] SCR 262.

150 *R. v. Fitton*, [1956] SCR 958.

151 Ibid., 962.

152 See *New Brunswick (Minister of Health and Community Services) v. G. (J.)*, [1999] 3 SCR 46 at para. 69.

153 *Hepton v. Maat*, [1957] SCR 606 at 607–8.

154 See *Minister of National Revenue v. Consolidated Glass*, [1957] SCR 167, and *Canadian Pacific Railway Co. v. Saskatchewan*, [1952] 2 SCR 231, respectively.

155 *Canada Safeway v. Minister of National Revenue*, [1957] SCR 717 at 727.

156 See D. Mullan, 'Mr. Justice Rand: Defining the Limits of Court Control of the Administrative and Executive Process' (1980) 18 *University of Western Ontario Law Review* 65.

157 Ibid., 68 and 112.

158 A. Mewett, 'Criminal Law and Procedure in the Decisions of Ivan C. Rand' (1980) 18 *University of Western Ontario Law Review* 51 at 62–63.

159 For a review of some of those cases, see Pollock, 'Mr. Justice Rand,' 519–43.

160 Bushnell, *The Captive Court*, 326.

161 *Brown v. Board of Education*, 347 U.S. 483 (1954).

162 See M.L. Dudziak, 'Desegregation as a Cold War Imperative' (1988) 41 *Stanford Law Review* 61.

163 Berger, *Fragile Freedoms*, 183.

164 F.A. Brewin, 'Criminal Law, *Boucher v. The King*' (1951) 29 *Canadian Bar Review* 193 at 202.

165 W.E. Conklin, *Images of a Constitution* (Toronto: University of Toronto Press, 1989), 233.

166 See A.A. Borovoy, 'A Rejoinder to Mr. Justice Berger' (1982) 62:720 *Canadian Forum* 6–7.

167 D. Dyzenhaus, 'The Deep Structure of *Roncarelli v. Duplessis*' (2004) 53 *University of New Brunswick Law Journal* 111 at 128–9.

168 Ibid., 140.

169 Laskin, 'Diefenbaker Bill of Rights,' 124.

170 Weinrib, 'The Supreme Court of Canada in the Age of Rights,' 711.

171 P. Girard, *Bora Laskin: Bringing Law to Life* (Toronto: Osgoode Society for Canadian Legal History and University of Toronto Press, 2005), 204. When Laskin was appointed, F.R. Scott could barely contain himself. 'There has not been a creative mind there since Rand left,' he said. See Girard, *Bora Laskin*, 365.

172 I. Rand, 'Legal Education in Canada' (1954) 32 *Canadian Bar Review* 387 at 417.

173 M. Cohen, 'The Judicial Process and National Policy: A Problem for the Canadian Federation' (1970) 16 *McGill Law Journal* 297 at 301–2.

174 P. Weiler, *In the Last Resort: A Critical Study of the Supreme Court of Canada* (Toronto: Carswell/Methuen, 1974), 192.

175 Gibson, 'And One Step Backward,' 629–30.

176 Ibid., 630.

177 T. Berger, 'The Charter: A Historical Perspective' (1989) 23 *University of British Columbia Law Review* 604.

178 See Weiler, 'The Supreme Court and Canadian Federalism,' 344.

179 A. Lajoie, P. Mulazzi, and M. Gamache, 'Political Ideas in Quebec and the Evolution of Canadian Constitutional Law, 1945 to 1985,' in I. Bernier and A. Lajoie, eds., *The Supreme Court of Canada as an Instrument of Political Change* (Toronto: University of Toronto Press, 1986), 19.

180 Interview with Robert McKay, 30 March 1990. See *Canadian Jewish News*, 25 April 2002. On the case itself, see Walker, *'Race,' Rights and the Law*, 182–245.

181 Peter Russell, *The Supreme Court of Canada as a Bilingual and Bicultural Institution* (Ottawa: Royal Commission on Bilingualism and Biculturalism, 1969), 192.

182 Interview with Glen How, 16 July 1988.

183 Rand Papers, Rand to Glen How, 5 October 1966: 'Please call me in Toronto for dinner and let's go somewhere where simple but good food is available and interesting discussion not barred.'

184 Glen How interview.

185 Interview with Kenneth Campbell, 23 January 1987.

186 Interview with William Jarvis, 2 April 1990.
187 Harvard University Archives, Griswold Papers, UA V. 512.26.15, box 55, file Holmes Lecture 1960, Memorandum to Faculty, 29 May 1959.
188 Ibid., Rand to Griswold, 24 June 1959. See also Rand Papers, Holmes Lecture File.
189 Rand Papers, Holmes Lecture File, Bora Laskin to Rand, 24 January 1960.
190 Rand, 'Some Aspects of Canadian Constitutionalism,' 136.

Chapter 5: Rand's Formula

1 The following section is derived from a number of sources, principally the *Windsor Star*, which covered the Ford strike and Rand arbitration in great detail. Also useful were S.C. Cako, 'Labour's Struggle for Union Security: The Ford of Canada Strike, Windsor, 1945,' MA thesis, University of Guelph, 1971; H. Colling, *Ninety-Nine Days: The Ford Strike in Windsor, 1945* (Toronto: NC Press, 1995); and D. Moulton, 'Ford Windsor 1945,' in I. Abella, ed., *On Strike: Six Key Labour Struggles in Canada, 1919–1949* (Toronto: James Lorimer, 1975).
2 *Financial Post*, 8 December 1945.
3 P. Martin, *A Very Public Life*, vol. 1 (Ottawa: Deneau, 1983), 215.
4 J. Fudge and E. Tucker, *Labour Before the Law: The Regulation of Workers' Collective Action in Canada* (Toronto: Osgoode Society for Canadian Legal History and Oxford University Press, 2004), 329–30.
5 L. Panitch and D. Swartz, *The Assault on Trade Union Freedoms* (Toronto: Garamond Press, 1988), 19.
6 RCMP Report, 23 April 1942, F.P. Varcoe to L. St Laurent, 24 April 1943, Department of Justice Papers, obtained under access request A90-00175.
7 D. Wells, 'The Impact of the Postwar Compromise on Canadian Unionism: The Formation of an Auto Worker Local in the 1950s' (1995) 36 *Labour/Le Travail* 156.
8 On England's communist affiliation see D.M. Wells, 'Origins of Canada's Wagner Model of Industrial Relations: The United Auto Workers and the Suppression of "Rank and File" Unionism' (1995) 20 *Canadian Journal of Sociology* 203. See also *RCMP Security Service Bulletin*, 18 September 1945, *Supplement to the September 1ˢᵗ Issue re Ford Strike* and *RCMP Security Service Special Section Monthly Bulletin*, 1 November 1945, re Ford Strike.
9 *Windsor Star*, 16 June 1945.
10 Ibid., 4 September 1945.
11 Ibid., 12 September 1945.
12 Alone, Professor Laskin also recommended 'maintenance of membership.'

13 B. Laskin, 'Union Recognition and Social Security' (1944) 8 *Public Affairs* 53.

14 H.D. Woods, 'Some Implications of Collective Bargaining' (1946) 10 *Public Affairs* 19.

15 *Windsor Star*, 12 September 1945.

16 Colling, *Ninety-Nine Days*, 18. See also, more generally, Moulton, 'Ford Windsor 1945.'

17 See 'Subversive Activity in UAW, Canada,' Library and Archives Canada [LAC], RG 146, RCMP Security Service files.

18 T.R. Berger, *Fragile Freedoms: Human Rights and Dissent in Canada* (Toronto: Clarke, Irwin, 1982), 149.

19 See Cako, 'Labour's Struggle for Union Security,' 18. This thesis was extremely valuable in reconstructing the background to the dispute and in the preparation of this narrative. On the communist issue, Cako states (at 105) that the UAW was 'a union whose principal officials were Communists or men influenced by Communist political policies.' See also J.S. Napier, 'Union Wins at Ford,' in *Memories of Building the UAW* (Toronto: Canadian Party of Labour, 1976), 56.

20 Eventually, belatedly realizing that communists were the enemy, he helped drive them from the UAW. See M. Lazarus, ed., *Up From the Ranks* (Toronto: Co-operative Press Associates, 1977), 21; C.A.B. Yates, *From Plants to Power: The Autoworkers Union in Postwar Canada* (Philadelphia: Temple University Press, 1993), 27–30, 66–7, 132–4; J.T. Morley, *Secular Socialists: The CCF/NDP in Ontario: A Biography* (Kingston and Montreal: McGill-Queen's University Press, 1984), 178; and I. Abella, *Nationalism, Communism and Canadian Labour* (Toronto: University of Toronto Press, 1973), 32, 38, 50, 62, 77, and 164–7.

21 G. Montero, *We Stood Together* (Toronto: James Lorimer, 1979), 103–4.

22 *Windsor Star*, 28 September 1945.

23 E.C. Awrey to C.L. Snyder, 15 September 1945, Ontario Archives [AO], RG 23, Series 4–02, box 36, file 36.6. See also affidavit of D.B. Greig, 22 September 1945, ibid.

24 Reaume to Blackwell, 15 September 1945, ibid.

25 Interview with Paul Martin, 11 May 1989; Martin, *A Very Public Life*, 390–7; Cabinet Conclusions, 7, 12, 14, and 28 November 1945, LAC, RG 2, Privy Council Office, Series A-5-a, vol. 2637, reel t-2364, file Labour Situation, entries for 7, 12, 14, and 28 November.

26 The section that follows is derived from the *Windsor Star* coverage of the strike together with the key sources set out in note 1.

27 Montero, *We Stood Together*, 104.

28 Ibid., 105.

29 House of Commons, *Debates*, 17 June 1948, 5371 [*Debates*].

30 Ibid., 9 October 1945, 864.

31 See for example, Reaume to Leslie Blackwell, 14 September 1945, OA, RG 23, Series 4–02, file 36.6, box 36.

32 Affidavits filed by Ford officials indicate clearly that police officers were instructed to offer no assistance to Ford employees attempting to enter the plant. 'I cannot break that picket line sir,' was the typical police response when a Ford executive attempted to drive to work: ibid.

33 Montero, *We Stood Together*, 106.

34 RCMP Access to Information Act request, 19 September 1990.

35 *Windsor Star*, 3 November 1945.

36 Ibid.

37 Ibid., 6 November 1945.

38 D. Jantzi, 'Ford Strike in Windsor, 1945,' in P. Craven and G. Teeple, eds., *Union Organization and Strikes* (Toronto: OISE, 1978), 54.

39 *Debates*, 5 November 1945, 1851.

40 Colling, *Ninety-Nine Days*, 32.

41 Ibid., 96, 122.

42 Cabinet Conclusions, 14 November 1945, LAC, RG 2, A–5–a, vol. 2637, reel T–2364.

43 *Windsor Star*, 7 November 1945; Cako, 'Labour's Struggle for Union Security,' 85.

44 *Windsor Star*, 7 November 1945.

45 Ibid., 10 November 1945.

46 Ibid., 12 November 1945.

47 RCMP Papers, LAC, RG 146, Ford Motor Company Strike, Access request AH-2001-00179.

48 *Debates*, 22 November 1945, 2402.

49 *Windsor Star*, 17 November 1945.

50 Colling, *Ninety-Nine Days*, 130.

51 *Debates*, 16 November 1945, 2182.

52 *Windsor Star*, 5 December 1945.

53 Ibid., 30 November 1945.

54 Colling, *Ninety-Nine Days*, 161.

55 *Windsor Star*, 18 December 1945.

56 Martin, *A Very Public Life*, 214.

57 Moulton, 'Ford Windsor 1945,' 147. In fact, it was the secretary-treasurer of the Canadian Congress of Labour, Pat Conroy, who suggested to Martin

that a Supreme Court of Canada judge be appointed to the job. The minister of justice, Louis St Laurent, independently believed that a high-profile appointment was necessary: see Martin, *A Very Public Life*, 395.

58 Colling, *Ninety-Nine Days*, 138. On Martin's role, see Martin, *A Very Public Life*, 388–97, and Paul Martin interview.

59 A. MacNamara to Rand, 18 December 1945, LAC, Rand Papers, MG 30 E77, vol. 1.

60 G.N. Chaison and E.D. Maher, 'An Interview with Horace Pettigrove,' unpublished ms., University of New Brunswick, 8 July 1974, 12.

61 Ibid., 12, 84ff.

62 Transcript of Evidence, 9 January 1946, in *Proceedings of hearings held before Honourable I.C. Rand, appointed as Arbitrator under Order in Council P.C. 7151, of November 23, 1945, to settle points of difference between the Ford Motor Company of Canada and Local 200, United Automobile, Aircraft and Agricultural Workers of America (CIO). Hearings held at Windsor, January 9 to January 15, 1946*, 3–4 [Transcript of Evidence].

63 Ibid., 25.

64 Ibid., 32.

65 See A. Seager, '"A New Labour Era?" Canadian National Railways and the Railway Worker, 1919–1929' (1992) 3 *Journal of the Canadian Historical Association* 171; H.M. Cassidy, 'Labour Co-operation on the Canadian National' (1926) *Canadian Forum* 42; and J. Corbett, 'Union-Management Co-operation' (1946) 25 *Trades and Labour Congress Journal* 6.

66 Transcript of Evidence, 9 January 1946, 42–3.

67 Ibid., 11 January 1947, 197.

68 Ibid., 10 January 1946, 66.

69 Ibid., 70.

70 See M. Leier, 'Cranks, Commies and Conformity: The Case of Kuzych versus White et al.,' in J. Judge and E. Tucker, eds., *Canadian Labour Law Stories* (Toronto: Osgoode Society for Canadian Legal History and Irwin Law, forthcoming, 2010).

71 Transcript of Evidence, 10 January 1946, 72.

72 See M. Lazarus, *Years of Hard Labour* (Don Mills: Ontario Federation of Labour, 1974), 50; Martin, *A Very Public Life*, 296; and Abella, *Nationalism, Communism and Canadian Labour*, 66–85, 95, 98, 120, 160, 174–5, 179, 204, and 214.

73 Transcript of Evidence, 10 January 1946, 80.

74 Ibid., 80–1.

75 Ibid., 83.

76 Ibid., 89.
77 Ibid., 274.
78 Ibid., 129.
79 Ibid., 142.
80 Ibid., 154.
81 Ibid., 194.
82 Ibid., 204.
83 Ibid., 204.
84 Ibid., 386–7.
85 Ibid., 204.
86 Ibid., 519, 525, 531.
87 Interview with Horace Pettigrove, 27 November 1989.
88 Chaison and Maher, 'An Interview with Horace Pettigrove,' 39.
89 Interview with Horace Pettigrove, 27 October 1989. According to Pettigrove, Rand was influenced by Herbert Agar and his book *A Time for Greatness* (Boston: Little, Brown, 1942). Agar was likewise opposed to the closed shop, where the union 'is almost a state within a state with the power to collect taxes and to destroy a man's livelihood.' Monopolies, he observed, were no more healthy for labour than they were for business. Agar had come up with a solution (179–80):

> By law, the union represents all the employees, both members and nonmembers. When the union, through collective bargaining or through strikes, obtains benefits in the way of wage increases, shorter hours, vacations with pay, grievance procedure, seniority and the like, these benefits accrue to all the employees. Yet the union members are forced to pay their monthly dues, while the non-union members obtain the benefits without any of the burdens. This sense of unfairness might be diminished by requiring a service fee from non-union members in return for the benefits which come to them from the work of the union. Such a fee would not force anyone to join the union, or to take part in its activities, or to go on strike when the union ordered. It would also preserve the right of seccession from the union. But it would prevent a group of non-union workers from a getting a 'free ride' at union expense.

What Rand seems not to have taken note of was Agar's cautionary remarks about extending the role of the state: 'There is already a demand from supporters of the closed shop that the government should register the unions and assume responsibility for seeing to it that there is no abuse of power.' To this John Chamberlain has given the classic conservative answer. 'Every time the state assumes more responsibility in the labor-management scheme of things,' he writes, 'we are just one step closer to the corporative set-up that is the basic structure of fascism.' Ibid., 180.

90 *Windsor Star*, 29 January 1946.

91 Transcript of Evidence, 15 January 1946, 689. For the text of the formula and for references to the quotations below, see 'Award on Issue of Union Security in Ford Dispute' (1947) 46 *Labour Gazette* 123–31.

92 Pettigrove to Marshall Pollock, 9 April 1976, Pettigrove Papers.

93 *Memo re Ford Co. and UAW*, ibid.

94 Ibid.

95 Canadian Congress of Labour, *The Case for Union Security and the Check-off* (Ottawa: The Congress, 1951), 41.

96 J. Fudge, 'Voluntarism and Compulsion: The Canadian Federal Government's Intervention in Collective Bargaining from 1900 to 1946,' D.Phil. thesis, Oxford University, 1988, 338–9.

97 Ibid., 344.

98 Rand to Pettigrove, 13 March 1946, Pettigrove Papers.

99 M.W. Bowman, 'Formula for Industrial Peace' (July 1949) *Manufacturing and Industrial Engineering* 26.

100 *Toronto Star*, 7 June 1946.

101 *Debates*, 6 April 1948, 2711.

102 Fudge and Tucker, *Labour before the Law*, 265.

103 M. Cohen, 'Case Comment, Re Labour Relations Board of Nova Scotia' (1952) 30 *Canadian Bar Review* 418.

104 Cited in S. Swartz, 'Hal Banks: The Rise and Fall of the Maritime Union Leader in Canada,' MA thesis, University of Illinois, 1968, 164.

105 Moulton, 'Ford Windsor 1945,' 153.

106 *Windsor Star*, 27 October and 27 April 1959.

107 E. Forsey, 'A Minority Report,' *The Canadian Unionist* (December 1946), 287–9. By the early 1950s, six provinces, for example, had enacted legislation providing for the voluntary revocable checkoff. See Canadian Labour Congress, 'Brief,' *The Canadian Unionist* (May 1953), 155.

108 Colling, *Ninety-Nine Days*, 175.

109 Cited in E. Tucker, 'Hersees of Woodstock v. Goldstein: How a Small Town Case Made it Big,' in Fudge and Tucker, eds., *Labour Law Stories*.

110 Horace Pettigrove interview, 27 October 1989.

111 Napier, 'Union Wins at Ford,' 60. See also Wells, 'The Impact of the Postwar Compromise.'

112 See, for instance, the *Globe and Mail* editorial published in the *Windsor Star*, 1 February 1946.

113 Transcript of Evidence, 9 January 1946, 5–6.

114 *Windsor Star*, 30 January 1946.

115 Rand to Pettigrove, 11 July 1946, 20 November 1957, Pettigrove Papers.

116 Ibid., 29 January 1947.

117 *Spun Rock Wools Limited v. Fiberglas Canada Limited*, [1943] SCR 565.

118 *Windsor Star*, 30 January 1946.

119 M.E. Baruth-Walsh & G.M. Walsh, *Strike: 99 Days on the Line* (Ottawa: Penumbra Press, 1995), 116.

120 Moulton, 'Ford Windsor 1945,' 129, 135.

121 *Debates*, 17 June 1948, 5370.

122 Moulton, 'Ford Windsor 1945,' 149.

123 *Debates*, 17 June 1948, 5372.

124 H.D. Woods, 'Some Implications of Collective Bargaining' (1946) 10 *Public Affairs* 19.

125 See J.A. Frank, 'The "Ingredients" in Violent Labour Conflict: Patterns in Four Case Studies' (1983) 12 *Labour/Le Travail* 87.

126 Ibid., 102.

127 *Lavigne v. Ontario Public Service Employees Union* (1991), 81 DLR (4th) 545 (SCC).

Chapter 6: Rand Tackles the Palestine Problem

1 The background to this chapter is drawn from a number of sources, including the work of the 'New Historians.' During the 1980s, some Israeli historians began to challenge traditional accounts and founding myths of their country's history, and they became known as the New Historians. They believed that Israel's 'Old Historians' had produced simplistic and consciously pro-Israel interpretations of the past which avoided mention of anything that reflected badly on Israel. The New Historians were critical and benefited from declassified archival materials that were used to evaluate the veracity of earlier scholarly accounts. Their critics claimed that they employed questionable methodology and were politically motivated in advancing a pro-Palestinian agenda, one that sought to delegitimize the state of Israel. Despite these and other criticisms, the New Historians gained a large following in Israel and abroad. See, for example, S. Flapan, *The Birth of Israel: Myths and Realities* (New York: Pantheon Books, 1987); I. Pappe, *Britain and the Arab-Israeli Conflict, 1948–51* (Basingstoke: MacMillan, 1988); B. Morris, *The Birth of the Palestinian Refugee Problem, 1947–1949* (Cambridge: Cambridge University Press, 1987); A. Shlaim, *Collusion across the Jordan: King Abdullah, the Zionist Movement, and the Partition of Palestine* (New York: Columbia University Press, 1988); and T. Segev, *The Seventh Million: The Israelis and the Holocaust* (New York: Hill and Wang, 1993).

2 Anglo-American Committee of Inquiry, *Report to the United States Govern-*

ment and His Majesty's Government in the United Kingdom (Lausanne, 1946).
See R. Crossman, *Palestine Mission: A Personal Record* (London: Hamish
Hamilton, 1947); C. Weizmann, *Trial and Error* (Westport: Greenwood
Press, 1949).

3 Cited in A. Hillmer, 'Canadian Policy on the Partition of Palestine 1947,'
MA thesis, Carleton University, 1981, 47. See, generally, E. Tauber, *Personal
Policy Making: Canada's Role in the Adoption of the Palestine Partition Resolu-
tion* (Westport: Greenwood Press, 2002).

4 Hillmer, 'Partition of Palestine,' 56.

5 William Lyon Mackenzie King Diary, 13 October 1944, Library and Archives Canada [LAC], MG 26, J13 [King Diary].

6 Ibid., 19 May 1947.

7 House of Commons, *Debates*, 28 May 1947, 3513 [*Debates*].

8 E.M. Pollock, 'Ivan Rand: The Talent Is the Call' (1980) 18 *University of
Western Ontario Law Review* 115 at 138. According to the Canadian ambassador to the United States, the Swedish government 'would issue no
instructions and offer no guidance to their representative.' Rand Papers,
Canadian Ambassador to the United States to Secretary of State for External Affairs, 22 May 1947.

9 Hillmer, 'Partition of Palestine,' 19.

10 D. Taras and D.H. Goldberg, 'Influencing Canada's Middle East Policy:
The Domestic Battleground,' in D. Taras and D.H. Goldberg, eds., *The
Domestic Battleground: Canada and the Arab-Israeli Conflict* (Montreal and
Kingston: McGill-Queen's University Press, 1989), 19.

11 Rand Papers, 'Historical Background of the Palestine Problem,' Memorandum for Mr Justice Rand, 31 May 1947.

12 'Good-time girls' were instructed to 'put in a good word about the *Yishuv*
at every opportunity': U. Milstein (ed. and transl. by Alan Sacks), *History of
the War of Independence: A Nation Girds for War*, 2 vols. (New York: University Press of America, 1996), vol. 1, 265.

13 J. García-Granados, *The Birth of Israel: The Drama as I Saw It* (New York:
Alfred A. Knopf, 1949), 107. On 'Emma,' see Bercuson Papers, Robert B.
Macatee to Gordon P. Merriam, 21 July 1947. The Bercuson Papers are
the research materials David Bercuson gathered for his book *Canada and
the Birth of Israel: A Study in Canadian Foreign Policy* (Toronto: University
of Toronto Press, 1985), which he generously shared with me and which,
along with the Rand and Pettigrove papers, have been deposited in the
University of Western Ontario archives.

14 García-Granados, *Birth of Israel*, 11.

15 See W. Khalidi, 'The Palestine Problem: An Overview' (1991) 21 *Journal of
Palestine Studies* 5 at 7.

16 N.E. Nashashabi, *Jerusalem's Other Voice: Ragheb Nashashibi and Moderation in Palestinian Politics, 1920–58* (Exeter: Ithaca Press, 1990), 188–90. Ragheb Nashashabi came from a prominent Palestinian family. He was mayor of Jerusalem and a political moderate with close British ties. This biography was written by his nephew and contains first-hand accounts of events. See also I. Khalaf, *Politics in Palestine: Arab Factionalism and Social Disintegration, 1939–48* (Albany: State University of New York Press, 1991), 144–58. As Khalaf's book observes, there is not an extensive literature, at least in English, on the last ten years of the mandate, and what there is does not discuss UNSCOP in much detail. It is probably a topic many Palestinians would prefer to forget. Moreover, critical introspection is not a hallmark of the little literature that exists.

17 Flapan, *The Birth of Israel*, 58. See also Shlaim, *Collusion across the Jordan*, 120.

18 Bercuson, *Canada and the Birth of Israel*, 81.

19 Interview with Marshall Pollock, 13 August 1990.

20 A. Eban, *An Autobiography* (New York: Random House, 1977), 76–8.

21 Rand to King, 8 June 1947, Mackenzie King Papers, LAC, MG 26 J1, vol. 428 [King Papers].

22 Eban, *Autobiography*, 76–7.

23 García-Granados, *Birth of Israel*, 12.

24 Ibid., 57.

25 I. Rand, 'Foreword,' in W.L. Hull, *The Fall and Rise of Israel* (Grand Rapids: Zondervan Publishing, 1954).

26 D. Horowitz, *State in the Making* (New York: Alfred A. Knopf, 1953), 167–8.

27 Pollock, 'Ivan Rand,' 122.

28 Eban, *Autobiography*, 83.

29 Horowitz, *State in the Making*, 170.

30 Marshall Pollock interview.

31 Horowitz, *State in the Making*, 177. On Weizmann, see Eban, *Autobiography*, 61, 79.

32 Cited in Tauber, *Personal Policy Making*, 16.

33 M. Cohen, *Palestine and the Great Powers, 1945–1948* (Princeton: Princeton University Press, 1982), 264.

34 Cited in Bercuson, *Canada and the Birth of Israel*, 87.

35 G. Meir, *My Life* (London: Putnam, 1975), 169.

36 King Abdullah later privately signalled that he would accept partition and, in that event, 'would be perfectly willing to give his full cooperation and to take over all the Arab areas of Palestine, or as much of them as were offered to him': Cohen, *Palestine and the Great Powers*, 266.

37 Ibid., 254.

38 García-Granados, *Birth of Israel*, 181.

39 Bercuson, *Canada and the Birth of Israel*, 86, 89.

40 Pollock, 'Ivan Rand,' 143. See also Horowitz, *State in the Making*, 200.

41 Horowitz, *State in the Making*, 186–7.

42 Ibid., 187.

43 Cited in Horowitz, *State in the Making*, 200.

44 See Rand Papers, Palestine File.

45 Horowitz, *State in the Making*, 200. See also 'Minutes of a Conversation be-
    tween Mr. Radak and Mr. Rand on 11.8.47,' cited in Tauber, *Personal Policy
    Making*, 26, 125.

46 'Minutes of UNSCOP's private meetings,' 7 August 1947, Bercuson Papers.

47 Memorandum by Mr Rand, confidential addendum to Plan on Partition
    with Economic Union Justification, UN Doc. A/AC. 13/82 (1947), cited in
    Pollock, 'Ivan Rand,' 144.

48 Memorandum to Trafford Smith, 20 August 1947, Bercuson Papers.

49 'Conversation with Dr. Bunche, 22 August 1947,' ibid.

50 Horowitz, *State in the Making*, 218–19.

51 Ibid., 162.

52 Ibid., 219–20.

53 *Report to the General Assembly by the United Nations Special Committee on Pal-
    estine* (Geneva, 1947), 81.

54 The Canadian Arab Friendship League saw things somewhat differently.
    Its president, in an address to the Montreal Optimist Club, said that the
    Arab world would 'remember' Pearson: Bercuson, *Canada and the Birth of
    Israel*, 136.

55 Horowitz, *State in the Making*, 223.

56 Cited in Tauber, *Personal Policy Making*, 110, 98.

57 Bercuson, *Canada and the Birth of Israel*, 105.

58 Horowitz, *State in the Making*, 225.

59 Bercuson, *Canada and the Birth of Israel*, 105. See also Memorandum of Con-
    versation between Ralph J. Bunche and James F. Green, 26 September 1947,
    Bercuson Papers.

60 Bercuson, *Canada and the Birth of Israel*, 105.

61 Milstein, *History of the War of Independence*, 97.

62 Rand Papers, 25 September 1947.

63 Taras and Goldberg, 'Influencing Canada's Middle East Policy,' 29.

64 Furlonge, *Palestine Is My Country: The Story of Musa Alami* (London: John
    Murray, 1969), 146.

65 Cited in Bercuson, *Canada and the Birth of Israel*, 110.

66 King Diary, 6 December 1947.

67 Eban, *Autobiography*, 90.
68 B. Morris, *The Road to Jerusalem: Glubb Pasha, Palestine and the Jews* (London: Tauris, 2002), 105.
69 See W. Khalidi, 'Revisiting the UNGA Partition Resolution' (1977) 27 *Journal of Palestine Studies* 5.
70 On 14 May 1947 the Soviet delegate to the UN, Andrei Gromyko, told the General Assembly that, while the Jews were entitled to a state of their own, no solution that ignored the lawful rights of either Arab or Jew could be justified. Gromyko, therefore, called for a single bi-national state but acknowledged that, if that was found impracticable, partition would have to be considered. See Cohen, *Palestine and the Great Powers*, 261. By March 1948 the USSR had begun a swing towards the Zionists, sanctioning Czechoslovakia's sale of arms to the Jews. According to Khalidi, 'The Palestine Problem,' 8, it was 'an extraordinarily fleeting convergence of interest between Washington and Moscow' that led to the partition resolution.
71 Rand Papers, Palestine File, letter dated 6 August 1967.

Chapter 7: King Coal

1 See I. Rand, *Report of the Royal Commission on Coal* (Ottawa: Queen's Printer, 1960), 10 [*Coal Report*].
2 On the $50 million, see *Report of the Royal Commission on Coal* (Ottawa: Queen's Printer, 1947), 562.
3 Ibid., 582–3.
4 Ibid., 75, 83.
5 J.T. Whetton, 'The Coal Problem in Great Britain and the World' (1960) *Transactions of the Mining Society of Nova Scotia* 742.
6 *Eleventh Annual Report of the Dominion Coal Board: Fiscal Year Ending March 31, 1959* (Ottawa: Queen's Printer, 1960), 18.
7 Canada, *Royal Commission on Canada's Economic Prospects, Final Report* [*Final Report*] (Ottawa: Queen's Printer, 1958).
8 Urwick, Currie Ltd., *The Nova Scotia Coal Industry* (Ottawa: Royal Commission on Canada's Economic Prospects, 1956), 3.
9 *Report of the Royal Commission on Mines* (Ottawa: Queen's Printer, 1947), 95–6.
10 Dosco might have simply adopted and adapted mining equipment from either the United States or Great Britain, instead of directing resources to the development of its own home-grown solution. The decision to do so was a mistake. The 'continuous miner' was an extremely complicated machine made up of 1,600 parts, the maintenance and replacement of which

were difficult and time-consuming. It was highly susceptible to break-down, among other problems directly affecting production.

11 *Royal Commission on Canada's Economic Prospects, Preliminary Report* (Ottawa: Queen's Printer, 1956), 103.

12 Ibid.

13 Ibid.

14 *Final Report*, 410–13.

15 *National Post*, 23 October 2008.

16 *Twelfth Annual Report of the Dominion Coal Board for the Fiscal Year Ending March 31, 1960* (Ottawa: Queen's Printer, 1962), 12.

17 W.C. Whittaker, 'The Twenty Years of the Dominion Coal Board,' in Dominion Coal Board, *Twentieth Dominion-Provincial Conference on Coal*, 1968, 78.

18 J.L. Granatstein, *The Ottawa Men: The Civil Service Mandarins, 1935–1957* (Toronto: University of Toronto Press, 1982), 260.

19 R.B. Bryce to Diefenbaker, 3 March 1959, Library and Archives Canada [LAC], RG 33/42, vol. 39.

20 'Nova Scotia Coal Industry,' 16 February 1959, ibid.

21 R.B. Bryce to Prime Minister, 27 April 1959, ibid.

22 *New Glasgow Free Press*, 10 March 1960.

23 Interview with Robert Stanfield, 9 April 1992.

24 Urwick, Currie Ltd., 'The Nova Scotia Coal Industry,' 19, 27.

25 House of Commons, *Debates*, 17 March 1959, 2009–10 [*Debates*].

26 *University of Western Ontario Gazette*, 6 October 1959.

27 He thought he was 'repulsive … a cheap country lawyer.' Interview with Robert and Margaret Rand, 26 October 1988.

28 Rand to Pettigrove, 18 October 1959, Pettigrove Papers.

29 H.R. Pettigrove to J.J. Ellis, 17 November 1960, ibid.

30 *Ottawa Citizen*, 8 October 1959.

31 *Halifax Chronicle-Herald*, 8 October 1959.

32 W. Keith Buck to Pettigrove, 29 December 1959, Pettigrove Papers.

33 See, generally, D. Smith, *Rogue Tory: The Life and Legend of John G. Diefenbaker* (Toronto: Macfarlane Walter & Ross, 1995).

34 R.B. Bryce to Rand, 16 March 1960, LAC, RG 33/42, vol. 37.

35 Much of the section on the commission's travels is derived from the newspaper log collected by commission staff. This section is from that log and from the report. See File, Newspaper Articles, Rand Royal Commission on Coal, ibid., vol. 13.

36 Secretary of State for External Affairs to Rand, 20 April 1960, ibid., vol. 39.

37 Submission by Stelco, 5 February 1960, ibid., vol. 3.

38 *Globe and Mail*, 4 January 1960.

39 *Victoria-Inverness Bulletin*, 23 March 1960.

40 Report of two meetings held in Ottawa, 20 October 1959, LAC, RG 33/42, vol. 39.

41 *Halifax Chronicle-Herald*, 23 January 1960.

42 G.N. Chaison and E.D. Maher, 'An Interview with Horace Pettigrove,' unpublished ms., University of New Brunswick, 1974, 211–12.

43 *New Glasgow News*, 18 March 1960; *Halifax Chronicle-Herald*, 24 March 1960; *New Glasgow Free Lance*, 31 March 1960.

44 *New Glasgow Free Lance*, 31 March 1960.

45 *Amherst News*, 19 March 1960.

46 *Antigonish Casket*, 18 February 1960.

47 *Hamilton Spectator*, 2 April 1960.

48 *Saskatoon Star Phoenix*, 3 February 1960.

49 *Toronto Star*, 30 March 1960.

50 *Halifax Chronicle-Herald*, 17 February 1960.

51 H.R. Pettigrove to J.J. Ellis, 17 November 1960, Pettigrove Papers.

52 Ibid.

53 *Coal Report*, 7.

54 Ibid.

55 The next few quotations are from ibid., 19–20, and the table at 94–5.

56 Ibid., 9.

57 The next few quotations are from ibid., 27–34.

58 It is not exactly clear that it was his idea. This was the thrust of the proposal made by the National Coal Association when Charles J. Potter presented its brief at the commission's hearings in Toronto. See *Brief*, LAC, RG 33/42, vol. 3.

59 *Coal Report*, 41.

60 Ibid., 37.

61 The following quotations are from ibid., 46–8.

62 *Cape Breton Post*, 3 September 1960.

63 Horace Pettigrove to Rand, 20 July 1961, Rand Papers.

64 *Financial Post*, 20 August 1960.

65 Interview with Horace Pettigrove, 27 October 1989. See J.J. Ellis to Pettigrove, 26 May 1960, Pettigrove Papers, where Rand arranged for Pettigrove to get a gratuity of $150 for all the hard work he did during six weeks of non-stop travel in March and April 1960.

66 *Globe and Mail*, 31 October 1960.

67 *Fredericton Gleaner*, 25 October 1960.

68 Rand to D.W. Gallagher, 9 January 1961, Rand Papers, Coal Report.

69 Ibid., 18 October 1960.
70 Ibid., 9 January 1961.
71 Ibid., 18 October 1960.
72 Rand to W. Keith Buck, 26 October 1960, ibid.
73 Rand to Pettigrove, 24 July 1961, Pettigrove Papers.
74 *Financial Post*, 1 October 1960.
75 *Globe and Mail*, 3 October 1960.
76 *Report of the Royal Commission on Dominion-Provincial Relations*, vol. 2 (Ottawa: King's Printer, 1940), 77.
77 Rand to Father A. Hogan, 13 October 1960, Rand Papers.
78 Walter Gordon to Rand, 14 September 1960, Rand Papers, Personal File, 1960–1.
79 *Saturday Night*, 12 November 1960, 25.
80 *Thirteenth Annual Report of the Dominion Coal Board for the Fiscal Year Ending March 31, 1961* (Ottawa: Queen's Printer, 1962), 13.
81 27 September 1960.
82 *Debates*, 23 November 1960, 111.
83 Pettigrove to Rand, 1 February 1962, Pettigrove Papers.
84 *Report of the Interdepartmental Committee on the Recommendations of the 1960 Royal Commission on Coal* [*Interdepartmental Committee*], Ottawa, 25 May 1961, 1–2.
85 W. Keith Buck to Rand, 8 June 1961, Rand Papers. 'This would,' Buck wrote, 'seem to be as much a difference in detail as a difference in substance.'
86 *Interdepartmental Committee*, 'Report 2: Research,' 15 October 1962, 2.
87 Cabinet Conclusions, 27 February 1962, Access to Information Act request 108–2/9293003(A) [AIA request].
88 *Debates*, 8 February 1962, 663.
89 Ibid., 4 April 1962, 2477.
90 Ibid., 21 February 1961, 2279, 2281.
91 W.V. Sheppard, 'Report,' April 1960, LAC, RG 33/42, vol. 30.
92 *Seventeenth Annual Report of the Dominion Coal Board for the Fiscal Year Ending March 31, 1965* (Ottawa: Queen's Printer, 1965), 10.
93 Ibid., 11.
94 J.R. Donald, *The Cape Breton Coal Problem* (Ottawa: Queen's Printer, 1966), 5–6.
95 Cabinet Conclusions, 22 November 1966, AIA request 108–2/9293028.
96 G.C. Van Kooten, 'The Coal Industry in Canada,' MA thesis, University of Alberta, 1974, 105.
97 R.K. Fletcher, 'The Development of an Energy Policy for the Maritime Provinces,' MA thesis, University of New Brunswick, 1965, 6.

98 Cabinet Conclusions, 6 June 1963, AIA request 108–2/9293003(A).
99 Cabinet Conclusions, 22 November 1963, AIA request 108–2/9293028.
100 Donald, *The Cape Breton Coal Problem*, 1.
101 Ibid., 4–5.
102 Ibid., 9.
103 Cabinet Conclusions, 4 October 1965, AIA request 108–2/9293028.
104 *Twentieth Annual Report of the Dominion Coal Board for the Fiscal Year Ending March 31, 1968* (Ottawa: Queen's Printer, 1968), 12.
105 Ibid., 13.
106 See *An Act to Establish the Cape Breton Development Corporation*, RSC 1985, c. C-25.
107 Pettigrove to Rand, 28 February 1961, Rand Papers.
108 Cabinet Conclusions, 22 April 1966.
109 *Globe and Mail*, 22 December 2001.
110 Donald, *The Cape Breton Coal Problem*, 34.
111 Robert Stanfield interview.
112 Rand to W. Keith Buck, 6 March 1964, Rand Papers.
113 E.M. Pollock, 'Ivan Rand: The Talent Is the Call' (1980) 18 *University of Western Ontario Law Review* 115 at 135.
114 *Toronto Star*, 27 October 2000.
115 *Maclean's*, 6 August 2001.
116 *Toronto Star*, 17 May 2001.
117 *Globe and Mail*, 22 December 2001.
118 'History Does Matter,' *Literary Review of Canada*, October 2008.
119 Letter to the Editor, ibid., November 2008.
120 *Toronto Star*, 17 May 2001.
121 *National Post*, 14 January 2000.

Chapter 8: A Founding Dean of Law

1 C.I. Kyer and J.E. Bickenbach, *The Fiercest Debate: Cecil Wright, the Benchers, and Legal Education in Ontario* (Toronto: Osgoode Society for Canadian Legal History and University of Toronto Press, 1987), 131.
2 Ibid.
3 On proposals for reform, see J. Frank, 'What Constitutes a Good Legal Education?' (1933) 19 *American Bar Association Journal* 723.
4 M. Cohen, 'The Condition of Legal Education in Canada' (1950) 28 *Canadian Bar Review* 267 at 278; W. Wesley Pue, 'Common Law Legal Education in Canada's Age of Light, Soap and Water' (1995) 23 *Manitoba Law Journal* 654–688 at 665ff. Possibly the benchers were reading Thorstein Veblen, who wrote: 'The law school belongs in a modern university no

more than a school of fencing': M. Cohen, 'The Condition of Legal Education in Canada: Fifteen Years Later, 1949–1964': (1964) *Canadian Bar Association Papers* 116 at 126.

5 J.D. Falconbridge, 'Legal Education in Canada' (1932) 9 *Journal of the Society of Public Teachers of Law* 32 at 35.

6 Kyer and Bickenbach, *The Fiercest Debate*, 145–6.

7 See R.C.B. Risk, 'Canadian Law Teachers in the 1930s: When the World
Was Turned Upside Down,' in G.B. Baker and J. Phillips, eds., *R.C.B. Risk:
A History of Canadian Legal Thought* (Toronto: Osgoode Society for Cana-
dian Legal History and University of Toronto Press, 2006), 344.

8 See R.C.B. Risk, 'The Many Minds of W.P.M. Kennedy,' in ibid., 314.

9 Kyer and Bickenbach, *The Fiercest Debate*, 148–9.

10 On Wright and Kennedy, see Risk, 'W.P.M. Kennedy' and 'Canadian Law
Teachers.'

11 I. Rand, 'Legal Education in Canada' (1954) 32 *Canadian Bar Review* 387 at
406.

12 Cohen, 'Condition of Legal Education in Canada,' 294.

13 Ibid., 295.

14 M. Cohen, 'Objectives and Methods of Legal Education: An Outline' (1954)
32 *Canadian Bar Review* 762 at 763.

15 Kyer and Bickenbach, *The Fiercest Debate*, 249.

16 See Federation of Law Societies, 'Task Force on the Canadian Common
Law Degree: Consultation Paper,' September 2008, appendix 2.

17 See J.J. Talman and R.D. Talman, *"Western," 1878–1953* (London, ON: University of Western Ontario, 1953), 40–2.

18 I am greatly indebted to Dr Margaret Banks and her book *Law at Western:
1959–1984* (London, ON: University of Western Ontario, 1984). See also
interview with Margaret Banks, 23 September 1989.

19 Rand to Scott, 16 May 1950, F.R. Scott Papers, Library and Archives Canada [LAC], MG 30 D 211, reel 1213, vol. 2, file 3, 'Association of Canadian
Law Teachers.' I would like to thank Philip Girard for bringing this reference to my attention.

20 Although Rand's piece had little to do with the survey, it did give him a
platform for the exposition of his views.

21 Rand, 'Legal Education in Canada,' 395.

22 Ibid., 390.

23 Ibid., 411.

24 Excellent lawyers were more than adept legal technicians, according to the
lawyer-statesman theory that originated in the nineteenth century. There
are many parts to the classical nineteenth-century ideal of the lawyer-

statesman. First, such a lawyer is a devoted citizen. In contrast to those who use the law to advance their own private agenda, lawyer-statesmen are prepared to sacrifice their own well-being in the face of the public good. They are said to have a 'special talent' for seeing where the public good lies 'and for fashioning those arrangements needed to secure it.' Not only would their clients look to them for guidance and advice, but other citizens would as well. In these situations, the lawyer is less concerned with specific means but offers advice about ends. A crucial part of this process is to help those being advised understand their own goals, ambitions, and interests. The lawyer-statesman was a 'paragon of judgment,' and he was looked to for leadership on account of his 'extraordinary deliberative power.' See A.T. Kronman, *The Lost Lawyer: Failing Ideals of the Legal Profession* (Cambridge, MA: Harvard University Press, 1993), and W.H. Rehnquist, 'The Lawyer-Statesman in American History' (1986) 9 *Harvard Journal of Law and Public Policy* 537.

25 Rand, 'Legal Education in Canada,' 391.
26 Ibid., 393.
27 Novice.
28 The quotations that follow all come from Rand, 'Legal Education in Canada,' 402–17.
29 Griswold to Rand, 9 September 1954, Griswold Papers, Harvard University Archives [HUA], UA V. 512.26.15, box 55.
30 W. French, 'A Monopoly the Lawyers Canceled Out of Court,' *Globe Magazine*, 23 April 1960.
31 The following section is derived from I. Holloway, '"You Must Learn to See Life Steady and Whole": Ivan Cleveland Rand and Legal Education,' unpublished paper, 19ff.
32 'Minutes,' 16 January 1959, Board of Governors fonds, University of Western Ontario Archives [UWOA], A807–063–002, reel 2 vol. 13, 124–5.
33 Ibid.
34 UWO, *Alumni Gazette*, April 1959.
35 Bora Laskin to Rand, 23 March 1959, Rand Papers, SCC file.
36 Faculty of Law, University of Western Ontario, 'Announcement 1959–60,' 16.
37 Faculty of Law, University of Western Ontario, 'Bulletin,' no. 2, 1960–1, 9.
38 *London Gazette*, 4 November 1960.
39 Faculty of Law, University of Western Ontario, 'Announcement,' 17.
40 I. Rand, 'The Student at Law School,' *Sesquicentennial Lectures* (University of New Brunswick, 1950), 3–4.
41 Ibid., 4–5.

42 Ibid., 6.

43 I. Rand, 'Some (Rather Harsh) Reflections on a Proposed Curriculum for the University of Western Ontario Faculty of Law,' n.d., Rand Papers, LAC, MG 30, E77, vol. 8.

44 Ibid.

45 Rand was obviously replying to an unsigned, undated document titled 'Policy Planning,' in which a member of faculty argued for faculty specialization and greater student choice in options. The document also called for regular faculty meetings. Ibid.

46 Ibid.

47 Rand to Horace E. Read, 11 January 1960, Rand Papers, Personal File, 1959–60.

48 Interview with Ronald Macdonald, 4 April 1989; interview with William Jarvis, 2 April 1990.

49 W. French, 'Law Takes a Chair at the Academic Table,' *Globe Magazine*, 30 April 1960.

50 Interview with Ralph E. Scane, 14 May 1990.

51 Interview with Albert Osterhoff, n.d.

52 Rand to G. Edward Hall, 19 December 1959, UWOA, Faculty of Law 1959–60, AFC40–38/59.

53 Interview with Robert Mackay, 30 March 1990; interview with Earl Palmer, 3 June 1990.

54 Interview with Margaret McNulty, 30 March 1990.

55 Cited in R. Yachetti, 'Ivan Cleveland Rand – The Teacher: A Student Viewpoint' (1980) 18 *University of Western Ontario Law Review* 145 at 151.

56 Rand to J. Noel Lyon, 25 April 1967, Rand Papers, SCC file.

57 Faculty of Law, 'Report of the Dean for the School Year 1959–60,' Rand Papers, LAC, MG 30, E77, vol. 8. Rand had read the literature before he wrote his *Canadian Bar Review* article and had at hand, because the author sent it to him, a copy of Maxwell Cohen's earlier *Canadian Bar Review* piece.

58 Ibid.

59 Rand, 'Legal Education in Canada,' 387.

60 Ibid., 406.

61 Interview with Dennis Brown, 22 May 1990.

62 Interview with David Steinberg, 7 May 1990.

63 Margaret McNulty interview.

64 Earl Palmer interview.

65 Ibid.

66 Interview with Robert Daudlin, 9 May 1990.

67 Albert Osterhoff interview.

68 Yachetti, 'Ivan Cleveland Rand,' 145.
69 William Jarvis interview.
70 Earl Palmer interview.
71 Robert Daudlin interview.
72 Interview with David Smith, 8 May 1990.
73 Harry Arthurs was invited to the dedication ceremony. In his recollection, the centrefold was unveiled at the ceremony: interview with Harry Arthurs, 7 October 2008.
74 Earl Palmer interview.
75 A.A. Fatouros to William Kaplan, 28 December 1990.
76 Robert Mackay interview.
77 Ibid., and Earl Palmer interview.
78 *Western Gazette*, 17 February 1961.
79 Ibid., 27 March 1962.
80 'Rand would sit in his office and speak quite matter-of-factly about his different prejudices': interview with Earl Cherniak, 12 August 2008.
81 Robert Mackay interview.
82 I. Rand, 'Foreword,' in W.L. Hull, *The Fall and Rise of Israel* (Grand Rapids: Zondervan Publishing, 1954).
83 Rand to Griswold, 21 February 1962, and Griswold to Rand, 28 February 1962, Griswold Papers, HUA, UA V 512.26.15, box 56.
84 Earl Palmer interview.
85 Ibid.
86 Robert Mackay interview.
87 R.S. Mackay, 'Ivan Cleveland Rand, 1884–1969' (1969) 47 *Canadian Bar Review* 155 at 159–60.
88 Kenneth Campbell to Rand, 6 July 1959, Rand Papers, Supreme Court, 1959–60. This was extremely odd advice. Wilfred Judson was among the most miserable of men and made the Ontario Court of Appeal judges of his day seem like gentlemen, which was quite a feat.
89 Earl Palmer interview.
90 Robert Mackay interview.
91 *Noble et al. v. Alley*, [1951] SCR 64.
92 Robert Mackay interview.
93 A.A. Fatouros to William Kaplan, 28 December 1990.
94 Earl Palmer interview.
95 I. Rand, 'Closing Remarks,' *French Canada Today* (Sackville: Mount Allison University, 1961), 109.
96 Earl Palmer interview.
97 A.A. Fatouros to William Kaplan, 28 December 1990.

98 W.H. Jarvis to Rand, 10 April 1962, Rand Papers, LAC, MG 30, E77, vol. 8.
99 'Tribute to Dean I.C. Rand' by Mr Justice J.R. Cartwright, 26 March 1964, 5, Rand Papers.
100 *Globe and Mail*, 28 March 1964.
101 Albert Osterhoff interview.
102 Interview with Alfred W.R. (Fred) Carrothers, 21 November 1988.
103 A.W.R. Carrothers, 'Legal Education at Western' (1965) 4 *Western Ontario Law Review* 1–6.
104 See, generally, Cohen, 'Condition of Legal Education in Canada,' 116–31, and *Law and Learning: Report to the Social Sciences and Humanities Research Council of Canada [Arthurs Report]* (Ottawa, 1983).
105 French, 'Law Takes a Chair.'
106 See B. Feldthusen, 'The Gender Wars: "Where the Boys Are"' (1990) 4 *Canadian Journal of Women and the Law* 66.
107 Rand, 'Legal Education in Canada,' 401.
108 Ibid. See also J. Frank, 'Why Not a Clinical Lawyer-School?' (1933) 81 *University of Pennsylvania Law Review and American Law Register* 907 at 916–17, where the 1918 Centennial History of Harvard Law School is cited.
109 M. Pollock, 'Mr. Justice Rand: A Triumph of Principle' (1975) 53 *Canadian Bar Review* 519 at 520–1.
110 *Arthurs Report*, 51, 52.
111 See, for example, W.B. Rayner, 'Western in the 1980s' (1989) 12 *Dalhousie Law Journal* 525.
112 Ibid., 526.
113 See Feldthusen, 'Gender Wars.'
114 Iredell Rand to Ruth Hébert, 6 December 1963, Rand Papers.
115 Rand to Ruth Hébert, 1964, Rand Papers.
116 Frank E. Archibald to Rand, 6 October 1964, Rand Papers.
117 *Moncton Transcript*, 25 September 1964.
118 Interview with Robert Rand, 29 November 1987.
119 Interview with Charles Rand, 10 September 1989.
120 Rand to Pettigrove, 14 October 1964, Pettigrove Papers.
121 Interview with Horace Pettigrove, 27 October 1989.
122 Alfred W.R. (Fred) Carrothers interview.

Chapter 9: Canadian Gothic Meets the Mambo King

1 What follows is largely a summary of W. Kaplan, *Bad Judgment: The Case of Mr. Justice Leo A. Landreville* (Toronto: Osgoode Society for Canadian Legal History and University of Toronto Press, 1996).

2 M. Bray and E. Epp, eds., *A Vast and Magnificent Land: An Illustrated History of Ontario* (Thunder Bay, ON: Lakehead University, 1984), 7.

3 Much of the following section is derived from ibid., 7–16; K. Coates and W. Morrison, *The Forgotten North: A History of Canada's Provincial Norths* (Toronto: Lorimer, 1992), 48–9; and L. Kimpton, *The Historical Development and the Present Situation of the French Canadian Community of Ontario* (Ottawa: Carleton University, Department of Sociology and Anthropology, 1984), 1–10.

4 M. Cousineau, 'Belonging: An Essential Element of Citizenship – A Franco-Ontarian Perspective,' in W. Kaplan, ed., *Belonging: The Meaning and Future of Canadian Citizenship* (Montreal: McGill-Queen's University Press, 1993), 137.

5 Quoted from B. Hodgins et al., *The Canadian North: Source of Wealth or Vanishing Heritage?* (Scarborough, ON: Prentice-Hall, 1977), 161–2.

6 Bray and Epp, *A Vast and Magnificent Land*, 14.

7 This section is drawn from W. Kilbourn, *PipeLine: TransCanada and the Great Debate, A History of Business and Politics* (Toronto: Clarke Irwin, 1970), 3ff.

8 Ibid.

9 Canada, *House of Commons Debates*, 13 March 1953, 2927–31 [*Debates*].

10 This account is substantially derived from R. Bothwell and W. Kilbourn, *C.D. Howe: A Biography* (Toronto: McClelland & Stewart, 1979), chap. 17.

11 *Re Trans-Canada Pipe Lines Ltd. and Western Pipe Lines, Alberta-Montreal Line* (1954), 73 CRTC 37.

12 A. Ross, 'The Life and Times of a Wheeler-Dealer,' *Maclean's*, September 1963, 18–19.

13 Ibid., 64.

14 However, see the evidence of C. Spencer Clark before the 1958 OSC investigation, in which he claimed, somewhat improbably, that it was a matter of relative indifference to NONG whether the northern or the southern route was chosen. While the former would involve, Clark claimed, a somewhat smaller capital expenditure, the scheme was feasible in either case, provided that monopolies were obtained throughout the north. *In the Matter of NONG Ltd.*, evidence of C. Spencer Clark, 29 May 1958, 21ff, Ontario Archives [OA], OSC Papers, RG 4–02, file 249.6.

15 *In the Matter of NONG, etc.*, evidence of Ralph K. Farris, 23 October 1962, in Leo Landreville Papers, University of Toronto Archives, Acc. No B 1995–054 [Landreville Papers]. This collection of materials, many of them given to me by Leo Landreville when I wrote *Bad Judgment*, was later deposited with the archives.

16 *R. v. Farris,* evidence of Gordon Kelly McLean, 10 April 1964, Landreville Papers, 442.

17 *Ottawa Citizen,* 25 January 1966. See also D.C. MacDonald, *The Happy Warrior: Political Memoirs* (Markham, ON: Fitzhenry and Whiteside, 1988), 76. Gordon Kelly McLean, however, insisted, at least for a time, that the idea was his, and that his uncle did not get involved until later. See *In the Matter of NONG Ltd.,* evidence of Gordon Kelly McLean, 2 June 1958, 62, OA, OSC Papers, RG 4–02, file 249–9.

18 Northern Ontario Natural Gas Company, *Annual Report,* 28 April 1958, 16.

19 North Bay *Daily Nugget,* 11 September 1956.

20 A 50 per cent interest was purchased in June 1956. Full control was obtained through a June 1958 share exchange. Ontario Securities Commission, *Final Report,* 22 July 1963 (Counsel: H.S. Bray), Landreville Papers, 10, 235ff.

21 See D.M. LeBourdais, *Sudbury Basin: The Story of Nickel* (Toronto: Ryerson Press, 1953), 1; C.M. Wallace, 'The 1880's,' in C.M. Wallace and A. Thompson, eds., *Sudbury: Rail Town to Regional Capital* (Toronto: Dundurn Press, 1993), 11.

22 Economic Council of Canada, *Performance and Potential: Mid-1950s to Mid-1970s* (Ottawa: Information Canada, 1970), 9.

23 O.W. Saarinen, 'The 1950s,' in Wallace and Thomson, *Sudbury,* 200; C. Dorian, *The First 75 Years: A Headline History of Sudbury, Canada* (Devon: Arthur H. Stockwell, 1959), 44–5; Economic Council of Canada, *Performance and Potential,* 196.

24 Dorian, *The First 75 Years,* 196; Saarinen, 'The 1950s,' 192.

25 Dorian, *The First 75 Years,* 88–92; Saarinen, 'The 1950s,' 207–8.

26 Report on the Economic Feasibility of Natural Gas Service to Designated Communities in Ontario, Canada, Phase 11, Fish Service & Management Corporation, Houston, 15 June 1956, 8–10, Landreville Papers.

27 Innis Christie, former dean of law, Dalhousie University, to William Kaplan, 9 August 1994.

28 P. Sypnowich, 'The Case of Mr. Justice Landreville' *Canadian Weekly,* 13 December 1965, 2–7.

29 *Ottawa Journal,* 1 November 1958.

30 L.B. Pearson to L.A. Landreville, 2 October 1953, Leo Landreville Private Papers. Justice Landreville allowed me to see these 'private' papers but retained them.

31 Landreville mayoralty speech, December 1954, ibid.

32 R.K. Farris to L.A. Landreville, 8 May 1956, Landreville Papers.

33 *In the Matter of NONG, etc.,* evidence of Ralph K. Farris, 17 October 1962,

Landreville Papers. Farris's evidence on this point was fully corroborated by both C. Spencer Clark and, of course, Leo Landreville.

34 R.K. Farris and C.S. Clark to L.A. Landreville, 20 July 1956, ibid.

35 L.A. Landreville to R.K. Farris, 30 July 1956, ibid. Landreville had by this time established a warm friendship with Farris. Visiting New York at the invitation of one of the directors of NONG, Landreville wrote to Farris about the trip, concluding, 'All the time thinking of our friendship and your kindness.' L.A. Landreville to R.K. Farris, August 1956, ibid.

36 The bubble eventually burst. Fabbro, who had taken the largest number of units for himself, held on to his shares for too long and watched them slip below his acquisition price. He arranged through Farris for John McGraw of Convesto to buy them back at $30 each when they were trading for much less. McGraw absorbed the loss. See Ontario Securities Commission, *Final Report*, 176.

37 Northern Ontario Natural Gas Company, *Annual Report*, 28 April 1958, 14.

38 Ibid., 9.

39 *Sudbury Star*, 30 August 1956, L.A. Landreville Scrapbook, Leo Landreville Private Papers.

40 Evidence of C. Spencer Clark, Vancouver, 14 March 1966, in *Proceedings of Inquiry into the Dealings of the Honourable Mr. Justice Leo A. Landreville with NONG Ltd., before the Honourable Ivan Cleveland Rand* (Ottawa: Queen's Printer, 1966), 132–3 [Proceedings of Inquiry].

41 L.A. Landreville to R.K. Farris, 19 September 1956, Landreville Papers.

42 R.K. Farris to L.A. Landreville, 1 October 1956, ibid.

43 *Minutes of Proceedings and Evidence of the Special Joint Committee of the Senate and the House of Commons respecting Mr. Justice Landreville* (Ottawa: Queen's Printer, 1967), no. 5, 9 March 1967 (Co-chairs: Daniel Lang and Ovide Laflamme), 165 [*Special Joint Committee*].

44 'Inter Alia' (1936) 6 *Fortnightly Law Journal* 1.

45 *Report of the Inquiry Re: the Honourable Mr. Justice Leo A. Landreville, Commissioner, the Honourable I.C. Rand* (Ottawa: Queen's Printer, 1966), 35 [*Landreville Report*].

46 J. McGraw to L.A. Landreville, 12 February 1957, Landreville Papers.

47 L.A. Landreville to Continental Investments Corporation, 16 February 1957, ibid.

48 *Special Joint Committee*, no. 5, 9 March 1967, 160.

49 For McLean's account of this event, see *R. v Farris*, Transcript, 10 April 1964, Landreville Papers.

50 Interview with Earl Cherniak, 20 March 1995.

51 *Time Magazine*, 28 January 1966.

52 Interview with John J. Robinette, 5 April 1991.
53 W.G. Morrow, *Northern Justice: The Memoirs of Mr. Justice William G. Morrow* (Toronto: Osgoode Society for Canadian Legal History and University of Toronto Press, 1995), 52–4.
54 *Proceedings of Inquiry*, evidence of Ralph Farris, 16 March 1966, 375–6, 354, 364.
55 Ibid., 378.
56 *Proceedings of Inquiry*, Vancouver, 15 March 1966, 221.
57 *Sudbury Star*, 23 March 1966.
58 *Proceedings of Inquiry*, Sudbury, 21 March 1966, 499.
59 Ibid., 621–4, 625–6, 658, 753.
60 J.D. Arnup to A.S. Pattillo, 13 February 1966, Law Society Papers, Law Society of Upper Canada Archives, Toronto.
61 A.S. Pattillo to J.D. Arnup, 4 March 1966, ibid.
62 J.D. Arnup to W.G. Morrow, 21 March 1966, ibid.
63 Ibid., 10 March 1966.
64 See, for example, RCMP Memorandum for File, 25 February 1966, Access to Information request, Library and Archives Canada, 94-A-00088.
65 A.A. Wishart to I.C. Rand, 16 March 1966, LAC, Rand Papers, E 77 Series, box 3, Landreville Correspondence file.
66 *Globe and Mail*, 26 April 1966.
67 *Proceedings of Inquiry*, Ottawa, 25 April 1966, 1082–3.
68 Ibid., 26 April 1966, 1138.
69 The next few quotations all come from ibid., 27 April 1966, 1270–90 and 1322.
70 J. Batten, *Robinette: The Dean of Canadian Lawyers* (Toronto: Macmillan, 1984), 188.
71 *Proceedings of Inquiry*, Ottawa, 27 April 1966, 1325–6.
72 Ibid., 1329.
73 L.A. Landreville to J.J. Robinette, 29 April 1966, Landreville Papers. This, of course, was both literally and figuratively correct.
74 *Landreville Report*, 4.
75 The next few quotations all come from ibid., 4, 17, 65–81, 92–108.
76 E.M. Pollock, 'Ivan Rand: The Talent Is the Call' (1980) 18 *University of Western Ontario Law Review* 115 at 136.
77 Interview with Ronald St J. MacDonald, 4 April 1989.
78 Privy Council Office, Cabinet Minutes, 23 August 1966, LAC, Access to Information requests 9293029 and 9495083.
79 *Globe and Mail*, 25 August 1966.
80 *Toronto Telegram*, 25 August 1966.

81 *Globe and Mail*, 26 August 1966.
82 *Landreville v R.*, Agreed Statement of Facts, Landreville Papers. See also L.A. Landreville to L. Cardin, 21 September 1966, ibid.
83 Privy Council Office, Cabinet Minutes, 29 August 1966, Access to Information requests 9293029 and 9495083.
84 Privy Council Office, Cabinet Minutes, 25 August 1966, Privy Council Office, ibid., 9293029.
85 *Debates*, 29 August 1966, 7742.
86 See L.A. Landreville to L. Cardin, 21 September 1966, Landreville Papers.
87 *Sudbury Star*, 30 August 1966.
88 M.L. Tyrwhitt-Drake, 'Mr. Rand and the Public Interest' (1967) *Law Society of Upper Canada Gazette*, 15.
89 'Editorial,' ibid., 4.
90 *Ottawa Journal*, 30 August 1966.
91 P. Russell, *The Judiciary in Canada: The Third Branch of Government* (Toronto: McGraw-Hill Ryerson, 1987), 180.
92 *Landreville Report*, 70.
93 *Proceedings of Inquiry*, evidence of L.A. Landreville, Ottawa, 25 April 1966, 1047–8.
94 *Landreville Report*, 70.
95 *Debates*, 12 May 1966, 5063.
96 John J. Robinette interview.
97 *Sudbury Star*, 30 August 1966.
98 *Special Joint Committee*, no. 4, 9 March 1967, 184.
99 *Landreville v. R. (No. 2)*, [1977] 2 FC 726 at 759.
100 See *Report to the Canadian Judicial Council of the Inquiry Established Pursuant to Subsection 63(1) of the Judges Act at the Request of the Attorney General of Nova Scotia, August 1990*: 'Is the conduct alleged so manifestly and profoundly destructive of the concept of the impartiality, integrity and independence of the judicial role, that public confidence would be sufficiently undermined to render the judge incapable of executing the judicial office.'

Chapter 10: Rand's Disastrous Investigation into Labour Disputes

1 The following section is derived from J. Fudge and E. Tucker, *Labour before the Law: The Regulation of Workers' Collective Action in Canada, 1900–1948* (Toronto: Oxford University Press and Osgoode Society for Canadian Legal History, 2001), 302–15.
2 *Polymer* (1959), 10 LAC 51.

3 J. Fudge, 'After Industrial Citizenship: Market Citizenship or Citizenship at Work?' (2005) 60 *Relations Industrielles/Industrial Relations* 631 at 637.

4 Fudge and Tucker, *Labour before the Law*, 305.

5 See E. Tucker, '*Hersees of Woodstock v. Goldstein*: How a Small Town Case Made It Big,' in J. Fudge and E. Tucker, eds., *Labour Law Stories* (Toronto: Osgoode Society for Canadian Legal History and Irwin Law, forthcoming).

6 J. Fudge and E. Tucker, 'Law, Industrial Relations, and the State' (2000) 46 *Labour/Le Travail* 251 at 283. On the general labour unrest, see *Labour News*, September 1965 to September 1966, study prepared by M.T. Mollison for A.W.R. Carrothers, ed., 'Report of a Study of the Labour Injunction in Canada,' Toronto, 1966.

7 A select legislative committee considered the use of injunctions and, in its 1958 report, recommended that *ex parte* labour injunctions be prohibited except in the case of an emergency. Instead, the *Judicature Act* was amended, as noted in the text, to provide even broader grounds to issue an injunction than those recommended by the committee. See Ontario Legislative Assembly, *Report of the Select Committee on Labour Relations*, 1958.

8 Carrothers, 'Labour Injunction in Canada,' 436.

9 *Globe and Mail*, 23 July 1966.

10 See B. Laskin, 'The Labour Injunction in Canada' (1937) 15 *Canadian Bar Review* 270. It is noteworthy that Laskin argued, in 1937, that the entire injunction process was flawed based on affidavit evidence not supported by cross-examination. He also deplored the legal process that endowed the employer 'with a militant power' that placed the judiciary in 'the ranks of employers.'

11 Bruce Stewart to William Kaplan, 24 November 2008.

12 Ontario, Legislative Assembly, *Official Report of Debates* [*Ontario Debates*], 9 February 1966, 337.

13 *Globe and Mail*, 2 February 1966.

14 Ibid., 3 February 1966.

15 Ibid., 4 February 1966.

16 Ibid., 7 February 1966.

17 Ibid.

18 Ibid., 12 February 1966.

19 Cited in J. Sangster, 'We No Longer Respect the Law: The Tilco Strike, Labour Injunctions, and the State' (2004) 53 *Labour/Le Travail* 47 at 54.

20 *Ontario Debates*, 22 February 1966, 743.

21 See Sangster, 'We No Longer Respect the Law.'

22 *Ontario Debates*, 24 February 1966, 836; 6 July 1966, 5786.

23 Ibid., 24 February 1966, 836.

24 Ibid., 4 July 1966, 5568–9.

25 Ibid., 5574.

26 *Globe and Mail*, 12 March 1966. See also *Ontario Debates*, 4 July 1966, 5573.

27 *Ontario Debates*, 18 May 1966, 3616.

28 Ibid., 26 May 1966, 3853.

29 Ibid., 4 July 1966, 5569.

30 *Globe and Mail*, 8 June 1966.

31 *Ontario Debates*, 6 July 1966, 5791.

32 Interview with Sydney Robins, 20 August 2008.

33 Sangster, 'We No Longer Respect the Law,' 65.

34 *Globe and Mail*, 28 June 1966.

35 Sangster, 'We No Longer Respect the Law,' 69.

36 Ibid., 70.

37 Ibid., 48.

38 H. Arthurs, 'Law, Labour and Liberty,' 11 February 1967, 14–15, *Royal Commission on Labour Disputes*, Ontario Archives [OA], RG 18, B–135, box 16.

39 Ibid., 3.

40 *Globe and Mail*, 5 May 1966.

41 The Arthurs study, 'Memorandum on the Use of Injunctions in Labour Disputes,' 8 October 1964, is cited in Sangster, 'We No Longer Respect the Law,' 75, n. 91; Arthurs, 'Law, Labour and Liberty.'

42 Goldenberg knew how to make the system work, and that is, undoubtedly, why government after government turned to him to study public problems. While admittedly unorthodox, Goldenberg, for example, after completing most of his work on his study of the construction industry, met with Premier Frost, who had appointed him, to review his tentative conclusions and recommendations. The purpose of the meeting was to ensure that the government would actually be able to implement its recommendations, even though Goldenberg would look independent when he released his report. See J. Crispo with M.E. Raycheba, *Rebel without a Pause: Memoirs of a Canadian Maverick* (Toronto: Warwick Publishing, 2002), 131. Goldenberg's approach ensured that, when *his* commission reported, the recommendations did not end up gathering dust on some shelf. Violence disappeared from the industry.

43 Interview with H. Carl Goldenberg, 7 November 1987.

44 *Royal Commission on Labour Disputes*, OA, RG 18, B–135, box 19, Press Release, 19 August 1966.

45 *Globe and Mail*, 1 February 1967.

46 *Toronto Star*, 17 January 1967.

47 *Toronto Telegram*, 19 January 1967.

48 Ibid., 7 April 1967.

49 'Speech Given in Windsor,' n.d., Rand Papers. See also I. Rand, 'Responsibility of Labour Unions,' *Special Lectures of the Law Society of Upper Canada* (Toronto: Richard de Boo, 1954).

50 'Observations on Labour Relations in Canada Today,' speech to the annual conference of the Canadian Association of Administrators of Labour Legislation, Ottawa, 12 September 1967; Rand to Pettigrove, 5 October 1962, Pettigrove Papers.

51 So was their mutual friend William F. Ryan, the dean of law at the University of New Brunswick: 'I can't help feeling that the very complicated matter of wage determination will never be as neat and well ordered as Dean Rand hopes it may become': William F. Ryan to H.R. Pettigrove, 8 April 1965, Pettigrove Papers.

52 *Time*, 20 January 1967.

53 *Royal Commission on Labour Disputes*, OA, RG 18, B–135, box 3, Transcript, January 10, 1967, 2–4.

54 *Kingston Whig Standard*, 12 January 1967.

55 *Toronto Star*, 12 January 1967.

56 Ibid.

57 *Toronto Telegram*, 13 January 1967.

58 Ibid.

59 *Globe and Mail*, 13 January 1967.

60 Ibid.

61 Wilf List, 'Youth and Age Stir Fresh Air' (1967) *Engineering and Contract Record* 39.

62 Interview with Edwin Stringer, 30 July 2008.

63 *Globe and Mail*, 19 May 1967.

64 Ibid.

65 *Toronto Star*, 19 January 1967.

66 *Globe and Mail*, 1 June 1967.

67 *Toronto Star*, 12 May 1967.

68 *Globe and Mail*, 12 May 1967.

69 Ibid., 25 January 1967.

70 *Royal Commission on Labour Disputes*, OA, RG 18, B–135, Box 44.

71 *Toronto Telegram*, 31 January 1967.

72 *Globe and Mail*, 8 May 1967; *Toronto Telegram*, 11 May 1967; *Maclean-Hunter's Construction Weekly*, 15 May 1967.

73 See, for example, 'Labour Law and Practice in Sweden,' July 1967, OA, RG 18, B–135, box 51.

74 Ibid., boxes 28–31. Harry Arthurs outlined the kind of social science research that was required in his 11 February 1967 speech, and Rand elaborated on it in the questionnaire. Rand wanted to know such things as the number of employees involved in the strike, the nature of the workplace, the most significant issues in dispute, whether a strike vote was held during negotiations, and conciliation – during the waiting period after conciliation or otherwise. He wanted to know whether the employer was able to maintain production, whether picketing occurred and where, and the conduct on the picket line. He was interested in the remedies sought, the legal applications commenced, and whether there were criminal proceedings in the aftermath of the strike or disciplinary ones. He also asked what grievances were filed and the result. Finally, he wanted to know about the outcome – whether it differed greatly or at all from the employer's final offer, the union's final demand, or the recommendations of the conciliation officer. A parallel study was made of injunction applications. Because of skewed response rates between labour and management, the research did not meet social science norms for validation.

75 Ibid., box 11, file, Harry Arthurs.

76 *Toronto Star*, 20 January 1968.

77 Interview with Marshall Pollock, 13 August 1990.

78 See H.J. Glasbeek, 'Restraints on Trade Union Activity in Australia,' in Carrothers, *Labour Injunction in Canada*, 706.

79 See Ibid.

80 W. List, 'Panacea Sought for Labour Ills' (1967) *Engineering and Contract Record* 25.

81 E. Marshall Pollock to Kaplan, 2 September 2008.

82 Ibid., 3 September 2008.

83 Marshall Pollock interview.

84 'Observations on Labour Relations in Canada Today.'

85 J. Crispo, 'A Memorandum on the Rand Commission Picketing Proposals,' January 1968, 4, OA, RG 18, B–135, box 21.

86 Ibid., 8.

87 Ibid.

88 Confidential Memorandum, 18 March 1968, ibid.

89 Ibid., 10–12.

90 See for example, Pollock to Rand, 10 June 1968, ibid.

91 Marshall Pollock interview.

92 Interview with William Ryan, 16 June 1991.

93 Marshall Pollock interview.

94 E.M. Pollock, 'Ivan Rand: The Talent Is the Call' (1980) 18 *University of Western Ontario Law Review* 115 at 125.

95 *Report of the Royal Commission Inquiry into Labour Disputes* [*Report*] (Toronto: Queen's Printer, 1968), 6.

96 The next few quotations come from ibid., 7–11.

97 The next few quotations come from ibid., 30–41.

98 This and the following quotation come from ibid., 114 and 121.

99 Notes on Labour Disputes File, Judge J.C. Anderson to Rand, 17 June 1968, Rand Papers.

100 Marshall Pollock interview.

101 *Toronto Star*, 6 September 1968.

102 D. Fisher and H. Crowe, 'Rand: A Kangaroo Report,' *St John's News*, 19 September 1968.

103 Interview with Shirley Goldenberg, 19 January 2000.

104 See D. Fisher and H. Crowe, 'Muddled Rand Report,' *Toronto Telegram*, 17 September 1968.

105 *Report*, 67.

106 G.N. Chaison and E.D. Maher, 'An Interview with Horace Pettigrove,' unpublished ms., University of New Brunswick, 1974, 218–19.

107 Ibid., 103.

108 Rand had earlier made it clear that he knew nothing about business, or, at best, that he had forgotten what he once understood. Bemoaning the fact that too many lawyers were using the profession of law as a 'stepping stone to high-paid jobs in business,' he went on to say: 'I must concede there is a need for them there to help executives to clarify their thinking. Many businessmen can't think an idea through to its logical conclusion, and need a lawyer's trained mind to direct them.' W. French, 'Law Takes a Chair at the Academic Table,' *Globe Magazine*, 30 April 1960.

109 E. Finn, 'Objectivity Difficult in Weighing Rand,' *Toronto Star*, 9 September 1968.

110 *Labour Gazette*, December 1968.

111 E. Finn, 'The Rand Report,' *Canadian Dimension*, September–October 1968, 7.

112 *Kingston-Whig Standard*, 6 September 1968.

113 *Toronto Star*, 6 September 1968.

114 Sangster, 'We No Longer Respect the Law,' 83.

115 'Comment on Recommendations – Rand Commission, Ontario,' CBC, 8 September 1968, Pettigrove Papers.

116 Sangster, 'We No Longer Respect the Law,' 54. *Ontario Debates*, 22 February 1966, 79.

117 M. Hikl, CUPE Research Director, 'Rand: Retreat from Glory,' unpublished paper, Pettigrove Papers.

118 The *Toronto Star* reported on 20 January 1969 that 'Rand's ideas hint at drastic labor changes.' See also Sangster, 'We No Longer Respect the Law,' 79, and M. Hikl, 'Rand: Retreat from Glory.'

119 *Labour Gazette*, December 1968, 687.

120 'Unions "Reactionary" in Handling of Rand Commission Findings?' *Financial Post*, 19 October 1968.

121 Arthurs, 'Law, Labour and Liberty,' 18.

122 *Globe and Mail*, 20 December 1968.

123 *Financial Post*, 28 December 1968. The CMA had no objection, however, to arbitration of public-sector disputes: 'This is one of the reasons why it is critical that private sector bargaining be free – so that the benchmarks for the public service have been arrived at fairly and in a manner acceptable to both sides.'

124 *Toronto Star*, 4 December 1968.

125 Fudge and Tucker, 'Law, Industrial Relations, and the State,' 285–6.

126 Ibid., 288.

127 See *RWDSU, Local 558 v. Pepsi-Cola Canada Beverages (West) Ltd.*, [2002] 1 SCR 156.

128 Arthurs, 'Law, Labour and Liberty,' 14.

129 Ibid., 14–15.

130 *Ontario Debates*, 15 May 1968, 2993.

131 H.C. Goldenberg, 'The Law and Labour Relations: A Reaction to the Rand Report' (1969) 24 *Relations Industrielles/Industrial Relations* 308.

132 E. Marshall Pollock to William Kaplan, 3 September 2008.

133 The total cost of the commission was $131,375: see *Ontario Debates*, 16 October 1969, 7155.

134 *Report*, 29.

135 *Globe and Mail*, 20 November 1968.

136 *Toronto Telegram*, 20 November 1968.

137 *Canadian Labour*, February 1969.

Conclusion

1 Maxwell Cohen was appointed to replace him. He submitted his report on 31 March 1972.

2 Rand to Pettigrove, 11 July 1967, Pettigrove Papers.

3 Ibid., 18 January 1966.

4 Ibid., Christmas 1967.

5 I. Rand, 'The Role of an Independent Judiciary in Preserving Freedom' (1951) 9 *University of Toronto Law Journal* 1 at 5.

6 Interview with Robert McKay, 30 March 1990.

7 I. Rand, 'Closing Remarks,' *French Canada Today*, Mount Allison University, 1961, 109.

8 J.E. Belliveau, *The Monctonians: Citizens, Saints and Scoundrels* (Hantsport, NS: Lancelot, 1981).

9 J.E. Belliveau, 'The Gentle Side of Ivan C. Rand,' *Globe and Mail*, 6 January 1969.

10 J.T. Saywell, *The Lawmakers: Judicial Power and the Shaping of Canadian Federalism* (Toronto: Osgoode Society for Canadian Legal History and University of Toronto Press, 2002), 252.

11 Dale Gibson, quoted in ibid., 252.

12 G. Blaine Baker, 'Willis on "Cultured" Public Authorities' (2005) 55 *University of Toronto Law Journal* 335–60. John Willis, a professor in the Law School at the University of Toronto, admired Rand, not because he was a great judge but because, as CN counsel, he helped to 'keep the trains running on time,' 337–8.

13 R.P.H. Balcome, E.J. McBride, and D.A. Russell, *Supreme Court of Canada Decision-Making: The Benchmarks of Rand, Kerwin and Martland* (Toronto: Carswell, 1990), 32.

14 Interview with Charles Rand, 10 September 1989.

15 His 1905 diary has his first reference to civilization: 'The civilization is like the pendulum – now low – now high like the wave of ocean. Man cannot maintain an even state at one extreme or the other.' Rand Papers, 1905 Diary, Memorandum, n.d.

16 *Jerusalem Post*, 8 April 1959.

17 See E. Adams, 'Constitutional Conceptions of a Different Order: Constitutional Thought and the Implied Bill of Rights,' unpublished paper, 51.

18 *Special Lectures of the Law Society of Upper Canada* (Toronto: Richard De Boo, 1954), 44–5.

19 I. Rand, 'Address to Graduates' (1945) 29 *Mount Allison Record* 47–9.

20 E.M. Pollock, 'Mr. Justice Rand: A Triumph of Principle' (1975) 54 *Canadian Bar Review* 519 at 523.

21 J.E. Belliveau, *Toronto Star*, 18 February 1950.

22 Rand to William F. Ryan, 27 April 1964, Rand Papers, Personal File.

23 Interview with William F. Ryan, 16 June 1991.

24 *Windsor Star*, 3 January 1969.
25 I. Holloway, '"You Must Learn to See Life Steady and Whole": Ivan Cleveland Rand and Legal Education,' unpublished paper, 25–6.
26 J.R. Cartwright, 'Ivan Cleveland Rand' (1969) 47 *Canadian Bar Review* 155 at 155.
27 I. Rand, 'The Student at Law School,' Sesquicentennial Lectures, University of New Brunswick, 1950, 9.

Index

2009 William Kaplan, *Canadian Maverick: The Life and Times of Ivan C. Rand*
R. Blake Brown, *A Trying Question: The Jury in Nineteenth-Century Canada*
Barry Wright and Susan Binnie, eds., *Canadian State Trials, Volume III: Political Trials and Security Measures, 1840–1914*
Robert J. Sharpe, *The Last Day, the Last Hour: The Currie Libel Trial* (paperback edition with a new preface)

2008 Constance Backhouse, *Carnal Crimes: Sexual Assault Law in Canada, 1900–1975*
Jim Phillips, R. Roy McMurtry, and John T. Saywell, eds., *Essays in the History of Canadian Law, Volume X: A Tribute to Peter N. Oliver*
Greg Taylor, *The Law of the Land: The Advent of the Torrens System in Canada*
Hamar Foster, Benjamin Berger, and A.R. Buck, eds., *The Grand Experiment: Law and Legal Culture in British Settler Societies*

2007 Robert Sharpe and Patricia McMahon, *The Persons Case: The Origins and Legacy of the Fight for Legal Personhood*
Lori Chambers, *Misconceptions: Unmarried Motherhood and the Ontario Children of Unmarried Parents Act, 1921–1969*
Jonathan Swainger, ed., *A History of the Supreme Court of Alberta*
Martin Friedland, *My Life in Crime and Other Academic Adventures*

2006 Donald Fyson, *Magistrates, Police, and People: Everyday Criminal Justice in Quebec and Lower Canada, 1764–1837*
Dale Brawn, *The Court of Queen's Bench of Manitoba, 1870–1950: A Biographical History*
R.C.B. Risk, *A History of Canadian Legal Thought: Collected Essays*, edited and introduced by G. Blaine Baker and Jim Phillips

2005 Philip Girard, *Bora Laskin: Bringing Law to Life*
Christopher English, ed., *Essays in the History of Canadian Law: Volume IX – Two Islands: Newfoundland and Prince Edward Island*
Fred Kaufman, *Searching for Justice: An Autobiography*

2004 Philip Girard, Jim Phillips, and Barry Cahill, eds., *The Supreme Court of Nova Scotia, 1754–2004: From Imperial Bastion to Provincial Oracle*
Frederick Vaughan, *Aggressive in Pursuit: The Life of Justice Emmett Hall*
John D. Honsberger, *Osgoode Hall: An Illustrated History*
Constance Backhouse and Nancy Backhouse, *The Heiress versus the Establishment: Mrs Campbell's Campaign for Legal Justice*

2003 Robert Sharpe and Kent Roach, *Brian Dickson: A Judge's Journey*

Jerry Bannister, *The Rule of the Admirals: Law, Custom, and Naval Government in Newfoundland, 1699–1832*

George Finlayson, *John J. Robinette, Peerless Mentor: An Appreciation*

Peter Oliver, *The Conventional Man: The Diaries of Ontario Chief Justice Robert A. Harrison, 1856–1878*

2002 John T. Saywell, *The Lawmakers: Judicial Power and the Shaping of Canadian Federalism*

Patrick Brode, *Courted and Abandoned: Seduction in Canadian Law*

David Murray, *Colonial Justice: Justice, Morality, and Crime in the Niagara District, 1791–1849*

F. Murray Greenwood and Barry Wright, eds., *Canadian State Trials, Volume II: Rebellion and Invasion in the Canadas, 1837–1839*

2001 Ellen Anderson, *Judging Bertha Wilson: Law as Large as Life*

Judy Fudge and Eric Tucker, *Labour before the Law: The Regulation of Workers' Collective Action in Canada, 1900–1948*

Laurel Sefton MacDowell, *Renegade Lawyer: The Life of J.L. Cohen*

2000 Barry Cahill, *'The Thousandth Man': A Biography of James McGregor Stewart*

A.B. McKillop, *The Spinster and the Prophet: Florence Deeks, H.G. Wells, and the Mystery of the Purloined Past*

Beverley Boissery and F. Murray Greenwood, *Uncertain Justice: Canadian Women and Capital Punishment*

Bruce Ziff, *Unforeseen Legacies: Reuben Wells Leonard and the Leonard Foundation Trust*

1999 Constance Backhouse, *Colour-Coded: A Legal History of Racism in Canada, 1900–1950*

G. Blaine Baker and Jim Phillips, eds., *Essays in the History of Canadian Law: Volume VIII – In Honour of R.C.B. Risk*

Richard W. Pound, *Chief Justice W.R. Jackett: By the Law of the Land*

David Vanek, *Fulfilment: Memoirs of a Criminal Court Judge*

1998 Sidney Harring, *White Man's Law: Native People in Nineteenth-Century Canadian Jurisprudence*

Peter Oliver, *'Terror to Evil-Doers': Prisons and Punishments in Nineteenth-Century Ontario*

1997 James W.St.G. Walker, *'Race,' Rights and the Law in the Supreme Court of Canada: Historical Case Studies*

Lori Chambers, *Married Women and Property Law in Victorian Ontario*

Patrick Brode, *Casual Slaughters and Accidental Judgments: Canadian War Crimes and Prosecutions, 1944–1948*

Ian Bushnell, *The Federal Court of Canada: A History, 1875–1992*

1996 Carol Wilton, ed., *Essays in the History of Canadian Law: Volume VII – Inside the Law: Canadian Law Firms in Historical Perspective*
William Kaplan, *Bad Judgment: The Case of Mr Justice Leo A. Landreville*
Murray Greenwood and Barry Wright, eds., *Canadian State Trials: Volume I – Law, Politics, and Security Measures, 1608–1837*

1995 David Williams, *Just Lawyers: Seven Portraits*
Hamar Foster and John McLaren, eds., *Essays in the History of Canadian Law: Volume VI – British Columbia and the Yukon*
W.H. Morrow, ed., *Northern Justice: The Memoirs of Mr Justice William G. Morrow*
Beverley Boissery, *A Deep Sense of Wrong: The Treason, Trials, and Transportation to New South Wales of Lower Canadian Rebels after the 1838 Rebellion*

1994 Patrick Boyer, *A Passion for Justice: The Legacy of James Chalmers McRuer*
Charles Pullen, *The Life and Times of Arthur Maloney: The Last of the Tribunes*
Jim Phillips, Tina Loo, and Susan Lewthwaite, eds., *Essays in the History of Canadian Law: Volume V – Crime and Criminal Justice*
Brian Young, *The Politics of Codification: The Lower Canadian Civil Code of 1866*

1993 Greg Marquis, *Policing Canada's Century: A History of the Canadian Association of Chiefs of Police*
Murray Greenwood, *Legacies of Fear: Law and Politics in Quebec in the Era of the French Revolution*

1992 Brendan O'Brien, *Speedy Justice: The Tragic Last Voyage of His Majesty's Vessel Speedy*
Robert Fraser, ed., *Provincial Justice: Upper Canadian Legal Portraits from the Dictionary of Canadian Biography*

1991 Constance Backhouse, *Petticoats and Prejudice: Women and Law in Nineteenth-Century Canada*

1990 Philip Girard and Jim Phillips, eds., *Essays in the History of Canadian Law: Volume III – Nova Scotia*
Carol Wilton, ed., *Essays in the History of Canadian Law: Volume IV – Beyond the Law: Lawyers and Business in Canada, 1830–1930*

1989 Desmond Brown, *The Genesis of the Canadian Criminal Code of 1892*
Patrick Brode, *The Odyssey of John Anderson*

1988 Robert Sharpe, *The Last Day, the Last Hour: The Currie Libel Trial*
John D. Arnup, *Middleton: The Beloved Judge*

1987 C. Ian Kyer and Jerome Bickenbach, *The Fiercest Debate: Cecil A. Wright, the Benchers, and Legal Education in Ontario, 1923–1957*

1986 Paul Romney, *Mr Attorney: The Attorney General for Ontario in Court, Cabinet, and Legislature, 1791–1899*
Martin Friedland, *The Case of Valentine Shortis: A True Story of Crime and Politics in Canada*
1985 James Snell and Frederick Vaughan, *The Supreme Court of Canada: History of the Institution*
1984 Patrick Brode, *Sir John Beverley Robinson: Bone and Sinew of the Compact*
David Williams, *Duff: A Life in the Law*
1983 David H. Flaherty, ed., *Essays in the History of Canadian Law: Volume II*
1982 Marion MacRae and Anthony Adamson, *Cornerstones of Order: Courthouses and Town Halls of Ontario, 1784–1914*
1981 David H. Flaherty, ed., *Essays in the History of Canadian Law: Volume I*